Advances in Human Evolution

A Prentice Hall College Division Series of Texts and Monographs

Advances in Human Evolution is committed to the timely publication of texts, monographs, and major edited works on all aspects of human evolution. The series' dedication to an interdisciplinary approach emphasizes new avenues of research in human evolution through biomolecular and DNA studies, developmental and evolutionary anatomy, paleoecological and paleobehavioral studies, ethnoarchaeological studies, as well as current debates on evolution from a biocultural perspective. Colleagues are invited to share these books with their undergraduate and graduate students as course texts or as supplemental readings. In addition to being of high scientific quality, books in this series advance our understanding of what it means to be human.

Series Titles:

Debating Humankind's Place in Nature, 1860–2000: The Nature of Paleoanthropology
Richard G. Delisle, McGill University (2007)

The Human Evolution Source Book, Second Edition (2006)
Russell L. Ciochon and John G. Fleagle (Editors)

The Epic of Evolution: Science and Religion in Dialogue (2004)
James B. Miller (Editor)

The New Physical Anthropology: Science, Humanism, and Critical Reflection (1999)
Shirley C. Strum, Donald G. Lindburg, and David Hamburg (Editors)

The Biological Basis of Human Behavior: A Critical Review, Second Edition (1999)
Robert W. Sussman (Editor)

Integrative Paths to the Past: Paleoanthropological Advances in Honor of F. Clark Howell (1994)
Robert S. Corruccini and Russell L. Ciochon (Editors)

Forthcoming:

The Primate Evolution Source Book
Russell L. Ciochon and John G. Fleagle (Editors)

Debating Humankind's Place in Nature 1860–2000

The Nature of Paleoanthropology

Richard G. Delisle

Anthropology, McGill University
Philosophy, Université de Montréal

With introductory and concluding essays by Milford H. Wolpoff and Bernard Wood

PEARSON
Prentice Hall

Upper Saddle River, New Jersey 07458

Library of Congress Cataloging-in-Publication Data

Delisle, Richard G.
Debating humankind's place in nature, 1860–2000 : the nature of paleoanthropology / by Richard G. Delisle; with introductory and concluding essays by Milford H. Wolpoff and Bernard Wood.
p. cm.—(Advances in human evolution series)
Includes bibliographical references and index.
ISBN 0-13-177390-9
1. Fossil hominids. 2. Human evolution. 3. Paleoanthropology. I. Title. II. Series.
GN282. D43 2006
599.93'8—dc22 2005054958

Publisher: Nancy Roberts
Editorial Assistant: Lee Peterson
Full Service Production Liaison: Joanne Hakim
Senior Marketing Manager: Marissa Feliberty
Assistant Marketing Manager: Andrea Messineo
Marketing Assistant: Anthony DeCosta
Manufacturing Buyer: Benjamin Smith
Cover Art Director: Jayne Conte
Cover Design: Bruce Kenselaar
Manager, Cover Visual Research & Permissions: Karen Sanatar
Cover Art: Courtesy University of Michigan Rare Books Collection
Composition/Full-Service Project Management: Ginny Somma/Stratford Publishing Services
Printer/Binder: The Courier Companies

Credits and acknowledgments borrowed from other sources and reproduced, with permission, in this textbook appear on appropriate page within text.

Pearson Education LTD., London
Pearson Education Singapore, Pte. Ltd
Pearson Education, Canada, Ltd
Pearson Education–Japan
Pearson Education Australia PTY, Limited
Pearson Education North Asia Ltd
Pearson Educación de Mexico, S.A. de C.V.
Pearson Education Malaysia, Pte. Ltd
Pearson Education, Upper Saddle River, New Jersey

PEARSON
Prentice
Hall

10 9 8 7 6 5 4 3 2 1
ISBN 0-13-177390-9

To the memory of my father Jacques Delisle
(1938–1992) who knew it all along

To Anik
for sharing her life with me

Contents

List of Figures

Acknowledgments

This long project has its roots in a Ph.D. thesis entitled *The Field of Human Evolution Within Evolutionary Biology and Anthropology: Historical and Epistemological Analyses since Inception* (1999) prepared in the Palaeoanthropology Research Group, University of the Witwatersrand, Johannesburg. It has been conducted under the supervision of Phillip V. Tobias, to whom I wish to extend my deepest admiration and my warmest affection. This research was then continued in different institutional settings. In 2000, I joined the Department of Anthropology of McGill University, Montréal, as a Lecturer. There, I received the unconditional support of Bruce G. Trigger and Michael Bisson. Thanks to the warm welcome of Henry de Lumley, I spent the academic year 2000–2001 at the Institut de Paléontologie Humaine in Paris as a postdoctoral fellow. Another postdoctoral stay brought me to the Department of Anthropology at the Université de Montréal during the academic years of 2001–2003. It has been for me a great pleasure to work with Norman Clermont during those years. The book was completed in a different institutional context as I felt the need for new intellectual tools in my quest to understand scholars' thinking about humankind's place in nature. This brought me to the preparation of another Ph.D. thesis, now in progress, in philosophy of biology at the Université de Montréal under the supervision of François Duchesneau. His credentials have been for me a genuine inspiration.

I am delighted that Milford H. Wolpoff and Bernard Wood so kindly accepted to write, respectively, an introductory essay and a concluding essay to this book. They were invited to do so in order to bring either complementary or contradictory viewpoints to the theses formulated here. Hopefully, this will contribute to stimulate further reflections on the much neglected history and philosophy of paleoanthropology. Bernard Wood was also very generous of his time in reading carefully the entire manuscript and suggesting numerous reccomendations to improve the quality of my writing. It is extremely difficult to fully master all the subtleties of a foreign language.

I am deeply indebted to the following institutions and the public agencies that kindly supported this research at one time or another: The University of the Witwatersrand (Burseries), the Foreign Affairs of the French Government (Bourses Chateaubriand), and the Government of Québec (Fonds FCAR). As there were years of financial drought in the early moments of this project, private funding was generously provided by Monsieur Georges Forest. He always profoundly believed in the intellectual quest pursued here. I express my warmest gratitude to him.

This book is also about consulting many books and articles that are difficult to find. This task was made much easier by the remarkable patience of the staff of the Interloan Service of the McLennan Library, McGill University. The assistance of Patrick Pollet at the Institut de Paléontologie Humaine was also invaluable. Many thanks for their much appreciated efforts. As this book is also about different languages, I received considerable help from Louis Bouchard of the *Das Buch* bookstore in Montréal for German translations.

My warmest gratitude must also be extended to numerous people who contributed innumerable services. Their generosity made all the difference in the preparation of this project: Christine Delisle, Stéphane Delisle, Claude Grondine, Robert Guay, David L. Hull, Anik Lebeau, Camille Limoges, Micheline Mayer, Paul Provost, the late Frank Spencer, and Ian Tattersall.

Lastly, I must express the joy I had working with Nancy Roberts at Prentice Hall and Russell L. Ciochon, the series editor. I would do it all over again if I could.

Richard G. Delisle

Paleoanthropology: A View from the Trenches

by Milford H. Wolpoff

I have the honor to introduce an exceptional history of paleoanthropology. Richard Delisle wrote his history as a paleoanthropologist with interests in history and the philosophy of science. His work raises many issues—some of these have been of deep concern to me through the years, and I appreciate the opportunity to discuss them.

It would be fair to expect that a history of paleoanthropology, especially a recent history, might look differently to different observers, and I write this as a practicing paleoanthropologist of almost forty years. Although my University of Illinois degree was in 1969, I wrote my first professional paper, on skeletal nasal aperture variation, in 1966. At sixty-two, thinking about my years in this profession sometimes makes me feel very old. But then I remind myself that sixty-two was the age at which Franz Weidenreich, my idol, left his recent appointment at the University of Chicago for Beijing, to replace Davidson Black who had just died unexpectedly. It was only then that he began the paleoanthropological work that resulted in numerous papers (including his polycentric theory) and the five major monographs on the Zhoukoudian remains that still stand as the finest exemplar for description and analysis of human fossils.

DATA DON'T SPEAK FOR THEMSELVES

In one of my first professional experiences in paleoanthropology I heard Louis Leakey present his views before a 1965 Wenner-Gren conference on "The Origin of Man" (DeVore, 1965). "Facts Instead of Dogmas on Man's Origin" was the title of his talk, and his theme was that theories shouldn't be allowed to masquerade as facts and that these facts, the data, speak for themselves. It left the opposite impression than intended on *this* young graduate student, playing to my growing conviction of the reverse, that the theories *were* the "facts" of the evolutionary world, and the data were more ephemeral, subjective, often unrepresentative and (as I later learned to describe data) of unknown distributional properties. I recognized that data played a role in the science, of course; actually a dual role. Data are the observations requiring explanation, while at the same time data are constantly auditioning for a part in an explanation's demise. But for me, the reality of paleoanthropology came to be the explanation: that is, the theory.

All paleoanthropologists share evolutionary theory (Mayr, 1982). Our common paradigm asserts that species and the populations that comprise them change over time, reflecting genetic change and in response to natural selection, mutation, genetic drift, and genic exchanges. But the way the evolutionary process works has never been resolved in a widely accepted manner. Lamarckian mechanisms were once considered valid, then discarded, and then brought back to acceptability. In one case this was through the resuscitation of the early twentieth-century vehicle of Lamarckian transmission, cytoplasmic inheritance along material lines that was part of dualist theories of evolution (dualist meaning Darwinism plus something else; see Wolpoff & Caspari, 1997). Dualist theories were prevalent in interwar Germany, exemplifying a style of thought in the German-speaking world that was developing before the Evolutionary Synthesis (Harwood, 1993). Dualism held that while some forms of variation were inherited, other more complex kinds of features changed when acted upon directly by the environment through the cytoplasm. This aspect of evolution reflected a then-accepted interpretation of Darwinism based on Darwin's own belief in the inheritance of acquired characteristics. There was no necessary contradiction perceived between Darwin's natural selection and the ability to inherit characteristics acquired during life. Selection was the mechanism that led to adaptation, while acquired characteristics were part of the variation that selection acted upon. The maternal inheritance of mitochondria and their DNA (both modifiable through life) is the dualism of modern biology.

A second instance of a Lamarckian evolutionary mechanism is the significant role now recognized for behavioral traditions in altering the pattern of selection acting on populations of many social mammals (Fragaszy, 2003; Nishida, 1987), including, of course, humans (Richerson & Boyd, 2004). Traditions are inherited outside the genome and are modified during life. Perhaps the altering acceptance of Lamarckian mechanisms reflect something less than alternative theories—one author (Harwood, 1993) uses the description of "styles of thought"—but their differing influence on the understanding of evolution is deep and significant.

Virtually all controversy in paleoanthropology is testament to the power of these styles of thought. Just in the past decades, competing models of evolutionary mechanisms, such as punctuated equilibrium and gradualism, are quite sufficient to frame such different interpretations that two scientists can literally interpret exactly the same data in opposite ways. Genetic studies in paleoanthropology almost invariably rest on the neutrality assumption for genetic changes, a simplifying and sensible assumption that allows generic variation to be interpreted as a reflection of past population history. Yet on the other hand, morphologists, with their focus on adaptive change, rarely evoke a neutral explanation, but will first assume that selection (or one of its consequences through exaptation) causes evolutionary change and seek to understand how. In these two applications of evolutionary theory, the starting assumption of one is the explanation of last resort for the other.

Even within the anatomical community there are vastly different interpretations of how evolution works. In one case the Evolutionary Synthesis was described as an orthogenic theory and explicitly equated with linear progressionism:

> [t]hanks to the overwhelming triumph of the Evolutionary Synthesis . . . human evolution, like that of other organisms, came to be seen as a gradual, linear process that, come hell or high water, continued doggedly along a path of inexorable betterment. (Tattersall, 2002, p. 81)

The same author asserts:

- "Most features will linger in a population as long as they simply don't get in the way." (p. 33)
- "Evolution is best described as opportunistic, simply exploiting or rejecting possibilities as they arise. . . . [t]here is nothing inherently directional . . . about this process." (p. 139)
- "For true innovations to arise and become permanently incorporated into some component of the human population, it will be necessary for that population to become fragmented." (p. 189)
- "There is no mechanism by which particular characteristics—still less, genes—can be singled out for favored or disfavored treatment." (p. 187)

These assertions are unrelated to the description of evolution developed in the Evolutionary Synthesis (e.g., Huxley, 1940; Mayr, 1963) and are at odds with the current understanding of many paleoanthropologists. The different interpretations these descriptions allow are more than sufficient to account for many of the different positions taken on issues of human evolution such as modern human origins, the fate of the Neandertals, and so on. And so it seems to me that a history of paleoanthropology must surely be a history of paleoanthropological theory, and we might profitably examine the questions of different understandings of evolutionary theory and even of different evolutionary theories, to unravel its pathway.

SCIENCE AS A HUMAN ACTIVITY

Do social factors have an impact on the development of paleoanthropology? Is science a human activity, as Jan Jelínek so often asserted? I must admit that for a good deal of my professional career I never seriously considered this possibility, until years after the Vietnam war was over when I read an essay pointing out that the partisans engaged in the australopithecine debate of that time—seed-eaters versus hunting carnivores—almost exactly divided into the doves and hawks of the

Vietnam debate. This really surprised me, all the more so because I was involved in both debates and the link never occurred to me.

But it shouldn't have been surprising (Proctor, 2003). Paleoanthropology, arguably more than most sciences, reflects the society paleoanthropologists live in and can quite significantly influence. Perhaps the strongest historical example of this is Ernst Haeckel. Haeckel supported the notion of common descent from a single ape ancestor for humans and did not derive races from different ape species as several of his contemporaries did. According to him, different human species each evolved from *Pithecanthropi* (different species of ape-men) living in different regions. Each attained human status; their human attributes were independently acquired through competition between them. [The ability of these species to interbreed was no impediment, like many other evolutionists of his time he accepted the notion that cross-species fertility was common in other animal species.] In the later decades of his life, Haeckel had a nationalist social agenda. His monism provided an interpretation of Darwinism within the Romantic framework of *Naturphilosophie*, romanticizing links between the human spirit, the land, and nature. Haeckel believed in a transcendental racial unity of the *Deutsche Volk*, a common spirit that bound them to the fatherland, and through Darwinism he found the mechanism explaining their natural racial superiority. Contrasting with the way that social Darwinism was used in Britain to justify laissez-faire capitalism by showing that *individual* competition was the natural way, Haeckel applied Darwinism through his theory of the competition between racial groups (species, for him) to explain why the extermination and exploitation of other racial groups were the inevitable and desirable consequences of natural selection. Haeckel's contribution to biological education in Germany included the conviction that natural selection would result in European superiority as other races (species) would be exterminated. Nazism, for the most part developing after his death, was applied biology.

OLD THEORIES NEVER DIE

Old theories, like old soldiers never die, they just fade away? Well actually they don't fade away at all; they continue to resurface, invigorated and with new audiences. Arguably the most corrosive example of this, given biological anthropology's significant role in creating the basis for the biopolicies so popular in twentieth-century political movements, is the continued re-emergence of polygenism (Hawks & Wolpoff, 2003). Polygenism is a theory that in paleoanthropology includes separate origins for different human races in different fossil primate species. Haeckel, discussed above, was a significant proponent of it (Haeckel, however, was *Darwin's* polygenist and believed that the different human species had their origin in a single primate species). Polygenism continued to be held by central figures within paleoanthropology such as Hooton (1946), Keith (1948), and Coon (1962), up to the middle of the twentieth-century (Bowler, 1986; Wolpoff & Caspari, 1997). This is reflected in the view that human geographic races have been essentially isolated from each other, and that their evolutionary histories are therefore mutually independent. Polygenist interpretations of human geographic diversity keep on reappearing long after separate primate origins for "races" have been thoroughly falsified (Brace, 1981). Some of today's scientists continue to explicitly or implicitly assume that human geographic races evolved independently from each other as separate clades, or lineages. This view is mostly assumed within parts of the genetics community, or by those who cite their publications, as a consequence of the belief that modern populations have a single, unique, recent origin, and quickly evolved to vary in proportion to the geographic distances between them (isolation by distance). Under this model, today's lower genetic diversity of non-Africans compared to Africans is taken to show the ancestors of the non-Africans left Africa with a small population size. For this bottleneck to have created the disparity in genetic diversity and allowed for the rapid evolution of the pattern of isolation by distance, there is a strong implication "that at least Africans and non-Africans are distinct evolutionary lineages" (Templeton 1998, p. 637). This implication is reflected in the continued use of evolutionary trees to express population relationships and history (Caspari, 2003).

Vince Sarich once quipped, "physicians bury their mistakes, paleoanthropologists rename theirs," and while he was addressing bones and not theories about them, he touched on an essential truth. Long-dead theories are continually resuscitated with new names, and one wonders whether the development of paleoanthropology is at all as Delisle describes it: "under the action of competing or successive theories"? Take the case of the Presapiens theory (Vallois, 1954), which claimed the existence of a human form within Europe during the Middle Pleistocene that had modern characteristics and showed a unique relationship to living people (Hammond, 1988). This ancient presapiens form existed alongside more "specialized" archaic human groups, most especially the Neandertals, in a kind of Pleistocene polygenic arrangement. Later events caused the overspecialized Neandertals to die out, leaving the descendants of the presapiens in sole dominion of Europe and (in this manifestly Eurocentric theory) its future colonial possessions elsewhere in the world. The original Presapiens theory built on fossils with incorrect dates like Galley Hill, fossils with partial and possibly incorrectly reconstructed anatomy, like Fontéchevade II, and the important Piltdown fossil that was an outright fraud, explains none of today's Middle Pleistocene evidence from Europe. Yet the Presapiens theory's core assumption that "modern" and archaic human species long coexisted with each other is an essential element in current theories of human origins, including some versions of the theory of recent African origin and the continued assertion that until a short time ago there were competing human species in Europe and other limited geographic areas (Tattersall, 2000). Some geneticists currently claim that our presapiens ancestors existed as a virtual "lost tribe," isolated from all archaic humans for a million years or more (Harpending et al., 1998). None of these are explicitly described as "Presapiens Theories" by their authors or proponents, but it is difficult to see them as anything else.

All of this raises the depressing question of whether paleoanthropologists can ever refute their theories; is there any sense that the profession can be seen to advance as one theory replaces another? One would think that in the Multiregional–Out-of-Africa (recent African speciation and worldwide replacement) debate a refutation should be possible, since contrary to some (Willermet & Hill, 1997), each of these is an unambiguous refutation of the other. The subject of the debate is the phylogenetic relationship of living humans to ancient humans known from the Pleistocene fossil record. Some have supported the hypothesis of a clear phylogenetic boundary between living people and some recent fossils on one side, and most ancient fossil humans on the other. Others have rejected the idea that such a phylogenetic boundary existed, and have supported the opposite idea that many living humans possess genes derived from ancient fossil humans spread widely across the Pleistocene Old World. Both of these hypotheses have numerous behavioral, material, anatomical, and genetic corollaries, so that the scope of inquiry has come to involve an impressive complexity. In their broadest interpretations, Multiregional evolution describes change within a species (within an evolutionary lineage) and Out of Africa describes change between species, change only when there are species splits. They could both be valid mechanisms of change during the evolution of a single clade, but not at the same time: They cannot account for the same set of observations.

But if theories don't replace each other but rather recycle under new descriptions of old ideas, can we at least expect that paleoanthropology makes progress because it is discovery driven and the discoveries accumulate? I remember many meetings of the American Association of Physical Anthropologists when Clark Howell would get up before the audience and exhort the young professionals to "dig, dig, dig!" How I wished it was appropriate to stand up and exhort them to "think, think, think," but the time never seemed right, and so I did this by teaching instead. I would like to believe that when my career is reviewed, my students are known first and foremost for thinking. Ironically, the scientist most strongly advocating the continued accumulation of fossils is the most strongly negative about their potential for resolving the main issues in the profession:

> Models and hypotheses of hominid diversification, including that of origins of genus *Homo* and of modern humans, are surely incomplete, and some more seriously flawed. . . . It is probably true that an encompassing scenario of hominin evolution is beyond our grasp, now if not forever (Howell, 1996, p. 31)

The modern human origins debate, as described above, has extended over a duration of more than sixty years; in spite of an explosive growth in the human fossil record and the incorporation of genetic studies of living populations and short fragments of ancient mtDNA into paleoanthropological considerations, the two opposing positions have been essentially the same during this entire time span (Wolpoff & Caspari, 1997; Hawks & Wolpoff, 2003). Their resolution, through the convincing refutation of at least one position, is much more likely to come from applying the proper, sophisticated theory.

PASSIVE CONSUMER OR INNOVATOR OF THEORY?

Are the conditions finally ripe for paleoanthropology "to receive deep theoretical inputs from specific evolutionary theories and/or to contribute genuinely to their elaboration?" David Pilbeam once described paleoanthropology as a consumer science, dependent on the observations and innovations of other sciences to make significant theoretical advances. I am not at all sure this is true, and in my doubt lies a source of optimism.

The theoretical changes that are key for the continued evolution of paleoanthropology are for the most part developments within paleoanthropology or in response posed by questions that arise out of paleoanthropological research. Karl Pearson, for instance, developed many of his descriptive statistics and multivariate procedures to cope with questions raised by the very large sample of varying human crania, and their relation to each other and the small fossil record. These approaches continue to fuel an inductivist interpretation of functional and phylogenetic relationships. The plethora of human data continues to grow, and well-funded research results in more details being known about evolution within the human species than about evolution within any other. Models of behavior and evolution have come to play a significant role in achieving this understanding. It could be argued that studies of no other species have combined so many complex interrelationships of genetic and anatomical variation at interspecies and intraspecies levels, for both ancient and modern genetic and anatomical data. Let's look again at which field is the consumer and which the innovator.

The observation of low variation among recent humans has been drawn into sharp relief both by the accumulation of genetic evidence during the past four decades and by the even longer-term statistical work on various anthroposcopic traits. Certainly humans are variable, particularly in an anatomical context, and humans are polytypic in a geographic context. But as great as the entire global range of human anatomical variation may be, it is so small that it fails to encompass most known hominid fossils from only 100,000 to 50,000 years ago (Hawks & Wolpoff, 2003). The variation among human genes, both within and among populations, is equally slight, and exactly the same can be said of the small but growing sample of ancient mtDNA: It all lies outside the range of modern variation. If selection on human anatomy and behavior, abetted by social or cultural factors, were the cause of our similarity, then the evolution of recent people may have involved a large population spread across large regions of the world. But if genetic drift was the cause, with only limited contributions of selection or other factors, then the evolution of recent people must have occurred within a very small population, one that must have been geographically restricted. This fundamental conundrum informs a far more general problem of evolutionary biology. Surely if the history of paleoanthropology in the twentieth century has any understandings to offer, it must include the insight that the resolution of this question, of the roles played by selection or drift in creating evolutionary change, is not likely to result from further accumulation of fossil data. As this resolution is worked out, as argued above, we can expect that insight will continue to come from the application of theory to the data at hand (i.e., Ackermann & Cheverud, 2004). And so I would argue, as I learned early in my professional career, that the true knowledge of human evolution is the knowledge of the theories explaining it.

REFERENCES

Ackermann, R.R., and J.M. Cheverud (2004). Detecting Genetic Drift Versus Selection in Human Evolution. *Proceedings of the National Academy of Sciences* (USA), 101(52): 17946–17951.

Bowler, P.J. (1986). *Theories of Human Evolution: A Century of Debate, 1844–1944.* Baltimore: John Hopkins University Press.

Bowler, P.J. (1997). Paleoanthropology Theory. In F. Spencer (Ed.), *History of Physical Anthropology. An Encyclopedia.* (New York: Garland). pp. 785–790.

Brace, C.L. (1981). Tales of the Phylogenetic Woods: The Evolution and Significance of Evolutionary Trees. *American Journal of Physical Anthropology*, 56(4): 411–429.

Caspari, R. (2003). From Types to Populations: A Century of Race, Physical Anthropology and the American Anthropological Association. *American Anthropologist*, 105(1): 63–74.

Coon, C.S. (1962). *The Origin of Races.* (New York: Knopf).

DeVore, P.L. (Ed.). (1965). The Origin of Man. Transcript of a symposium sponsored by the Wenner-Gren Foundation for Anthropological Research. (New York: Current Anthropology).

Fragaszy, D. (2003). Making Space for Traditions. *Evolutionary Anthropology*, 12(2): 61–70.

Hammond, M. (1988). The Shadow of Man Paradigm in Paleoanthropology, 1911–1945. In G.W. Stocking Jr. (Ed.), *Bones, Bodies, Behavior. Essays on Biological Anthropology.* University of Wisconsin Press, Madison. pp. 117–137.

Harpending, H.C., M.A. Batzer, M. Gurven, L.B. Jorde, A.R. Rogers, and S.T. Sherry (1998). Genetic Traces of Ancient Demography. *Proceedings of the National Academy of Sciences* (USA), 95(4): 1961–1967.

Harwood, J. (1993). *Styles of Scientific Thought: The German Genetics Community 1900–1933.* (Chicago: University of Chicago Press).

Hawks, J., and M.H. Wolpoff (2003). Sixty Years of Modern Human Origins in the American Anthropological Association. *American Anthropologist*, 105(1): 87–98.

Hooton, E.A. (1946). *Up From the Ape,* revised edition. (New York: MacMillan).

Howell, F.C. (1996). Thoughts on the Study and Interpretation of the Human Fossil Record. In W.E. Meikle, F.C. Howell, and N.G. Jablonski (Eds.), *Contemporary Issues in Human Evolution.* Wattis Symposium Series in Anthropology, California Academy of Sciences Memoir 21: 1–45.

Huxley, J.S. (Ed.). (1940). *The New Systematics.* (Oxford: Clarendon).

Keith, A. (1948). *A New Theory of Human Evolution.* (New York: Philosophical Library).

Mayr, E. (1963). *Animal Species and Evolution.* (Cambridge: Belknap Press of Harvard University Press).

Mayr, E. (1982). Reflections on Human Paleontology. In F. Spencer (Ed.), *A History of American Physical Anthropology 1930–1980.* New York: Academic Press. pp. 231–237.

Nishida, T. (1987). Local Traditions and Cultural Transmission. In B.B. Smuts, D.L. Cheney, R.M. Seyfarth, R.W. Wrangham, and T. Struhsacker (Eds.). *Primate Societies.* Chicago: University of Chicago Press. pp. 462–474.

Proctor, R.N. (2003). Three Roots of Human Recency. *Current Anthropology*, 44(2): 213–239.

Richerson, P.J., and R. Boyd (2004). *Not by Genes Alone: How Culture Transformed Human Evolution.* (Chicago: University of Chicago).

Tattersall, I. (2000). Paleoanthropology: The Last Half-century. *Evolutionary Anthropology*, 9(1): 2–16.

Tattersall, I. (2002). *The Monkey in the Mirror. Essays on the Science of What Makes Us Human.* (New York: Oxford).

TEMPLETON, A.R. (1998). Human Races: A Genetic and Evolutionary Perspective. *American Anthropologist*, 100(3): 632–650.

VALLOIS, H.V. 1954 Neanderthals and Presapiens. *Journal of the Royal Anthropological Institute*, 84: 111–130.

WILLERMET, C.M., AND B. HILL (1997). Fuzzy Set Theory and Its Implications for Species Models. In G.A. Clark and C.M. Willermet (Eds.), *Conceptual Issues in Modern Human Origins Research*. New York: Aldine de Gruyter. pp. 77–88, and combined bibliography on pp. 437–492.

WOLPOFF, M.H. (1999). *Paleoanthropology*. (2nd ed.) (New York: McGraw-Hill).

WOLPOFF, M.H., AND R. CASPARI (1997). *Race and Human Evolution*. (New York: Simon and Schuster).

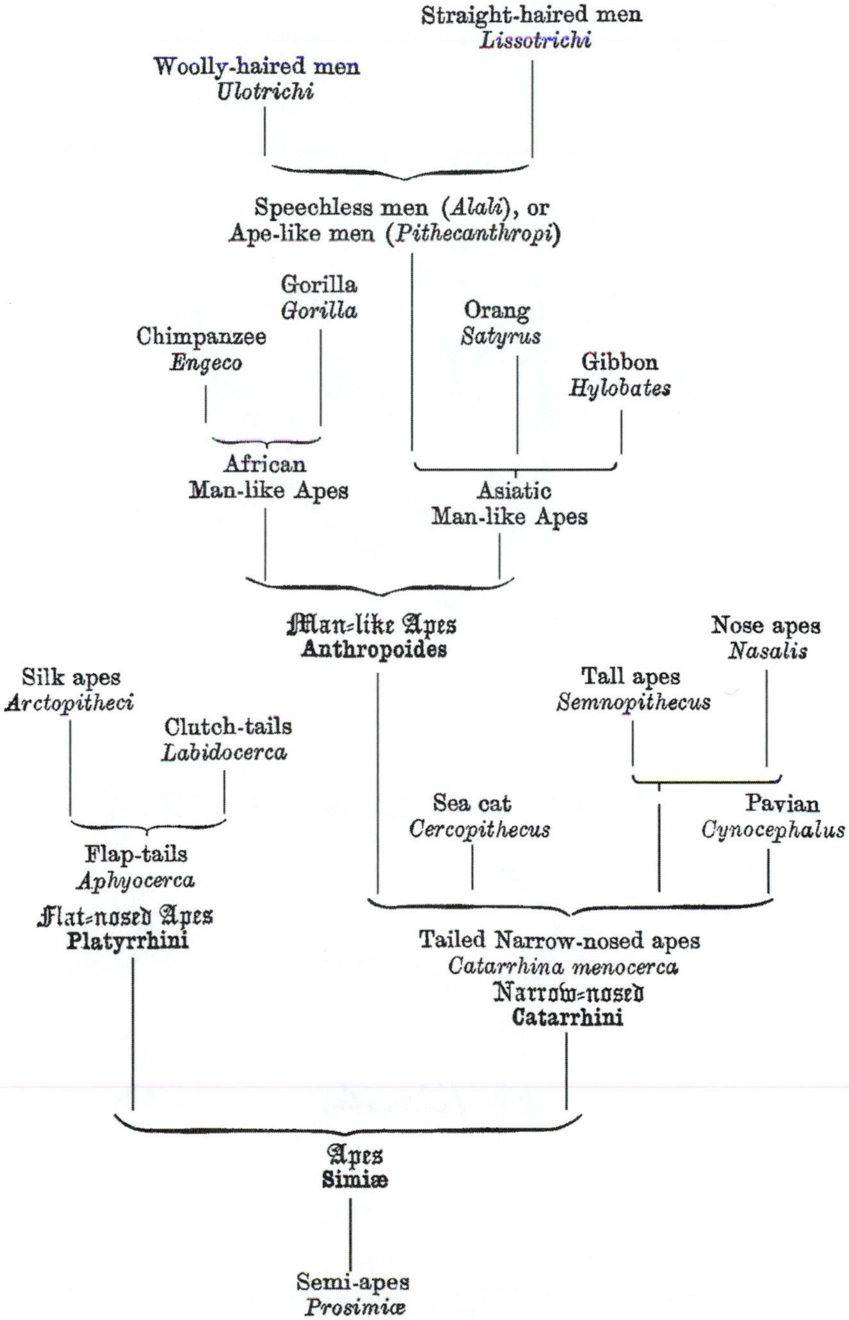

Figure 1 Ernst Haeckel's primate phylogenetic tree of 1876.

Figure 2 Charles Darwin's primate phylogenetic tree of 1868.

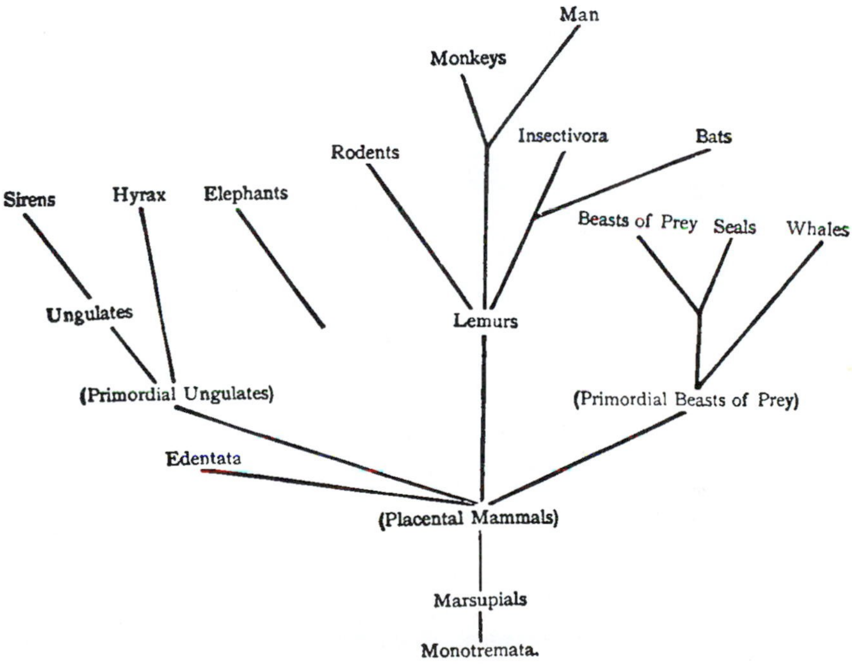

Figure 3 Oscar Schmidt's mammal phylogenetic tree of 1887.

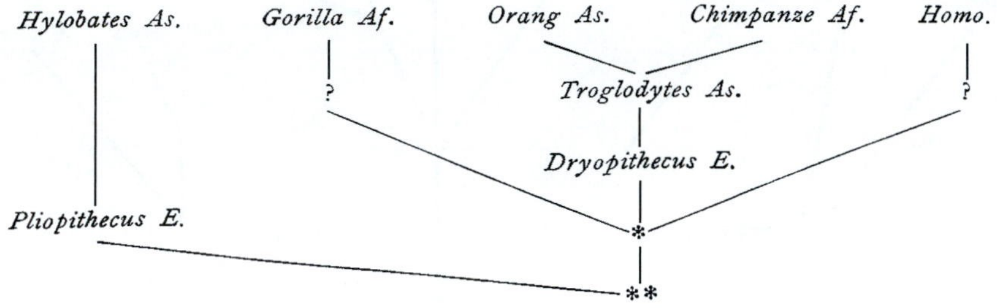

Figure 4 Max Schlosser's primate phylogenetic tree of 1888.

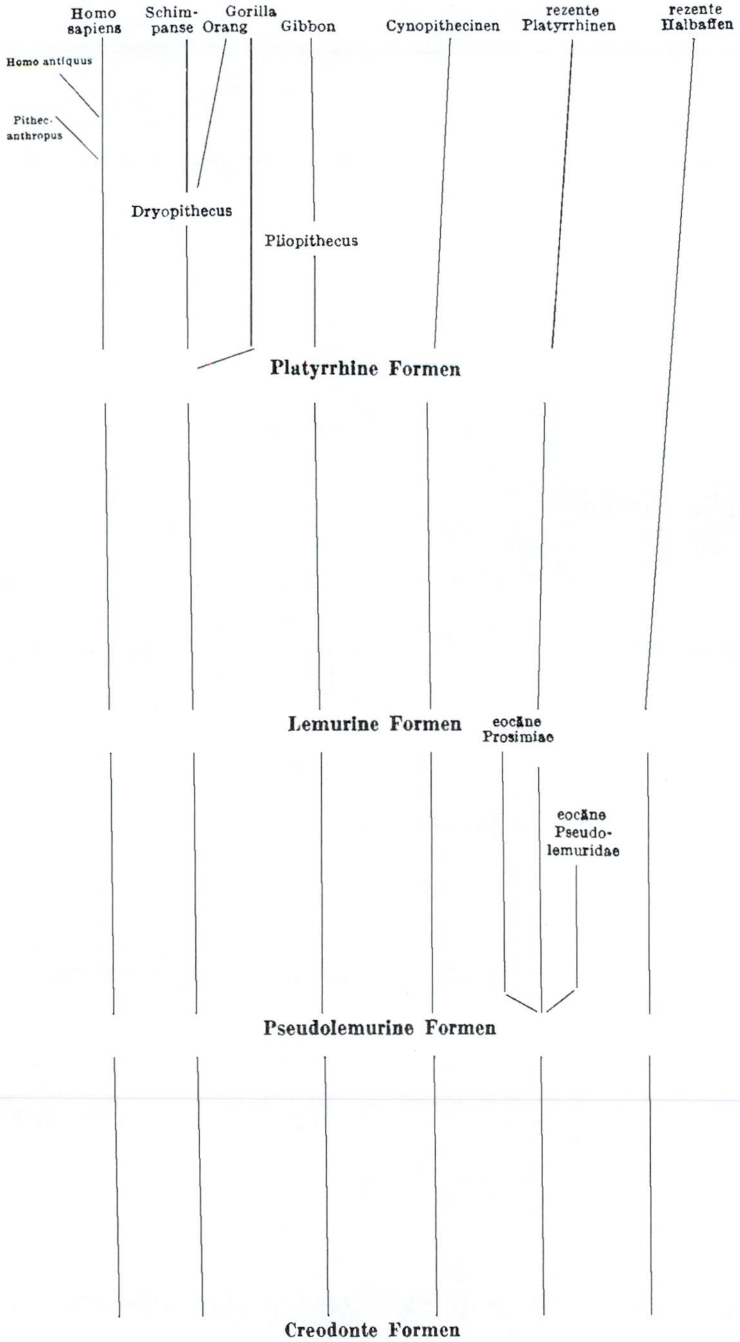

Figure 5 Paul Adloff's primate phylogenetic tree of 1908.

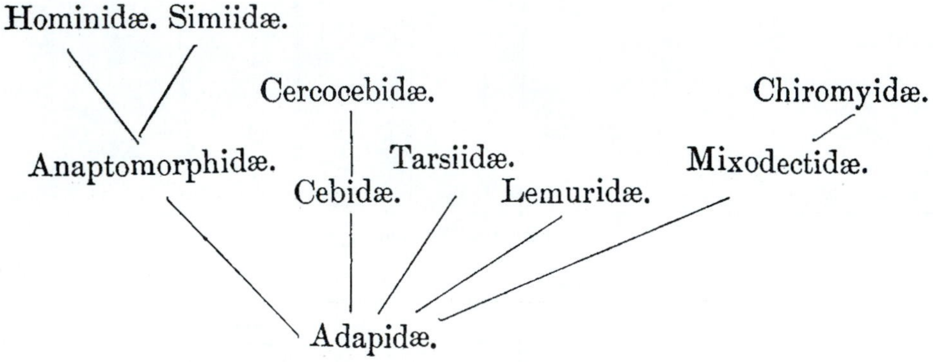

Figure 6 Edward Cope's primate phylogenetic tree of 1888.

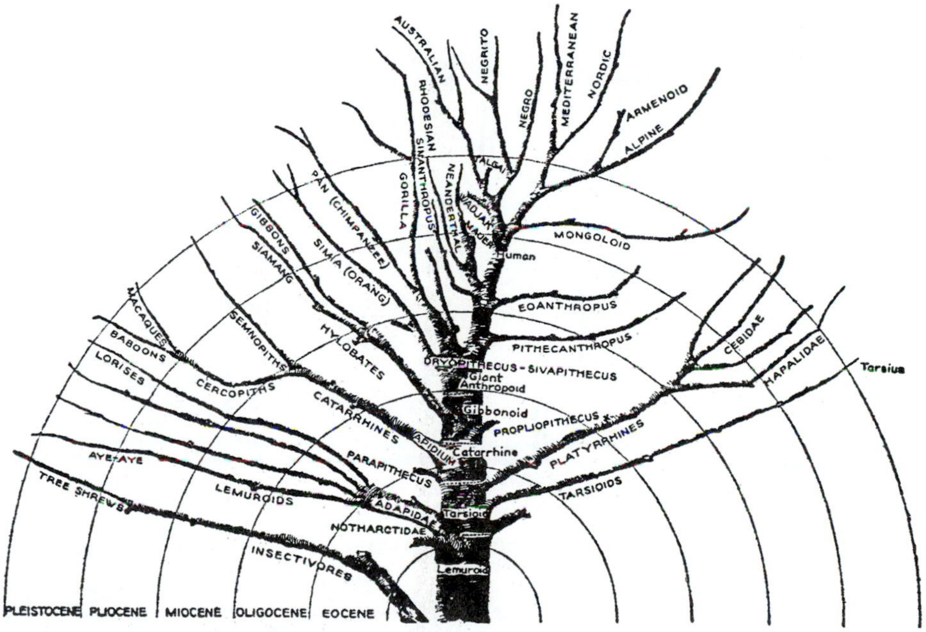

Figure 7 Albert Hooton's primate phylogenetic tree of 1931.

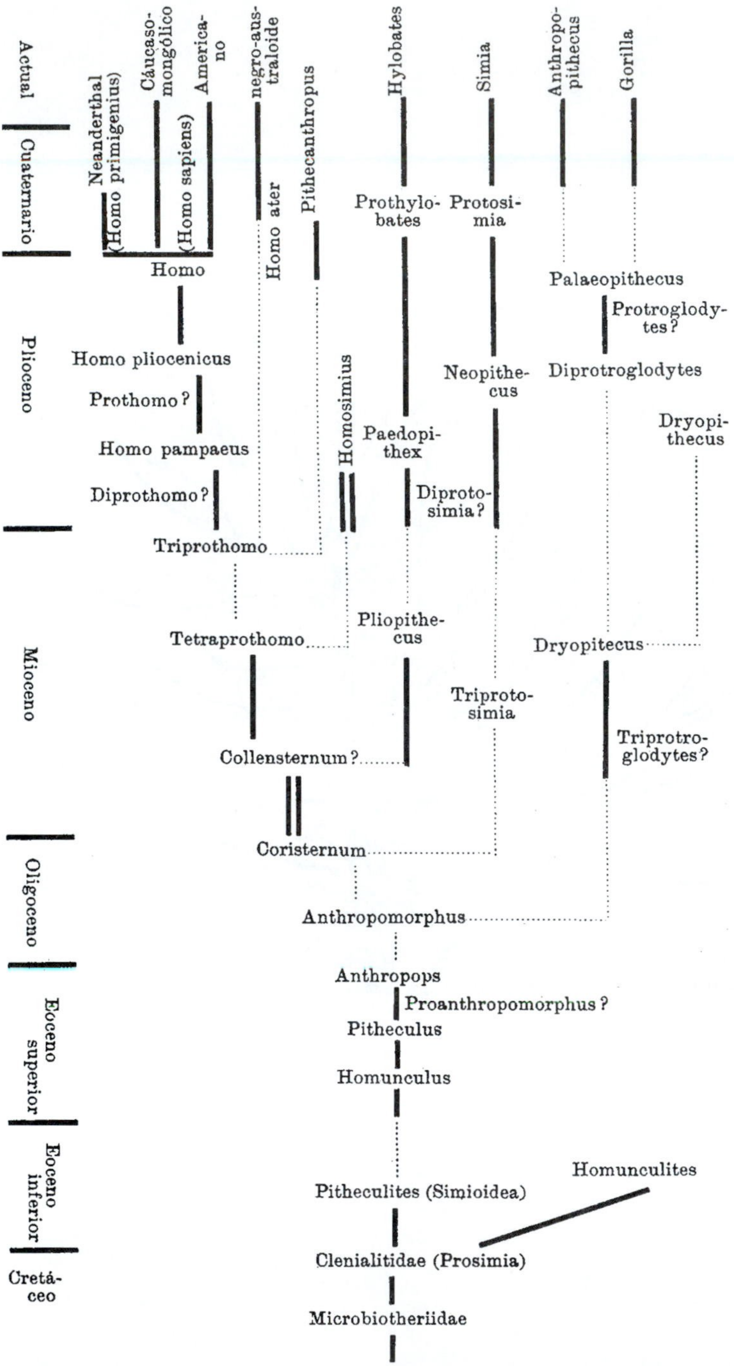

Figure 8 Florentino Ameghino's primate phylogenetic tree of 1907.

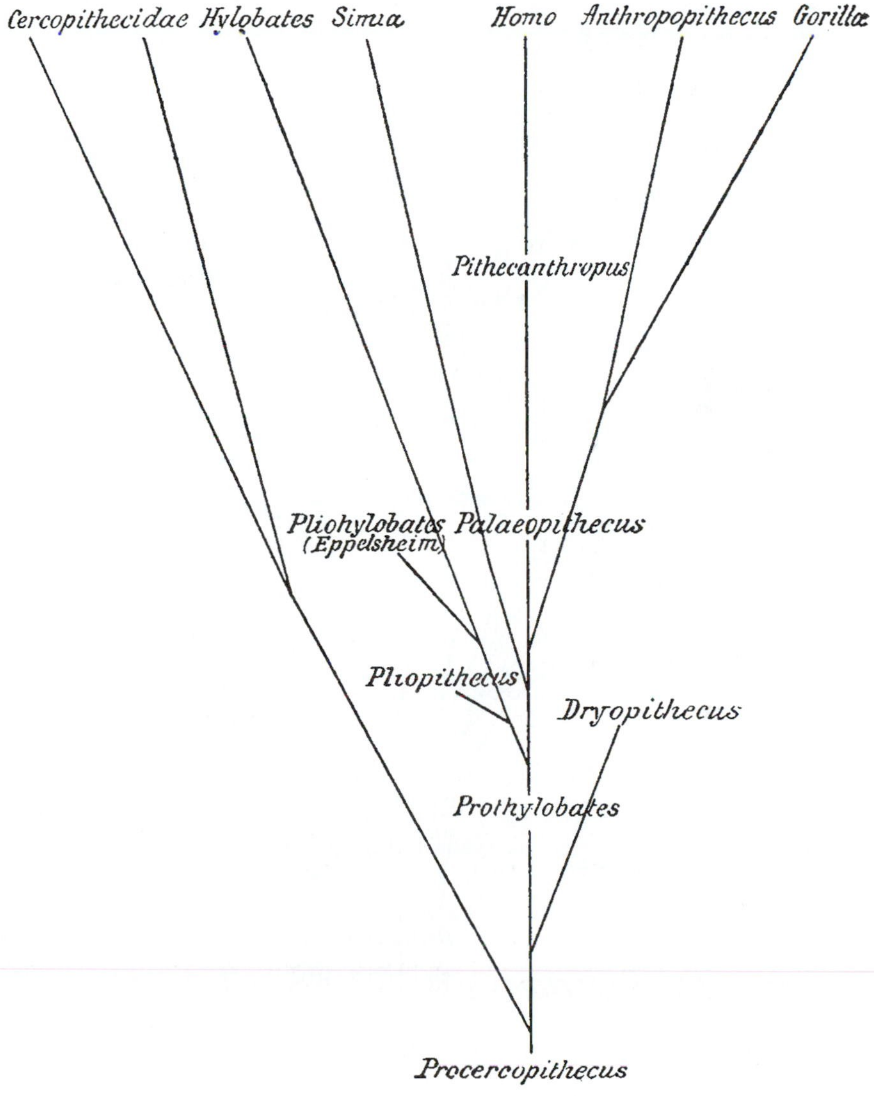

Figure 9 Eugène Dubois's primate phylogenetic tree of 1896.

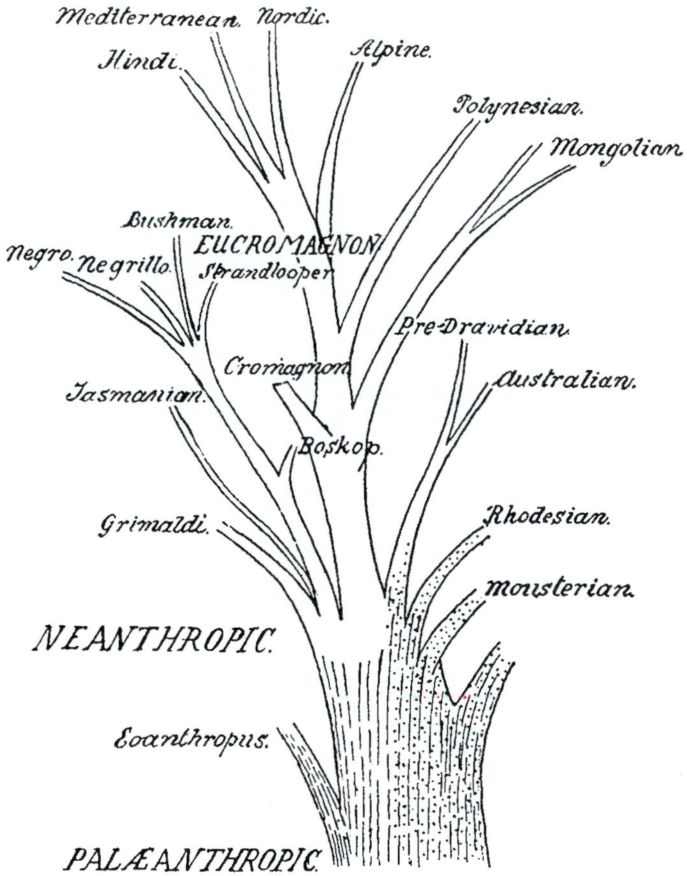

Figure 10 William Pycraft's parallel phylogenetic tree of 1925.

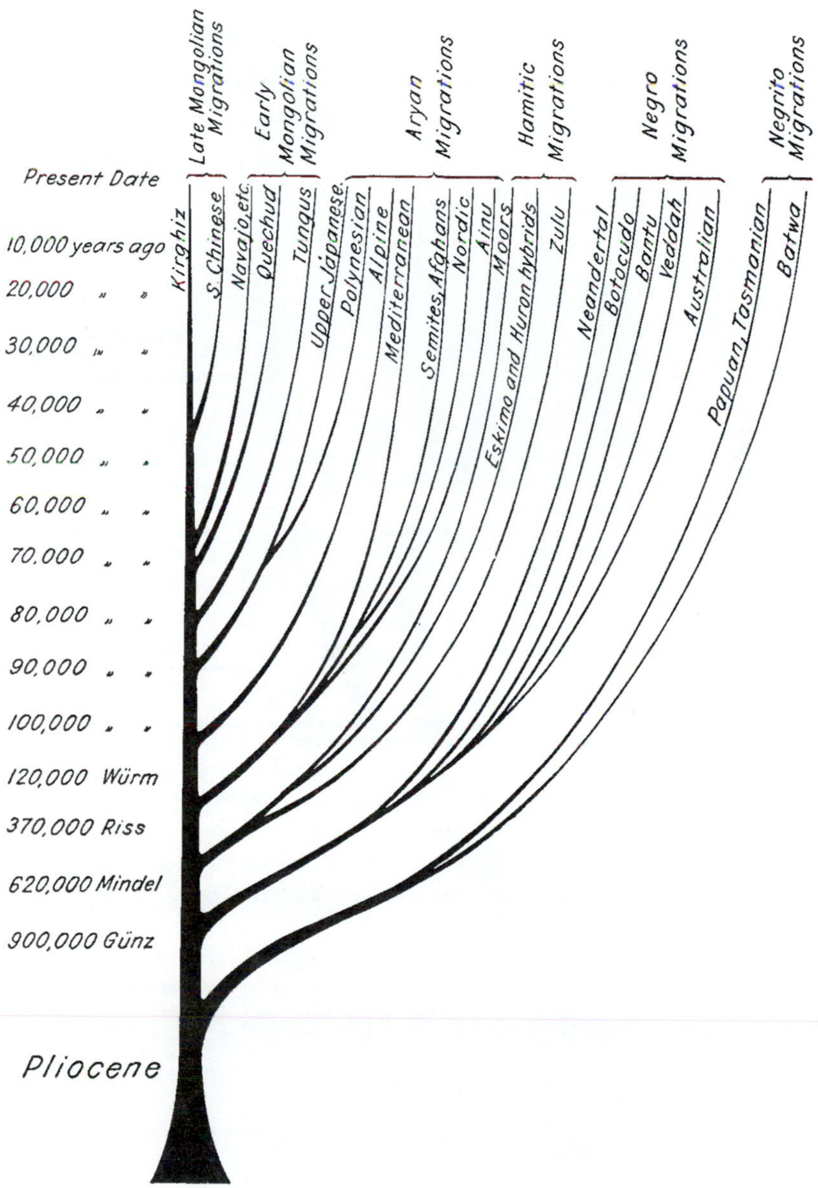

Figure 11 Griffith Taylor's parallel phylogenetic tree of 1919.

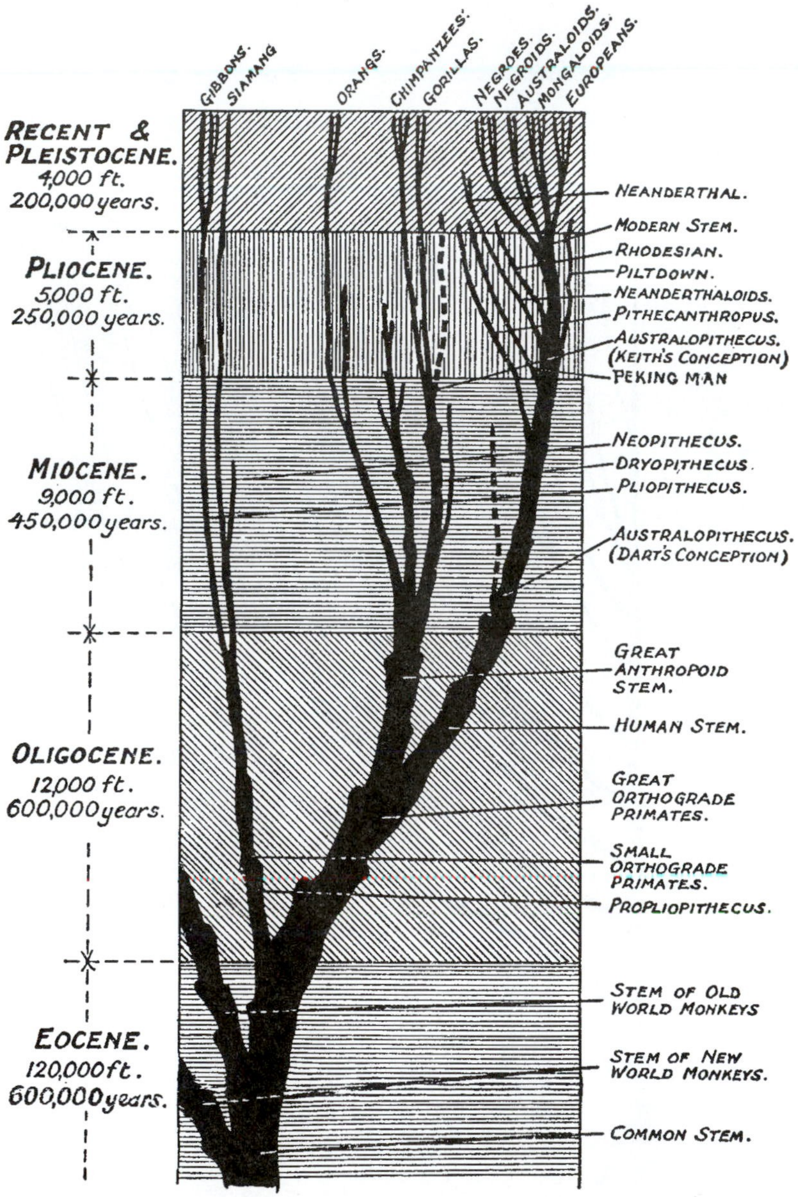

Figure 12 Arthur Keith's primate phylogenetic tree of 1931.

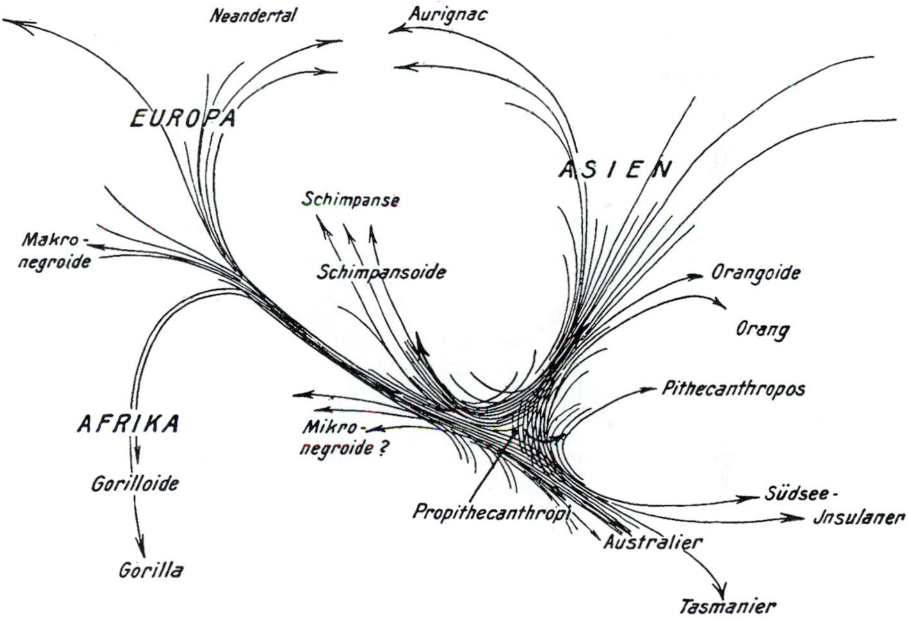

Figure 13 Hermann Klaatsch's polyphyletic tree of 1910.

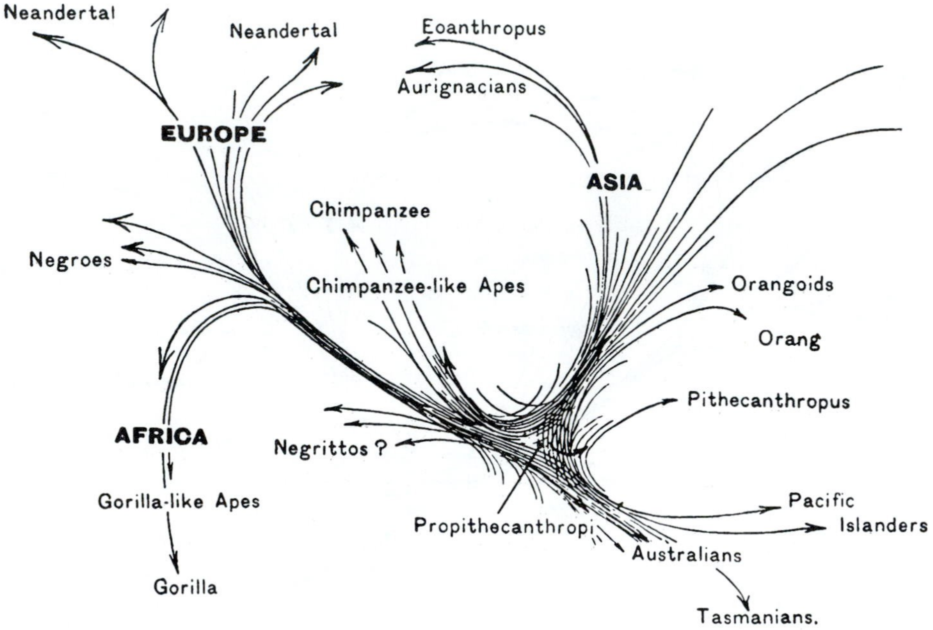

Figure 14 H. von Buttel-Reepen's polyphyletic tree of 1913.

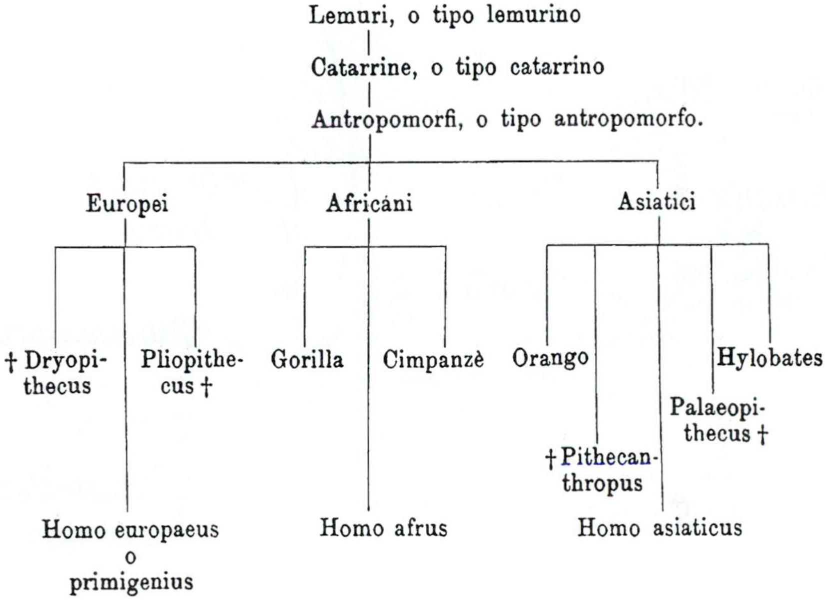

Figure 15 Giuseppe Sergi's polyphyletic tree of 1908.

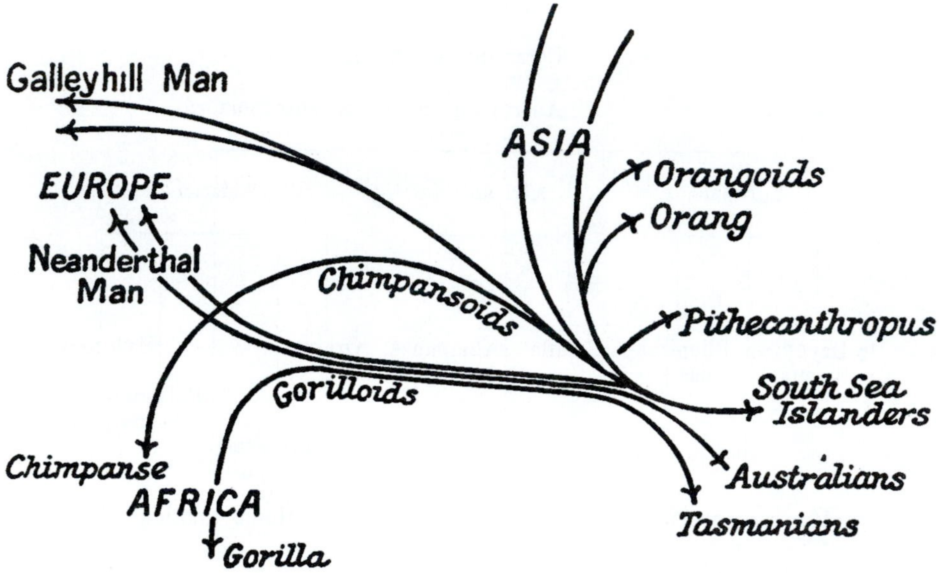

Figure 16 John Gray's polyphyletic tree of 1911.

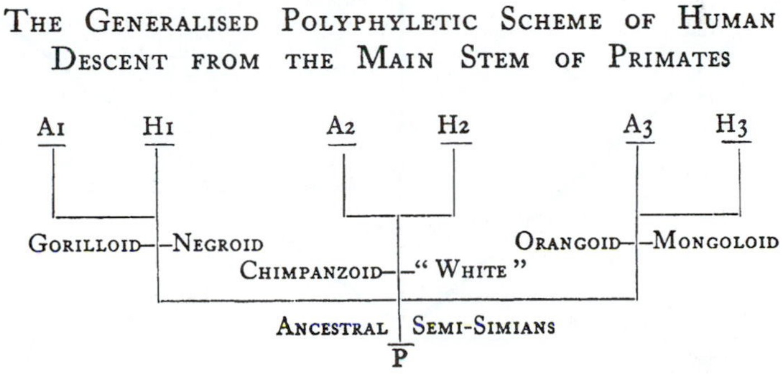

Figure 17 F.G. Crookshank's polyphyletic tree of 1931.

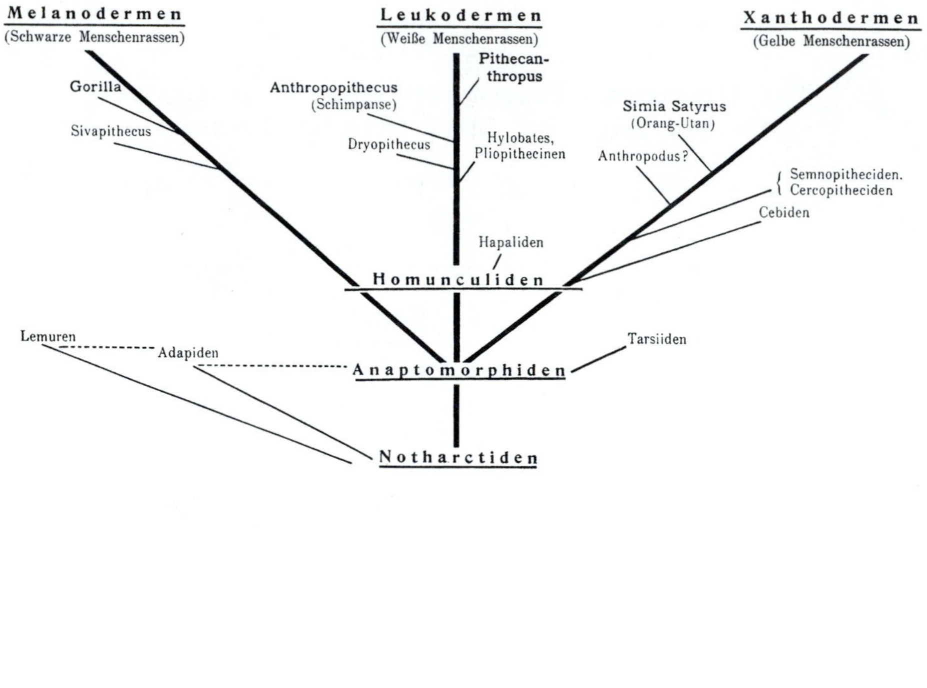

Figure 18 Theodor Arldt's polyphyletic tree of 1915.

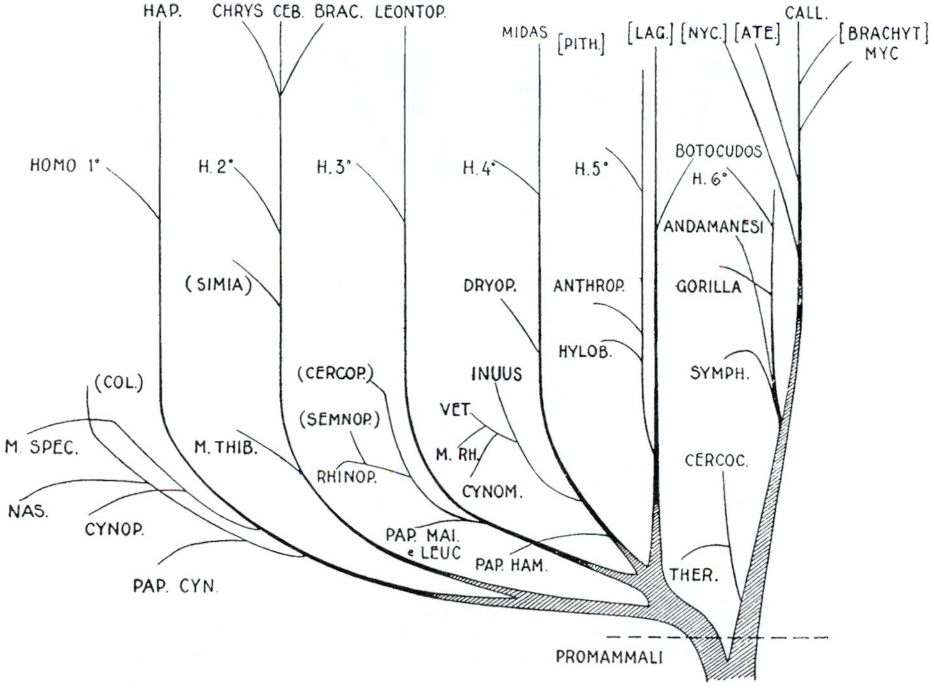

Figure 19 Gioacchino Sera's polyphyletic tree of 1918.

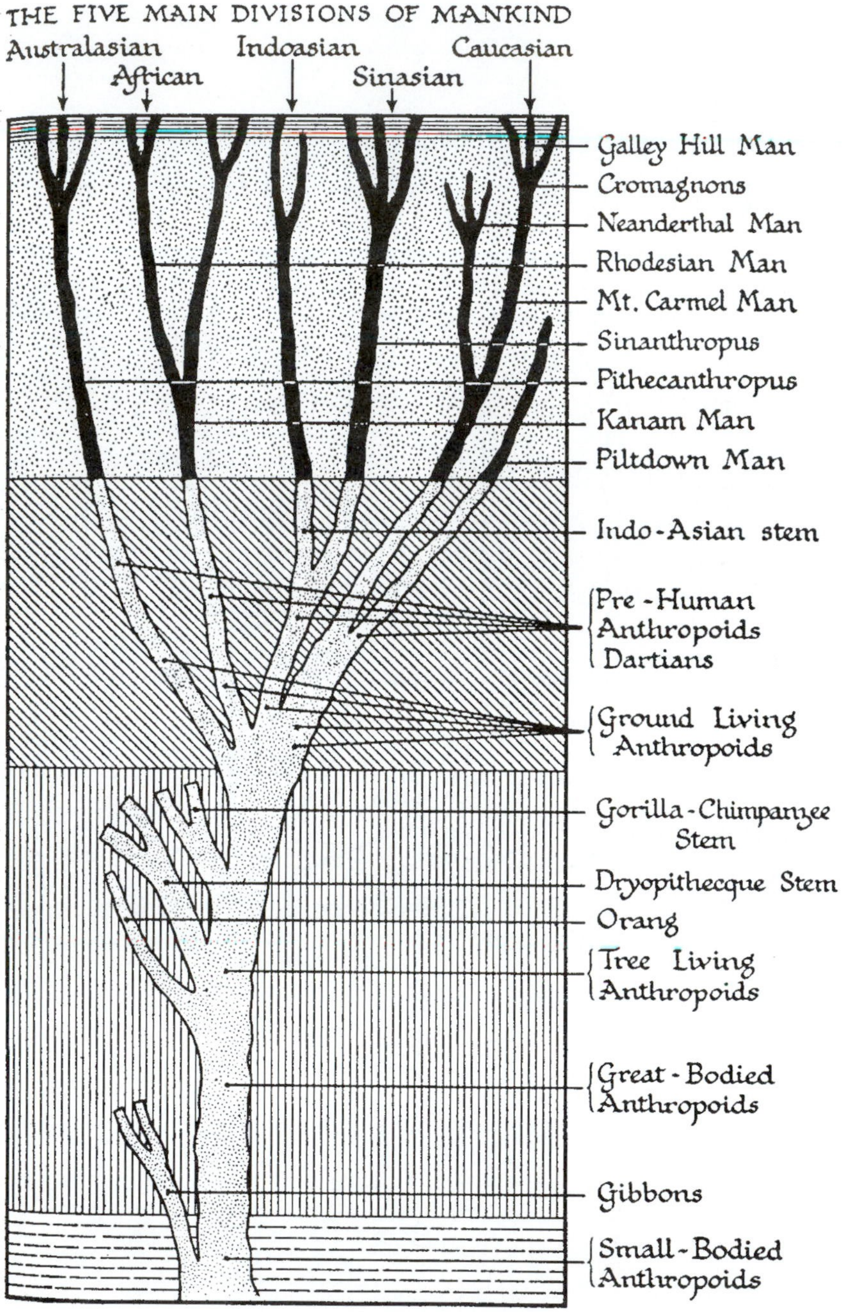

Figure 20 Arthur Keith's parallel phylogenetic tree of 1948.

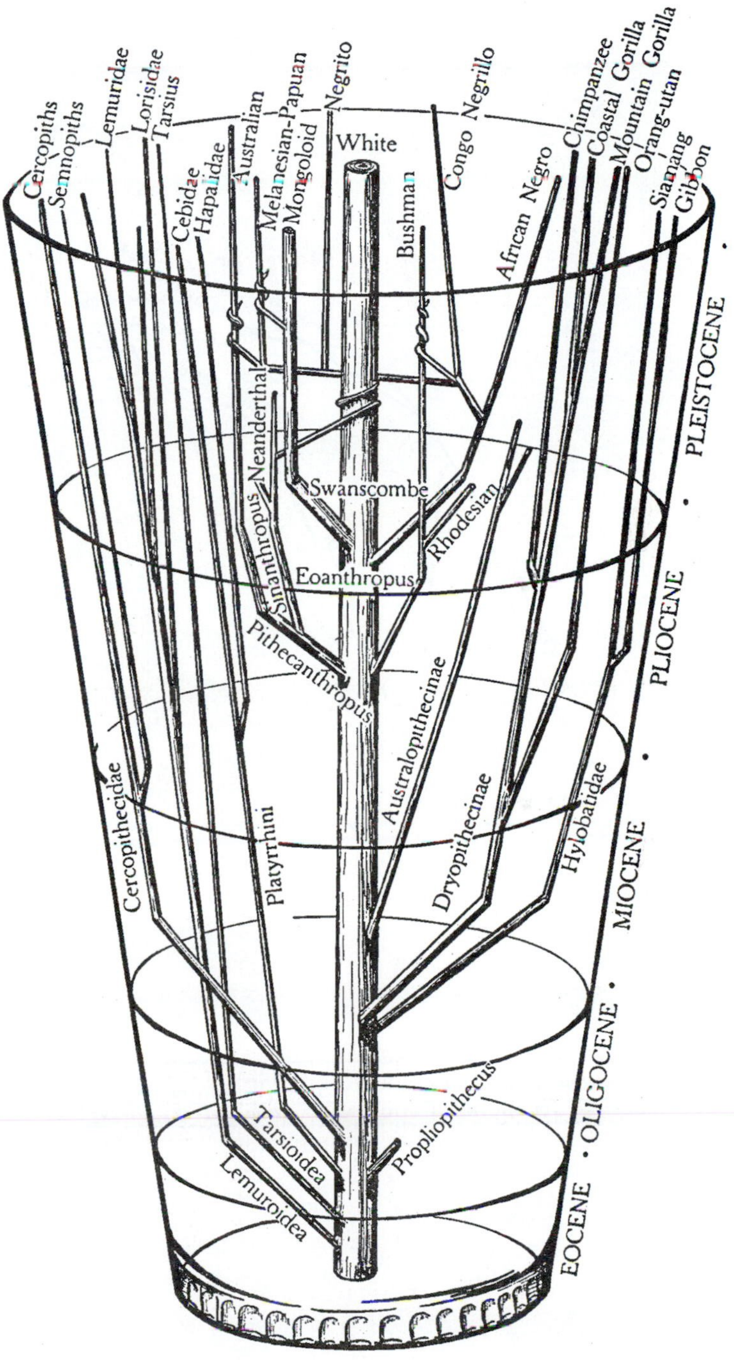

Figure 21 Albert Hooton's parallel phylogenetic tree of 1946.

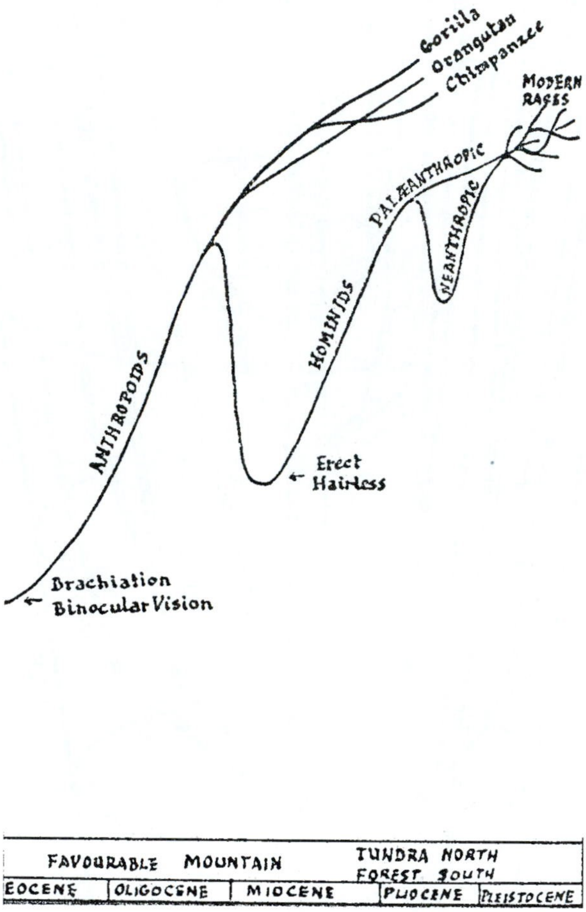

Figure 22 J.R. Marett's parallel phylogenetic tree of 1936.

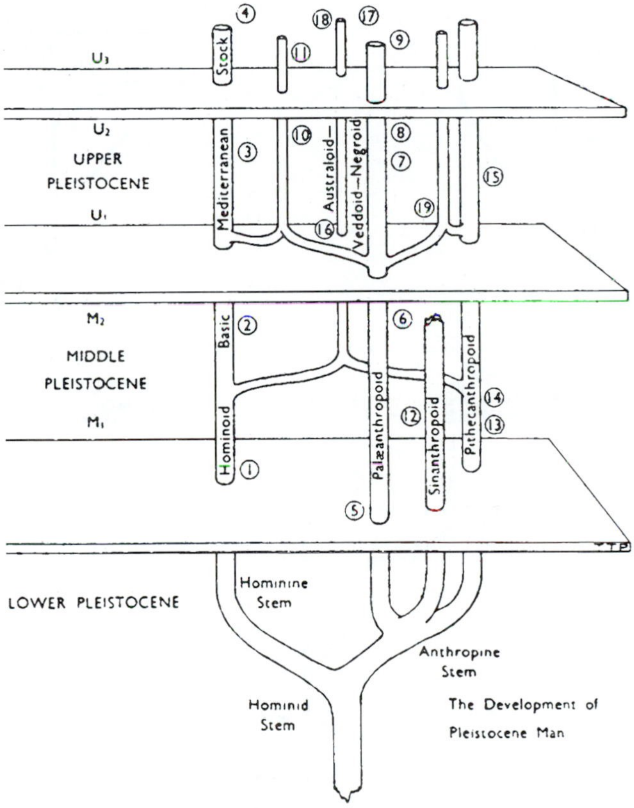

Figure 23 T.T. Paterson's parallel phylogenetic tree of 1940.

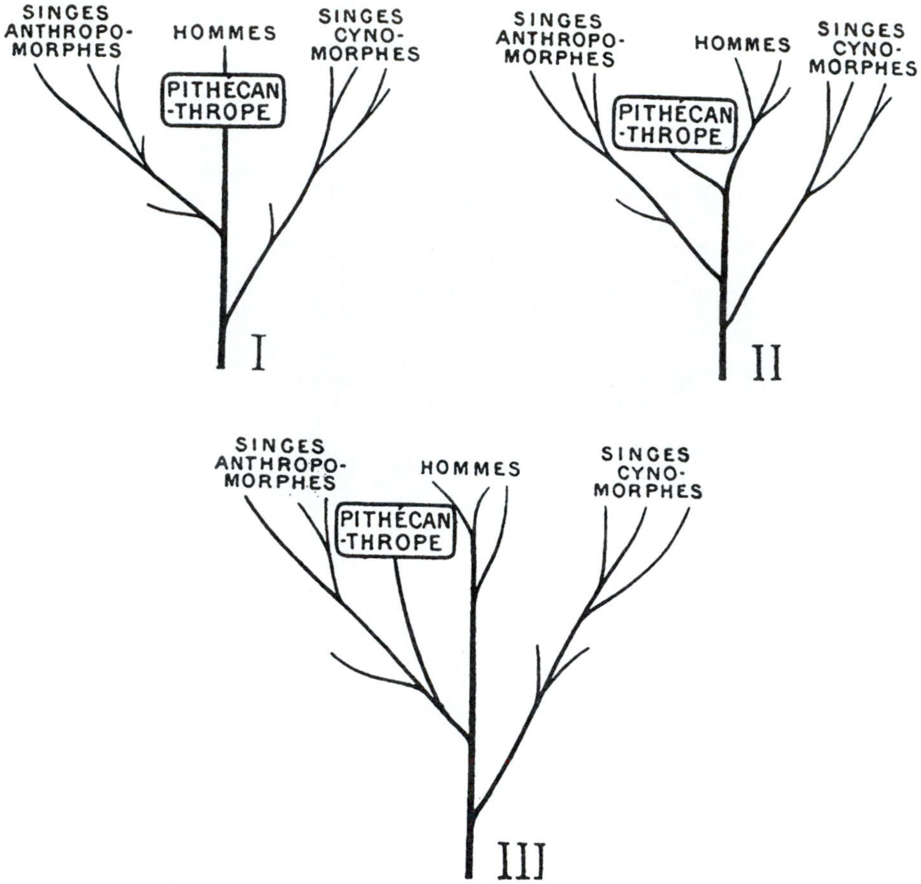

Figure 24 Marcellin Boule's changing perspective on *Pithecanthropus* in the 1930s and 1940s.

1

The History of Paleoanthropology

INTRODUCTION

Paleoanthropologists devote their lives to the search and the understanding of human origins. They do so because they are fascinated about this subject, no doubt, but also because they believe they can contribute to the resolution of a number of uncertainties pertaining to the biological and cultural evolution of humankind. After all, who would invest that much time and effort in a quest judged insoluble? Yet, the past few decades have been difficult ones for optimistic paleoanthropologists who contend that a resolution—quick or slow—of major questions relevant to human evolution is reachable. Apparently, the difficulties arise both from inside and outside the field of paleoanthropology.

Outside that field, several factors have converged to raise doubts about the progressiveness of the scientific enterprise in general. For instance, sociologists of science have been promoting the idea that the development of science is partly or entirely obstructed by the fact that the elaboration of knowledge is a social enterprise (e.g., Barnes, Bloor, & Heury, 1996). As such, science is influenced by the wider culture and the values of its time. In the sociologists's eye, objective scientific knowledge is something which is hard to come by.

Philosophers of science, on their part, have been promoting that the establishment of knowledge is anything but a straightforward process limited to collecting empirical facts. Instead, they hold that empirical facts do not stand on their own but need to be inserted in a wider theoretical context to take on their meaning. Empirical facts are meaningless when cut from the theoretical conditions which gave rise to them. According to this view, science is as much a business of gathering empirical facts as building theoretical context to interpret them. In addition to empirical facts, the scientific enterprise comprises theories per se, but also methodological principles, conceptual tools, and ontological issues. Competing explanations may therefore either involve differences of empirical facts and/or theoretical contexts.

To make things more complicated still, philosophers of science hold that the scientific enterprise is rarely about comparing competing explanations in order to decide once and for all which one is the more appropriate. Instead, it is argued that knowledge is a historical process being slowly elaborated over time by gathering empirical facts but also by building theoretical contexts. If this is the case, then the scientific quest is not so much about comparing full-grown theories but rather about comparing much more complex and changing entities best called paradigms (Kuhn, 1970), research programs (Lakatos, 1978) or research traditions (Laudan, 1977). In this perspective of science, it becomes difficult to fully and definitely prove or disprove an explanation, because future discoveries (empirical or theoretical in nature) may change the assessment we have of it.

Practicing scientists live in a scientific world rendered more complex by the studies made by the sociologists and the philosophers of science. According to this view, the establishment of an objective knowledge is everything but straightforward. If the most optimistic paleoanthropologists are not discouraged as yet about the possibility of resolving major questions in human evolution, then perhaps the historical studies made about their own field will. It will be seen that these studies convey the impression that the field of paleoanthropology is not a progressive one, but is rather largely at a standstill.

THE HISTORIOGRAPHY OF REPETITION

It is not uncommon to hear that the development of paleoanthropology has largely been characterized by the opposition and the alternation of two main phylogenetic hypotheses: unilinear versus multilinear. For instance, Kurtén (1981: 61) wrote:

> Our view of the fossil history of man is affected not only by study of the fossil remains but also by current theories . . . : 1) the single-species interpretation, 2) the multiple-species or branching interpretation . . . Historically, there has been a tendancy to alternation between these views.

Being more explicit than Kurtén on this alternation of phylogenetic hypotheses, Hammond (1988: 135) suggested that the field of human evolution was under fifty-year cycles: "[T]heory in human paleontology seems to move in fifty-year cycles. . . . Around 1910 the multilinear paradigm replaced this initial [unilinear] evolutionary model, and fifty years later it too was challenged." Hammond even conjectured that this alternation of models might also be true in the future. In yet another manifestation of the assumed importance of the opposition and the alternation of unilinear and multilinear phylogenetic hypotheses in paleoanthropology, Bowler (1997: 785, 789) wrote:

> One of the greatest theoretical divisions in the field has been that between the linear and the multilinear models of hominid evolution. . . . [D]ebates that have plagued

> paleoanthropology throughout its history continue to resurface in modernized forms. . . . [T]he basic issues of linearity versus divergence, and continuity versus displacement, remain.

Whether based on fossil discoveries, evolutionary theories, or social factors, these three distinct assessments depict the historical development of the field of human evolution as being characterized by recurring debates. Although this may or may not have been the intended goal pursued by these scholars, such assessments leave the reader with the strong impression that very little progress has been made over human phylogeny since the inception of the field, as this field seems trapped in endless debates over the very same phylogenetic hypotheses.

THE HISTORIOGRAPHY OF STAGNATION

Whereas a number of scholars evaluated the development of paleoanthropology through the unilinear/multilinear hypotheses of human phylogeny, others turned to scenarios of hominization. For instance, Stoczkowski (1994, [2002]) analysed a host of such scenarios in the nineteenth century and the late twentieth century by looking at both the individual features they are displaying (bipedality, big brain, small canines, tools, etc.) as well as the nature of the causal relationships postulated to bind them. On the basis of many recurrent features and causal relationships in these scenarios, Stoczkowski (2002: 127) concluded that the scenarios of hominization have changed little since the inception of paleoanthropology:

> It is obvious, therefore, that the core of the knowledge employed in hominisation scenarios is based on a relatively inert structure that prolongs the tradition of conjectural anthropology and has not been remodelled, in its broad outlines, either under the influence of new palaeontological and archaeological discoveries or as a consequence of the theoretical developments in biology.

Stoczkowski (2002: 35) was very explicit about the fact that he recognized in scenarios of hominization just one aspect of the field of paleoanthropology, and not the entire discipline itself. Yet, the reader is again left with the strong impression that paleoanthropology, in part or as a whole, is in a deep state of stagnation upon which any new empirical or theoretical inputs have had very little impact.

THE MAIN THESES OF THIS BOOK

This book will argue forcefully against any impression that the field of paleoanthropology is a nonprogressive research area. On the contrary, it will be seen that paleoanthropologists managed to resolve most of the major issues which plagued the quest to establish humankind's place in nature. This was done in less than 150 years. Today's debates in human evolution, no matter how acrimonious they might be, are near consensus in comparison to the pre-1935 debates. What is truly remarkable is that the number of defensible hypotheses in paleoanthropology has been continually decreasing throughout the twentieth century, whereas at the same time the number of scholars taking part in this quest has drastically increased. The notion that paleoanthropology has largely been at a standstill since its inception essentially rests on a very limited number of historical and epistemological analyses which are far too incomplete. It is unfortunate that such analyses have been neglected by historians and philosophers as well as paleoanthropologists. It is hoped that this book will contribute to filling in the gap.

This book promotes three main theses (and a host of minor and related theses). Although these are made more explicit in the remainder of the book, it is useful to enumerate them at this stage. First of all, there will be no attempt to evaluate the possible role of social factors on the development of paleoanthropology. It is unclear if such factors ever had any significant impact on the field. This question will be left to the sociologists of science. The first main thesis promoted in this book holds that the field of paleoanthropology—as defined by its quest to establish humankind's place within the tree of life—is not constituted of several competing theories, paradigms, research programs, or research traditions. Instead, it is argued that, since its inception around 1860, paleoanthropology has been founded on a single and general theory: the theory of biological evolution. This implies that a phylogenetic link exists between the living humans and the other animals. Assuming the biological evolution of humankind, paleoanthropologists have, from that time on, been debating over a number of key issues, such as humankind's closest relative among the nonhuman creatures; the antiquity of the human line; the geographical place of humankind's cradle, and so on.

The notion that the field of paleoanthropology could be founded on more than one theory (or paradigm, research program, research tradition, etc.) has been discarded on the basis that the entire quest to establish humankind's place in nature since 1860 has been remarkably coherent in its development. This is true regardless of the fact that there have been important differences of viewpoints on a number of key issues, especially prior to 1935. It has been somewhat fashionable of late to attribute any major differences of viewpoints in human evolution to differences in theories or paradigms. Although there are no objective criteria to define a theory or a paradigm, a number of philosophers of science recognize that a substantial amount of cognitive and logical differences are needed in order to justify their separateness (e.g., Hempel, 1966; Kuhn, 1970; Lakatos, 1978; Laudan, 1977; Nagel, 1979). It is not my intention here to get embroiled in a debate over how to define a theory or a paradigm as long as it is recognized that the so-called Presapiens theory, for instance, is cognitively and logically very different in nature from the Newtonian theory. I believe that the coherence with which the search for humankind's place in nature has been conducted since 1860 is best envisioned as deploying within a single theoretical context. It is on that basis that the differences of viewpoints held within this theoretical context are called here *hypotheses*. This last statement is not a commitment in any shape or form to Karl Popper's epistemology of science (see Chapter 11).

Three closely related epistemological implications flow from viewing the field of paleoanthropology as developing within a single theoretical context. First, instead of looking for a field of paleoanthropology which is characterized by tensions and oppositions between debates based on distinct theories, one is forced to look for continuities or similarities behind the distinct viewpoints or hypotheses. When viewed from this latter perspective, the three distinct epistemological stages (or time periods) through which the field of paleoanthropology has passed since 1860 becomes perfectly intelligible, cognitively and logically speaking. It will be seen that the scholars systematically exploited, during each main time period, all the possible hypotheses that were defensible on the basis of the facts that were known *then*. Hypotheses which were no longer defensible were eventually discarded, thus contributing to pushing forward the field of paleoanthropology into a new epistemological stage or time period.

The second epistemological implication is that some (though not all) of the difficulties related to knowledge building are avoided in paleoanthropology. We have seen that the philosophers of science promote that science is as much a business about gathering empirical facts as building theoretical context to interpret them. They also insist that knowledge in a research area is often carried through several competing and complex historical entities called paradigms or research programs, which need to continually renew their empirical bases as well as their theoretical foundation. It is promoted here that the remarkable successes obtained in paleoanthropology in less than 150 years are largely attributable to its simple theoretical structure—its single theoretical foundation based on the assumption of the biological evolution of humankind—which has not changed since its inception in 1860. As this has been settled from the very beginning, there was no need for paleoanthropologists to engage in existential questions over competing theoretical divergences in their field. Instead, most of the efforts were channelled along resolving practical problems.

The third epistemological implication which flows from recognizing that paleoanthropology is developing within a single theoretical context is that this field has been largely impermeable to competing evolutionary theories. Because paleoanthropologists early on accepted the theory of biological evolution, they have been more committed to a general conception of evolution than to any specific theory of evolution. Assuming this general conception of evolution, most paleoanthropologists have been devoting all their time to establish humankind's place in nature with the help of the method of comparative anatomy and the fossil record, and not to evaluate human evolution in the light of specific competing evolutionary theories (Darwinism, orthogenesis, neo-Darwinism, etc.). This is not to say that paleoanthropology has been entirely impermeable to changes in evolutionary theories, but simply that the impact of such theories has been limited or well circumscribed. We will come back, on more than one occasion, to this important question.

The second main thesis promoted in this book denies that the field of paleoanthropology is trapped in endless and recurring debates over unilinear or multilinear phylogenetic hypotheses. The traditional historiography, which has focused on the assumed centrality of this debate for the development of the field, neglected important portions and aspects of the discipline. By so doing, it is only natural that this historiography produced both a partial and a distorted vision of its development. What is needed is a broader conception of paleoanthropology. First, if one focuses on the unilinear/multilinear debate it then becomes impossible to understand the events in human evolution prior to the twentieth century, as this debate only arose with the new century. Second, the unilinear and the multilinear hominid phylogenetic hypotheses were only two brands of hypotheses among two others promoted during the 1900–1935 period: parallel and polyphyletic hypotheses. It is only by reinserting them in the analysis of the discipline that one gets a real impression of progress in human evolution. Therefore, a special effort will be devoted to expose the viewpoints of the scholars promoting these neglected or forgotten hypotheses.

Still, the reintegration of these other brands of hypotheses does not sufficiently contribute to broaden the conception of the field of paleoanthropology. As their name implies, these hominid phylogenetic hypotheses are merely concerned with human phylogeny proper. The history of paleoanthropology has too often been equated only with the debates on human phylogeny proper. It is argued here that the quest to establish humankind's place in nature has also been concerned with the nature of the phylogenetic link between the hominids and the other nonhuman animals. That is why a significant portion of this book is devoted to the aspects of the debates on primate phylogeny which are directly relevant to human phylogeny. Only a field of paleoanthropology broadly conceived can reveal the true progressiveness of its development since 1860, as the signs of this progression also need to be sought in aspects other than human phylogeny proper. Let us insist on key examples.

First, the early phylogenetic viewpoints searched for humankind's closest relatives among a remarkably wide diversity of nonhuman primate forms. This diversity of forms was gradually reduced to comprise the great apes only. Second, it was once debated whether humankind and its closest nonhuman primate relatives were evolved from a human-like ancestor or from an ape-like one. The debate was resolved in favor of the latter position. Third, the time range suggested to derive humankind from his nearest relatives used to vary considerably to comprise the entire Tertiary era and even beyond. Now, this time range has been substantially reduced to the very last portion of the Tertiary era. Fourth, the geographical range proposed as humankind's cradle once included the entire surface of the earth. This cradle is now restricted to the Old World only.

Note that the four debates just enumerated are closely related, as they are largely mutually dependent on each other. If the human line is directly derived from a prosimian form, then its cradle could be placed in North America during the early Tertiary era. On the other hand, if the human line is derived from a great ape form, then its cradle could be placed in Africa during the late Tertiary era. The coherence and integrity of all these key debates suggest that it is fruitful to conceive the development of paleoanthropology as occurring within a single and flexible theoretical context, as already suggested above.

The third main thesis promoted in this book holds that the empirical content of paleoanthropology is cumulative and has been increasing since its inception. Again, this thesis is consistent with the view that paleoanthropology has been deploying within a single theoretical context, as scholars have been investing much more time building the empirical content of the field rather than questioning its theoretical foundation. In the early stages of its development, the empirical content of paleoanthropology was essentially restricted to the living forms, which were viewed as terminal points of undocumented evolutionary branches. The method of comparative anatomy was used to infer phylogenetic proximity among these living forms. As time went by, the fossil record gradually came to play a role in such phylogenetic inferences. At first, this record served the purpose of merely confirming or disproving the assumed relationships elaborated on the basis of the living forms. Later, the fossil record became a key source of information in the process of phylogeny building.

The implication of this thesis is that hominid phylogenetic hypotheses, as well as scenarios of hominization, were getting better empirical foundations as the twentieth century progressed. This contributed powerfully to the elimination of a number of phylogenetic hypotheses once believed to be defensible. This also contributed to an increase in the empirical robustness of a number of scenarios of hominization, although it is well known that scenarios are more speculative by their very nature. This being said, a number of elements once contained in scenarios of hominization eventually became so well documented, empirically speaking, that they came to be directly incorporated in standard hominid phylogenetic analyses. For instance, to speak of an increasing brain size in human evolution was, in the nineteenth century, entirely conjectural and more appropriately part of scenarios of hominization rather than of hominid phylogenetic hypotheses. With time, the rather precise documentation of the increasing brain size of the various hominid species permitted to incorporate this knowledge in standard phylogenetic trees. On this view, there is a certain connection between scenarios and phylogenetic hypotheses, although the link is not always as strong as desired. There is no reason not to believe that things will continue to improve. Regardless of whether or not the constituting elements of the scenarios of hominization and their causal relationships have not significantly changed since the inception of paleoanthropology, as suggested by Stoczkowski (1994, [2002]), their scientific credibility has nonetheless been slowly improving.

To support the theses presented here, a special effort was made to reconstitute the thoughts of as many scholars as possible. The views of too many scholars who took part in this quest are incompletely presented in the traditional historiography, if presented at all. In an attempt to fill this void, considerable space is sometimes devoted to the presentation of the scholars' viewpoints. Accordingly, this book is also a reference book. When information was found, biographical notes were added for the authors reviewed before 1960 in a biographical appendix to be found at the end of the book. More information can also be found in Spencer's two-volume *History of Physical Anthropology: An Encyclopedia* (1997). It is always possible to quicken the pace at which the book is read because it is systematically organized in the same fashion: Most of the key ideas and theses are presented in the introductory comments of each division, chapter, section, and subsection, as well as in the historiographical notes and the concluding comments.

Readers should be warned that this book deliberately looks at paleoanthropology from a broad scale or a wide angle. This approach has the great advantage of permitting a synthetic view of the development of the field. Yet, it also has the important disadvantage of overlooking small scale events. This is merely a consequence of the scale chosen to work from.

Many fossil discoveries are referred to in this book. The reader can find more information about them in Hartwig's *The Primate Fossil Record* (2002), Szalay's and Delson's *Evolutionary History of the Primates* (1979), and Schwartz's and Tattersall's four-volume *The Human Fossil Record* (2002–2005).

Part I

A SYNTHESIS OF APPROACHES TO HUMAN EVOLUTION, 1860–1890

In the early nineteenth century, Lamarck was probably the only scholar who promoted a general theory of evolution and applied it to humankind. His view of human evolution was surprisingly modern. Lamarck (1802, 1809, 1820) explained how humankind sprang from the primates by passing through a series of anatomical and intellectual changes. Lamarck imagined that a sophisticated primate form such as the orang of Angola (the chimpanzee) could well have been gradually transformed into the human shape if constrained to live not in the trees but on the ground. This new life style would have instigated a cascade of anatomical changes: the replacement of the grasping foot useful in climbing by a supporting foot more stable in walking; the reconfiguration of the leg shape to permit a bipedal gait; the loss of the projecting snout and the large frontal teeth which were no longer required to either fight or tear food apart because of the freed hands. This last feature, in turn, permitted the use of tools. From there, humans successfully spread all over the world and diversified into six different varieties or races, as seen today. It is during this process of geographical expansion that our ancestors, facing new challenges, developed the need for articulated language. This only contributed to enhance further humankind's superiority and intelligence over the other animals.

Lamarck's view is modern in that it is fairly close to what we believe today to be true. Yet, it epitomizes powerfully the lack of knowledge that he and his contemporaries faced on the question of human origins. Although Lamarck established a close proximity between the humans and the chimpanzees, as we do today, this should not distract us from the fact that everything remained to be done at the time to investigate the anatomy of the living primates, including the humans. During Lamarck's time, many living primate species were either still unknown to science or were simply not well identified, thus causing confusion between two or more such species (Huxley, 1863; Zaborowski, 1881; Hartmann, [1883] 1885; e.g., Delisle, 2004).

Much remained to be done to identify, name, and classify properly all the living primates. As will be seen, this need of information led to an intense period of studies in comparative anatomy after 1860. It is thus clear that Lamarck established a very close genealogical link between the humans and the chimpanzees on a scientific basis that was meagre, to say the least. Many scholars after him disagreed about this assumed proximity.

We also saw that Lamarck recognized several races among the living humans. Yet, it is not possible to determine from his writings whether or not he intended to derive them from a single source (monogeny) or from several of them (polygeny). What is sure, however, is that throughout the rest of the nineteenth century and during the first third of the twentieth century scholars disagreed profoundly on this question. Without more studies in comparative anatomy, the monogeny/polygeny debate remained open. The lack of a decent fossil record made it also impossible to determine if humankind's genealogical roots were shallow or immensely deep, geologically speaking.

Facing so many gaps of knowledge about human evolution, Lamarck had to resign himself to speculate about the anthropogenesis process which made possible the transformation of an ape-like creature into a human-like form. This evolutionary process is usually presented under a scenario of hominization. Various types of such hypothetical reconstructions were performed during the rest of the nineteenth century and throughout the twentieth century. Many years after Lamarck clearly took position in favor of a hypothetical ape-like ancestor for humankind, scholars were still debating whether this ancestor was more ape-like or more human-like in conformation. As it may now be clear, the only thing that was really modern about Lamarck's viewpoint on human evolution was his conclusion. Like an empty shell, the empirical foundation that was required to justify Lamarck's conclusion was entirely lacking. It is the purpose of this book to reconstitute how this scientific basis was gradually improved after 1860.

Knowledge about human evolution was so fragmentary during the 1860–1890 period that it was imposssible to tackle the question in its entirety. Instead, scholars directed their efforts on a number of more or less independent debates. It is a distinctive feature of the development of paleoanthropology at the time that knowledge had to be gathered from distinct avenues in order to establish a picture which was the least incomplete. It is best to envision paleoanthropology at the time not as a monolithic field of research but rather as a fragmented one characterized by several debates being conducted in parallel, each throwing a very partial light on human evolution.

The fragmented nature of the field was not only the result of a fragmentary knowledge about our origins, as alluded to, but also the heritage of a field which arose around 1860 from the meeting of several distinct debates which had already taken shape in the pre-1860 era. The important point here is that paleoanthropology is not merely a by-product of the rise of evolutionary biology. During the 1850s and especially the 1860s, the idea of a universal transmutation of species gained increasingly in support. This situation has prompted a number of historians to interpret the rise of the field of human evolution as being a logical consequence of the acceptance of transformism. In this perspective, it seemed natural to turn to this period of history and expect that scholars would be busy establishing human ancestry by searching for intermediate forms between humankind and the animals. Such commentators assumed that if scientists, or some of them, were not working on filling up this agenda, it must be because they had not yet been converted to evolution. This view completely misses the point that we should not speak of a single source for the rise of paleoanthropoplogy around 1860, but of its multiple sources (e.g., Delisle, 1998).

It is incontestable that the acceptance of the general theory of evolution played an active role in the constitution of paleoanthropology. However, other very important sources also played a crucial role. At least three different sources converged or contributed to the rise of paleoanthropology around 1860. One came from the advent of the transmutation theory itself. Supposed evolutionary links between humans and animal forms, usually primates, could thus be postulated. Considering the state of the fossil record at the time, comparative anatomy and embryology of the living forms were extensively used to postulate such relationships. The second source came from the monogeny/polygeny debate; an old debate completely uncoupled from the transmutation theory prior to 1860. This debate over whether or not the living human races were derived from one or several sources was rapidly recasted in an evolutionary perspective after 1860. This was easily done because the monogeny/polygeny debate was largely consistent with transformism. The third source to give rise to paleoanthropology derived from the considerations over the peopling of Europe as first evidenced by the studies of languages (philology) in the first half of the nineteenth century, and later by more or less ancient human remains. This latter source was also completely uncoupled from questions pertaining to transmutation in the pre-1860 era. After 1860, debates on the peopling of Europe continued without any fundamental change, as their nature made them not particularly central to the new and broader scientific context introduced to the field of human evolution by the general theory of biological evolution. Yet, the debates on the peopling of Europe and the transmutation theory were anything but inconsistent with each other. It was easy to harmonize the former with the general context of the latter without impinging on the nature of the debates on the peopling of Europe.

The distinct sources which contributed to the rise of paleoanthropology around 1860 played different roles in the debates on human origins between 1860 and 1890. This is best seen in the distinction made here between the *global* and the *local* debates. On the one hand, three such global debates were conducted after 1860: (1) the debate on humankind's place among the primates; (2) the monogeny/polygeny debate; and (3) the debate on both the hypothetical reconstruction of humankind's ancestors and the anthropogenesis processes (scenarios of hominization). Owing to the state of the fossil record at the time, such global debates were almost entirely based on the comparative anatomy and embryology of the living forms. The global debates, as their name imply, were concerned with the broad evolutionary questions in human evolution.

On the other hand, the ancient human remains evaluated between 1860 and 1890, though fairly abundant, were judged by most scholars to be essentially of modern appearance, in addition to being almost exclusively restricted to Europe. Although of no or limited use in global debates, these ancient human remains were of great value in the local debates, that is, in debates which were centered on the prehistoric peopling of Europe. Because of their fairly modern appearance, these prehistoric human remains were most fruitfully compared to the living human races and not interpreted as ancestral links between the humans and the other primates.

It is suggested here that in order to understand the development of paleoanthropology during the 1860–1890 period, it would be best to analyse it through the glasses of a research area organized around two main analytical levels, one concerned with the global debates and the other with the local debates. While the former level will be discussed in the next chapter, the latter will be presented in Chapter 3.

2

Comparative Anatomy

INTRODUCTION

Remarkably, the 1860–1890 period saw the rather sudden rise of key debates in human evolution, especially those concerned with humankind's place among the primates and with the hypothetical reconstructions of humankind's early ancestors. It is not that such debates were totally without pre-1860 antecendents—think of Lamarck, for instance—it is rather that they presented themselves during this time period in full-blown scale, with well-articulated arguments and already with an impressive diversity of viewpoints. Although the establishment of the precise birth date of paleoanthropology is a moot question (e.g., Delisle, 1998)—which might not necessarily be of supreme importance—a good argument could be mounted in favor of the view that the field was fully constituted between 1860 and 1890 as seen by the surprising vitality and robustness of the debates then being conducted. The value of this argument is further increased when considering that many of the 1890–1935 debates found their roots in the 1860–1890 ones.

HUMANKIND'S PLACE AMONG THE PRIMATES

The first global debate which shall concern us is the one on humankind's place among the primates. During the 1860–1890 period, scholars profoundly disagreed on the phylogenetic place of the humans in the primate family tree. It is useful to regroup the scholars under three main hypotheses: (1) humans are not closely related to the anthropoid apes; (2) humans are closely related to the anthropoid apes; and (3) humans are so closely related to the anthropoid apes that some human races are more closely related to specific primate species than to other human races. In order to avoid a possible confusion between the hominoids and the anthropoids—a distinction not clearly made in the literature at the time—the anthropoid apes are defined in this book as comprising the hominoids, the Old World monkeys, and the New World monkeys, while the hominoids themselves are defined as comprising the humans, the chimpanzees, the gorillas, the orangutans, and the gibbons.

Not descended from the anthropoid apes. At least three scientists, Owen, Mivart, and de Quatrefages, inclined to think that humans were not linked to the anthropoid stem. For instance, in the late 1850s and early 1860s, Owen (1857, 1861) classified humankind in a separate subclass from all the other primates, *Archencephala*, on the basis of structural peculiarities of his brain.[1] Although Owen never specified precisely the phylogenetic implication of his taxonomic view, it seems doubtful that he would have agreed with a close phylogenetic link between humans and the anthropoid apes, at least to judge by his position in the 1830s, when he strongly rejected the idea of an ape ancestry for humankind (e.g., Desmond, 1985). While Owen recognized that humans and the anthropoids shared many anatomical similarities, he evaluated the psychological or mental gap separating them to be enormous.

Owen was often falsely considered an anti-evolutionist. In fact, he was already in favor of transmutation prior to 1860 (e.g., Bowler, 1976; Richards, 1987). Owen (1863: 89–96, 1868: 799–809) promoted after that period a law called the derivative law, which derived species from one another by a preordained and innate tendency to change independently of external conditions. Under such a law, it becomes possible to justify why humans and anthropoids shared many similarities without necessarily being closely related, phylogenetically speaking, for such similarities could be explained by parallel evolution and not by common descent.

If Owen refrained from explicitly embracing this conception, Mivart (1873) explicitly applied it to primate evolution. Mivart contended that human structural characters were shared by a great many living forms, primates and nonprimates alike. He held that the "lines of affinity existing between different Primates construct rather a network than a ladder" (1873: 176). Accordingly, Mivart argued in favor of numerous morphological similarities acquired without any genetic affinity through parallel evolution. Humankind's phylogenetic position remained unspecified under such circumstances, but Mivart probably had in mind an independent origin of humans and anthropoid apes, just as he postulated that the primates of the Old and New Worlds had been created independently of one another. This is how Mivart (1873: 185–186) supported his view:

> [V]ery frequently indeed similarity of structure may arise without there being any genetic affinity between the resembling forms, as also that it is much rather to an internal cause or principle than to any action of surrounding external conditions that the origin of new specific forms is due.

Like Owen and Mivart, de Quatrefages (1870: 366–367) recognized the general morphological similarity between the humans and the other living primates, although he insisted that, whereas all the primates were structurally built for climbing, humankind, for its part, was built for walking, thus demonstrating that they had developed structurally in opposite directions (e.g., Blanckaert, 1995). Taxonomically, de Quatrefages (1905) classified humankind alone in a kingdom of its own, the human kingdom, for he thought that morality and religion were exclusive attributes that justified it. Phylogenetically speaking, de Quatrefages granted that some anatomical, physiological, and embryological facts could be interpreted in favor of a common ancestry between humans and the living anthropoids. Yet, when turning to the fossil record, he insisted that no evidence could bring any support to the rapprochement between the most ancient human races and the twenty-one fossil species of primates that were then known (de Quatrefages, 1894: 192–194).

Not denying completely the theoretical possibility of a common ancestry between the humans and the primates, de Quatrefages excluded it on the basis of a lack of any directly observable data. De Quatrefages (1894: 194) stated that:

> [W]e have not found yet the *common ancestor* from which Man and the apes would have sprung; and it is not even possible to show a single link of a series of intermediary beings supposedly linking Man and apes. The notion of a *collateral affinity* between the human species and the other primates [cannot] appeal to a single experimental and observational fact. Consequently . . . this very explanation of humankind's origins cannot be accepted by anyone who would take into account the proper standards of modern science.[2] [My translation; the italics are not mine.]

Although de Quatrefages rejected all the transformist theories of his time, he cannot be classified among the anti-evolutionists. He argued that two distinct causes acting at two different levels were responsible for evolutionary change: (1) the origins of species are explained by a yet unknown cause, which manifests itself intermittently during important geological events; (2) changes within species are molded by factors such as natural selection, acclimatization, crossbreeding, and so on (de Quatrefages, 1867: 242, 1894: 288, 1905: 75).

Owen, Mivart and de Quatrefages were all rather vague in their views on human evolution. However, they were apparently inclined to think that humankind had stemmed either from an early and primitive form unrelated to the anthropoid stem, or maybe from a nonprimate ancestor altogether. Their views probably implied that humankind's phylogenetic roots were to be found in extremely ancient geological times, and that the general conformation of humankind's remote ancestor was probably not ape-like.

Up from the anthropoid apes. If a small group of scholars thought that humans were unrelated to the anthropoid apes, a much more important group of them promoted just that view. This latter view is also unanimously supported today. However, as far as the pre-1890 period is concerned, it should be noted that humankind's precise place among the anthropoid apes was widely disputed at the time. This contrasts sharply with the current situation. It is therefore possible to distinguish at the time several hypotheses within the broader thesis of humankind's place among the anthropoids.

For scholars like Haeckel, humans were, phylogenetically speaking, more closely related to some hominoid apes than to others. The living hominoid apes and humans were very closely related, maintained Haeckel, as evidenced by comparative anatomy and embryology. He thought this assertion to be reinforced by the ape-like features seen in most living human races. In his writings, Haeckel (1876: 267–277, 291–297; 1896: 177–183) suggested that humans stemmed from the branch leading to the living man-like apes (hominoid apes) probably during the Miocene or the Pliocene period.[3] In drawings, however, Haeckel was even more explicit and suggested that humans were more closely related to the Asian man-like apes (the orangs and gibbons) than the African man-like apes (chimpanzees and gorillas). In fact, he even hinted that the orang was probably humankind's closest living relative (see Figure 1).[4] On the basis of human and animal biogeography, Haeckel speculated that humankind's cradle may be traced back to a sunken continent of southern Asia called Lemuria, although he did not completely exclude Africa from being this cradle.

For other scientists like Huxley, Darwin, and Wallace, humankind's evolutionary link with the primates is to be found near the base of the hominoid branch. For instance, Huxley defended the taxonomic conclusion, based on embryology and comparative anatomy, that the "structural differences which separate Man from the Gorilla and the Chimpanzee are not so great as those which separate the Gorilla from the lower apes" (Huxley, 1894: 144). On that basis, Huxley favored, in 1863, classifying humankind in a family of its own, *Anthropini*, within the order *Primates*. From there, Huxley (1894: 146–147) drew the evolutionary implication that "there would be no rational ground for doubting that man might have originated by the gradual modification of a man-like ape; or as a ramification of the same primitive stock as those apes."

Darwin's view of human phylogeny was fairly similar to that of Huxley. We have seen that Haeckel inclined to think that the Asian hominoid apes were humankind's closest living relatives. Darwin, for his part, favored the African hominoid apes. Although Darwin published *The Origin of Species* in 1859, he was to wait until 1871 before publicly expressing his opinion about humankind. In considering the human place in relation to other primate forms, Darwin acknowledged that some characteristics of the human structure may claim the rank of a suborder, or probably a higher grade, if mental faculties were considered. However, Darwin (1871: 195) contended that "under a genealogical point of view it appears that this rank is too high, and that man ought to form merely a Family, or possibly even only a Sub-family." Darwin's (1871: 197, 199) phylogenetic assessment of humankind's place among the primates reads as follows:

> If the anthropomorphous apes [hominoid apes] be admitted to form a natural sub-group, then as man agrees with them . . . we may infer that some ancient member of the anthropormorphous sub-group gave birth to man. . . . It is therefore probable that Africa was formerly inhabited by extinct apes closely allied to the gorilla and chimpanzee; and as these two species are now man's nearest allies, it is somewhat more probable that our early progenitors lived on the African continent than elsewhere.

In an unpublished drawing dated April 21, 1868, kept today among the Darwin papers at the Cambridge University Library,[5] we can see that Darwin thought that the human branch departed from the primate family tree before all the hominoid apes (chimpanzee, gorilla, orangutan, and gibbon) started to diverge from one another (see Figure 2). This implies that although, taxonomically speaking, the chimpanzee and the gorilla were humankind's closest living relatives in Darwin's mind, phylogenetically speaking, it is the four hominoid apes which were more closely related to each other, with the humans being slightly more distant. Darwin speculated that humans might possibly have stemmed from the primates as early as the Eocene period.[6]

In a phylogenetic view similar to that of Huxley and Darwin, Wallace recognized the close affinity between the humans and the hominoid apes. More precisely, he asserted that the three great apes (chimpanzee, gorilla, and orangutan) had diverged less from one another than all of them from humans. The phylogenetic implication was that "the [humans] must, therefore, have diverged from the common ancestral form before the existing types of anthropoid apes [hominoid apes] had diverged from each other" (Wallace, 1889: 455–456). Wallace then introduced two distinct series of facts to specify his phylogenetic scheme. The first one concerned the discovery of fossil apes:

> Now, this divergence almost certainly took place as early as the Miocene period, because in the Upper Miocene deposits of Western Europe remains of two species of ape [*Pliopithecus* and *Dryopithecus*] have been found allied to the gibbons . . . We seem hardly, therefore, to have reached, in the Upper Miocene, the epoch of the common ancestor of man and the anthropoids [hominoid apes]. (Wallace, 1889: 456).

In order to support humankind's great antiquity, Wallace then referred to a second series of facts: Tools and human fossils in Europe. First, he pointed to ancient tools found both in the Old and New Worlds that allegedly had been dated to the Pliocene period (but see below). Second, Wallace thought that the discovery of fairly ancient and modern looking skulls at Engis and Neandertal prior to 1860 further supported the case that humankind's ancestor is to be found in very ancient geological horizons.

For another group of scholars, comprising Schmidt and Topinard, humankind's link with the primates remained unspecified, although they believed that this phylogenetic quest should be conceived in a broader framework to include not only the hominoid apes but also the other anthropoids. For instance, Schmidt (1887: 282–310) made clear that he believed that humans and anthropoids were descended from a common root.[7] This is clearly seen in his phylogenetic tree (see Figure 3).[8] More specifically, Schmidt viewed this common ancestor between the humans and the anthropoids to be either with the Old World monkeys, if not with the hominoid apes, thereby probably excluding the New World monkeys from this ancestral position. By 1884, Schmidt reinforced his conviction that humans were, phylogenetically speaking, related exclusively to the Old World anthropoids by discarding his previous monophyletic conception of primate phylogeny in favor of a polyphyletic one. In this new view, prosimians (*Halbaffen*), New World monkeys, and Old World anthropoids (including humans) all independently arose from primitive mammals (Schmidt, 1884: 265–273).

If Schmidt excluded the New World monkeys from any consideration over human phylogeny, Topinard will leave this option open. Topinard (1888; 1891; 1892) united all the anthropoids (hominoids, Old and New World monkeys) into the same taxonomic category, leaving humankind standing by itself in a suborder of the *Primates*. But this particular taxonomic disposition did not prevent Topinard from postulating a simian descent for humans, probably not from the hominoid stem but rather directly from an undetermined anthropoid form, possibly of monkey-like conformation and dated to the early Miocene period. Topinard (1891: 349) stated:

> To summarize ourself on Man, the Anthropoids [hominoid apes] and the Monkeys [Old and New Worlds], we will compare the primate order to a tree. The lemurs constitute the roots which give rise to one or several stems. One of these stems is the Monkey one, from which a higher branch is projecting, the Anthropoid [hominoid ape] one. Another branch, which origins or contact points with the previous one is uncertain, will give rise to the branch of the living humans, by running in parallel to the Anthropoid [hominoid ape] branch, without being in relation to the latter while going beyond it.[9] [My translation]

Topinard found support for the idea that humans were derived from the anthropoid stem by recognizing what he thought to be some simian features in the Neandertal skull and the La Naulette jaw. Although Topinard would not derive the humans from the hominoid stem—as he thought they both had evolved in parallel—he nevertheless recognized that, taxonomically speaking, the hominoid apes in general and the chimpanzees in particular were human's closest living relatives.

For yet another group of scholars like Broca and Hartmann, humans were probably affiliated with the anthropoids, should they be hominoids or not, although they judged premature any final decision on this question. Unsurprisingly, their presented views were rather vague. For instance, Broca held that, taxonomically speaking, humans represented only a distinct family within the order *Primates*; a family which shared many similarities with the family of the hominoid apes. Phylogenetically speaking, however, Broca (1869) did not interpret this as necessarily strong evidence for their common ancestry. For him, the anatomical similarities did not constitute necessary evidence for a common origin. Whether or not humankind's origins were at all related to simian ancestors was, in Broca's mind, an unresolved question as yet. However, he recognized that the gap separating humans from the other primates had been bridged to some extent by the few simian features seen in the Neandertal skull and the La Naulette jaw. He therefore expected that future discoveries should close the gap further.

Broca's cautious attitude on the question of humankind's ancestral connection with the other primates may not be unrelated to his general evolutionary conception called *polygenetic transformism*, in which populations are believed to have developed in parallel (Broca, 1870b; Blanckaert, 1989a). Instead of a single or a very limited number of stocks from which life on earth originated, Broca believed it more probable that numerous such origins had occurred in different places and times. Broca never believed in the great modifying power of external conditions as often expounded by monogenists and many evolutionists. Races and species were not, in his mind, endowed with great flexibility to change. What Broca (1867) envisaged, instead, was the production of variability through crossbreeding and hybridization of races and species.

In a cautious attitude not unlike that of Broca, Hartmann (1885) was apparently inclined to believe that the humans and the hominoid apes were descended from a common ancestor.[10] However, this ancestor remained, in Hartmann's view, unspecified considering that none of the living or fossil primate species thus far discovered represented such an ancestor. Hartmann was against any hypothetical reconstruction of that common ancestor, as he clearly indicated that all the attempts performed to this date were just a stretch of imagination without much significance. That hypothetical common ancestor, continued Hartmann, still awaited its actual discovery by paleontologists.

Whereas the scholars reviewed in this subsection agreed that humans were affiliated with the anthropoid stem, they were not agreed on the precise nature of humankind's link within this group of primates. Similarly, the question of the conformation of this common ancestor linking the humans and the other anthropoids was everything but settled. While Haeckel and Darwin seemed to believe that this common ancestor was a sort of ape-like creature, it is unclear if Broca, Schmidt, and Hartmann would have agreed with this characterization. After all, it is not inconsistent to promote, on the one hand, that humans sprang from the anthropoid stem and, on the other hand, that this common ancestor is more human-like than ape-like. This latter view was frequently assumed in the first third of the twentieth century (see Chapter 4).

Polyphyletic hypotheses. All the scholars reviewed thus far debated about whether or not humankind was affiliated with the anthropoids. Although not in agreement on this question, they agreed on the question of the unity of the human species as defined in the following terms: No living human races were thought to be more closely related to some living primate species than to other living human races. For other scholars like Vogt, Schaaffhausen, Hovelacque, and Hervé, this latter view of human evolution—the polyphyletic view—was considered to fit more neatly the facts than the monophyletic view. Probably the most important scholar promoting a polyphyletic view during the second half of the nineteenth century was Carl Vogt, who clearly and authoritatively opted for this viewpoint in the early 1860s. He subsequently strongly inspired Hovelacque and Hervé, as will be seen.[11]

According to Vogt (1864a: 461–468), humans and apes were built on the same morphological plan, which testified to their genetic relationship.[12] He thought the evidence of such a genetic link was threefold. First, he recognized in human races (especially the "Negroes") a number of characteristics approaching the ape-type.

Second, he identified among the ancient human remains ape-like characteristics, such as the elongated form and the low arching of the skull (Engis and Neandertal skulls). Third, he recognized in human microcephalics a morbid arrest of development, which might indicate the existence of a now extinct intermediate form between the humans and the apes (see also Vogt, 1867a).

However, far from suggesting a single ape-type ancestor for humankind, Vogt favored a polyphyletic origin. On the one hand, he held that the differences between some human races, which he sometimes called species, were greater than those between some species of apes. He contended that this distinctiveness or plurality of the human races could be traced back into the prehistoric period, as demonstrated by the cave men of Belgium and the Rhenish provinces, and the Lapps of the Stone Age. On the other hand, Vogt held that the distinct hominoid lines developed not from a single ape type but in parallel from distinct monkey stocks. From there, Vogt contended that the various human races sprung worldwide in distinct and parallel lines going through, first, a monkey-like stage, and later, an anthropomorph-like stage.

From a general perspective, Vogt's conception of parallel evolution of life forms on earth was consistent with the notion of polygenetic transformism already alluded to (see Broca above). From a more specific perspective, Vogt's conception partly rested on his conviction that each living hominoid species was more closely related to a specific monkey species than to other hominoid species. In his view, orang-utans, gibbons and *Semnopithecus* were genealogically related; chimpanzees had evolutionary links with the macaques; and gorillas shared a common ancestry with the baboons. On that basis, Vogt (1864a: 466–467) held that:

> If the Macaci in the Senegal, the baboons on the Gambia, and the gibbons in Borneo could become developed into anthropoid apes [hominoid apes], we cannot see why the American apes [monkeys] should not be capable of a similar development! If in different regions of the globe anthropoid apes [hominoid apes] may issue from different stocks [monkeys], we cannot see why these different stocks should be denied the further development into the human type, and that only one stock should possess this privilege; in short, we cannot see why American races of man may not be derived from American apes, Negroes from African apes, or Negritos, perhaps, from Asiatic apes!

As no hominoid apes but only New World monkeys were known in America when Vogt wrote these lines—a fact he recognized, as we do today (excluding the prosimian-like forms of North America)—his phylogenetic view implied that living human races in America directly sprung from a monkey-like ancestor. More specifically, Vogt was inclined to believe that some branches of the New World monkeys developed into anthropomorph-like forms (not necessarily into hominoid ones) before reaching the human stage.

To fully understand the implication of Vogt's phylogenetic view, it should first be noted that he insisted on the fact that monkeys of the Old and New Worlds had been separated for a long time. Later, he made clear that he viewed the monkeys of the Old and New Worlds not to be descended from a common ancestor (Vogt & Specht, 1887: 73–76, 94–95).[13] In Vogt's view, therefore, living human races in the Old and New Worlds had been separated for a substantial amount of time, in addition to being derived from totally distinct evolutionary roots. Under this evolutionary conception, how were the similarities between the distinct living human races to be explained? Vogt turned to a process of convergence that took place in the later stages of human evolution. On this thinking, the gaps existing between the distinct and original ape-man stocks were gradually filled by the rise of mongrel races through admixture and interbreeding.

Like Vogt, Schaaffhausen (1868) was a proponent of the polyphyletic thesis. He too believed that the traces of the ascent of the human type from a lower one were threefold: (1) As seen in the lower organization of some human races approaching the ape conditions; (2) as evidenced by the primitive characters of a number of human fossils (the forehead of the Neandertal skull, the dentition and shape of the La Naulette jaw, and the prognathism of some juvenile jaws of the Stone Age); and (3) as seen in the clues provided by human embryological development. When turning to human phylogeny, Schaaffhausen clearly hinted at a preference for a polyphyletic hypothesis, although he based his view on a different data set than Vogt's. It is worth quoting him at some length:

> Setting aside the changes the human skull undergoes by culture, there remain two rude types—the dolichocephalic and the brachycephalic skull. We possess no facts for their common origin; but that they are of different descent may be deduced from the circumstance that those regions of the globe in which the above types are strongly represented, namely, equatorial Africa and South Asia, are also the homes of two species of anthropoid apes [hominoids], who differ similarly in cranial structure. . . . Duvernoy was the first who opposed the dolichocephalic Chimpanzee to the brachycephalic Orang. Agassiz has pointed out that in Asia and Africa the large apes and the human races have the same colour of the skin. I myself have drawn attention to the fact that the gorilla is also dolichocephalic, and that the approximation of two human races to the apes of the same countries in colour and cranial form appears the most formidable objection to the unity of the human species in the present state of our knowledge. (Schaaffhausen, 1868: 418)

It is unclear if Schaaffhausen ultimately derived the various anthropomorph-like creatures, which distinctively gave rise to the living human races, from monkey-like ancestors, like Vogt did. It is also unclear if Schaaffhausen's view regarding the rise of human races equally applied to the primates of the Old and New Worlds, like Vogt's conception, or if his was restricted to the Old World only.

Hovelacque and Hervé explicitly embraced Vogt's polyphyletic conception of distinct and parallel lines of human races evolving through monkey-like and hominoid-like stages. Hovelacque and Hervé stated (1887: 202, 205):

> Almost all the difficulties which have faced the notion of evolutionism, when concerning the constitution of the human races, vanish when one accepts that the main natural divisions of humanity developed independently, in both distinct geographical centres and times, in addition to being descended from distinct species and genera . . . Nothing is against the notion that, during the Miocene, regions of the earth were once inhabited by anthropoids [hominoids] which evolutionary stages went beyond the

> stage of the living anthropoids [hominoids] . . . It is likely that they constituted several distinct groups, species or even genera, living in different habitats, and stemming themselves from distinct monkey types. On this view, the plurality of origins would explain the diversity of the human types.[14] [My translation]

Hovelacque and Hervé supported the parallelism of their view by appealing to the evolutionary conception of polygenetic transformism, that is, the multiple rise of life forms in different places and in different time horizons. They argued that humans sprang from definite simian-like creatures belonging to different species or genera in which conformation is intermediary between humans and hominoid apes, not unlike the hypothetical creature imagined by Gabriel de Mortillet and called by him *Anthropopithecus* (see below). Contrary to Vogt, who believed that the human races had sprung from several distinct centres throughout the Old and New Worlds, Hovelacque and Hervé restricted these centres of evolution to the Old World only. Their polycentric view comprised four such geographical regions: Europe, Palearctic, Ethiopic, and Oriental.

What was the state of the debate on humankind's place among the primates in the 1860–1890 period? It is clear that this question remained totally unsettled. Many key issues were still very much in the air:

1. While scholars like Haeckel suggested that humankind may have stemmed from the primates as late as the Pliocene period, others like Darwin evaluated that it might have been as early as the Eocene period.

2. If many scholars assumed a monophyletic origin for humankind, others promoted a polyphyletic one.

3. Scholars were not agreed about whether humankind's common ancestor with the primates was more ape-like or human-like in conformation.

4. Some scholars promoted that humankind had sprung from a single geographical zone (Haeckel and Darwin) while others that it arose from several geographical zones (Vogt, Hovelacque, and Hervé).

5. Lastly, numerous phylogenetic hypotheses were proposed at the time to link humankind with the primates: Some suggested a close link with the hominoid apes (Huxley, Haeckel, Darwin, Wallace); others with possibly the monkeys (Topinard); still others suggested that a link existed between only some living human races and some anthropomorph-like or monkey-like species (Vogt); while some might have alluded to the possibilty of finding no link at all between the humans and the other primates (Owen, Mivart, de Quatrefages).

An interesting point to note about the 1860–1890 period is the relatively weak link which apparently existed between taxonomy and phylogeny in the minds of most scholars (though not all, see de Quatrefages below). For instance, Darwin clearly stated that chimpanzees and gorillas were humankind's closest living allies, although he held, at the same time, that the human line had split from the base of the hominoid branch before the four living hominoid apes had differentiated from one another. The same with Topinard who thought that the chimpanzees were humankind's closest living relative, while promoting, at the same time, that humans may possibly have directly evolved from the monkey stem without going through a hominoid ape stage. The assumed weak link between taxonomy and phylogeny during that period is a clear indication of the scholars's awareness that anatomical similarities between organisms may be either caused by common descent or by parallel and/or convergent evolution. We have seen that scholars like Broca, de Quatrefages, Hervé, Hovelacque, Mivart, Owen, Schaaffhausen, and Vogt were strongly inclined to believe that human phylogeny and/or primate phylogeny had been largely shaped by parallel evolution. This situation was not unique to the field of human evolution at the time. Zoologists and palaeontologists alike had been busy debating the impact of common ancestry versus parallel evolution in all major taxonomic groups ever since transformism has been widely accepted (e.g., Bowler, 1996).

MONOGENY OR POLYGENY?

While scholars were debating over humankind's place among the primates, another debate was being simultaneously conducted in the 1860–1890 period: Were the living human races derived from a single or several sources? Several of the scholars just reviewed were also engaged in this other debate, which also contributed to what has been called here the global debates (as opposed to the local ones). The monogeny/polygeny debate, which was in principle not unrelated to the one on humankind's place among the primates, was nevertheless largely conducted independently of it mainly because of a lack of any material link between the humans and the other primates. It will be remembered that this debate has a long pre-1860 history which cannot be presented here (e.g., Blanckaert, 1996; Grayson, 1983; Poliakov, 1971; Popkin, 1978–79). During an earlier phase, this debate was conducted in a fairly restricted time frame, which extended somewhere between a few to several tens of thousands of years, in addition to being couched in nonevolutionary terms by most scholars. After 1860, the monogeny/polygeny debate was recast in an evolutionary context, for it was largely consistent with an evolutionary worldview. From that time on, its time frame was also greatly expanded, geologically speaking. We will take the debate from there.

The monogenists. For a number of scholars like Wallace, Huxley, Haeckel, and Darwin, the rise of an evolutionary context after 1860 permitted to resolve the ancient monogeny/polygeny debate in favor of monogeny, but not without incorporating some empirical facts traditionally restricted to the polygenist camp. In reality, the monogenetic views of these four scholars, which were entirely remolded in the light of evolutionism, may best be called *monophyletism*.

For instance, Wallace (1864) thought that the monogeny/polygeny debate could be reconciled under the theory of evolution by means of natural selection. He conceded to the polygenists that they had the better of the argument, at least to judge by the apparent existence of human races in ancient times and the lack of evidence that these ancient races converged towards each other as we go deeper in time. Like the monogenists, however, Wallace held that the humans originated from a single type. He argued that humankind had been, at a very early period, probably a widely distributed and homogeneous race living in warm climates. As some populations migrated to other parts of the world and became exposed to new and varied conditions, numerous populations would have differentiated and adapted under the pressure of natural selection. Thus arose the characteristics which distinguished the living human races. As humankind's mental faculties gradually developed through time, Wallace thought that humans would have been able to cope with the demand of conditions by mental skills only (weapons, shelters, division of labor, etc.). At this juncture, Wallace conjectured that the effect of natural selection would have shifted from advantageous physical features to advantageous mental faculties, bringing the tranformation of the former almost to a stop, thus fixing permanently the physical characteristics of the main human races. According to this view, Wallace argued that the presence of humans in remote geological times was not only rendered possible but necessary. He therefore saw no theoretical reason against our finding human fossils or artefacts in Tertiary deposits.

Like Wallace, Huxley (1865) recognized that the application of Darwinian principles could reconcile the strong points of both monogenetic and polygenetic hypotheses. On the one hand, Huxley thought he could identify among the living humans eleven distinct groups or stocks on the basis of their skin complexion, head conformation, and morphology of hair.[15] He asserted that these stocks remained mostly unchanged in time, even under the effect of migrations and intermixtures as determined by the historical and archaeological records. Huxley (1894 [1865]: 240) stated that to "sum up our knowledge of the ethnological past of man; so far as the light is bright, it shows him substantially as he is now; and, when it grows dim, it permits us to see no sign that he was other than he is now." On the other hand, Huxley contended that it was unnecessary to postulate multiple simian origins for humankind. He wrote that "it may safely be affirmed that, even if the differences between men are specific, they are so small, that the assumption of more than one primitive stock for all is altogether superfluous" (Huxley, 1894 [1865]: 248). Huxley assumed that humankind probably arose in a single locality, from which it spread under the pressure of the changing conditions. Such conditions permitted the action of natural selection, and thus created instances of isolation among groups which permitted the hereditary fixation of the characteristics now distinguishing the various human stocks.

Not unlike Wallace and Huxley, Haeckel looked upon the monogeny/polygeny debate from an evolutionary viewpoint and reduced it to this:

> [I]n a *wide sense*, the monophyletic opinion is the right one. For even supposing that the transmutation of Man-like Apes into Men had taken place several times, yet those Apes themselves would again be allied by the one pedigree common to the whole order of Apes . . .. In a *narrower sense* . . . the polyphylist's opinion would probably be right

> in as much as the different primaeval languages have developed quite independently of one another. . . . Still they [the different races of men] would of course be connected further up or lower down at their root, and thus all would finally be derived from a common primaeval stock. (Haeckel, 1876: 303–304)

Haeckel's conception of life on earth rested on the notion of a single or very few original and primitive life forms from which all the other life forms gradually diverged.[16] Haeckel's view, therefore, contrasted sharply with the notion of several origins of life forms in time and space (polygenetic transformism) characterized by distinct parallel evolutionary lines as promoted by other scholars.

In his monophyletic view, Haeckel made clear that he believed that the different groups of speechless primeval forms were all derived from a common and single ape-like human form. From there, Haeckel suggested that various speechless "species" (races) of men, most of which are now extinct, developed from the original ape-like man. Among these ancient species of men two quite distinct forms, the straight-haired and the woolly-haired (the latter being more ape-like), survived to eventually contribute to the two main groups of human species (races) now living: The latter form gave rise to the Papuans, the Hottentots, and the "Negroes," while the former to the Australians, the Malays, the Mongols and the Mediterraneans.

Following several scholars of the time, Darwin also evaluated the monogenetic and polygenetic views as being far from contradictory. Darwin (1871: 235) asserted that when the reality of evolution was accepted, "the dispute between the monogenists and the polygenists will die a silent and unobserved death." Darwin insisted that the living human races diverged from a single common ancestor. He also insisted on the arbitrary nature of the taxonomic question that often accompanied the monogeny/polygeny debate at the time. Darwin (1871: 229–230, 235) stated:

> When the races of man diverged at an extremely remote epoch from their common progenitor, they will have differed but little from each other; . . . consequently they will then . . . have had less claim to rank as distinct species, than the existing so-called races . . .. In a series of forms graduating insensibly from some ape-like creature to man . . . it would be impossible to fix on any definite point when the term "man" ought to be used . . .. So again it is almost a matter of indifference whether the so-called races of man are thus designated, or are ranked as species or sub-species; but the latter term appears the most appropriate.

By promoting a view in which the living human races are seen as the result of a process of divergence from a common ancestor, Darwin (1871: 230–231) was openly and explicitly opposed to Vogt's view, which recognized the great importance of parallelism and convergence in human evolution.[17] Accordingly, Darwin and Haeckel sided together against the conception based on polygenetic transformism.

If several scholars took advantage of the rise of an evolutionary context after 1860 to rethink the monogeny/polygeny debate, a scholar like de Quatrefages, however, continued this debate in a fashion that was somewhat reminiscent of the pre-1860 period, at least to judge from some of the arguments he deployed. This is understandable when considering that de Quatrefages (1860–1861, 1861) was already in 1860 (and before) a devout monogenist. Furthermore, he remained very critical of all evolutionary theories promoted during his life time, without being an anti-evolutionist, strictly speaking. De Quatrefages's brand of monogenism was somewhat different from the one proposed by the other scholars just reviewed. It is perhaps best to distinguish between de Quatrefages's *monogenetic* view, and the *monophyletic* views of Darwin, Haeckel, Huxley, and Wallace.

It will be remembered that de Quatrefages identified two distinct causes of change acting at two different levels. An unknown cause was responsible for the origin of species and another for changes within the species. According to de Quatrefages (1905), it is under this latter cause exclusively that human evolution was molded, for he held that humankind constituted a single species, as demonstrated especially through the fluidity of the crossbreedings taking place among its living representatives. It is precisely such arguments over the number of living human "species" and the possibility of successful interbreeding between them that are, in de Quatrefages's approach, reminiscent of the monogeny/polygeny debate prior to 1860.

For de Quatrefages, the living humans were all part of the numerous races or varieties belonging to a single human species; races or varieties derived from, or affiliated with, a single primitive stock that lived in a single and restricted geographical area, probably somewhere in Asia. That original stock, it will be remembered, was not necessarily affiliated with the primates in de Quatrefages's view (see above). He envisaged that an early single human primitive type was gradually superseded in time through the action of changing conditions. Such natural agencies were responsible for the formation of the primary human races. Then, through crossbreeding, these primary human races were transformed into secondary races or varieties. If the original human type was completely superseded, several of its traits persisted until today. The initial human type was not profoundly transfigured, meaning that all the changes that occurred to humankind since its origin took place within the limits of the same species. De Quatrefages (1905: 220) stated: "Dolichocephalic or brachycephalic, tall or small, with prognathism or without it, Quaternary man is human in the full meaning of the word." [my translation][18]

The polygenists. Other scholars would not subscribe to the notion that the living human races were descended from a single source. We have already seen that Vogt, Schaaffhausen, Hovelacque, and Hervé promoted a polyphyletic view of human phylogeny. For them, some living human races were, phylogenetically speaking, more closely related to some living primate species than to other human races. Similarly, for scholars like Broca and Topinard, more than one source may have contributed to the rise of the living humans. In this sense, this latter view is also a kind of polyphyletism. However, it is only a very weak one in comparison to the form promoted by Vogt, Schaaffhausen, Hovelacque, and Hervé. Broca and Topinard were not promoting that some living human races were more closely related to some living primate species than to other living human races. In order to distinguish the strong polyphyletic thesis from the weak one, we will continue to refer to the former as *polyphyletism*, whereas the latter will be called *polygenism*.

As a well known polygenist, Broca made clear that he would not accept without convincing demonstration that humankind originated and diverged from a single stock (e.g., Blanckaert, 1989a). It will be remembered that Broca never believed in the great modifying power of external conditions. On such arguments, Broca held that things presented themselves as if humankind was descended from several distinct stocks. To support this view, he mentioned that the known Quaternary human races were as distinct as modern races were, thus providing no evidence of convergence, as should have been expected if they were indeed derived from a single stock (Broca, 1867, 1870b, 1870c).

Topinard's polygenetic view was more explicitly stated than Broca's. When considering the dispute between the monogenists and the polygenists, Topinard (1890: 531) flatly declared that "[i]t no longer has any interest."[19] What he meant, of course, was that, within an evolutionary framework, the question took a different meaning and was now only of relative importance. This being said, Topinard (1890: 531–532) expressed a preference for polygeny:

> As to the question of the most elementary human types to which we might go back, types utterly irreducible, . . . are they the issue of many Anthropoid ancestors, Pithecoids or others; or are they derived from a single stock . . . ? The anthropological data given in this work appear to us more favorable to the former opinion, if we accept the transformation theory. The most characteristic races, whether living or extinct, do not form one single ascending series, such as may be compared to a ladder or a tree, but . . . to a series of frequently parallel lines.

Later, Topinard (1891: 345–348) was apparently more unsettled than ever on the monogeny/polygeny question. Yet, he insisted that if the polygenetic hypothesis turns out to be the right one, then he would be inclined to believe that two distinct primate sources gave rise to all the living human races, two sources which originated either from the same or two distinct geological time horizons.

Just like the debate on humankind's place among the primates, the monogeny/polygeny debate remained unsettled during the 1860–1890 period. It is interesting to note that both debates faced the same major difficulty: the lack of a fossil record that could help narrow down the number of phylogenetic hypotheses generated by an approach that was, after all, exclusively based on the comparative anatomy of the living forms. Such a fossil record would not be at scientists' disposal until the second third of the twentieth century. In front of such a grim perspective, a number of scientists attempted to fill the void by either reconstructing hypothetical ancestors or by suggesting scenarios of hominization. It is easy to understand why the studies in comparative anatomy created a sense of anticipation about both the physical conformation of humankind's earliest ancestors as well as the process of anthropogenesis.

RECONSTRUCTING HYPOTHETICAL ANCESTORS

Two different sources were used during the 1860–1890 period to reconstruct humankind's hypothetical ancestors. The first one, suggestively used by Haeckel, Darwin, and Hovelacque, directly derived from comparative anatomy, as might have been expected. The second source came, maybe somewhat unexpectedly, from the field of prehistoric archeology. This latter source was explicitly exploited by Roujou, but also especially by de Mortillet.

Comparative anatomy. Remember that as early as the first decade of the nineteenth century Lamarck proposed a scenario of hominization. This hypothetical approach to human evolution continued after 1860. For some scholars, this procedure was entirely a by-product of comparative anatomy.[20] For instance, we have already seen that Haeckel (1876: 292–300) held that humans stemmed from the hominoid apes. Haeckel imagined a hypothetical intermediate stage between this man-like ape and the living humans. He created *Pithecanthropus*, a speechless ape-like man. Haeckel argued that the development of the man-like ape into modern humans through *Pithecanthropus* occurred in two major adaptational steps. The first step saw the specialization of the upper and the lower parts of the body: The upper part adapted to the function of grasping and handling, while the lower part adapted to standing and walking. These new adaptations instigated changes to the vertebral column, the pelvic girdle, and the shoulders. At this *Pithecanthropus* stage, the body was assumed to be already modern in conformation, with the exception of the brain. Haeckel described this creature as possessing a long skull, thick woolly hair, a dark skin, long and strong upper limbs, short and thinner lower limbs. The gait of this creature was said to be a semi-erect one. The second adaptational step was related to speech. With the development of an articulate language, humankind was believed to have completed its transformation from *Pithecanthropus*. This last step was accompanied by the development of the brain and the mental skills.

Like Haeckel before him, Darwin also proposed a reconstruction of humankind's earliest ancestors. It will be remembered that Darwin argued that humankind was descended from an ape-like form that stemmed from the base of the hominoid ape branch. Darwin (1871: 206–207) contended that the early progenitors of humans were covered with hair, possessed pointed ears capable of movement, had a tail, a prehensile foot, great canine teeth (especially in males), and lived in the trees. Darwin (1871: 140–151) also conjectured on the possible process of anthropogenesis. He explained that as soon as some primate forms came to live on the ground, owing to the changing conditions or to new strategies in food gathering, such forms would have become modified to adapt either to a quadrupedal or a bipedal locomotion. Human ancestors, continued Darwin, exploited the latter avenue. This new bipedal adaptation would have instigated a series of morphological transformations in the course of time. Freed hands and arms being advantageous, the progenitors of humans became more and more erect. The upper part of the body was modified for prehension skills, while the lower part for firm support on the ground. Indirect modifications then followed from the free use of the upper limbs and hands. First, these permitted the use of tools for defense, thus allowing the size reduction of the large jaws and teeth once needed during such an activity. Ultimately, the prognathism of the face was also reduced. Eventually, the brain was also enlarged and the mental faculties increased.

Dissatisfied with the previous efforts of Haeckel and Darwin, Hovelacque (1877) tried to present a better reconstruction of the precursor of humankind (e.g., Richard, 1993). Hovelacque reconstructed the ape-like creature of the Tertiary period that produced crude artefacts and was referred to by de Mortillet as *Anthropopithecus* (see below). Hovelacque made it clear that this original human form was a general morphological type already composed of several distinct races that were the source of the present human diversity. Hovelacque's method of reconstruction rested on the systematic use of comparative anatomy. Two basic assumptions were among his premises. First, no particular living apes were closer to the humans than any others. Secondly, some human races presented more primitive features than others, thus taking them closer to a simian ancestor. However, he made it clear that more primitive human races were not links between the more advanced ones and a simian ancestor. The salient features of Hovelacque's reconstruction are summarized as follows. Like the hominoid apes and the human races, some human precursors had dolichocephalic skulls, while others had brachycephalic ones. They all had a lower mean endocranial capacity than any modern human races, but one that was probably higher than the highest mean endocranial capacity values among the living hominoid apes. The frontal portion of this precursor's cranium was greatly reduced and flattened, as seen among the "lower" human races and the apes. The same applied to the supraorbital torus which was salient, as seen in the fossil crania of Neandertal, Eguisheim, Engis, and Gibraltar.

According to Hovelacque (1875), the simian traits identified on the ancient human remains of the Quaternary period, thus far discovered, constituted positive proof for both the transmutation theory and the origin of the human races from a stem shared in common with the hominoid apes. Indeed, our precursors also had a greater prognathism, large canine teeth, and a simian-like mandible, as seen in the fossil jaw of La Naulette. Although bipedal, Hovelacque insisted that humankind's precursor could not have been entirely erect as yet.

Squeezing blood out of stone tools.[21] The other avenue exploited to conceive humankind's hypothetical ancestor appealed not to the method of comparative anatomy but rather to prehistoric archeology. A particular feature of the research about human origins has always been that artefacts recovered are substantially more abundant than the human remains themselves. The field of prehistoric archeology has been instrumental in the establishment of the presence of intelligent beings in ancient times. After repeated claims of prehistoric finds during the first half of the nineteenth century, the scientific community finally recognized around 1860, after crucial and careful discoveries made in France and England, that human artefacts were found in contemporaneity with extinct animals of the Quaternary or the

Pleistocene period (e.g., Cohen & Hublin, 1989; Grayson, 1983; Trigger, 1989; Van Riper, 1993). From that time on, scholars saw an important input of empirical data coming from the numerous excavations then being conducted in Europe, especially in Western Europe. They were confronted with the tasks of identifying lithic industries and of placing them in their proper temporal context. Debates erupted on both counts. Within a few decades, an archaeological framework for prehistoric Europe, which persisted well into the twentieth century, was established. By the last few decades of the nineteenth century, prehistoric Europe was commonly divided into the Palaeolithic period (with industries such as the Chellean, Acheulean, Mousterian, Solutrean, and Magdalenian) and the Neolithic period (with industries such as the Robenhausian).

If most scientists from the 1860s on agreed that the existence of humankind could be positively documented in the Quaternary era, others believed that this could also be the case for the much older deposits of the Tertiary era (e.g., Bourgeois, 1872; Capellini, 1876; Prestwich, 1892; Ribeiro, 1880). Two issues kept recurring in what was first called the controversy over Tertiary man, and later as the controversy over the Eolith tools. First, the nature of the supposed artefacts was disputed because their crudeness made them look like natural objects. Were they man-made or not? Second, the geological provenance of the material was often questioned. Were they as ancient as some claimed? This debate persisted well into the twentieth century (e.g., Grayson, 1986; Spencer, 1988, 1990: 1-28). Undoubtedly, this situation contributed to the creation of a sense of anticipation about the eventual recovery of the fossil remains of these ancient tool-makers. But for some scholars, the recovery of such artefacts was more than just a sign of the presence of toolmakers, for it was also a valuable source of information about the toolmakers themselves. These latter scholars assumed that biological evolution was a mirror of cultural evolution. This assumption has not been uncommon in the field of human evolution (e.g., Delisle, 2000a). This particular approach was especially exploited by Roujou and de Mortillet during the 1860–1890 period.

According to Roujou (1867, 1873), the existence of artefacts in the Tertiary era only confirmed the expected presence of humankind in these ancient times. This was a predictable outcome of the theory of evolution, continued Roujou, considering that humankind was derived from a simian form. It was argued that just as the faunas had changed in the course of time, so did humankind. Roujou believed that this was probably an indication that humankind was probably of a different conformation in Tertiary times from what it is today. The primitive state of early humans seemed to be confirmed, in Roujou's (1873: 677) mind, by the crudeness of their artefacts in the Tertiary era: "As far as the crudeness of the stone tools of the Miocene period is concerned, it can easily be explained by recognizing that mankind was, at this early time, a much more inferior being . . . "[22] [My translation]

More clearly than Roujou, de Mortillet fully exploited the assumption that biological evolution was a mirror of cultural evolution. Of all the scientists who considered artefacts to be a most valuable source of information about the toolmakers themselves, de Mortillet was the one who made the greatest use of it. Not unlike Roujou, de Mortillet's synthesis pulled together elements from geology, paleontology, and prehistoric archaeology (de Mortillet, 1873, 1879, 1883, 1892; e.g., Pautrat, 1993). For lack of sufficient fossil material to fill up the agenda of documenting human biological evolution, de Mortillet relied heavily on prehistoric archaeology.

De Mortillet subscribed to a view of transmutation that was derived from geology and paleontology: The succession of strata showed that the constitution of the faunas and the floras had inevitably changed with time. Such changes were commonly believed not to be radical between two successive strata but rather partial and gradual, thus establishing phylogenetic links between them. De Mortillet referred to this process as the "paleontological law." From there, he enshrined the fossil and the artefactual material he judged relevant to the understanding of human evolution within this evolutionary and geological framework.

Europe, for instance, was believed to be the seat of a gradual co-evolution of a simian form into modern human type, as seen by its fossil remains, but especially by the transformation of crude and primitive industries into complex ones. Indeed, de Mortillet turned to the oldest artefactual material, considered by him to be of the Tertiary era (Miocene), and thought it justified to recognize the hypothetical fabricators of these supposed artefacts as belonging to a different genus, for which he adopted the name of *Anthropopithecus*. Furthermore, he recognized three hypothetical species of the genus *Anthropopithecus* on the basis of both the time dimension and the distinctions among the artefacts themselves. It is worth quoting de Mortillet (1883: 105–106) at some length:

> This genus obviously had to contain several species. Actually, the *Anthropopithecus* of Thenay [*A. bourgeoisii*], found in the Aquitanian time horizon, cannot belong to the same species than the one found at Cantal [*A. ramesii*], dated to the Tortonian. Between these two geological periods, the upper and the lower parts of the Miocene, there was a complete renewal of the fauna. We can also assert that the *Anthropopithecus* from Portugal [*A. ribeiroii*] is not similar to those of France. Its industry is very peculiar. Therefore, we have to recognize three distinct species of *Anthropopithecus*. . . . The only information that one has about the anatomical conformation of these creatures, is that they were sensibly smaller than humans. This characteristic was especially true of *Anthropopithecus bourgeoisii*. The stone tools of Thenay are remarkable by their small size. . . . The stone tools from Portugal, equally too small for living humans, indicate nonetheless a form of *Anthropopithecus* which is more similar to the human proportions.[23] [My translation]

If, as it was supposed, the Tertiary era was characterized by very crude stone and bone tools not very clearly distinguished from one another, the Quaternary era, continued de Mortillet, saw a succession in time of complex and very definite industries like the Chellean, the Mousterian, the Solutrean, the Magdalenian and the Robenhausian. De Mortillet used this succession of industries in time as chronological markers for the scarce human fossil record. The fossil remains from Neandertal, Canstadt, Eguishem, Olmo, and La Naulette, which were associated with the Chellean industry and possibly the Mousterian one, were united in the Neandertal race. De Mortillet recognized a number of simian features in this Neandertal race, thus demonstrating clearly that humans were related to other primates. Furthermore, de Mortillet saw in the Neandertal "race" a species distinct from that of the living humans. While de Mortillet specified that a yet undiscovered human race was associated with the Solutrean industry, he promoted that the fossils from d'Arcy and Laugerie-Basse (Laugerie race) were associated with the Magdalenian industry, and those from Cro-Magnon (Cro-Magnon race) with the Robenhausian industry.

CONCLUSION

The three global debates in human evolution between 1860 and 1890—humankind's place among the primates, the monogeny/polygeny debate and the hypothetical reconstruction of humankind's ancestor—show clearly that evolutionary considerations were vigorously applied to humankind during that period, no matter what the different bases of this evolutionism were and regardless of the assessment of some recent commentators (see Chapter 3). It is remarkable that as soon as transmutation was accepted by most scientists, all the key questions pertaining to human origins were rapidly and openly debated in evolutionary terms. By far the most impressive feature of this period is the diversity of viewpoints held about humankind's place among the primates. Considering such a level of disagreement among the scholars, it became apparent that these debates would not be resolved rapidly. This is especially true when considering that so much remained to be done, at the time, to gather the necessary empirical information, even among the living primates (including the humans).

Key evolutionary questions remained unsettled, partly because of a lack of a suitable fossil record. It is true that scientists like Broca, de Mortillet, Hovelacque, Schaaffhausen, Topinard, and Vogt identified a number of so-called simian features among the human fossils. It was believed that these features might be indicative of humankind's ascent from a lower type of primate. This being said, a consensus prevailed at the time that the hominid fossil record was virtually devoid of any specimen which could represent an intermediate form between the modern humans and a supposed primate ancestor.[24] That is why some scholars turned to the reconstruction of a hypothetical intermediate form to fill the void. We will see in the next chapter that the human fossil record was intensively exploited during the 1860–1890 period. However, considering the very nature of that record, questions raised in the global debates remained largely unanswered by it. This explains why the field of human evolution was not, at the time, a unified or a monolithic research area. Instead, it was characterized by a multileveled disciplinary structure which corresponded both to the empirical reality of the time as well as to the multiplicity of the research traditions which contributed to its rise around 1860.

This multileveled structure of paleoanthropology can easily be overlooked if the field is entirely envisioned as being merely a by-product—a sort of outgrowth—of transformism. In this latter and more traditional perspective, viewpoints debated within human evolution are seen as simply echoing—on a smaller scale—larger issues being debated in evolutionary biology. This is one of the assumptions held by the historian of science Peter J. Bowler (1986). This view leads Bowler to reduce the debates on human phylogeny to considerations over the evolutionary patterns as influenced by the evolutionary processes (theories). In Bowler's conception, human fossil discoveries are unimportant in determining the views on human phylogeny, as fossils are simply inserted in evolutionary patterns which are themselves suggested by evolutionary processes. It is true that the impact of the fossil record had been greatly limited during some historical periods of paleoanthropology. As will be seen in Chapter 5, this is especially true for the first third of the twentieth century. However, the limited impact of the human fossil record is barely attributable to the assumed influence of the evolutionary processes and theories. What's more, the fossil record genuinely loomed large in debates over human phylogeny during the 1930s and 1940s (see Chapter 6). The next chapter will shown that this was also the case during the 1860–1890 period, to the extent that the modern observer applies the proper analytical perspective to the field. Considering Bowler's conception of the nature of paleoanthropology, it is not surprising that he completely overlooked the debates which powerfully appealed to the human fossil record between 1860 and 1890.

It is not that the global debates presented in this chapter were entirely uncoupled from questions pertaining to evolutionary patterns and processes. This is clearly seen in the standpoints of Broca, Hervé, Hovelacque, and Vogt in favor of polygenetic transformism and those of Darwin and Haeckel in favor of monophyletism. Once this is recognized, however, it does not imply that the global debates in human evolution were necessarily determined by broader considerations on evolutionary patterns and processes. In fact, the reverse may well be true, at least in some instances. It is apparent that several proponents of polygenetic transformism opted for this general conception of evolution because of their understanding of human evolution. For these scholars, the differences between the living human races were so important that they could not convince themselves to explain it by monophyletism. The field of human evolution cannot be reduced to a passive role in front of the rise of evolutionary biology and its accompanying theories. I surmise that the former contributed, at least to some extent, to the development of the latter. More important for our thesis here than the possible impact of paleoanthropology on the development of evolutionary biology is the notion that many debates in paleoanthropology at the time were not by-products of specific evolutionary theories but were rather merely consistent with them. This consistency argument will be further developed in Chapters 5, 9, and 10.

NOTES

1. For some discussion of Owen's view see T.H. Huxley, "On the Zoological Relations of Man with the Lower Animals," *Natural History Review*, 1 (1861): 67–84; P. Broca, "Réponse aux observations de M. le professeur Richard Owen," *Bulletins de la Société d'Anthropologie de Paris*, 2e série, 5 (1870): 592–605. For an account of the confrontation between Owen

and Huxley on this matter see A. Desmond, *Archetypes and Ancestors: Palaeontology in Victorian London, 1850–1875* (London: Blond & Briggs, 1982), pp. 74–83.

2. The original text reads as follow: "... on n'a pas encore découvert l'*ancêtre commun* d'où seraient issus l'Homme et les singes; et on ne peut pas montrer un seul terme de la série d'êêtres intermédiaires, qui est censée avoir existé entre lui et nous. La conception d'une *parenté collatérale* entre l'espèce humaine et les autres primates ... [ne peut] en appeler au moindre fait d'expérience ou d'observation. Par conséquent ... cette explication des origines humaines ne peut être acceptée par quiconque tiendra compte des justes exigences de la science moderne" [not my italics]. On this particular conception of de Quatrefages see also G. Laurent, "Idées sur l'origine animale de l'homme en France au XIXe siècle," in R. Corbey and B. Theunissen (eds.), *Ape, Man, Apeman: Changing Views since 1600* (Leiden University: Department of Prehistory, 1995), pp. 157–171.

3. Haeckel's 1876 book was originally published as *Natürliche Schöpfungsgeschichte* (Berlin: Georg Reimer, 1868), while his 1896 book was originally published as *Anthropogenie oder Entwicklungsgeschichte des Menschen* (Leipzig: Wilhelm Englemann, 1874).

4. See Haeckel's phylogenetic trees in *The History of Creation: Or the Development of the Earth and Its Inhabitants by the Action of Natural Causes*, Vol. 2 (London: H.S. King, 1876), p. 271 and *The Evolution of Man: A Popular Exposition of the Principal Points of Human Ontogeny and Phylogeny*, Vol. 2 (New York: Appleton, 1896), p. 189. Haeckel published a phylogenetic tree of the primates in relation to humankind as early as 1866 in his *Generelle Morphologie der Organismen*, 2 Vols (Berlin: Georg Reimer, 1866). The latter tree is among several other phylogenetic trees of plants and animals at the end of the second volume. This is perhaps the earliest tree on human phylogeny ever to be published.

5. Darwin's tree is reproduced in H.E. Gruber, *Darwin on Man* (New York: E.P. Dutton, 1974), p. 197.

6. It should be noted that during most of the second half of the nineteenth century no intermediary geological period between the Miocene and the Eocene was recognized. The Oligocene period was created and placed between the Miocene and Eocene periods only at the end of the nineteenth century or early in the twentieth century.

7. O. Schmidt's book of 1887 was first published in German as *Descendenzlehre und Darwinismus* (Leipzig, 1873).

8. O. Schmidt, *Descendenzlehre und Darwinismus* (Leipzig, 1873), p. 250 or O. Schmidt, *The Doctrine of Descent and Darwinism*, 7th edition (London: Kegan Paul, Trench, 1887), p. 269.

9. The original text reads as follow: "Pour nous résumer sur l'Homme, les Anthropoïdes [hominoids] et les Singes [Old and New World monkeys], nous prendrons la comparaison de l'ordre des Primates à un arbre. Les Lémuriens en sont les racines donnant naissance à une ou plusieurs souches. L'une de celles-ci est la souche des Singes, dont l'une des branches émet un rameau plus élevé, celui des Anthropoïdes [hominoids]. Une autre, dont le point d'origine ou de contact avec la précédente nous échappe, donne le rameau humain actuel, qui s'élève parallèlement à celui des Anthropoïdes, sans relation avec lui, et le dépasse."

10. Hartmann's book was originally published as *Die menschenähnlichen Affen und ihre Organization im Vergleich zur menschlichen* (Leipzig: F.A. Brockhaus, 1883).

11. At least another scholar was apparently greatly influenced by Vogt's polyphyletic conception. See E. Dally, "Introduction," in T.H. Huxley, *De la Place de l'Homme dans la Nature* (Paris: J.B. Baillière, 1868), pp. 1–95. It is interesting to note that Dally envisioned the common ancestor between the humans and the apes to be more human-like than any simian form yet known or discovered.

12. Vogt's book was originally published as *Vorlesungen über den Menschen, seine Stellung in der Schöpfung und in der Geschichte der Erde*, 2 Vols. (Giessen, 1864a).

13. Vogt's and Specht's book was originally published as *Die Säugethiere in Wort und Bild* (München, 1882).

14. Hovelacque's and Hervé's original text reads as follows: "Presque toutes les difficultés auxquelles s'est notamment heurté le transformisme, quand il a dû rendre compte de la formation des races humaines, disparaissent, si l'on admet que les grandes divisions naturelles de l'humanité se sont développées isolément, en des centres géographiques séparés, à plusieurs époques, et

qu'elles descendent d'espèces ou de genres différents. . . . Rien ne s'oppose d'une façon absolue à ce qu'il y ait eu, à l'époque miocène, des régions du globe habitées par des anthropoïdes [hominoids] dont l'évolution aurait dépassé le stade auquel se sont arrêtés les anthropoïdes [hominoids] actuels. . . . Il y a lieu de penser qu'ils formaient plusieurs groupes, d'espèces ou même de genres différents, à habitats séparés, et dérivant eux-mêmes d'autant de formes distinctes de singes pithéciens [monkeys]. Ainsi s'expliquerait, par la pluralité des origines, la diversité des types humains."

15. A few years later, Huxley recognized only four distinct races among living humans. See T.H. Huxley, "On the Distribution of the Races of Mankind, and Its Bearing on the Antiquity of Man," *Congrès International d'Anthropologie et d'Archéologie Préhistoriques*, 3e session (1868): 92–97.

16. See Haeckel's phylogenetic trees in his *Generelle Morphologie der Organismen*, Vol. 2 (Berlin: Georg Reimer, 1866). The trees are at the end of this volume.

17. Darwin's principle of divergence is clearly seen in his diagram, which appeared in *On the Origin of Species* (London: John Murray, 1859). In the first edition of 1859, this diagram is on the page next to p. 116.

18. De Quatrefages's original text goes as follow: "Dolichocéphale ou brachycéphale, grand ou petit, orthognathe ou prognathe, l'homme quaternaire est toujours homme dans l'acception entière du mot".

19. Topinard's book was first published as *L'Anthropologie* (Paris: Reinwald, 1876).

20. Among other scholars of some interest not discussed here and which insisted on some features of humankind's hypothetical ancestor see H. Schaaffhausen, "On the Primitive Form of the Human Skull," *Anthropological Review*, 6 (1868): 412–431; and G. Hervé, "L'homme descend-t-il d'un animal grimpeur," *L'Homme*, 3 (1886): 513–523; and "Les prétendus Quadrumanes," *Bulletins de la Société d'Anthropologie de Paris*, 3e série, 12 (1889): 680–717.

21. This very suggestive subtitle is borrowed from an archeologist, the late Glynn L. Isaac.

22. Roujou's original text reads like this: "Pour ce qui est des formes grossières des silex taillés miocènes, elles peuvent très-bien s'expliquer en admettant que l'homme de cette époque était extr[ehat]mement inférieur. . . ."

23. De Mortillet's original text reads as follows: "Ce genre évidemment devait contenir plusieurs espèces. En effet, l'anthropopithèque de Thenay [*A. bourgeoisii*], qui est aquitanien, ne peut appartenir à la même espèce que celui de Cantal [*A. ramesii*], qui est tortonien. Entre ces deux époques géologiques, la base et le sommet du miocène, il y a eu changement complet de faune. Nous pouvons aussi affirmer que l'anthropopithèque de Portugal [*A. ribeiroii*] ne se rapporte pas à ceux de France. En effet, son industrie a un caractère tout particulier. Nous devons donc admettre trois espèces d'anthropopithèques. . . . La seule donnée comme description anatomique que nous puissions avoir sur ces anthropopithèques, c'est qu'ils étaient sensiblement plus petits que l'homme. Ce caractère existait surtout dans l'Anthropopithecus Bourgeoisii. En effet, les silex taillés de Thenay sont remarquables par leurs petites dimensions . . . Les pierres taillées de Portugal, trop petites aussi pour l'homme actuel, dénotent pourtant un anthropopithèque se rapprochant des proportions humaines."

24. On this last point, among others, see T.H. Huxley, *Evidence as to Man's Place in Nature* (London: Williams & Norgates, 1863), reprinted in *Thomas Henry Huxley. Collected Essays (1893–1894)*, Vol. VII (Hildesheim: Georg Olms Verlag, 1970), p. 205; C. Vogt, *Lectures on Man: His Place in Creation, and in the History of the Earth* (London: Longman, Green, Longman, and Roberts, 1864a), p. 463; H. Schaaffhausen, "On the Primitive Form of the Human Skull," *Anthropological Review*, 6 (1868), p. 431; C.R. Darwin, *The Descent of Man, and Selection in Relation to Sex*, Vol. 1 (London: John Murray, 1871), p. 185; E. Haeckel, *The History of Creation: Or the Development of the Earth and Its Inhabitants by the Action of Natural Causes*, Vol. 2 (London: H.S. King, 1876), p. 326; P. Topinard, "Les dernières étapes de la généalogie de l'homme," *Revue d'Anthropologie*, 3 (1888), p. 332.

3

The Human Fossil Record

A HISTORIOGRAPHICAL NOTE

The human fossil record was of little use during the 1860–1890 period in the process of establishing a broad perspective on the question of humankind's place in nature, as seen in the so-called global debates. This does not mean, however, that the fossil record was useless during that period. To evaluate its profound significance, one needs to understand at what level of analysis it was interpreted. Its full potential was exploited in the establishment of the prehistoric peopling of Europe, as these fossils were largely restricted to this geographical area. This was done through what we call here the local debates (as opposed to the global debates). A useful way to grasp the situation at the time in the field of human evolution is to compare it with the practice of vertebrate palaeontology. Rainger (1985) argued convincingly that vertebrate palaeontologists were often constrained to produce phylogenetic trees of higher taxonomic levels (genera, families), because of the paucity of the vertebrate fossils, among other reasons. In human evolution, on the contrary, the nature of the fossil material at scientists' disposal constrained them to investigate human phylogeny at lower taxonomic levels (individuals, populations, races). Not only was this fossil record largely restricted to Europe, it was also composed of fairly numerous and modern-looking specimens.

Two assumptions made in the recent literature about the study of the human fossil record during the 1860–1890 period should be qualified. First, as human fossils were often interpreted as being representative of ancient European races rather than of evolutionary stages in human evolution, it has sometimes been assumed that it is because the idea of evolution was not widely spread or accepted yet. Thus, Tattersall (1995: 15) asserts:

> But as long as the idea of the mutability of species (as opposed to varieties of species) was entertained only as an abstraction, as a philosophical concept rather than an

> organizing principle of the diversity of life, what . . . [everyone] necessarily lacked was the idea of common descent among species. . . . That the Neanderthaler . . . might represent not a variety but a relative—perhaps even an ancestor—of modern humankind was totally foreign to the prevailing mindset.

This alleged opposition between an evolutionary perspective and one concerned with the establishment of human's racial past is maintained also by Leguebe (1986: 19):

> This viewpoint [to consider the Neandertal as a race and not as a distinct species from modern humans] is the one which is adopted by numerous naturalists at the time: It constitutes a means to reduce the possible impact of the increasing support in favor of evolutionism on the genealogy of the human species.[1] [My translation]

As far as the application of evolutionism to humankind is concerned, we have seen in the previous chapter how the transmutation theory was widely embraced after 1860. Therefore, we should look elsewhere to explain why ancient human remains were interpreted as representatives of prehistoric European races.

Another frequent assumption made about the reception given to the human fossils at the time is that they were interpreted either as representing an early stage of human evolution by evolutionists or as modern humans deformed by a pathology according to anti-evolutionists. For instance, Reader (1981: 25) wrote:

> Broadly speaking there were two points of view. The physical peculiarities of Neanderthal Man represented either an early stage of human evolution linking man to an ape-like ancestor, or pathological deformities of modern man more gross than any medical science had ever encountered. . . . Those willing to accept the theory [of evolution] believed the remains were very old and freely discussed their primitive, 'barbarous' and ape-like characteristics in evolutionary terms. Those opposed to the theory of evolution . . . believed the remains were of modern man and sought a modern, medical explanation for their peculiarities.

This thesis was also supported by Trinkaus and Shipman (1993: 53, 58, 59–60) in the following terms:

> [Considering the discovery of the Neandertal skull, Schaaffhausen] thought he had found direct evidence supporting his theory of the mutability of species and the descent of humans from apes. . . . [Whereas] the Neandertal remains were pathological in Virchow's terms in that they were unlike modern humans. . . . Underlying all this was his deep dislike of evolutionary ideas. . . . In this regard, he fought acceptance of the Neandertals because they implied that evolution occurred. . . . Virchow tried to suppress the acceptance of evolutionary ideas or any hominid fossils by every means possible until he died in 1902.

Some anti-evolutionists might have held that some human fossils were modern pathological forms. However, it must be noted that some sympathizers of the transmutation theory, such as Blake (1863, 1864a, 1864b) and Hunt (1866, 1867), also held that the Neandertal skull was pathological (Blake, 1862: 207; Hunt, 1864: XV). Two points must be insisted upon here. First, scientists repudiating a simian ancestry for humankind should not be considered as necessarily anti-evolutionists. After all, humankind could have been derived from nonsimian forms, as alluded to by Owen, Mivart, and de Quatrefages (see Chapter 2). In fact, it is surprisingly difficult to find clear and open anti-evolutionary statements after 1870 in the circle of human evolution. Without being avowed evolutionists, a number of scientists after 1860 considered transmutation to be either a valid hypothesis or accepted it in principle as being highly probable, although perhaps insufficiently documented or explained as yet. Of great value here is the distinction introduced by Harvey (1983) between materialist scientists who judged hypothetical statements to be a crucial part of the scientific enterprise, versus positivist scientists who refrained from speculative statements, preferring more solid grounds to build science on. We should also keep in mind that as the nineteenth century progressed and the doctrine of evolution was being accepted, it became more and more difficult for scientists to take a truly anti-evolutionary stance without suggesting a valid scientific alternative.

The second point which must be insisted upon is that besides an anti-evolutionary stance, there were positive scientific reasons to defend the interpretation that the Neandertal remains were pathological. For instance, Davis held that the apparent simian configuration of the Neandertal skull was caused by a pathological deformation such as synostosis, that is, premature closing of cranial sutures. He referred to Virchow, Lucae, and Welcker as authorities who contributed brilliantly to the study of such processes. Far from being of rare occurrence according to Davis (1863–1864, 1864), it was pointed out that ancient races in Italy and Britain seemed to have been affected by synostosis to an uncommon frequency, thus breaking the apparent isolation of this phenomenon in the Neandertal specimen. The understanding of the growth and development of skulls was considered at the time to be a great achievement of the science of craniology (e.g., Retzius, 1874).

Furthermore, pathology could also serve as a basis for support of an evolutionary perspective. For instance, Étienne Geoffroy Saint-Hilaire and Richard Owen were both inspired, before 1860, by teratology (the study of abnormal ontogenetic development) as a possible mechanism of transmutation (e.g., Fischer, 1972; Laurent, 1977; Richards, 1987). For Virchow, similarly, every variation was a disruption of the organism and was therefore pathological by definition. But if such variations or deviations were passed on through the inheritance of acquired characteristics, the passage from one type to another could thus be completed. By such means, new varieties, species, and maybe genera could have been formed (e.g., Churchill, 1976). This being said, Virchow (1872, 1882) considered human fossils such as the Neandertal skull and the La Naulette jaw to be only isolated instances of individual pathology, for he (1874) insisted that they were not to be confused with new races that originated from pathology. Virchow (1867) contended that, although it was possible to imagine that new human races may arise by such a process, still there were no positive observations to support this.

However, there is more to it. As will be seen below, ancient human remains were largely used to establish the prehistoric peopling of Europe during the 1860–1890 period. How could the so-called anti-evolutionists try to counteract the evolutionary interpretation of human fossils, if the so-called evolutionists themselves were not engaged in research activities that could be considered to be "typically" evolutionary? That is to say, they were not engaged in identifying evolutionary stages of humankind with the assistance of the fossil record. It might even be argued that there was no need at all to be an evolutionist in order to study the prehistoric peopling of Europe.

In fact, it is not clear who were the scientists that supposedly proposed such "typical" evolutionary interpretations. For instance, when considering the Neandertal skull, Blake (1864a: cxliv; 1865–1866: 80), by no means an anti-evolutionist, wrote that some "writers authoritatively declared that we had at last discovered the 'missing link' which binds man and the apes," although he failed to identify these writers. In the same fashion, Pruner-Bey (1869: 674), having in mind the Neandertal skull and the La Naulette jaw, declared that ". . . we speak of crania, simian jaws or intermediary beings between man and ape . . . which gives the impression that . . . the ape-man is a reality" [my translation], without referring to any scientist who supposedly held such a view.[2] For his part, Davis (1863–1864: 281; 1864: 714) contended that some authors seemed to be disposed to interpret the Neandertal skull as a link between humankind and the other primates, although he specified that this position had not been clearly stated by anyone, and also failed to name any scientist who might have alluded to it. Lastly, Mayer (1864) mentioned that Huxley and others would have held that the Neandertal skull was a kind of intermediate link between man and the apes. Huxley (1864) rightly replied to this misconstrued view. What Huxley (1894 [1863]: 157–208) had stated was simply that the Neandertal skull was the most pithecoid yet discovered, although he had asserted that in no sense could this fossil be regarded as intermediate between humans and apes.

It is true that scientists like Broca, de Mortillet, Hovelacque, Huxley, Schaaffhausen, Topinard, and Vogt identified a number of so-called simian features among human fossils. These were interpreted as support for the hypothesis of the human's simian ancestry, but everyone agreed that no intermediate form or stage between humans and a putative simian ancestor had yet been discovered. Also, it should be noted that terms such as "pithecoid," "ape-like" and "simious" were often used at the time in a strictly descriptive sense without any real evolutionary implication, as Spencer (1984: 6–7) correctly noted.[3] In fact, most if not all human fossils discovered during the 1860–1890 period were considered to be, generally speaking, modern looking. Among the few clear statements to the contrary was King's proposition to classify the Neandertal skull in a new species (if not a new genus) called *Homo neanderthalensis*. King (1864) judged the Neandertal skull to have the closest affinity to the apes, especially the chimpanzee. Unfortunately, he failed to specify the evolutionary implications of his position, if there were any. We already saw that de Mortillet (1883) also followed King in attributing the Neanderthal skull with the status of a new and distinct species (*Homo neanderthalensis*). This being said, it is clear that too much weight must not be given to the naming of new human fossil species in a historical period that was, after all, often relativising the distinction between human races and species (see below).

Let us simply insist upon the fact that whether human fossils were interpreted as modern pathological forms or as more or less ancient and relatively modern-looking human representatives with so-called simian features, the gulf which separated these two views was far from being as irreconcilable as some modern observers have claimed.

THE ARYAN ORIGIN MODEL

A number of modern observers have tried to understand the rise of paleoanthropology by focusing on the reception given to a limited number of human fossil discoveries (e.g., Delisle, 1998). By so doing, they have extracted the field from its proper historical context. It is true that some discoveries made during the nineteenth century generated considerable discussion at the time. This is especially true of the Engis skull discovered in Belgium in 1833, the Neandertal skull discovered in Germany in 1856, and the La Naulette jaw discovered in Belgium in 1866.[4] These three remains were interpreted along the following lines: They were held as being within the normal variation of the human species; as instances of human pathological variation; as human variation previously unknown; or, as combination of such variants. But I surmise that the real interest of such discoveries lies not in their individual evaluation but rather in their collective evaluation. Indeed, the remains from Engis, Neandertal, and La Naulette, far from being isolated, belonged to a fairly important fossil sample, which was interpreted in a wider context that needs to be addressed. This wider context was not the worldwide monogeny/polygeny debate, as already alluded to. The more local consideration for the peopling of Europe constituted such a framework. Several scholars who contributed to the global debates were also among the leading figures in the local debates.

One model of the peopling of Europe widely held during the first part of the nineteenth century suggested that most peoples of Europe originated in Asia. This view was based on the results of comparative philology which indicated that the Indo-European tongues were affiliated. This conception was often referred to as the Aryan origin. It led to the assumption that European races which belonged to the Indo-European family were all derived from a single stock. The non-Aryan tongues in use among Europeans, being sometimes affiliated with the Mongoloid or Touranian family, were attributed to remnant populations of past races that inhabited Europe before the arrival of the Aryans. This view was strengthened when an anatomical dimension was added to it around the mid-nineteenth century. The first anatomical investigations of the living races of Europe belonging to these two alleged ethnic groups (pre-Aryans and Aryans) by Retzius in the 1840s and 1850s tended to demonstrate that the first inhabitants of Europe were brachycranial (the Finns, the Lapps, the Basques, etc.) or round-headed, while the invaders of the Aryan races were dolichocranial (the Celts) or long-headed (Blanckaert, 1989b). In Retzius's own words (1850: 86):

> This paper consisted in the Application of the theory of Arndt, Rask and others, as to the general diffusion of a race akin to the Finns over the Whole of Europe anterior to

> the immigration of the Indo-European tribes. The Celt, generally considered as the earliest inhabitants of the British Isles, has a skull remarkable for its diameter from front to back [dolichocrany]. Such, also, are the skulls found in barrows of secondary antiquity. In the most ancient, however, the skull has its chief development from side to side [brachycrany]; the conformation of the aboriginal nations hypothetically allied to the Finns and Laplander.

This view of the peopling of Europe as a superposition of two or more main ethnic groups was to provide a framework for organizing the discoveries of the ancient human remains, at least for a number of scientists such as Schaaffhausen, Spring, Pruner-Bey, and de Quatrefages, during the late 1850s and throughout the 1860s. It should be noted, however, that the precedence in geological times of the brachycranial type over the dolichocranial one, as Retzius maintained, was not always accepted by proponents of this model.

Schaaffhausen held that the peculiar conformation of the Neandertal skull exceeded the known morphological range and was not known to exist even in the most "barbarous" races. Schaaffhausen promoted that the Neandertal skull belonged to an individual who was probably derived from one of the wild races of northwestern Europe at a period prior to the arrival of the Celts and the Germans, but encountered by the German immigrants on arriving in Europe. Far from being completely isolated in Schaaffhausen's (1861 [1858]: 171–172) mind, the Neandertal skull was compared to other more or less ancient remains:

> The fragments of crania from Schwaan and Plau [Germany] . . . may probably be assigned to a barbarous, aboriginal people, which inhabited the North of Europe before the *Germani*; and, as is proved by the discovery of similar remains at Minsk in Russia, and in the Neanderthal near Elberfeld, must have been extensively spread—being allied, as may be presumed from the form of the skull, with the aboriginal populations of Britain, Ireland, and Scandinavia.

Recognizing in some living humans traces of a markedly prominent supraorbital region, Schaaffhausen contended that this trait represented the vestiges of a primitive type, which was manifested in the Neandertal skull.

More clearly than Schaaffhausen, Spring (1864) recognized that Europe had been inhabited by successive ethnic waves. When turning to the question of humankind during the Quaternary period, Spring suscribed to the evolutionary approach promoted by the palaeontologist d'Omalius d'Halloy. This approach recognized that species slowly transmuted from one stratum to another, with the introduction and extinction of a number of species in each time period (e.g., Laurent, 1987: 395–403). Not unlike de Mortillet at a later time, Spring (1864) was to rely heavily on archaeological remains to establish both a chronological framework and the means to trace back the ancient races of Europe.

The most ancient human form Spring identified in the Quaternary period was called by him the Engis race. This race, essentially composed of the remains from Engis, Engihoul, Maestricht, and Moulin-Quignon, was described as being dolichocephalic and orthognathic. Spring conjectured that this race migrated into the north-western part of Europe from the south. After a long period of transition during which the modern fauna and flora of Europe took shape, Spring identified a new human race characterized by its small stature and its brachycephalic and orthognathic conformation which he named the Chauvaux race. This latter race, believed to be a Nordic one that spread toward the south of Europe, was represented by the remains of Chauvaux, Bruniquel, and a host of remains from France, Switzerland, Ireland, and Denmark. The Basques, the Finns, and the Lapps were, in Spring's view, all affiliated with this ancient race. After some time, the Chauvaux race was confronted by the invasion of Aryan peoples (the Celts and the Germans) of dolichocephalic conformation, who were equipped with superior technologies. Spring excluded the Neandertal skull from his discussion because he contended that it had as yet no known equivalent. Under such circumstances, he judged it preferable not to rely on the Neandertal skull when considering questions pertaining to transmutation.[5]

Pruner-Bey was possibly the most influential scientist who promoted the Aryan origin model, which rested on the notion of a succession of waves which populated Europe. He inserted into this model most human fossils known by the 1860s. Pruner-Bey (1863, 1866a, 1866b, 1867) recognized two morphological types in prehistoric Europe. The most ancient race of Europe, constituted essentially of brachycranial skulls and associated remains, was of short stature and was affiliated with the mongoloid stem that included numerous inhabitants living today in Europe, Asia, and America. The other prehistoric race of lesser antiquity, mostly represented by dolichocranial skulls and associated remains, was of tall stature and was affiliated with the migration that brought the Celts (and their civilization) to Europe. In the ancient mongoloid type, Pruner-Bey included human remains from d'Arcy, Aurignac, Bruniquel, Furfooz (trou du Frontal), La Naulette, and Solutré. In the Celtic type, he gathered the remains from Engis, Lombrive, Moulin-Quignon, Neandertal and Vauréal.

After the discovery of the Cro-Magnon remains in 1868, Pruner-Bey linked these skulls to his mongoloid type (being affiliated to the living Estonians) regardless of their dolichocranial conformation. He justified this latter view by arguing first that their dolichocrany differed from the Celts', and secondly that it became clear as the science of craniology progressed that the brachycrany-dolichocrany dichotomy was of limited value because both forms often existed in a single race. Pruney-Bey (1868a, 1868b) argued that other morphological features needed also to be considered to establish race identity.

Pruner-Bey held that far from being limited to the ancient period of Europe, the two morphological types he identified persisted through time until today, although they both underwent some morphological change. For instance, he argued that the ancient Celts (including the Neandertal skull) had a sloping forehead, whereas their modern representatives greatly attenuated this feature. Pruner-Bey (1867: 353–357) also acknowledged that intermediate forms between the two morphological types existed, although he contended that their recognition depended first on the proper assessment of the types' limits, and secondly on the evaluation of the effect of their admixture.

In essence, de Quatrefages (1867: 251, 257–270, 480–487) was to agree with Pruner-Bey's conception of the peopling of Europe. According to this view, the Neandertal skull was that of a Celt and brachycranial skulls antedated dolichocranial ones. Although agreeing that the peopling of Europe had occurred as a superposition of two distinct ethnic elements, de Quatrefages was to suggest, not unlike Pruner-Bey, that the first inhabitants of Europe might have been represented by both types of skull conformation (although brachycranial skulls greatly predominated), thus possibly explaining the discoveries of ancient dolichocranial skulls at Engis and Eguisheim. In other words, what de Quatrefages envisaged was the possibility of an early peopling of Europe from a polymorphic mongoloid stem comprising both brachycranial and dolichocranial races, followed by a somewhat later and similarly polymorphic Celtic stem.

The models suggested by Retzius, Schaaffhausen, Spring, Pruner-Bey, and de Quatrefages to explain the peopling of Europe were rapidly challenged. They were challenged both by new empirical evidence against the view that brachycrany antedated dolichocrany, and by a new conception that envisioned prehistoric Europe not as a superposition of two or more distinct ethnic elements but as a complex cohabitation of several more or less ancient and distinct racial elements. Early in the 1860s, it was realized that brachycrany did not antedate dolichocrany everywhere (e.g., Blake, 1862; His, 1864; van Düben, 1865). At the same time, it was realized also that some living populations, thought at first to be either dolichocephalic or brachycephalic after the preliminary investigations of small samples by Retzius (and on which the Aryan origin model was founded), were in reality of the opposite morphological type (e.g., Broca, 1863b; Welcker, 1868). These challenges were easily bypassed or incorporated by the proponents of the Aryan origin model or the so-called Mongoloid theory, by either holding that the Mongoloid and Celtic stems were polymorphic, or by simply dismissing the supposed antiquity of some dolichocranial skulls. The latter procedure was far from illegitimate, considering the great uncertainty surrounding the dating of the human remains at the time (e.g., Oakley, 1964a). However, some scientists like Thurnam, Vogt, and Broca were unconvinced by these accommodations and ventured into another conception of the peopling of Europe during the 1860s.

BEYOND THE ARYAN ORIGIN MODEL

For Thurnam (1863–1864a), more data were required before the origins of the different peoples of Europe could be properly settled. He pointed out several elements that demonstrated the complexity of the task. These were of two orders. First, populations such as the Basques, which were previously thought to be brachycephalic, had now been demonstrated to be dolichocephalic. The reverse was true for populations such as the Germans. Second, the linkage between a morphological type and a linguistic family was broken as populations of both head shapes were speaking Aryan or Indo-European languages and non-Aryan or allophylian tongues. Thurnam would not discard the possibility of a migration into Europe of dolichocranial peoples of Indo-European origins from Asia or one of brachycranial peoples of Mongoloid origins, although he discarded the Aryan origin and Mongoloid models as explaining satisfactorily the peopling of Europe. Having demonstrated that in Britain a pre-Celtic, dolichocranial race was more ancient than the Celtic, brachycranial one (and not the reverse), Thurnam tried to explain the presence of these two types in Britain by deriving the older type from north Africa. It is worth quoting him at some length:

> A few observations may be allowed on the possible or probable affinities of the two British types. . . . I had the advantage of examining the series of sixty Basque skulls. . . . I was at once struck with their great resemblance to the dolichocephalic skulls from the long barrows of this country. . . . That they are [the Basques] the lineal descendants of the ancient Iberians, is now generally admitted by scholars. That the Iberians had their origin in northern Africa . . . is an opinion not without able advocates . . . . Altogether, the doctrine of an Iberian, or Ibero-Phoenician origin of a very early, perhaps the earliest, population of at least part of Britain, though not as yet proved, derives much additional weight from the comparison here instituted of the skulls of the British dolichocephali of the stone period with those of the Basques. That the brachycephalic skull-form of the bronze-period in Britain was introduced into this island from Gaul, and was the type of the Celtic skull, at least that of the dominant race, appears to me to be proved. What may have been the origin of this "Turanian" type of skull, and how it became that of a Celtic-speaking and so-called Indo-European people; or, conversely, how the Celtic became the language of a people with such a skull-form; are important questions for the investigation of the anthropologists of Europe. (Thurnam, 1863–1864a: 160–166).

At first, Thurnam's view was limited to the historical or immediately prehistoric times of Europe. Of even greater interest was Thurnam's (1863–1864b) reaction, a year later, to truly ancient human discoveries of Europe at Engis, Furfooz, Lombrive, and Neandertal. Now, facing this new evidence, he wondered if his conclusions regarding the presence of two morphological types in Britain could not be reinterpreted by deriving them both directly from these ancient human remains found in Europe:

> Is it not probable that the long and short skulls found in the two classes of the most ancient tombs of England . . . are the direct and but slightly modified descendants of those truly primeval long-heads and short-heads whose remains . . . are found in the bone-caves of western Europe, in England, Belgium, Germany, France, and the Spanish peninsula? (Thurnam, 1863–1864b: 519)

In a view which was more synthetic than Thurnam's, Vogt (1864a: 370–401) attempted to present what was then known about the prehistoric races of Europe. Although he did not discard completely the possibility of some ethnic elements having migrated into Europe from Asia, his conception rested on the recognition of a complex cohabitation of several morphological types that developed and persisted in Europe. In other words, his conception of the peopling of Europe was not rooted within the Aryan origin or Mongoloid models. Vogt recognized at least four ancient prehistoric races in Europe:

1. a dolichocranial and prognathous Rheno-Belgian race of the cave-bear period represented by the Engis and Neandertal skulls;
2. a somewhat dolichocranial race with a high forehead of the reindeer period (following the cave-bear period) represented by the skulls of the Lombrive cave;
3. a somewhat brachycranial race of the later Stone Age of Denmark represented by skulls from Borreby; and
4. a somewhat mesaticranial race represented by numerous skulls from the Stone and Metal Ages of Switzerland.

When considering the morphological differences that separated the Lombrive remains from those of Engis and Neandertal, Vogt judged it inadmissible to establish a relationship of descent or any type of affinity between them. He also held that the four prehistoric races identified above all had living representatives: The Rheno-Belgian skulls had their cognates in the long, narrow heads of Dutchmen, the skulls of Lombrive were allied to those of Basques, the ancient skulls from Denmark were linked to those of the Lapps and the Finns, while the ancient skulls from Switzerland persisted locally until today. Relying on the above facts, Vogt (1864a: 391–392) concluded that:

> We thus find in the oldest prehistoric times everywhere very diversified races . . . but nowhere do we find proof of migrations or radiations from a common centre over the habitable globe. Though the short-heads [brachycranial] might be derived from Asia, it would not apply to the narrow heads, which claim the highest antiquity, as no such heads are met with in Asia. Thus, the facts we adduce from the earliest periods, merely represent man as an original product of the soil he then inhabited and still inhabits. In every such old race there is presented a remarkable constancy of form, the fundamental type of which is not obliterated, though various intermixtures have taken place with later immigrants.

When considering later the persistence of the Neandertal type, Vogt (1867b: 213) explained that, although this ancient race disappeared through gradual extinction or by transmutation, it surely intermixed with other ancient races so that remnants of the former reappeared today partly through atavism.

Like Thurnam and Vogt, Broca eventually joined the scholars who promoted a complex and long cohabitation of several morphological types in Europe. Although Broca thought that brachycrany antedated dolichocrany until 1862, he was soon to become a vocal opponent of the Aryan origin and Mongoloid models. Broca (1964a, 1964b) held after that time that Europe had been inhabited for a long time by a host of non-Asian peoples comprising brachycranial races as well as dolichocranial ones. Broca further contended that when the Celts or the Aryans arrived from Asia at a later period, they found in Europe a human population not substantially different from the one we find today. If the Aryans were of dolichocranial conformation when they first arrived in waves in Europe, they slowly mixed with the indigenous populations to the point where their morphological type disappeared without having changed significantly the local types. Although the Aryans themselves changed morphologically, they nevertheless managed, step-by-step, to impose their cultures, that is, their Indo-European languages and material cultures, such as the working of metals. The Aryan invasion led to the transmission of cultures and ideas rather than the substitution of a morphological type by another.

To support his assertion that Europe had been inhabited for a long time by both brachycranial and dolichocranial races, Broca, in 1867, considered the remains from Furfooz and Solutré as representing the former type, and those from Bruniquel, Eguisheim, Engis, Lahr, and Neandertal, as representing the latter (Broca, 1867). In 1868, Broca added to his list the remains from Cro-Magnon, a dolichocranial race he evaluated to be different from all other known races, ancient and modern (Broca, 1868).

THE PEOPLING OF EUROPE AND THE MONOGENY/POLYGENY DEBATE

Let us pause to reflect on one aspect of the thesis presented here. We have argued that the monogeny/polygeny debate would not constitute the framework within which the ancient human remains were mainly interpreted during the 1860–1890 period. We have said that a more restricted framework was needed and that considerations over the peopling of Europe constituted such a framework. The discussion presented above, it is suggested, favors this interpretation. Yet, is it not possible that some scientists might have been influenced in their conception of the peopling of Europe by their respective position in the monogeny/polygeny debate? Conversely, were models of the peopling of Europe used to favor a particular side in the monogeny/polygeny debate? Here, the nature of the link between the monogeny/polygeny debate and models of the peopling of Europe is raised. From what follows, it is clear that debates over the peopling of Europe were not just debates on the European portion of the monogeny/polygeny debate.

It is true that Broca (1870c: 518), the polygenist, held that the present knowledge of the ancient human remains did not favor the view that the human races stemmed from a single stock. Whether or not he judged this to constitute strong evidence in favor of multiple origins of the human races is an entirely different matter. Considering Broca's positivist inclination, it seems doubtful that he would have thought so, no matter how strongly he believed this. Even if some scholars promoted a particular conception of the peopling of Europe because of their position in the monogeny/polygeny debate, a distinction should be made between their motive and their capacity to demonstrate it on a scientific basis. This last point is clearly seen when Broca and de Quatrefages were eventually to share a similar view of the peopling of Europe after 1870 (see below), regardless of the fact that they clung to opposite positions in the monogeny/polygeny debate. If the human fossil record suggested that the oldest human races yet found were as distinct from one another as the living ones—a view widely recognized at the time—this constituted in itself everything but a crucial argument in favor of polygeny or polyphyly. After all, it could be argued that the proof for monogeny or monophyly lay still deeper in time and/or would eventually be found in other regions of the world, a view that, for instance, Wallace (1864) and Huxley (1894 [1865]) were perfectly prepared to accept.

Pruner-Bey clearly understood that. As someone who promoted the Mongoloid model, Pruner-Bey (1866b) explained, after Broca accused him of being a monogenist, that his conception of the peopling of Europe could not be taken as supporting the monogenist hypothesis because the search for the ancient human remains, which had barely started in Europe, needed also to be expanded to other regions of the world. Pruner-Bey anticipated that the eventual discovery of ancient human races all over the world would either show signs of convergence as we go deeper into time, in which case the monogenist hypothesis would be greatly supported, or would show no signs of convergence. He admitted that the human remains discovered thus far in Europe showed that very little morphological change had occurred during the ancient times. Pruner-Bey concluded by saying that much remained to be done by the doctrinaires to demonstrate either view. He perfectly understood that, empirically speaking, there was only a very weak connection between models of the peopling of Europe and the monogeny-polygeny debate.

THE ESTABLISHMENT OF PARALLEL MODELS OF PEOPLING

If the 1860s were characterized by the confrontation of two main models of the peopling of Europe, the 1875–1890 period was one of relative unanimity. Most scientists now discarded the Aryan and Mongoloid origin models in all their rigidity. These models implied strong ties with Asia, ties which could not be strongly supported in the 1870s when the wealth and antiquity of the empirical material found in Europe, relative to other parts of the world, were considered. The immigration of ancient ethnic elements into Europe from Asia was sometimes assumed but remained to be documented. The 1875–1890 period was very much one of evaluation by scholars like Broca, Fraipont, Lohest, and Huxley of the conclusions reached in a piece of work of unprecedented breadth presented by de Quatrefages and Hamy.

In a series of studies made in the first half of the 1870s, de Quatrefages and Hamy (1873, 1874a, 1874b, 1875) attempted a synthesis of all the ancient human remains known at the time. Published collectively in the first part of their *Crania Ethnica* (1882: 1–146), these studies recognized at least three morphological types in Europe during the Quaternary period.

The most ancient type largely distributed in the substratum of Europe, which they named the Canstadt race, was composed of skulls and jaws from Canstadt, Eguisheim, Brüx, Neandertal, Gibraltar, Denise, Staengenaes, Olmo, La Naulette,

Arcy, Clichy, and Goyet. They described the Canstadt race as a dolichoplatycephalic and prognathous one with considerable variability, which was characterized also by a more or less developed supraorbital ridge and a low receding forehead. The law of atavism was judged responsible for occasional reappearances of such a physical type among the living populations throughout a large part of the Old World. However, noting a close morphological resemblance between the Canstadt race and some living populations of Australia and India, de Quatrefages and Hamy alluded to a possible affiliation between them.

The second prehistoric type they identified was the Cro-Magnon race, which was thought to have lived essentially in contemporaneity with the Canstadt race. The Cro-Magnon race was said to be restricted to western Europe. This race was represented by crania and jaws from Cro-Magnon, Laugerie-Basse, Bruniquel, Menton, Isola del Liri, Grenelle, Solutré, Engis, La Madeleine, Engihoul and Smermaas. Also a dolichocephalic but not a platycephalic race, the morphology of the forehead and the facial regions was described as being completely different from that of the Canstadt race. The Cro-Magnon type was said to be found erratically among the living Europeans. However, this type, it was contended, was found in more pronounced form and more frequently in the populations of north-western Africa; the law of atavism explaining again such occurrences.

The third prehistoric type identified by de Quatrefages and Hamy comprised crania and jaws from Furfooz, La Truchère, Grenelle, Moulin-Quignon, and Nagy-Sap. This type was in reality a group of brachycephalic and mesaticephalic remains that comprised possibly four races. Believed to have been contemporaneous at some times with the Canstadt and Cro-Magnon races, these former races persisted into the more recent times. Traces of them were said to be found among recent and living populations. De Quatrefages and Hamy affiliated the remains from Grenelle and La Truchère, but not those of Furfooz, to a Mongoloid stem. According to de Quatrefages (1988 [1883]: 77), all the morphological types and races that he and Hamy described persisted distinctly throughout the Quaternary period, regardless of admixture. However, they were diluted when successive waves of migrations of dolichocranial and brachycranial races occurred in Europe during and after the Neolithic period.

In essence, Broca (1877) was to agree with the characterization of at least three fossil races in prehistoric Europe (Canstadt, Cro-Magnon, and Furfooz) after de Quatrefages and Hamy. In 1873, Broca himself contributed to the establishment of affiliations between the tall Cro-Magnon type of the second half of the Quaternary period and the medium-size race of the Neolithic period, represented in the cave of l'Homme-Mort. Broca (1873) believed that this lineage might have had some living representatives among the Basques and the Berbers, thus demonstrating that it was submitted to morphological changes owing to external conditions and admixtures. By so doing, Broca hypothesized the possible migration of the Cro-Magnon type into Europe from northern Africa.

We have seen that de Quatrefages and Hamy recognized in the Furfooz type possibly four races of brachycephalic and mesaticephalic conformations. For Broca, the Furfooz type comprised only a single brachycephalic stem that lived first in eastern Europe late in the Quaternary period only to migrate later into western Europe. Broca (1877: 24–25) explained the presence of a mesaticephalic race in Belgium by an encounter and admixture between dolichocephalic Cro-Magnon races and the new brachycephalic comers in western Europe.

In the 1880s, new fossil discoveries fueled the debate on the prehistoric peopling of Europe. Indeed, two skeletons closely resembling the Neandertal remains found in Germany in 1856 were discovered at Spy (Belgium) in 1886. By comparing the differences between the skulls of Spy 1 and 2, Fraipont and Lohest (1887) suggested a redefinition of the Canstadt race as previously defined by de Quatrefages and Hamy. Fraipont and Lohest held that if the two Spy skulls were those of a male and a female respectively, then the Canstadt race was more likely to be represented by the skulls from Brüx, Denise, Eguisheim, Canstadt, and Spy, whereas the skulls from Castenedolo, Clichy, Olmo, and Staengenaes (females of the Canstadt race according to de Quatrefages and Hamy) would have to be attributed to another race.

Fraipont and Lohest (1887) directly addressed the question of the relationship between the Canstadt, the Cro-Magnon, and the Furfooz races. They wondered if these races could somehow all be related. They asked: ". . . can we link directly to the Neanderthal or Canstadt race the one of Cro-Magnon, and to the latter the Furfooz race?" (1887: 726) [my translation].[6] They answered this question affirmatively by suggesting a scheme linking the ancient Neandertal race to the Cro-Magnon race, and the Cro-Magnon race to the more recent Furfooz race. In support of this, they tried to bridge the morphological gap separating the Cro-Magnon type from the Neandertal or Canstadt type by establishing a morphological gradation from the females of the Cro-Magnon race, the remains from Hamoir and the females of the Canstadt race (as defined by de Quatrefages and Hamy). The affiliation between the dolichocephalic Cro-Magnon type and the brachycephalic Furfooz type was easily demonstrated, they believed, by the discovery of intermediate forms. This whole phylogenetic scheme represented a complex reticulate pattern which postulated the possible existence of at least two ancient, unamed and unknown human races as yet. Fraipont and Lohest (1887: 728–729) stated:

> This type [Neanderthal] or another type older than the former one gave rise, at one time in Asia, probably to the men whose descendents appeared under the ethnic type of Cro-Magnon which arrived in Europe with its specific features. As far as the Furfooz races are concerned . . . it is no less certain that at some point the two types [Cro-Magnon and Furfooz] went through some interbreeding. Is this the starting point of one of the Furfooz races? Or is it the result of a mixing between the pure type of Cro-Magnon and another invading and equally pure race from another region?[7] [My translation]

According to Fraipont and Lohest, an appreciable number of individuals living today in Belgium were directly descended from the Furfooz races, whereas the Cro-Magnon and the Canstadt features occasionally found among the living Europeans were not transmitted by direct inheritance but arose by atavism.

Although Fraipont and Lohest recognized that the Spy remains were characterized by an unmatched number of pithecoid traits, they contended that an abyss still separated those fossils from any living ape. However, having noted the morphological transformation that the human races underwent in Europe throughout the Quaternary era, they supposed that it should be possible to pursue the ancestral type of humankind and that of the apes much further into the past, possibly as far back as the Eocene period or even earlier. Later, Fraipont (1889) made it clear that he believed that humankind and the apes descended from a common stem.

In the light of all these human fossil discoveries, Huxley brought, in 1890, some precision to his view on human phylogeny. Remember that Huxley (1863) once stated that the Neandertal skull found in Germany in 1856 was the most pithecoid form yet discovered, although he had asserted that in no sense could this fossil be regarded as an intermediate between the humans and the apes. Now, in the light of the Spy discoveries, Huxley (1890) restated his view and asserted that the genus *Homo*, and possibly the species *Homo sapiens*, had existed as early as the Pliocene or even the Miocene period. After noting that skulls occasionally approach the neandertaloid type among the living dolichocephalic races, Huxley tried to explain such a continuity in the following way (1970 [1890]: 327–328):

> It may be taken to be a pretty sure indication of the physiological continuity of the blond long-heads [dolichocephalic] with the pleistocene Neanderthaloid men. But this continuity may have been brought about in two ways. The blond long-heads may exhibit one of the lines of evolution of the men of the Neanderthaloid type. Or, the Frisians [a living dolichocephalic race] may be the result of the admixture of the blond long-heads with Neanderthaloid men . . . The same alternatives present themselves when Neanderthaloid characters appear in skulls of other races. If these characters belong to a stage in the development of the human species, antecedent to the differentiation of any of the existing races, we may expect to find them in the lowest of these races, all over the world, and in the early stages of all races. I have already referred to the remarkable similarity of the skulls of certain tribes of native Australians to the Neanderthal skull . . . Neanderthaloid features are to be met with, not only in ancient long skulls; those of the ancient broad-headed people [brachycephalic] entombed at Borreby in Denmark have been often noted.

CONCLUSION

In order to explain why the human fossil record was interpreted within the framework of the prehistoric peopling of Europe, a number of recent observers have suggested that it was because the ancient human remains were interpreted in a sort of race-succession paradigm, in which the prehistoric morphological types of Europe were not transmuting into one another but rather were merely replacing one another (Leguebe, 1986: 19; Smith, 1997a: 712; Spencer, 1984: 10–11; Tattersall, 1995: 15; Trinkaus and Shipman, 1993: 109–110, 119). This race-succession paradigm implies that the human fossil record was not being interpreted in evolutionary terms. Yet, we have seen above how avowed evolutionists such as Schaaffhausen,

Vogt, Broca, Fraipont, Lohest, and Huxley, among others, all interpreted the ancient human remains by inserting them in complex phylogenetic hypotheses about the peopling of Europe, involving both the replacement and the transformation of races in the time dimension. Therefore, it is argued here that the race-succession paradigm, assuming that such a concept is judged of any utility, was by no means the main framework within which most scientists interpreted the human fossil record at the time.

From our contemporary viewpoint, this throws a different light than expected on the nature of the link between intraspecific and interspecific changes during the 1860–1890 period. We might have expected that, whereas phylogenies of the peopling of Europe were concerned with changes of human races (intraspecific changes), the transformation of one species into another (interspecific changes) was left out only to be explained by phylogenies debated among the global debates. However, things were not that simple. For several scholars of the time, among whom Darwin and Huxley figured, the question whether all the living humans were part of the same species was of minor importance. What really mattered to them was the recognition that the morphological types changed through time, whether these were called races or species. As we have seen, this is exactly what many scientists recognized when they assessed the phylogeny of the European peoples. That is not to say that no scientist posed a clear distinction between intra- and interspecific changes, for de Quatrefages did just that. But it must be recognized that the species question, to use a modern expression, was not a key issue in human evolution during the 1860–1890 period.

Let us conclude the first part of this book by insisting on what we believe is the key feature of the 1860–1890 period in paleoanthropology: the chasm that separated the studies based on the human fossil record from those based on the comparative anatomy of the living primate forms. The profound implication of this chasm meant that human evolution had to be approached from two sides at the same time, sides which were barely, if at all, in contact with one another. If the fossil record was restricted to Europe exclusively, in addition to only comprising relatively recent and modern-looking human specimens, the studies in comparative anatomy were, on the other hand, based on living organisms which were distributed worldwide and which comprised both living human forms and the other primates.

The assessment of humankind's place in nature was therefore arrived at only by attempting a synthesis of the results of these two levels of analysis. Unsurprisingly, the general picture was only very incomplete. In 1895, Keith admitted that the evolutionary studies based on neontological data or living forms, which were at first expected to resolve the question of human descent, yielded results of general nature only. Keith (1895) concluded that only the fossil record could establish with some precision the human line of descent from the primates, a fossil record he judged, at the time, simply too incomplete for that matter. Keith's frustation was, from our contemporary viewpoint, partly understandable, knowing, as we do, that the earliest and most primitive hominids are probably only to be found in Africa, while Europe had been occupied only at a later stage of human evolution.

NOTES

1. Leguebe's original text reads like this: "Une telle position est celle adoptée par beaucoup de naturalistes de l'époque: elle constitue un moyen de réduire l'impact que pourrait avoir, sur la généalogie de l'espèce humaine, la faveur grandissante que connaissent les thèses évolutionnistes. . . ."

2. Pruner-Bey's original text reads like this: ". . . on parle de crânes, de mâchoires simiennes ou intermédiaires à l'homme et au singe . . . qui laisse supposer que . . . l'homme pithécoïde . . . est un fait accompli."

3. To be convinced of the real limitations regarding the words "pithecoid," "ape-like," and "simious" in the minds of the scholars at the time, see the exchange that occurred in P. Denicker, A. de Quatrefages, J. Fraipont, L. Manouvrier, and P. Topinard in "Discussion," *Congrès International d'Anthropologie et d'Archéologie Préhistoriques*, 10e session, 1889: 348–362.

4. In addition to the literature already cited regarding such hominid finds, see C. Blake, "On a Human Jaw From the Cave of La Naulette, Near Dinant, Belgium," *Anthropological Review*, 5 (1867): 294–303; P. Broca, "Observations sur le crâne de Néanderthal," *Bulletins de la Société d'Anthropologie de Paris*, 4 (1863a): 322–323; "Sur la mâchoire humaine de la Naulette (Belgique)," *Bulletins de la Société d'Anthropologie de Paris*, 2e série, 1 (1866): 593–601; T.H. Huxley, *Evidence as to Man's Place in Nature* (London: Williams & Norgates, 1863); F. Pruney-Bey, "Observations sur le crâne de Néanderthal," *Bulletins de la Société d'Anthropologie de Paris*, 4 (1863): 318–322; "Sur la mâchoire humaine de la Naulette (Belgique)," *Bulletins de la Société d'Anthropologie de Paris*, 2e série, 1 (1866): 584–593; H. Schaaffhausen, "On the Crania of the Most Ancient Races of Man," translated from Müller's Archiv (1858) with remarks by G. Busk, *Natural History Review*, 1 (1861): 155–176; P. Topinard, "Les caractères simiens de la mâchoire de la Naulette," *Revue d'Anthropologie*, 3e série, 1 (1886): 385–431; and W. Turner, "On Human Crania Allied in Anatomical Characters to the Engis and Neanderthal Skulls," *Quarterly Journal of Science*, 1 (1864): 250–259; "Additional Note on the Neanderthal Skull," *Quarterly Journal of Science*, 1 (1864): 758–760.

5. A. Spring, "Les hommes d'Engis et les hommes de Chauvaux," *Bulletin de l'Académie royale des sciences, des lettres et des beaux-arts de Belgique*, 2e série, 18 (1864), footnote #3 on pp. 489–490.

6. Fraipont's and Lohest's original text reads as follows: ". . . pouvons-nous rattacher directement à la race de Néanderthal ou de Canstadt celle de Cro-Magnon et à celle-ci celle de Furfooz?"

7. Fraipont's and Lohest's original text reads like this: "Ce type [Neandertal type] ou un autre type antérieur à celui-ci a donné naissance, à un moment donné en Asie, probablement à ces hommes dont les descendants ont réalisé le type ethnique de Cro-Magnon qui à gagné l'Europe avec ses caractères distinctifs. Quant aux races de Furfooz.. il n'est pas moins acquis qu'en certains points . . . les deux types [Cro-Magnon and Furfooz] ont été mélangés. Est-ce là le point de départ de l'une des races de Furfooz? Ou bien le résultat du métissage entre la race pure de Cro-Magnon et une autre race non moins pure envahissante et d'une autre région?"

Part II

COMPETING APPROACHES TO HUMAN EVOLUTION, 1890–1935

In the first stage of development of paleoanthropology between 1860 and 1890 an unbridgable gap separated the global debates from the local ones. Because this situation started to gradually change after 1890, the field entered a second stage of development which lasted until about 1935. During this new phase, a new empirical reality was instituted by the gradual increase of primate and hominid fossil discoveries. This contributed to reduce the gap that separated the research being conducted on humankind's place among the primates from that on human phylogeny proper. Therefore, it is no longer appropriate to speak of two distinct levels of analysis in the human evolutionary studies after 1890. This does not mean, however, that a complete integration of the two areas had occurred by then. Certainly not. After all, this integration process is not fully completed as of today. As far as the 1890–1935 period is concerned, the situation is different, to the extent that it is not as easy to draw clearly the frontier between these two research areas as it was in the previous time period.

As will be seen, the new empirical reality which was instituted by the gradual increase of the primate and the hominid fossil discoveries did not contribute in any way to reduce the diversity of viewpoints about humankind's place in nature. On the contrary. While the scholars promoted an even greater diversity of hypotheses about humankind's place among the primates than during the previous time period, this diversity of viewpoints now spread to debates on human phylogeny proper. This is easily understood. The debates on the phylogeny of the European peoples during the 1860–1890 period were constrained within these geographical limits, for obvious empirical reasons. The new empirical context which now also covered non-European regions after that period opened up many more phylogenetic possibilities. These were fully exploited between 1890 and 1935. Never in the entire history of the field of human evolution, before or after, will such a level of disagreement be entertained about our origins.

Although the fossil record gradually improved, in no way was it determinant in strongly orienting phylogenetic views at the time. Two interrelated reasons may explain this. First, the fossil discoveries were still too few in number to really constrain the number of divergent phylogenetic hypotheses. Second, the same fossils could be used to promote new and divergent phylogenetic hypotheses. Apparently, paleoanthropology was at that time still largely dominated by the comparison of the living forms (comparative anatomy). It seems that the fossils were used to promote phylogenetic views which were based on conclusions largely derived from the studies in comparative anatomy. The continuing influence of comparative anatomy in the post-1890 period is perhaps not surprising when considering that this approach was, prior to 1890, largely responsible for the establishment of a global phylogenetic framework. It was only natural that when primate and hominid fossil discoveries with global implications (as opposed to local ones) were at last recovered after 1890 that they should have been incorporated into phylogenetic hypotheses largely based on the living forms. Accordingly, the fusion process at work between the two main empirical chains during the 1890–1935 period—the knowledge acquired through the fossil record and comparative anatomy—was somewhat superficial, being largely unidirectional in favor of comparative anatomy.

In the 1860–1890 period, the assessment of humankind's place in nature was arrived at only by synthesizing the results of comparative anatomy and the human fossil record. This approach served the purpose of presenting a view of human evolution which was as incomplete as possible. But as the gap separating the two approaches was being gradually filled between 1890 and 1935, this new period was no longer characterized by a spirit of synthesis but rather by one of competition of perspectives. At first, of course, this only contributed to increase further the level of disagreement about humankind's origins. However, far from constituting a step backward, this new level of uncertainty represented a crucial step forward beyond the previous time period only because the field of human evolution had to start integrating the results from both comparative anatomy and the fossil record. This was a necessary step in the development of paleoanthropology toward a resolution of humankind's place in nature. The apparent confusion that came along with this time period is merely an illusion that hides a necessary epistemological phase. It is convenient to divide the analysis of the 1890–1935 period into two chapters, one concerned with human phylogeny proper (Chapter 5) and the other, to which we now turn, with primate phylogeny.

4

Primate Phylogeny

INTRODUCTION

None, or very few, primate fossils were used in human phylogenetic hypotheses from 1860 to 1890. Among the scholars reviewed in the previous chapters, only Wallace referred to two primate fossils (*Pliopithecus* and *Dryopithecus*) which he affiliated with the gibbon line. Wallace used them merely as chronological or geological markers in order to establish the probable time of separation between the humans and the hominoid apes.

The primate fossils were of no or little use in the reconstruction of human phylogeny prior to 1890, mainly because those that had been recovered were judged to be only remotely related to humans, if at all. Although the primate fossil record was not exhaustive in 1890, the diversity of specimens recovered between 1820 and 1890 was by no means insignificant, as testified by the attempts made to survey the record at the time (e.g., Flower and Lydekker, 1891; Trouessart, 1892; von Zittel, 1926 [1893a]; see also Fleagle & Hartwig, 1997; Hartwig, 1995; Kennedy and Ciochon, 1999).[1] Yet, starting with the late 1870s, one finds occasional statements to the effect that primate fossils could shed light on humankind's origins. This constitutes the starting point of a slow and still incomplete process of fusion between the results generated by the fossil record and comparative anatomy.

For instance, in 1878, Gaudry held that *Dryopithecus*, a fossil hominoid ape of the European Miocene, presented some resemblances to humankind. Gaudry (1878: 235–241) even suggested that *Dryopithecus* might have been responsible for the stone tools in supposedly Tertiary deposits. Following more fossil discoveries of *Dryopithecus*, however, Gaudry (1890) retracted his previous view and declared that *Dryopithecus* showed more differences from the humans than he had expected.

In 1879, Lydekker identified a fossil hominoid ape of the Pliocene of India which he called *Palaeopithecus sivalensis*. Lydekker (1879) found that this ape differed from all known living and fossil anthropoid apes, although it had some resemblances to the orang, *Dryopithecus*, to man, and particularly to the chimpanzee. On morphology and geographical distribution, Lydekker conjectured that all these forms might have had a common parentage and ancestral home in Lemuria, a continent presumed to be sunken in the Indian Ocean. This implied that missing links binding humankind to the anthropoid apes might be lost forever, argued Lydekker.[2]

Yet another example is Schlosser who in 1888 promoted a phylogenetic hypothesis involving the humans and all the hominoid apes which appealed to the primate fossil record (see Figure 4). According to Schlosser (1888), the humans and the three great apes shared a common ancestor in the late Miocene or early Pliocene period. In his view, the fossil discovery of *Pliopithecus* is directly and uniquely ancestral to the gibbons, while fossils such as *Dryopithecus* and *Troglodytes* constitute ancestral stages of both the living orangs and the chimpanzees.[3] Schlosser derived the common ancestor of all the hominoids (including humans) directly from an ancestor shared with the New World monkeys rather than with the Old World monkeys.[4]

In the last two decades of the nineteenth century and in the early portion of the twentieth century, a number of primate fossil discoveries which could bring light on humankind's place among the primates were reported.[5] Among such recoveries frequently referred to at the time were *Dryopithecus*, *Pliopithecus*, *Propliopithecus*, *Palaeopithecus*, *Palaeosimia*, *Sivapithecus*, and *Hesperopithecus*. Primate fossils such as *Gryphopithecus*, *Neopithecus*, *Pliohylobates*, *Anaptomorphus*, *Pitheculites*, and *Homunculus*, were also referred to, but less frequently. With this new empirical input one would have had expected an important effect on the debates on humankind's place among the primates during the 1890–1935 period. Although this is true to a certain extent, the nature of the effect must be qualified.

Scholars like Ameghino and Pilgrim were, indeed, especially inspired by these new primate fossil discoveries. However, for a majority of scholars the nature of the link between humankind and his closest living relatives was still being worked out largely on the basis of comparative anatomy. It is not that the primate fossils were ignored by these scholars, though Schultz disregarded them. Rather, it is that the primate fossil record was judged to be still too fragmentary to seriously disrupt the phylogenetic hypotheses originally based on comparative anatomy. For these scholars, the primate fossils were neither crucial nor central to their phylogenetic arguments, but, instead, constituted a complementary source of information. For instance, primate fossils could be useful as chronological markers of lineages and for splitting events already identified or assumed on the basis of comparative anatomy. Such fossils could also be useful to assess the conformation of humankind's remote ancestors, although the incompleteness of the fossil individuals themselves limited that procedure to partial results only.

It is therefore easy to understand why comparative anatomy still loomed large in the process of building phylogenetic hypotheses after 1890. The primate fossils were, for a majority of scholars, more or less enshrined in phylogenetic hypotheses which were largely pre-established by the method of comparative anatomy. That is why the fusion process at work between the studies based on comparative anatomy and the fossil record was somewhat superficial in addition to being unidirectional in favor of comparative anatomy.

THE CASE FOR THE NEW WORLD

The 1890–1935 period differed from the previous one because of the rise of a new geographical dimension in human evolution: the New World. The primate fossils and embryology played a key role in favor of this new perspective. Prior to 1890, only Vogt and Schlosser postulated that some or all of the living humans shared a phylogenetic connection with the New World primates. At that time, the question of humankind's place among the primates was tackled almost exclusively in terms of the Old World primates. This situation was to change, at least in the minds of a number of scholars. For instance, Klaatsch would not derive humans from an Old World monkey-like ancestor on the basis that it is the New World monkeys which retained more features in common with the humans. Using similar arguments and the support of a number of primate fossils, Ameghino held that humankind and the New World monkeys were more closely related to each other than either of them was to the Old World monkeys. For his part, Sergi derived some portions of humanity directly from distinct and ancient American ancestors; portions of humanity which were not related to a common hominid ancestor. We will come back to the viewpoints of these scholars later in this book.

The interest in the New World during the 1890–1935 period is easily explained. It is recognized today that humankind's ascent from the primates passed through stages that were all connected to the Old World, except perhaps for the earliest prosimian-like stage of North America. It is true that a majority of scholars then were convinced that the scientific evidence was strong enough to definitely exclude the New World from being the theater of humankind's ascent.[6] In the minds of other scholars, however, this was not definitely established. This latter conception was made possible partly because biogeography and geology were conceived differently at the time.

Remember that both Haeckel and Lydekker hypothesized that the cradle of humankind may have been in Lemuria, a presumed sunken continent in the Indian Ocean. This conception was not an imaginary fantasy; it was based on a theory recognized by many scholars between 1860 and 1930 which postulated that the geographical distribution of the living organisms throughout the history of the earth had been continually disturbed by the subsidence of landmasses below sea level, including during a significant part of the Tertiary era (e.g., Bowler, 1996: 371–418). The geographical distribution of the living and extinct species which were separated by wide oceans could be explained by the subsidence of major portions of landmasses; the islands themselves being the visible parts of such sunken continents. With regard to this theory, scholars postulated the existence of earlier and much larger hypothetical continents than those seen today. For instance, one such great southern continent was alleged to have united Australia, Africa, Antarctica, and South America. Also, this theory permitted the scholars to hypothesize about the existence of now vanished land bridges, such as the long one which was thought to have directly linked Africa and South America across the Atlantic ocean.

The fairly popular theory of the sinking continents was not unanimously accepted at the time. An alternative theory suggested that the continents and the oceans had been stable and permanent entities for a very long time (e.g., Fichman, 1977). From the perspective that the continents were stable, the irregular or broken-up geographical distribution of the living forms is explained by the combination of three distinct historical processes: (1) by appealing to massive migration of biomass followed by subsequent local extinctions; (2) by the accidental transport of plant and animal species by ocean currents, winds, or floating devices; and (3) by changes in the height and extent of the landmasses caused by climate changes (i.e., glaciations).

Yet, a third theory at the time could explain the geographical distribution of the living forms, a theory based on the drifting continents. However, this theory had to wait for the scientific elaboration of plate tectonics and its accompanying mechanisms of long-distance drift before receiving serious consideration later in the twentieth century (e.g., Stewart, 1990; LeGrand, 1988). Continental drift explains the geographical distribution of the living forms by assuming that continuous populations spread over a single landmass were gradually separated during the break-up process of that continent into several parts.

This brief incursion in the biogeographical conceptions of the time makes clear that the scholars then were considerably less constrained than those of today in their explanation of the ancient distribution and migration of the primate and hominid forms. The discipline of biogeography offered them many alternatives, and thus considerable flexibility, in the explanation of the geographical distribution of organisms. Thereby, it should come as no surprise that several hypotheses on primate and human phylogeny at the time apparently relied on what are merely unusual biogeographical explanations. This is especially true for the scholars who incorporated the New World in their human phylogenetic hypotheses, as they often implicitly relied on an alleged ancient great southern continent that united Australia, Africa, Antarctica, and South America.

In addition to the biogeographical dimension behind the case for the New World in human evolution were a number of empirical aspects which added credence to it. Three independent events in the first third of the twentieth century demonstrate that several scholars may have been wise to not turn away too quickly from the case of the New World. The first event relates to prehistoric archeology. As already stated, prehistoric archeology has always been instrumental in indicating the presence of intelligent creatures in geological deposits. We have seen that an archeological framework of prehistoric Europe had been established in the last decades of the nineteenth century with the recognition of several Palaeolithic and Neolithic industries (see Chapter 2). Debates at the time centered on the possible existence of hominids before the Quaternary era (or the pre-Paleolithic period), as seen in allegedly primitive tools. Debates raged over what became known as the controversy over Tertiary man or the eoliths. This controversy continued during the first third of the twentieth century and was disseminated to other regions of the world.

The reality of Eolithic industries or Tertiary man in Europe was supported by a small number of energetic scholars (e.g., Rutot, 1904–05, 1909, 1918; Moir, 1919, 1927; see also Grayson, 1986). The prospect of eventually finding the makers of eoliths in the Tertiary era must have contributed to questions about early creatures' physical conformation and their genealogical connection with both the primates and the humans. Keep in mind that de Mortillet (1883) imagined, on the basis of a distinction between Eolithic tools or cultures, several hypothetical ape-like creatures that he called *Anthropopithecus*, and later *Homosimius* (de Mortillet and de Mortillet, 1900). For de Mortillet, *Anthropopithecus* was a phylogenetic link between the apes and the humans. For his part, Rutot (1900–1901) spoke of a doomed humanity in the Miocene of Europe that was responsible for the earliest eoliths before going extinct because of insufficient intelligence. But the actual humanity would have arisen later, as seen in the Pliocene eoliths and subsequent Paleolithic and Neolithic industries.[7]

It is not surprising that the debates in European prehistoric archeology inspired similar research in other regions of the world, especially in South and North America. In this context, a number of scholars assumed a parallelism of cultural stages between Europe and other regions, thus expecting the eventual discovery of similar or equivalent cultural stages in such regions. As evidenced in Europe, debates erupted on the validity and the chronology of such cultural vestiges and sequences. As early as 1879, Ameghino held that Tertiary tools from South America had been recovered. At that time, Ameghino (1879) also alluded to the fact that there should be consideration that de Mortillet's *Anthropopithecus* first arose in the Americas rather than in Europe. By the early twentieth century, Ameghino (1910a, 1910b, 1910c) had described cultural vestiges from time horizons he attributed to the Pliocene, the Miocene, and even to the Oligocene periods.

The case for the great antiquity of humankind in North America also found a number of adherents in the late nineteenth and early twentieth centuries (e.g., Foster, 1873; Abbott, 1881; Balch, 1917; Cook, 1927). The case for eoliths or Tertiary man in North America was less often promoted than in Europe. In North America, debates largely resolved to dating controversies over well-anthenticated tools rather than possible eoliths. In fact, many scholars at the time argued that the presence of humans during the Paleolithic of North America had not even been clearly demonstrated as yet (e.g., Meltzer, 1983). Proponents of the great antiquity of humankind in North America chose to rely more on the anticipation of eventual eolith discoveries in the light of an assumed Pliocene migration from the Old World (e.g., Hay, 1918). From the above discussion, we start to understand why prehistoric archeology could have contributed to support the case for the New World in human evolution, at least in the minds of a number of scholars. With time, however, it became clear that the Americas had been inhabited only during a relatively recent geological period (see also Chapter 6).

The second event supporting the case for the New World relates to paleontology. Between 1922 and 1927, two worn teeth, apparently belonging to a highly evolved ape of the early- or mid-Pliocene period of North America (Nebraska), were discovered. This led to the creation of a new fossil species called *Hesperopithecus haroldcookii* by Osborn (e.g., Osborn, 1922a, 1922b; Gregory and Hellman, 1923a, 1923b). Osborn considered that more discoveries were needed to determine whether *Hesperopithecus* belonged to the hominoid ape stem or to the hominid stem. On the other hand, Gregory and Hellman were apparently more established about the phylogenetic place of *Hesperopithecus* because they thought it represented an extinct branch that evolved out of the same Miocene stock as humans, chimpanzees, and gorillas.[8] Also sure about the place of *Hesperopithecus*, Elliot Smith (1924: 6–10) assessed that it was in all probability an extinct branch of the hominid family tree.[9]

Notwithstanding such enthusiasm, many scholars judged the diagnosis of this new primate species to be either premature or simply wrong. For instance, Smith Woodward (1922) and Pycraft (1922) suggested that *Hesperopithecus* may not be a primate at all but rather a primitive member of the bear. The detractors of *Hesperopithecus* will no longer be a concern for us here. For advocates of this new primate discovery—whether *Hesperopithecus* was judged to be closely affiliated to the hominoid apes or to the hominids—this find indicated that North America had been occupied by evolved primates as early as the first half of the Pliocene period. This discovery opened up several possibilities for human phylogeny. First, it could be an indication that hominoid apes or hominids arrived earlier than expected in North America, after having stemmed from an Old World ancestor. Osborn, Gregory, Hellman, and Elliot Smith were inclined to favor this view. Second, it could suggest that hominoid apes and/or hominids evolved independently in the Old World as well as in the New World. As will be seen, Sergi and Klaatsch promoted views based on this theme in the early portion of the twentieth century, but without the benefit of *Hesperopithecus*. Third, it could support the view that the hominoid apes or the hominids first appeared in the New World, as seen in the early presence of *Hesperopithecus* in North America, before migrating to the Old World. In the first decade of the twentieth century, Ameghino presented a similar view, but again without the benefit of *Hesperopithecus*.

All the possible implications of the discovery of *Hesperopithecus* to support the case of the New World were never fully realized because enthusiasm was short-lived. In 1927, one of its most vocal advocates, Gregory (1927a), recognized that new fossil discoveries showed that *Hesperopithecus* was in all probability not a primate but an extinct representative of a form related to the modern peccaries (pigs). It is irrelevant for our thesis here that *Hesperopithecus* turned out to be something other than an evolved primate. What is significant is that a number of scholars were prepared to accept the presence of such a primate in North America on such limited empirical bases. This strongly suggests that a number of basic ideas about primate and human evolution were not perfectly established as yet during the 1890–1935 period. Had they been, scholars like Osborn, Gregory, Hellman, and

Elliot Smith would have required much more empirical evidence to disturb what they would have considered to be a resolved question.

The third event in favor of the case for the New World relates to zoology. In 1929–1930, there was the discovery of a living primate form in South America (Venezuela) which apparently presented many similarities with both the living hominoid apes and the humans. This living primate was first discovered between 1917 and 1920 by the geologist François de Loys during a scientific expedition in forested areas. Only a single photograph of a shot animal survived the expedition; the remains of the primate in question could not be brought back. This primate was described in the following terms: a tall and ground-living primate; a body similar to the gibbons; limbs and fur resembling the orangs; a human-like face; presence of thirty-two teeth only (most New World monkeys have thirty-six teeth); the complete absence of a tail (all New World monkeys have tails); a nose, a thumb, and sexual parts similar to some New World monkeys. Montandon (1929a, 1929b, 1929c, 1930) named this new living primate species *Amer-anthropoides loysi* (e.g., Honoré, 1929).

Needless to say, many scholars at the time refused to recognize the validity of *Amer-anthropoides* and its anthropomorph-like status. For instance, Keith (1929) declared that *Amer-anthropoides* was merely a common spider monkey of the New World, and that no new name was needed for it. He was unable to determine, on the basis of a single photograph, whether or not this was a new species of spider monkey. The notion that *Amer-anthropoides* was a form akin to the *Ateles* was shared by many scholars then (e.g., Anonymous, 1929a; Ashley-Montagu, 1929; Oppenheim, 1929; Remane, 1929). As in the case of *Hesperopithecus*, we shall not be concerned further with the detractors of *Amer-anthropoides*.

More interesting for our purposes here are the two groups of scholars who were open-minded about the possibility of finding hominoid-like primates in the Americas. For the first group, the discovery of *Amer-anthropoides* was indeed a fascinating discovery that required further confirmation. Although cautious about this initial discovery, such scholars were not closed at the idea of eventually finding or recognizing hominoid-like creatures in the Americas (e.g., Anonymous, 1929b; Bourdelle, 1929; Urbain and Rode, 1948: 36).

The second group of scholars believed that the discovery of *Amer-anthropoides* was convincing enough to explore its evolutionary implications. For Montandon, this new primate species of South America clearly indicated that many human-like and hominoid-like features developed in parallel in both the Old World and New World primates by independently going through similar evolutionary stages. In Montandon's (1929b, 1929c) view, *Amer-anthropoides* was of the same evolutionary level or grade as the Old World hominoids. He argued that this new discovery confirmed that highly evolved primates probably developed independently throughout the entire world in accordance with the Ologenetic theory of evolution (see Chapter 5). Joleaud concurred with Montandon that *Amer-anthropoides* was indeed an important discovery. He affiliated it with the New World monkey stem, especially to the genus *Ateles* (spider monkeys), but of a new and giant kind. Joleaud (1929) held that some New World monkeys, including this new species, had attained an evolutionary level or grade which was more or less equivalent to some Old World hominoid species. In fact, Joleaud argued that just as the ground-living *Pithecanthropus* was a more evolved form stemming from the tree-living gibbon lineage, the ground-living *Amer-anthropoides* was a more evolved form derived from the tree-living *Ateles* stem. Joleaud's view implied parallel evolution between the primates of the Old and New Worlds.

Without referring to the discovery of *Amer-anthropoides*, several other scholars recognized, in the post-1930 period, that the primates of the New World evolved in a direction that approached the hominoid ape or the human condition. For instance, Hooton (1931: 85; 1946: 82) insisted that although the New World monkeys do not present us with an evolutionary stage through which humankind's ancestors had passed, it must be recognized that in "the spider monkey (Ateles) alone of all the Cebidae, the habit of swinging by the arms from bough to bough brought about certain bodily modifications that suggest those of the anthropoid apes [hominoids]." For his part, Wood Jones (1948: 22) concurred with Joleaud that although no hominoid-like primates arose from the New World stock, he insisted that woolly monkeys (*Lagothrix*) reached a level "that permits them to rank at least with the gibbons of the Old World." Gregory was even more explicit. He alluded that some New World monkeys might have been prevented from taking the dominant place of humankind in the world not by lack of brain power or manipulative skill but rather because they stayed in the trees and failed to adapt to ground-living conditions. In Gregory's (1951: 467) own words:

> If the prize of world dominance had been awarded by natural selection solely on the criterion of the size of the brain in relation to the total body weight, then the New World monkeys, or some of them, might well have overspread the habitable earth. In course of geologic time they might conceivably have risen to high levels of intelligence. In that case the history of the primates might even have been investigated and recorded by some big brained descendant of the [New World] Capuchins, rather than by distant cousins [humans] of the [Old World] rhesus monkeys and baboons . . . In the forests of Brazil and Central America this expanded brain is busied chiefly in keeping the feeble monkey folk in the trees . . . In short a wider dispersal of the New World monkeys seems to have been limited rather by their genetic failure to develop new adaptations for ground-living. . . .

For his part, Schultz (1969: 244) recognized the extraordinary amount of parallelism seen in the Old and New World primates, as seen in other instances in the rise of gibbon-like New World monkeys:

> Some of the latter [Cebidae monkeys] have acquired new modes of locomotion, particularly the closely related spider monkeys and woolly monkeys which have become highly expert brachiators with a correspondingly great elongation of their upper limbs. In this respect, as also in their remarkably large relative brain size, they correspond quite closely to the Hylobatidae [gibbons] of Asia.

A remarkable parallel seems to exist between the interpretations given to *Hesperopithecus* and to *Amer-anthropoides* from the part of their respective proponents.

Like Osborn, Gregory, Hellman, and Elliot Smith in the previous case, Montandon and Joleaud were also prepared to accept the presence of forms approaching the hominoid level of evolution in the Americas on the basis of very limited empirical evidence, in this case a single photograph. This strongly indicates that a number of basic ideas about primate and human evolution were still open to question during the 1890–1935 period. Apparently, the role of the Americas in human evolution was not completely excluded at the time. Should this have been the case, Montandon and Joleaud would have required much more empirical evidence before changing their minds about what they would have probably considered a nonissue.

Remember that in the 1860s, Vogt hypothesized that the living human races in the New World had sprung from anthropomorph-like forms, although no evidence was clear at the time. In the 1880s, Schlosser offered a different perspective: that humans and hominoid apes shared a common ancestor with the New World monkeys rather than with the Old World monkeys. Again, no evidence, besides the similarities of the living forms, was used then. If these conceptions were very much a minority view at the time, they have persisted well into the twentieth century, during which time they were expressed more explicitly and with more vigor than in the past. Apparently, these conceptions were now considered to be empirically founded, at least for an increasing number of scholars. The persistent idea of a rise of a human-like or hominoid-like form in the Americas can be explained, in part at least, by the association of two ideas: (1) The idea held by numerous scholars at the time (and after) of a sort of evolutionary parallelism between the Old World and New World primates, although these two groups had been separated for a considerable amount of time; (2) As more evolved forms such as the hominoid apes and the hominids somehow sprung from, or succeeded to, the Old World monkeys, it was thought by a small number of scholars not to be unreasonable to expect that something similar had also occurred in the New World.

We have already stressed that the 1890–1935 period constituted a second phase of development for paleoanthropology. However, the discontinuity between the pre-1890 and the post-1890 periods should not be overstressed. Several aspects debated in the latter time period were also debated in the former one. It is not that such debates were continued without any change; several of them took on a new dimension. The evidence put forward to promote the case for the New World during the 1890–1935 period epitomizes very well this situation. This is also seen in other aspects such as the persistent diversity of viewpoints about hypotheses concerned with humankind's place among the primate, a divergence which increased after 1890. All these aspects inherited from the 1860–1890 period were not merely continued after that period, but were also presented with more clarity than previously, as if the 1890–1935 period permitted the crystalization of such viewpoints. If the 1890–1935 period was a period of continuity with the previous one, it was also a period during which the debates were amplified. The following review of the debates on humankind's place among the primates between 1890 and 1935 exemplifies this situation.

PARALLEL EVOLUTION

In the 1860–1890 period, scholars like Owen, Mivart, and de Quatrefages were inclined to believe that the humans had stemmed either from an early primate form unrelated to the anthropoid stem or from a nonprimate ancestor altogether. Although these scholars were rather vague in their views of humankind's origins, it is clear that they appealed to an important degree of parallelism in order to explain a number of similarities between humankind and the other primates. In other words, such similarities were not explained by common descent, but by parallel evolution. At least two scholars in the early period of the twentieth century, Adloff and Sergi, continued this tradition of interpretation. Contrary to their forebears, however, they were able to promote this view without much ambiguity.

According to Adloff (1908), primate phylogeny is entirely explained by a process of parallel evolution of six primate evolutionary lines: prosimians, New World monkeys, Old World monkeys, gibbons, great apes (chimpanzee, gorilla, and orang) and humans. These six evolutionary lines have evolved, in Adloff's view, in complete independence of one another throughout the entire Tertiary and Quaternary eras, ever since they independently arose from creodont mammals in the late Secondary era (see Figure 5).[10] This view was largely dominated by the weight of comparative anatomy so that the primate fossils were merely placed along such independent evolutionary lines, either as direct ancestors or as extinct side branches. For instance, *Pithecanthropus* and *Homo antiquus* (Neandertals) were interpreted by Adloff as side branches of the human line doomed to extinction. *Dryopithecus*, placed on the great apes line, was believed to be a direct ancestor of both the chimpanzees and the orangs (but not gorillas), while *Pliopithecus* was assumed to be a direct ancestor situated on the gibbon line.

In order to explain the similarities between some of the living representatives of the distinct primate evolutionary lines, Adloff postulated that they went through similar evolutionary stages. For instance, the human line, the great apes line, and the gibbon line all independently passed through lemur-like and monkey-like stages. Furthermore, Adloff explained the ressemblances between the humans and the anthropomorph-like apes by the similarities that were already present in their distinct creodont-like ancestors. The living representatives of the prosimian and the New World monkey lines have not proceeded very far down the line of evolutionary change, thus retaining much of their primitive conditions. The implication of Adloff's conception of primate evolution is that although humans are, phylogenetically speaking, totally unrelated to any other primate lineages, the human evolutionary line had nonetheless passed through several ape-like stages.

Like Adloff, Sergi recognized many parallel and unrelated evolutionary lines in the primate family tree. Unlike Adloff, however, Sergi also applied this type of parallelism to humankind itself by breaking it up into several distinct human lines, thus promoting a kind of polygenism. From undetermined primate ancestors, Sergi (1911, 1913, 1914) independently derived three main primate groups, *Cercopithecidae*, *Simiidae* and *Hominidae*, each being represented by several and independent evolutionary lines.[11] In the human group, for instance, Sergi recognized several evolutionary lines or genera (themselves often composed of several "species") which either led to living representatives such as *Notanthropus* (Black races), *Heoanthropus* (Asian races) and *Hesperanthropus* (American races), or to extinct members such as *Eoanthropus* (Piltdown), *Palaeanthropus* (Neandertals) and *Archaeanthropus* (*Homo pampaeus*), the latter being an assumed fossil form from South America.

These hominid evolutionary lines were not, in Sergi's mind, derived from a common ancestor, nor were they related in any way to the hominoid apes or any other primate lineages. These were apparently distinct ever since they arose from unknown ancestors, and have since evolved and persisted in distinct geographical areas, worldwide. As far as can be determined, Sergi's conception of relatively stable and independent evolutionary lines seems to imply that humankind's ancestors are more human-like than ape-like in conformation.

Although very few scholars will make use of the concept of parallel evolution to the extent seen in Adloff's and Sergi's views, this concept was, implicitly or explicitly, widely used at the time in a way which is unparalleled today. This situation illustrates well the diversity of viewpoints that could be promoted on the basis of comparative anatomy (the living forms). The absence of a primate fossil record of any significance could not contribute to trimming down the number of phylogenetic hypotheses.

UNRELATED TO THE HOMINOID APES

Adloff and Sergi completely cut off the humans from the other primates. But for scholars like Cope, Boule, and Wood Jones, not unlike Topinard prior to 1890, a genealogical connection existed between humankind and the other primates near the base of the primate family tree. In so doing, they promoted that the human stem had directly evolved from ancient and primitive primate forms, thus avoiding completely a hominoid ape stage of evolution. This makes it easy to understand why proponents of this phylogenetic view rejected the idea that humankind's earliest ancestors were too hominoid-like in conformation.

Cope (1885, 1888), for instance, believed the humans were not descended from the hominoid apes because both were independently derived from a common Eocene stock of lemurs (see Figure 6). Cope (1888: 661) stated that "man was derived directly from Lemuroids without the intervention of the Anthropoid apes [hominoids]." On this view, the human and the hominoid ape stems both avoided going through a monkey-like stage of evolution.[12] Cope traced back the distant ancestor of the humans and the hominoid apes to the Eocene lemuroid family called *Anaptomorphidae*, the latter being known notably by the fossil genus *Anaptomorphus* of North America.[13]

While Cope once looked for humankind's direct ancestors among the lemur-like forms, Boule preferred the monkey-like types. According to Boule (1911–1913, 1921), although the humans shared many anatomical similarities with the hominoid apes, the former were not derived from the hominoid stem. In his view, these similarities were acquired through parallel evolution and not common descent. Boule held that humankind and the hominoid apes were both probably independently derived early from the base of the Old World monkeys' stem. However, Boule would not discard completely the possibility of independently deriving the human line from the very base of the anthropoid stem, which includes both the Old World and New World monkeys.[14] Although *Pithecanthropus* shows some human-like features, continued Boule, its real affinity is with the hominoid ape stem, more specifically with the gibbon line. Boule also placed *Troglodytes dawsoni* (Piltdown's jaw) with the hominoid ape group. Although Boule reviewed the key primate fossil discoveries of his time, his view of primate phylogeny relied exclusively on the comparison of the living forms. He stated that too few primate fossils were known as yet to be of any serious use in phylogeny reconstruction.

For his part, Wood Jones believed that humankind's direct ancestors would be found among the tarsioid-like forms. For Wood Jones (1918, 1919, 1929), humankind's evolutionary history never went through a monkey-like or a hominoid-like stage. Instead, he argued that the humans, the hominoid apes, and the Old World monkeys all diverged from a common primitive tarsioid-like group of the early Oligocene period. While the monkeys and, to a lesser degree, the hominoid apes developed pithecoid features during their evolution, the human stem retained more features of this early and primitive common ancestor. According to Wood Jones's polygenetic stance, the main living human races are not descended from a common stock, but rather gradually and independently departed from a proto-human stem. This latter stem was, in Wood Jones's view, also probably characterized by extinct offshoots.

HUMANKIND'S LINK WITH THE HOMINOID APES

For scholars like Adloff, Sergi, Boule and Wood Jones, humankind's ancestry is in no way linked to the hominoid ape stem. It is true that this viewpoint was held by a minority of scientists between 1890 and 1935. Yet, this minority stance is nonetheless significant for the understanding of the field of human evolution during that period. It is a clear indication that the situation was still very unsettled about humankind's place among the primates. The majority of scholars at the time promoted that the humans were, indeed, phylogenetically linked to the living hominoid apes. Genealogically speaking, these scholars continued the tradition already established by Darwin, Haeckel, Huxley, Lamarck, and Wallace prior to 1890. This conception is also the one held by all students of human evolution today. Unlike today's conception, however, an outstanding diversity of hypotheses was being promoted at the time on the general theme of humankind's link with the hominoid apes. On this view, the context of interpretation between then and now is quite dissimilar.

For instance, scholars then disagreed about humankind's closest living relative(s) among the hominoid apes: gibbon, orang, gorilla, or chimpanzee? It is certainly another specificity of this time period that the gibbon played such an important evolutionary role. Indeed, the gibbon appears to hold the key to the nature of the link between the humans and the other hominoids for scholars such as Ameghino, Klaatsch, Osborn, Pilgrim, and Schultz.[15] This fact is certainly not totally unrelated to the episode surrounding the discovery and interpretation of *Pithecanthropus erectus* at the turn of the twentieth century (see Chapter 5). Besides the question regarding the nature of the human/hominoid ape link, scholars during the 1890–1935 period also disagreed about the conformation of this common ancestor: ape-like or human-like? This is another important difference in the context of interpretation with the present time. Proponents of an ape-like ancestry for the humans simply needed to explain in what way a single group (humans) lost the ape-like features originally shared in common with the other hominoids. The issue was quite different for the proponents of a human-like ancestor because they needed to explain the rise of ape-like features in several distinct primate groups (hominoid apes). In other words, although the *phylogenetic* conceptions of all the scholars reviewed in this subsection were fairly close, the interpretations given to the polarity of the characters—the direction of the evolutionary change—were diametrically opposed: Were the humans descended from the apes or were the apes descended from the humans? This simple reversion of polarity has had a tremendous impact on the understanding of human evolution in the 1890–1935 period.

Ape-like ancestors. The majority of the scholars who promoted the idea that the humans and the hominoid apes are closely related held that this common ancestor is more ape-like than human-like in conformation. Humankind, therefore, had to be descended from the apes. However, even if agreed on this last point, they were unable to reach a consensus on the exact nature of humankind's connection with the other hominoids.

Humans and one hominoid ape. For Pilgrim, Schultz, Elliot Smith, and Weinert, the humans are more closely related to only one living hominoid ape. While the first two scholars established a link with the gibbon, the third assumed a connection with the gorilla, and the last connected the humans with the chimpanzee.

Pilgrim (1915) described a number of new primate fossil discoveries from the Siwalik Hills of India, notably three new species of *Dryopithecus* and two new genera he called *Sivapithecus* and *Palaeosimia*. On that basis, Pilgrim argued that the humans evolved out of the hominoid ape stem, a stem which he apparently derived from the common anthropoid stem (comprising the Old World and New World monkeys). In Pilgrim's conception, the three great apes separated early from the base of the hominoid stem (early Oligocene). Fossil forms such as *Propliopithecus, Pliopithecus, Gryphopithecus, Palaeopithecus, Dryopithecus*, and *Palaeosimia* were all part of this ramified stem which has today only three surviving species: the orang, the gorilla, and the chimpanzee.

The other main lineage which constituted the hominoid radiation, in Pilgrim's view, has today only two surviving species, the gibbon and humankind. It is from this gibbon line that Pilgrim derived the human lineage which went through a

Sivapithecus stage in the late Oligocene or early Miocene period.[16] *Eoanthropus* (Piltdown), *Homo neanderthalensis, Neopithecus, Sivapithecus,* and *Pithecanthropus* were among the extinct side branches of this hominid stem. Later, Pilgrim (1927) removed *Sivapithecus* from the human lineage, although he maintained that the humans were more closely related to the gibbon line than to any other living hominoid apes.[17] Pilgrim proposed that humankind evolved out of ape-like creatures which presented less specialization than the living hominoid apes.

Not unlike Pilgrim, Schultz also closely associated the humans and the gibbons, although he did so from a different perspective. On the basis of comparative anatomy and embryology of the living forms exclusively, Schultz (1924, 1927, 1930, 1936) presented a view of primate evolution which contrasted the remarkably homogeneous group of the Old World monkeys with the immensely variable group of the hominoids, as seen in their body size, mode of locomotion, and sexual dimorphism. It was held that the adaptive plasticity of the hominoids permitted evolutionary experiments which either carried them into widely differing levels along the same directions (the gradual acquisition of the semi-erect and erect posture), or toward greatly diverging directions (increase in brain size).

Phylogenetically speaking, Schultz held that the hominoid stem sprung from a common Old World primate stock. From there, the gibbons first departed from this common hominoid stem in the direction of an extremely arboreal niche, soon to be followed by the human stem which opted for the terrestrial bipedal niche. The humans and the gibbons are therefore closely linked at the base of the hominoid stem. The three great apes, for their part, continued their evolution as a single evolutionary unit for some time before the orang line departed in the direction of an extremely arboreal niche, leaving the gorilla and the chimpanzee lines exploiting the terrestrial arboreal niche.[18]

According to Elliot Smith (1924), humankind's closest living relative was not to be found among the gibbons (as just seen in Pilgrim's and Schultz's views) but rather among the gorillas. Elliot Smith held that the gorilla branch was the last one to have split from the stem leading to the humans. Elliot Smith's conception of primate evolution is largely derived from comparative anatomy. He promoted the view that the evolution of the primates is characterized by the ascent of a main evolutionary line which went through a gradual increase in mental faculties. By proposing this concept, he believed the brain led the way in primate evolution. Elliot Smith suggested that the adaptability of the human line lay in its capacity to avoid specialization—by retaining its plasticity through its primitiveness—contrary to all other primate forms. He envisioned the line leading to the humans as one having passed through a series of stages that are characterized by the primitive and the ancestral forms of the extant primates: a prosimian-like stage, a tarsioid-like stage, a New World monkey-like stage, an Old World monkey-like stage and a hominoid-like stage. All the other nonhuman primate forms developed at one time or another from this main evolutionary line leading to the humans.[19]

Elliot Smith believed that the earliest primates such as the lemurs, the tarsioids and the monkeys were nurtured in North or Central America before migrating throughout the world. It is during this journey to the ancient continent that the Old World monkeys (Eocene period), and later the hominoid apes (Eocene and Miocene periods), departed from the main line leading to the humans. Elliot Smith (1930) was inclined to believe that the human stem, just like its closest living relatives, the chimpanzee and especially the gorilla, had appeared first in Africa during the Miocene period. From there, Elliot Smith argued that humankind's ancestors reentered the New World as early as the Pliocene period as seen in *Hesperopithecus* of Nebraska (see above). He also held that the humans and the great apes shared a common Miocene ancestor (among the Siwalik apes) that was ape-like in conformation. His commitment to the view that the brain led the way in primate evolution should not be interpreted as meaning that this common ancestor was human-like in conformation. For Elliot Smith, *Hesperopithecus, Pithecanthropus, Homo heidelbergensis, Homo rhodesiensis*, and *Homo neanderthalensis* are extinct hominid side branches which successively went down the path of specialization, like the other primate evolutionary lines.[20]

For Weinert (1932), humankind's closest living relative was to be found among the chimpanzees, the less specialized of all the hominoid apes, especially in comparison to the Asian ones, the orangs and the gibbons. It is from this chimpanzee-like branch that the human line emerged. Like many of his contemporaries, Weinert relied almost exclusively on comparative anatomy and embryology to establish phylogenetic connections. He proposed a phylogenetic tree of the primates in which all the main living primate groups budded one after the other from a common trunk: First were the prosimians followed later by the New World monkeys in the Eocene period; then the Old World monkeys were followed by the gibbon in the Oligocene period; next came the orang-utan during the Miocene period, while the gorilla budded in the mid-Pliocene period; finally the last split occurred between the chimpanzee and human lines at the turn of the Pliocene/Pleistocene periods.[21] It is a specificity of Weinert's conception at the time that he believed that the truly human form appeared as recently as the early Pleistocene.

Weinert made use of the fossil discoveries in the elaboration of his primate family tree, but only to the extent that they were enshrined in lineages leading to the living forms. For instance, fossil discoveries such as *Palaeopithecus, Sivapithecus, Gryphopithecus*, and some specimens of *Dryopithecus* were affiliated to the gorilla line, while *Neopithecus* (*Anthropodus*), *Australopithecus* (Taung), and some specimens of *Dryopithecus* were affiliated to the lineage leading to the chimpanzee. Although Weinert was apparently not sure about the place the cradle of humankind in the Old World in 1932, a few years later he was inclined to believe that Europe could have constituted such a place (Weinert, 1938).

Humans and two hominoid apes. If some scholars thought that the humans were more closely related to only a single living hominoid ape, others judged that humankind shared a genealogical link with two living hominoid species. For Gregory and Hooton, for instance, the two African great apes (chimpanzee and gorilla) constituted these closest living relatives.

For Gregory (1916, 1922, 1925, 1927b, 1930a, 1930b, 1934), humankind and the two African great apes shared a last common ancestor in the mid-Miocene period; the ancestral human-chimpanzee-gorilla stock being represented by the fossil *Dryopithecus-Sivapithecus* group. In Gregory's view, the orang line was a bit more distant from the human-chimpanzee-gorilla common stock, and the gibbon line still further removed from all of them. This being said, Gregory was apparently not entirely fixed about the exact phylogenetic place of the orang and the gibbon lines.[22] Gregory derived all the hominoids from an Old World stock also shared in common with the Old World monkeys.

In 1916, Gregory clearly inserted a number of fossil primate forms in the hominoid tree. *Pliopithecus* and *Gryphopithecus* were related to the gibbon line, *Palaeosimia* was associated with the orang line, *Palaeopithecus* was placed on the gorilla line and *Pan vetus* (the jaw of Piltdown) led to the living chimpanzees. Gregory positioned the extinct *Hesperopithecus* ape of Nebraska between the human stem and the African great apes stem. Gregory held that humankind's evolution went through a lemuroid stage, an early anthropoid stage (Old World) and a large hominoid stage. In this view, he strongly opposed those who favored that the humans and the hominoid apes acquired most of their similarities through parallel evolution, rather than by direct kinship. In Gregory's conception, *Pithecanthropus* and Neandertals were extinct side branches of the stem leading to the living humans.

Like Gregory, Hooton also closely linked the humans, the chimpanzees, and the gorillas. Although taking into account the primate fossil record, Hooton's conception of primate phylogeny is much more indebted to comparative anatomy than Gregory's. Deriving all the primates from an arboreal mammalian ancestor of the Secondary era, Hooton (1931) envisioned the main primate trunk at the root of humankind as having proceeded through the following stages (see Figure 7): lemuroid, tarsioid, gibbonoid, and giant hominoid (orang, gorilla, and chimpanzee).[23] At each of these evolutionary stages, groups of primates departed from this main primate trunk leading to living humans in order to give rise to the other nonhuman living primates. This happened through a process of specialization. Humankind's precursors, therefore, benefited from new adaptations gradually developed during these stages: handling (lemuroid), sitting up (tarsioid), erect posture of the upper body (gibbonoid), increased body size and exploitation of terrestrial resources (giant hominoid). The human lineage departed from the chimpanzee-gorilla branch in the mid-Miocene period, possibly from a common ancestor to be found in the *Dryopithecus-Sivapithecus* group.

Humans and three hominoid apes. For a scholar like Keith, humankind's closest living relatives were to be found among the three great apes: orangs, chimpanzees, and gorillas. Keith (1915, 1925a) promoted that the common ancestor of those three forms is to be traced back as far as the mid-Oligocene period. Keith's conception of primate phylogeny rested essentially on comparative anatomy. For him, humankind's ascent went through five primate stages: tarsioid, small monkey, small hominoid, large hominoid, and early humanoid. The human stem went its own way by the late Oligocene period in order to enter its early humanoid stage, thus leaving behind its large hominoid stage.[24] Keith made clear that he believed that humankind's last common ancestor with the great apes were ape-like creatures with small brains and developed supraorbital ridges. As far as the primate fossils were concerned, Keith put *Propliopithecus*, *Pliopithecus* and *Neopithecus* on the line leading to the living gibbons, while he thought *Dryopithecus* to be closely associated to the three great apes, to the exclusion of the human line.

Humans and all the hominoid apes. For other scholars like Osborn and Le Gros Clark, humankind's closest living relatives are to be found among all the hominoid species. Their view consisted of presenting that the humans and all the hominoid apes had departed from each other at about the same time period.

For instance, Osborn (1915) derived all the hominoids (including humans) from an early common gibbon-like ancestor (*Propliopithecus*) from which they subsequently departed from each other around the mid-Oligocene period. This common ancestor was held to have sprung from an unknown stem of the Old World primates. Osborn assumed this common ancestor to have probably originated among the forests and flood-plains of southern Asia, after which some of its descendants migrated early into Africa and western Europe. Osborn explicitly stated that although no evidence of direct relationship was recovered between humankind and the living and fossil hominoid apes, the proof of their common ancestry is found in the hominoid-like features of the living and the fossil human races.[25]

Osborn proposed that the primate fossil forms such as *Pliopithecus* and *Pliohylobates* were evolutionary stages through which the gibbon line had passed, while *Dryopithecus* is probably closely related to the ancestral stock of the three great apes exclusively. In 1922, Osborn hesitated about placing *Hesperopithecus* of Nebraska on the human stem or on the hominoid ape stem. Osborn (1915: 489–491) conceived humankind's family tree as being composed of a number of entirely separate branches with two main stems: one stem grouped *Pithecanthropus*, *Homo heidelbergensis*, and *Homo neanderthalensis*, all evolving separately toward extinction, while another stem led to the modern human types and was represented by the fossil races of the Upper Palaeolithic (Cro-Magnon, Brünn, Grimaldi, Furfooz).

Le Gros Clark's (1934, 1935, 1936) conception of primate phylogeny rested much more deeply on comparative anatomy than Osborn's. Le Gros Clark viewed the evolutionary history of the primates as being characterized by several adaptive radiations: lemurs, tarsiers, and anthropoids. Within the anthropoid radiation, the New World monkeys, the Old World monkeys, and the hominoids all stemmed from a common protarsioid stock during the Eocene or the early Oligocene period. In Le Gros Clark's view, the distinct hominoid species (including humankind) started to differentiate from one another in the Oligocene period, although the chimpanzee-gorilla line remained fused together much longer than the other ones.[26] Because the various hominoid lines differentiated from one another quite early and from a rather generalized anthropomorph form, Le Gros Clark explained the similarities among the living forms by appealing to the pervasive effect of parallel evolution. This parallelism was explained by the principle of orthogenesis, that is, by the inherent tendency of organisms that are closely related to vary along similar, definite, and limited evolutionary lines, regardless of environmental factors. Natural selection, on this view, is not a creative force in evolution but merely an arbiter of what is good or bad.

Although Le Gros Clark paid little attention to the primate fossil record, he recognized in *Parapithecus* and *Propliopithecus* early Oligocene forms situated near the base of the hominoid stem, and again in *Propliopithecus* and *Pliopithecus* forms near the gibbon line. As far as the fossil remains of *Dryopithecus, Palaeopithecus, Sivapithecus*, and *Australopithecus* (Taung) were concerned, Le Gros Clark (1934: 280) stated:

> While most of these fossils have been regarded as bearing a not very distant relation to the recent anthropoid [hominoid] apes, some at least exhibit certain human features which make it probable that they are early derivatives of a stock which may also have given rise to Man's ancestors.

In fact, Le Gros Clark (1935) made clear that he believed that the human line went through a dryopithecine phase of evolution, as those seen in the Miocene period, although its time of departure from the hominoid stock was much more earlier than that. Le Gros Clark held that while the other hominoid lineages went along the path of specialization, as seen in their long arms (in relation to their legs) and their large canines, the human lineage avoided such specializations by retaining a more generalized and primitive condition.

Human-like ancestors. The group of scholars we are about to review believed that the humans were indeed closely related to the hominoid apes. However, their viewpoints diverged from the scholars just reviewed in that they assessed that the common ancestor binding the humans and the hominoid apes is not ape-like but rather human-like in conformation. As already stated, this simple reversion in the interpretation of the polarity of the characters—the direction of the evolutionary change—throws a totally different light on the understanding of primate and human phylogeny. In this reversed perspective, it is the apes which are descended from the humans, so that one has to explain the rise of ape-like features in several distinct hominoid branches.

For several proponents of this latter view, embryology and ontogeny were used in a new way. By so doing, they changed the conventional use of this approach in the field of human evolution. Prior to 1890, embryology and ontogeny were used exclusively to give information about the phylogenetic relationship between humankind and its closest living relatives.[27] In other words, embryology and ontogeny only served the purpose of giving information about phylogenetic inferences. During the 1890–1935 period, this approach continued to serve its original purpose but a new dimension was added to it: It was also taken to indicate the actual conformation—the physical appearance—of the common ancestor between humankind and its closest living relatives. Because the earliest stages of the ontogenetic development of the living hominoids show a conformation more reminiscent of the human state than the ape state, this was interpreted to indicate that the common ancestor between the living humans and the hominoid apes was more human-like than ape-like in conformation. For proponents of this new perspective, the dictum which stated that "ontogeny recapitulates phylogeny" was interpreted in its literal sense.[28]

As would be expected, this new use of embryology and ontogeny was not unanimously approved at the time. For instance, Le Gros Clark accorded little attention to embryological evidence on the basis that such a scientific knowledge proved too general. Le Gros Clark (1934: 3) stated:

> Embryological evidence of evolutionary paths has not proved of great scientific value. Unhappily, however, it has often been drawn upon with a too rash assurance to give verisimilitude to theories of one kind or another. The proposition that ontogeny recapitulates phylogeny is no doubt true in a very general way, but the recapitulation is not so specific that it may form a basis of argument for any particular theory of evolutionary descent unless the evidence is of a very positive nature.

Such a critical evaluation of this use of embryology was not surprising when considering that Le Gros Clark himself derived humankind and all the other living hominoid apes from an ape-like common ancestor. Apparently, Le Gros Clark was not against the use of embryology per se in phylogenetic analyses, but more against the conclusion that on such a basis humankind could be said to have sprung from a human-like ancestor rather than an ape-like ancestor. Indeed, a few years later Le Gros Clark (1939a) recognized the usefulness of comparative embryology for establishing phylogenetic relationships.[29] Clearly, then, Le Gros Clark assumed that embryology was valid for phylogenetic inferences, at least to a certain extent, but not for establishing the conformation of humankind's ancestor.[30] He tried to explain his view in the following words:

> There is, as a matter of fact, abundant evidence from the study of the development of the human body to suggest that Man evolved initially from a primitive and generalized mammalian ancestor, but surprisingly little to indicate the nature of his immediate progenitor. (Le Gros Clark, 1934: 3)

Unmoved and unconvinced by such distinctions at the time, scholars like Ameghino, Klaatsch, Hill-Tout, and Osborn (after the mid-1920s) all ventured in this new approach to embryology and ontogeny, in conjunction with other scientific arguments.

For Ameghino, humankind's closest living relative was to be found among the gibbons (see Figure 8). His conception of primate phylogeny was based both on allegedly very ancient South American primate and hominid fossil discoveries and the assumed proximity between the humans and the New World monkeys. Ameghino held that South America had nurtured the very first mammals, including the first primates in the late Secondary era (Cretacean period), before they migrated throughout the world. Ameghino was not alone in believing at the time that South America could have possibly been the cradle of all or some of the mammals which then spread through the assumed great southern continent (e.g., von Zittel, 1893b; Smith Woodward, 1908).

Ameghino (1891, 1897, 1906, 1907, 1909) described the earliest primates as small prosimian-like creatures (*Clenialitidae*) from which stemmed, successively, all the other primate lineages before their migration throughout the world. On this view, the two stems of the New World monkeys and the hominids/hominoids were both derived from a common ancestor (*Pitheculites*) of the early Eocene period, while the Old World monkeys stem evolved from a separate ancestor (*Homunculites*) of the same time period.[31] By the late Oligocene or early Miocene period, primates now living in the Old World had left South America.

Ameghino's conception of primate phylogeny was rooted in his conviction that all the earliest primate forms were not pithecoid or ape-like in conformation. From that primitive state they all subsequently went through, to various degrees, a bestialization process with notable exceptions among some of the New World monkeys and especially the hominids. For Ameghino, the hominids and the hominoid apes were directly derived from South American fossil homunculid forms such as *Homunculus* (not to be confused with *Homunculites*) and *Anthropops*, which, Ameghino hypothesized, were characterized by human-like features in the head conformation. These fossil forms were at the base of a lineage which gradually evolved towards increased encephalization and humanization. The ancestral prototype of this main lineage would best be represented today by the modern genera of the *Cebus* and the *Saimiris* of the New World monkeys.

This explains why Ameghino thought that the hominids/hominoid apes' lineage and the New World monkeys' lineage were both more closely related to each other than either of them was to the Old World monkeys. While this common lineage to the hominids and the hominoid apes evolved towards a humanization process, continued Ameghino, several stems nonetheless diverged from it in the direction of a bestialization: The living hominoid apes diverged early from this main evolutionary stem, while the extinct hominid forms such as *Pithecanthropus*, Neandertals, and Heidelberg man diverged at a later period.[32] On this conception of primate phylogeny, the gibbon line was the last of the hominoid apes to have departed from the human stem, preceded by the orang line and at an even earlier time by the chimpanzee-gorilla line.

Ameghino's view implies that although the humans and the hominoid apes are descended from a common ancestor, the former never went through a hominoid stage. On this last point, Ameghino clearly stated that humankind is not a perfected ape, for it is the apes which are degenerated humans. To confirm his view, Ameghino turned to embryology and ontogeny which clearly indicated that the skulls of young hominoid apes and monkeys were more human-like than ape-like in conformation, as seen in their earliest stages of development. Ameghino also hypothesized that the human line went directly from a quadrupedal gait to a bipedal one, without going through a climbing phase. The living hominoid apes, for their part, also went through this evolutionary sequence before adopting very recently—after they had split from the lineage leading to the humans—their actual habit of living almost completely in the trees.

According to Ameghino, the hominid line (or lines) has been going its separate way from the hominoid ape line (or lines) since at least the early Miocene period and probably before. Accordingly, *Tetraprothomo argentinus*, *Diprothomo platensis*, *Homo pampaeus,* and *Homo pliocenicus* all constituted Miocene or Pliocene South American hominid fossils heading in the direction of the humanization process of most, though not all, of the living human races. Ameghino (1906: 450) envisaged the possibility of recognizing a polygenetic origins of the living human races from separate Old World and New World precursors. All of them would, of course, be ultimately derived from a common South American trunk.

If Ameghino closely linked the humans and the gibbons, a number of other scholars, who were advancing the idea that the humans and the hominoid apes descended from a common human-like ancestor, were rather vague about the exact nature of this relationship. Among them are found Hubrecht, Klaatsch, and Hill-Tout. For instance, Hubrecht (1897) proposed a view of primate phylogeny which appealed extensively to parallel evolution. Hubrecht held that humankind's ascent was not the result of a succession of evolutionary stages such as lemur-like, monkey-like and hominoid-like stages. First of all, the prosimians and all lemur-like forms were not, in Hubrecht's mind, primates. Their ancestry was more aligned with the pigs, the horses, and the ungulates in general. Second, Hubrecht held that the monkeys and the hominoids (including humans) each independently evolved from insectivore-like creatures of the Secondary era. As far as the living humans and hominoid apes were concerned, Hubrecht (1897: 22–23) imagined the following hypothetical situation:

> [A] direct ancestor of the anthropoids [hominoid apes] and man, differing from Simiae Catarhinae, Platyrhinae, and Tarsiae, must have existed throughout the Tertiaries, and must have directly sprung from a Mesozoic insectivorous ancestor, small in size, but already more or less erect in posture, provided with a spacious brain cavity, with a decidua reflexa, and with a discoid placenta of the Erinacean type of development.

Hubrecht apparently affiliated the lower Eocene *Anaptomorphus homunculus* of North America to this human/hominoid apes stem. He assumed that humankind avoided going through a hominoid-like stage of evolution, implying therefore that the common ancestor to the living humans and the hominoid apes was more human-like than ape-like in conformation.

In the conception of Klaatsch, humankind's place among the primates was largely derived from comparative anatomy and embryology and, to a lesser degree, from fossil discoveries such as *Pithecanthropus*.[33] According to Klaatsch (1905 [1902]), humans, hominoid apes, and monkeys are all derived from a common ancestor, although the exact nature of this evolutionary split is not perfectly clear from his writings. However, Klaatsch made clear that he did not believe that the human lineage derived from an Old World monkey-like ancestor. He further added that the modern way of looking at this question harmonizes perfectly with the fact that the New World monkeys retained more features in common with the humans and the hominoid apes than with the Old World monkeys. In fact, Klaatsch insisted that although there were, strictly speaking, no hominoid ape forms in the New World, he promoted that monkeys which belonged to the *Ateles* and *Mycetes* genera could be considered to represent such anthropomorph-like forms in the New World.

When considering the relationship between the humans and the hominoid apes, Klaatsch held that they were descended from a common hypothetical form he called *Proanthropus*. He maintained that the human line had been separated from all the other hominoids since the Eocene or Oligocene period. Klaatsch imagined this common ancestor to be more human-like than ape-like, a fact he said to be supported by the comparative ontogeny of the living hominoids. Each of the hominoid evolutionary lines is envisioned as having proceeded independently further down the path of apeness and degeneration, unlike the human line. However, Klaatsch recognized that the living gibbons and especially the fossil specimen of *Pithecanthropus* have proceeded less toward that apeness. For him, *Pithecanthropus* is not on the human line because it is already too committed in the ape direction. Klaatsch contended that all the living and the fossil human races could be traced back to a single human-like ancestor who lived in an unknown and restricted geographical area. Klaatsch was visibly inquisitive about either Australia or a now-disappeared and fragmented great southern continent being the cradle of humankind.

Unlike Klaatsch but not unlike Ameghino, Hill-Tout's (1921) conception of primate phylogeny was largely based on his assessment of new hominid fossil discoveries and primate embryology. Hill-Tout explicitly opposed the view which envisioned the gradual transformation of a hominoid-like creature into a human form through stages such as *Pithecanthropus* and Neandertals. Hill-Tout put forth the idea, on the basis of embryology, that Old World monkeys, New World monkeys, hominoid apes, and humans were all descended from a common ancestor that was more human-like than ape-like in conformation, especially in skull shape. On this view, simian features such as large jaws and teeth, well-developed muscular crests and tori, and projecting faces were morphological traits that gradually evolved independently, to various degrees, in each anthropoid lineage with the exception of the humanoid one. In Hill-Tout's view, *Pithecanthropus* was a form affiliated to the hominoid ape stem, rather than the human stem, but which presented more human-like features than any other such forms by having been less committed in the pithecoid direction. Conversely, extinct forms such as the Neandertals and Heidelberg man were affiliated to the hominid stem but with more ape-like traits than any other hominids. Hill-Tout believed that Piltdown man—dated to the late Pliocene or early Pleistocene period—may possibly be the earliest known representative of the main human line. According to Hill-Tout, this human line may well be traced back to a mid-Miocene hypothetical common ancestor coming between the humans and the hominoid apes. He named this hypothetical form *Homosimius precursor*.

The last three scholars reviewed here were rather vague about the exact nature of the link they saw between the humans and the hominoid apes, but Osborn's view to which we now turn was presented without much ambiguity. Osborn clearly insisted that none of the living hominoid apes was more closely related to humankind only because the human line departed from all the hominoid forms quite early. We have previously seen that during the 1910s, Osborn promoted a view that derived the humans from a hominoid-like ancestor. By the mid-1920s, however, Osborn (1927a, 1927b, 1929, 1930) favored a different view of human evolution. He now discarded the "Ape-Man" hypothesis and replaced it by the "Dawn-Man" hypothesis. This view independently derived the humans and the hominoid apes from a common Oligocene neutral stock. Osborn now argued that the so-called simian features of the human lineage were acquired either because of a very remote common inheritance with the apes or because of a convergence of the ape type toward the human shape, not the reverse.

Osborn now held that human features such as a large brain, an erect posture, the proportions of the upper and lower limbs, the configuration of the hands and feet, were all acquired as early as the Pliocene. Although Osborn recognized that the human stem had passed through an arboreal stage, he insisted that this stage did not progress so far as to carry this stem into a state approaching that of the hominoid apes. He turned to embryology in order to demonstrate that there was no evidence of the human form having passed through an ape-like prehensile lower limb stage. Furthermore, Osborn sought support for his Dawn-Man hypothesis in paleontology by arguing that the living members of mammalian families were already often represented in the Pliocene period by fairly modern-looking forms. However, this new view would not significantly alter Osborn's phylogenetic tree of human evolution.[34] What changed, instead, was his interpretation of the morphological characters of the human fossils. He now insisted on the human and the non-ape traits of all the human fossils. Osborn held that the human characteristics were acquired early. He insisted on the fact that he had supposedly predicted the discovery of a large-brained pre-man in the Pliocene period, a discovery he now claims to be proven by the alleged earlier dating given to the Piltdown remains. The relatively small brain of *Pithecanthropus*, which contradicted Osborn's new conception of human evolution, was explained by him as a case of arrested development (pathology).

HYPOTHETICAL RECONSTRUCTIONS AND SCENARIOS

Prior to 1890, a small number of scholars expressed views about the hypothetical reconstruction of humankind's ancestors and the scenarios of hominization. On the one hand, attempts at reconstruction of humankind's ancestors were made by Hovelacques on the basis of comparative anatomy and by de Mortillet with the assistance of prehistoric archeology and so-called paleontological laws. It is under such an approach that de Mortillet imagined the hypothetical ancestor named *Anthropopithecus*. On the other hand, scenarios of hominization were proposed by

Lamarck, Haeckel, and Darwin on the basis of comparative anatomy. It will be remembered that Haeckel conceived a series of transformational stages between humans and nonhuman primates, one of which was represented by the hypothetical form named by him, *Pithecanthropus alalus*. The 1890–1935 period saw the naming of new hypothetical forms as seen in Klaatsch's *Proanthropus* and Hill-Tout's *Homosimius precursor*.[35] This being said, there was no need to create new names in order to be able to imagine hypothetical creatures or stages.

All the scholars who attempted such hypothetical reconstructions or scenarios prior to 1890 postered the idea that humankind had sprung from ape-like creatures. It is not that everyone agreed with this view at the time, for scholars like Owen, Mivart, and de Quatrefages were probably inclined to see this ancestor as being more human-like in conformation. However, these latter scholars only presented their views in a vague fashion, and thus have not contributed to hypothetical reconstructions or scenarios. It is another distinctive feature of the 1890–1935 period that the diversity of viewpoints expressed about humankind's place among the primates also found its way into hypothetical reconstructions and scenarios of hominization. This may well have been a sign that this diversity of viewpoints was now well-entrenched in the field of paleoanthropology.

Another specific advancement of the 1890–1935 period was the occasional use of fossils in hypothetical reconstructions and scenarios of hominization. It will be remembered that prior to 1890, all the scholars agreed that no intermediary form had been found yet to connect the humans with the other primates. It is not surprising that it is during the 1890–1935 period that fossils were occasionally used for this purpose. This has been the case of Piltdown man and/or *Pithecanthropus* by Elliot Smith, Morton, and Hill-Tout. Two reasons may explain this occurrence: (1) because the primate fossils entered, at last, the debates on humankind's place among the primates for the first time during this time period; (2) Because the diversity of viewpoints promoted at the time increased considerably the possibility of such a use by one author or another.

It is true that at a superficial level, all hypothetical reconstructions and scenarios of hominization may look alike. After all, once it is admitted that the humans and some other primates are, genealogically speaking, closely related, there are only a limited number of ways to express this relationship. However, the differences should not be underestimated as these are found in the details of the explanation. It is remarkable that scenarios of hominization suggested by Lamarck, Haeckel, and Darwin prior to 1890 were fairly similar to each other, in that they derived humankind from ape-like ancestors and insisted that what made us human was instigated by a new locomotive adaptation: bipedality. During the 1890–1935 period, more variables were added to, and debated in, the hypothetical reconstructions and the scenarios of hominization. At least three sets of antinomic variables were important at the time: ape-like versus human-like; small-brained versus big-brained; and nonbipedal versus bipedal. It is useful to divide the analysis of this topic into two main issues: (1) the hypothetical reconstruction of humankind's ancestors, and (2) the hypotheses proposed to explain the sequence and the cause of the transformation of humankind's ascent from the other primates, that is, the scenarios of hominization proper.

Reconstructing humankind's ancestors. Among the scholars who contributed to forging an image about humankind's remote ancestors, a number of them depicted it as an ape-like creature. Once agreed on this, however, they were not necessarily agreed on its body size, its brain size, nor its posture. For instance, Gregory (1925, 1927b, 1930a, 1930b) envisioned the precursors of the humans as semi-arboreal, semi-erect, and semi-quadrupedal apes of large size with a small brain and a tendency for a bipedal posture. While the chimpanzee-gorilla group retained most of this ancestral condition, humankind's forerunners went through profound structural changes. For his part, Le Gros Clark (1934, 1935) believed that the human stem had diverged from the hominoid apes at a stage during which the common ancestor is a gibbon-like creature of small size and of orthograde (semi-erect) posture. This ancestor was seen as being of a generalized hominoid conformation not yet committed to specialized body proportions (short legs and long arms) and with a not too specialized grasping foot for living in the trees, rather than a supporting one as assumed by Gregory. This view supports the idea that the human line, during its evolutionary history, avoided many of the specializations of the living hominoid apes. In yet another view, Keith (1915, 1925a) concurred with Gregory and Le Gros Clark in believing that humankind's ancestor was an ape-like creature with a small brain, although he insisted that the humans had acquired early their large brain capacity. Keith evaluated that since the early Pliocene period the human stem had been characterized by ancestors that presented brains as large as modern humans, while they retained skulls, teeth, and mandibles which were still ape-like in conformation.[36]

For other scholars, however, the image of humankind's remote ancestor has more to do with a human-like creature rather than a hominoid ape-like form. Although they too were unable to agree on the details of the image of our hypothetical ancestor, they were all agreed on at least one key feature: the relatively large brain size of that ancestor. For instance, Hubrecht (1897) assumed that the hominid evolutionary line acquired very early an increased brain size and an erect posture. Hubrecht contended that humans had avoided going through a hominoid ape-like stage of evolution, although he insisted that the living hominoid apes shared a common ancestor with the human line at some point in time. As far as can be determined from Hubrecht's writing, this common ancestor was apparently more human-like than ape-like in conformation. For his part, Klaatsch (1902 [1905]) hypothesized that the common ancestor to the humans and the hominoid apes, which he called *Proanthropus*, was an arboreal, semi-erect creature, with legs and arms of equal length, prehensile extremities (hands and feet), a relatively large and rounded skull and a moderately developed dentition. From this more-or-less human-like initial point, Klaatsch further hypothesized that the human line adapted to a fully bipedal gait by developing a supporting foot, while going through an encephalization process. In another view, Ameghino (1906, 1909) insisted that all the earliest primate forms were not pithecoid in conformation but were rather characterized by a relatively large, high, and rounded skull, had a reduced prognathism, and had little or no browridges. The lineage leading to living humans retained many of these ancestral features while evolving towards an increased encephalization, contrary to humankind's closest living relatives, the hominoid apes. In yet another view, Hill-Tout (1921) suggested that the hominoid apes and the humans were descended from a common ancestor which was more human-like than ape-like in conformation, especially in skull shape. This common hypothetical form, it is argued, could be foreseen in the ontogeny of young human and hominoid ape forms. Hill-Tout referred to this hypothetical ancestor as *Homosimius precursor*. It was described as being chinless, with limb proportions similar to that of the living hominoid apes, and more pronounced canines and developed mandibles than the living humans. Hill-Tout saw in Piltown man—with its rounded and well-developed braincase and moderate simian features in the jaw and teeth—a form which probably approached that hypothetical common ancestor.

For a third group of scholars, the ape-like/human-like dichotomy presented in this chapter is of limited value to assess their hypothetical reconstructions, only because they argued that human evolution is entirely unrelated to the hominoid apes. For these scholars, humankind's remote ancester could not be too ape-like in conformation. For instance, Wood Jones (1918, 1919, 1929) assumed that the protohuman stock arose from a small-bodied and large-brained tarsier-like form committed to arboreal bipedalism. This form evolved in the general direction of a larger gibbon-like stage (with no genealogical implication) devoid of pithecoid features and early committed to both terrestrial bipedalism and to an increased encephalization.

Scenarios of hominization. Scholars who reconstructed humankind's hypothetical ancestors either remained silent on the anthropogenesis process or presented their views in an implicit way exclusively. The procedures were quite different for those who proposed scenarios of hominization. Scenarios are, by definition, dynamic explanations constituting explicit arguments about the sequence and the cause of the evolutionary change responsible for the rise of the modern human form. All the scholars who proposed such scenarios in the 1890–1935 period held that humankind's ancestors were ape-like forms. It is not clear if this is simply a coincidence or not. Perhaps the scholars who favored the ape-like thesis felt compelled to explain the major evolutionary changes that were required for the unique rise of the human shape? Indeed, how could the human line avoided the fate that awaited the several distinct ape-like lineages? Conversely, perhaps the scholars who insisted that humankind's ancestor was already more human-like than ape-like in conformation thought that the hominization process was too obvious to require any explanation. After all, the anatomical gap separating the living humans from this ancestor is narrower if it is not assumed that this ancestor is ape-like in conformation.

Scholars who favored the ape thesis were neither agreed on the sequence of the evolutionary change in time nor agreed on its cause. For instance, Elliot Smith (1924) held that the earliest hominid members were apes in the face, teeth, and body configuration, but with an overgrown brain. The Piltdown man with its large brain and pithecoid jaw was, he continued, just such a confirmation. These early simian features in human evolution persisted for a considerable length of time after the brain had noticeably increased and the hind limbs adapted for an erect posture. Here lies the heart of Elliot Smith's scenario of hominization: It is a bigger and better brain which permitted good manipulative skills of the hands, which in turn required their full liberation through a bidedal gait.

For Morton (1927), it is not the brain but bipedality which was the key change that instigated the hominization process. Morton held that the rise of humankind from a tarsioid stock proceeded in two main evolutionary phases. First, an early arboreal phase which lasted between the mid-Eocene and the late Oligocene periods during which the common ancestor of the living humans and the hominoid apes were of small size and had short arms. Second, a late terrestrial phase which followed the split of the human stock from the hominoid ape one in the mid-Miocene period.[37] In Morton's view, the humans had clearly evolved out of ape-like creatures. In fact, he envisioned humankind's common ancestor with the great apes to be a dryopithecine-like creature with a small brain. It is the bipedal adaptation of the early hominids which instigated the gradual development of all the other human morphological and intellectual features. This hominization process was assumed to have started in the lower portion of the body (feet and legs adapted for bipedality), only to be gradually extended with time to the entire body frame. This, in turn, favored what Morton (1927: 194) called "a wider scope of interdependent action between the hands and the brain," or a positive feedback loop, as we would say today. Once early hominids had freed their hands from the function of locomotion, this permitted the development of the brain and, eventually, the loss of ape-like facial features. Clearly, Morton saw the rise of most human attributes to be a by-product of a new kind of locomotion: terrestrial bipedality. He used the hominid fossil remains of *Pithecanthropus* and Piltdown to confirm his assertion that the brain increased only once bipedality had developed. These remains showed a smaller brain capacity than the living humans while already being erect creatures, as seen in the femur of *Pithecanthropus.*

Elliot Smith and Morton believed that one factor in particular had instigated the hominization process. For Hooton, Osborn, and Weinert, however, the hominization process was the result of several, mutually reinforcing factors with not one clearly defined prime mover. In their views, two or more factors were involved in a synergetic system. For instance, Hooton (1931) insisted on the dual influence of intelligence and bipedality in the anthropogenesis process. He held that once the chimpanzee-gorilla branch had departed from the one leading to the humans in the mid-Miocene period, humankind's immediate precursors gradually developed specific adaptations related to, first, a fully bipedal gait and, later, to a much larger brain capacity. In Hooton's view, humankind's ancestor was clearly an ape-like creature with arms proportions and jaw conformation approaching that of the living chimpanzees, but with a slightly bigger brain size as well as with longer and stronger legs. Hooton recognized that the scenario of hominization which involved liberated hands and increased brain capacity must be true to some extent, but remained cautious about facile mechanistic or functional interpretations. Although Hooton (1930) recognized that we are quite unable to explain the causes of human evolution, he was apparently inclined to believe that when humankind's ancestors first adapted to live on the ground, they did so successfully only because they were already more intelligent than the chimpanzees. This initial mental superiority, he seemed to have believed, was a key factor in instigating the other anatomical and intellectual changes in the course of human evolution (Hooton, 1931: 143–164).

For his part, Osborn (1915) explained the specificity of human evolution during the Miocene and Pliocene periods as a coincident development of four structural changes: Erect attitude, opposable thumb, growth of the brain, and power of speech. Osborn (1915: 60) explained the entire hominization process—and the effect it had on humankind's ancestor in the late Pliocene—in the following terms:

> A similar action and reaction between foot and brain developed the erect gait which released the hand from its locomotive and limb-grasping function, and by the resultant perfecting of the motion of thumbs and fingers turned the hand into an organ ready for the increasing specialization demanded by the manufacture of flint implements. This is the stage reached, we believe, in late Pliocene times . . . The attitude is erect, the hand has a well-developed opposable thumb, the centres of the brain relating to the higher senses and to the control of all motions of the limbs, hands, and fingers are well developed. The power of speech may still be rudimentary. The anterior centres of the brain for the storing of experience and the development of ideas are certainly very rudimentary.[38]

Together with Hooton and Osborn, Weinert (1932) also insisted on the positive feedback loop of several mutually reinforcing features involved in the rise of the human line. Weinert held that because of changing environmental conditions, humankind's chimpanzee-like ancestor was able to adapt to these new conditions only because he was not too specialized, while being slightly more intelligent than his competitors. These preconditions permitted the instigation of a cascade of anatomical and behavioral changes: the adaptation to a bipedal gait, the freed hands, the domestication of fire, the reduction of the face and teeth, and language and socialization (see also Weinert, 1940).[39]

CONCLUSION

The main goal of this chapter has been to present the extent of the disagreement over humankind's place among the primates between 1890 and 1935. It is argued here that it is not possible to understand properly the development of paleoanthropology without understanding this broader interpretative context. Unfortunately, historians of the field have too often focused exclusively on human phylogeny proper. How can one assess the progress made in the research on humankind's place in nature if one excludes the considerations of the insertion of the humans among the other primates? After all, debates on human phylogeny are usually only concerned with the placing of hominid fossils in the human family tree. Such debates rarely explicitly present the evolutionary connections between the humans and the other animals. It is therefore difficult to assess the views of the scholars on the question of humankind's place in nature only through their conceptions of human phylogeny proper. In a sense, the nature of humankind's link with the other animals is a much more determinant factor for the resolution of the question of humankind's place in nature than the nature of the link between humankind and its close hominid relatives.

Let us briefly summarize the key elements which contributed to entertain a remarkably high level of uncertainty about humankind's place among the primates during the 1890–1935 period. We have seen that three main phylogenetic hypotheses were proposed: (1) humankind's complete absence of a link with the other primates as seen in Adloff's and Sergi's parallel hypotheses; (2) humankind's link with early and primitive primates which were unrelated to the hominoid apes as promoted by Cope (before 1890), Boule, and Wood Jones; and (3) humankind's link with the hominoid apes as held by many scholars, although they were unable to agree on the exact nature of this relationship.

In addition to these three main phylogenetic hypotheses, scholars were also divided on the fundamental issue concerning the conformation of humankind's remote ancestors: ape-like or human-like? We have seen that this has been a dominant underlying theme for the entire 1890–1935 period. Important implications flowed from this disagreement in the assessment of the polarity of the characters or the direction of the evolutionary change.

Scholars were also unable to agree on the geological moment when the human stock had departed from its closest relatives. It is useful to regroup these views in three geological time periods: (1) the scholars who assumed that the human stem had immensely deep phylogenetic roots which go back as early as the very late Secondary or very early Tertiary eras (Hubrecht, Adloff, Cope); (2) the scholars who placed the rise of the human stem at about the mid-Tertiary era, that is, during the Oligocene period (Le Gros Clark, Osborn [after 1925], Keith, Wood Jones); and (3) the scholars who thought that the humans had arisen later during the Miocene period (Hill-Tout, Hooton, Gregory, Osborn [before 1925], Elliot Smith) or even as late as the turn of the Pliocene/Pleistocene periods (Weinert).

There was yet another important subject of dispute among the scholars at the time: the geographical site proposed as humankind's birthplace. Remember that Sergi held that the human races had sprung from different geographical areas distributed worldwide; Elliot Smith took a clear position in favor of Africa; Osborn hypothesized that South Asia was the location; Ameghino placed South America at the heart of all key primate evolutionary events, including humankind's ascent; Hubrecht turned to North America as the whereabouts of humankind's earliest and probably direct ancestor; Weinert would not exclude Europe from being that cradle; and Klaatsch wondered whether Australia or an assumed great southern continent might be the site.

The level of disagreement about humankind's place among the primates was indeed very considerable during the 1890–1935 period. Yet, it may be added that this level of uncertainty was even more important than presented in this chapter. A number of scholars at the time also proposed that the humans had shared an intertwined evolutionary history with some other primates, as seen in their polyphyletic hypotheses. In order to avoid repetition, these views are presented in the next chapter.

NOTES

1. K. von Zittel, *Textbook of Palaeontology* (London: Macmillan, 1926) was originally published as *Handbuch der Palaeontologie* (Leipzig: R. Oldenbourg, 1893).
2. Lydekker later referred *Palaeopithecus* to *Troglodytes*, and still later to *Anthropopithecus*. See R. Lydekker, "Indian Tertiary and Post-Tertiary Vertebrata. Siwalik Mammalia—Supplement I," *Memoirs of the Geological Survey of India*, 10th series, 4 (1886): 1–21; W.H. Flower and R. Lydekker, *An Introduction to the Study of Mammals Living and Extinct* (London: Adam and Charles Black, 1891), pp. 736–738.
3. See Schlosser's phylogenetic tree in "Die Affen, Lemuren, Chiropteren, Insectivoren, Marsupialier, Creodonten und Carnivoren des Europäischen Tertiärs," *Beiträge zur Paläontologie Österreich-Ungarns und des Orients*, 6 (1888), p. 9.
4. See Schlosser's phylogenetic tree, "Die Affen, Lemuren, Chiropteren, Insectivoren, Marsupialier, Creodonten und Carnivoren des Europäischen Tertiärs," *Beiträge zur Paläontologie Österreich-Ungarns und des Orients*, 6 (1888), p. 54.
5. For instance, E.D. Cope, "The Lemuroidea and the Insectivora of the Eocene Period of North America," *American Naturalist*, 19 (1885): 457–471; M. Schlosser, "Die Affen, Lemuren, Chiropteren, Insectivoren, Marsupialier, Creodonten und Carnivoren des europäischen Tertiärs," *Beiträge zur Paläontologie Österreich-Ungarns und des Orients*, 6 (1888): 1–224; F. Ameghino, "Les formations sédimentaires du Crétacé supérieur et du Tertaire de Patagonie," *Anales del Museo Nacional de Buenos Aires*, 3rd series, 8 (1906): 1–568; M. Schlosser, "Beiträge zur Kenntniss der Oligozänen Landsäugetiere aus dem Fayum: Ägypten," *Beiträge zur Paläontologie und Geologie Österreich-Ungarns und des Orients*, 24 (1911): 51–167; G.E. Pilgrim, "New Siwalik Primates and Their Bearing on the Question of the Evolution of Man and the Anthropoidea," *Records of the Geological Survey of India*, 45 (1915): 1–74; R. Fourteau, *Contribution à l'étude des vertébrés miocènes de l'Égypte* (Cairo: Government Press, 1918). Other references are given in the main text of this chapter.
6. Among those who addressed direct criticisms at the empirical foundation of this conception, especially in South America, see G. Schwalbe, "Studien zur Morphologie der südamerikanischen Primatenformen," *Zeitschrift für Morphologie und Anthropologie*, 13 (1910): 209–258; V. Giuffrida-Ruggeri, "Il supposito centro antropogenico sud-americano," *Monitore Zoologico Italiano*, 22 (1911): 269–286; K. Stolyhwo, "Contribution à l'étude de l'homme fossile sud-américain et de son prétendu précurseur le Diprothomo platensis," *Bulletins et Mémoires de la Société d'Anthropologie de Paris*, 6ième série, 2 (1911): 158–168.
7. Later, Rutot no longer spoke of the rise of a failed humanity responsible for the earliest eoliths. Instead, he attributed these earliest tools to a very primitive and almost ape-like segment of humanity which arose as early as the Eocene period and survived to modern day in the Tasmanians and evolved through fossil representatives such as Mauer, Grimaldi, and Neandertals. See A. Rutot, "Une industrie éolithique antérieure à l'Oligocène supérieur ou Aquitanien," in *Congrès préhistoriques de France, Compte rendu de la quatrième session, Chambéry 1908*, 1909, pp. 90–104.
8. See their primate family tree, W.K. Gregory and M. Hellman, "Notes on the Type of *Hesperopithecus Haroldcookii* Osborn," *American Museum Novitates*, No. 53 (1923), p. 15.

9. See Elliot Smith's primate family tree, *The Evolution of Man: Essays* (London: Oxford University Press, 1924), p. 3.

10. See Adloff's primate family tree, *Das Gebiss des Menschen und der Anthropomorphen* (Berlin: Julius Springer, 1908), p. 131.

11. See Sergi's graphic representation of those primate parallel evolutionary lines in *L'Evoluzione Organica e le Origini Umane: Induzioni paleontologiche* (Torino: Fratelli Bocca, 1914), p. 206.

12. See Cope's primate family tree, "Archaeology and Anthropology," *American Naturalist*, 22 (1888), p. 663.

13. It should be noted that after 1890, Cope modified his view of humankind's place among the primates and now derived the human stem from some undetermined anthromorph-like creatures, see E.D. Cope, "The Genealogy of Man," *American Naturalist*, 27 (1893): 321–335.

14. See Boule's primate family tree, *Les hommes fossiles: éléments de paléontologie humaine* (Paris: Masson, 1921), p. 448.

15. It will not be possible to present here all the scholars who promoted a close phylogenetic link between the gibbons and humankind during the 1895–1935 period. Among others not reviewed here see E.-R. Lenoir, "L'homme et le gibbon," *Revue Anthropologique*, 36 (1926): 427–460 and E. Werth, *Der Fossile Mensch: Grundzüge einer Paläanthropologie* (Berlin: G. Borntraeger, 1928). See Werth's hominoid family tree on p. 874.

16. See Pilgrim's primate family tree situated at the very end of his paper, "New Siwalik Primates and Their Bearing on the Question of the Evolution of Man and the Anthropoidea," *Records of the Geological Survey of India*, 45 (1915), 1–74.

17. See Pilgrim's new primate family tree, "A Sivapithecus Palate and other Primate Fossils from India," *Memoirs of the Geological Survey of India, Palaeontologia Indica*, 14 (1927), p. 17.

18. See Schultz's primate family trees, "Studies on the Growth of Gorilla and of other Higher Primates With Special Reference to a Fetus of Gorilla, Preserved in the Carnegie Museum," *Memoirs of the Carnegie Museum*, 11 (1927), p. 66; "The Skeleton of the Trunk and Limbs of Higher Primates," *Human Biology*, 2 (1930), p. 402; "Characters Common to Higher Primates and Characters Specific for Man," *Quarterly Review of Biology*, 11 (1936), p. 451.

19. See Elliot Smith's primate family tree, *Essays on the Evolution of Man* (London: Oxford Univerity Press, 1924), p. 3.

20. See Elliot Smith human family tree, *Essays on the Evolution of Man* (London: Oxford Univerity Press, 1924), p. 2.

21. See Weinert's primate family tree, *Ursprung der Menschheit* (Stuttgart: F. Enke, 1932), p. 351.

22. Compare Gregory's primate family trees, W.K. Gregory, "Studies on the Evolution of the Primates," *Bulletin of the American Museum of Natural History*, 35 (1916), p. 337 and W.K. Gregory and M. Hellman, "Notes on the Type of *Hesperopithecus haroldcookii* Osborn," *American Museum Novitates*, 53 (1923), p. 15.

23. See Hooton's primate family tree, *Up From the Ape* (London: George Allen & Unwin Ltd, 1931), p. 391.

24. See Keith's primate family trees, *The Antiquity of Man* (London: William and Norgate, 1915), p. 509; *The Antiquity of Man*, 2nd edition (London: William and Norgate, 1925), Vol. 1, frontispiece.

25. See Osborn's primate family tree, *Men of the Old Stone Age: Their Environment, Life and Art* (New York: Charles Scribner's Sons, 1915), p. 54.

26. See Le Gros Clark's primate family tree in *Early Forerunners of Man: A Morphological Study of the Evolutionary Origin of the Primates* (Baltimore: William Wood, 1934), p. 275. Le Gros Clark never explicitly and directly stated that the human branch had departed from the hominoid stock in the Oligocene period but this can easily be deduced from his writings. For instance, Le Gros Clark (1935: 4) argued that if the chimpanzee branch was already differentiated in the Lower Miocene, one has to look for the rise of the human branch in a much earlier time because he assumed that the latter branch differentiated from the hominoid stock before the former branch. In another instance, Le Gros Clark (1934: 279) recognized in *Propliopithecus* of the Lower Oligocene a form almost at the base of the hominoid radiation just before the moment when the gibbon and the human lines split from the common hominoid stock, as can be seen in his phylogenetic tree on p. 275.

27. See, for instance, T.H. Huxley, *Evidence as to Man's Place in Nature* (London: Williams & Norgate, 1863); H. Schaaffhausen, "On the

Primitive Form of the Human Skull," *Anthropological Review*, 6 (1868): 412–431; C.R. Darwin, *The Descent of Man, and Selection in Relation to Sex*, Vol. 1 (London: John Murray, 1871); E. Haeckel, *The Evolution of Man: A Popular Exposition of the Principal Points of Human Ontogeny and Phylogeny*, 2 vols. (New York: Appleton, 1896).

28. For a discussion of the various kinds of connections between ontogeny and phylogeny promoted at the time consult D. Ospovat, "The Influence of Karl Ernst von Baer's Embryology, 1828–1859: A Reappraisal in Light of Richard Owen's and William B. Carpenter's Palaeontological Application of Von Baer's Law," *Journal of the History of Biology*, 9 (1976): 1–28; S.J. Gould, *Ontogeny and Phylogeny* (Cambridge: Harvard University Press, 1977); N. Rasmussen, "The Decline of Recapitulationism in Early Twentieth-Century Biology: Disciplinary Conflict and Consensus on the Battleground of Theory," *Journal of the History of Biology*, 24 (1991): 51–89.

29. Le Gros Clark (1939a: 53) argued that the method of comparative anatomy (including embryology and physiology) permitted to establish that the human line was derived from a common ancestral group also shared with the modern hominoid apes.

30. It should be noted that although Le Gros Clark (1939a: 56–57; 1947a: 384) always recognized the usefulness of comparative anatomy and embryology, he gradually became aware of the limitations of their resolution in phylogenetic inferences. Prior to that, however, Le Gros Clark (1934: 4) declared that comparative anatomy was the main source of evidence in phylogenetic inferences.

31. See Ameghino's primate family tree in "Les formations sédimentaires du Crétacé supérieur et du Tertiaire de Patagonie," *Anales del Museo Nacional de Buenos Aires*, 3rd series, 8 (1906), p. 451.

32. For more detail about Ameghino's phylogenetic view of the living human races, hominid fossils, and hominoid lineages, see his family trees in "Notas preliminares sobre el Tetraprothomo argenticus: Un precursor del hombre del Mioceno superior de Monte Hermoso," *Anales del Museo Nacional de Buenos Aires*, 3rd series, 9 (1907), pp. 222 and 224; and "Le *Diprothomo platensis*: Un précurseur de l'homme du Pliocène inférieur de Buenos Aires," *Anales del Museo Nacional de Buenos Aires*, 3rd series, 12 (1909), p. 206.

33. Klaatsch's publication of 1905 in French was orignally published as "Entstehung und Entwickelung des Menschengeschlechtes," in H. Kraemer (ed.), *Weltall und Menscheit: Geschichte der Erforschung der Natur und der Verwertung der Naturkräfte im Dienste der Völker*, Vol. 2 (Berlin: Bong & Co., 1902), pp. 1–338.

34. Compare Osborn's phylogenetic trees in "The Discovery of Tertiary Man," *Science*, 71 (1930), p. 3, and his previous diagram in *Men of the Old Stone Age: Their Environment, Life and Art* (New York: Charles Scribners' Sons, 1915), p. 491.

35. Eugène Dubois also imagined a hypothetical ancestor he called *Prothylobates*. See Chapter 5.

36. Later, however, Keith held that the hominids had reached a modern brain size only much later in time, that is during the Pleistocene; see A. Keith, *The Construction of Man's Family Tree* (London: Watts & Co., 1934).

37. See Morton's family tree in D.J. Morton, "Human Origin: Correlation of Previous Studies of Primate Feet and Posture With Other Morphologic Evidence," *American Journal of Physical Anthropology*, 10 (1927), p. 192.

38. It should be remembered that after the mid-1920s, Osborn no longer held that the humans had stemmed from a genuine ape-like creature.

39. Weinert presented in greater detail his conception of the hominization process in *Der geistige Aufstieg der Menschheit: Vom Ursprung bis zur Gegenwart* (Stuttgart: F. Enke, 1940). This book was translated in French as *L'ascension intellectuelle de l'humanité: Des origines aux temps présents* (Paris: Payot, 1946).

5

Human Phylogeny

A HISTORIOGRAPHICAL NOTE

Modern observers have often asserted that the debate over human phylogeny during the first third of the twentieth century was polarized by two alternatives: a unilinear conception and a multilinear conception (e.g., Bowler, 1997; Hammond, 1988; Smith, 1997a; Spencer, 1984). This chapter presents an alternative view to this traditional historiography. This reinterpretation has the following implications. While the Neandertals held a pivotal role in the unilinear and multilinear hypotheses, these remains were not always judged crucial for the assessment of human phylogeny at the time. A number of scientists, then, used interpretative frameworks in which the Neandertals merely figured as contributors among many others. In their view, the Neandertals constituted only a small part of the problem of the human descent. These phylogenetic interpretations constituted genuine alternatives to both the unilinear and the multilinear hypotheses. Consequently, the historiography based on this dichotomy is too narrow to serve as a proper analytical framework for the debate on human phylogeny during the 1890–1935 period. In short, this traditional historiography is wrongly biased toward the place of the Neandertals in human descent.

In order to understand the need to go beyond the unilinear/multilinear dichotomy during this time period, it is perhaps not irrelevant to raise the question of how knowledge is acquired in the field of human evolution. It is true that the previous three chapters make our evaluation of the epistemological strategy used by paleoanthropologists fairly clear. However, this should be presented in an even more explicit way. Two different assessments of the epistemology used in paleoanthropology are of interest to us. In the first one, knowledge about human descent is judged to be largely contingent upon the occasional discovery of human fossils and the interpretation given to them by their discoverers (e.g., Reader, 1981). According to Reader (1981: 16), the "study of fossil man has been restricted to a slowly accumulating collection of diverse specimens." In the other assessment, to which we have already alluded, knowledge about the course of human evolution is judged to be largely contingent upon the patterns suggested by evolutionary theories (e.g., Bowler, 1986). According to Bowler (1986: 5), "it is obvious from the differing interpretations offered by scientists at the time that the fossils had meaning only to the extent that they could be fitted into theories of how human evolution occurred."

These two distinct assessments bring forth insights on the process of knowledge acquisition in the field of paleoanthropology since 1860. However, it will be shown in this chapter that isolated fossil discoveries as well as evolutionary patterns suggested by evolutionary theories had a limited and well circumscribed impact on the general development of the field during the 1860–1935 period. A more determinant factor was at work in this reconstruction process: the interpretative frameworks within which human fossils were inserted. The building of evolutionary hypotheses is not unlike putting together a jigsaw puzzle, meaning that the scholars can only place new pieces (fossil discoveries) by comparing them to the pieces which are already known to them. This well-known metaphor of the jigsaw puzzle among the evolutionists has been insufficiently explored as yet, when thinking about the historical development of paleoanthropology.

In paleoanthropology, the pieces of the jigsaw puzzle which are already known to the scholars are the living human races and the living nonhuman primate species judged relevant to assess human phylogeny. We have seen in the previous chapter that although comparative anatomy was not the only source of information used to establish humankind's place among the primates between 1890–1935, it still continued to loom large in that period. The same conclusion applies to the specific research on human phylogeny. Through this continued influence of comparative anatomy, the hominid fossil discoveries were placed in genealogical trees by relating them to either: (1) the living human races; (2) some of the living nonhuman primate species; or (3) a combination of both groups. This obvious procedure in evolutionary studies constituted a natural starting point for the establishment of human phylogeny in the early phase of the development of paleoanthropology.

This chapter will show that quite divergent phylogenetic hypotheses resulted when the researchers compared the hominid fossil discoveries to the living human races, to the nonhuman primate species, or to both groups. This procedure generated a number of human phylogenetic hypotheses which cannot be accommodated within the unilinear/multilinear framework. Before proceeding with the presentation of these phylogenetic hypotheses, it will be useful first to illustrate how human fossil discoveries are inserted in what is called here "interpretative frameworks." This is exemplified by the reception given to the discovery of *Pithecanthropus erectus*.

PITHECANTHROPUS: IN THE MIDST OF COMPETING INTERPRETATIVE FRAMEWORKS

The episode following the discovery of *Pithecanthropus* in Java in 1891–1892 provides a good case to illustrate the impact of the competing interpretative frameworks on the development of paleoanthropology during the 1890–1935 period.[1] Let us examine the context in which *Pithecanthropus* was first interpreted. For Dubois, the discoverer of *Pithecanthropus*, this form was more a primate fossil resembling the humans than a human fossil approaching the apes. For that reason, Dubois interpreted *Pithecanthropus* by comparing it to the nonhuman primates rather than the humans. Indeed, when Dubois discovered *Pithecanthropus*, he first attributed its remains to a fossil ape he called *Anthropopithecus* (Theunissen, 1989: 54–58). He was convinced that he had discovered a kind of fossil chimpanzee from Java, a form not unrelated to the creature from the Siwalik Hills of India described previously by Lyddeker, but more human-like than any known hominoid ape because it was characterized by a bipedal gait. Dubois considered his fossil to be an intermediate form which linked humankind more closely with his next of kin among the mammals. At this stage, it is not entirely clear if Dubois intended his fossil ape to be a genuine precursor of humankind. After all, it should not be forgotten that scholars like Boule evaluated Dubois's fossil as intermediate between humankind and the hominoid apes without holding, however, that it was ancestral to humankind (see below). Instead, Boule insisted that Dubois's fossil was an ape that evolved some humanoid features in parallel to the true human stem or stems. In other words, "intermediate" and "ancestral" should not be equated. The view that Dubois's fossil was that of an ape not ancestral to humans was not without able advocates at the time. Among them we also find Hill-Tout (1921), Joleaud (1929), Klaatsch (1899), Kollmann (1895), Krause (1895), Sergi (1914), and Virchow (1895).

As shown by Theunissen, and after realizing that the endocranial capacity of his fossil specimen was larger than previously evaluated, Dubois changed its name to *Pithecanthropus erectus*. From *Anthropopithecus*, the man-ape chimpanzee of Java, Dubois now evaluated his fossil specimen as *Pithecanthropus*, the ape-man from Java (Theunissen, 1989: 58–60). After 1894, Dubois (1894, 1896a, 1896b) made it clear what he thought the place of *Pithecanthropus* should be in the human family tree (see also Theunissen, 1989: 65–66, 94–95). Dubois conjectured that all the hominoids, including the humans, stemmed from a hypothetical Tertiary gibbon-like form he called *Prothylobates* (see Figure 9).[2] From this form, the human line went through a *Pithecanthropus* stage before giving rise to *Homo sapiens*. Maybe not unexpectedly, Dubois's phylogenetic view was supported by de Mortillet (1896) and Haeckel (1898). However, Dubois's view also gained the support of Mahoudeau (1912), Manouvrier (1895, 1896), Marsh (1896), and Schwalbe (1899), among others.

As may already be clear, Dubois arrived at his phylogenetic view regarding *Pithecanthropus* by comparing it almost exclusively to the other nonhuman primate forms, and not to the living human races. The nature of Dubois's approach is nicely captured by Theunissen (1989: 71) when he states that:

> Dubois thought of his missing link as an ape-like form which because of its development in the direction of Man could be regarded as a transitional form, rather than as a human-like form still at too low a stage of development to be called *Homo*.

I subscribe to Theunissen's (1989: 108–117) view that *Pithecanthropus* was important for the development of the field of human evolution. This discovery was indeed instrumental in promoting what Theunissen calls a "phylogenetic interpretation" of the hominid fossil record, that is, the incorporation of some human fossil remains into a framework of analysis that also exploited knowledge from comparative anatomy and embryology of primates in order to assess human phylogeny. We have already seen that scholars like Gaudry (1878) and Lydekker (1879) were already committed to this approach prior to the discovery of *Pithecanthropus* in 1891–1892. However, I do not agree with Theunissen when he states that the discovery of *Pithecanthropus* gave rise to what he calls an "evolutionary paleoanthropology." The notion of a pre-evolutionary palaeoanthropology supposedly displaced by a truly evolutionary one at the turn of the twentieth century is untenable, as already demonstrated in the two previous chapters.

If a number of scholars evaluated *Pithecanthropus* to be a nonhuman primate more or less closely related to the humans, others judged it to be a representative of humankind. In contradistinction to Dubois's approach, the latter scientists compared *Pithecanthropus* to modern humans. For instance, Turner (1895) made it clear that this approach revealed that the skullcap of *Pithecanthropus* presented many similarities with both the living human races now dwelling under "savage" conditions (Australians) and the prehistoric races of Europe (e.g., Neandertals). *Pithecanthropus*, declared Turner, is no missing link because it is a human. Among the scholars who promoted a human status for *Pithecanthropus* were Houzé (1895–1896), Lydekker (1895), Martin (1895), Pettit (1895), and Topinard (1895). This view was also expounded by Pycraft and Dixon in the first third of the twentieth century (see below).

It is true that the incompleteness of the *Pithecanthropus* remains—composed of a skull cap, a femur, and a tooth—permitted a variety of opinions about its status and phylogenetic position. This factor should not be underestimated in this episode of the history of paleoanthropology. However, it is argued here that the *Pithecanthropus* episode reveals, above all, that this fossil discovery was caught in the midst of divergent and competing interpretative frameworks in order to establish its place in human phylogeny. Although only two such frameworks were briefly presented here, the 1890–1935 period also saw the promotion of a third one. These three interpretative frameworks constituted profoundly divergent ways of looking at the human fossil record.

PARALLEL SCHEMES

A number of scholars believed that all the hominid fossil discoveries should be compared to the living human races. Proponents of this approach, for whom the nature of the evolutionary link between the humans and the nonhuman primates was of little consequence for their views of human phylogeny, held that all or most human fossils could comfortably be accommodated in a scheme within which they were phylogenetically related to one or several of the living human races. In the tradition of the scholars who contributed to the local debates and established local phylogenies prior to 1890, they did not necessarily hold that the human fossils fitted well within the modern human range of variation. True, some of them held such a view. More importantly, however, they held that the morphological features of the hominid fossils made them suitable ancestors of one or several of the living human races. From phylogenies essentially restricted to Europe prior to 1890, the post–1890 period saw a number of phylogenies with worldwide implications. This conception of human phylogeny has been largely neglected in the traditional historiography, which is essentially committed to the unilinear/multilinear dichotomy in the first third of the twentieth century. In order to re-establish the diversity of the viewpoints entertained about human phylogeny at the time, one must restore this conception which comes in two main versions.

Two distinct contributors. The first version consists of the recognition that at least two distinct morphological types, one ape-like and one human-like, simultaneously contributed to give rise to different portions of humanity. This is seen in the views of Verneau and Pycraft. It is sometimes held that Verneau was a proponent of the unilinear hypothesis. This view is incorrect. For Verneau, the Neandertal type was not *a stage* in human evolution but merely a form among others leading to living humans. As early as 1906, Verneau (1906a: 316) stated his position:

> . . . it seems that the Spy race [Neandertals] and the one from Grimaldi are two collateral branches from a common trunk which is still difficult to recognize with some precision, but which must have resembled to a certain extent *Pithecanthropus*. The evolution of these two branches occurred in opposite directions. . . .[3] [My translation]

According to Verneau, Spy or Neandertal man retained in its cranium most of his ancestral features, but lost his exaggerated prognathism. On the other hand, the Grimaldi type went through considerable development in the size of the braincase, but his face has not evolved in accordance with the other features, as seen especially by its prognathism. For Verneau (1886, 1902, 1906b), prehistoric Europe has been successively inhabited by the Spy race (Neandertals), the Grimaldi race and much later, the Cro-Magnon race. As we come closer to the present time these races were further removed from the ancestor that might have looked like *Pithecanthropus*; the Grimaldi race being an intermediate (though not a phylogenetic link) between the Neandertal and Cro-Magnon races. All these races, contended Verneau, still possessed some living representatives that retained, sometimes in attenuated form, features of the original type. Verneau's (1924) conception of human phylogeny rested on the conviction that humankind was constituted, at a very early period, by one or several ape-like "negroid" types which evolved and spread. The prehistoric races of Neandertal and Grimaldi were considered as two distinct branches of this evolving "negroid" type, a type still represented today in attenuated form in Australia and Neo-Caledonia, and which could be followed in time through the Talgaï (Australia) and Wadjak (Java) remains, and which is found only scattered in Europe. In Verneau's view, the origins of races of dark complexion preceded everywhere those races of lighter complexion.

For Pycraft (1925), most living "species" of humankind were directly descended from a common and differentiated trunk of the Upper Palaeolithic period. The fossil remains of Boskop, Cro-Magnon, and Grimaldi were part of this trunk. However, these living human species were said to have interbred to a certain extent with the Mousterian or Neandertal element. Pycraft further argued that the living Australians and Dravidians showed a conspicuous strain of Neandertal blood; a phylogenetic line which also gave rise to the Rhodesian Man (Kabwe or Broken Hill of Zambia). Not unlike Verneau, Pycraft (1925: 193–194) explained the origins of living humans in the following way:

> . . . we may fairly postulate the divergence of the human race, at a very early stage of its development, into two branches, one with relatively feeble, and the other with strongly developed brow-ridges: *Eoanthropus* stands for the one, *Pithecanthropus* and Neander-man for the other. . . .

Pycraft envisioned that the "beetle-browed" form had been for some time the dominant race, as seen by the fact that all the skulls of the Lower and Middle Palaeanthropic Periods were of the Neander type. In Europe, however, this form had been preceded by the "smooth-browed" race as represented by *Eoanthropus*. It was suggested by Pycraft that these two types had lived in close proximity throughout a prolonged period, permitting interbreeding between them. Pycraft's view of human phylogeny was clearly presented in a phylogenetic tree (see Figure 10).[4]

Racial admixtures. The other version used to promote a parallel conception of human phylogeny envisioned human evolution as a complex process of interactions between several racial types which all contributed, by various degrees, to segments of humanity. Dixon and Taylor favored this alternative. According to Dixon (1923), the problem was to determine how many human races were to be recognized, their origin, distribution, and interaction. On the basis of exclusively three skull indices (cephalic, altitudinal, and nasal), Dixon tentatively defined eight fundamental types or races from which all the living ones were derived by blending. These fundamental races were: Caspian, Mediterranean, Proto-Negroid, Proto-Australoid, Alpine, Ural, Palae-Alpine, and Mongoloid. When considering the hominid fossil remains, Dixon comfortably inserted all of them in his racial system. In Europe, for instance, the Neandertal race (Le Moustier, La Chapelle-aux-Saints, La Quina) was judged to belong to the Proto-Australoid type; the early brachycephalic element to the

Mongoloid type (La Chapelle-aux-Saints); the Grimaldi race to the Proto-Negroid type; dolichocephalic skulls of the Palaeolithic period in France to the Caspian type (Chancelade and Combe Capelle); and late Palaeolithic remains to the forerunners of the Mediterranean type (Cro-Magnon, Laugerie-Basse, Combe Capelle). Dixon (1923: 27–33, 46–48) contended that the great Neolithic migrations into Europe of the Mediterranean and Palae-Alpine types shattered and destroyed the people of the older Proto-Australoid and Mongoloid types, although some traces of them still survived while some admixture also took place. Dixon (1923: 180) held that the Palaeolithic populations of Africa had been represented by four main racial elements (Proto-Australoid, Proto-Negroid, Mongoloid, and Palae-Alpine types), as seen by the fossil remains of Gibraltar, Boskop, Broken Hill, and some Egyptian palaeoliths. As for southeast Asia, Dixon (1923: 475–476) recognized it as the probable homeland of the Proto-Australoid type, and alluded to *Pithecanthropus erectus* as a very early representative of this type before it migrated to Australia as reflected by the Talgai skull.

Describing himself as a polygenist, although he recognized ultimately a single ancestral prototype for humankind, Dixon (1923: 504–505) thought of his fundamental human racial types as arising in definite areas at different times:

> . . . from the phylum which branched off from that of the anthropoid apes, a number of distinct types arose, just as among the anthropoids; and that just as the latter varieties and species spread from their several areas . . . , so did these originally distinct forms. The degree of divergence in the human phylum was less great than in that of the apes, the separate varieties were fertile *inter se* and have blended and crossed in every imaginable fashion to produce the existing races of man.

For his part, Taylor (1919, 1921, 1927, 1930, 1934, 1936, 1937) promoted a conception of racial evolution in which the very early history of human races was evaluated in the light of their migration and differentiation under the changing environmental conditions of the Pleistocene. In Taylor's view, the living human races (Negritos, "Negroes", Australoids, Mediterraneans, and Alpines) were distributed in a series of racial zones centering around south central Asia. This pattern was explained by the following process: Ever since the Pliocene or early Pleistocene, after humankind had split from the anthropoids, central Asia has been, throughout this period, the cradle from which the main racial movements have sprung, successively and repeatedly, to people the world. Taylor held that central Asia constituted a stimulating milieu producing, continually, more advanced human types that pushed more primitive ones to the periphery. This explained why, generally speaking, the more primitive human types were found at the periphery of the Asian cradle. This also explained why the distribution of the human forms through time could be seen as a succession of ancient primitive types being gradually replaced by more recent advanced ones. This explained both the early date and the distant location of *Pithecanthropus* (Java) and of Piltdown man (England) relative to that cradle.

Taylor accommodated within this racial model all or most of the hominid fossil remains known at the time by relating them to one of the main living human races.

At first, Taylor (1919) was inclined to favor a single Asian trunk (with *Pithecanthropus* possibly at its base), from which all subsequent living and fossil human forms stemmed and migrated (see Figure 11). Later, following the discovery of so-called neandertaloid fossils throughout the Old World (Galilee, Broken Hill, Wadjak, Talgaï), Taylor affiliated the Neandertal type to most, but not all, the living races. He wrote (1937: 272) that it was logical "to assume two precursors of modern man living in middle Palaeolithic times . . . These two were Neanderthal man and Proto-Negrito (Grimaldi?) type." Taylor established the Neandertals at the base of four living races ("Negroes", Australoids, Mediterraneans, and Alpines), while the Negrito race was independently derived from another type, possibly the Grimaldi one. On this view, the Neandertal type gave rise to the Negroid and Australoid types, from which in turn the Mediterranean and Alpine types later sprung. In Taylor's (1937: 131–134, 158–166, 255–258) scheme, Europe constituted a marginal land that received successive and interrupted migrations of all the racial types, the European fossil record being filled with representatives of these various races which still have some living members. The possibility of a triple origin for the living human races was not completely discarded by Taylor (1937: 261–262):

> I think that the simplest explanation is that the ancestors of the Negrito and Neanderthal types developed independently from the primitive Catarrhine ape-stock, in Pliocene or even Miocene times. They lived side by side in Asia until the immense climatic changes of the Pleistocene greatly quickened evolution. Whether the negro [not to be confused with the Negrito] and later races [Australoids, Mediterraneans and Alpines] developed in Asia from a Neanderthaloid man, as seems probable to the writer, or whether there was a third 'Proto Cro-Magnon' type must be left to the future to decide.[5]

LINEAR AND MULTILINEAR SCHEMES

The interpretative framework which permitted the elaboration of the parallel schemes just reviewed is part of a tradition of interpretation that goes back to at least the 1860s. The next interpretative framework to which we now turn was largely established in the wake of the *Pithecanthropus* discovery in 1891–1892. It is to this conception of human phylogeny that the traditional historiography has turned to analyse the field of paleoanthropology in the first third of the twentieth century. The basis of this second interpretative framework is apparently founded on the following elements. For an increasing number of scholars after 1890, hominid fossils were compared to living and fossil nonhuman primates, as they seek to establish the phylogenetic link binding humans and the other primates. The nature of this very connection was often judged important for the establishment of human phylogeny, as it served the purpose of identifying a morphological series evolving from a simian to a human state. There could thus be only one true evolutionary line bridging living humans to a nonhuman primate ancestor. Scholars expressed this conception in linear evolutionary hypotheses. However, this interpretative framework is not only characterized by linear schemes. If some hominid fossils were judged not to be representatives of a stage leading to the living humans, these were relegated to side and extinct branches. The dating of fossil specimens was often considered crucial to the determining of phylogenetic relationships. This view of human evolution was expressed in multilinear phylogenetic hypotheses.

The linear and multilinear schemes are regrouped here in the same interpretative framework because both conceptions are grounded in the same logic. After all, a linear interpretation can be transformed into a multilinear one by simply disposing some hominid fossils not in a directly ancestral position to the living humans, but rather as indirect contributors or offshoots. The fact that the same logic underlies these two phylogenetic conceptions can perhaps best be seen in the work of a scholar like Schwalbe who easily conceived human phylogeny as either a linear or a multilinear hypothesis. Indeed, there was, in his mind, no chasm separating these two hypotheses. Possibly another indication that these two phylogenetic versions are logically connected is seen in a scholar like Keith who first promoted a linear scheme and later revised his view in favor of a multilinear one. Yet another indication of this connection is seen in the fact that proposed linear schemes at the time were rarely perfectly unilinear, as seen in the views of Keith (before 1912), Mahoudeau, and Hrdlicka. Proponents of this latter view sometimes recognized that particular fossil specimens may not be exactly directly ancestral to the living humans although such fossils provided clear evidence in favor of an assumed ancestral stage. It is argued here that the traditional historiography has overestimated the logical gap separating the linear and the multilinear hypotheses at the time.

Linear hypotheses. For a number of scholars, the discovery of *Pithecanthropus* in 1891–1892 constituted the first hominid fossil specimen that could be interpreted as a genuine intermediary link binding all the living humans to an ape ancestor, as Dubois did. Remember that after 1894, Dubois (1894, 1896a, 1896b) made it clear that he believed that all the hominoid apes, including humans, stemmed from a hypothetical Tertiary gibbon-like form he called *Prothylobates*. From this form, the human line alone went through a *Palaeopithecus* stage as seen in the Sawilik Hills of India in the late Miocene and a *Pithecanthropus* stage in the late Pliocene before giving rise to *Homo sapiens* (see Figure 9).[6] In Dubois's view, the ascent of humankind constituted a gradual emancipation from a gibbon-like condition. Dubois considered *Pithecanthropus* to be, most likely, directly ancestral to the humans and, if not, very nearly related to such an ancestral form.

If Dubois's linear conception primarily centered on a single hominid fossil specimen, other scholars like Keith, Schwalbe, Mahoudeau, and Hrdlicka thought that this conception could be reinforced by taking into account the numerous fossil specimens now attributed to the Neandertal group, as seen especially in the discoveries at Spy (Belgium) in 1886, Krapina (Croatia) between 1899 and 1905, and those at several French sites during the 1908–1909 period, including La Chapelle-aux-Saints, Le Moustier, La Quina, and La Ferrassie. The *Pithecanthropus* and Neandertal remains, they contended, could well represent two different stages of a single evolving lineage, the former being older and more primitive than the latter. This conception of human phylogeny was sometimes designated as the "Neandertal Phase Hypothesis."

For instance, Keith (1895) held that only four fossil hominid specimens were complete enough to permit an anatomical reconstruction: *Pithecanthropus*, Neandertal, and the two Spy specimens. From there, Keith became convinced that humankind has not changed much since the end of the Tertiary period, although brain size increased while the masticatory system was reduced, features that linked humankind to other primate ancestors.[7] Bringing some precision as to the phylogenetic implication of this view later on, Keith (1911a) argued that *Pithecanthropus* (which he called *Homo javanensis*) and Neandertal types represented stages in the evolution of modern humans from the apes. Keith (1911: 78–79, 136–137) contended that the Neandertal type was both an extinct precursor and a direct ancestor to the modern humans, while he judged *Pithecanthropus* to be either a true ancestral link or a late surviving form of a more ancient stage in human evolution.

For Schwalbe (1899, 1906, 1909), humankind's closest living relative had to be sought among the hominoid apes as evidenced by comparative anatomy, embryology, and physiology (blood relationship).[8] While Darwin had been without any serious candidate to link humans and the apes, contended Schwalbe (1909: 135), we are now in possession of transitional forms presenting ape-like characters in *Pithecanthropus* and *Homo primigenius* (Neandertals): "I consider [*Pithecanthropus*] as the root of a branch which has sprung from the anthropoid ape root and has led up to man." In this scheme, continued Schwalbe (1909: 129):

> *Homo primigenius* must also be regarded as occupying a position in the gap existing between the highest apes and the lowest human races, *Pithecanthropus*, standing in the lower part of it, and *Homo primigenius* in the higher, near man.

In Schwalbe's mind, this morphological series (hominoid apes, *Pithecanthropus*, *Homo primigenius*, and *Homo sapiens*) did not necessarily constitute a phylogenetic series. He proposed two possible phylogenetic hypotheses: (1) a unilinear scheme directly linking *Pithecanthropus*, through *Homo primigenius*, to *Homo sapiens*; and (2) a multilinear scheme putting *Pithecanthropus* and *Homo primigenius* on side branches not directly leading to humans, but revealing nonetheless important clues as to the evolutionary stages through which humankind had passed.[9] Schwalbe's phylogenetic viewpoint rested on two key elements: the morphological value of fossil specimens and their stratigraphic position. For instance, Schwalbe held that *Homo primigenius* represented either a true phylogenetic link or the remnant of an intermediate stage between the humans and the apes. This view was based both on the recognition of a morphological hiatus separating *Homo primigenius* from *Homo sapiens* and a chronological gap separating the former (early Diluvium) from the latter (late Diluvium). It must be noted that Schwalbe first restricted the definition of the Neandertals or *Homo primigenius* to the fossil specimens of Neandertal, Spy, Krapina, and possibly Gibraltar. Later, he added other specimens to this list.

Not unlike Schwalbe, Mahoudeau also analyzed human phylogeny by combining the results of comparative anatomy of living primates, primate paleontology, and chronological markers. Mahoudeau (1904, 1912, 1914) derived the hominid lineage from an ancient hominoid ape that closely resembled the gibbon. Mahoudeau contended that *Pliopithecus*, the Miocene ape of Europe, and *Propliopithecus*, the Oligocene ape of Egypt, were two indications of a common stem linking the humans and the hominoid apes. Stating this view, *Pithecanthropus* was intermediate between humans and apes, thus providing a clear indication as to the morphological stages of the prehominid form. However, Mahoudeau insisted that *Pithecanthropus* was not a true phylogenetic link because it was probably too late in time and too generalized a form to constitute such a direct connection leading to the European races of the Quaternary period. When considering the prehistoric races of Europe, Mahoudeau recognized in them numerous ape-like features in somewhat attenuated form, especially as far as the Neandertal type was concerned. Recognizing a morphological hiatus between the early Quaternary Neandertal type and the late Quaternary Cro-Magnon type, Mahoudeau left open both possibilities that the former directly gave rise to the latter or that the latter replaced the former.

If Schwalbe and Mahoudeau were somewhat hesitant, at one time or another, to claim with certainty that the Neandertals were directly ancestral to *Homo sapiens*, Hrdlicka unambiguously championed this view in the 1910s and later, under the concept of the "Neanderthal Phase of Man" (e.g., Spencer and Smith, 1981). According to Hrdlicka (1914, 1921, 1926, 1927, 1930), *Homo sapiens* could not have stemmed from a hominoid stock (which he assumed) without having passed through a phase similar to that of the Neandertal type. Like several of his contemporaries, Hrdlicka insisted on the numerous simian features of the Neandertals. He also based his argument in favor of the Neandertal phase of man, among other things, on the chronological position of this fossil group. Hrdlicka argued that the traces of a modern human type never preceded or coexisted with the Mousterian Man (Neandertals), but always followed it. On this view, the diversification of the living human races was judged to be a fairly recent event. Hrdlicka postulated that the Neandertals were not a homogeneous group, but a variable one whose most advanced segments evolved into primitive *Homo sapiens* (Krapina, La Ferrassie, La Quina), while its less progressive ones (Neandertal, Spy, La Chapelle-aux-Saints, Le Moustier) might have become extinct. It should not be assumed, however, that Hrdlicka necessarily defended a perfectly unilinear interpretation of human phylogeny. When speaking of humankind's early precursors, Hrdlicka (1914: 494) stated that:

> [S]ome strains of them . . . lacked also in vitality or in sufficient adaptability to changing conditions and have disappeared; but others kept on modifying in the upward direction until in the course of long ages they reached the various somewhat unequally advanced types of man of the present day.[10]

Clearly, Hrdlicka evaluated *Pithecanthropus* to be intermediate between apes and humans, a form which he believed might or might not have been directly ancestral to humankind, although he favored the latter alternative. The rationale for this argument apparently rested on the following basis. Hrdlicka considered southwestern Europe to be the cradle of humankind's latest stages of evolution, as evidenced by the fossil remains of Europe and their almost complete absence in Asia. It is on that basis that he favored a western and African origin for the earliest stages of human evolution, thus probably implying that *Pithecanthropus* became extinct (Hrdlicka, 1921: 541).

Multilinear hypotheses. We have indirectly reviewed in Chapter 3 a number of scholars who promoted a multilinear hypothesis of human evolution in the first third of the twentieth century. Adloff, Ameghino, Elliot Smith, Gregory, Hill-Tout, Pilgrim, Osborn, and Wood Jones all promoted one form or another of this hypothesis. To avoid repetition here, these scholars will not be discussed again.

To an increasing number of scholars after the turn of the twentieth century, all the hominid fossil discoveries could not easily be accomodated in a single evolving line. Instead, they believed that several of them should be relegated to extinct side branches. One after the other, fossil specimens such as *Pithecanthropus*, Neanderthals, Heidelberg man, Rhodesian man, and *Sinanthropus* were all put on side branches. Two interrelated reasons apparently contributed to favor this hypothesis, especially after 1910: (1) These hominids were judged to be either too specialized, too ape-like, or too committed in an evolutionary direction to directly lead to living humans (assuming that they were all related to the human family tree, which was denied by Boule); (2) More human-like fossils thought to be either contemporaneous or older than the other hominids were believed to be the genuine ancestors of the living humans. This latter idea was reinforced by the use of embryology by a number of scholars in order to reconstruct the conformation of humankind's ancestors (see Chapter 4). The notion which derived the living humans from ancient and modern-looking representatives at the expense of the more ape-like candidates came later to be designated the "Presapiens theory." Scholars like Boule, Keith, Hooton, and Leakey adopted this perspective. The discovery of Piltdown man played a role in the promotion of this perspective. This very question is postponed to a later section in this chapter. This being said, it should not be assumed that the multilinear hypotheses needed, necessarily, to be based on ancient and modern-like ancestors, as clearly demonstrated in the viewpoints of Adloff, Gregory, and Osborn (before 1925) in the previous chapter.

For Boule, the human evolutionary history was conceived by applying the principles of paleontology (e.g., Laurent, 1995b). Boule took them to say that the human line was closely related to the hominoid apes, although it was not derived from this stem, meaning that the living humans and the apes have long been separated. Boule (1908, 1911–1913, 1914, 1915, 1921) held that *Pithecanthropus* and *Homo neanderthalensis* were intermediate morphological forms between humankind and the apes as testified by their numerous ape-like features, but insisted that the distinct evolutionary trees leading to the living humans and the apes were highly branched ones characterized by numerous extinct branches not leading directly to their living forms, among which *Pithecanthropus* and *Homo neanderthalensis* figured (see also Boule and Anthony, 1911).

In fact, Boule affiliated *Pithecanthropus* to the hominoid ape stem exclusively, but recognized that it evolved, in parallel, a number of human-like traits. When considering the human stem, Boule hypothesized at least two distinct and long-separated lineages. The first lineage led to *Homo neanderthalensis*, possibly through *Homo heidelbergensis* (the Mauer jaw). This lineage was described as morphologically homogeneous and clearly distinguished from the living humans by numerous primitive and ape-like features. The fact that *Homo neanderthalensis* has not genealogically contributed to the rise of the living humans was further indicated, contended Boule, by its contemporaneity with more advanced forms such as the Grimaldi type. The second lineage Boule recognized in the human family tree was considered truly ancestral to *Homo sapiens*. It might have been represented at an early time by the Piltdown cranium exclusively, for Boule believed the jaw to belong to a fossil chimpanzee. This lineage could be followed toward the end of the Pleistocene in Europe through the Cro-Magnon, Grimaldi, and Chancelade races, by which time the major racial divisions of the living humans already existed.

We have seen that Keith was at first inclined toward a linear hypothesis of human phylogeny. However, he eventually changed his mind and proposed a multilinear one. Keith (1912, 1915) now concurred with the view that the Neandertal type was totally distinct from all the living human races by virtue of its numerous simian traits, and so placed it on an extinct side branch of human evolution. Simultaneously, he held that the existence of fossil remains of modern appearance such as Galley Hill, Bury St. Edmunds, Moulin Quignon, Grenelle, Clichy, Denise, Olmo, Castenedolo, Grimaldi, and Combe Capelle—which Keith assumed were contemporaneous with or older than the Neandertal remains—meant that the modern human types had started their differentiation as early as the late Pliocene or early Pleistocene period (see also Moir and Keith, 1912). Instrumental in Keith's shift of view from a linear to a multilinear phylogeny was the discovery at Piltdown of presumably very ancient remains of a creature called *Eoanthropus* with modern features (e.g., Spencer, 1990). In 1915, Keith (1915: 505, 506) distinguished at least three major branches on the human stem:

> The common Pliocene ancestor which gave origin to three such types could not be of a very low form. At least in Eoanthropus [Piltdown], as in Neanderthal man, the brain was equal in size to that of modern man. If we suppose that in an early part of the Pliocene period there was a form of man in which the brain had attained a human size, but in which the mandible, the teeth, and the skull still remained anthropoid in conformation, we have such a type as would serve as a common ancestor . . . It will thus be seen that I look on Eoanthropus, as on Neanderthal man, as a representative of an extinct form of man . . . Further, we realise that the three or four human types so far discovered represent but a few fossil twigs of the great evolutionary human tree. We may hope to find more branches.

According to Keith, *Pithecanthropus* figures as a late representative (late Pliocene or early Pleistocene) of an extinct stem that split as early as the Miocene period from the humanoid stem.[11] In 1925, Keith recognized that the fossil material he relied on to prove the great antiquity of the modern human types turned out to be unreliable. He also mentioned that the anticipated length of time of the geological periods had been overestimated. Consequently, Keith (1925a, vol. 1: xiii) held that "evolution has proceeded at a more rapid pace in the fashioning of man than some of us have hitherto thought." This being said, Keith's conception of human phylogeny remained unchanged. To his previous scheme, he added another extinct side branch represented by the Rhodesian specimen, while fossil remains such as Wadjak, Talgaï, Boskop, Galley Hill, Grimaldi, Combe Capelle, Cro-Magnon, and Obercassel were all affiliated to the living human races or *Homo sapiens*. A few years later, Keith (1931) added yet another important extinct side branch to his phylogenetic scheme, the one represented by *Sinanthropus* or Peking Man (see Figure 12).[12]

In the early 1930s, Hooton (1931) envisioned human phylogeny as being characterized by a number of distinct side branches leading toward extinction (*Pithecanthropus, Eoanthropus, Sinanthropus*, Neandertals). He also held that the human stem leading to the living human races appeared quite early, perhaps as early as the mid-Pliocene (see Figure 7).[13] To students of human evolution who held that modern humans evolved through a generalized Neandertaloid stage, Hooton replied that *Homo sapiens*, as seen through fossil remains such as Kanjera, Kanam, Galley Hill, Olmo, and Castendolo, is of great antiquity. This view implied, for Hooton (1935), that forms such as *Sinanthropus*, Heidelberg man, and all the Neanderthaloids be relegated to extinct blind alleys branching away from the main stem of human evolution.

For L.S.B. Leakey (1934), the conviction that the real ancestors of the living humans would eventually be found in deposits as old as the early Pleistocene period rested on the notion that the present differentiation of humankind into races could only have occurred through a slow and gradual evolutionary process for which plenty of time was required.[14] Related to this thinking, Leakey held that hominid forms of the Pleistocene characterized by massive browridges such as *Pithecanthropus, Sinanthropus*, and all the Neandertaloid ones (Europe, Palestine, and Rhodesia) represented distinct lineages part of a hominid stem, that he called *Palaeoanthropidae*, which evolved towards extinction. On the *Neoanthropidae* stem which evolved into the main races of *Homo sapiens*, Leakey recognized as early contributors in East Africa *Homo kanamensis* (Kanam jaw). An even earlier side branch of this stock leading to the living humans may be represented by *Eoanthropus*. In Leakey's view, the *Palaeoanthropidae* and *Neoanthropidae* stems shared a common ancestry in the early Miocene, while the entire hominids had a common ancestor with the hominoid stem as early as the mid-Oligocene period.[15]

Let us conclude this section on linear and multilinear schemes by insisting on the role played by hominid fossil discoveries in this interpretative framework. In general, it seems that as more hominid fossils were being gradually recovered during the 1890–1935 period, the more difficult it was to promote a linear hypothesis *within* that interpretative framework. This may explain why so few scholars were able to promote such a linear scheme after 1910. It is therefore argued here that the hominid fossil record had an important impact on the interpretations of human phylogeny within this framework. As seen in this chapter, however, the same fossil discoveries had either no, or a totally different impact on the other two interpretative frameworks.

POLYPHYLETIC SCHEMES

Scholars like Vogt, Schaaffhausen, Hovelacque, and Hervé promoted a polyphyletic conception of human phylogeny during the 1860–1890 period. This tradition of interpretation continued during the 1890–1935 period with more vigor than ever and with more diversity of viewpoints than in the past. The polyphyletic thesis has never been more popular than during that time period and this is seen by the large number of its adherents. It is true that this conception always remained a minority stance. Yet, the fact that it could not be ignored by the majority of scholars in the field of human evolution is perhaps best seen in the criticisms directly addressed at polyphyletism (e.g., Keith, 1910, 1911b; Stolyhwo, 1912; Giuffrida-Ruggeri, 1918; Mendes-Corrêa, 1923; Vallois, 1927, 1929). The traditional historiography largely overlooked the proponents of polyphyletism at the time. Again, it is only by rehabilitating them in the main narrative that one can understand properly the development of the field of paleoanthropology.

Remember that proponents of polyphyletism held that the humans and the other primates shared not a more or less distant common ancestor, but rather literally had an intertwined evolutionary history. For these scholars, human phylogeny is established by comparing human fossils to both the living human races and the living and fossil primates. This approach gave rise to complex evolutionary schemes in which some human races had a closer genealogical link with some nonhuman primate species than with other living or fossil human races. While some polyphyletists advocated that the human races shared an intertwined genealogy with the hominoid apes only, others extended this relationship to include the other primates. The proponents of polyphyletism established their phylogenetic connections by often appealing to one or several of the following four factors:

1. the differences observed among the living human races themselves;
2. the minute anatomical or behavioral similarities noted between specific human races and one primate species in particular;
3. the divergence which occurred between two distinct affiliated forms (a human and an ape) under distinct adaptive conditions; and
4. the geographical distribution of the human races and the other primate species.

The geographical dimension of the polyphyletic thesis finds its rationale in the recognition, at the time, of distinct zoological provinces on earth (e.g., Bowler, 1996: 379–389). Although not agreed on the precise frontiers of such zoological provinces, many scholars recognized that the geographical distribution of animal types could be circumscribed in geographical zones which contained some animal types and not others. It should be noted that the recognition of these zoological provinces is entirely independent of the polyphyletic thesis, as it was established by scholars interested in biogeography. For the proponents of the polyphyletic thesis in human evolution, however, the recognition that specific human races and nonhuman primate species were geographically restricted to local zones could be used as an argument in favor of genealogical connections between the members of each zoological province, human and nonhuman primate alike. This argument was previously used by polyphyletists prior to 1890 (see Chapter 2), and was used again after that period, implicitly or explicitly, in the works of Sergi, Kurz, and Horst.

Intertwined with the hominoid apes. Many proponents of the polyphyletic conception during that period favored a close link between the human races and the hominoid apes, although they disagreed on how many distinct evolutionary stems should be recognized. Scholars like Klaatsch, von Buttel-Reepen, and Frassetto recognized only two such evolutionary stems.

We have already seen that at the turn of the twentieth century, Klaatsch was committed to a monophyletic view of human phylogeny (see Chapter 4). By 1909, however, Klaatsch (1910a, 1923) was fully supportive of the polyphyletic thesis (see Figure 13).[16] Having compared the Neandertal type with the Aurignacian type (*Homo aurignacensis hauseri*: Combe Capelle, Brünn I, Chancelade, Galley Hill, Krapina, and Engis), Klaatsch became convinced that these two fossil human types had originated from two distinct stocks; stocks which were believed to have given rise to both hominoid ape and human forms. Klaatsch now postulated the origin of all these forms during the early Tertiary era from a common south Asian stock of man-like apes (not ape-like men) he called *Propithecanthropus*, although he remained elusive about the precise birthplace of this common ancestor. Klaatsch described this hypothetical ancestor as being human-like both in its dentition and body proportions. On the other hand, it was insisted that its foot was still more a grasping appendage than a fully supporting apparatus, while its general aspect may have looked like a generalized hominoid-like form unlike the living hominoid apes. In Klaatsch's view, the projecting canines, the shape of the skull, and the relatively long arms and short legs are all specializations that independently developed to various degrees in all hominoid ape branches, taking them away from both the conformation of the common ancestor and the human type.

From this common primeval group, Klaatsch postulated repeated outpourings of populations over Asia and Africa, these being organized around two main stems, and each being composed of several distinct evolutionary branches. Representatives of these two stems subsequently reached Europe: (1) An eastern stem was said to have given rise to the orang, the Aurignacian type, and several human races such as the Mongoloids and some white races (including some races of black complexion); (2) a western stem gave rise to the gorilla, the Neandertal type and the "negroid" races of humankind.[17] Klaatsch argued that both stems fused or hybridized to some extent in at least some of their segments, thus possibly giving rise to some human European races. Furthermore, it was hypothesized that the living Australians might have stemmed directly and independently from the common primeval group. In Klaatsch's view, for instance, the Neandertals were not derived from the gorilla. Rather, both were derived from a common stock of man-like apes that split into a form that degenerated (gorilla), while another developed further along the humanoid direction (Neandertals). On this view, the hominoid apes are failed experiments to becoming human because of their life conditions.

Having clearly identified at least two main evolutionary stems in human phylogeny, Klaatsch hypothesized that we might eventually find that the chimpanzee and the gibbon belong to two distinct stems—the former being associated with the great Western stem and the latter with the great Eastern stem—from which distinct human races might also have sprung. Klaatsch alluded to the fact that the *Pithecanthropus* extinct offshoot may well represent the human-like type of a branch shared in common with the gibbon, the latter being, of course, the hominoid ape type of this stem. It should be noted that Klaatsch's view of human phylogeny was not unfavorably received by a number of scholars at the time (e.g., Wegner, 1910; Seal, 1911; von Bonin, 1911; Heilborn, 1923; Duckworth, 1912).

Klaatsch's phylogenetic hypothesis inspired some scholars to add new fossil discoveries to this scheme. For instance, von Buttel-Reepen (1913: 72–77) added the newly discovered Piltdown man to Klaatsch's stem which gave rise to the Orangutan and the Aurignacian type (see Figure 14).[18] Von Buttel-Reepen made clear that he believed that when the Neandertal and the Aurignacian types met in Europe—types that, it should be remembered, are derived from two distinct human/hominoid ape stems—they probably gave rise to the Grimaldi and the Cro-Magnon types through interbreeding.

Not unlike von Buttel-Reepen, Frassetto (1927) used the discovery of Piltdown man to promote what seems to be a polyphyletic conception based on two main lineages. Frassetto held that Piltdown man represented a primitive human race belonging to the same genus as the orang-utan type. Also belonging to this group is the living human Mongoloid type. On the other hand, Frassetto reunited the chimpanze, Neandertal man, and the Black human races in the same group.

For other proponents of the polyphyletic conception involving hominoid species only, at least three main evolutionary stems could be recognized. This is seen in the works of Sergi, Gray, Kurz, and Crookshank. After 1911, it will be remembered, Sergi envisioned human phylogeny as a series of parallel evolutionary lines not derived from a common ancestor (see Chapter 4). In 1908, however, Sergi (1908) believed that the human races and the hominoid apes shared an intertwined evolutionary history as they were descended from a hominoid-like common ancestor itself derived from the Old World monkeys stem (see Figure 15). From this common ancestor, insisted Sergi, three geographically distinct evolutionary stems developed, each being represented by one main living human race and several living or extinct hominoid ape species: The European stem diversified and comprised *Homo europaeus* (living European human races), *Dryopithecus*, and *Pliopithecus*; the African stem gave rise to *Homo afrus* (living African human races) the gorilla, and the chimpanzee; and the Asian stem, which was the most diversified, included *Homo asiaticus* (living Asian human races), the orang-utan, the gibbon, *Pithecanthropus*, and *Palaeopithecus*.[19]

Gray (1911) held that Klaatsch's phylogenetic tree should be modified (see Figure 16). Gray maintained the phylogenetic link between the Neandertal type and the gorilla, but considered that the Aurignacian type (called the Galley Hill type) was more closely related to the chimpanzee than to the orang-utan. Like Klaatsch, however, Gray seems to have affiliated the orang-utan with the Mongoloid human races, but by so doing he created a third evolutionary stem which was not clearly recognized by Klaatsch.[20] In order to explain the morphological similarities between the two distinct human races (Neandertal and Galley Hill)—races which are not genealogically related because they evolved out of two independent human/hominoid ape stems—Gray turned to a process of convergent evolution. This convergence process, it was argued, occurred through the similarity of the life conditions which these two distinct races faced when they both entered a terrestrial niche, thus leaving behind the life in the trees they had shared with their respective hominoid ape ancestors. Gray explained the differences between the Galley Hill and the Neandertal types by assuming that the former had differentiated at an earlier time from its chimpanzoid stock, while the latter separated from the gorilloid stock at a more recent time. This explained why the Galley Hill type is more modern in conformation than the Neandertal one.

Kurz's (1924) support in favor of the polyphyletic thesis largely comes from his studies of the similarities between the orang-utan and the Asian living human races. Kurz took these resemblances to indicate an affiliation between these two types. Extending his analysis to cover other regions in the Old World (largely on the basis of the works of other scholars), Kurz recognized two other main evolutionary stems. One united the chimpanzee, fossil forms such as *Gryphopithecus*, *Dryopithecus*, Piltdown, Mauer, Spy, Le Moustier, and Combe Capelle, and the living human races of Europe (white races) while another stem affiliated the gorilla, fossil forms such as *Sivapithecus* and Talgaï (Australia), and the living human races of dark complexion. In Kurz's hypothesis, the common ancestor of each of these three main evolutionary stems is more hominoid-like than human-like in conformation. For instance, the living human races of white complexion, which shared a common ancestor with the chimpanzee, were believed to have evolved out of chimpanzoid-like ancestor.

In contradistinction to the other polyphyletists, Crookshank's (1913, 1924, 1931) conception was largely inspired by a medical viewpoint rather than an anatomical one. Crookshank drew a parallel between the three main living human types (Black, White, and Yellow) and specific diseases associated with each of them (Black and the type of idiot called the "Ethiopic" variety; White and a mental illness called Dementia Precox; Yellow and the Mongolian imbecile). Taking these diseases to represent remnants of past evolutionary stages for each main human race, Crookshank established another parallel between such diseases and three great apes: gorilla, chimpanzee, and orang-utan. By so doing, Crookshank hypothesized phylogenetic links between, respectively, the Black and the gorilla, the White and the chimpanzee, and the Yellow and the orang. In Crookshank's view, these forms were ultimately all descended from a common ancestor (see Figure 17).[21]

Crookshank tried to reinforce his postulated phylogenetic links by noting numerous homologies in morphology and behavior. The presence of Mongolian imbeciles among the White human races was explained, for instance, by historic or prehistoric crossing with the Yellow or the Mongolian human races. Furthermore, the human fossil record was also exploited in this evolutionary conception: The Grimaldi remains were associated with the Black-gorilla branch; the Cro-Magnon and Piltdown remains with the White-chimpanzee branch, and the Chancelade and Mauer remains with the Yellow-orang branch. Like several polyphyletists of the time, Crookshank believed that each of the three main phylogenetic branches was characterized by a progressive form (human) and a degenerate one (ape).

As a proponent of the polyphyletic thesis which intertwined the hominoids exclusively, Melchers (1910) argued that this thesis is best supported by recognizing at least four distinct evolutionary stems. Melchers insisted that regardless of the fact that all the living human races could interbreed with one another, they always remained widely distinct entities with separate origins. Their separate origins are confirmed, continued Melchers, by the morphological similarities observed between some human races and one of the four hominoid ape species. The first evolutionary stem identified by Melchers affiliated the gorilla, fossil remains such as Spy, the Neandertal specimen, the La Naulette jaw, and living human races of mostly black complexion such as the Zulus and the Bantus (although human races of white complexion like the Finns were also included). The second evolutionary stem reunited the chimpanzee, fossil remains of Heidelberg, Gibraltar, Le Moustier, and Combe Capelle, and living human races of dark as well as light complexion (Bushmen, Berbers, Mediterraneans, Lapps). The third stem derived from a common ancestor the orang-utan, the fossil remains of the Aurignac man, and living human races of Australia, Tasmania, Indonesia, and the southeast region of Europe. Last, the fourth evolutionary stem affiliated the gibbon, the fossil of *Pithecanthropus*, and living human races from Asia. Melchers explained the differences between a human type and an ape type which are affiliated with the same evolutionary stem by the adaptation of the former to ground conditions and the latter to tree conditions. In Melchers's view, the hominoid apes retained most of the ancient and primitive conditions, meaning that it is the human types that went through a greater morphological transformation.

Intertwined with the primates. Proponents of the polyphyletic thesis were not all agreed that this evolutionary scheme should exclusively comprise the hominoids. Indeed, a number of them promoted that the evolutionary history of the living human races should also be intertwined more closely with the primates. On this view, monkeys of the Old World and New World, and more rarely prosimians, were also seen as possible contributors to human phylogeny. This situation is perhaps not as surprising as it seems when considering that the 1890–1935 period saw important debates on the nature of the link between humankind and all the other primates (see Chapter 4). Remember that scholars like Adloff, Boule, and Wood Jones promoted the view that the hominoid apes were not necessarily humankind's closest living relatives. Furthermore, it should not be forgotten that the seemingly parallel evolution of the Old World and New World primates prompted some scholars to anticipate or establish evolutionary links between New World monkeys and local human races. We have seen that this latter idea has been expressed under different shapes and forms in the works of Ameghino, Joleaud, Klaatsch (before 1908), Montandon, Sergi, and Vogt. Thereby, polyphyletists like Sergi, Horst, Arldt, and Sera, who also incorporated the non-hominoid primates in their conceptions, were merely exploiting commonly discussed ideas at the time. This being said, they did not all agree on the number of distinct evolutionary stems which should be recognized.

Remember that in 1908 Sergi supported a polyphyletic view which was restricted to the Old World and to the hominoid apes. Now, Sergi (1909–1910, 1910) extended this conception, geographically and phylogenetically speaking, to include the New World monkeys. Like the Old World monkeys stem, Sergi now held that the New World monkeys stem also gave rise to forms approaching the hominoid grade of evolution, as seen in the fossil remains of *Tetraprothomo argentinus* (late Miocene) and *Diprothomo platensis* (early Pliocene). This New World hominoid grade, continued Sergi, probably directly evolved out of the *Cebidae* group rather than the *Hapalidae* one, because the latter budded too early from this stem. It was argued that this main stem ultimately led to the humans as testified by the fossil remains of *Homo pampaeus* (mid-Pliocene). Sergi's broader perspective now recognized two major evolutionary stems independently evolving in the Old and New Worlds, each giving rise to numerous extinct and living nonhuman primate species and human races. Ultimately, these two evolutionary stems would have had a common parentage in the early mammals of the Secondary era, perhaps in a geographical place now located in South America. After 1911, Sergi extended the parallelism of each main human and nonhuman primate groups to the extent that they were no longer connected through a common ancestry.

For his part, Horst's (1913) viewpoint promoted that distinct portions of humanity had shared their evolutionary history with three hominoid ape stocks, although at least one such stock also shared a phylogenetic connection with some Old World monkeys.[22] The first stem identified by Horst apparently has its cradle in the southwest of Europe, from where it expanded in the entire west portion of the Old World. This stem linked together the chimpanzee, primate fossils such as *Dryopithecus*, a host of hominid remains in Europe (Neandertal, Heidelberg, Gibraltar, Aurignac, Grimaldi), and living human races, many of which are of black complexion. The second evolutionary stem was assumed to have arisen in India before spreading out in Asia and in Europe. This stem affiliated the gorilla, fossil remains like *Pithecanthropus*, Galley Hill, Cro-Magnon, and a host of living human races including some black races and some white races in Europe. In Horst's view, this second stem was also genealogically connected with Old World monkeys. The third evolutionary stem identified by Horst finds its birthplace in the eastern portion of the Old World. This stem regrouped the orang-utan, human fossil remains like La Truchère, Grenelle, and Furfooz, and living human races of Mongoloid affinities, among others.

In 1913, it is not entirely clear from which form or forms Horst intended to derive the three main evolutionary stems he identified. However, Horst's (1918–1919) view was made clearer a few years later when he prolonged the independent evolutionary roots of these main evolutionary stems deeply in time by incorporating genuinely primitive or prosimian-like primate forms at their very base. The first stem which gave rise to the chimpanzee and several living human races of black complexion was originally derived from *Microchoerus* (*Necrolemur*), but not before having passed through an Old World monkey phase (*Macacus*). Similarly, the second evolutionary stem which diversified to incorporate the baboons, the gorilla, and a host of distinct living human races finds its origins in *Palaeolemur* (*Adapis*). Lastly, the third evolutionary stem which bound the orang-utan and several living human races from Asia now incorporated the gibbon. This entire stem was derived from an early *Anaptomorphus* phase (*Tarsius*).

According to Arldt (1915, 1917), the intertwined evolutionary history of the human races and the anthropoid primates can be conceived as three main evolutionary stems, commonly derived from an *Anaptomorphidae* stock of the Eocene period of North America (see Figure 18). From this common ancestor, all three evolutionary stems independently passed through a *Homunculidae* stage in South America before evolving in three different directions. A first stem gave rise to the Black human races, the gorilla, and *Sivapithecus*. A second stem diversified into the White human races, the chimpanzee and the gibbon, and the fossil remains of *Pithecanthropus*, *Dryopithecus*, and *Pliopithecus*. Apparently, some New World monkeys (*Hapalidae*) are more closely related to this stem than the other two. A third stem contributed to the Yellow human races, the orang-utan, some New World monkeys (*Cebidae*), most of the Old World monkeys and possibly fossil forms such as *Anthropodus*.[23] In Arldt's view, while the human forms affiliated to the three stems evolved toward a modern type, the three great apes (chimpanzee, gorilla, orang) associated with each of them independently went through a bestialization process. Arldt believed that the split between the human and the ape types that were part of the same human/anthropoid stem had occurred by the Pliocene period, if not before.

The last polyphyletist reviewed here, Sera (1918), identified no less than six main evolutionary stems which gave rise to all the human races and the anthropoid apes (see Figure 19). Sera's phylogenetic hypothesis is by far the most shattered one by affiliating within the same evolutionary stem a host of anthropoid forms from throughout the world, specific human races, hominoid apes, and Old World and New World monkeys. Sera established these genealogical connections on the basis of minute anatomical details. Sera's six evolutionary stems are the following: A first stem gave rise to the human races of Polynesia, colobines, and marmosets (New World monkeys [NWm]), baboons and some macaques species (Old World monkeys [OWm]); a second stem diversified into the Mongolian human races, *Cebus* (NWm), and orang-utan; a third stem regrouped the Euro-asiatic human races, *Semnopithecus* and *Cercopithecus* (OWm); a fourth stem evolved into the European human races, *Midas* (NWm) and Cynomorphs (OWm); a fifth stem gave rise to the Black human races, the *Lagothrix* (NWm), most gibbon species, and the chimpanzee; and the last stem diversified to comprise the human races of South Africa (Bushmen), *Ateles* and *Brachyteles* (NWm), *Cercopithecus* and *Theropithecus* (OWm), and the gorilla and some gibbon species.[24]

PILTDOWN MAN: RETHINKING ITS IMPACT

The 1890–1935 period was not only characterized by an outstanding diversity of viewpoints on the question of humankind's place among the primates, but this level of disagreement also extended to debates on human phylogeny proper. This situation may come as a surprise in light of the traditional historiography which, it should be remembered, only recognizes a tension between unilinear and multilinear phylogenetic hypotheses in the first third of the twentieth century. In this historiography, it has sometimes been assumed that a number of key fossil discoveries weighed heavily on the interpretation of human phylogeny. This thesis has been most strongly promoted by Reader (1981), among other scholars. The discovery of Piltdown man, for instance, is thought to represent such a crucial discovery. In fact, the discovery of Piltdown man is often assumed to epitomize the very thesis that isolated fossil discoveries created a profound impact on the development of paleoanthropology. A closer look at this thesis is in order here.

Today's attitude toward the Piltdown discovery is apparently not entirely unrelated to the fate of that discovery. Hopefully, the following analysis will help to dispel the strange combination of fascination and guilt on the part of paleoanthropologists regarding the Piltdown question, as seen in the prolific literature published in the last few decades. Indeed, perhaps the time has come to exorcize what has been more an illusion than a reality. This brief analysis will reveal how every fossil discovery was, at one time or another, literally swallowed up by the three competing interpretative frameworks identified in this chapter, thus considerably reducing the importance of each isolated fossil discover *no matter what it looked like or what its datation was.*

Between 1908 and 1915 near Piltdown, England, fossil remains of supposedly very ancient hominids were recovered. We know today that these remains were part of a scientific fraud or hoax that combined cranial remains of a modern human type and a jaw bone which belonged to a living pongid of the genus *Pongo* (orang). However, until 1953 when the hoax was exposed, the Piltdown remains were thought to be genuine fossils (Weiner et al., 1953). Piltdown man, also named *Eoanthropus dawsoni*, is incontestably an integral part of the history of paleoanthropology during the first half of the twentieth century, in the sense that scholars had to consider it in their quest to establish humankind's place in nature. This is not the place to recount in any detail the Piltdown episode (e.g., Weiner, 1955; Spencer, 1990).[25] It will suffice to mention that most scholars evaluated the Piltdown remains in one of the two following ways: (1) as fossil remains which all belonged to the same fossil type, meaning that Piltdown represented a very ancient hominid form which was characterized by a combination of a modern-looking braincase and an ape-like jaw; or (2) as fossil remains which belonged to two distinct fossil types, the jaw bone being an ancient fossil hominoid ape and the cranial pieces an ancient fossil hominid. In either view, Piltdown was an indication that a very ancient hominid type was characterized by a large and relatively modern-looking braincase. This certainly constrasted with the other ancient hominid types of the time, such as *Australopithecus* (Taung),

Pithecanthropus, and the Neandertals, types which were often depicted as possessing numerous ape-like traits in their cranial anatomy.

Piltdown was discovered at a moment when a number of scholars began to promote multilinear hypotheses of human phylogeny, in which most human fossils were put on extinct side branches. Some proponents of this view supposed that the living humans had descended from ancient fossil types which were less ape-like and more human-like in conformation than *Australopithecus*, the Neandertals, or *Pithecanthropus*. This view of human phylogeny, eventually dubbed the "Presapiens theory," is sometimes considered today to constitute a paradigm. It is easy to understand why Piltdown either fitted nicely with this view or contributed to its rise. It is on that basis that a number of modern observers have claimed that Piltdown played a major role in orienting the views on human phylogeny during the first half of the twentieth century. For instance, Hammond (1988: 117–118) states that:

> . . . the period between 1911 and the end of World War II was striking in that mankind was left virtually ancestorless. One by one, all major fossil populations were assigned to dead-end branches in our evolutionary tree . . . So powerful was this model that for four decades it is possible to predict the scientific response to new finds by leading theorists and by the majority of the physical anthropological community. If a fossil indicated that the morphological modernization of the lower face and the body had preceded the modernization of the braincase, then the discovery was attributed to a dead-end branch. On the other hand, if a fossil showed the opposite pattern . . . then even if it was fragmentary in the extreme, it was likely to be regarded as a potential human ancestor . . . The two pillars of the shadow man paradigm were Marcellin Boule's rejection of ancestral status for Neandertals, and the infamous Piltdown forgery . . . Its importance [Piltdown] lay not in its claim to ancestral status, but rather in its role as a signpost, pointing clearly to the existence of other populations evolving in our distant past with distinctly un-Neandertal-like characteristics.

In a similar spirit, Tobias (1992: 243) evaluated that the impact of Piltdown on the interpretation of human phylogeny was so important that it delayed the progress of the field of paleoanthropology for more than a quarter of a century. Tobias argued that the morphological features of the Taung skull (*Australopithecus*) discovered in South Africa in 1924 were the antithesis of the Piltdown remains. He assessed the situation in the following way:

> [I]f Taung and *Australopithecus* proved to be correctly appraised as early hominids . . . , Piltdown could not have been an ancestor . . . [I]f Piltdown were correctly seen as a very early (Pliocene) fossil hominid ancestor, then Taung would have had to be relegated to the status of no more than an unusual ape. . . . (Tobias, 1992: 259–260)

It is not denied here that Piltdown created an impact on the process of building human phylogenetic hypotheses in the first decades of the twentieth century. We have already seen in this chapter the role played by Piltdown in the multilinear schemes proposed by Boule, Keith, and Osborn. However, it is argued here that the impact of

Piltdown on the field of paleoanthropology was confined essentially to proponents of the Presapiens hypothesis, and not to proponents of other views of human phylogeny. In other words, its impact was felt to a certain extent but only within a single interpretative framework, the one first characterized by linear schemes and subsequently dominated by multilinear ones. As already stated, Piltdown either contributed to, or was consistent with, the rise of such multilinear interpretations.

However, the discovery of Piltdown neither created disruption in, nor contributed to reinforce, the other two interpretative frameworks. Few examples will make this point clear. Many scholars believed at the time that the humans and the other primates shared an intertwined evolutionary history, thus explaining their polyphyletic schemes in which some human races had a closer genealogical link with some nonhuman primate species than with other living or fossil human races. For instance, Crookshank hypothesized phylogenetic links between, respectively, the Black and the gorilla, the White and the chimpanzee, and the Yellow and the orang. In Crookshank's (1931: 243, 386–392) view, the orangoid feature of the Piltdown jaw, in addition to the smooth and poorly developed browridges of the Piltdown cranium, only constituted further proof for his alleged evolutionary link between the Yellow human races and the orang-utan. The notion that the peculiar conformation of Piltdown man demonstrated its exclusive affiliation with the orang-utan—thus confirming the polyphyletic thesis—was also supported by von Buttel-Reepen (1913: 72–77; see Figure 14) and Frassetto (1927). For his part, Kurz (1924) believed that Piltdown permitted the linking, polyphyletically, of the white human races and the chimpanzee.

A number of other scholars believed that all or most of the hominid fossils could comfortably be accommodated in a scheme within which they were phylogenetically related to one or several living human races. For proponents of this view, the discovery of Piltdown created no disruption of their broad evolutionary conception because it simply constituted another fossil useful for tracing the genealogy of a specific living human race. For instance, Dixon recognized eight fundamental human types or races from which all the living ones were derived by blending: Caspian, Mediterranean, Proto-Negroid, Proto-Australoid, Alpine, Ural, Palae-Alpine, and Mongoloid. Dixon (1923: 63–64) easily inserted all the human fossils in his racial system, including Piltdown which he attributed to a blend between the Proto-Australoid and the Mongoloid types. Another example is Pycraft's view of human phylogeny in which he postulated the divergence, at an early stage, of two branches leading to living humans: one with relatively poorly developed browridges (Piltdown), and the other with strongly developed browridges (*Pithecanthropus* and Neandertals). Pycraft (1925) held that these two types lived in close proximity for a long period of time, during which they occasionally interbred. In Pycraft's view, Piltdown is easily incorporated in human phylogeny by becoming one of the two main stems which gave rise to humanity (see Figure 10).

Pycraft's view contradicts Hammond's and Tobias's assessment of the impact of Piltdown on the development of paleoanthropology. The latter two hold that if Piltdown was recognized to be ancestral to living humans, then the other more ape-like human fossils would be either put on side branches evolving toward extinction or excluded altogether from human ancestry. According to Hammond and Tobias, it is inconceivable that two completely distinct morphological types could have contributed to giving rise to the living humans. Yet, Pycraft did just that. In fact, far from being a marginal interpretation, Pycraft's view of two main ancestral lineages leading to the living humans, one relatively modern-looking and the other more ape-like, will be supported from several perspectives by Marett, Coon, Paterson, and Gates in the 1930s and 1940s (see Chapter 6). For those scholars, there were no contradictions in this view of human phylogeny. It is remarkable how historical analyses continually reveal to modern observers a combination of ideas which they had assumed were unthinkable.

It is argued here that the Piltdown hoax demonstrates, above all, that the fossil discoveries were relatively easily incorporated in the three main interpretative frameworks identified in this chapter. Fossil discoveries were shuffled and reshuffled in them with remarkably little difficulty. To speak of the Presapiens "theory" as a paradigm, after Hammond, in which Piltdown played an important role during the first half of the twentieth century, should not obscure the fact that a considerable number of scholars at the time worked under different premises which made this so-called paradigm meaningless to them. When the Piltdown hoax was exposed in 1953, it was pointed out that its elimination rendered human evolution more coherent. Weiner et al. (1953: 145–146) stated:

> 'Piltdown Man' (*Eoanthropus*) was actually a most awkward and perplexing element in the fossil record of the Hominidae, being entirely out of conformity both in its strange mixture of morphological characters and its time sequence with all the palaeontological evidence of human evolution available from other parts of the world.

Similarly, Sherwood L. Washburn insisted recently that Piltdown man was in the 1940s making absolutely no sense in the light of the other fossil discoveries, to the point of declaring that: "I remember writing a paper on human evolution in 1944, and I simply left Piltdown out. You could make sense of human evolution if you didn't try to put Piltdown into it" (quoted in Lewin, 1987: 75).

On the basis of the above discussion, however, it is clear that such statements can be true from hindsight only. Piltdown created no problems of interpretation for many scholars interested in human phylogeny at the time, because it simply constituted another fossil to incorporate in one interpretative framework or another. The 1930s and 1940s were also remarkable in that Piltdown man was again very easily incorporated in most hypotheses of human phylogeny. In fact, during this latter time period its importance was continually reduced because of a rapidly growing worldwide fossil record, and this is true even for the proponents of the Presapiens hypothesis such as Vallois (see Chapter 6). Perhaps the easiest way to understand why the discovery of Piltdown had such a limited and well-circumscribed impact on the field of paleoanthropology, is by looking at the bewildering diversity of viewpoints entertained at the time about both human phylogeny and humankind's place among the primates. From this perspective, it is difficult to see how any single fossil discovery—genuine or fake, expected or unexpected in conformation—could have had any major impact on the development of the field. It seems, on the contrary, that the assumed impact of the Piltdown discovery on the development of the field by the modern observers is more the product of their current commitment to a particular view of human evolution rather than a historical reality.

EVOLUTIONARY THEORIES: DARWINISM AND ORTHOGENESIS

If individual hominid fossil discoveries were not that important for the assessment of human phylogeny in the first third of the twentieth century, what about the impact of evolutionary theories? According to Bowler, the most important factor determining the interpretation of human phylogeny is contingent upon the patterns suggested by the evolutionary theories. Bowler (1986: 5–6) stated that:

> . . . it is obvious from the differing interpretations offered by scientists at the time that the fossils had meaning only to the extent that they could be fitted into theories of how human evolution occurred . . . Whatever the potential interest of the actual [fossil] discoveries, it seems obvious that a comprehensive study of how understanding of human evolution has developed must focus on the theories, not on the fossils.

Bowler argued that specific theories of biological evolution, such as Darwinism and Orthogenesis, which recognized multiple lines of evolution, explained the widely held multilinear hypotheses of human phylogeny at the time. Furthermore, Bowler (1986: 12–13) argued that scholars interested in human evolution widely adopted non-Darwinian concepts of evolution such as Orthogenesis, for they believed in the existence of irreversible and predetermined trends characterized by parallel evolutionary lines evolving in a common direction and driven by an internal drive. This view of evolution is contrasted with the haphazard or branching (divergent) evolution of the Darwinians which is based on the undeterministic process of natural selection, that is, on the adaptation of populations to local environment only. Bowler (1986: 46–47) explained the distinction between the Darwinian and Orthogenetic theories of evolution in the following way:

> In Darwin's theory of branching evolution, similarity of structure indicates community of descent: the modified descendants of a single ancestor still preserve an underlying similarity of structure inherited from that ancestor. But the Americans' theory [Orthogenesis] supposed that a number of similar forms might actually belong to lines of development that had been separate for a long time, each independently acquiring the same new characters as the result of a shared tendency to vary in the same direction . . . If one applied this concept to human evolution, it might be argued that the similarities between humans and apes were acquired independently, so there was no close link between them. If one applied the same principle in a different way, it might be argued that the human races were the products of separate lines of evolution that had merely converged so closely together that they could now interbreed.

Bowler is certainly right to stress that some interpretations of human phylogeny promoted at the time benefited from the patterns suggested by these evolutionary theories. However, this factor is anything but as generalized as Bowler would have it. This section aims to demonstrate that the impact of the evolutionary theories on the human phylogenetic hypotheses during that period has to be put in its proper context.

One ambiguity with Bowler's thesis is that parallelism in human evolution, which might be indicative of the influence of nonDarwinian theories, can also be generated by taxonomic procedures only. It has been argued in the introductory section of this chapter that the building of evolutionary hypotheses is an exercise similar to fitting a puzzle together, meaning that one can only place new pieces (new fossil discoveries) by comparing them to the pieces which are already known. In the case of the human evolutionary studies, new fossil discoveries were compared either to (1) living human groups, (2) living and fossil nonhuman primate groups, or (3) to both groups. For instance, the simple insertion of hominid fossil discoveries in the three interpretative frameworks presented in this chapter generated parallelism. If one judges that the differences between the living human races are so important that they can only have arisen through a long and separate evolutionary process, then parallelism is merely a by-product of this view. This is seen in the parallel schemes already presented within which all hominid fossils were related to one or several living human races. Furthermore, if one evaluates that each main living human race shares with a particular living primate species more similarities than those seen between this human race and another, then the similarities between these two living human races can only be explained by parallel evolution. Again, parallelism here is merely a by-product of this conception. This is seen in the polyphyletic schemes already reviewed in this chapter.

The difficulty of Bowler's thesis is seen in his attempt to explain all proposed human phylogenetic hypotheses by appealing to evolutionary theories. Therefore, when such schemes did not conform to the anticipated patterns of specific evolutionary theories, Bowler felt compelled to explain this situation by appealing to extra-scientific factors. In one such instance, when referring to scholars who held a unilinear interpretation of human phylogeny, Bowler (1986: 79–80) asked:

> . . . why did the grossly oversimplified image of a single line leading toward modern mankind become so popular around 1900, despite the fact that it was inconsistent with all known evolution theories?. . . A whole host of influences thus turned late-nineteenth-century evolutionism into a form of linear progressionism, against which the logic of the Darwinian theory struggled in vain. It was thus almost inevitable that the first human fossil would be fitted into the simplest possible linear sequence of evolution . . . The collapse of the linear view of human evolution in early twentieth century was a necessary prerequisite for further development in the field, since it paved the way for a more sophisticated interpretation in tune with the broader principles of evolution theory.

No one doubts that extra-scientific factors have always played one role or another in the development of scientific disciplines. However, one cannot refer to such factors only when one tries to save an argument. There must be a more consistent way of addressing this. Bowler seems to get in trouble because he argues that all the phylogenetic interpretations must be explained by evolutionary theories. First of all, this view makes sense only if one assumes that the field of human evolution is entirely a by-product of evolutionary theories, which is certainly not the case (see also Chapter 2).

There is an alternative way to explain the promotion of linear schemes in human evolution. Evolutionists like Dubois, Keith (before 1912), Schwalbe, Mahoudeau, and Hrdlicka who favored, at one time or another, a linear view of human phylogeny might have judged this interpretation to be defensible on the following two bases: (1) Living humans are descended from a hominoid ape ancestor, as seen by the morphological similarities between the living humans and the hominoid apes; (2) the human fossil material now available (especially *Pithecanthropus* and Neandertals) shows intermediate morphological features between the modern humans and an alleged hominoid-like ancestor. On this view, the linear interpretation of human phylogeny is explained by referring to taxonomic procedures only.

In order to evaluate the possible impact of the evolutionary theories on human phylogeny in the first third of the twentieth century, it will be necessary to analyze and compare the work of some scholars. Let us first consider the work of scholars who were clearly influenced by evolutionary theories. George Montandon is a case in point. According to Montandon, the pattern of human phylogeny is best explained by the evolutionary theory of Ologenesis or Ologenism, as first proposed by Rosa (1923, 1931 [1918]).[26] In Rosa's view, life originated in as many places as it possibly could, thus giving rise to an extraordinary multitude of identical primitive life forms over a large territory. From such a multitude of primitive life forms or stem species, and after periods of relative stability, evolution occurred during episodic splitting events, through mutation, as each stem transformed itself into precisely one advanced and one retrogressive stem. The occurrence of such mutational events in the evolutionary history of each stem is explained by an inherent property of the living matter itself, and repeats itself until exhaustion of the stem's driving force leads it to extinction. On this theory, the history of life on earth from the very beginning is not explained by the migration and expansion of life forms into uncharted territories, only because habitable zones are already occupied by more or less complex life forms. Instead, the two stems which arise from every splitting event live in geographical zones which are always more restricted as time goes by. In Rosa's evolutionary conception, as may now be clear, similarities among different stems are more often than not explained by parallel evolution.

In the light of Rosa's theory, Montandon (1928, 1929d, 1933) held that the first hominids were represented by a largely distributed *Pithecanthropus* stage. From this initial stage or stem, human evolution occurred during splitting or dichotomic events, through mutation, as the mother stem transformed itself into two daughter stems: an advanced evolutionary segment and a retrogressive one. From there, the pattern was repeated again, as each daughter stem went throught the same process. Montandon held that the original hominid stem split into two segments, the retrogressive portion being represented by Heidelberg man and the advanced one being represented by Piltdown. This former retrogressive portion split again into two unequal segments before they both went extinct, as seen on the one hand by the Neandertal man and on the other by Broken Hill. The advanced portion of the segment represented by Piltdown continued its evolution through the same dichotomic process until it gave rise to all living human races.[27]

Montandon's case constitutes a clear example of the influence of an evolutionary theory on the interpretation of human phylogeny. Besides Montandon's view, however, it is remarkably difficult to find scholars who derived *entirely* their view of human phylogeny from an evolutionary theory. This situation may be explained, in part at least, by the nature of the relationship between the evolutionary mechanisms and the evolutionary patterns. Although Darwin's mechanism of evolution is theoretically associated with a pattern of divergence from a common ancestor, it is far from clear that proponents of Darwinism are obliged to establish phylogenies by appealing to the divergence principle. It is one thing to state that natural selection is the main mechanism of evolutionary change in human evolution, and quite another to establish the pattern of human phylogeny along the principle of divergence. Obviously, there is no necessary connection between an alleged mechanism of evolutionary change and the pattern that results from studying the empirical data.

The same conclusion is valid for the other evolutionary mechanisms often proposed between 1860 and 1950, should it be neo-Lamarckism, Theistic evolutionism, Mutation theories, Hybridization theories, Orthogenetic theories, etc. There is always a possibility that a link can be found between the evolutionary mechanisms and the evolutionary patterns, but it is important to recognize that the nature of this link can be of two different orders: (1) The mechanism(s) may directly guide the reconstruction of a phylogeny; (2) the mechanism(s) may come only once a phylogeny is established in order to explain, justify or be consistent with that phylogenetic reconstruction. It is argued here that, as far as the field of human evolution is concerned, most scholars who maintained a link between the evolutionary mechanisms and the evolutionary patterns in the first third of the twentieth century approached it from the second perspective.

Bowler suggested that the impact of the evolutionary theories on the field of human evolution is especially acute as far as Orthogenesis is concerned. The comparison of the work of Osborn, Boule, and Keith, which presents many similarities, will be useful to put Bowler's thesis in perspective. Osborn has been a leading exponent of Orthogenesis in the first third of the twentieth century (e.g., Rainger, 1988; Bowler, 1983: 174–176). Is it possible to detect in his view of human phylogeny the influence of his evolutionary conception? In 1915, Osborn (1915) held that the humans and the hominoid apes were descended from a common stock of the late Oligocene or early Miocene period. Osborn viewed humankind's family tree as being composed of a number of entirely separate branches with two main stems: One stem regrouped *Pithecanthropus, Homo heidelbergensis*, and *Homo neanderthalensis*, all evolving separately toward extinction, while another stem led to modern human types.[28] By the mid-1920s, however, Osborn had somewhat modified his view of human phylogeny. He now discarded the "Ape-Man" ancestry of humankind and replaced it by the "Dawn-Man" hypothesis of human descent, that is, the view that humans had sprung from an Oligocene "neutral" stock. Osborn (1927a, 1927b, 1929, 1930) now believed that the so-called simian features of the human lineage were acquired either by parallel evolution or by a common inheritance with all the other primates. However, Osborn's new view would not alter significantly his phylogenetic tree of human evolution.[29] Here, it is likely that the parallelism found in Osborn's view of human phylogeny is related to his promotion of the theory of Orthogenesis. Yet, it is not easy to demonstrate that link, at least to judge by Osborn's writings. Bowler (1986: 113–114, 187, 199) readily acknowledged this situation, for he noted that Osborn did not extend his theory to humankind. Although it is not clear if Osborn applied the theory of Orthogenesis to human evolution, it is certainly not detectable by looking at his human phylogenetic scheme. After all, several scholars at the time promoted similiar views, although they were clearly not influenced by Orthogenesis.

For Boule, for instance, human evolutionary history was to be conceived by applying the principles observed in palaeontology (e.g., Laurent, 1995b). Boule took palaeontology to say that evolution was a complex and multilinear pattern with numerous instances of parallel evolution of phyletic lines, as living members of mammalian families were often represented as early as the Pliocene period by fairly modern-looking representatives. Boule's view of human phylogeny, which is not unlike Osborn's, is interesting precisely because in his mind a multilinear human phylogeny characterized by parallel evolution is uncoupled from any evolutionary theory. Instead, Boule was merely inspired by a general pattern of evolution thought to be found in the mammalian fossil record. For Boule (1911–1913, 1921), living humans and apes have long been separated, their resemblances being explained more by the similarity of the evolutionary stages they went through (parallelism) than by their retention of characteristics from a common ancestor.

Like Osborn and Boule, Keith viewed human phylogeny after 1912 as being characterized by a multilinear pattern with instances of parallel evolution of distinct hominid lines. Keith (1912, 1915) recognized at least three major branches on the human stem, two of which were extinct (Neandertal man and *Eoanthropus*). However, Keith's view of human phylogeny after 1912 was merely consistent with Orthogenesis, as it was founded on a different basis that appealed to the hominoid fossil record and considerations about social evolution (e.g., Bowler, 1986: 91–99).

The comparison of the work of Osborn, Boule, and Keith reveals that the recognition of parallel evolution in human phylogeny does not necessarily flow from a commitment to any specific evolutionary theory. It is not argued here that evolutionary theories such as Orthogenesis had no impact on the field of human evolution, but only that their influence must be greatly relativized. In fact, it seems that only a very limited number of scholars derived *entirely* their view of human phylogeny from a specific evolutionary theory, such as Montandon did. In the case of scholars like Boule and Keith, their views of human evolution were *merely* consistent with Orthogenesis. It is certainly not unreasonable to believe that the promotion of evolutionary theories characterized by parallel evolution contributed, at the time, to create a climate of opinion which was not against the recognition of such parallelism in human evolution. Yet, this is not the same as to state, as Bowler (1986: 12–13) does, that scholars widely recognized such a parallelism in human evolution because they adopted non-Darwinian concepts of evolution such as Orthogenesis.

This entire discussion should not distract us from the fact that for a majority of scholars interested in human evolution at the time, the reconstruction of human phylogeny was not established with the help of evolutionary theories but rather with the assistance of the taxonomic procedure only. For such scholars, parallelism was not an assumption of their theories but merely a by-product of their procedures. It is precisely for that reason that we have stressed throughout this chapter the importance of the three interpretative frameworks in determining the views on human phylogeny during the 1890–1935 period.

CONCLUSION

It is a remarkable fact that as recently as 1930 the question of humankind's place in nature was still totally unsettled. It is barely an exaggeration to say that almost every possible phylogenetic hypothesis involving the humans and the other primates has been promoted at one time or another between 1860 and 1935. In a sense, to look back at this period is, for a modern observer, to look at a different field of paleoanthropology. It is not good enough to deny the existence of the scholars who seem today to be so completely wrong about human evolution. Present paleoanthropologists cannot select their forefathers in accordance to their current views. If one wants to understand the development of paleoanthropology, one is obliged to rationalize what seems to be strange early phases of development. Of course, this strangeness is only an illusion. If many scholars of the time promoted what seems to be incredible hypotheses, it is only because there were no obvious starting or referential points. This can only contribute to our appreciation of the immensity of the task that lay before these scholars. It gives us a sense that what we consider today to be so obvious is, after all, anything but obvious. These efforts will only bear fruit for the establishment of the truly modern research structure in paleoanthropology in the post-1935 period. This turning point was made possible only because earlier scholars tested and exploited many avenues which ultimately resulted in the conceptions which we take for granted today. It is clear from what we have seen in this book thus far that the quest to establish humankind's place in nature was much harder than one would have imagined.

NOTES

1. The list of papers published on the *Pithecanthropus* discovery before 1930 is impressive. For a good start consult G.S. Miller, "The Controversy over Human Missing Links," *Annual Report of the Smithsonian Institution* for 1928, pp. 413–465.

2. See Dubois's phylogenetic tree in "On *Pithecanthropus erectus*: A Transitional Form Between Man and the Apes," *Scientific Transactions of the Royal Dublin Society*, 6 (1896), p. 17 and "The Place of Pithecanthropus in the Genealogical Tree," *Nature*, 53 (1896), p. 245.

3. Verneau's original text reads as follows: " . . . on dirait que la race de Spy [Neanderthals] et celle de Grimaldi soient deux branches collatérales d'un tronc qu'il est encore difficile de préciser, mais qui devait ressembler dans une certaine mesure au *Pithecanthropus*. Chez elles, l'évolution s'est faite en sens divergents."

4. See Pycraft's human phylogenetic tree in "On the Calvaria Found at Boskop, Transvaal, in 1913, and Its Relationship to Cromagnard and Negroid Skulls." *Journal of the Royal Anthropological Institute*, 55 (1925), p. 193.

5. Taylor presented again his entire conception of human evolution in the mid–1940s with no visible change in *Environment, Race and Migration*, 2nd edition (Toronto: University of Toronto Press, 1945).

6. See Dubois's phylogenetic tree in "On *Pithecanthropus erectus*: A Transitional Form Between Man and the Apes," *Scientific Transactions of the Royal Dublin Society*, 6 (1896), p. 17, and "The Place of Pithecanthropus in the Genealogical Tree," *Nature*, 53 (1896), p. 245.

7. A glimpse of Keith's linear conception in 1900 can be seen in a phylogenetic tree, at least as it was presented several years later. See A. Keith, *The Construction of Man's Family Tree* (London: Watts & Co., 1934), p. 13.

8. Several scholars have already discussed Schwalbe's contribution to the field of human evolution. See P.J. Bowler, *Theories of Human Evolution: A Century of Debate, 1844–1944* (Baltimore: Johns Hopkins University Press, 1986), pp. 68–70, 83–85; F.H. Smith, "Gustav Schwalbe: Neandertal Morphology and Systematics, 1899–1916," *Physical Anthropology News*, 6 (1987): 1–5; F.H. Smith, "Schwalbe, Gustav (1844–1916)," in F. Spencer (ed.), *History of Physical Anthropology: An Encyclopedia*, vol. 2 (New York: Garland Publishing, 1997b), 916–918; E. Trinkaus and P. Shipman, *The Neandertals: Changing the Image of Mankind* (New York: Alfred A. Knopf, 1993), pp. 156–158.

9. These two phylogenetic possibilities were expressed graphically in G. Schwalbe, *Studien zur Vorgeschichte des Menschen* (Stuttgart: E. Schweizerbartsche, 1906), p. 14.

10. See also A. Hrdlicka, "The Peopling of Asia," *Proceedings of the American Philosophical Society*, 60 (1921), p. 541, and "The Peopling of the Earth," *Proceedings of the American Philosophical Society*, 65 (1926), p. 151.

11. See Keith's phylogenetic tree in *The Antiquity of Man* (London: Williams and Norgate, 1915), p. 501.

12. See Keith's new phylogenetic tree in *New Discoveries Relating to the Antiquity of Man* (London: Williams and Norgate, 1931), frontispiece.

13. See Hooton's phylogenetic tree in *Up from the Ape* (New York: Macmillan, 1931), p. 391.

14. For biographical and autobiographical information on Louis Leakey, consult L.S.B. Leakey, *By the Evidence: Memoirs, 1932–1951* (New York: Harcourt, Brace and Jovanovich, 1974); S. Cole, *Leakey's Luck: The Life of Louis Seymour Bazett Leakey, 1903–1972* (London: Collins, 1975), V. Morell, *Ancestral Passions: The Leakey Family and the Quest for Humankind's Beginnings* (New York: Simon and Schuster, 1995).

15. See Leakey's phylogenetic tree in *Adam's Ancestors: An Up-To-Date Outline of What Is Known About the Origin of Man*, 2nd edition (London: Methuen, 1934), p. 227. The first three editions of this book appeared in 1934.

16. Klaatsch's book *The Evolution and Progress of Mankind* (London: T. Fisher Unwin, 1923) was originally published posthumously under the title *Der Werdegang der Menschheit und die Entstehung der Kultur* (Berlin: Bong & Co., 1920).

17. See Klaatsch's phylogenetic tree in "Die Aurignac-Rasse und ihre Stellung im Stambaum der Menschheit," *Zeitschrift für Ethnologie*, 42 (1910), p. 567.

18. See von Buttel-Reepen's phylogenetic tree in *Man and His Forerunners* (London: Longmans, Green and Co., 1913), p. 73.

19. See Sergi's phylogenetic tree in *Europa* (Milano: Fratelli Bocca, 1908), p. 82.

20. See Gray's modified phylogenetic tree in "The Differences and Affinities of Palaeolithic Man and the Anthropoid Apes," *Man*, 11 (1911), p. 120.

21. See Crookshank's phylogenetic tree in *The Mongol in Our Midst*, 3rd edition (London: Kegan Paul, Trench, Trubner & Co., 1931), p. 380.

22. See Horst's graphic representation of his three main evolutionary stems in, *Die natürlichen Grundstämme der Menschheit* (Hildburghausen: Thüringische Verlags-Anstalt, 1913), placed at the end of the text.

23. See Arldt's phylogenetic tree in "Die Stammesgeschichte der Primaten und die Entwicklung der Menschenrassen," *Fortschritte der assenkunde*, 1 (1915), p. 50.

24. See Sera's phylogenetic tree at the end of the text in "I caratteri della faccia e il polifiletismo dei primati," *Giornale per la Morfologia dell'Uomo e dei Primati*, 2 (1918): 1–296.

25. For some important references gathered on the Piltdown discovery before 1930 see G.S. Miller, "The Controversy over Human Missing Links," *Annual Report of the Smithsonian Institution* for 1928, pp. 413–465.

26. D. Rosa, *Ologenesi. Nuova teoria dell'evoluzione e della distribuzione geografica dei viventi* (Firenze: Bemporad, 1918). This book was translated into French under the title *L'ologénèse. Nouvelle théorie de l'évolution et de la distribution géographique des êtres vivants* (Paris: Alcan, 1931).

27. See Montandon phylogenetic tree in his *L'ologenèse humaine* (Paris: Alcan, 1928), pp. 204–205.

28. See Osborn's phylogenetic tree in *Men of the Old Stone Age: Their Environment, Life and Art* (New York: Charles Scribners's Sons, 1915), p. 491.

29. Compare H.F. Osborn's phylogenetic tree in, "The Discovery of Tertiary Man," *Science*, 71 (1930), p. 3, with his previous diagram in *Men of the Old Stone Age: Their Environment, Life and Art* (New York: Charles Scribner's Sons, 1915), p. 491.

Part III

TOWARD THE MODERN RESEARCH STRUCTURE IN PALEOANTHROPOLOGY, 1935–2000

The gradual increase of primate and hominid fossil discoveries during the 1890–1935 period contributed to reducing the gap that separated the research being conducted on humankind's place among the primates from those on human phylogeny proper. However, because of a paucity of fossils at that time we have seen how phylogenetic hypotheses based on inferences of the living forms (comparative anatomy) continued to loom large. This situation was to change significantly starting in the 1930s. It is not that the fossil record became so well-documented as to definitely exclude the influence of comparative anatomy on the field of paleoanthropology. It is simply that, at last, the fossil record contributed powerfully to a number of debates to such an extent that in some instances it became either a respectable or even a prime source of information in the phylogenetic analyses. This new empirical reality propelled the field of paleoanthropology in its third epistemological stage.

The opening event of this new era was the downfall of the polyphyletic thesis which received a fatal blow that was delivered by the rapidly improving hominid fossil record in the 1930s (see Chapter 6). The elimination of such a thesis immediately impacted both the debates of humankind's place among the primates (see Chapter 7) and also those of human phylogeny proper (see Chapter 9), as this thesis had direct implications in these two research areas. It is certainly significant that it is fossil discoveries which belonged to the hominid fossil record (and not to the nonhuman primate fossil record) that eventually contributed to the downfall of hypotheses also of relevance for the debates on humankind's place among the primates. This constituted only the beginning of a complex process in paleoanthropology during which discoveries in one research area influenced another research area. After the late 1940s, the australopithecine discoveries, particularly, played a pivotal role in driving forward this integrating process (see Chapters 8 and 10).

From a field originally organized around largely isolated debates, paleoanthropology gradually lost its dislocated structure in favor of a fairly integrated one with important overlapping research areas. The 1935–2000 period was particularly significant in permitting the institution of such a new level of coherence in paleoanthropology's research program. The rapidly improving fossil record since the 1930s and the molecular studies since the 1960s were at the very heart of this cohesion process. This new empirical reality confined the main debates relevant to the quest of humankind's place in nature within more restricted or better circumscribed frameworks. Not only were the scholars constrained to work with a smaller set of defensible phylogenetic hypotheses, but also it permitted them to test the hypotheses more thoroughly. After the pre-1935 period which consisted of the elaboration of an ever greater number of hypotheses, the trend was reversed in the post-1935 period as scholars engaged in the elimination of these hypotheses. The modern research structure in paleoanthropology was developed on this very process of elimination.

6

The Constriction of Human Phylogenetic Hypotheses, 1935–1950

INTRODUCTION

Hominid phylogenetic hypotheses in the 1890–1935 period were profoundly divergent. This was the direct product of scholars working within three competing interpretative frameworks. This situation was to change dramatically during the 1935–1950 period. Two main factors explain the rise of this new research context. First, the interpretative framework which was responsible for the polyphyletic hypotheses disappeared. Second, the two remaining interpretative frameworks started to generate phylogenetic hypotheses that were very close to each other, conceptually and empirically. In fact, these two surviving frameworks were now overlapping in their interpretations of human phylogeny to such an extent that it is no longer relevant to refer to them as "interpretative frameworks." This latter concept served its purpose well in the first third of the twentieth century at a time when viewpoints on human phylogeny were separated by important differences. This concept has now outlived its utility. Regarding this new situation, after 1935, the field of paleoanthropology saw a considerable reduction both in the distinctiveness of the viewpoints about human phylogeny as well as in the taxonomic diversity entertained about such hypotheses. This led to the proposition of human phylogenetic hypotheses which were less and less distinct from one another. In this chapter, this process has been called the "constriction" of phylogenetic hypotheses.

We have seen that the impact of individual hominid fossil discoveries was very limited during the 1890–1935 period. This was clearly seen in the reception that was given to the discovery of Piltdown by the scholars working within any of the three interpretative frameworks. Fossil discoveries then known were simply shuffled and reshuffled within these frameworks. This situation was to change significantly during the 1930s. Indeed, never in the entire history of the field of paleoanthropology, before or after, will hominid fossil discoveries so profoundly affect the views of human phylogeny than those recovered during the 1930–1940 decade. Remember that the vast majority of hominid fossils recovered prior to the 1930s were found in Europe. The most important exceptions to this situation were *Pithecanthropus* in Java, Talgaï in Australia, Broken Hill in Southern Africa, *Hesperopithecus* in North America, and several disputed discoveries in South America (*Tetraprothomo argentinus*, *Diprothomo platensis*, *Homo pampaeus*, and *Homo pliocenicus*). It is remarkable that the great diversity of opinions expressed about human phylogeny at the time were made on the basis of a fossil record that was essentially restricted to a small territory called Europe. Perhaps this phenomenon could be better understood if the perspective were to be reversed: This diversity of opinions was made possible only because the fossil record was essentially restricted to Europe, thus imposing very few contraints on the formulation of these phylogenetic hypotheses. In sharp contrast to the previous time period, it will be seen that most hominid fossils recovered during the short time span of the 1930–1940 decade were found outside Europe. Furthermore, few major debates erupted on the validity of their hominid status or on their geological provenance. All this contributed to significantly change the role played by the human fossil record in the process of phylogeny-building.

In the view of an increasing number of scholars, these new fossil discoveries permitted them to push deeper into the geological past and the roots of the living human races. It is, thus, easy to understand why such discoveries greatly contributed to strengthen the hypotheses in which all the human fossils are phylogenetically related to one or several living human races. Conversely, it contributed to putting the proponents of multilinear hypotheses on the defensive, especially following the abandonment of this option by scholars like Keith, and eventually Hooton. But perhaps the most important impact of the discoveries made during the 1930–1940 decade is that the discoveries strengthened the notion of the unity of the human races, thus blocking the way to the polyphyletic hypotheses. Polyphyletists, it will be remembered, believed that the similarities observed among the main living human races were superficial in nature, and that they had to be explained by parallel or convergent evolution. Their views were based on minute anatomical details which were thought to link specific living and fossil human races with particular nonhuman primate species. However, if it could be shown that all the main living human races had deep genealogical roots in time taking them back to a more primitive (and possibly common) primate-like condition, then it would be much harder to hold that they independently reached their human status by arising from stocks shared in common with distinct hominoid or anthropoid forms.

It is unclear if the recovery of hominid fossils during the 1930–1940 decade was the only cause that contributed to the downfall of the polyphyletic thesis. What is clear, however, is that such a thesis had been completely abandoned by the 1930s by lack of new adherents (e.g., Delisle, 2004). Apparently, these new fossil recoveries prevented or discouraged any eventual continuation of this tradition of interpretation in the future. Although the fall of this interpretative framework greatly contributed to reduce the diversity of viewpoints about human phylogeny, its impact was also felt in the debates concerned with humankind's place among the primates, as the polyphyletic thesis also had direct phylogenetic implications for this question. This paved the way for the rise of the modern research structure in paleoanthropology.

HOMINID FOSSIL DISCOVERIES IN THE 1930–1940 DECADE

The hominid fossil discoveries which contributed to the establishment of a new research context in human evolution came from distinct geographical areas: Southeast Asia, South and East Africa, the Middle East, Europe, and, from a negative perspective, the Americas. In some instances, discoveries of the 1930s were only the latest stage of a series of such recoveries made in the previous decades which finally reached a point where they could instigate a shift of interpretation.

Southeast Asia. In the second half of the nineteenth century, a number of scholars had already recognized the similarities between some European fossil remains and the living human races in Southeast Asia. For instance, Huxley (1863) held that the Neandertal skull found in Germany in 1856 shared remarkable similarities with some native tribes of Australia. Similarly, de Quatrefages and Hamy (1882) noted a close resemblance between the fossil race they named Canstadt and the living populations of Australia and India. This genealogical proximity between the European fossils and the living humans in this region of the world was sometimes maintained in the early twentieth century (e.g., Sollas, 1908; Burkitt and Hunter, 1922–1923; Sarasin, 1924). For a number of scholars, however, this proximity was denied for it was argued that both living Australians and Tasmanians had deep genealogical roots that must go back to the late Pliocene or early Pleistocene period (e.g., Klaatsch, 1908, 1923; Sergi, 1912; Berry and Robertson, 1913–1914). Yet, without any further fossil evidence, this debate on the genealogy of the living populations of Southeast Asia remained unsettled. This situation was to change gradually after the 1910s. Discovered in 1884, but brought to scientific attention only in the 1910s, the Talgaï skull (Australia) was described as a Proto-Australian specimen with a number of ape-like characters, some of which were clearly differentiated from the Neandertal type, and with an antiquity which was presumably of Pleistocene age (Smith, 1918). Discovered in 1889–1890 but not brought to the scientific attention until 1920, the two Wadjak specimens (Java) presumably dated to the early Pleistocene were also described as being of Proto-Australian conformation, with features that distinguished them from *Homo neanderthalensis* (Dubois, 1921).

Until the 1920s, the genealogy of the living races of Southeast Asia remained unspecified as long as it was based on so few fossil remains of uncertain antiquity, such as Talgaï and Wadjak. The 1930s were responsible for a giant leap forward on this very question, and it is in this light that Talgaï and Wadjak became important. The discovery of *Sinanthropus* remains near Beijing in China (Black, 1927, 1934; Pei, 1936, 1937), of a rich collection of *Homo soloensis* (Ngandong Man) in Java (Oppenoorth, 1937; von Koenigswald, 1937; Weidenreich, 1951), and other skulls of *Pithecanthropus* in Java (von Koenigswald, 1949; von Koenigswald and Weidenreich, 1939), all contributed significantly to the establishment of a possible genealogical link between the living human races of Southeast Asia and hominids of the early Pleistocene. In this new empirical context, several scholars were able to establish ancient genealogical roots for the inhabitants of this region of the world.

South and East Africa. Important discoveries were also made in South and East Africa. In South Africa, three discoveries are of special interest to us. Found in 1913, the Boskop skull was often interpreted as a representative of a fossil race of some antiquity which might be ancestral to the living Bushmen (e.g., Broom, 1918, 1923; Dart, 1923; Pycraft, 1925; Galloway, 1937–1938a). A second discovery occurred in 1921 at Broken Hill, Rhodesia, where a skull sometimes referred to as *Homo rhodesiensis* was recovered. Debates soon erupted on its place in human phylogeny. Some scholars argued that it constituted a possible link between *Homo sapiens* and *Homo neanderthalensis* (Smith Woodward, 1921). Others postulated that it was remotely ancestral to the living Hottentots (Broom, 1923). Still others believed that it was ancestral to the aboriginal Australians (Pycraft, 1928). A third discovery was made at Florisbad, South Africa, in 1932. This fossil skull was thought to be more ancient than the Boskop skull (Dreyer, 1935). While some scholars believed the Florisbad skull to be related to the Neandertals (Drennan, 1935), most of them insisted on its genealogical connection with the living populations of South Africa (Dreyer, 1936; Galloway, 1937–1938b; Keith, 1937–1938).

In East Africa, three discoveries are also of special interest. In 1932, a jaw was discovered at Kanam and parts of three skulls at Kanjera. These specimens of debated antiquity were sometimes interpreted as representatives of *Homo sapiens* in the early Pleistocene period (Leakey, 1934, 1936a). Furthermore, a skull of great antiquity which was believed to present some similarities with *Sinanthropus* of Peking was discovered in 1935. This skull was sometimes referred to as *Africanthropus* (Leakey, 1936b; Weinert, 1939a).

On the basis of the fossil discoveries made in South and East Africa, possible genealogical links between the living human races of Africa and hominids of the early Pleistocene were proposed in the 1930s and after (e.g., Galloway, 1937; Dart, 1940; Broom, 1943). Not unlike the situation found in Asia, this also permitted a number of scholars to trace ancient genealogical roots to the inhabitants of Africa.

The Middle East. In 1931–1932, numerous fossil remains were found at Mount Carmel, Palestine. At first, these remains of the mid-Pleistocene period were divided in groups which were thought to share a kinship with either the Cro-Magnon type or the Neandertal group (Keith and McCown, 1937). Later, however, all these remains were pulled together in a single fossil population presenting a great variability. The place of this fossil group in human phylogeny was evaluated as a collateral branch of the Cro-Magnon stock which presented Neandertaloid features (McCown and Keith, 1939). The significance of the Mount Carmel discoveries lies not so much in the argument that a direct kinship existed between the Neandertal and the modern human types, but rather in the demonstration that the morphological chasm thought to exist between these two forms was not as important as sometimes believed in the first third of the twentieth century. The Mount Carmel discoveries contributed to weaken the view that human phylogeny had been characterized by many important extinct and isolated side branches.

Europe. In Europe, a possible evolutionary sequence linking very ancient hominids and the living humans had also been suggested. In 1935, a hominid skull dated to the mid-Pleistocene period was uncovered at Swanscombe, England. This specimen was depicted as an ancient representative closely akin to *Homo sapiens* (Marston, 1937; Hinton et al., 1938). In the light of the Swanscombe skull, Keith (1938–1939) ventured a proposed lineage comprising Piltdown and Swanscombe, among other specimens.

The new world. If a number of scholars ventured to propose possible evolutionary sequences linking the living human races and ancient hominid forms in the Old World in the 1930s, the situation was quite different in the New World. Repeated claims have been made since the beginning of the twentieth century about discoveries of more or less ancient human remains in the Americas (e.g., Barbour, 1907; Sellards, 1916; Stock, 1924; Jenks, 1932; Bowden and Lopatin, 1936; Howard et al., 1936; Bryan, 1945; Cressman, 1946). These claims, however, have been disputed (e.g., Hrdlicka, 1907, 1918, 1937; Hrdlicka et al., 1912). Irrespective of the validity of these claims, no hominid evolutionary sequence resulted from these investigations. Perhaps the only clear exceptions to this were the views promoted by Ameghino (1909) and Sergi (1910) very early in the century (see Chapter 4). However, the fossil discoveries needed to further support these assumed evolutionary sequences never materialized, except perhaps for the brief episode in the early 1920s when a very ancient hominoid and/or hominid tooth named *Hesperopithecus* (Osborn, 1922a, 1922b) was believed to have been found in Nebraska (see also Chapter 4). This wrongly identified fossil specimen was soon discarded. By the middle of the twentieth century, the idea that the hominids entered the New World only at the very end of the Pleistocene period was now profoundly entrenched in the field of paleoanthropology.

THE OBVIOUS AND IMMEDIATE IMPACT

By far the most visible impact of the evolutionary sequences proposed to link the living human races and the ancient hominids in the Old World during the 1930s was the change of heart of scholars such as Keith and Hooton. Both scholars were once strong proponents of the multilinear hypotheses in which several main hominid extinct branches were recognized. Keith, and later Hooton, eventually exercised a complete retreat from this position in favor of parallel hypotheses in which most hominid fossils were linked to distinct portions of humanity. By so doing, Keith and Hooton contributed to weaken the multilinear conception of human phylogeny by depriving this view of their support while simultaneously contributing to reinforce the parallel conception of human phylogeny through their recent adherence.

Beginning in 1912, Keith was promoting the idea that numerous human fossils were not leading toward the living human races (see Chapter 5 and Figure 12). In this view, *Pithecanthropus*, Peking man, Piltdown, Rhodesian man, and the Neandertals were all put on different side branches leading toward extinction. Keith (1934) held to this view until 1934. By 1935, Keith (1935) alluded to a new view of human phylogeny, to which he fully adhered the next year (Keith, 1936). From then on, Keith maintained that the separation of the main human races was a very ancient event (early Pleistocene), as these races underwent a series of parallel evolutionary changes in teeth, jaws, and brain, independently from each other in distinct geographical areas. Their similarities were explained, Keith insisted, by a process of convergence that took place during the Pleistocene period. Keith's (1936: 194) new view implied that "throughout the Pleistocene period the separated branches of the human family appear to have been unfolding a program of latent qualities inherited from a common ancestor of an earlier period." Later, Keith (1949: 125–135, 243–244) insisted that the mechanism of evolution responsible for such parallel trends was rooted in the rapid transformation of small evolutionary units (populations) propelled by the competition and selection of gene combinations. Because ancient human populations were more often than not attached to specific territories, this permitted a distinction or a regionalization of the features of the main human races.

To students of human evolution who saw in *Pithecanthropus, Sinanthropus* and the Neandertals an ascending series or a succession of stages, which culminated, without a break, in *Homo sapiens*, Keith (1944a) objected that these Pleistocene types merely represented separate evolutionary products, each being at a different stage of evolution. In Keith's new perspective, most human fossils were directly related to the main living human races (see Figure 20). One such line was the *Pithecanthropus*, Solo man, Wadjak, Talgaï, Keilor, and living Australasians. Among other such lines or stems, Keith identified an African stem leading to the living Africans through fossil specimens such as *Africanthropus*, Kanam, Kanjera, Broken Hill, Boskop, and Florisbad. *Sinanthropus* was identified as an ancestor of the living Sinasians, while the Caucasians were directly derived from the Mount Carmel and the Cro-Magnon types, meaning that the Caucasians shared a close relationship with the Neandertals, this latter form being without living representatives. Keith (1949: 256–265) put Piltdown on a separate line leading towards extinction.[1]

What prompted Keith to change his view of human phylogeny in the mid-1930s? During the 1930s, Keith was involved in the study of the fossil remains discovered at Mount Carmel, Palestine (Keith and McCown, 1937; McCown and Keith, 1939). From this study, Keith concluded that these remains presented traits that were found in Neandertal and modern human types alike, thus establishing a possible evolutionary link between the two. However, it seems that the Mount Carmel recoveries were not the main triggering factor that prompted Keith to change his view of human phylogeny. After all, his pre-1935 view depicted the Neandertals as a side branch of the main human stem evolving toward extinction, while his new view depicted them as a side branch of the Caucasian stem still leading toward extinction. Rather, it seems that the repeted discoveries of hominid fossils in Java between 1891 and 1935, which permitted the establishment of a possible evolutionary link between *Pithecanthropus* and the living Australians, was the key factor that made Keith change his mind (Keith, 1944b). In his pre-1935 scheme, *Pithecanthropus* was put on a side branch evolving toward extinction like many others. However, it also represented the most primitive form and the earliest one to diverge from the main human stem leading to the living humans. The establishment of a possible connection between *Pithecanthropus* and the living Australians was by far the worst thing possible that could have happened to Keith's view of human phylogeny at the time. Apparently, Keith's multilinear hypothesis simply collapsed in front of this possible evolutionary sequence. Keith (1944b: 742) confessed that:

> [A] decade ago . . . [most of us] believed that we should find, some day, the remains of a type which would serve as an ancestor for all living races . . . this ancestral type spreading abroad in the world, exterminating the other early pleistocene types; all the evidence has gone against this supposition.

In contradistinction to Keith, it is more difficult to find out what prompted Hooton to change his mind about human phylogeny. In the early 1930s, Hooton (1931, 1935) envisioned human phylogeny as being characterized by a number of distinct side branches leading toward extinction (*Pithecanthropus, Eoanthropus, Sinanthropus*, Neandertals). He also held that the human stem leading to the living human races appeared as early as the mid-Pliocene on the basis of a number of allegedly ancient and modern-looking specimens (see Chapter 5 and Figure 7). In 1937, Hooton maintained his view of human phylogeny, although by that time a major figure like Keith had retreated from it, and although the antiquity of modern-looking fossil discoveries in East Africa (Kanam and Kanjera) could not be confirmed:

> Nevertheless, I am of the opinion that Dr. Leakey was probably right and that he did actually find the ancestor of modern man in an Early Pleistocene deposit, but that he was unfortunate . . . in not securing [the] evidence which is essential for the proof of such critical cases . . . For many years I have adhered to Sir Arthur Keith's view that *Homo sapiens* is geologically very ancient and did not spring from the Neanderthaloids or from any other known archaic and apelike form of fossil man. Sir Arthur has been wavering in that opinion for the past few years, and now he seems to be in full retreat from his palaeontological Verdun . . . I think that Keith's former position is still tenable . . . I am sitting in it. (Hooton, 1937: 97)

In 1940, Hooton still maintained a clear distinction between the "ape-like" hominid types (*Pithecanthropus, Sinanthropus*, and the Neandertals), which he apparently regrouped in a single evolutionary stem, and the ancient and modern-looking ancestors of *Homo sapiens*. By then, Hooton (1940: 57–85) declared that the question about the great antiquity of a modern type of man had been answered definitely in the affirmative, following the discovery of the Swanscombe remains of Middle

Pleistocene period in England in 1935. Following the discoveries at Mount Carmel during the 1930s, Hooton still denied the possibility of an evolution of *Homo sapiens* from the Neandertals, although he now recognized that an early hybridization between members of the *Homo sapiens* and Neandertal species had occurred.

By 1946, Hooton's view of human phylogeny had changed significantly (see Figure 21).[2] Now, numerous human fossils were directly or very nearly related to the stems leading to the living human races. Hooton (1946: 410–414) presented an evolutionary scheme in which numerous instances of hybridization occurred among various stems. *Pithecanthropus*, Solo, and Wadjak were related to the living Australians. Broken Hill was a side branch of a stem leading to the living Bushmen (*San*) through the Florisbad and Boskop remains. *Sinanthropus* was presented as the ancestor of the Neandertal type; portions of the latter type went extinct while others were absorbed and swamped by a dominant *Homo sapiens* type. For Hooton, all these stems derived directly or secondarily from the main Pliocene *Homo sapiens* trunk that led directly to the basic "white" stock through *Eoanthropus*, Swanscombe, Galley Hill, and Combe Capelle. In this new view of human phylogeny, Hooton managed to preserve some aspects of his previous one: (1) that *Homo sapiens* is not, formerly speaking, derived from the Neandertals, because only a portion of the latter interbreed with the former; (2) that the *Homo sapiens* type, through the *Eoanthropus* and Swanscombe segment, is of great antiquity. Yet, generally speaking, Hooton's view of human phylogeny was no longer characterized by several side branches evolving toward extinction.

It is difficult to pinpoint exactly what made Hooton change his mind about human phylogeny. It seems reasonable to think that the discoveries made at Mount Carmel in the 1930s broke the chasm that Hooton maintained between the "apelike" (*Pithecanthropus, Sinanthropus*, Nendertals) and the "modern-looking" (*Eoanthropus*, Swanscombe, Kanam, Kanjera) hominid types until at least 1940. Once this evolutionary chasm has been filled, it becomes possible to speculate that the establishment of a possible link between *Pithecanthropus* and the living Australians, through intermediate fossils, was rendered more acceptable and convincing to Hooton after 1940. What seems almost sure is that fossil discoveries made in the 1930s created a great impression on Hooton (1946: vii): "I think it is safe to assert that the finds of fossil man since 1931 exceed in number and importance all that had been made in the whole period before that date."

PARALLEL AND LINEAR HYPOTHESES

It took Keith and Hooton a number of important fossil discoveries to change their mind about human phylogeny. By so doing, they joined an increasing number of scholars for whom most, if not all, hominid fossils are related to the living human races. Besides Keith and Hooton, it is not entirely clear if most scholars who embraced this conception in the 1930s and after did it expressly because of the new fossil discoveries made in the 1930s or simply because they were convinced that this view was alreay well-founded. After all, it will be remembered that this tradition of interpretation has deep historical roots (see Chapters 3 and 5). What is clear, however, is that this conception now received considerable support from the hominid fossil discoveries made during the 1930s, thus continuing to bolster this very tradition of interpretation by adding an empirical robustness to it. Indeed, a new dimension was added to this tradition with the rise of a very broad spectrum of phylogenetic hypotheses in which hominid fossils were linked to the living human races.

This new and broad conception of human phylogeny became possible in part because the linear hypotheses and the parallel hypotheses met and fused under a single tradition. Whereas the linear hypotheses had been closely associated to the multilinear hypotheses during the previous time period, the former now became a natural ally to the parallel hypotheses. This directly contributed to the rise of a spectrum of closely related phylogenetic hypotheses; a spectrum that was broader than ever. The close proximity of the linear and the parallel hypotheses in the 1930s constitutes one of the founding blocks of the modern research structure in paleoanthropology that is still in place today.

Polymorphic contributors. We have seen that there has been more than one way to promote the view that all or most of the human fossils are related to the living human races (see Chapter 5). One of them, held by Verneau and Pycraft in the first decades of the twentieth century, recognized that at least two distinct morphological types—one ape-like and one human-like—simultaneously contributed to give rise to different portions of humanity. This viewpoint was still championed in the 1930s and 1940s by scholars like Marett, Coon, and Paterson. This was also the new view expounded by Hooton in 1946 (see above). For those scholars, the more modern-looking strain in the fossil record constituted the most important contributor to humanity, although it was by no means the only one. It was held that intermixture played an active part in this conception of human evolution.

Marett's (1936) view of human phylogeny largely stemmed from his investigation of how mineral changes in the soil and the resulting vegetable food could have influenced human evolution. He insisted that mineral deficiencies in living organisms, beside causing pathologies, also led to cases in which the size and the rate of growth in animals had been altered. On that basis, Marett argued that the reduced bone growth of the modern human type was the direct result of a selection for an economy of bone-forming material. He insisted that the robust skeletal development of Palaeoanthropic hominids (Neandertals and other earlier robust hominids) has been caused by a former abundance of bone-forming material. The variation in the rate of metabolic and developmental change, continued Marett, constituted the most important aspect of the difference between the Palaeanthropic and the Neanthropic (modern-looking) strains, although numerous racial admixtures have occurred between them. Indeed, admixtures of these strains explained certain associations of bodily characters in the living humans.

Marett assumed that the earliest hominids were developed out of large hominoid apes during the changes of habitats in Central Asia during the Miocene. He believed that a single and short period of severe mineral shortage, which required a rapid physiological response, precipitated the large anatomical change from ape to human, by selecting for a small size, an erect posture, the expansion of the brain and skull, and the loss of body hair. Marett's picture of early hominids is that of a small, short-limbed, and achondroplastic figure—virtually a pygmy. Not unlike Verneau and Pycraft before him, Marett held that two distinct evolutionary stems (Neanthropic and Palaeoanthropic) were at the base of all the living human races (see Figure 22). His view of human phylogeny can best be summarized from his own words (Marett, 1936: 194–197, 214):

> [T]he known [hominid] fossils are probably all the products of unions between more specialized and unknown species or sub-species . . . The [Neanthropic and southern] strain may be held responsible for most of the genes now predominant in modern man . . . The stock adapted to cold and aridity [Palaeoanthropic] would tend to develop . . . a massive skeleton . . . The Southern stock, on the other hand, would tend towards small size of fine bone . . . [I]t remains necessary to remember the possibility of a Proto-neanthropic inheritance having contributed towards the development of all or any of the extinct forms. This will be definitely suggested in the case of the large-brained Piltdown and Neanderthal races; and it cannot be altogether ruled out even in the case of such small-brained specimens as Sinanthropus and Pithecanthropus . . . On this theory a complete Modern Man, with a chin and thin long legs, and probably with a 'smooth' high-vaulted skull, must be presumed to have been already in existence in the late Pliocene or early Pleistocene.[3]

In Marett's (1936: 209–213) view, the evolutionary history of humankind is filled with extinct races such as Piltdown, Neandertal man in Europe, Broken Hill, and possibly both *Pithecanthropus* and *Sinanthropus*. However, for him, all the hominid fossils discovered were inserted either in the Palaeoanthropic or in the Neanthropic stocks; stocks which went through numerous interbreeding during the Pleistocene period. On this view, both stocks have lived in coexistence throughout the Pleistocene and contributed to various degrees to the rise of the living human races (Marett, 1936: 217–235).

Like several scholars before him, Coon's (1939: 1–3) phylogenetic view recognized two distinct hominid stems which contributed to the living humans:

> During the Pleistocene one species, at least, had developed in the manner of a foetalized terrestrial ape, and it is that species which carries today the main stem of *Homo sapiens*. Other species, including the fossil men of Java, of Peking, and *Homo neanderthalensis*, had developed at the same time into a heavier [form] . . . [T]hese non-foetalized species did not wholly die out . . . at least one of them was absorbed into the main human stem . . . [T]he present races of Europe are derived from a blend of (A) food-producing peoples from Asia and Africa, of basically Mediterranean racial form, with (B), the descendants of intergracial and glacial food-gatherers, produced in turn by a blending of basic *Homo sapiens*, related to the remote ancestor of the Mediterraneans, with some non-*sapiens* species of general Neanderthaloid form. The actions and interactions of environment, selection, migration, and human culture upon the various entities within this amalgam, have produced the white race in its present complexity.

Coon dated the appearance of a fully *sapiens* hominid type in the Old World to the Middle Pleistocene, as seen in the remains of Galley Hill, Piltdown (excluding the jaw), Swanscombe, and possibly also by Clichy, Kanam, Kanjera, Olmo, and Moulin-Quignon. When turning to non-*sapiens* fossil specimens—*Pithecanthropus, Sinanthropus, Homo* (*soloensis, heidelbergensis, neanderthalensis, rhodesiensis*)—Coon evaluated that most of them were of Middle Pleistocene age, thus apparently excluding the possibility that this heavy browridged group of non-*sapiens* could have evolved directly into the earliest known form of *Homo sapiens*. However, Coon was inclined to believe that these non-*sapiens* forms contributed to the living human stock through admixtures with genuinely modern forms.[4] For instance, Coon recognized that the Neandertals of western Europe constituted a primitive and marginal group of that species, whereas the specimens of the Middle East (Galilee and Mount Carmel) showed beyond doubt that this Neandertal strain did not become extinct, but survived into the genetic stock of the modern humans. On the basis of the case of the Neandertal strain exclusively, Coon (1939: 28) was now inquisitive about similar occurrences in other regions of the Old World:

> We now know that the Neanderthal strain did not become extinct, but passed over into the genetic stock of modern man. If this occurred once, it could have occurred a number of times. The field is now open to discover survivals of non-*sapiens* accretions in modern races in other parts of the earth. This privilige must, however, be used with caution.

Eventually, Coon himself went on to identify numerous non-*sapiens* contributors to the living human races in the 1950s and 1960s (see Chapter 9).

Like Marett and Coon, Paterson (1940) recognized two main polymorphic stems contributing to the rise of living humans. Paterson submitted the idea that just as the cultural development showed mixture of cultures, so have the various hominid stocks in the Pleistocene periods. Because of such admixtures, Paterson held that the classification of the human Pleistocene fossils could not follow the normal zoological method. Instead, he suggested the application of a pedigree system of cross-bred domesticated animals. He adopted a nomenclature in which hominids of the Lower Pleistocene were classified in two distinct subfamilies (*Hominінae* and *Anthropinae*) and those of the Middle Pleistocene in three distinct genera (*Homo*, *Palaeoanthropus* and *Pithecanthropus*). He then classified all the hominid species of the Upper Pleistocene within the genus *Homo*, while the living forms were all included as varieties of *Homo sapiens*.

Translating this system of classification into a phylogeny, Paterson (1940) divided his tree into two main stems descended from a common ancestor in the Lower Pleistocene (see Figure 23).[5] The modern-looking *Homininae* stem linked Piltdown in the early Middle Pleistocene to the living Mediterranean stock, through the intermediary of remains such as Swanscombe, Kanjera, Bury St. Edmunds, Galley Hill, and Combe Capelle. The second main stem, the primitive-looking *Anthropinae* stem, was divided into three lines: (1) The Palaeoanthropoid line linked some living forms to early Pleistocene ones through Neandertaloid forms (Mauer, Steinheim, Tabun,

Krapina, etc.); (2) the Pithecanthropoid line linked some living forms to early Pleistocene ones through fossil remains such as *Homo modjokertensis*, *Pithecanthropus erectus* and *Homo soloensis*; and (3) the Sinanthropoid line went extinct in the Middle Pleistocene. In Paterson's view, most of these stems or lines mixed during the Middle or the Upper Pleistocene in order to give rise to the living human races. This being said, he insisted that, of all the lines, the modern-looking *Homininae* one contributed more to the living humans than the others.

Polymorphic contributors and evolutionary stages. Another group of scholars, including Poisson and Gates, believed that the evolutionary history of humankind is also to be understood in terms of modern-looking as well as primitive-looking ancestors contributing genealogically to living human races, but with the addition of the concept of evolutionary stages. For these scholars, the double recognition of the concepts of polymorphic ancestors and of evolutionary stages was not contradictory, although it must be recognized that their views of human phylogeny paid only lip service to the concept of evolutionary stages. In contradistinction to Marett, Coon, and Paterson, Poisson, and Gates apparently believed that it is the more primitive or "ape-like" stems which contributed the most to the ancestry of the living human races rather than the more modern-looking ones. In fact, it is perhaps easier to be committed to the notion of evolutionary stages in human evolution if convinced that the most important contributors to living humans are not modern-looking in conformation. At the same time, Poisson and Gates were, perhaps, only committed superficially to this notion of evolutionary stages because they recognized several distinct polymorphic stems in human phylogeny. Not unlike Marett, Coon, and Paterson, Poisson and Gates also recognized that interbreeding had occurred between the various polymorphic ancestors during the process of the rise of the living humans.

In Poisson's (1939) view of human phylogeny, early hominid forms were originally characterized by a marked geographical uniformity in their morphology, only to diverge from one another and reach the actual racial differentiation. Poisson also recognized that human phylogeny was characterized by a succession of three evolutionary stages: Anthropians, Hominians, Humans. Regarding the Pleistocene, Poisson identified at least three distinct and ancient hominid lineages: (1) the *Pithecanthropus–Homo soloensis*–Wadjak–Australians lineage; (2) the *Sinanthropus*–Mongolian lineage; and (3) the *Eoanthropus*–Galley Hill lineage. Also stemming from the *Pithecanthropus* type, some strains of the polymorphic Neandertal stem (which differed in Europe, Palestine, and Rhodesia) possibly gave rise to some living black races. Poisson judged the extinction of all the Neandertal strains to be unlikely. Turning to the peopling of Europe in the Upper Pleistocene, Poisson identified at least two distinct races. The first one, which Poisson conjectured might be related to the *Eoanthropus*–Galley Hill lineage, was the Cro-Magnon race. The second one, the Combe Capelle race, might somehow be related to the Neandertal strain and the "negro" races. According to Poisson, these two distinct racial types of prehistoric Europe contributed to the present races of Europe, although they were somewhat modified or diluted by later racial migrations coming into Europe.

In Gates's (1948: 4) conception of human phylogeny, "the old idea that man as we know him on the different continents diverged simultaneously from a single common ancestry is no longer tenable . . . [for] there have been multiple centers of man's evolution, involving again a certain amount of parallelism." In Gates's view, evolutionary parallelism has been a common phenomenon in the history of life. This, contended Gates, tallies well with the fact that mutations of organisms tend to occur in certain directions and not in others. For Gates, isolation in some areas and crossing in others have both played their part throughout human evolution, not to mention local evolution. Gates (1944) saw the evolution of humankind has being characterized by three more or less successive evolutionary grades, which he considered to be successive genera (*Pithecanthropus*, *Palaeoanthropus*, and *Homo*), each being represented by several species. On this thinking, he recognized five living human species: *Homo australicus*, *H. capensis*, *H. africanus*, *H. mongoloideus*, and *H. caucasicus*. Apparently, Gates traced back the origins of all the hominids either to the dryopithecine or the australopithecine group or both of them (Gates, 1948: 72–73, 78–79).[6] In Gates's (1948: 141–142) conception of human phylogeny, human evolution was characterized by two main hominid stems which had occasionally crossed:

> . . . there have been two more or less independent streams in human evolution. One of them began with heavy brow ridges and occipital tori, as in Pithecanthropus. These were gradually reduced to the condition seen in the Australian aborigines . . . The other line, beginning with Eoanthropus and Kanam man, evolved without these heavy skull ornamentations, but has hybridized from time to time with representatives of the other line, such as Neanderthal man.

Within these two main hominid stems, Gates identified a number of evolutionary lines. Stemming from the *Pithecanthropus* type, Gates saw at least three lines:

1. *Pithecanthropus–Javanthropus soloensis–Homo wadjakensis*–Talgaï skull–living Australians;
2. *Africanthropus njarensis–A. rhodesiensis*–Florisbad–*Homo capensis*–Hottentots;
3. *Sinanthropus pekinensis*–Amerindians and Eskimos.

Stemming from the *Eoanthropus* type and the Kanjera man, Gates recognized two evolutionary lines:

1. *Eoanthropus*–Galley Hill–London skull; and
2. *Homo kanamensis*–Mount Carmel remains.[7]

Although not all the evolutionary lines led to living humans in Gates's scheme, most of them did directly or indirectly (interbreeding).

Several nonpolymorphic ancestors and evolutionary stages. Weidenreich proposed yet another interpretation out of the spectrum of hypotheses linking the hominid fossils and the living human races. On the one hand, Weidenreich agreed with Poisson and Gates in recognizing distinct evolutionary lineages leading to living humans as well as evolutionary stages in human evolution. On the other hand, Weidenreich believed that the living human races were not descended from polymorphic contributors. By so doing, he excluded from human evolution the notion of ancient and modern-looking representatives, so that all the living human races had evolved from distinct ancient and ape-like contributors. This view contrasts with those of the several authors just reviewed who insisted on ancient modern-looking representatives in human evolution. This permitted Weidenreich to put a greater stress than Poisson and Gates on the concept of evolutionary stages in human evolution. In fact, Weidenreich (1940, 1943a, 1943b, 1946a, 1947a) explained the morphological disparity between all the evolutionary lines at each evolutionary stage not by polymorphic contributors, as already alluded to, but rather by differential rates of evolution in each main lineage leading to living humans. Weidenreich (1940: 380-382) explained his conception of human phylogeny in the following terms:

> While man was passing through different phases, each one of which was characterized by certain features common to all individuals of the same stage, there existed, nevertheless, within such community different types . . . [which can be] rated as regional differentiation [corresponding] to the racial dissimilarities of present man. . . .

Weidenreich explained the morphological and the chronological discrepancies in the fossil record this way. In his view, human evolution was not going on simultaneously everywhere but was occurring at various paces. Weidenreich recognized three successive evolutionary stages through which passed all hominid forms: *Archanthropinae* (Prehominids); *Paleoanthropinae* (Neandertals); and *Neoanthropinae* (modern humans). Human evolution is viewed as being characterized by an orthogenetic trend, that is, by a unidirectional evolution devoid of important deviations (Weidenreich, 1947b). Within this succession of stages, Weidenreich identified at least four human branches evolving more or less in parallel in different geographical areas (Weidenreich, 1943a: 246–256). In the first branch, Weidenreich linked *Pithecanthropus–Homo soloensis*–Wadjak–the living Australians. Weidenreich (1943a: 249–250) insisted that this "does not mean, of course, that I believe all the Australians of today can be traced back to *Pithecanthropus* or that they are the sole descendants of the *Pithecanthropus–Homo soloensis* line." In the second branch characterized by a yet undiscovered *Paleoanthropinae* stage, Weidenreich linked *Sinanthropus*–Choukoutien Upper Cave–the living Mongolians. Again, he mentioned that this "does not mean that modern Mongols derived exclusively from *Sinanthropus* nor that *Sinanthropus* did not give origin to other races" (Weidenreich, 1943a: 253–254). In the third and fourth branches, of which no *Archanthropinae* forms were yet known, Weidenreich linked, on the one hand, Rhodesian Man–Florisbad–Boskop–the living South Africans, and on the other hand, Tabun–Skhul–Cro–Magnon–the living Eurasians.[8]

According to Weidenreich (1946b), human evolution entirely occurred within the limits of a single evolving species, although this species has been divided in several distinct races since the mid-Pliocene period; races characterized by an obvious tendency to exchange acquired features. Weidenreich held that the hominid and the hominoid ape stems diverged from one another at an early stage (see also Chapters 7 and 8).[9]

Linear hypotheses and evolutionary stages. At the other end of the spectrum of hypotheses connecting the hominid fossils and the living human races were the linear hypotheses. From a certain perspective, the conception of Weidenreich that has just been reviewed constitutes a form of linear hypothesis, as each distinct evolutionary line imperatively went through evolutionary stages which were common to all the other lines. This reasoning can be pushed to the extreme by arguing that all the evolutionary lines are fused together in a common and widely geographically distributed thread with some regional varieties; varieties all going through the same evolutionary stages. This argument will be promoted.

At this stage of our inquiry, it is perhaps not out of place to ask why the linear hypotheses are no longer as closely associated with the multilinear hypotheses as by the past. It will be remembered that scholars like Dubois, Keith (before 1912), Schwalbe, Mahoudeau, and Hrdlicka all promoted, during the first third of the twentieth century, linear hypotheses (see Chapter 5). Their views were based on a handful of fossils scattered in time and almost exclusively restricted, geographically speaking, to Europe. This permitted envisioning only a partial and thin thread binding the living humans from an ape ancestor. The empirical fragility of this position perhaps explains why it has been easy to change a linear hypothesis into a multilinear one in the 1910s and 1920s by simply arguing that a number of fossil discoveries did not conform to the anticipated evolutionary sequence of an assumed thread binding humans and other primates. Apparently, the scholars promoting linear hypotheses prior to 1930 were lacking a robust empirical basis which came only with the hominid fossil discoveries made during the 1930–1940 decade. It is such discoveries that permitted the meeting of parallel and linear hypotheses. Indeed, these new fossil recoveries opened up two important possiblities: (1) the extension into the past of the genealogical roots of the main living human races, thus recognizing evolutionary stages common to all these evolutionary lines; (2) the establishment of evolutionary stages on the basis of fossil discoveries now spread more evenly in time as well as in space throughout the Old World, thus establishing a much thicker and more robust evolutionary thread binding the living humans and the other primates. The views of von Eickstedt and Weinert examplified, from two different perspectives, the new dimensions added to the linear hypotheses.

For von Eickstedt (1934 [1950]), the evolutionary history of humankind is best envisioned as a dynamic and complex racial process involving migration, transformation, replacement and fusion.[10] In a sense, this conception of human evolution is not unlike that of Dixon and Taylor already reviewed in Chapter 5. At the heart of von Eickstedt's view is the notion that crustal movements and climatic shifts in Central Asia constituted favorable conditions for the appearance of ever more progressive hominid forms expanding in waves to the edges of the Old World from their Asian cradle, thus destroying or pushing more primitive forms to the periphery or into isolated areas:

> [The marginal forms of primal men] were capable of penetrating into and even through the forest belts, when in the oldest part of the species' dwelling-space [Central Asia]

> the process of differentiation had moved on to produce . . . yet more active and resistant races. And finally, no less significant than the capacity of adaptation to climate and economy has been the fertility of the early Hominidae, which is considerable, and attached to no particular periods . . . These marginal forms, possessing as they did the lesser intellectual and physical resistivity, sustained at last heavy destruction only from members of their own species who had attained a higher degree of differentiation . . . Pushed back by the major-races who surpass them in population, intellect, and impetus, today they lie round about the region of distribution of these others like a slag-dump from the formative process of humanity . . . To this day they demonstrate in their lesser degree of differentiation the stages of developmental potentials once obtaining, and which the higher races have left behind. (Von Eickstedt, 1950: 504)

Von Eickstedt (1934: 84) derived the humans from a common ancestor shared with the chimpanzee. From this early generalized form, he (1950: 505–506) conceived the rise of humankind as rapidly presenting geographical distinctions:

> Now, in every animal species the distinctive kind of life-expression results in a distinctive kind of anatomical construction; and it could not have been otherwise with the Prehominidae. Therefore later humanity fell apart into physiomorphic groups, into races, even before it had actually become "humanity". This in no wise forbids our placing at its root, perhaps as far back as the Miocene or Pliocene . . . a basic form that was little specialized, [and] relatively homogeneous . . . But this form could not have resembled even remotely . . . the physical picture of modern "humanity"; nor even the Prehominidae, as these demonstrate by virtue of a differentiation attested by the finds of Trinil, Heidelberg, and Peking [that is *Pithecanthropus*, Mauer and *Sinanthropus* respectively].

Von Eickstedt recognized the succession in time of at least three main phyletic outbursts or successive stages from an assumed Asian cradle: *Prehominidae* or *Praehomo*, *Homo primigenius*, and *Homo recens*. Each of these outbursts was presumably being represented by both primitive as well as progressive phyletic segments. From a general perspective, von Eickstedt's scheme binds, genealogically speaking, all living and extinct hominid forms through this common Asian thread. For a better understanding of von Eickstedt's view, however, one needs to look more closely at his interpretation of the human fossil record in three geographical areas: Europe, southern Africa, and South Asia. However, the light thrown by von Eickstedt himself on the earliest known hominid fossils is rather dim, being restricted to the recognition of distinct geographical variants as seen in *Pithecanthropus*, Mauer, and *Sinanthropus*, although he alluded to the fact that connections existed between this first phyletic outburst and the following one (von Eickstedt, 1934: 346, 409–411). More light is cast on von Eickstedt's conception of human phylogeny by looking at the nature of the connections he established between the second (*Homo primigenius*) and the third (*Homo recens*) phyletic outbursts.

In Europe, the typical Neandertals of western Europe were judged not to be directly ancestral to modern European types, although a limited amount of interbreeding may have occurred between them. Von Eickstedt (1950: 490) stated that "[p]erhaps the limited reproductive capacity of species-bastards is precisely what explains the meager survival of Neanderthal traits in modern European man." In eastern Europe, however, the Neandertals which presented some attenuated traits established potential connections with the living Europeans. This was made possible either by a direct transformation of a form into another, or more probably by a metamorphosis through the encounter (interbreeding) of primitive types of modern races now extinct such as the Aurignac type. On this view, the Neanderthal–Aurignac–Cro-Magnon morphological series indicated the stages of development toward the living humans. The succession in time of such stages of development occurred, in part only, by direct local kinship, but more importantly by waves of invasions which stemmed from the common Asian thread. Von Eickstedt (1934: 338, 346, 415–426) made clear that he believed that the modern Europeans stemmed from ancient neanderthaloid-like forms.

In southern Africa, von Eickstedt recognized in Rhodesian man a neanderthaloid form which probably arrived quite early in Africa through a pre-neanderthaloid phase. The direct ancestors of the black races of Africa, the pre-"negroids", were themselves described as neanderthaloid-like forms. Von Eickstedt established a morphological parallel between the precedence in time of the Neandertal type on the Aurignac type in Europe, with the precedence of the Rhodesian man on the Cape-Flats type in southern Africa. Therefore, the modern-like (though still primitive and probably extinct) Cape-Flats type established a morphological series between Rhodesian man and the living human types in this region of the world, as seen in Boskop man, Strandloopers, Khoisands, Hottentots, and Bushmen (von Eickstedt, 1934: 347, 416, 580–590).

In South Asia, von Eickstedt recognized in Ngandong man (*Homo soloensis*) a neanderthaloid form, thus establishing again a morphological series with Ngandong man, Talgaï, Cohuna, Wadjak (a pre-Australian type), and the living Australians. The Australian type was described as a form which presented many similarities with the Aurignac type of Europe, although its conformation was judged to be less primitive. The recognition of more primitive types among living humans (i.e., Australians) by von Eickstedt is not surprising considering that he identified both primitive and progressive segments in each phyletic outburst. Von Eickstedt held that the primitive living human races of Oceania stemmed from a pre-neanderthaloid form, a form which arrived from Asia (von Eickstedt, 1934: 346, 416, 669–670, 768).

Weinert's linear hypothesis differs in nature from that of von Eickstedt. For Weinert (1938 [1939b], 1941 [1944]), the course of human evolution can be established by linking its known terminal forms (the living human races) to its allegedly single source of origin (an undiscovered late Pliocene hominoid form). Not only was this unknown form postulated to have its birthplace in Europe, but it was also proposed that it shared a common ancestry with the chimpanzee and the extinct *Dryopithecus*.[11] Weinert held that the monophyletic origins of humankind are clearly seen in the numerous traits binding together the ancient and the living human forms alike. Furthermore, he held that at all times the hominid stocks were capable of interbreeding. Based on this view, the evolutionary history of humankind from its outset is one of a single evolving and diversifying threads which resulted in the living human races. The quest to establish human phylogeny consisted, for Weinert, in the identification of the most ancient representatives to all living human races.

To achieve this task, Weinert surveyed the hominid fossil record in a chronological fashion by starting with the most ancient remains. In each geological period, Weinert asked if any fossil remains could be particularly linked to one or more living human races. He arrived at two conclusions: (1) Hominids were already spread throughout most of the Old World by the early Pleistocene; (2) the single hominid stem evolving throughout the Pleistocene period remained homogenous until it diversified quite late in the Pleistocene in order to give rise to the living human races. For Weinert, therefore, the evolution of humankind is essentially characterized by a succession of several stages. Weinert's earliest and most homogeneous stage was represented by the fossil remains of *Pithecanthropus*, *Sinanthropus*, *Africanthropus* and the Mauer jaw. Weinert included in a subsequent stage all the Neandertaloid remains. And last, all the modern-looking remains of a still later stage were regrouped in *Homo sapiens*. According to Weinert, the living human races could not be traced back to particular races of the Neanderthaloid stage, although this latter stage was already divided into a few broad geographical races, namely, *Homo neanderthalensis africanus*, *H. neanderthalensis asiaticus*, and *H. neanderthalensis europeus*. Whether or not all Neandertaloid groups transformed themselves into *Homo sapiens* was a moot question for Weinert, as long as it was recognized that the Neandertals are the ancestors of the living humans races.

Weinert's conception of human phylogeny implied that all the living human races had passed through the same evolutionary stages. However, this conception of human phylogeny did not prevent Weinert from holding that it was possible to recognize that the living Australians had a particular kinship with *Pithecanthropus* of Java through the intermediary of remains such as Ngandong (*Homo soloensis*) and Wadjak. In Weinert's (1944: 85–90) view, this did not mean that only the Australians could trace back their ancestry to *Pithecanthropus*, but rather that the former retained more traits from the latter than all the other living human races. By holding this view, Weinert managed to fuse the concept of a deep ancestry for the Australians (the only such instance in human phylogeny according to him) with the concept of common stages to all hominid forms.

MULTILINEAR HYPOTHESES

Undoubtedly, the hominid fossil discoveries made during the 1930–1940 decade gave a boost to the various hypotheses which established a genetic continuity between the hominid fossils and the living humans. However, during the 1935–1950 period, not everyone agreed with this view. The tradition which recognized that the human family tree had been characterized by several major extinct lineages—multilinear hypotheses—was maintained during this time period. Yet, proponents of multilinear hypotheses were somewhat on the defensive not least because Keith and eventually

Hooton had completely retreated from this viewpoint. Perhaps more importantly, however, proponents of multilinear hypotheses such as Boule, Vallois, Le Gros Clark, and maybe Leakey had to recognize, implicitly or explicitly, that the new empirical evidence recovered during the 1930s created some problems for their conception. They thus introduced a number of modifications to their multilinear hypotheses. This instigated a taxonomic compression or phylogenetic constriction of phylogenetic views: It was now recognized that the human family tree was not as bushy as previously expected. This created a profound effect on the field of paleoanthropology.

Starting with the 1930s, the human phylogenetic hypotheses, whether multilinear, parallel, or linear, started to blend more and more imperceptibly into one another, meaning that there were fewer differences between extreme options such as multilinear and linear hypotheses. The ease with which Keith and Hooton switched viewpoints makes clear that the cognitive gap between these various options was anything but insurmountable. In this new scientific context, the potential consensual basis for human phylogeny had considerably increased in the 1930s and 1940s. This generated a genuine coherence for the research on human phylogeny, thus solidly grounding one of the pillars of the modern research structure in paleoanthropology.

Proponents of multilinear hypotheses responded differently to the new empirical challenge of the 1930s. Remember that during the 1910s and 1920s, Boule held that the two distinct evolutionary trees leading to the living humans and the hominoid apes were both highly branched ones being characterized by numerous extinct branches not leading to living forms, among which *Pithecanthropus* and *Homo neanderthalensis* figured. At the time, Boule affiliated *Pithecanthropus* (and later *Sinanthropus*) not to the human stem but rather to the hominoid ape stem, although he recognized that it had evolved, in parallel, a number of human-like traits. When considering the human stem, Boule hypothesized at least two distinct and long separated lineages. The first lineage led to *Homo neanderthalensis*, possibly through *Homo heidelbergensis* (the Mauer jaw). The second lineage was considered to be truly ancestral to *Homo sapiens* and might have been represented at an early time by the Piltdown cranium (excluding the jaw).

Boule held to this conception until about the mid-1930s (Boule and Piveteau, 1935: 811–850). By 1937, however, Boule had modified his view (Boule, 1937; Boule and Vallois, 1946).[12] He still maintained that human phylogeny was characterized by two distinct and long separated lineages: the Neandertaloid stem evolving towards extinction and the other stem evolving towards the living human races, with possibly Piltdown and now Swanscombe as early representatives. However, he now displaced *Pithecanthropus* and *Sinanthropus* from the hominoid ape stem to the human stem (see Figure 24), and believed them to be probable ancestors of the Neandertaloid stem. Boule made clear that recent hominid fossil discoveries found in Australia, Java, and Africa showed that *Pithecanthropus* and *Sinanthropus* should be inserted into the human family tree (Boule and Vallois, 1946: 127–128).

For his part, Vallois (1927) once held that it was possible to recognize several distinct hominid stems evolving in parallel during the Pleistocene, such as the

Neandertals, *Eoanthropus*, and possibly Heidelberg man. In Vallois's view, therefore, at least one of these lineages was more ape-like while another was more human-like in conformation. It was held that a form approching the modern human type had already been established by the early Pleistocene period. At the time, Vallois contended that at least one hominid evolutionary stem (possibly more), the Neandertals, evolved toward extinction.

Vallois was to maintain this conception of human phylogeny throughout the 1930s and 1940s, although he later conceived that some of the stems previously thought to have been evolving toward extinction might after all have had some living representatives. For instance, in the mid-1930s Vallois (1935) was inclined to recognize only two polymorphic evolutionary stems evolving in parallel during the Pleistocene period. In one such stem, called *Homo neanderthalensis*, he included the Neandertals of Europe, the Galilee man (Palestine), the Rhodesian man, and the new discoveries of Java (*Homo soloensis* or *Javanthropus*). In the other stem, called *Homo sapiens*, Vallois included among its possible ancient representatives Piltdown man and fossils from Kenya (presumably Kanam and Kanjera). Whereas he had previously clearly excluded the Neandertals from the human ancestry, Vallois (1935) now left open the possibility of a transformation of a portion of the Neandertal stem into *Homo sapiens*, as seen in the transitional features of the Galilee specimen.

Furthermore, by the late 1940s and early 1950s Vallois recognized not two but at least three distinct hominid evolutionary stems evolving in parallel during the Pleistocene (Vallois, 1949a, 1949b, 1950; Boule and Vallois, 1952).[13] The third stem now recognized was represented in the Lower and Middle Pleistocene by the various forms of the *Pithecanthropus* type (*P. erectus*, *P. robustus*, *Meganthropus*, and *Sinanthropus*) and the Solo type. In Vallois's new view, all these hominid forms went through an adaptive radiation which resulted in numerous extinctions, with the exception perhaps of the line leading to Solo man. Although Vallois apparently doubted that the Solo line could have directly contributed to the living humans, he nonetheless conceded that the hypothesis of its extinction was premature and uncomfirmed as yet. For him, Solo man belonged to a group of Asian Neandertals that was not as isolated from the modern human type as the classic European Neandertals were. It seems that Vallois was ready to recognize, implicitly, that some living humans indirectly sprang from this Asian evolutionary stem, perhaps through a sort of "pre-Neandertal" stage. As for the Neandertal stem itself, which extended back to the Lower Pleistocene as seen in Mauer jaw, Vallois now confirmed that if its more recent and specialized portion left no descendants (the classic Neanderthals), it was far from impossible to believe that more ancient and generalized representatives, called Preneandertals (Steinheim), had transformed themselves into *Homo sapiens* through the intermediary of the Palestine remains. In the second hominid stem recognized by Vallois represented by individuals approching the modern human type, the fossils of Fontéchevade and Swanscombe of the Middle Pleistocene were added to Piltdown of the Lower Pleistocene. This lineage, now called *Presapiens*, was believed to be a continuous one.

According to Vallois, the unilinear stages through which humankind had allegedly passed (Prehominids, Neandertal, and *Homo sapiens*) were, in reality, different portions of several lineages evolving in parallel during the Pleistocene. Vallois's (1949b: 359) view of human phylogeny is well-summarized by his own words:

> [T]he family Hominidae doubtless rapidly produced several phyla which evolved in parallel, giving out branches of which certain ones became extinct more or less quickly . . . Several of them, perhaps, contributed to the formation of Homo sapiens, whose races would therefore have a much more ancient origin than is generally supposed.

In Vallois's recent view, it is clear that the *Presapiens* were not the only contributors to the living human races. The constriction of Vallois's human phylogenetic hypothesis continued in the early 1950s. Indeed, all the parallel evolutionary lines he recognized were now more frequently pointing toward the direction of the various living human races, although they did not necessarily all contribute to their rise (Vallois, 1952).[14]

Like Boule and Vallois, Le Gros Clark also eventually presented a view of human phylogeny with less ramifications and extinct evolutionary lines than previously. For instance, in the mid-1930s Le Gros Clark (1935, 1936) held that human evolutionary history, like the one of the other primates, was characterized by several branches evolving in parallel. When considering human phylogeny, Le Gros Clark (1935: 5) wrote:

> [The most archaic forms of hominids] are represented by *Pithecanthropus, Sinanthropus* and *Eoanthropus*. In view of the discovery that a modern type of Man apparently existed in Africa very early in the Pleistocene times [presumably Kanam and Kanjera], however, it may be doubted whether these other fossils bear any close relation to the evolutionary development of *Homo*.

At that time, Le Gros Clark was apparently inclined to put *Pithecanthropus, Sinanthropus,* and *Eoanthropus* on extinct side lines. As far as the Neandertals were concerned, he insisted that they must have arisen late in the Pleistocene from a stock akin to *Homo sapiens*.

After 1940, however, Le Gros Clark (1940, 1945, 1946a) changed his mind and now promoted a less ramified human phylogeny. This change of heart is apparently related to the realization that many fossil discoveries showed that hominid fossil groups presented substantial variability which made it possible to identify a rough evolutionary line or trend going from the earliest pithecanthropines to the living humans (e.g., Le Gros Clark, 1939a, 1940).[15] Le Gros Clark now recognized that the *Pithecanthropus* group (comprising also *Sinanthropus* and possibly *Africanthropus*), which evolved into the generalized Neandertaloid type, provided the basis for the development of the later human types. At this juncture, two separate evolutionary lines developed: one toward the collateral and extinct Neandertal branch (including Rhodesian and Solo men) and the other toward *Homo sapiens* through Swanscombe man.

It is clear that Boule, Vallois, and Le Gros Clark were now more cautious about their defense of a multilinear hypothesis. The case of L.S.B. Leakey is more difficult to assess. Leakey (1934, 1948) held that hominid forms of the Pleistocene which were characterized by massive browridges, such as *Pithecanthropus*, *Sinanthropus*, and all the Neandertaloid ones (Europe, Palestine, and Rhodesia), represented distinct lineages part of a single hominid stem which evolved towards extinction. This stem was called *Palaeoanthropidae*. On the *Neoanthropidae* stem which evolved into the main races of *Homo sapiens*, Leakey recognized as early ancestors in East Africa the Kanam jaw of the Lower Pleistocene and the Kanjera skull of the Middle Pleistocene. Leakey (1934) saw in Piltdown man an even earlier side branch of this stem leading to the living humans.[16] In Leakey's view, the *Palaeoanthropidae* and *Neoanthropidae* stems shared a common ancestor as early as in the early Miocene.[17]

Throughout the 1930s and 1940s, Leakey maintained that numerous hominid lineages evolved towards extinction. However, he did so not without ambiguity. In one instance, Leakey (1953: 186) stated:

> . . . in this chapter we will deal with the extinct types of man; specialized side branches from the stock which gave rise to *Homo sapiens*, which have no descendants living in the world today. In my original edition of *Adam's Ancestors* [of 1934] I regarded the majority of these extinct types as members of a distinct sub-family, the *Palaeoanthropida*e, which broke away from the stock which gave rise to *Homo* possibly as far back as the Miocene. I treated Peking man, Java man, and the Neanderthaloids as all belonging to this sub-family, more closely related to each other than to man as we know him today. In this I believe that I was wrong. I think that the more likely interpretation in the light of present-day knowledge is that all of these extinct types, as well as some others, are really nothing but various aberrant and over-specialized branches that broke away *at different times* from the main stock leading to *Homo*. [The italics are not mine]

This passage seems to suggest that Leakey now recognized that the human family tree was not as ramified as he first thought. Apparently, he no longer believed that the human family tree was divided into two main stems long separated, but rather that the various extinct branches broke away from the main stock leading to modern humans, each at a different time as he insisted. This view would suggest that the empirical input of the hominid fossil discoveries made in the 1930s forced Leakey to bring the massive browridges types such as *Pithecanthropus*, *Sinanthropus*, and the Neandertaloids closer to the stem leading to living humans. However, in the same book of 1953 Leakey also restated his previous view of 1934 in the following words:

> . . . I believe that the evidence suggests a major division at least as early as the Middle Pliocene and perhaps earlier, with one branch leading up to *Homo sapiens* races of today via Kanam man, and Kanjera and Swanscombe, etc., with the other leading to the stock represented by Java man, the Mauer jaw, and *Meganthropus*, in the early stages, and by Neanderthal man, Eyasie man [*Africanthropus*], Rhodesian man, and Solo man as end-products just before extinction. (Leakey, 1953: 212)[18]

This latter view of Leakey was further substantiated by a phylogenetic tree. If this corresponded to Leakey's view of human phylogeny in 1953, it would mean that the fossil discoveries made in the 1930s were simply incorporated into his previous tree without creating any impact on his view. It is not possible here to resolve this apparent ambiguity in Leakey's conception of human phylogeny in 1953, except perhaps to mention that by the 1960s Leakey favored a significantly constricted hominid evolutionary tree (see Chapter 9).

CONCLUSION

The nature of the research on human phylogeny was profoundly modified in the 1930s and 1940s. Suffice to say for the moment that the new empirical input of the 1930s instigated a constriction of the hominid phylogenetic trees (other changes are discussed in Chapter 9). At last, the human fossil record had a genuine and major impact on the entire human phylogenetic debate. Never in the history of the field of paleoanthropology, before or after, will the hominid fossil discoveries contribute to determining to such an extent the orientation of the future debates. Two independent events led to the constriction of the human phylogenetic hypotheses during that time period.

In the first event, the polyphyletic hypotheses were entirely abandoned. This powerfully contributed to a simplification of the debates on human phylogeny by centering them around multilinear, parallel, and linear hypotheses exclusively. Yet, more than just a period of simplification, the demise of the polyphyletists' thesis permitted the anchoring of one of the pillars at the base of the modern research structure in paleoanthropology: the unity of humankind (e.g., Delisle, 2004). With the refutation of the polyphyletic thesis, the spectrum of scientifically defensible hypotheses about human phylogeny was considerably reduced. In other words, the playground for paleoanthropologists' phylogenetic proposals had been substantially reduced by being much better cirscumscribed than in the past. Future generations of scholars had to play within these tightened boundaries as far as human phylogeny was concerned. But in addition to a better defined area of research, investigations on human phylogeny became a more coherent area too.

If the downfall of the polyphyletic hypotheses constituted the first constriction event in the hominid research area, the constriction of the multilinear hypotheses constituted the second one. By being less ramified, the new multilinear hypotheses were closer in idea to other phylogenetic hypotheses, that is, the parallel and linear views. This significantly closed the gap that separated all the human phylogenetic hypotheses. This instituted a relatively coherent spectrum of hypotheses grading more or less insensibly into one another. The breakdown of the relative barriers which separated the various kinds of hypotheses certainly contributed to facilitate the changing of viewpoints, thus explaining perhaps how scholars like Keith and Hooton abandoned so easily their original multilinear hypotheses in favor of parallel ones (see also Chapter 11).

This newly gained coherence in the hominid research area gave rise to a robust scientific framework which contributed to the establishment of the modern research structure in paleoanthropology. Interestingly, the coherence and robustness of the hominid fossil record was such in the 1930s and 1940s that it also created an impact on questions pertaining to humankind's place among the primates. By that time, the quest to both establish humankind's place among the primates and human phylogeny proper represented research areas that were less isolated from one another. This is again perhaps best demonstrated in the 1930s by the fall of the polyphyletic thesis. The critical mass of hominid fossil discoveries made in the 1930s demonstrated convincingly the unity of humankind, thus blocking the way to polyphyletic viewpoints which involved not only human forms but also other primate species. No doubt, the stage was set for the human fossil record to occasionally impact directly on the debates concerned with humankind's place among the primates.

NOTES

1. See Keith's new hominid phylogenetic tree in *A New Theory of Human Evolution* (New York: Philosophical Library, 1949), p. 159.
2. See Hooton's new hominid phylogenetic tree in *Up from the Ape*, revised edition (New York: Macmillan, 1946), p. 413.
3. For an approximation of Marett's view of human phylogeny see his *Race, Sex, and Environment: A Study of Mineral Deficiency in Human Evolution* (London: Hutchinson, 1936), pp. 142 and 227.
4. See Coon's phylogenetic tree in *The Races of Europe* (New York: Macmillan, 1939), p. 290.
5. See Paterson's hominid phylogenetic tree in "Geology and Early Man," *Nature*, 146 (1940), p. 50.
6. See Gates's primate phylogenetic tree in *Human Ancestry From a Genetical Point of View* (Cambridge: Harvard University Press, 1948), p. 56.
7. See Gates's hominid phylogenetic tree in *Human Ancestry From a Genetical Point of View* (Cambridge: Harvard University Press, 1948), p. 161.
8. See Weidenreich's diagram of human phylogeny in *Apes, Giants and Man* (Chicago: University of Chicago Press, 1946), p. 30.
9. See Weidenreich's primate tree in *Apes, Giants and Man* (Chicago: University of Chicago Press, 1946), p. 24.
10. E. von Eickstedt, *Rassenkunde und Rassengeschichte der Menschheit* (Stuttgart: F. Enke, 1934). A small part of this book has been translated into English. See E. von Eickstedt, "The Science and History of the Human Races," in E.W. Count (ed.), *This Is Race: An Anthology Selected from the International Literature on the Races of Man* (New York: Henry Schuman, 1950), pp. 489–514.
11. H. Weinert, *Entstehung der Menschenrassen* (Stuttgart: F. Enke, 1938). This book was translated into French as H. Weinert, *L'homme préhistorique: des préhumains aux races actuelles* (Paris: Payot, 1939). The second German edition of 1941 was also translated into French in 1944. I used here the two French editions.
12. It should be noted that Boule died in 1942. While the third edition of *Les hommes fossiles: éléments de paléontologie humaine* (Paris: Masson, 1946) had been completed by Vallois, it was made clear by Vallois himself in the Foreword of the book that it is Boule who made the changes in the first eight chapters between 1934 and 1939. Only those chapters are considered here, as they represent Boule's last view on human phylogeny.
13. It should be noted that although the name of Boule still figures on this edition, it had been reworked substantially by Vallois after Boule's death in 1942. In that sense, the 4th edition of *Les hommes fossiles: éléments de paléontologie humaine* (Paris: Masson, 1952) represents well Vallois's view of human phylogeny.
14. Compare Vallois's phylogenetic diagrams in "The Fontéchevade Fossil Men," *American Journal of Physical Anthropology*, 7 (1949), p. 355 and in "Monophyletism and Polyphyletism in Man," *South African Journal of Science*, 49 (1952), p. 77.

15. This rough evolutionary line or trend linking the earliest pithecanthropines to the living humans was more easily established by putting aside the remains of Kanam, Kanjera, and Piltdown. See the discussion on Le Gros Clark in Chapter 8.

16. Leakey (1946) was strongly inclined to believe that whereas the Piltdown skull was a genuine ancient and modern-looking hominid representative, the jaw, for its part, probably belonged to a fossil great ape.

17. See Leakey's phylogenetic tree in *Adam's Ancestors: An Up-To-Date Outline of What is Known About the Origin of Man*, 2nd edition (London: Methuen, 1934), p. 227.

18. See Leakey's phylogenetic tree in *Adam's Ancestors: An Up-To-Date Outline of the Old Stone Age (Palaeolithic) and What is Known About Man's Origin and Evolution*, 4th edition (London: Methuen, 1953), p. 212.

7

Primate Phylogeny, 1935–1965

INTRODUCTION

During the 1935–1965 period, the debates about humankind's place among the primates were greatly simplified or circumscribed, as the debates on human phylogeny had been.[1] This followed the abandonment of two distinct theses that were promoted in the 1860–1935 period. First, no adherent continued to embrace the tradition of polyphyletic hypotheses in which it was held that some living human races had a closer phylogenetic link with some primate species than with other human races. Interestingly enough, the specter of this thesis continued to hang over the field of paleoanthropology in the late 1940s and early 1950s in the writings of Wood Jones and Osman Hill, only to be discarded or falsely applied by them (see below). Second, nobody followed in the steps of Adloff and Sergi in promoting parallel hypotheses in which the human line (or lines) had no phylogenetic link whatsoever with any primate form. It is unclear what contributed to the demise of this latter viewpoint besides the fact that it has always been a very marginal one. Apparently, scholars presenting ideas after the 1930s all agreed that irrespective of the geological time horizon when, or the evolutionary stage at which, the human line departed from its last common ancestor, this ancestor was a primate.

The fall of the polyphyletic and parallel hypotheses greatly restricted the number of acceptable or defensible viewpoints after 1935. This instigated important changes on a number of counts. First, phylogenetic debates would revolve around only three main hypotheses: (1) The human line evolved from a very generalized and early primate form which avoided going through a hominoid ape stage; (2) the human line evolved out of a hominoid ape stage but at a generalized level; (3) the human line evolved straight out of a somewhat specialized and recent hominoid ape stage. These main phylogenetic hypotheses constituted, in reality, a spectrum of hypotheses sometimes blending into one another, thus making it more difficult to render a neat classification of them into one category or another. This reinforces the impression that the phylogenetic hypotheses during the 1935–1965 period were part of a much more coherent or united group of hypotheses, when compared to the pre-1935 period.

A second important change concerned the pre-1935 question of whether or not humankind's last common ancestor with the primates was ape-like or human-like in conformation. This question was replaced after 1935 by hypotheses describing this last common ancestor as ranging from a very generalized primate to a somewhat specialized primate. In other words, the idea that it is the apes that are descended from the humans and not the reverse was abandoned. Concomitantly, the notion that a human-like ancestor could be found in very ancient geological strata was no longer defended, being valid only in the later phases of human evolution. This last question was now being debated in the research area concerned only with human phylogeny proper (see Chapters 6 and 9).

The third important change concerned the geographical dimension of the debates on humankind's place among the primates which were now restricted to the Old World only. The conception was that not only was the New World discredited as a possible cradle for the evolution of the human line, but the possible phylogenetic connections between humankind and the New World monkeys were also excluded.

All these changes contributed to forge a new context of research. By that time, the key question centered entirely around the hominoid ape radiation: Was the split of the human line before, in the early phase of, or in the later phase of this radiation? This well cirscumcribed framework of research constrained all the scholars to raise issues around themes such as: (1) the generalized versus the specialized conformation of the form linking humankind and the other primates; (2) whether or not the human line arose from a quadrupedal form, a prebrachiator form, or a brachiator one.

It has not been possible to reach such a level of resolution in the debates of the pre-1935 period as the issues were just too diffuse. Scholars were dispersed over divergent phylogenetic hypotheses such as polyphyletism, parallel evolution, and humankind's link with the hominoid apes. There were even major debates at the time among the proponents of a close link between humankind and the hominoid apes, as far as the conformation of that common ancestor was concerned: more human-like or more ape-like? Another important disputed issue of the pre-1935 period was the potential geographical areas relevant to human evolution. With the uncertainties surrounding the South American living primate *Amer-anthropoids* and the North American assumed primate fossil *Hesperanthropus*, the Old World could not be the only place to look in order to understand human evolution. Hesitations of this nature opened up the possibility of pulling in all the New World primates, living and fossil, into questions pertaining to human phylogeny. Indeed, a number of scholars have not hesitated to do so. No doubt, the pre-1935 period constituted a very different scientific context in comparison to the post-1935 one. Although it is certainly possible to recognize debates on humankind's place among the primates in the 1920s that continued to be conducted in the post-1935 period (e.g., Fleagle and Jungers, 1982), it is argued here that the former period cannot and should not be entirely analyzed in light of the post-1935 developments.

Ultimately, it is the increasing number of fossil discoveries in the 1930s and after—hominids or nonhuman primates alike—which forged a new and restricted framework of analysis for the debates on humankind's place among the primates, should it be phylogenetic hypotheses, biogeographical questions, or behavioral inferences. Interestingly, this new era of the development of paleoanthropology saw, for the first time, a genuine integrating process between the research areas concerned with humankind's place among the primates and human phylogeny proper. This is clearly seen when fossil discoveries of primary concern in one research area also powerfully impacted in the other. For instance, it was largely because of hominid fossil recoveries made in the 1930s that the polyphyletic thesis became very difficult, if not impossible, to defend. We have seen in Chapter 6 how a critical mass of hominid fossil recoveries made in the 1930s demonstrated convincingly the unity of the living human races, thus blocking the way to polyphyletic viewpoints involving human races and nonhuman primate species. In fact, the 1935–1965 period was characterized by an impressive number of fossil discoveries, whether they were hominids, australopithecines, or hominoid apes. These could only have contributed to break the relative isolation between the two research areas just mentioned above. Furthermore, such fossil discoveries bolstered the importance of the fossil record in the process of phylogeny building, thus somewhat decreasing the importance of comparative anatomy (living forms) for that matter. This constituted an important change with the pre-1935 period.

The number of nonhuman primate fossil discoveries directly relevant to the debates on humankind's place among the primates increased during the 1935–1965 period.[2] It is perhaps useful to regroup them in a number of categories:

1. The dryopithecines were represented at one time or another by *Dryopithecus*, *Sivapithecus*, *Sugrivapithecus*, *Ramapithecus*, *Kenyapithecus*, *Hispanopithecus*, *Ankarapithecus*, *Palaeosimia*, etc. These primates of the Mio-Pliocene period were often seen as more or less specialized hominoid apes closely related to the three great apes, but sometimes also to humankind.

2. *Pliopithecus*, *Epipliopithecus*, and *Limnopithecus* were more often than not considered to be part of the gibbon evolutionary line, a line which extended from the Oligocene period to the present.

3. *Propliopithecus* of the Oligocene period was usually either exclusively associated with the gibbon line or seen as a generalized hominoid ape form which could also be ancestral to the humans and/or to the great apes.

4. *Proconsul* of the Oligocene period was also usually seen as a generalized hominoid ape form which could be ancestral to the humans and/or to the great apes.

5. *Parapithecus* and *Apidium* of the Oligocene period were often believed to represent primitive anthropoid forms of the Old World. A number of scholars appealed to them to explain the rise of the human line.

6. *Oreopithecus* of the Miocene period was a form which was either classified with the Old World monkeys or the hominoid apes, but also attracted the attention of several scholars as a possible phylogenetic link confined exclusively to the human evolutionary line.

Although scholars were not agreed on the proper phylogenetic place or on the evolutionary significance of all these primate fossils, it is largely through their use that the debates on humankind's place among the primates were conducted at the time. Indeed, the influence of such primate fossils were felt even among the proposed scenarios of hominization at the time.

BYPASSING THE HOMINOID APE PHASE

We have seen that scholars such as Topinard, Cope, Boule, and Wood Jones, prior to the 1930s, promoted that the human line evolved from a very generalized primate form which avoided going through a hominoid ape stage. This tradition of interpretation continued in the 1935–1965 period and was well-represented by Schepers, Osman Hill, Wood Jones, Straus, Piveteau, and Genet-Varcin. Convinced that the human line avoided altogether the hominoid phase of evolution, these scholars searched deeply into the past for a common ancestor between the human line and the other primates, that is, in the Oligocene period or before, and even sometimes as early as the Cretaceous period of the Secondary era as seen in the case of Genet-Varcin. Nobody considered looking for a common ancestor that was prosimian-like in conformation. Instead, this ancestor was conceived to be a tarsoid-like form, a generalized catarrhine primate or an unspecialized monkey-like form. In short, all small bodied primates. On this view, the rise of the bipedal posture in humans was not believed to have been preceded by a brachiation or a pre-brachiation phase, but rather by a quadrupedal one (monkey-like ancestor) or only possibly by a leaping one (tarsoid-like ancestor). What characterized the viewpoints of these scholars is that all or most primate fossils discovered thus far were thought to be largely irrelevant to human evolution. In other words, a negative use of the fossil record was made as this record indicated that the human line had not sprung from the relatively abundant hominoid fossil record. Therefore, it is not surprising to see that these scholars relied heavily on comparative anatomy and/or embryology in their phylogenetic analyses, as no, or very few, fossil specimens were known to substantiate the rise of the human line from a genuinely early primate form.

For scholars like Schepers and Osman Hill, the rise of the human line from the other primates can be explained, in part at least, by the notion that humans are generalized primates that retained many juvenile features (pedomorphic traits). In so doing, they avoided over-specializations (gerontomorphy) and retained their evolutionary plasticity to face the challenges of the environment. According to Schepers (1946), humans avoided altogether a hominoid phase of evolution because in the Oligocene or Lower Miocene period humankind's ancestor must have been a plastic and generalized primate form. It is from this generalized form, and through a process of rapid specialization, that the various hominoid apes arose. A form such as *Dryopithecus* was believed not to constitute a phylogenetic link testifying to the rise of the humans from the hominoid apes, but rather the other way around.

Unable to use the known fossil record, which he thought was showing forms that were too specialized, Schepers turned to embryology. Noting that the human fetus does not at any stage of its ontogenetic development approach the condition of the adult living hominoid ape—the two groups being the closest only in the early months—Schepers goes on to insist that the proximity is even closer when the embryos of humankind and the archaic *Tarsoidea* are compared, thus reinforcing the notion of an ancient differentiation of the human stock. Schepers envisioned humankind's remote ancestor as a small and frail-bodied creature with delicate teeth, one committed to an early differentiation of the upper and lower extremities, respectively involved in prehensible and supporting functions: in short, "a being more Tarsoid than Anthropoid" (Schepers, 1946: 262).

Schepers conceived the evolution of the primates as being under two important actions: (1) the gradual increase in brain size over time in some primate evolutionary lines but not in others; (2) the tendency of the primates to be either pedomorphic (retaining juvenile features in adulthood) or gerontomorphic (developing large and bestial features). According to Schepers, the Eocene period saw the rise of a terrestrial primate called *Paratarsioidea* from a prosimian-like ancestor. This *Paratarsioidea* form constituted the stock from which the Old World monkeys, the hominoid apes, and the humans all differentiated from each other in the Upper Eocene or Lower Oligocene period. While the Old World monkeys' stem departed first in the direction of both tree-living and ground-living forms, the remnants of this paratarsioid stock, which avoided the arboreal specialization, constituted the genuine ancestor of the hominoid apes and the humans. Schepers referred to this form as *Anthropomorpha primitivae*. This creature was believed to be characterized by a bipedal cursorial mode of locomotion. From there, the relatively large-brained hominoid apes diverged from one another in various directions: One evolutionary line represented by *Propliopithecus*, *Pliopithecus*, and the gibbon developed longer arms and gave rise to fully brachiating forms, while another evolutionary line became gerontomorphic by developing larger and more bestial bodies, as seen in the chimpanzee but especially in the gorilla.

Another portion of *Anthropomorpha primitivae* of the Lower Oligocene period avoided the hominoid ape phase of evolution, with its over-specialization in respect to a large body size and, relatively speaking, limited cerebral evolution. It is this progressive portion of *Anthropomorpha primitivae* which continued its evolution towards the living humans through a *Pithecoid homunculi* phase:

> [T]hese transition forms lived during the whole of the Lower Miocene on the plains of Africa; and the variety of combinations between pedomorphic and gerontomorphic trends, between large and small-brained forms, will reveal that this phase of evolution was the most critical in human evolution. For, while gerontomorphism would still exert

> tremendous influence to produce gigantic forms, the advance in cerebral evolution would always give advantage to the more agile, more skillful types. Never again would any of these forms be able to degenerate into Apes . . . This then is the significance of the discovery of the *Australopithecinae*. They have crystallized for us this critical phase in the evolution of *Pithecoid homunculi* (Schepers, 1946: 270).[3]

For Schepers, therefore, the australopithecines are pedomorphic creatures when compared to the hominoid apes, but are gerontomorphic creatures relative to the other hominids.

Not unlike Schepers, Osman Hill also appealed to the opposition between gerontomorphy and pedomorphy in order to explain primate phylogeny. For Osman Hill (1950, 1954), the human line could not have directly sprung from the stock of the hominoid ape. If humankind remains today a relatively generalized primate form little changed from his immediate ancestors, this is not the case for the hominoid apes which were subjected to numerous specializations, thus confining them to restricted ecological niches. Osman Hill explained that humankind's generalized status is largely due to pedomorphism or fetalization, that is, the retention into adulthood of features that are usually only transient during infancy or fetal life. Relative to humankind, the hominoid apes, especially the great apes, are gerontomorphic, that is, they evolved by modifying or pushing further the stages associated to specialized features in adulthood. According to Osman Hill, the gorilla is the gerontomorphic creature *par excellence*, as seen in the highly developed bony structures on its skull (nuchal and sagital crests), projecting face, and huge canines. Osman Hill recognized that the living hominoid apes presented similarities with the humans; for instance, their ability to adopt an upright posture (though not a fully bipedal gait). Many of these similarities between humankind and the hominoid apes, however, could be explained easily by convergent evolution: the manifestation of latent and similar trends in distinct evolutionary lines originally inherited from a common stock that did not itself exhibit these traits.

Although Osman Hill recognized that some of the Miocene apes (*Proconsul*, *Dryopithecus*, *Sugrivapithecus*, *Ramapithecus*, and *Sivapithecus*) were less specialized than their living counterparts, thus being closer to living humans, he insisted that they were already too committed in the direction of the three great apes to have given rise to the human branch. "That man branched off from the main Primate stock at an earlier date then the apes," contended Osman Hill (1950: 162), "seems almost certain." Convinced that the human lineage had genealogical roots in more ancient times than usually assumed, he was inclined to seek such an ancestor in a generalized catarrhine primate. Osman Hill (1950: 162) made clear that his conception of humankind's place among the primates was similar to Straus's (1949) view, and could even possibly be reconciled with that of Wood Jones (1948). Osman Hill (1954: 163) stated:

> Straus concludes that a non-anthropoid [hominoid] hypothesis of Man's origin fits the facts better than the anthropoid-ape-hypothesis; and with this conclusion the present author, on the basis of his own researches, agrees. The hominid line, after emerging from the common Eocene pool of tarsoids must have been represented by an unspecialized

> quadrupedal monkey-like Primate, possibly represented by *Parapithecus*. The line leading to the apes [hominoid apes] separated from that which gave rise to Man probably in the Oligocene.

For Osman Hill, *Parapithecus* of the early Oligocene period of Egypt was a small and very generalized primate which descended from the Eocene tarsoids and could well be the progenitor of the Old World monkeys, the hominoid apes and the humans as well.

When considering the evolution of the human line itself, Osman Hill raised, not unlike Wood Jones before him (see above), the question of the polyphyletic hypothesis. It is worth quoting him at some length:

> Of course it is conceivable, since large-brained, semi-erect anthropoids [hominoid apes] have survived both in Asia and Africa, and that each continent produced at any rate fossil forms exhibiting evolutionary trends in a human direction . . . , that Man arose independently in both places, the two stocks having, thereafter, undergone parallel development, or even convergent evolution . . . Early forms of the polygenist attitude are represented by the Digenic theory of Klaatsch . . . who believed that Asiatic Man arose from the orang-utan . . . whereas the Negro was regarded as originating from a common stock with the African anthropoids [hominoids]. It is true that there are parallelisms between Asiatic Man and the orang, and between the Negro and the chimpanzee-gorilla assemblage; but that these resemblances are due to common origin or to exhibition of latent common trends, or may be similar adaptations to a common environment are disputed questions. (Osman Hill, 1954: 115)

Osman Hill's view on the polyphyletic thesis seems to be everything but straightforward. However, when other elements of his thinking are taken into account it is possible to get a better understanding of it. First, it is interesting to note that Osman Hill is apparently not prepared to definitively rule out the polyphyletic thesis in a period as late as the early 1950s. This being said, his openness towards this thesis is probably more theoretical than anything else. Considering that Osman Hill derived the human branch early from a generalized catarrhine primate, thus avoiding altogether the hominoid ape phase of evolution, it is fairly clear that he did not promote that the various living human races had independently evolved from distinct stems leading to the living hominoid apes. As will be seen below (see Chapter 9), Osman Hill was indeed prepared to recognize that the various human lineages are derived from distinct ancestors. But following the distinction already made in Chapter 2, Osman Hill's conception is a polygenetic view rather than a polyphyletic one. Because of the ambiguity of his own writings, Osman Hill only created confusion between these two theses.[4]

Whereas Schepers and Osman Hill viewed the evolution of the primates through the lenses of the pedomorphic-gerontomorphic dichotomy, others like Wood Jones, Straus, and Piveteau established the place of humankind among the primates by comparing the three main radiations of the Old World primates: the Old World monkeys, the hominoid apes, and the humans. This comparison allowed them to define both the time and the conformation of the last common ancestor to these three radiations. Wood Jones (1948) held that the relationships of the primates do not constitute a simple ascending series in grade complexity going from the lemurs to the humans, passing through the monkeys and the hominoid apes. Rather, he believed primate phylogeny to be a complex assemblage profoundly marked by parallel evolution. First of all, Wood Jones denied the primate status to the lemurs. He argued that the *Strepsirhini* (lemurs) and the *Haplorhini* (tarsiers, monkeys, apes, and humans) represented two separate mammalian stocks not phylogenetically related, with both retaining common primitive features and adaptations to arboreal life. This being said, continued Wood Jones, it must be recognized that the lemur stock once gave rise, independently from the primates, to monkey-like representatives as seen in extinct forms such as *Nesopithecus* and *Mesopropithecus*. Wood Jones also promoted that the monkeys of the Old World and New World developed most of their monkey-like features independently from a common and very ancient primitive *Haplorhini* primate which cannot be commonly called a monkey. Monkey-like creatures thus independently arose twice among the primates and once among the lemurs. We have already seen that Wood Jones argued that although no hominoid-like primates arose from the New World stock, woolly monkeys (*Lagothrix*) had nevertheless reached a similar level of organization approaching the gibbons in the Old World (see Chapter 4).

Wood Jones conceived the evolution of the Old World primates as a radiation which culminated in the phylogenetic trend of specialized monkey-like forms, although several forms avoided going through such a level of specialization. The hominoid apes (gibbons, orangs, chimpanzees, and gorillas) are too generalized in conformation to have been the end product of such a phylogenetic trend, meaning that they departed from several distinct conservative stocks situated nearer the base of this entire Old World radiation. Indeed, Wood Jones insisted on the lack of homogeneity and the superficial similarity (related to a large size) of the hominoid apes, which testified to their not too close ancestry:

> The Gorillas might be regarded as giant survivors of the radiation that is represented today by the African baboons. The Chimpanzees might well be the conservative survivors of the large type developed on the ancestral line of the modern African Cercopithecus; while the Asiatic anthropoids [orangs and gibbons] might similarly be regarded as descendants of the more primitive members of the stock that ultimately culminated in the production of the present Asiatic Langurs . . . [The] "Anthropoid Apes" [hominoids] have been developed more than once from the stem of the Catarrhines. (Wood Jones, 1948: 28)

Wood Jones apparently believed that the Asiatic hominoid apes were more generalized than the African ones, for he recognized that the former departed earlier from the common Old World primate stem than the latter. If the hominoid apes are viewed as less developed Catarrhines than are the Old World monkeys, continued Wood Jones, then the humans must be viewed as forms more generalized still. This implied that the human stock or stocks departed from the common Old World primate stem at an even earlier period than any of the hominoid apes. Recognizing that fossil forms such as *Dryopithecus*, *Sivapithecus*, and *Propliopithecus* were dated to the Miocene and Oligocene periods, in addition to being related to the living hominoid apes exclusively, Wood Jones evaluated that the human line or lines departed from the Old World primate stem during the Eocene period. He hinted that tarsioid forms devoid of their present specializations (saltatory locomotion and vision), which are known in the Eocene period of North America and Western Europe in *Anaptomorphidae*, could constitute such a generalized common ancestor to the human line (or lines). It is clear from Wood Jones's conception that living and fossil hominoid apes were already too specialized to have been ancestral to the human line. On this view, a long-armed, short-legged, and brachiating ape could not be ancestral to a bipedal human form.

Turning to the living humans, Wood Jones recognized that the main living groups (Black, Caucasian, Mongol) were separated by major features which probably took considerable time to get established. Considering the importance of parallel evolution in primate phylogeny, he wondered if the polyphyletic conclusion of the rise of humankind could be escaped. Yes, he insisted, but only if his conception of primate evolution was embraced:

> If both monkeys and Anthropoid apes [hominoids] have been produced on more than one occasion in the evolutionary story of the Primates, is it not possible that Man has been begot more than once from the primitive radiations of the catarrhine stock? . . . *There is only one alternative to admitting the possibility of polyphyletic human origin and yet escape from the difficulty of rebutting the evidence of the "Polygenists", and that is to postulate that the emergence of the human type from a very primitive Primate form took place at a period so far distant that an enormous interval was available for the profound degree of differentiation that has occurred in an originally homogeneous stock.* (Wood Jones, 1948: 42, 44–45) [Not my italics]

Straus's (1949) conception of the link between the Old World monkeys, the hominoid apes, and the humans was significantly different from that of Wood Jones's. Impressed by the specialized features of the living and fossil hominoid apes relative to the humans, Straus believed it was more appropriate to derive the human line not directly from the hominoid stock, but rather from a more generalized catarrhine or Old World primate probably from no later than the end of the Oligocene period. Straus insisted that many of the human primitive features were shared with the Old World and New World monkeys, but also with the gibbons, thus indicating that this latter form retained much of the ancestral proto-catarrhine type. Although Straus excluded the New World monkeys from any consideration on human phylogeny, he insisted that humankind and the New World monkeys retained many features in common from a distant ancestor whose exact nature remains unspecified.

Straus believed that the human line had departed from the primitive catarrhine stock before there even existed hominoid apes, that is, before the predryopithecine stage and before the differentiation of the *Hylobatidae* stock (gibbons and siamangs). Whether humankind's earliest ancestors should be called proto-cercopicoids or proto-hylobatioids matters little, insisted Straus, for the early protean catarrhine primates were incipiently both. In Straus's conception of primate phylogeny, the similarities between the humans and the hominoid apes had to be explained by parallel evolution rather than by direct kinship. Whereas Wood Jones (1948) held that the Old World monkeys were the most specialized of all the catarrhine primates, Straus promoted, on the contrary, that they were the most primitive of the living catarrhines. Therefore, the hominoid apes, especially the great apes, are the most specialized of the catarrhines, with the humans being somewhat intermediate between the Old World monkeys and the hominoid apes. Straus argued that the human line had passed through a monkey-like stage during its evolutionary history. In his phylogenetic conception, while the Old World monkeys were the first group to depart from the common catarrhine primate stem, they were later followed by the human line, thus leaving a third and still later departure to the hominoid apes. The gibbons were the first to depart from this common ape stem, followed by the orang and later by the chimpanzee-gorilla group. Straus's view implied that the two African great apes are the most specialized of all the Old World primates. In the early 1950s, Straus's view of primate phylogeny was modified (see below).

In contradistinction to the views of Wood Jones and Straus, Piveteau was not interested in establishing whether or not the Old World monkeys had been the most primitive or the most specialized Old World primates. Presumably, Piveteau believed that this morphological polarity had no bearing on the question of the rise of the human line. Piveteau (1954, 1957, 1958, 1962, 1963) derived the human line from a common ancestor shared with the other hominoid apes. This common ancestor was, in Piveteau's mind, not too remotely related to the earliest members of the Old World monkeys stem. Piveteau imagined three distinct stems diverging from one another, each exploiting its own evolutionary road: The human line adopted early the bipedal gait, the ape line adopted late the brachiating mode of locomotion, and the Old World monkeys line retained the quadrupedal mode of locomotion, which apparently was the primitive condition of all these Old World anthropoid lines. Piveteau (1957: 647) stated:

> The marked similarities observed between the Hominids and the Pongids [hominoid apes], and the similarities observed between these two lineages on the one hand and the Old World monkeys lineage on the other hand, implies almost indubitably the existence of a common and ancestral group which can be called proto-catarrhine, from which the three evolutionary lines diverged, each at it own pace: Old World monkeys, apes and hominids. [The translation is mine][5]

Piveteau advanced the idea that the human line never went through a brachiating mode of locomotion, only because the bipedal gait directly developed out of a quadrupedal one. Piveteau made clear that the human line had not been derived from a monkey-like ancestor but simply that the common stock to the catarrhines was a quadrupedal creature (Piveteau, 1962, 1963). Once committed to their new mode of locomotion, the human and the ape lines evolved in opposite directions. The hominoid apes developed long arms and short legs while these proportions were reversed in the human line. Furthermore, while the hominoid apes developed large canines and incisors, humankind's earliest ancestors retained the small canines and incisors of the more primitive condition. For Piveteau, it is clear that the earliest hominoid apes were creatures less specialized than their living counterparts.

Turning to the fossil record, Piveteau recognized in the dentition of *Propliopithecus* of the Oligocene period of Egypt a form which was already committed in the ape direction. For that reason, he held that the human line must have already been distinct by that geological time period. It was speculated that the rise of the human line could have occurred in the tropical and subtropical regions of the southern zone of the Mediterranean Sea. Piveteau saw in *Propliopithecus* a convenient early representative of the hominoid apes, though perhaps not a fully developed one when compared to the living representatives. In the Miocene and Pliocene phase of the ape radiation, Piveteau recognized fossil apes which already presented features seen later among their living representatives: larger frontal teeth and adaptations to the brachiating mode of locomotion. If *Proconsul* and *Dryopithecus* were perhaps directly ancestral to the living chimpanzees and gorillas, *Sivapithecus* may have been related to the living orangs, while *Pliopithecus* and *Limnopithecus* could somehow be linked to the living gibbons. On the other side of the divide, Piveteau (1957, 1958) recognized in *Oreopithecus* of the late Miocene of Italy a probable early representative of the hominid stem, as seen by its reduced frontal dentition, the molarization of the premolars, the short face, and the configuration of the pelvic region, which indicated a tendency for an erect posture. However, more fossil discoveries eventually showed that the body proportions of *Oreopithecus* (long arms and short legs) were more reminiscent of the ape condition. Regardless of these new facts, Piveteau (1962, 1963) still leaned toward the view of *Oreopithecus* being an extinct and specialized side branch of the human stem not directly ancestral to the living humans.

Unlike Wood Jones, Straus, and Piveteau, Genet-Varcin would evaluate the place of humankind among the primates not by comparing the three main Old World radiations—Old World monkeys, hominoid apes, and humans—but by comparing only the last two. For Genet-Varcin (1963, 1969a), the hominoid apes and the hominids had departed very early from a common ancestor. In fact, Genet-Varcin derived all the main primate groups independently from a very early common ancestor.[6] At first, Genet-Varcin (1963) postulated that this separation had occurred in the early Paleocene period. Later, however, she suggested that this separation had occurred at an even earlier time period, that is, in the early or middle Cretaceous period of the Secondary era (Genet-Varcin, 1969a). The justification for such an early separation time between the hominoid apes and the humans is revealed, she insisted, by the fact that the hominoid apes had been clearly committed to their own specific evolutionary road by the Oligocene period, as seen in the dental remains of *Propliopithecus* and *Aegyptopithecus*. These fossil types, it was contended, already showed the beginning of a dental specialization that was avoided in the human line: larger canines and incisors and canine-like first lower premolars.

This hominoid ape stem went through an important diversification of forms and geographical expansion in the Miocene and Pliocene periods before declining rapidly. Genet-Varcin saw in *Pliopithecus*, *Epipliopithecus*, and *Limnopithecus* representatives of the radiation leading to the living gibbons. These early forms indicated that hominoid apes were once generalized primates with a quadrupedal mode of locomotion. With fossil forms of the Miocene period such as *Proconsul*, Genet-Varcin argued that we have in them the rise of a great ape type already in the process of developing a brachiating mode of locomotion. While *Dryopithecus* was perhaps more generally affiliated to the African great apes, *Proconsul*, *Hispanopithecus*, and *Ankarapithecus* were possibly more closely related to the living chimpanzees, while *Sivapithecus* was connected to the living orangs. The hominoid ape radiation was, for Genet-Varcin, a series of smaller and distinct radiations. The two radiations leading the living gibbons and the great apes, respectively, had been separated since the late Paleocene period. At first, Genet-Varcin (1963: 212) was open to the idea of *Ramapithecus* being a possible representative of the human line.[7] However, she insisted that more fossils were needed to confirm this view. Later, Genet-Varcin (1969a: 95–103) was inclined to view the dental and gnathic remains at our disposal as indicators that *Ramapithecus* probably belonged to the hominoid ape radiation exclusively. She now doubted the human-like reconstruction of the *Ramapithecus* remains suggested at the time, although she left open the possibility that new fossil remains might eventually show its hominid status.

Genet-Varcin described the earliest representatives of the human line as very generalized creatures. The original ascent of this line was presented as being very marginal, taxonomically and geographically speaking, until quite late in the Tertiary era. Indeed, the human line had its apogee only in the Pleistocene period. The only tangible sign of this marginal evolutionary line throughout the long Tertiary era was seen in *Oreopithecus* of the late Miocene of Europe. Although it was held that *Oreopithecus* only constituted an extinct branch of the stem leading both to the australopithecines and to the living humans—as seen in its adaptation to a brachiating mode of locomotion—that fossil was nonetheless indicative of a number of key morphological features already present in the ascent of humankind: molar-like premolars, a broad pelvis, a tendency toward a bipedal gait, a nonprojecting face, a lack of strong cresting patterns on the skull, a relatively large brain size for the geological time period, etc. Genet-Varcin believed that *Oreopithecus* had already departed from the main hominid stem by the mid-Oligocene period.[8] She explained the similarities between the long-separated human and hominoid apes lines (increased brain size, loss of the tail, large upper body, tendendy toward erectness of the body) by two factors: the heritage from their common ancestor and convergent evolution.

UP FROM A GENERALIZED HOMINOID STOCK

For other scholars like Hürzeler, Arambourg, Schultz, Straus (after 1953), Le Gros Clark, Vallois, Leakey, and Heberer humankind sprang directly from a hominoid ape but at a fairly generalized level, thus avoiding the dryopithecine radiation, narrowly defined. In their view, the human line avoided going through a specialized hominoid phase seen today among the three living great apes. These scholars continued the tradition of interpretation already carried on by Osborn (before 1925), Schultz, and Le Gros Clark before 1935. Proponents of this view in the 1935–1965 period were unable to agree on the geological moment when the human line departed from the other primates. Evaluations were ranging from as late as the middle Miocene period to as early as the Paleocene period. When turning to the conformation and the behavior of this common ancestor it was agreed that it was certainly not a large-bodied brachiating creature, meaning that it was seen as a rather small-bodied form (either a generalized quadrupedal form or a prebrachiating one).

Among the several primate fossils relied upon to articulate this viewpoint, *Oreopithecus*, *Propliopithecus*, and *Proconsul* were especially important. Interestingly, scholars like Arambourg (before 1959), Schultz, Straus, Le Gros Clark, and Vallois turned to the gibbon evolutionary line to shed some light on either the timing of the separation of the human line from the other primates or the stage at which this separation had occurred. We have already seen that the gibbon played such a role for many scholars in the pre-1935 period. Clearly, then, the gibbon continued to be important in the debates on humankind's place among the primates during the 1935–1965 period.

For Hürzeler and Arambourg (after 1959), the human line departed from the hominoid stock before the other hominoid forms had diverged from one another. Indeed, Hürzeler believed he had found proof for this in the fossil record and not in comparative anatomy. Hürzeler (1956, 1960) insisted that it would not be possible to arrive at a consensus on humankind's place among the primates through the comparison of the living forms exclusively. He surmised that there were simply too many ways to interpret the relationships of forms on that basis. It was Hürzeler's contention that only the fossil record could settle these questions. Hürzeler (1954a, 1956, 1958, 1960, 1962, 1968) believed that he had identified an early ancestor of the human line in *Oreopithecus*, a Miocene primate of Europe. Traditionally, *Oreopithecus* had been interpreted as a member belonging to the Old World monkeys. For Hürzeler, however, the monkey features of *Oreopithecus* are merely traces or primitive traits of a shared ancestry with the entire catarrhine primates. Hürzeler saw in the premolars, the relatively small canines, and the nonprojecting face of *Oreopithecus* sure signs of its exclusive affiliation to the human branch.

Hürzeler argued that although the humans shared a common ancestor with all the other hominoids, the latter had been exploring a divergent evolutionary road than the one taken by humankind. Hürzeler saw in *Proconsul*, and all the dryopithcines in general, ancient forms directly ancestral to the three living great apes, whereas he recognized in *Pliopithecus*, *Limnopithecus*, and *Propliopithecus* forms directly ancestral to the living gibbons. Thus humankind could only have diverged from the common and primitive hominoid stock at an early period and stage when the hominoid apes were not as yet distinct from each other. In other words, the human branch had not been derived from a more or less specialized form approaching one of the living hominoid apes. As *Oreopithecus* of the Miocene period was already committed in the human direction, Hürzeler assumed that the earliest hominid forms would be found in a still deeper time period. Hürzeler placed the time of the separation of the hominid line from the rest of the hominoid stock in the Eocene or the Paleocene period.[9]

Following more discoveries of *Oreopithecus*, Hürzeler (1960) recognized that its body proportions (long arms and short legs) were quite the opposite of the human type. He argued that such a feature was probably due to parallel evolution rather than direct descent with the other hominoid apes. More importantly, Hürzeler pointed out that the short and broad pelvis of *Oreopithecus* indicated that it was on its way to acquire an erect posture, thus clearly demonstrating that the entire human line had been committed early to the hominization process. Hürzeler always favored the view that *Oreopithecus* was probably not directly ancestral to living humans, but rather constituted an extinct side branch that departed from the main human stem, perhaps as early as the Oligocene or the Eocene period. The australopithecines were yet another side branch of this main lineage leading to living humans which diverged at a later period than had the *Oreopithecus* line.[10] Although he never presented a clear view on the place of the australopithecines, Hürzeler (1962) first established that they had diverged from the human branch in the late Pliocene, only to suggest in 1968 that they had done so as early as the early Miocene period.

Not unlike Hürzeler, Arambourg held in the late 1950s and early 1960s that the human line was the first one to depart from the hominoid radiation, although its basis to support this was not entirely similar to Hürzeler's. Remember that this has not always been Arambourg's viewpoint (see below).[11] Arambourg (1959, 1960, 1961, 1965) promoted that the human line departed from the hominoid stock before all the other hominoids had passed through a gibbon-like *Propliopithecus* phase. He held that *Propliopithecus* was a representative of the gibbon line that could also possibly be a common ancestor to all the other nonhuman hominoids. It was held that humankind had sprang from a hominoid form that was more primitive and more generalized in conformation than *Propliopithecus*.

Excluding *Limnopithecus* from such an ancestral position, Arambourg held that *Parapithecus* was to be put at the base of the human line. He presented *Parapithecus* to be a small creature with a reduced prognathism, small frontal teeth, and reduced canines. Arambourg also added to the human line the Late Miocene form of *Oreopithecus*. He insisted that *Oreopithecus* was a fully bipedal creature of the size of a chimpanzee with a relatively large brain and a reduced snout. But because of its body proportions, *Oreopithecus* showed it was fully adapted to living in the trees. Arambourg considered *Oreopithecus* to be an aberrant and extinct side branch of the hominid stock, as it represented a bipedal brachiator. Furthermore, *Apidium* was also put at the very base of this extinct hominid branch leading to *Oreopithecus*.[12]

Between 1943 and 1965, Arambourg gradually pushed back in time the rise of the human line from the other primates. Although at first he stated that the human line had been separated from the rest of the hominoid radiation by the early

Miocene, he later wrote that this separation had occurred in the Oligocene if not the late Eocene.[13]

For scholars like Schultz, Arambourg (before 1959), and Straus (after 1953) it was believed that the human line had departed from the hominoid stock not before but, rather, just after the gibbon line had split. This shared phylogenetic interpretation was, however, variably interpreted by these authors. Schultz's conception in the 1950s and 1960s remained unchanged when compared to his view of the 1920s and 1930s (see Chapter 4). More studies on the anatomy and embryology of the living primates only convinced him that his early view was essentially correct. Although Schultz continued to base his interpretation largely on comparative anatomy, he now also incorporated some of the primate fossil recoveries. This being said, it is hard not to have the impression that he essentially shoehorned such fossils in a phylogenetic conception based on the living forms. The predominance of comparative anatomy over the fossil record is, in Schultz's mind, founded on the conviction that all the phylogenetic changes are caused largely by the alterations of the ontogenetic development, changes which can best be studied through comparative anatomy.

Schultz (1950a, 1953, 1969) now made clear that he believed that the hominoids originated from an early and extinct primate of the *Cercopithecinae* group (macaques, baboons) in the Oligocene period or before, although this could not as yet be proven by paleontological evidence. In Schultz's (1969: 245) own words, the "hominoids had evolved from the basal, very early and unspecialized stock of monkeys". He envisioned the hominoid radiation as being represented by three distinct living phylogenetic groups which had departed from this common generalized hominoid stock. From there, each took different evolutionary roads which were largely determined by their posture and locomotion. The gibbon group was the earliest one to diverge in the Oligocene period and took to the trees by gradually perfecting the brachiating mode of locomotion. The small body size of the group helped bridge the gap that separated the Old World monkeys from the hominoids.

Very shortly after the gibbon line had departed, the human group diverged from the common hominoid trunk in an opposite evolutionary direction by fully exploiting very early the bipedal terrestrial niche. The great apes group was the last one to dissolve, with the orangutans diverging first in the Miocene period by developing, not unlike the gibbons, specific adaptations for brachiation. These adaptations developed in parallel. For their part, the chimpanzees and the gorillas split from one another later in the Pliocene period and adopted conservative adaptations by a sort of compromise between arboreal and terrestrial life styles.[14]

In Schultz's view, the first and most decisive specialization of the human line which instigated all the others—an early and fully bipedal locomotion—was made possible only because the earliest hominoids were endowed with potentialities for an erect posture, as seen especially in their upper body. While this potentiality had been exploited to various degrees by all the living hominoids, only the human line had fully done so. In fact, Schultz (1950a) once alluded to the possibility that some extinct hominoid apes may have been more deeply committed to the upright posture than any of their living counterparts. Fundamental to Schultz's (1950b, 1963, 1965, 1968, 1969) conception of hominoid evolution was the notion that all the forms were built on the same morphological plan: Only the frequency and the extent of the features and systems in question varied. For him, the enlargement and perfection of the brain so characteristic of the later phase of human evolution was also a feature developed to various degrees in all the other hominoid lines.

In Schultz's phylogenetic view, the proximity of the human and gibbon lines had no special meaning beyond the timing of this separation. This was not the view expounded by Arambourg prior to 1959, for whom the gibbons throw vivid light on the evolutionary stage at which the human line departed from the other primates. Arambourg (1943a, 1943b, 1947, 1957) held that humankind did not spring directly from the Mio-Pliocene dryopithecine group, already too committed in the direction of the specialized living great apes. The rise of humankind had to be sought in an earlier time period and among more generalized hominoid apes. Arambourg derived the humans and the hominoid apes from a common stem which departed from the Old World anthropoids in the mid-Eocene. By the mid-Oligocene, this common hominoid stem divided in two branches: one evolving toward the three living great apes after going through a dryopithecine phase (including *Proconsul*, *Palaeopithecus*, *Sivapithecus*, *Palaeosimia*), another evolving toward the living gibbons after having passed through a *Pliopithecus* stage. In Arambourg's view, it is from the very base of this latter gibbon-like lineage that the human line had departed. Arambourg saw in the living gibbons a form which retained many primitive features of the common ancestor to all the living hominoids, including the humans. In fact, *Propliopithecus* could well represent such a generalized common hominoid ancestor. By the late Oligocene, therefore, the human line had sprung from a small gibbon-like form. Arambourg recognized in the humanoid teeth of *Limnopithecus* from Kenya a form that announced the rise of the humans, so that the human line has in *Limnopithecus* an early representative in the Lower Miocene period.[15] For Arambourg (1945, 1948a), Africa— not Asia— had been at the heart of human evolution.

From such a small, generalized, and gibbon-like ancestor such as *Propliopithecus*, which presented a v-shaped mandible, a moderate size of the canines, and a relatively short face, Arambourg (1948b, 1952, 1956) maintained that the hominoid radiation proceeded in two opposite evolutionary directions. On the one side, the rise of the ape conformation was subjected to a great deal of morphological change. The development of the anterior dentition, the increase in the size of the canines, and the development of a forward projection of the snout led to the rise of the hominoid ape type, as best represented today in the three great apes. On the other side, the rise of the human conformation was not subjected to such profound morphological changes. Indeed, the living humans retained many features from the common hominoid ancestor. All that was needed to instigate the rise of the human type was a further reduction of the canines and of the face in general. Arambourg modified his view somewhat after 1959 (see above).

Not unlike Arambourg, Straus also exploited the close phylogenetic proximity between the human and gibbon lines. For Straus, however, the true evolutionary significance of this relationship was more directly related to the rise of bipedality rather than changes in skull anatomy. Remember that Straus's view of primate phylogeny was somewhat different in the late 1940s (see above). Now, taking into account new primate fossil discoveries, Straus (1953, 1961, 1962, 1963) recognized that he had "overemphasized the 'nonanthropoid' [nonhominoid] nature of hominid ancestry" (Straus, 1962: 103). On this new basis, Straus became a proponent of the thesis that the human line sprang from a very primitive and generalized hominoid form, although he retained many features of his previous viewpoint. Instrumental in this shift were the fossil remains of *Proconsul* and *Limnopithecus*, which showed that the earliest representatives of the hominoid stock presented a mixture of cercopithecoid and hominoid features. Previously, Straus had assumed that the earliest hominoid apes were already specialized forms. Now, Straus was at liberty to postulate that the human line had diverged from the earliest portion of the hominoid radiation, while maintaining the view that the human stock had retained many primitive monkey-like features, as well as maintaining the notion that this stock had never passed through a genuine brachiating phase of evolution (Straus, 1940). Only implicit in Straus's previous writings, and now made explicit, was the idea that an unspecialized proto-brachiating stage would constitute a preadaptation to the acquisition of a perfectly bipedal posture. This is where the significance of the gibbon evolutionary line comes in.

The primate fossil discoveries of *Limnopithecus* and *Oreopithecus*, the former being possibly affiliated with *Proconsul* as well as with the gibbon evolutionary line, also contributed to modify Straus's view: "I do not feel as convinced as I did in 1949 that the hominid line of evolution must have branched off and become independent before the departure of the hylobatid line" (Straus, 1962: 104; see also Straus, 1961: 761). Straus was now inclined to think that the gibbon line departed first from the hominoid radiation immediately followed by the human line. This new view might imply that the human stock arose at a later period than first evaluated, although Straus still placed that moment in the Oligocene period. This phylogenetic proximity of the human and gibbon lines, the latter being the brachiator *par excellence*, could be established in Straus's mind only because he recognized that the genuine adaptation for brachiation developed quite late in the gibbon evolutionary history. Furthermore, Straus also recognized that brachiation, as a mode of locomotion, developed independently in several distinct evolutionary lines and at different times. This enabled Straus (1957, 1962, 1963) to hold that *Oreopithecus* was an aberrant and extinct side branch of the human line not directly ancestral to humans. Regardless of its genuine brachiating locomotion which was probably not shared with its immediate ancestor, *Oreopithecus* shows that truly hominid features had appeared as early as the late Miocene or early Pliocene period. For Straus, *Oreopithecus* showed clear signs of a preadaptation to an erect bipedal gait.

For yet other scholars like Le Gros Clark, Vallois, and Leakey, the nature of the split of the human line from the other primates can best be understood in the light of the great apes. This is not to say that the gibbon line lost all of its interest for them. At least this is not the case for Le Gros Clark and Vallois. This is perhaps not entirely surprising considering that all these scholars promoted that the human line had departed from a generalized hominoid stock. The gibbons could justifiably figure among such generalized hominoids in more than one aspect. Remember that in the mid-1930s Le Gros Clark (1934, 1935, 1936) held that the human branch had departed from the hominoid apes at the very base of this radiation in the Oligocene period, from a quite generalized form (see Chapter 4). A few years later, however, Le Gros Clark modified his view. Such changes were apparently largely instigated by taking the fossil record into consideration more fully. Previously, Le Gros Clark held that the primate fossil record was too incomplete to permit any precise phylogenetic inferences, so that one had to rely much more heavily on comparative anatomy. He stated:

> Unfortunately, palaeontological records even approaching such completeness are very rare, and they can hardly be said to exist so far as the evolution of the Primates is concerned. The major part of the evidence upon which zoologists have perforce to depend for the reconstruction of the phylogenetic lines of the Primates is therefore derived from the study of the comparative anatomy of existing forms and of such fossil forms as have hitherto been discovered. (Le Gros Clark, 1934: 4)

Now, Le Gros Clark assessed that the tables had turned and that comparative anatomy could no longer establish the phylogenetic relationships with any more precision than it already had. He stated:

> The question now arises whether we are likely to gain any more certain knowledge regarding the genetic affinities of Man and the anthropoid [hominoid] apes by further comparative anatomical studies of existing forms. The answer to this is—probably not . . . (Le Gros Clark, 1939a: 56–57).

This method, insisted Le Gros Clark, is unable to distinguish clearly between similarities related to kinship from those resulting from parallel evolution. In the future, he continued, this will have to be done through the fossil record. It is precisely what Le Gros Clark set out to do in the late 1940s and early 1950s by getting firsthand knowledge of the East African hominoids of the Miocene and the South African australopithecines of the Plio-Pleistocene.[16] Starting in 1940, Le Gros Clark's viewpoint on humankind's place among the primates already showed some modifications following either the fossil discoveries or the reevaluation of *Limnopithecus*, *Proconsul*, and *Ramapithecus*. Such changes were then confirmed and developed throughout the 1940s, 1950s, and 1960s. Among the most important changes were the following:

1. Le Gros Clark still maintained that the human line had split from the hominoid stock at a stage when that ancestor was a generalized anthropomorph-like form, although he now alluded that such a form was perhaps not as generalized and as small as he previously believed. Above all, his conception of this common ancestor was

presented with much more clarity than in the past. This ancestor was no longer exclusively a generalized tree-living creature but rather a generalized quadrupedal one, not exclusively confined to the trees.

2. Le Gros Clark previously held that the human line had split from the hominoid stock at the very base of this radiation in simultaneity with the gibbon line. Now, he argued that the human line had split at the base of the stem which regrouped the three great apes, thus introducing a slightly earlier split between the gibbons, on the one hand, and all the other hominoids, on the other hand.[17]

3. Whereas Le Gros Clark had previously placed this split event in the Oligocene period, he now placed this segregation process in the Miocene period, although he was perhaps not prepared to definitely exclude the Pliocene period for such a splitting event.[18]

4. Le Gros Clark no longer insisted on the pervasive effect of parallel evolution in hominoid phylogeny, as if the fossil record had convinced him that such a parallelism was present but was certainly not as important as he once believed. Le Gros Clark now somewhat downplayed parallelism in hominoid phylogeny in favor of structures which were inherited from a common generalized ancestor.

In Le Gros Clark's (1950a, 1955, 1960a, 1964, 1967, 1971; Le Gros Clark and Leakey, 1951) modified view, a small and generalized gibbon-like form perhaps not unlike *Propliopithecus* of the Oligocene period probably gave rise in the Lower Miocene period to two distinct evolutionary stems: one evolving toward the adaptive radiation of the gibbons through forms such as *Pliopithecus*, and another evolving toward the adaptive radiation of the larger great apes and the living humans.[19] Le Gros Clark placed near the base of the great ape radiation a form like the Lower Miocene *Proconsul* (later sunk in *Dryopitecus africanus*), an assumed sign post on the road to the living great apes and humankind.[20] *Proconsul* was believed to be sufficiently generalized to indicate how the evolutionary split between the specialized great apes and the more generalized humans could have occurred. *Proconsul* was described as having monkey-like limb proportions (equal in size) adapted for a quadrupedal locomotion, a moderate prognathism, a poorly developed supraorbital torus, and middle-sized canines and incisors.

From this original state, the great apes developed a number of specilizations as seen in their relatively long arms now adapted for brachiation, their projecting face, their well-developed canines and incisors, and their important supraorbital torus (excluding the orangs). At one time or another, Le Gros Clark recognized among fossils such as *Dryopithecus*, *Palaeopithecus*, and *Palaeosimia* forms near the ancestry of the three living great apes, the former two being related to the African great apes and the latter to the orang-utan. For Le Gros Clark, the hominoid apes (including the gibbons) developed a number of similar traits in parallel, especially their adaptation to brachiation. From a *Proconsul*-like form, the human branch adapted to a bipedal locomotion and avoided the development of many specialized ape-like structures seen in the living hominoid apes and in their immediate ancestors. However, if the earliest ancestors of the human line had canines not as developed as the living great apes, it should not be assumed that they were necessarily small or absent. Although Le Gros Clark remained vague in the 1940s and 1950s about Miocene or Pliocene hominid ancestors, he recognized in the 1960s that *Ramapithecus* might possibly constitute such a link (Le Gros Clark, 1967: 129; 1971: 344).[21] It was argued that East Africa was probably in the Oligocene and Miocene periods the cradle of all the living hominoids, with India being a later and secondary center of dispersal.

Not unlike Le Gros Clark, Vallois worked out a way between the gibbons and the great apes in order to understand the departure of the human line from the other primates. One has to wait for the second half of the 1950s to get a clear presentation of Vallois's conception of humankind's place among the primates. Prior to that, Vallois's view was rather vague although he was inclined to believe that the human stem had departed early from the other primates near the junction point where the Old World monkeys and the hominoids had also split (e.g., Boule and Vallois, 1952).[22]

By the mid-1950s, Vallois (1955a, 1956, 1961) had changed his mind about the proximity of humankind and the hominoid apes, although he continued to believe that the human stem had sprung from a generalized form and not from a specialized living hominoid ape. He now promoted that all the hominoids, including the humans, arose in the early Oligocene period from a primitive tree-living gibbon-like form not unlike *Propliopithecus*, that was certainly not yet too committed to a brachiating mode of locomotion, if at all. From this common source, the gibbon line evolved through *Limnopithecus* and *Pliopithecus*, while the great apes and the humans all individually sprang later from a common generalized *Proconsul*-like ancestor in the late Oligocene or early Miocene period. For Vallois, the great ape lines gradually went through a specialization process and developed long arms for a fully brachiating mode of locomotion, large frontal teeth and canines, and a projecting face.

On the other side of the divide, the human line not only avoided such specializations but either kept its generalized conformation or gradually went through a reduction of the canines and of the face in general. This line also developed early long legs for a bipedal locomotion followed only much later by an increase in brain size. It was held that the dryopithecines were extinct evolutionary lines too specialized to have contributed to the ascent of humankind, although forms such as *Sivapithecus* and *Ramapithecus* showed a number of human-like traits that were evolved independently of the human lineage. In Vallois's phylogenetic hypothesis, the African great apes—the chimpanzee and the gorilla—were humankind's closest living relatives.[23] Unable to pinpoint the exact location of humankind's birthplace, Vallois identified the African or Asian lands surrounding the Indian Ocean to be such a place.

More than Le Gros Clark and Vallois, Leakey assessed the separation of the human line from the other primates in the light of the great apes exclusively, thus giving no consideration to the gibbons. For Leakey (1943, 1948, 1953; Le Gros Clark and Leakey, 1951), humankind and the three great apes were derived from a common ancestor during the first half of the Miocene period.[24] Leakey insisted that the early Miocene primates of East Africa called *Proconsul* were instrumental in shedding light on the nature of this separation. Leakey saw in *Proconsul* a very primitive ape-like form. On the one hand, this form presented several monkey-like features in the anatomy of its brain case and in the proportions of the arms and legs, clearly showing that this creature still possessed a quadrupedal mode of locomotion once shared in common with the Old World monkeys in the Oligocene period. On the other hand, it was argued that *Proconsul* was already clearly committed in the ape direction as seen in the morphology of its dentition and jaw conformation. What this ape form revealed above all, insisted Leakey, was that its generalized features placed it in the ancestral position to both the living great apes line and the living humans line.[25]

The lack of a supraorbital torus, the general lightness of the body structure of the skull, and the absence of a genuine simian shelf in the jaw were all interpreted as generalized ape features. This implied that the specialized features of the living great apes such as an important supraorbital torus (except in the orang), large frontal teeth, massive simian shelf, long arms relative to the legs, etc., were all gradually developed since the early Miocene. For Leakey, the dryopithecines departed from the ape stem before the ape/hominid divergence had occurred, although the dryopithecines evolved many features in parallel to the living great apes.[26] When turning to the branch leading to the living humans, Leakey fostered the idea that it altogether avoided a brachiating phase of evolution, meaning that the bipedal gait directly developed out of a quadrupedal mode of locomotion. Leakey saw in the generalized features of *Proconsul* a suitable ancestral stage to the human line. Although Leakey first stated that *Sivapithecus africanus* of the early Miocene of East Africa was probably ancestral to the European and Asian dryopithecines (Le Gros Clark and Leakey, 1951), he soon changed his mind and suggested that the fragmented remains of *Sivapithecus africanus* may prove to be a candidate directly ancestral to the human line, while *Sivapithecus indicus* of the Pliocene of India was part of an extinct hominid side branch shared with *Ramapithecus*, which itself departed from the main human stem in the mid-Miocene (Leakey, 1953). Leakey stressed that more discoveries of *Sivapithecus* could throw much light on the later phases of human phylogeny.

In the 1960s, Leakey added and slightly modified some components of his view. This change was brought about mainly by some primate fossil recoveries. Leakey (1960a, 1961a, 1961b, 1962, 1963) now recognized in the early Miocene deposits of Kenya two unnamed mandibles of genuine great apes with a well-developed simian shelf and canine-like third premolars. Remember that Leakey previously assumed that these morphological features had developed only during the later stages of the evolutionary history of the great apes. The discovery of such unnamed forms showed, in Leakey's mind, that the specialized features of the great apes were already fully developed by the early Miocene period. On that basis, Leakey no longer proposed that *Proconsul* was a generalized form from which stemmed both the living great apes and the humans. Rather, Leakey (1960a, 1961a, 1962, 1968a) excluded *Proconsul* from the great apes evolutionary line and put it exclusively at the base of the human line. Now, the human and great apes evolutionary lines were thought to have been separated from each other since the late Oligocene period, thus leaving their common ancestry unspecified (Leakey, 1963).[27]

As far as the human line is concerned, Leakey (1961c, 1963, 1967, 1968a, 1970) recognized in the newly discovered primate fossil remains called *Kenyapithecus africanus* and *Kenyapithecus wickeri*, respectively of the early Miocene and early Pliocene periods, what he believed constituted the oldest known hominids.[28] Leakey (1968b) even held that *Kenyapithecus* had been making use of stone tools. Among the assumed hominid features of *Kenyapithecus* were the reduced upper canines, the shovel-shaped upper incisors, the shape of the dental arcades, and a less prognathous face. For Leakey, *Kenyapithecus* and *Ramapithecus* were both early hominids, which indicated that the roots of the human evolutionary line was a deep one, geologically speaking. Leakey (1967: 155) stated:

> [As *Ramapithecus* and *Kenyapithecus*] were already present in India and East Africa respectively, in Mio-Pliocene times we should expect to find still earlier ancestral members of the family Hominidae either in the Middle or even in Lower Miocene deposits . . . [T]he origin of the family Hominidae may even be found to extend back to the Oligocene.

Although Leakey remained open about finding the earliest hominids outside Africa, he repeatedly claimed that all the major evolutionary steps in the rise of the human line probably occurred in Africa.

In a conception showing many similarities to Leakey's view of the 1950s, Heberer (1952, 1955, 1956, 1959a [1962], 1959b, 1965) also evaluated the rise of the human line in relation to the three great apes exclusively. Heberer placed the departure time of the human line from a primitive pongid type either in the Early Miocene or no later than in the Middle Miocene period.[29] Heberer insisted that the Mio-Pliocene dryopithecines were probably already too committed in the direction of the living great apes to constitute also a proper ancestor to the living humans. This was seen especially in their specialized frontal teeth, a specialization which probably announced their future evolution toward a fully brachiating mode of locomotion. Recognizing in *Ramapithecus* some human-like features, Heberer believed them to have been merely acquired independently from the human line under parallel evolution. Turning to *Proconsul*, the idea was advanced that this Early Miocene form nearly approached the morphological type shared in common by the great apes and humankind. By being a tree-living quadrupedal creature with grasping hands and feet which was not adapted to a brachiating mode of locomotion, as seen by its legs and arms of about equal length, *Proconsul* reveals some clues as to how the brachiating great apes and the bipedal humans could have independently arisen. In fact, Heberer saw in *Proconsul* a sort of generalized brachiator that could occasionally adopt brachiating behaviors without, however, being structurally adapted to, or specialized for, brachiation.

It is in this sense only that Heberer (1959b: 237) dubbed his own conception of human evolution the "prebrachiation-hypothesis", meaning that bipedality had arisen not from a genuine brachiation phase but rather from a tree-living quadrupedal one. For further proof of the lack of a brachiating phase in human evolution, Heberer turned to the postcranial remains of the Plio-Pleistocene australopithecines that not only indicated that these creatures were fully bipedal but also lacked traces of brachiation. Looking for primitive pongid forms to establish a phylogenetic link between the proconsuloids and humankind, Heberer identified in *Oreopithecus* of the Late Miocene or Early Pliocene period a form which clearly indicated that, by that time, the human line had been on its own. The exclusively hominid status of *Oreopithecus* was confirmed, contended Heberer, by a combination of features such as the absence of canine-like first premolars, lack of an upper diastema, a somewhat parabolic jaw shape, and wide hip bones. This being said, Heberer saw in *Oreopithecus* not a direct ancestor to the living humans but a somewhat early specialized extinct offshoot of the human stem. Considering the wide geographical distribution of the hominoid fossil remains, Heberer was unable to pinpoint the cradle of the human line in the Old World.

OUT OF A SPECIALIZED HOMINOID STOCK

A third group of scholars, well-represented by Washburn, Hooton, Gregory, Weidenreich, von Koenigswald, Patterson, Simons, Pilbeam, and Simpson, thought the human line departed from the primates from either a not too generalized or a somewhat specialized hominoid form. Through the promotion of this view, the tradition of interpretation to which Keith, Hooton, Gregory, and Pilgrim contributed in the 1890–1935 period was continued. Although not agreed on the exact moment when the human line departed from the hominoid radiation, the scholars of the 1935–1965 period placed this event in the Oligocene, the Miocene, or even as late as the Pliocene period. As far as the conformation and the behavior of this last common ancestor are concerned, it was generally believed to be a somewhat large hominoid ape committed either to a prebrachiating or a brachiating mode of locomotion, rather than a small-bodied quadrupedal hominoid.

For proponents of this view, the human line arose from within the dryopithecine radiation, broadly defined. This being said, they did not agree on the exact relationship between humankind and the other hominoid apes. Although the gibbon line was usually excluded from their considerations, this was not always the case. Very few scholars were prepared to clearly commit themselves to the view that humankind is phylogenetically speaking (not morphologically) more closely related to the two African great apes exclusively. This implies that the orang-utan had a role to play in many phylogenetic analyses of the 1935–1965 period. This situation was to change after 1965 (see Chapter 10). The order of our presentation here is made according to the number of living hominoid apes judged relevant to analyze the rise of humankind, starting with the scholars who included all of them and ending with those who were inclined to exclude all of them except the two African great apes.

For Washburn, the human line departed from the other primates at the base of a hominoid radiation which comprised all the hominoid apes.[30] This conception is, phylogenetically speaking, similar to the views of several scholars already reviewed. However, it differs in that this divergence event is envisioned not to have occurred at a generalized evolutionary stage but at a somewhat specialized one. This is a clear indication that phylogeny and morphology are not necessarily tightly related in the phylogenetic analyses. After all, it is possible to promote simultaneously that two forms are morphologically very similar and yet phylogenetically distant from one another, the reverse also being true. Several factors can explain this discrepancy, including parallel evolution and adaptive pressures. It is for the evolutionists to try to interpret the mixed signals displayed by nature. The viewpoints of the scholars reviewed in this section will highlight the flexibility of the conceptual relationship between phylogeny and morphology in the context of hominoid evolution.

Of all the scholars who promoted that humankind directly sprang from a rather specialized hominoid ape, Washburn's view was perhaps the most extreme one in the sense of allowing for a specialized ape form to transform itself in a human form quite rapidly. For Washburn (1950, 1963a), the adaptive radiation of the hominoids depended on a locomotion adaptation: brachiation. This new mode of locomotion instigated profound anatomical and behavioral changes in the upper body taking the hominoids away from the quadrupedal manner of the monkeys. In Washburn's view, humankind shared with the other living hominoids every essential detail of the brachiation adaptive complex, humankind being merely a modified brachiator. It was contended that the human radiation, itself based on an adaptation to live on the ground (bipedality), is entirely founded on the brachiation adaptive complex. On this view, the principal question to be resolved is how a brachiating ape was transformed into a fully bipedal human.

To bolster the thesis that humankind had sprung directly from a fairly specialized or committed brachiator, Washburn turned to comparative anatomy.[31] For instance, a shorter pelvis and a slight reconfiguration of the accompanying muscles would be needed for a gibbon type to complete a powerful extension of the leg required in a fully bipedal creature. Similarly, because the morphology of the gorilla's foot approaches the human condition, no major evolutionary change is needed to transform it to a fully bipedal foot. Likewise, the leg muscles used by the hominoid apes in climbing need no radical alteration of form and function to become a fully functional complex required in bipedality, thus clearly demonstrating that climbing is a preadaptation to human walking. In Washburn's view, therefore, a relatively small adaptive shift in the mode of locomotion would have been enough to instigate a divergence between all the hominoid apes (including the gibbons) and humankind. Indeed, Washburn promoted that the human stock departed from the common hominoid stock as recently as the very last portion of the Pliocene period. This implied that the differentiation now observed between the gibbons, the orangutans, the chimpanzees, the gorillas, and the humans essentially took place during the Pleistocene period.[32]

Whereas Washburn incorporated the gibbon line in his phylogenetic considerations, Hooton, Gregory, Weidenreich, von Koenigswald, and Patterson excluded it. The real issues for them were the precise role of the orang line in understanding human evolution, the chronological framework of the departure of the human line, and the morphological state at which this separation had occurred. For his part, Hooton envisioned that the rise of the human line from the hominoid radiation had occurred through a not too specialized ancestor and at a not too late divergence date. Although Hooton (1931) had previously established a closer phylogenetic proximity between the African great apes and the humans, with the orangs being slightly more distant, he later incorporated the orang line with the African great apes lines. In Hooton's (1946) latest view, the differentiation of the hominoid stock occurred from a tarsioid type soon after the earliest Old World monkeys were developed. This is seen in *Propliopithecus* of the Lower Oligocene in Egypt, the first hominoid ape, which is also the nearest representative of a gibbon-like stock which gave rise to all the hominoids. Hooton viewed this gibbon-like common ancestor of all the hominoids to be a small, generalized, and arboreal form. He insisted that in both the posture and in the mode of locomotion, the gibbon presented us with an important step in the humanoid direction. It is not that Hooton believed that the gibbon line gave rise to the humans, for he insisted that this now specialized line could be traced back directly to *Propliopithecus* through *Pliopithecus* of the Lower Pliocene of Germany. Rather, Hooton believed that the bipedal gait was made possible in the human line only because earlier it went through a generalized gibbon-like stage of evolution.

In Hooton's view, the next stage in human evolution is to be found in the giant and primitive hominoid stage of the Miocene period, thus approaching the present condition of all the great apes, and in some cases, of the humans. Hooton believed that the orang was probably the first line to diverge from the common great apes/human stock in the Lower Miocene period, as seen in the mid-Miocene fossil remains of *Palaeosimia*. Although Hooton apparently derived the gorilla and the chimpanzee lines directly from the dryopithecine group, he recognized that more fossil evidence was needed to either confirm or refute the idea of the rise of humankind from a primitive *Dryopithecus* stock. This raised uncertainties regarding the phylogenetic place of humankind relative to the three great apes. Previously, Hooton (1931) had embraced unequivocally the idea of deriving the human line from the dryopithecines. Perhaps the recovery of more fossil remains of *Proconcul* in East Africa opened up new evolutionary hypotheses in Hooton's (1946: 280) mind:

> Instead of being ancestral to the chimpanzee, this fossil ape [*Proconsul*] seems to have been nearer to the main ancestral line from which man ultimately was derived. It appears probable that the ancestral chimpanzee diverged from the main giant primate stock before the differentiation of the more specialized Proconsul form in early Miocene times.

As far as can be determined from Hooton's (1946: 411) phylogenetic tree, he believed that the human line had been separated from all the other great apes lines by the early Miocene period only to later pass through a sort of australopithecine-like phase.[33]

Whereas Hooton held that the human line evolved out of a specialized ancestor somewhat early, Gregory, Weidenreich, and von Koenigswald envisioned this ancestor to be slighly more specialized, although they were not agreed on the exact time of its divergence. We have already seen that prior to 1935, Gregory promoted the thesis that humankind had sprung from a relatively late hominoid-like ancestor shared in common with especially the two African great apes, the chimpanzee, and the gorilla (see Chapter 4). Although he was to hold to this view, he was now apparently less inclined than in the past to exclude the orang-utan from humankind's closest living relatives. Gregory (1938, 1951) believed that the human stem had derived from a chimpanzee-like ancestor perhaps as recently as the Lower Pliocene period. But what was the nature of the relationship of this human line with the other hominoids? Gregory saw in the oldest representative of the very diversified and widely distributed dryopithecine group, *Proconsul*, a form closely affiliated to the common stock from which all the living hominoids emerged. He also saw in the Mio-Pliocene forms such as *Dryopithecus* and *Sivapithecus* signs of dental changes which recorded the transformation of the hominoid group which ultimately gave rise to the three great apes and humankind.

Gregory apparently thought of the chimpanzee as a sort of prototype for these latter forms. Indeed, the chimpanzee was believed to be the less modified and the most generalized form of all the living descendants of the dryopithecines. For instance, Gregory insisted that the chimpanzee avoided the limb changes observed in the orang (long arms and long hands), and also avoided going through the size increase seen in the gorilla. It is therefore from such a proto-chimpanzee condition that the human stock developed its own specializations (long legs and short arms), a chimpanzee-like form itself evolved from a semibipedal and gibbon-like ancestor.

More clearly than others, Weidenreich refused to discard the potential importance of the orang line in the rise of humankind, as he conceived the possibility of gene exchanges between all the great apes and the humans. Weidenreich (1943b, 1946) thought that hominid forms like *Pithecanthropus* and *Sinanthropus* could be useful in throwing some light on the question of humankind's phylogenetic link with the hominoid apes, a comparison which showed that the orang line could not be excluded:

> If man could have derived from a common man-chimpanzee stem or a common man-chimpanzee-gorilla stem . . . one would expect the primitive features displayed by *Pithecanthropus* and *Sinanthropus* to reveal a much closer approach to chimpanzee or gorilla than to orang-utang. . . . (Weidenreich, 1943b: 260)

According to Weidenreich, the human line is not closer to the African great apes than to the orang line. He insisted that the separation between the human and the hominoid apes lines occurred at an early hominoid ape stage, that is, before the differentiation of *Dryopithecus* and related forms took place. Because Weidenreich believed that gigantic forms such as *Gigantopithecus* and the australopithecines were akin to the human line—therefore postulating that massiveness was a primitive condition of this line—he was inclined to believe that the gorilla line was perhaps, morphologically speaking, the nearest to the human branch.[34] This being said, Weidenreich would not exclude the possibility that interbreeding took place before a complete separation of the different human and great apes lines had occurred, thus permitting the exchange of features between all of them, including the orang. Weidenreich postulated that the human line had departed from the other three great apes lines perhaps as early as the Lower Miocene period.

For his part, von Koenigswald held that the rise of the human line from within the great apes radiation was achieved through a not too specialized ancestor. Von Koenigswald (1953, 1963) promoted that humankind sprang from the hominoid stock in the Upper Miocene or the Lower Pliocene period at a time when there were many geological and climatological changes. Although at first von Koenigswald (1956: 145) recognized that there existed a fairly close link between the dryopithecines (including *Sivapithecus* and *Ramapithecus*) of the Mio-Pliocene period and the human evolutionary line, he insisted that the former were somewhat over-specialized forms.

Later, however, von Koenigswald (1960 [1962], 1963, 1964, 1976 [1968]) made clear that he derived humankind from within the dryopithecines, but from the less specialized portion of this important and widely distributed adaptive radiation.[35] This less specialized portion was now believed to be constituted of representatives such as *Ramapithecus*, *Sivapithecus,* and *Kenyapithecus*. According to von Koenigswald, the human line had sprung from a form not as specialized as the living great apes, for it retained more primitive features, as seen notably in the lack of a specialized feature such as a simian shelf. Von Koenigswald (1960 [1962]: 58) stated:

> We consider that the hominoidea must have consisted of three groups. A neutral, completely extinct group, unlike any living species of anthropoid ape [hominoid], derived from unspecialized forms [*Propliopithecus*, *Proconsul*]. The anthropoid apes [hominoids] branched off from this group through overspecialization of canines and better adaptation to arboreal life, and the Hominidae branched off through reduction of the canines and by the assumption of an erect posture.[36]

This being said, in no way was the human line derived from a human-like ancestor. On the contrary, since von Koenigswald (1956: 162) stated that we "may assume that, to begin with, the hominids . . . parted from the anthropoids [hominoids] without, at first, developing into something fundamentally different." Indeed, von Koenigswald (1953, 1955, 1963, 1964) assumed that the unknown Miocene or Pliocene direct ancestors of humankind possessed lower molars characterized by the dryopithecine pattern, a diastema and fairly large canines; features still present, it was argued, in some of the pithecanthropines of the Lower Pleistocene. Although *Ramapithecus* was at first considered by von Koenigswald (1956) probably too specialized to have been ancestral to the human line, he (1958) was soon to hold that such a form, of all the known fossil higher primates, presented a conformation that may have approached the Pliocene representatives of the human line.[37] However, von Koenigswald (1962 [1960], 1976 [1968]) was unable at this stage to determine with any certainty whether or not *Ramapithecus* had been truly ancestral to the human lineage. On the basis of the numerous discoveries of genera of higher primates made in India, von Koenigswald inclined to believe that Asia had been the cradle of the human stem.

More than the scholars just presented, Patterson (1954) was prepared to derive the human line from a specialized evolutionary state. Patterson held that the hominoids arose during the Oligocene period and were all quadrupedal creatures at this early stage of their development. This early mode of locomotion was replaced throughout the Miocene period or the Pliocene period by various kinds of brachiating modes of locomotion. Whereas Patterson apparently recognized that the gibbon line had differentiated early from the rest of the hominoid radiation, as seen in the probable ancestral position of *Propliopithecus* of the Oligocene, the two African great apes and the humans were believed to have started their differentiation from one another later in the Miocene period during a dryopithecine phase. Patterson promoted that the human line evolved out of a brachiating ancestor:

> There would seem to be nothing in the known structure of the earlier pongids [great apes] to indicate that they did not brachiate to some extent, and, as Gregory has long insisted, a moderate amount of brachiation seems to be the best explanation of how the hominid line got up on its hind legs. (Patterson, 1954: 207)

Patterson insisted, however, that the brachiating ancestor of the hominids was not as specialized as the living hominoid apes were. The time of the split of the human line from the great apes line was placed at a relatively late date. Because he conceived this event to constitute a rapid evolutionary change, there were no obstacles to placing it as late as the early Pliocene period.[38]

For the last group of scholars reviewed here, the rise of the human line is to be understood largely in light of the African great apes, although references to other hominoid apes were sometimes included. For instance, Simons (1961, 1963, 1964a, 1964b, 1965, 1967) held that the human line arose from within the dryopithecine radiation itself, broadly conceived. In promoting this view, Simons was soon joined by Pilbeam (Simons and Pilbeam, 1965; Pilbeam and Simons, 1965). In fact, Simons and Pilbeam reduced this radiation usually recognized to be composed of many forms to three genera only: *Gigantopithecus*, *Dryopithecus*, and *Ramapithecus*. *Gigantopithecus* was believed to constitute an aberrant extinct side branch which departed from the main dryopithecine group in the Miocene or the Pliocene period. It was argued that the genus *Dryopithecus* was composed of several species distributed throughout a large portion of the Old World, two of which directly led to the chimpanzees and the gorillas. Indeed, Simons (1967) and Pilbeam (1968) later made clear that *Dryopithecus africanus* and *Dryopithecus major* were such respective ancestors. The genus *Ramapithecus* of the late Miocene or early Pliocene period, which was also believed to be widely distributed geographically, was seen as a form directly and exclusively ancestral to the living humans. In fact, *Ramapithecus* was described as an early hominid. This link with the living humans was thought to be reinforced by the similarities seen between *Ramapithecus* and the australopithecines.

Ramapithecus was described as a creature with reduced canines, a parabolic dental arch, a nonprojecting face, and a tendency toward an erect posture.

Simons and Pilbeam established a close genealogical connection between the living humans and the two African great apes, with the living orang-utans being possibly more distantly related. Although the ancestors of the orang-utans were unidentified, it was argued that they probably departed from the *Dryopithecus* stock as early as the Oligocene or the early Miocene period. Simons and Pilbeam had insisted, at first at least, that the orang line had departed from the dryopithecine group before the African great apes and the human lines had differentiated from each other:

> Tentatively, then, one can postulate that an early hominoid line gave rise to the ancestors of *Pongo* [orangs] and the late Oligocene or early Miocene species of *Dryopithecus*-like apes, at present unknown, which were ancestral to *Pan* [chimpanzees], *Gorilla*, and perhaps to *Homo*. (Simons and Pilbeam, 1965: 139)

Later, however, Pilbeam (1967) was perhaps less inclined to believe that the orang line had departed earlier than the other two great apes from the common dryopithecine stock. Simons and Pilbeam were uncertain if the human line had directly evolved from a dryopithecine-like or a *Propliopithecus*-like creature. Indeed, another candidate proposed later as being such a possible last common ancestor between the humans and the great apes was *Aegyptopithecus*. The fact of this uncertainty, and new fossil discoveries, eventually encouraged Simons (1965, 1967) and Pilbeam (1967) to place the rise of the human line still deeper in time, that is, in the Oligocene period.[39]

If Pilbeam had his doubts about the relevance of the orang line for the rise of humankind, Simpson (1945, 1949) was originally inclined to include both the gibbon and the orang lines in his own understanding of this evolutionary process. By the early 1960s, however, Simpson (1962–1963, 1963a, 1966) now evaluated the phylogenetic situation by appealing exclusively to the African great apes, although he felt that the morphological similarities uniting the orangs and the two African great apes had to be explained in one way or another. In Simpson's new view, the gibbon line (*Propliopithecus*, *Pliopithecus*) departed early from the hominoid stock at a stage when the other living hominoids were not yet distinct from one another. The *Apidium-Oreopithecus* line was also believed to have departed from the hominoid stock at such an early stage, evolving toward an evolutionary dead end.

Simpson supported his own early view and continued to promote that the three great apes and humankind had probably sprung from the polymorphic dryopithecine group. But now, Simpson made clear that he believed that the orang line departed first from this assumed dryopithecine group followed next by the human line, thus leaving the chimpanzee-gorilla line fused together for some time before their eventual separation. It was held that, humankind shared a last common ancestor with the chimpanzees and the gorillas, probably in the Miocene period. Simpson assessed that humankind's relationships with the two African great apes were about equal, although the gorilla became somewhat more specialized with respect to the common ancestor. Simpson insisted that the common ancestor of *Homo* (humans) and *Pan* (chimpanzee, gorilla) was more *Pan*-like than *Homo*-like in conformation, although this common ancestor was less specialized than the two African great apes. But because Simpson believed that the gorilla was more specialized than the chimpanzee, it is logical to assume that he saw this common ancestor to be more chimpanzee-like than gorilla-like.

Regardless of the close phylogenetic proximity between humankind and the two African great apes, Simpson clearly stated that the three great apes were, morphologically speaking, much more similiar to each other than either of them was to the humans. Such dissimilarities between humankind and the three great apes were explained by the invasion and adaptation of the human line to an ecological niche which differed from that of the other hominoids (including the gibbons). The human line soon developed an upright posture and a bipedal gait following its divergence with the common stock. It was held that forms such as *Ramapithecus* and possibly *Kenyapithecus* may be near the ancestry of the human line exclusively.[40]

SCENARIOS OF HOMINIZATION: THE IMPACT OF NONHUMAN PRIMATE FOSSILS

As had happened in each time period, scenarios of hominization were appealed to during the 1935–1965 period in order to explain the rise of humankind. Scenarios, remember, are conjectural explanations about the causes or the evolutionary sequence of the rise of humankind's key features. They serve the purpose of filling a void in our knowledge, a void, it is hoped, that will eventually be partially filled by a more complete fossil record and a better understanding of the evolutionary processes and mechanisms at work in human evolution. No doubt, the situation had somewhat improved in the 1935–1965 period as far the fossil record was concerned. This was immediately felt in the scenarios of hominization proposed during that period. Whereas only occasional use of fossil discoveries were made in the 1890–1935 period essentially because of a lack of them, it became common to do so in the 1935–1965 period. Scenarios of hominization proposed after 1935 had a better empirical foundation than most suggested prior to that. This is not to say that they were, empirically speaking, well-founded. Certainly not. Yet, the fossil record started to play a role in suggesting possible evolutionary pathways and perhaps eliminating others, albeit diffidently.

In this new context, it is perhaps not surprising to see that the number of variables being debated in the scenarios of hominization were less anatomic than during the 1890–1935 period. Remember that three sets of such antinomic variables were important during this latter time period: ape-like versus human-like; small-brained versus big-brained; nonbipedal versus bipedal. The meaning of these sets of antinomic variables had subtly changed in the 1935–1965 period. By then, the notion of a genuinely ancient human-like creature with a big brain and a bipedal gait had been completely discarded. The fossil record had showed that this event only occurred during a fairly late geological time horizon. For that reason, when scholars exploited the variables such as human-like, big-brained, and bipedal when referring to ancient forms during the 1935–1965 period they usually meant: a very generalized creature rather than a human-like form; an intelligent creature or a slightly increased brain size rather than a big-brained one; and a semi-erect creature preadapted to bipedality rather than a habitual biped. It is important not to lose sight of the fact that all sets of antinomic variables are relative, so that their meaning could change and, indeed, has changed with the development of paleoanthropology.

Of all the scenarios of hominization reviewed in the 1935–1965 period, it is interesting to note that bipedality is always the earliest feature to appear in human evolution, either alone as the instigating factor of the subsequent rise of the other features or in conjunction with a number of them.[41] Bipedality never arises once the hominization process is well under way.[42] Perhaps scholars could not conceive that all the other attributes usually accompanying the hominization process (big brain, small canines, stone tools, etc.) could have arisen without the liberation of the hands.

Fossil-free scenarios. With the increase of the nonhuman fossil discoveries, it became customary for the students of human evolution to incorporate them in their scenarios of hominization between 1935 and 1965. For scholars like Wood Jones and Hooton, however, no primate fossils were used in their explanation of the hominization process. Presumably, they believed that no discovery made yet could throw any light on this process. Their shared attitude regarding the fossil record in scenario building cannot be explained by a common view of humankind's place among the primates. Whereas Wood Jones promoted an early separation of the human line from a very generalized nonhominoid form, Hooton argued for a later separation from a more specialized hominoid form. For Wood Jones (1948), it is the acquisition of the bipedal gait or the orthograde posture that separated humans from the rest of the primates. Such a change in function and structure instigated a host of changes such as freed hands, the enlargement of the brain case, and the possibility of manufacturing tools for defense. In other words, this new mode of locomotion powerfully contributed to open up new adaptive possibilities and thus constituted the triggering factor which permitted the rise of humankind's own attributes. It is only once the key elements of this new functional package were in place that some structural adaptations were perfected to adjust them to the demands of this new posture.

Wood Jones denied the possibility of a successful and gradual rise of a bipedal gait from a quadrupedal pronograde. For him, this new mode of locomotion is part of an entirely distinct evolutionary package that could not have arisen from an ancestral hominoid-like state. On the contrary, the bipedal gait could only have arisen from a very ancient and much more generalized state, excluding brachiation and saltatory modes of locomotion. The human foot was, for Wood Jones, a definite specialized structure in affording a support for a bipedal gait. Yet, he insisted that such a structure was also a primitive mammalian condition. Similarly, Wood Jones postulated that the bipedal locomotion of the human stock came so early in time that such early ancestors possessed a primitive and simple vertebrate hand type. The unspecialized hand of living humans is therefore an ancient and primitive structure that was liberated from the constraint of locomotion during this primitive state. The arboreal grasping abilities of the hominoid apes were developed in direct opposition to the human pattern toward a more specialized mode of locomotion. Wood Jones viewed the earliest ancestors of the line leading to humans as small and active animals which were not hairy, slouching, or ape-like in conformation.

In contradistinction to Wood Jones, Hooton (1946) envisioned humankind's earliest ancestors at the ape stage as a kind of arboreal creature not yet as large in body size as the present great apes and the humans, although large in comparison to the other primates. Less specialized than the progenitors of the present great apes, these early human ancestors were described as being more versatile in their locomotion with a moderated taste for brachiation in addition to being able to walk biped on branches and perhaps, occasionally, walk on all fours. Faced with a cramped environment, continued Hooton, humankind's earliest ancestors were able to abandon the arboreal life for a life on the ground. They achieved this successfully for these apes were unusually intelligent and daring, had skillful hands and powerful jaws, had a body size which was too large to really benefit from the arboreal life style, and also desired to diversify their diet.

For Hooton, both a modern human body size and a significant brain size were antecendent to, or prerequisite for, humankind's career as a fully bipedal creature on the ground. These changes, insisted Hooton, could not have been attained before the mid-Miocene period. Once on the ground, humankind's earliest and intelligent representatives soon developed implements or tools to prepare the food, thus decreasing the importance of powerful and projecting jaws which permitted the anatomical reduction of this entire functional complex. Similarly, the use of manipulative skills contributed to increase further their brain size. This being said, Hooton warned that not every arboreal ape could have taken the path borrowed by humankind. If the human line diverged from the ape line, insisted Hooton, it was not only because the former went through the hominization process—which involved the positive interactions of a number of key elements—but also because humankind's earliest representatives were already endowed with certain inherent differences and genetic potentialities not present in the other hominoids.

Fossil-based scenarios. Regardless of what could be said of the paucity of the non-human primate fossil record in the 1935–1965 period, it has to be recognized that its influence was significantly felt regarding the debates concerned with humankind's place among the primates. There is perhaps no better demonstration of this than in their use in scenarios of hominization. Indeed, scholars like Arambourg, Piveteau, Pilbeam, and Simons unhesitatingly referred to various fossils in their scenarios of hominization. Considering that a number of other scholars at the time largely based their scenarios on the australopithecines, these observations will be reviewed in the next chapter.

At first, Arambourg's view of the hominization process appealed to *Propliopithecus* and *Limnopithecus*. Arambourg always maintained that the human line had sprung and modified from a generalized hominoid ape since about the Oligocene period. Arambourg (1943a, 1945, 1947, 1948b, 1952) held in the

1940s and early 1950s that the human line departed from the very base of the lineage leading to the living gibbons. For Arambourg, *Propliopithecus* represented such a generalized hominoid ancestor, with its gibbon-like conformation, small size, moderated canines, and relatively short face. From such an ancestor presenting many human-like features, Arambourg argued that the hominization process occurred in the direction of a further reduction of the canines, jaw, and the face in general. *Limnopithecus* was believed to be at the very base of this hominization process in the early Miocene period, already announcing the future arrival of the australopithecines and the living humans.

By the late 1950s and early 1960s, Arambourg's (1959, 1960, 1961, 1965) view of the hominization process was slighly modified on several counts and was now based on *Parapithecus* and *Oreopithecus*. He now believed that the human line sprang out of a hominoid form which was more primitive, more generalized, and less gibbon-like than *Propliopithecus*. *Parapithecus*, a small creature with a reduced prognathism, small frontal teeth, and reduced canines, was to be put at the base of the human line. The hominization process could also be followed in the late Miocene period with *Oreopithecus*, a fully bipedal creature the size of a chimpanzee with a relatively large brain and a reduced snout, but body proportions clearly indicating that this creature was also adapted for brachiation. Although *Oreopithecus* was an aberrant and extinct side branch of the early hominid stock, it nonetheless represented a sign post in the hominization process.

Furthermore, Arambourg now held that the hominization process went directly through the more ancient and more generalized australopithecines of the late Pliocene and early Pleistocene period. Although Arambourg had previously insisted on the correlation between the hominid evolutionary stages (pithecanthropine, Neandertal, and *Homo sapien*) and the gradual advancement of the stone tools industries, he now clearly envisioned the hominization process as being under the key evolutionary factor of the increasing brain size. Indeed, if the liberation of the hands was made possible because of a bipedal locomotion, thus contributing to accelerate the pace of human evolution, it is the enlargement of the brain which constituted the primordial factor that instigated all the other anatomical and intellectual changes, as seen in the gradual complexity of material culture.

For his part, Piveteau essentially referred to *Oreopithecus* in his scenario of hominization. Piveteau (1954, 1957, 1958, 1962) promoted that the hominization process was made possible because of several developments. The acquisition of a new mode of locomotion—the erect posture—was the very reason why the human stem first departed from the ancestor shared in common with the hominoid apes. It was postulated that a bipedal gait started perhaps to be gradually developed as early as the Oligocene period. Piveteau contended that the reduced frontal dentition and the molarization of the premolars typical to all hominids might also be coincident with the rise of a bipedal gait. Thus, the frontal dentition in the human line avoided going through an increase mainly because of a coincident development of a bipedal gait. Piveteau saw in *Oreopithecus* of the late Miocene period a form which showed such a dentition and some anatomical traits associated with an erect posture, a state fully reached by the australopithecines at the turn of the Plio-Pleistocene period. Once the fully bipedal gait was achieved, the hands were totally and permanently liberated. However, Piveteau insisted that the freed hands were only truly instrumental for the hominization process once an enlarged brain was developed, an event which did not occur until a much later time period.

By that time, Piveteau postulated a mutually reinforcing relationship between the freed hands and the brain enlargement, thus contributing to bring the hominization process to its completion. Piveteau (1962) thought that the hands/brain relationship was obvious enough to postulate that the unfamiliar hands of the small-brained australopithecines were surely not yet fully human in conformation. At first, Piveteau (1957) believed that the small-brained australopithecines had failed to reach the level of a thinking being as well as failed to manufacture stone tools. Later, he recognized that they had, in fact, achieved both probably because their small brains had already gone through a reorganization (Piveteau, 1962). By so doing, Piveteau was able to maintain the primacy of the hands/brain relationship in the rise of a truly thinking being.

Pilbeam and Simons made use of another primate fossil—*Ramapithecus*—in their scenario of hominization (Pilbeam, 1967; Pilbeam and Simons, 1965; Simons, 1964a; Simons and Pilbeam, 1965). They held that the earliest hominoids—whether brachiators or proto-brachiators—probably showed a high degree of trunk erectness implying that they spent considerable time walking and running bipedally, either on the ground or in the trees. Humankind's earliest ancestors already possessed, therefore, some preadaptations to a fully bipedal gait. By turning to the fossil record, Pilbeam and Simons established that by the early Pliocene period the human facial and dental features were already developed as seen in *Ramapithecus*.

The anatomical features of *Ramapithecus* were used by Pilbeam and Simons to promote that humankind's ancestors were already, in the Miocene period, tool users. This conjecture was based on the notion that the reduced face and canines of *Ramapithecus* indicated that it was making a living in a different way from the other apes, most probably through a greater use of the hands. Freed hands, in turn, indicated that such a creature was standing upright. Although direct fossil evidence for an increased hand use and a bipedal gait was still wanting, these suppositions were incorporated in a theoretical conception which comprised at least some empirical elements. In Pilbeam's and Simons's scenario of hominization, the rise of the human line was associated to an important evolutionary shift involving a new way of life. It is this evolutionary shift involving anatomical, behavioral, and cultural features—a positive feedback system—which allowed the rapid and profound differentiation of the human line from the other apes.

CONCLUSION

The rise of a better circumscribed and more coherent framework of analysis from which the debates on humankind's place among the primates were conducted undoubtedly constitutes the major feature of the 1935–1965 period. This greater coherence is clearly seen in the various phylogenetic hypotheses which were fusing more or less insensibly into one another. By that time, the phylogenetic hypotheses were being elaborated on implicit consensual principles which were devoid of any breach of fundamental premises.

The fall of the polyphyletic and parallel hypotheses prior to 1935 rendered the elaboration of this new scientific context possible (see Chapters 4 and 5). Remember that whereas the former stipulated that some human races had a closer phylogenetic connection with some primate species than with other human races, the latter promoted that the human evolutionary line was entirely unrelated to the other primates. These theses rested on principles and premises which differed significantly from the ones underlying the interpretative context of the 1935–1965 period. Indeed, scholars now restricted their debates to whether the human line had sprung from a generalized nonhominoid (and nonprosimian) primate, a generalized hominoid ape, or a somewhat specialized hominoid ape. If the diversity of these phylogenetic hypotheses strikes the contemporary reader as unusual, it must nonetheless be appreciated that they were part of a framework of analysis which offered a brand new level of coherence in comparison to the previous time period.

This new scientific context was made possible largely because of a significantly improved fossil record—hominids and nonhuman primate fossils alike. In the light of today's litany that ever more fossils are needed, it is easy to overlook the extent to which the fossil record had improved during the 1935–1965 period. Fossils were, for the first time, extensively used in the elaboration of phylogenetic hypotheses, thus genuinely contributing to reduce the importance of comparative anatomy. Needless to say, the fossil record was still too scarce to really impose a narrow research agenda. If the recovery of nonhuman primate fossils was important during the 1935–1965 period, the recovery of australopithecine fossils in particular was, for its part, simply spectacular. The significance of this latter event in the eyes of a majority of scholars was twofold. First, it permitted extending more deeply into the past the hominid fossil record, thus revealing a more primitive evolutionary stage than the one being represented by the pithecanthropines. Second, it contributed to forging a link between the two research areas respectively concerned with humankind's place among the primates and human phylogeny proper, thus slowly dissolving their relative isolation and contributing to an integrative process of the various research areas in paleoanthropology. Scholars' views regarding the significance and the place of the australopithecines are treated in the next chapter.

NOTES

1. For a different and able analysis of the debates on primate phylogeny between 1930 and 1980 see J.G. Fleagle and W. L. Jungers, "Fifty Years of Higher Primate Phylogeny." In F. Spencer (ed.), *A History of American Physical Anthropology, 1930–1980* (New York: Academic Press, 1982), pp. 187–230.
2. In addition to the references already presented in the previous chapters and throughout the main text of this one, new primate fossil discoveries

between 1935 and 1965 were described and discussed in many papers. Among the most important are the following: D. Allbrook and W.W. Bishop, "New Fossil Hominoid Material From Uganda," *Nature*, 197 (1963): 1187–1190; P.M. Butler and J.R.E. Mills, "A Contribution to the Odontology of *Oreopithecus*," *Bulletin of the British Museum of Natural History*, 4 (1959): 1–26; E.H. Colbert, "A New Primate From the Upper Eocene Pondaung Formation of Burma," *American Museum Novitates*, 951 (1937): 1–18; E.H. Colbert, "Fossil Mammals from Burma in the American Museum of Natural History," *Bulletin of the American Museum of Natural History*, 74 (1938): 255–434; M. Crusafont-Pairo and J. Hürzeler, "Les Pongidés fossiles d'Espagne," *Comptes Rendus de l'Académie des Sciences*, 252 (1961): 582–584; D. Ferembach, "Les Limnopithèques du Kenya," *Annales de Paléontologie*, 44 (1958): 151–249; L. Ginsburg, "Découverte de *Pliopithecus antiquus* Bl. dans le falun savignéen de Noyant-sous-le-Lude (Maine-et-Loire)," *Comptes Rendus de l'Academie des Sciences*, 252 (1961): 585–587; D.A. Hooijer, "Prehistoric Teeth of Man and of the Orang-Utan From Central Sumatra, With Notes on the Fossil Orang-Utan from Java and Southern China," *Zoologische Mededeelingen*, 29 (1948): 175–301; D.A. Hooijer, "Some Notes on the Gigantopithecus Question," *American Journal of Physical Anthropology*, 7 (1949): 513–518; D.A. Hooijer, "Questions Relating to a New Large Anthropoid Ape From the Mio-Pliocene of the Siwaliks," *American Journal of Physical Anthropology*, 9 (1951): 79–94; A.T. Hopwood, "Miocene Primates From Kenya," *Journal of the Linnean Society of London*, 38 (1932–1934): 437–464; J. Hürzeler, "Neubeschreibung von Oreopithecus bambolii Gervais," *Schweizerische Palaeontologische Abhandlungen*, 66 (1949): 1–20; J. Hürzeler, "Contribution à l'étude de la dentition de lait d'Oreopithecus bambolii Gervais," *Eclogae Geologicae Helvetiae*, 44 (1952): 404–411; J. Hürzeler, "Contribution à l'odontologie et à la phylogénèse du Genre *Pliopithecus* Gervais," *Annales de Paléontologie*, 40 (1954): 5–63; J. Hürzeler, "Oreopithecus bambolii Gervais: A Preliminary Report," *Verhandlungen der Naturforschenden Gesellschaft in Basel*, 69 (1958): 1–48; L.S.B. Leakey, "A Miocene Anthropoid Mandible From Rusinga, Kenya," *Nature*, 152 (1943): 319–320; L.S.B. Leakey, "A New Lower Pliocene Fossil Primate From Kenya," *Annals and Magazine of Natural History*, 4 (1961): 689–696; L.S.B. Leakey, "An Early Miocene Member of Hominidae," *Nature*, 213 (1967): 155–163; L.S.B. Leakey, "Upper Miocene Primates From Kenya," *Nature*, 218 (1968): 527–528; W.E. Le Gros Clark and L.S.B. Leakey, "The Miocene Hominoidea of East Africa," *Fossil Mammals of Africa*, 1 (1951): 1–117; G.E. Lewis, "Preliminary Notice of New Man-Like Apes From India," *American Journal of Science*, 27 (1934): 161–179; G.E. Lewis, "A New Species of Sugrivapithecus," *American Journal of Science*, 31 (1936): 450–452; G.E. Lewis, "Taxonomic Syllabus of Siwalik Fossil Anthropoids," *American Journal of Science*, 34 (1937): 139–147; D.G. MacInnes, "Notes on the East African Miocene Primates," *Journal of the East Africa and Uganda Natural History Society*, 17 (1943): 141–181; J.R. Napier and P.R. Davis, "The Fore-Limb Skeleton and Associated Remains of Proconsul Africanus," *Fossil Mammals of Africa*, 16 (1959): 1–69; W.-C. Pei, "Giant Ape's Jaw Bone Discovered in China," *American Anthropologist*, 59 (1957): 834–838; W.-C. Pei and Y.-H. Li, "Discovery of a Third Mandible of *Gigantopithecus* in Liu-Cheng, Kwangsi, South China," *Vertebrata Palasiatica*, 2 (1959): 198–200; K.N. Prasad, "Fossil Primates From the Siwalik Beds Near Haritalyangar, Himachal Pradesh, India," *Journal of the Geological Society of India*, 3 (1962): 86–96; K.N. Prasad, "Upper Miocene Anthropoids From the Siwalik Beds of Haritalyangar, Himachal Pradesh, India," *Palaeontology*, 7 (1964): 124–134; C. Rusconi, "Las especies de primates del oligoceno de Patagonia (gen., Homunculus)," *Revista argentina de paleontologia y antropologia, Ameghinia*, 1 (1935): 71–123; E.L. Simons, "Two New Primate Species From the African Oligocene," *Postilla*, 64 (1962): 1–12; E.L. Simons, "New Fossil Apes From Egypt and the Initial Differentiation of Hominoidea," *Nature*, 205 (1965): 135–139; E.L. Simons, "The Earliest Apes," *Scientific American*, 217 (1967): 28–35; E. Thenius, "Tertiärstratigraphie und tertiäre Hominoidenfunde," *Anthropologischer Anzeiger*, 22 (1958): 66–77; G.H.R. von Koenigswald, "Eine fossile Säugetierfauna mit Simia aus Südchina," *Proceedings of the Section of Sciences*, 38 (1935): 872–879; G.H.R. von Koenigswald, "Remarks on Indopithecus: A Reply," *American Journal of*

Physical Anthropology, 9 (1951): 461–464; D.N. Wadia and N.K.N. Aiyengar, "Fossil Anthropoids of India: A List of the Fossil Material Hitherto Discovered From the Tertiary Deposits of India," *Record of the Geological Survey of India*, 72 (1938): 467–494; J.-K. Woo, "*Dryopithecus* Teeth From Keiyuan, Yunnan Province," *Vertebrata Palasiatica*, 1 (1957): 25–31; J.-K. Woo, "New Materials of *Dryopithecus* From Keiyuan, Yunnan," *Vertebrata Palasiatica*, 2 (1958): 38–42; J.K. Woo, "The Mandibles and Dentition of Gigantopithecus," *Palaeontologia Sinica*, 146 (1962): 63–94; H. Zapfe, "The Skeleton of Pliopithecus (Epipliopithecus) Vindobonensis Zapfe and Hürzeler," *American Journal of Physical Anthropology*, 16 (1958): 441–455; H. Zapfe, "A New Fossil Anthropoid From the Miocene of Austria," *Current Anthropology*, 1 (1960): 428–429; H. Zapfe, "Die Primaten funde aus den miozänen Spaltenfüllung von Neudorf on der Maach (Devinska Nova Ves), Tschechoslowakier," *Schweizerische Paläontologische Abhandlungen*, 78 (1960): 1–293; H. Zapfe, "Ein Primatenfund aus der miozänen Molasse von Oberösterreich," *Zeitschrift für Morphologie und Anthropologie*, 51 (1961): 247–267.

3. See Schepers's primate family tree in *The South African Fossil Ape-Men: The Australopithecinae, Part II, The Endocranial Casts of the South African Ape-Men* (Pretoria: Transvaal Museum Memoir No. 2, 1946), p. 265.

4. Osman Hill's conception of humankind's place among the primates was, by the early 1970s, clearly based on the notion that humans were directly derived from Miocene apes, as especially established through the connection with *Ramapithecus*. See Osman Hill's hominid family tree in *Evolutionary Biology of the Primates* (London: Academic Press, 1972), p. 194.

5. The original text reads as follows: "Les ressemblances si marquées que nous observons entre Hominidés et Pongidés, entre ces deux phylums d'une part et celui des Cynomorphes d'autre part, impliquent, d'une manière à peu près indubitable, l'existence d'un groupe ancestral commun, que l'on peut désigner sous le nom de proto-catarhinien, à partir duquel, selon un rythme évolutif différent, se seraient individualisées, par une divergence de plus en plus accentuée, les trois lignées: Cynomorphes, Pongidés, Hominidés."

6. See Genet-Varcin's primate phylogenetic tree in *Les singes actuels et fossiles* (Paris: N. Boubée & Cie, 1963), pp. 220–221. The writing style of Genet-Varcin in 1963 is rather vague when questions pertaining to phylogenetic relationships are concerned. Gladly, much more precise information can be found on this topic in her primate phylogenetic tree.

7. See the two places of *Ramapithecus* in Genet-Varcin's primate phylogenetic tree, *Les singes actuels et fossiles* (Paris: N. Boubée & Cie, 1963), pp. 220–221.

8. See the place of *Oreopithecus* on the human stem in Genet-Varcin's phylogenetic trees, *Les singes actuels et fossiles* (Paris: N. Boubée & Cie, 1963), pp. 220–221, and *À la recherche du primate ancêtre de l'homme* (Paris: Boubée et Cie, 1969), p. 304.

9. See Hürzeler's two hominoid family trees in "Quelques réflexions sur l'histoire des anthropomorphes." In, *Problèmes actuels de paléontologie, évolution des vertébrés*, No. 104 (Paris: Colloques internationaux du Centre National de la Recherche Scientifique, 1962), p. 448 and "Questions et réflexions sur l'histoire des anthropomorphes." *Annales de Paléontologie*, 54 (1968), p. 229.

10. In fact, in 1968 Hürzeler pushed more deeply into the past all the main speciation events in the hominoid phylogeny as compared to his 1962 viewpoint. Compare his two hominoid family trees in "Quelques réflexions sur l'histoire des anthropomorphes." In, *Problèmes actuels de paléontologie, évolution des vertébrés*, No. 104 (Paris: Colloques internationaux du Centre National de la Recherche Scientifique, 1962), p. 448 and "Questions et réflexions sur l'histoire des anthropomorphes." *Annales de Paléontologie*, 54 (1968), p. 229.

11. Arambourg's slight shift of interpretation can be clearly seen by comparing his two primate family trees in *La genèse de l'humanité*, 5th edition (Paris: Presses Universitaires de France, 1957), p. 123 and *La genèse de l'humanité*, 6th edition (Paris: Presses Universitaires de France, 1961), p. 117. It is perhaps significant of this changing period in Arambourg's mind that he presented us a primate family tree in 1959 in which the names of the primate fossils did not appear. See C. Arambourg, "Les données de la paléontologie humaine." In, A. Varagnac (ed.),

L'homme avant l'écriture (Paris: Armand Colin, 1959), p. 57. Indeed, although Arambourg's general view of primate phylogeny was to change only slightly, there will be some important changes regarding the positions of the primate fossil specimens. Between 1943 and 1957, Arambourg attributed the following places to primate fossils: *Limnopithecus* was an early hominid exclusively, *Propliopithecus* was the common ancestor to all the hominoids (including humans), *Parapithecus* was a generalized form not unlike *Propliopithecus*, *Oreopithecus* was absent and *Apidium* was an early form leading to the Old World monkeys. By the first half of the 1960s, Arambo urg changed their positions: *Limnopithecus* disappeared, *Propliopithecus* was the possible common ancestor to all the ho minoids except the humans, *Parapithecus* was an early representative of the human line exclusively, *Oreopithecus* was part of an extinct hominid side branch and *Apidium* was at the base of this *Oreopithecus* branch.

12. For a more precise view of the relationship between the *Parapithecus*-human line and the *Apidium-Oreopithecus* line within the hominoid stock, see C. Arambourg, *La genèse de l'humanité*, 7th edition (Paris: Presses Universotaires de France, 1965), p. 119.

13. In fact, Arambourg always maintained in his phylogenetic trees that such a separation had occurred in the Oligocene. But in his texts, he went from the early Miocene to the late Oligocene to the Oligocene in general. Compare, C. Arambourg, *La genèse de l'humanité*, (Paris: Presses Universitaires de France, 1943), p. 126; *La genèse de l'humanité*, 4th edition (Paris: Presses Universitaires de France, 1955), p. 118; *La genèse de l'humanité*, 6th edition (Paris: Presses Universitaires de France, 1961), p. 120. The reference to the idea that such a separation had occurred as early as the late Eocene can be found in Arambourg's primate family tree in *La genèse de l'humanité*, 7th edition (Paris: Presses Universitaires de France, 1965), p. 119. This edition contains two different primate family trees which present some small discrepancies. This time, such discrepancies are not between the content of the text and the illustrations but rather between two different illustrations in the same book.

14. See Schultz's primate family tree in "Man's Place among the Primates." *Man*, 53 (1953), p. 8. See also Schultz's family tree of the hominoids in *The Life of Primates* (New York: Universe Book, 1969), p. 251. In this latter tree, Schultz reduced to antiquity of some speciation events involving the hominoids. For instance, whereas Schultz placed the separation of the human line from the hominoid stock in the early Oligocene period in 1953, he placed it at the turn of the Oligocene/Miocene period in 1969.

15. See Arambourg's primate family trees in *La genèse de l'humanité* (Paris: Presses Universitaires de France, 1943), p. 130 and "La classification des primates et particulièrement des hominiens," *Mammalia*, 12 (1948a): 123–135.

16. It is significant that Le Gros Clark's paper of 1940 is precisely entitled "Palaeontological Evidence Bearing on Human Evolution." *Biological Reviews*, 15: 202–230.

17. See Le Gros Clark's family tree of the hominoids in *The Antecedents of Man: An Introduction to the Evolution of the Primates* (Chicago: Quadrangle Books, 1960a), p. 344. This book was first published by the Edinburgh University Press in 1959. See also Le Gros Clark's family tree of the hominoids in *The Antecedents of Man: An Introduction to the Evolution of the Primates*, 3rd edition (Chicago: Quadrangle Books, 1971), p. 346. Although the latter tree was identical with the previous one of 1959, the names of *Limnopithecus* and *Proconsul* were removed from this 1971 tree. Le Gros Clark now sunk *Limnopithecus* under the name *Pliopithecus*, and *Proconsul* was sunk under *Dryopithecus*. Such a taxonomic revision followed the great reduction of names involving the fossil hominoids promoted by Elwyn Simons and David Pilbeam in the 1960s.

18. In 1939 Le Gros Clark (1939a: 58) already indicated that the human line had split from the hominoid stock in the Lower Miocene period and not in the Oligocene period. It should be noted that this paper is by many aspects, most notably by its vagueness, reminiscent of Le Gros Clark's previous conception. In my view, Le Gros Clark's slightly modified conception of humankind's place among the primates starts only to be clearly established in 1940 and after. In 1955, Le Gros Clark (1955: 169) speaks of the separation of the *Pongidae* and the *Hominidae* in the Lower or Middle Miocene period. In 1971, Le Gros Clark (1971: 345) speaks of such a separation in the Miocene or perhaps the very early part of the Pliocene.

19. In fact, Le Gros Clark (1950a; Le Gros Clark and Leakey, 1951) once placed *Limnopithecus* and not *Propliopithecus* in the ancestral position to the gibbon line, on the one hand, and the great apes and humans line, on the other hand. By 1955, he had apparently confined *Limnopithecus* to the gibbon line exclusively (Le Gros Clark, 1955: 168).

20. The connection between the human line and the dryopithecines apparently changed through the years in Le Gros Clark's view. For a time, Le Gros Clark (1950a, 1955, 1960a; Le Gros Clark and Leakey, 1951) was apparently setting apart *Proconsul* from the dryopithecine group giving the impression that this later group was directly ancestral to the living great apes but not to the living humans. This is reinforced by the fact that Le Gros Clark (1947a: 331), speaking of the many specializations of the dryopithecine apes, mentioned that "it appears very doubful whether the conception of a 'dryopithecine phase' in human evolution is any longer tenable". This was contrary to his previous view (Le Gros Clark, 1935, 1939a, 1940) which stated that the human branch sprang from the dryopithecine radiation but during its most early and generalized phase. But following the taxonomic revision of the fossil hominoids in the 1960s, to which Le Gros Clark concurred, *Proconsul* was now part, taxonomically speaking, of this dryopithecine radiation (Le Gros Clark, 1964, 1967, 1971). On this new view, the human line did, after all, spring from the dryopithecine radiation.

21. Prior to that, Le Gros Clark (1940; 1955: 164; 1964: 179) recognized the numerous human-like features of *Ramapithecus* but alluded that it was a fossil hominoid form.

22. It will be remembered that following Boule's death in 1942 this 4th edition of *Les hommes fossiles: éléments de paléontologie humaine* (Paris: Masson, 1952) was entirely reworked by Vallois alone. It is therefore legitimate to take its content to fully and exclusively represent Vallois's own view.

23. See Vallois's primate family trees in "L'ordre des primates." In, P.-P. Grassé (ed.), *Traité de zoologie: Anatomie, systématique, biologie*, Tome XVII, 2ième partie (Paris: Masson, 1955a), p. 2082 and "L'origine de l'homme: État actuel de la question." *Le Concours Médical*, 83 (1961), p. 4909.

24. Previously, Leakey maintained that the four hominoid apes (gibbons, orangs, gorillas, and chimpanzees) and not only the three great apes departed all together from the main human stem. At the time, Leakey placed this separation in the Oligocene period. See L.S.B. Leakey, *Adam's Ancestors*, 2nd edition (London: Longmans, Green and Co., 1934). By 1953, Leakey held that the gibbon line departed alone from the main ape stem in the Oligocene period while the three great apes departed together from the stem leading to the humans in the Miocene period.

25. In 1946, Leakey was apparently more inclined to view *Proconsul* as being already committed in the human direction rather than representing an ancestral form to both the living humans and the great apes. See L.S.B. Leakey, "Fossil Finds in Kenya: Ape or Primitive Man?" *Antiquity*, 20 (1946): 201–204.

26. See Leakey's primate family tree in *Adam's Ancestors*, 4th edition (London: Methuen & Co., 1953), p. 212.

27. It is not clear if Leakey maintained throughout the 1960s the idea that the *Proconsul* group was at the base of the human line. For instance, Leakey once alluded to the possibility that the human line (*Hominidae*) might have been developing in parallel with the *Proconsul* group (*Proconsulidae*) in the late Oligocene period, without specifying the nature of their relationship. This suggestion opens the theoretical possibility that the human line is merely evolving in parallel with the *Proconsul* group without stemming from it. See L.S.B. Leakey, "East African Fossil Hominoidea and the Classification Within this Super-Family." In, S.L. Washburn (ed.), *Classification and Human Evolution* (Chicago: Aldine, 1963), pp. 32–49.

28. Leakey sank or incorporated in his newly created species of *Kenyapithecus africanus* the fossil remains of what he formerly called *Sivapithecus africanus*.

29. See Heberer's hominoid family tree in "Das moderne Bild der Abstammungsgeschichte des Menschen." *Berliner Blätter für Vor- und Frühgeschichte*, 4 (1955), p. 4 and in "Die Abstammung des Menschen," in L. von Bertalanffy and F. Gessner (eds.), *Handbuch der Biologie*, Vol. 9, *Der Mensch und seine Stellung im Naturganzen* (Akademische Verlagsgesellschaft Athenaion Konstanz, 1965), p. 310.

30. For a biographical note on Sherwood L. Washburn see A.L. Zihlman, "In Memoriam: Sherwood Washburn, 1911–2000," *American Journal of Physical Anthropology*, 116 (2001): 181–183.

31. Note that Washburn also extensively used the australopithecines to throw some light on the evolutionary transition from a brachiating ape to a fully bipedal human (see Chapter 8).

32. See Washburn's hominoid family tree in "Tools and Human Evolution." *Scientific American*, 203 (1960), p. 67.

33. There was no mention of the Taung skull or of *Australopithecus* in the first edition of Hooton's *Up from the Ape* (New York: Macmillan, 1931).

34. See Weidenreich's phylogenetic tree of the hominoid group in *Apes, Giants and Man* (Chicago: University of Chicago Press, 1946), p. 24.

35. Von Koenigswald's book *The Evolution of Man* (Ann Arbor: University of Michigan Press, 1962) was first published in German as *Die Geschichte des Menschen* (Berlin: Springer-Verlag, 1960). Similarly, von Koenigswald's book *The Evolution of Man*, revised edition (Ann Arbor: University of Michigan Press, 1976) was first published in German as *Die Geschichte des Menschen* (Berlin: Springer-Verlag, 1968).

36. A few years later, von Koenigswald (1976 [1968]: 61) used the exact same words to describe his viewpoint. See von Koenigswald's primate family tree in *Meeting Prehistoric Man* (New York: Harper & Brothers, 1956), p. 202. This book also appeared in German under the title *Begegnungen mit dem Vormenschen*.

37. In von Koenigswald's (1958: 75) own words: "De tous les Primates supérieurs fossiles connus, ce *Ramapithecus* est *le plus proche* du type représentatif des Hominidés au Pliocène, tel que nous pouvons l'imaginer." The italics are not mine.

38. See Patterson's primate family tree in "The Geologic History of Non-Hominid Primates in the Old World," *Human Biology*, 26 (1954), p. 204.

39. Compare Simons's hominoid family trees in "The Early Relatives of Man." *Scientific American*, 211 (1964b), p. 55 and "The Earliest Apes." *Scientific American*, 217 (1967), p. 35. See Pilbeam's hominoid family trees in "Man's Earliest Ancestors." *Science Journal*, 3 (1967), p. 53 and *The Evolution of Man* (London: Thames and Hudson, 1970), p. 83 and 113.

40. See Simpson's two hominoid phylogenetic trees in "The Meaning of Taxonomic Statements." In S.L. Washburn (ed.), *Classification and Human Evolution* (Chicago: Aldine, 1963), pp. 26–27.

41. The notion that bipedality arose first either alone or in conjunction with other features is also promoted in the scenarios of hominization of Dart, Weidenreich, Washburn, Robinson, and von Koenigswald. These are reviewed in Chapter 8.

42. A possible exception to this is von Koenigswald (see Chapter 8). However, this exception is valid only because the hominization process is defined in a specific way. Von Koenigswald recognized that bipedality was the earliest feature which appeared but not the instigator of the hominization process. For him, the definition of this process only started when the brain grew and when stone tools appeared.

8

The Place of the Australopithecines, 1925–1965

A HISTORIOGRAPHICAL NOTE

The story of the australopithecines starts in 1925 when the first fossil discovery was made public. This story is recounted here in the 1935–1965 period because its impact on paleoanthropology only started to be significantly felt in the 1940s and after. How can this delayed impact be explained? Until 1936 there was only one known representive of the australopithecine group: the Taung child or *Australopithecus africanus* of South Africa. It is common to hear today that the impact of the australopithecines on the field was delayed because the Taung skull was in the wrong geographical place, Africa rather than Asia, and its small brain was the wrong morphological combination because a bigger brain was expected (e.g., Cartmill et al., 1986; Hammond, 1988; Lewin, 1987: 47–62; Tobias, 1984: 45–46, 1992; Washburn, 1985).[1] According to this historiographical interpretation, the field of paleoanthropology was dominated then by two "theories" which, when combined, could only have contributed to reduce the importance of the Taung recovery. Let us take them in turn from a critical perspective.

In one such "theory", it was argued that it is the brain which led the way in human evolution. It seems logical to assume that proponents of this hypothesis would believe that the Taung skull had a brain too small to be ancestral to the living humans. Indeed, Keith (1931: 67–71), who embraced this view, was apparently inclined to exclude the Taung skull from human ancestry on the basis of brain size, among other reasons. However, what seems logical to a modern observer need not be obvious for scholars in a different scientific context.

First of all, it is hard to see how the small brain of the Taung skull could have been such an insurmountable obstacle to its placing near the human line when considering that the young age of this specimen instigated debates about the size it would have reached by adulthood (e.g., Alsberg, 1934; Broom, 1933: 122–123; Dart, 1926; Keith, 1925b, 1931: 67; Sollas, 1925; Zuckerman, 1928). Scholars accepted that the Taung skull had an actual brain capacity of somewhere between 450 cc and 520 cc, but according to the evaluated age of the specimen and the model used to extrapolate the rest of the growth (human, chimpanzee, or gorilla) they arrived at figures ranging from 515 cc to 750 cc depending on the assumed sex of the specimen. This certainly provides a lot of flexibility of interpretation, even for a proponent of the hypothesis that it is the brain which led the way in human evolution.

Indeed, a strong proponent of this hypothesis like Elliot Smith (1927: 167–168) argued that the Taung skull may show both an increase in brain size relative to the other hominoid apes as well as a reorganization of brain structures that was only completed later by other forms in human evolution. If brain size was one issue, brain structure was another. It is one thing to exclude the Taung skull from human ancestry because of its supposedly insufficient brain size but what about the possible reorganization of its brain structures? Again, this offers more flexibility for the interpretation of this fossil discovery. For his part, Elliot Smith (1927) was not prepared to exclude the Taung skull from human ancestry.

But there is more to it. It is not even clear if the notion that the Taung skull presented the wrong morphological combination was such a determinant factor in its dismissal from human ancestry. We have already seen how scholars like Dixon, Pycraft, Marett, Coon, Paterson, and Gates have been able to accommodate widely divergent morphological types such as *Pithecanthropus* and Piltdown man within evolutionary stems that contributed to the rise of living humans (see Chapter 5). The least that can be said is that the notion of a so-called expected morphological combination was rather flexible in the field of human evolution during the 1890–1935 period. This certainly could be applied when considering the immature state of the Taung specimen. After all, who could really predict what an adult specimen would have looked like?

The other "theory" which supposedly dominated the field of paleoanthropology in the first part of this century stipulated that Asia was the cradle of humankind because the Tertiary environmental changes related to the uplift of the Himalaya mountains constituted challenging conditions ideal for the rise of the versatile and capable human line (e.g., Barrel, 1917; Black, 1925; Lull, 1917: 671–672; 1929, 672–673; Osborn, 1926). Clearly, this hypothesis has the merit of proposing an environmental context explaining the split of the human line from the other primates. Yet, its great weakness resides in the fact that many places on earth were known to have constituted challenging environments during these same geological periods. Why then should Asia be the birthplace of humankind rather than Africa or anywhere else? Indeed, Dart (1925a, 1926) himself, who recognized early the importance of the Taung skull, pointed out that South Africa presented to the australopithecines a stimulating milieu which contributed to their evolution out of apedom.

It cannot be denied that only a limited number of scholars located the cradle of humankind in Africa at the time. This is understandable considering the limited number of African primate fossils known in the 1920s. However, this situation was to change drastically in the following decades. We have already seen that every part of the habitable globe has been held by one scholar or another to constitute humankind's birthplace during the 1890–1935 period (see Chapter 4). In this scientific context, it is difficult to imagine that the African location of the Taung skull could have been an insurmountable obstacle to its placement in human ancestry. In fact, the contrary may sometimes be true. As more australopithecine fossils were recovered in Africa starting in the mid-1930s, scholars in the 1940s, 1950s, and 1960s started to either anticipate or even recognize that the australopithecines were probably widely distributed throughout the Old World. This will be clearly seen in this chapter. It is certainly interesting to note how discoveries of australopithecines in Africa eventually aroused the interest for the same fossil group in Asia and maybe even in Europe. Clearly then, the assumed location of humankind's cradle is a factor which cannot be so restrictive in the evaluation of new fossil discoveries.

When looking at the field of paleoanthropology in the 1920s, it is not obvious at all that the two so-called theories just discussed have had an important role in the dismissal of the Taung child from the human ancestry. We have seen more than once in this book that the history of paleoanthropology has often been misconstrued because it was based on a selection of a small number of specimens that scholars thought to represent the view of an entire time period. Remember that the Taung skull was discovered at a historical moment when a diversity of viewpoints about humankind's place in nature reached a peak never seen before or after (see Chapters 4 and 5). This diversity of viewpoints concerned not only the nature of the phylogenetic link between the living humans and the other beings but also the timescale of such evolutionary events as well as the geographical areas covered by them. The fact that no less than four scholars (Dart, Broom, Adloff, and Alsberg) before 1935 were clearly prepared to place the Taung skull near the human line is not an insignificant event in itself. To this, we must also add the scholars who were awaiting more fossil recoveries before openly embracing this view (e.g., Elliot Smith, 1927; Sollas, 1926).

An obvious problem with the reception given to the Taung child relates more to the expectation of the modern observers than to the scholars of the time. Believing as we do today that the autralopithecines are both closely related to the human line and probably geographically restricted to Africa, it is certainly tempting to expect that the scholars of the time should have believed the same. As already stated, however, the scientific context then was entirely different from ours.

In fact, it would have been entirely abnormal for them to so readily embrace the Taung skull as if they knew what to expect from future discoveries. The diversity of the viewpoints at the time attests precisely that no one agreed about the supposed expectations. It is therefore difficult to believe that *Australopithecus* was dismissed by a majority of scholars only because it had a small brain and was discovered in Africa. It is argued here that the reception given to the Taung skull in the 1920s and 1930s must be taken at face value: the discovery of a single immature specimen not well dated. Furthermore, it must not be forgotten that the Taung skull arrived on the scene at a moment when there were many interesting fossil discoveries being made and evaluated (Rhodesian man, *Sinanthropus*, *Hesperopithecus*, etc.). Considering the general turmoil of the time, perhaps the perspective should be reversed: It is the amount of attention which the Taung skull managed to attract which is genuinely remarkable, not the other way around.

THE 1925–1935 PERIOD

We have seen in Chapter 7 that a number of primate fossil discoveries were used between 1935 and 1965 to establish a phylogenetic connection between humankind and the other primates. Among such discoveries frequently referred to at the time were *Propliopithecus*, *Oreopithecus*, *Proconsul*, *Ramapithecus*, and *Kenyapithecus*. Such primate fossils were believed to throw some light on human evolution, but only during the relatively ancient time periods of the early Pliocene, the Miocene, and the Oligocene. The value of these discoveries in providing possible genealogical connections between humankind and the other primates during the 1935–1965 period was increased significantly by another series of discoveries dated to the Pliocene and/or Pleistocene periods: the australopithecines. These only added to the hominid fossils already discovered. Together, all these fossil remains reinforced themselves and helped to blur or break the relative isolation of the two research areas respectively concerned with humankind's place among the primates and human phylogeny proper.

From that time on a number of milestones were available, materially speaking, for scholars to propose a range of phylogenetic hypotheses linking the living humans to the other primates throughout the Oligocene, the Miocene, the Pliocene, and the Pleistocene periods. It is true that such potential milestones were scarce in number and were scattered both in the immensity of the geological times and throughout the geographical area of the entire Old World. Yet, this constituted a genuine and major progress on the pre-1935 period for the field of human evolution.

The impact of the australopithecines on paleoanthropology occurred in two main historical phases. The first phase between 1925 and 1935 saw a majority of scholars being highly reserved if not squarely opposed to the notion that the australopithecines were directly or nearly related to the human line exclusively. This skeptical phase was perhaps understandable considering that this fossil group was being only represented at the time by a single and immature specimen, the Taung child discovered in South Africa in 1924. It was a widely known fact then that immature individuals of the human and great apes species are quite anatomically similar during their early age. This situation changes as the individuals age. This is yet another sign of mistrust from the part of several scholars regarding the use of embryology or ontogeny in the process of phylogeny building in the field of human evolution. However, this view was not shared by everyone.

A small number of scholars like Dart, Broom, Adloff, and Alsberg recognized in the single australopithecine specimen a form shedding considerable light on the place of humankind in nature. According to them, the empirical gap separating the nonhuman primate fossil record and the hominid fossil record was reduced because of this single fossil specimen. When Dart (1925a, 1926, 1929) first described the Taung skull—called by him *Australopithecus africanus*—he was explicit about its place and significance for human evolution. Dart recognized in this specimen a number of hominoid-like features which testified that its membership was to this taxonomic group, broadly defined. Above all, however, he insisted that *Australopithecus* was provided with humanoid features: the teeth and their parabolic arrangement, the nonprojecting face, some brain structures (as seen in the natural endocranial cast), the forwardly positioned foramen magnum, and the general shape and large size of the cranium.

These features, insisted Dart, indicated that this new extinct form was morphologically intermediate between the living hominoid apes and humankind and that it was a man-ape representative of a prehuman stock filling the gap with the most primitive of the ape-men (i.e., *Pithecanthropus*). *Australopithecus* was neither ancestral to any of the living hominoid apes nor a member of the dryopithecines. Its genuine place, he continued, is at the very base or near the ancestry of the human line, depending on its geological position:

> If the deposit at Taungs is not of Tertiary age, but is recent or Pleistocene, then the Australopithecidae represent the later offshoot of the stock which gave rise to man . . . The Australopithecidae gave birth to the Hominidae and South Africa was the land of their travail. (Dart, 1929: 649, 658)

Dart was inclined to believe that *Australopithecus* was Pliocene in age and that Africa had been the cradle of humankind. The significance of *Australopithecus* in human evolution, for Dart (1926), was that it filled an evolutionary stage that had to be theoretically and logically assumed until its discovery. If Dart (1926) recognized that humankind had passed through a hominoid phase of evolution, he made clear that the human line arose from a generalized form which budded from the main hominoid stem before the three great apes departed from it in the Pliocene period in a direction toward greater specialization (Dart, 1929).[2] In fact, Dart (1934) later insisted that although *Australopithecus* is closest among the living apes to the chimpanzee, he specified that the former also shared many features with the orang and especially the gibbon. This incited him to promote the idea that the human line diverged from a pre-gibbonoid stage not unlike *Propliopithecus* of the Oligocene period of Egypt and avoided altogether the dental specializations of the living hominoid apes:

> [T]he dental conditions in Propliopithecus, Australopithecus and primitive men are such that the forms bridging these gaps need never have passed through nor have given rise to any dentitional stage . . . associate[d] with living apes and all the known fossil anthropoids [hominoids] of the dryopithecid genus . . . (Dart, 1934: 220)

Dart promoted that the Oligocene *Propliopithecus* may well represent an ancestral stage to the Pliocene *Australopithecus* through unknown Miocene forms. There was little doubt in Dart's mind that these unknown Miocene intermediate ancestors had small canines just like *Australopithecus* and also probably *Propliopithecus*.

Broom soon joined Dart in the defense that *Australopithecus* is an evolutionary link between the lowest human types (i.e., *Pithecanthropus*) and the hominoid apes. For Broom (1925a, 1925b), *Australopithecus* is a large hominoid ape which presented many features in common with the living African great apes but whose humanoid features, though not entirely developed, clearly pointed toward humanity as seen in a relatively large brain capacity, a human-like dentition and an imperfect erect attitude.[3] Broom (1925b, 1929, 1933) continually changed his mind about the exact age of *Australopithecus*: Pleistocene, Pliocene, or maybe even Miocene? This raised the possibility that Taung might have been too late in time to be directly ancestral to the living humans:

> [T]hough *Australopithecus* may have lived quite recently and thus could not have been the ancestor of *Pithecanthropus* or *Eoanthropus*, the endeavor is to show that these latter and the higher human types have all been descended from an *Australopithecus*-like type but not necessarily from *A. africanus*. (Broom, 1925b: 417–418)[4]

Irrespective of Broom's uncertainties about whether the chimpanzee or the gorilla is the closest living relative to *Australopithecus*, he derived the living humans from within this large ape group in the Miocene or the Lower Pliocene period, with *Dryopithecus* (Europe) near the common ancestry, and through the intermediary of a form approaching *Australopithecus*.[5] This is in sharp contrast to Dart's view which rested on the notion that *Australopithecus* was too generalized in conformation to have entertained such a phylogenetic proximity with the great apes, living or fossil. *Australopithecus* showed, insisted Broom (1925b), that Africa was the cradle of humankind.

Dart and Broom were not alone at the time in believing that the Taung child was significant for human evolution. They soon received the support of Adloff and Alsberg in the early 1930s. Adloff chose dental anatomy to lend support. Adloff (1932) agreed that the molar and the canine morphology of the Taung's specimen was sufficient to show that *Australopithecus* was on the human side of the ape radiation. Adloff explained the ape features of Taung as merely remnants of an ancestry shared in common with the hominoid apes.

For his part, Alsberg appealed to his so-called biological method to attribute a place to the Taung child. Alsberg (1934) concurred with the idea that *Australopithecus* was at the very base or near the human line. He arrived at this conclusion on the basis of the "biological method" which he opposed to the "morphological method". Instead of merely weighing the differences and similarities between organisms in order to assess their phylogenetic relationships, one needed to think in terms of integrated life systems adapted to specific strategies. When applying this principle to human evolution, Alsberg (1934: 158) held that there existed two opposite strategies, the animal kind or the human kind: "The construction of the body must always be based upon a central dominating plan that is adjusted to the evolutionary principle of either animal or man. An ape that is half or quarter of a man is a biological misunderstanding." Whereas the apes developed large teeth and projecting faces for their defense, humankind developed tools for that purpose, thus reducing the necessity for such aggressive anatomical structures. This latter strategy, insisted Alsberg, could only be accompanied by freed hands and a bipedal gait.[6]

The phylogenetic place of the Taung child was established by determining on which side of the divide it fell. With its small canines, reduced face and large brain size, Alsberg evaluated that *Australopithecus* was already committed to the biological strategy of humankind. Thus, *Australopithecus* of the Lower Pliocene represented the first materialized primitive stages that had previously been theoretically conceived to lead to the later hominids (i.e., *Pithecanthropus*). Although Alsberg derived humankind and the hominoid apes from a common ancestor, and although he assumed that the chimpanzee was the closest relative, it is not possible from his writing to establish with any precision the phylogenetic place of *Australopithecus* relative to the hominoid radiation.

Few scholars were prepared at the time to follow Dart, Broom, Adloff, and Alsberg regarding the place of the Taung child in human phylogeny. We have already mentioned that the juvenile status of the specimen certainly contributed to this skepticism. Indeed, Dart (1940b: 170) himself recognized several years later that our ignorance concerning the anatomy of juvenile hominoids justified this attitude to a certain extent. Similarly, Broom (1941a: 10) had to confess that some striking human-like features of the Taung child were indeed only attributable to his young age. Another problem which plagued the case of *Australopithecus* being on the human side of evolution was the admitted difficulty of establishing the datation of the specimen with any precision.

Based on such uncertainties, it is perhaps not surprising to find an important literature between 1925 and 1935 simply unable to take a firm position on the question of *Australopithecus*. Initially, at least, some of these scholars held that more information and more fossil discoveries were needed before determining if *Australopithecus* was an ape or a primitive human (e.g., Boule, 1925; Duckworth, 1925; Elliot Smith, 1925; Romer, 1930). Eventually, however, it became possible to recognize two distinct tendencies among what could be called the uncertain scholars. Some of them were apparently not closed to the idea that *Australopithecus* might eventually be recognized to be related to the living humans. For instance, it was agreed that *Australopithecus* possessed some interesting human-like features that might be indicative of an evolutionary stage in human evolution, although it was impossible to confirm this view as yet (e.g., Sollas, 1925, 1926; Elliot Smith, 1927). This cautious attitude is perfectly understandable considering that it is entirely possible to conceive of a hominoid ape which approached the human condition not so much because of phylogenetic proximity but because of independent parallel evolution. It is precisely on that basis that another group of scholars were more inclined to believe that *Australopithecus* was not phylogenetically related to the human branch, though at this point they were unable to fully confirm this view (e.g., Boule and Piveteau, 1935; Hrdlicka, 1925; Keith, 1925b; Romer, 1933; Smith Woodward, 1925; Zuckerman, 1928).

From uncertainties to certainties, a number of scholars finally took a clear position in favor of the view that *Australopithecus* was phylogenetically related to the hominoid apes and not to the human branch. For instance, Keith (1925c, 1925d, 1925e, 1931) clearly recognized in the Taung child many features which showed that it was phylogenetically related to the two living African great apes, the chimpanzee and the gorilla. *Australopithecus* is an extinct cousin of the African great apes which only presented more human-like features than any other known hominoid ape. It was argued that this should not surprise us considering that humankind and the great apes have a common parentage. In Keith's view, the place of *Australopithecus* in the primate family tree is apparently greatly determined by the datation of the specimen itself. It is worth quoting Keith (1931: 116) at some length:

> If the geological evidence had been such as would have permitted us to attribute Australopithecus to a miocene date, then we should have had to consider seriously . . . that in Australopithecus we have a representative of a prehuman stage of man's ancestry. For most of us who have inquired into the evidence relating to man's evolution are convinced that man has passed through an anthropoid [hominoid] stage, and of all the fossil apes yet discovered Australopithecus comes nearer to our expectation of what our anthropoid [hominoid] ancestor should be like . . . All the evidence bearing on Australopithecus is best explained by supposing it to have sprung as a branch of the phylum which gave us the gorilla and chimpanzee, and not . . . from the root of the human phylum . . . [W]e may regard the gorilla, chimpanzee and Australopithecus as a series in which the chimpanzee represents the older and more primitive form. From this central type the gorilla has evolved in the direction of increased brutalization, while Australopithecus has branched in an opposite direction, thus assuming many human traits.

Not unlike Keith, Weinert (1932) recognized in Taung a form which presented similarities with both the gorilla and the chimpanzee, although he insisted that *Australopithecus* was essentially a chimpanzoid form of the later Pliocene period of South Africa which was not ancestral to the living humans. Weinert stated that the human line was more closely related to a chimpanzoid form of Europe (*Dryopithecus*), a form believed to be probably older than Taung.

If scholars like Keith and Weinert placed *Australopithecus* near a chimpanzee-like line, others favored the gorilla stock. W. Abel (1931a, 1931b) recognized in the dentition of *Australopithecus* a form which presented a number of human-like features. But on the basis of other cranial and dental features—especially the specialization of the milk dentition—W. Abel advanced the idea that the Taung child was clearly affiliated with the two African great apes, the chimpanzee and the gorilla. For him, *Australopithecus* was too specialized to have been near or on the human line. It was held that *Australopithecus* arose from the hominoid stock near the line which gave rise to the gorilla branch, although it never reached the kind of dental (canines) and facial (prognathism) specializations seen in the living gorillas.

O. Abel (1934) concurred with W. Abel's conception that *Australopithecus* was more nearly related to the gorilla line than the other hominoids. Indeed, O. Abel envisioned the Taung child as being a representative of a side branch of the gorilla evolutionary stem that diverged from it in the mid-Pliocene period before going extinct in the Lower Pleistocene.[7] For O. Abel, humankind and the two African great apes were closely related as they all sprang from the dryopithecine group of the Miocene period. Because O. Abel promoted that the human line was more likely to be directly derived from *Dryopithecus darwini*, the chimpanzee line from *Dryopithecus germanicus*, and the gorilla line from *Dryopithecus fontani*, his view implied that *Australopithecus* was more closely related to this latter fossil form.

Similarly, Schwarz (1934, 1936) recognized in a series of morphological features of *Australopithecus* many gorilla-like traits, as seen in the teeth as well as in the skull conformation. On that basis, Schwarz held that *Australopithecus* was a gorilla, but of a pigmy or dwarfed kind. He explained the small canines of the known *Australopithecus* as evidence that such remains are female.[8]

In contradistinction to the previous authors, Le Gros Clark refrained from identifying which living hominoid ape was more closely related to the australopithecines. Le Gros Clark (1934, 1939b, 1940) was content to hold that the extinct australopithecines were merely apes—part of the hominoid radiation which produced a number of forms presenting certain human-like features. The usefulness of these forms unrelated to the human branch, he continued, was to show that they were derived from a primitive and generalized hominoid stock which was endowed with a potentiality for an evolutionary development in the human direction.

The debate on the place of the australopithecines entered a second historical phase starting in 1936. In a sense, this second phase continues to this very day. This time period saw the gradual acceptance, or conversion, of an overwhelming majority of scholars to the thesis that the australopithecines are indeed directly or very closely related to the human line exclusively. This conversion phase—which occurred mainly throughout the 1940s and 1950s—was largely related to the ongoing process of recovery of australopithecine fossils in South Africa between 1936 and the early 1950s (Broom, 1936a, 1936b, 1937a, 1938a, 1938b, 1938c, 1941b, 1942a, 1946, 1947a, 1947b, 1949, 1950b; Broom and Robinson, 1947a, 1947b, 1949a, 1949b, 1949c, 1950a, 1950b, 1950c, 1952; Dart, 1948a, 1948b, 1949a, 1949b, 1949c, 1954, 1955).

Such discoveries comprised specimens of various ages (juvenile, adolescent, and adult) as well as specimens represented by cranial and postcranial parts. It was estimated that at least sixty-five different individuals were represented in this fossil sample (Robinson, 1954a: 183), including several almost complete crania. In addition to *Australopithecus africanus* named in 1925, the 1936–1950 period saw the identification of four new species and two new genera, as seen respectively in *Plesianthropus transvaalensis*, *Paranthropus robustus*, *Australopithecus prometheus*, and *Paranthropus crassidens*.

Far from being restricted to South Africa, the australopithecine fossils were once believed to be widely distributed. Numerous scholars in the 1940s, 1950s, and

1960s had been prepared to recognize that the australopithecines might have had an extended geographical range covering the tropical and subtropical portions of the entire Old World, comprising also Java, China, Israel, Central Africa, and East Africa (e.g., Coppens, 1961a, 1961b, 1962; Leakey, 1959; Leakey and Leakey, 1964; Robinson, 1953a; Simons, 1963; von Koenisgwald, 1952, 1976 [1968]). As it turned out, presumed australopithecine fossils from Java, China, Israel, and Central Africa were all eventually discarded (e.g., Coppens, 1965; Tobias, 1965a, 1966a; Tobias and von Koenigswald, 1964). Since 1959, however, their presence was clearly confirmed in East Africa with the discovery of *Zinjanthropus* (*Australopithecus boisei*). Subsequent discoveries in this region after 1970 comprised forms such as *Australopithecus afarensis* and *Australopithecus* (*Paranthropus*) *ethiopicus*, to name just two. One has to wait until 1995 for a confirmation of their presence in Central Africa (Tchad) as seen in *Australopithecus bahrelghazali* (see Chapter 10).

This is not the place to write a detailed history of the australopithecines' discoveries between 1935 and 1965 (e.g., Dart and Craig, 1959; Morell, 1995; Reed, 1983; Tobias, 1984). More important for our thesis here is their epistemological utility in paleoanthropology during that time period. As already stated, such discoveries contributed to significantly reduce the relative isolation of the research areas respectively concerned with the debates on humankind's place among the primates from those on human phylogeny proper.

WITHIN THE APE RADIATION?

It must not be assumed, however, that unanimity had been achieved in the 1940s and 1950s regarding the phylogenetic place of the australopithecines. This was not the case. Wood Jones, Osman Hill, Zuckerman, and Straus were still either uncertain or unconvinced that the australopithecines should be placed on the human line rather than on the ape line. For them, the recoveries of australopithecine fossils added little or nothing to our understanding of the rise of humankind. How could they deny the hominid status of the australopithecines? It is sometimes believed that the bipedality of the australopithecines should have been recognized as soon as enough postcranial bones were recovered by the late 1940s. Once this bipedality is identified—the argument goes—the hominid status of the australopithecines should have been pretty obvious.

This kind of reasoning assumes that bipedality is unique to the human line. If bipedality was often believed to be primordial in the hominization process, it was not necessarily argued that bipedality was unique to humankind. We saw in the previous chapter that several scholars recognized that the hominoid apes were endowed with a potentiality for an erect posture. In their view, this constituted a common evolutionary background that was only fully exploited in the human line in order to reach a complete and permanent liberation of the hands. But maybe the road to bipedality could have also been travelled by another extinct non-human hominoid ape called the australopithecines. Conversely, must a hominid imperatively be a bipedal creature? If the direct ancestor of the living humans needed to be so, maybe not all the members belonging to this nonhominoid ape family had to be bipedal. After all, it might be argued that it is possible to establish the hominid status of the australopithecines on cranial features only, irrespective of their gait. As will be seen in this chapter, the questions of the gait (bipedal/nonbipedal) and the status (hominid/hominoid ape) of the australopithecines were not necessarily tightly linked. The australopithecines were therefore not excluded from the hominid radiation exclusively because of their nonbipedal locomotion. If Zuckerman and Straus appealed to this factor, it was not the case for Osman Hill.

Two distinct attitudes were used in the 1940s and 1950s to deny that the australopithecines were part of the hominid radiation. One such attitude consisted of adopting a firm stance. Without much ambiguity, Wood Jones (1948: 36, 44, 86) insisted that the australopithecines were situated exclusively on the evolutionary line leading to the hominoid apes. In his view, the australopithecines were extinct and generalized hominoid apes. The australopithecines carried the evolutionary history of the hominoid apes back to a stage during which they had acquired still less catarrhine specializations than their living counterparts. Remember that Wood Jones thought of the evolution of the Old World primates as a radiation which culminated in the phylogenetic trend of specialized monkey-like forms, although forms such as the hominoid apes variably avoided going through such a level of specialization (see Chapter 7). Because the australopithecines were merely apes which fell short of acquiring all the specializations of the living hominoids, Wood Jones assumed that they had split from the Old World primate stem at an even earlier time than the lines leading to the living hominoid apes.

Like Wood Jones, Osman Hill took, at first, a firm stance against the hominid status of the australopithecines, although his view softened during the 1950s. In 1950, Osman Hill (1950) fostered the idea that the australopithecines were not on the human line but rather on the ape line. He explained the similarities between humankind and the australopithecines by appealing to two distinct factors. The first relates to the distinction between pedomorphic and gerontomorphic forms. Remember that Osman Hill explained that humankind's generalized status is largely due to pedomorphism or fetalization, that is, the retention into adulthood of features that are usually only transient during infancy or fetal life (see Chapter 7). On the other hand, Osman Hill held that the hominoid apes are gerontomorphic forms because they evolved by modifying their specialized features of adulthood. Although Osman Hill drew such a clear distinction between the separate evolutionary roads taken by humankind and the hominoid apes, he also allowed for the existence of both pedomorphic and gerontomorphic forms within each of these main evolutionary stems. Osman Hill argued that the australopithecines had a number of human-like features not because they were affiliated to this stem but rather because they represented pedomorphic apes who merely shared this morphological feature with the human line. The second factor used by Osman Hill (1950: 162) to explain the morphological similarities between humankind and the australopithecines consisted of appealing to the concept of parallel evolution:

> There is no reason to suppose that the Pliocene Australopithecinae were nearer than the Miocene *Proconsul* and its allies [dryopithecines] to the human stem . . . [Their human-like features] are merely parallel manifestations of latent trends.

A few years later, however, Osman Hill (1954) was no longer as affirmative about the nonhominid status of the australopithecines, although one still gets the impression that he still favored this view. For instance, he classified the subfamily of the *Australopithecinae* among the fossil forms of giant apes next to the subfamily *Dryopithecinae*. But as already stated, it is difficult to assess a phylogenetic conception on the basis of a taxonomic position exclusively, simply because there is not necessarily direct connection between taxonomy and phylogeny. Osman Hill's recent ambiguity can be seen in his assessment that the australopithecines were essentially apes, as seen by their relatively small brain size and lesser projecting face and jaw, but apes that avoided the specializations of the living hominoid apes and progressed beyond their structural level, just like humankind did, probably because they too adapted to a terrestrial and bipedal mode of locomotion.

Were the australopithecines merely apes that approached the human condition quite closely or were they ape-like hominids that failed to become human? A cogent argument against them being accepted as progenitors of the human line, according to Osman Hill, is their geological age which makes them too late in time to be ancestral to the prehumans (*Pithecanthropus*, etc.). Yet, Osman Hill believed that the australopithecines provided useful clues as to the structural level attained by the more or less immediate precursors of humankind. As bipedal creatures, Osman Hill recognized that the australopithecines had freed hands that could be used for exploring the environment, although he found it questionable to attribute to them the ability to manufacture stone tools. In the 1950s, although Osman Hill did not support the view that the australopithecines were part of the hominid radiation, he also no longer clearly supported that they were restricted to the ape radiation exclusively.[9]

A second approach used to deny the hominid status of the australopithecines was to adopt a cautious attitude—if not squarely an ambiguous one—not unlike Osman Hill's (1954). Zuckerman (1933, 1950, 1954), for instance, maintained that the primate fossil remains at our disposal—including both the dryopithecines and the australopithecines—shed no light whatsoever on the point of divergence of the human line with the other hominoid apes. This situation prompted Zuckerman (1933: 178) to once state that the "available evidence cannot even deny the possibility of man's independent evolution from as far back as the Oligocene," a conclusion he claimed was still valid several years later (Zuckerman, 1950: 476; 1954: 302).

According to Zuckerman, the hiatus in humankind's evolutionary history between the early Miocene period and the Middle Pleistocene period has been filled by speculations only. This lack of evidence prompted him to infer that the human line had probably been distinct ever since the Oligocene period. As far as the australopithecines are concerned, Zuckerman (1954) denied that they bridged any of the three main morphological complexes involved in the hominization process: (1) the development of the brain, (2) the decrease in the size of the teeth and of the face, and (3) the rise of an upright posture. On all of these counts, continued Zuckerman, the australopithecines were ape-like creatures. Zuckerman (1954: 347) stated:

> [T]he *Australopithecinae* were predominantly ape-like, and not man-like creatures . . . [T]hey provide no clear indication of the major anatomical changes one would expect in the transformation of a non-human Primate into a big-brained bipedal animal possessing articulate speech, and the capacity to use his hands to work with artificially-fashioned tools.

This being said, Zuckerman apparently did not entirely close the door on the australopithecines. He stated that it is as likely that some australopithecines represented forerunners of the two African great apes as it is that they are somehow related to the ancestors of humankind. However, he made clear that australopithecines were in no way proto-hominids themselves.[10]

Straus also adopted a cautious attitude toward the place of the australopithecines, one that was not entirely devoid of ambiguity. According to Straus (1949, 1953), it is possible that the australopithecines constituted a link in human evolution, although this had to wait confirmation. Straus's cautious attitude was, perhaps, not entirely unrelated to his broader conception of humankind's place among the primates. Remember that Straus (1949) derived the human line directly from an ancient generalized monkey-like stage, avoiding altogether a more specialized hominoid-like stage of evolution (see Chapter 7). The question of the place of the australopithecines in primate phylogeny was therefore crucial to his phylogenetic conception. Support for the thesis that the human line had passed through a hominoid-like phase would have been increased if the australopithecines were assessed to present a combination of human-like and hominoid-like traits. If such an interpretation eventually turned out to be right, we may speculate that Straus would have been forced to either abandon his monkey-like thesis to accomodate the australopithecines in human phylogeny, or to argue that the australopithecines were merely extinct hominoid apes unrelated to the human line which presented several human-like features developed in parallel.

At this stage of the debate, Straus apparently decided to leave the question open. But far from being a passive spectator, Straus (1948a, 1948b, 1949; Kern and Straus, 1949) insisted that the australopithecines showed that there never was a genuine brachiating stage in the course of human evolution, as seen in the monkey-like features of their limb bones. On the basis of such monkey-like features, Straus also questioned the validity of the assertion that the australopithecines were incontestably bipedal creatures not using their upper limbs for locomotion. On the other hand, Straus (1957, 1962, 1963) recognized in *Oreopithecus* of the late Pliocene period a form which presented preadaptations to an erect bipedal locomotion, regardless of its monkey-like body proportions.

Although Straus slightly modified his view about humankind's place among the primates after 1949—as he now recognized that the human line had sprung from a generalized hominoid ape and not a monkey-like one (see Chapter 7)—his viewpoint on the place of the australopithecines apparently remained unchanged. Straus (1962) even insisted that his main thesis regarding humankind's place among the primates was only reinforced by the additional discoveries and the further analyses of the australopithecines. The implications of this statement for the place of the australopithecines in Straus's view is not clear.

Opposition to the notion that the australopithecines belonged to the hominid radiation in the 1950s was rather weak. Very few scholars, if any, after 1960 were able to clearly and unambigously hold that the australopithecines were entirely unrelated to this radiation. It seems that by that time the empirical evidence was such that it was no longer possible or reasonable to do so. While the debate on the status of the australopithecines gradually receded in the background during the 1940s and 1950s, another debate replaced it.

WITHIN THE HOMINID RADIATION

The increasingly strong movement of approval of the place of the australopithecines within the hominid radiation was further reinforced by the change of heart of scholars like Romer (1941), Keith (1947, 1949), Le Gros Clark (1947a, 1947b), and Weinert (1951) who were all once against this relationship (see above). For that reason, the substance of the debate in the 1950s and 1960s was therefore not on whether or not the australopithecines were affiliated to the human line but rather what was the nature of this relationship. The profound epistemological significance of the australopithecines for the field of paleoanthropology resides in the fact that they powerfully contributed to drive forward a fusion process between the research areas concerned with humankind's place among the primates and human phylogeny proper. If it is true that the other nonhuman primate fossils discovered in the 1935–1965 period had their part to play in this integrating process (see Chapter 7), the impact of the australopithecines was greater still. The recovery of australopithecine fossils (1) were impressive because of their number; (2) were from a crucial temporal stage that pushed back in time the existing hominid fossil record; and (3) presented possible intermediate morphological features linking humankind to other nonhuman primate fossils.

In 1935, the two research areas concerned with humankind's place among the primates and human phylogeny proper were still largely united through inferential analyses based on the comparative anatomy of the living forms. We have seen how phylogenetic analyses almost exclusively based on this approach in the pre-1935 era generated a plethora of hypotheses. The field of paleoanthropology lacked at that time a coherent research agenda and a reliable empirical foundation. This situation was to change rapidly after 1935 following a series of fossil discoveries, among which the australopithecines figured. Considering the importance of the australopithecines for the integrating process of paleoanthropology's distinct research areas, we will review how scholars responded to two distinct questions not always easily separated: (1) What was the evolutionary relationship between the australopithecines and the other nonhuman primates? and; (2) What was the evolutionary relationship between the australopithecines and the living humans? Let us take them in turn.

The rise of the australopithecines. It was seen in Chapter 7 that scholars debated, during the 1935–1965 period, the evolutionary stage or grade at which the human line had sprung from the other primates: was it at the generalized nonhominoid stage, at the generalized hominoid ape stage, or at the somewhat specialized hominoid ape stage? Unsurprisingly, the australopithecines were an integral part of this debate. How were they used to resolve whether the human line arose from a generalized ancestor or from a specialized ancestor?

Generalized ancestors. In the view of a number of scholars, the recoveries of australopithecine fossils either brought support for, or were not contradictory to, the notion that the human line departed from the nonhuman primates at a generalized evolutionary stage. For these scholars, the australopithecines were inserted in phylogenetic hypotheses deriving them from a very generalized ancestor either near the base of all the hominoids or even before that. This idea was often associated with the notion that this generalized form was also very ancient, that is, of Oligocene period if not older. This can be explained by the fact that one must look deeply into the evolutionary past to identify an ancestor which avoided altogether the specializations of the hominoid apes. Among the proponents of a human line which evolved out of a generalized nonhominoid form, several of whom, such as Wood Jones, Osman Hill, and Straus either rejected the australopithecines from the hominid radiation or entertained certain doubts about their place in this radiation (see above). Presumably, they were inclined to believe that the australopithecines were either too specialized or too ape-like to occupy this phylogenetic position. However, this interpretation was not shared by Robinson, Genet-Varcin, and Piveteau who also derived humankind from a generalized nonhominoid ancestor.

Robinson's conception of the place of humankind among the primates seems to have been directly influenced by the australopithecines.[11] Robinson (1956, 1962, 1963, 1968) recognized in the australopithecines many morphological features—especially in the teeth and the pelvis—which could not easily be derived from a great ape type or most of the dryopithecines. On that basis, Robinson apparently hesitated between two alternatives: (1) The human line arose from an early and generalized hominoid stock to which *Proconsul* belongs; (2) the human line arose from a very early stock which avoided altogether the hominoid phase and has been independent since the prosimian stage. Robinson (1956: 175) was inclined to favor this second alternative:

> If, then, one postulates a pre-pongid or very early pongid hominid ancestor in the Oligocene, which has a relatively short ilium, never developed especially large canines and had a tendency toward molarisation . . . the further evolution of the hominid would be relatively easy to understand . . . On this view the two monkey lines and the pongid and hominid ones would all have arisen at about the same time from very

similar sorts of prosimians with probably the same one common to the pongid and hominid groups.

At one time, it was believed that this view received further support from the assumed near-hominid status of *Oreopithecus* of the early Pliocene of Italy (Robinson, 1962, 1963).[12]

Like Robinson, Genet-Varcin found in the australopithecines some evidence for a long separated evolutionary history of the human line in complete independence from the hominoid apes. Genet-Varcin (1963, 1969a) postulated that the hominoid apes and the hominids departed very early from a very generalized common ancestor. Placed at first in the early Paleocene, this separation time was later put more deeply in time in the early or middle Cretaceous period of the Secondary era. In Genet-Varcin's (1963, 1967, 1969a) conception, the australopithecines are situated on this human stem which runs throughout the entire Tertiary era.[13] In her view, the known australopithecines of the late Pliocene and early Pleistocene originally presented less specialized features, features which contributed to throw some light on the yet largely unknown and marginal human evolutionary line.

Also postulating the rise of the human line from a nonhominoid ape, though perhaps not from an ancestor as ancient as that suggested by Robinson and Genet-Varcin, Piveteau found support for his view in the australopithecines. Piveteau (1954, 1957, 1958, 1962, 1963) derived both the human line and other hominoid apes from a quadrupedal creature common to all the catarrhines. He argued that the human line must have already been distinct by the Oligocene time period, thus avoiding altogether the specializations of the other hominoids. Piveteau saw in the generalized australopithecines a signpost on the road to the living humans. He (1954, 1957, 1958) insisted that their ape features were merely primitive ones inherited from an ancient state shared in common with the hominoid apes and perhaps also with the Old World monkeys. The australopitheicines, continued Piveteau, had already acquired a bipedal gait and possessed a human-like dentition, key signs of the hominization process. It was believed that such key human features were developed much earlier in time than the second half of the Pliocene or in the early Pleistocene, these periods being attributed to the known australopithecines.

Like Robinson, Genet-Varcin, and Piveteau, Broom and Le Gros Clark also derived the human line from a generalized ancestor. Unlike the former, however, they derived this ancestor from a generalized hominoid ape rather than a generalized nonhominoid form. In their view, the australopithecine fossils supported this conception. In fact, Broom apparently found in the continuing recovery of such fossils a reason to modify his previous idea. We have already seen that in the 1920s and early 1930s Broom promoted the view that the australopithecines were near or at the very base of the human branch which itself was closely related to the African great apes, all of which sprang from the dryopithecine group in the Miocene period. Broom (1936a, 1937a, 1937b, 1939, 1941a) held to this view until the early 1940s.[14] By 1942, however, Broom had an important change of heart in favor of a much more ancient and much more generalized ape-like ancestor to the human line. The australopithecines were apparently instrumental in this change:

> Until recently I inclined to [believe] that man has been derived from a primitive Dryopithecid; but as the living anthropoids [hominoids] and most of the fossil Pliocene forms have teeth characters not found in man and the Australopithecines, I now think likely that man and the Australopithecines came from a pre-Dryopithecid. . . . (Broom, 1942a)

Interestingly, just prior to 1942 Broom (1941a, 1941b) had started to insist on the more numerous monkey-like features in humankind and the australopithecines than in the hominoid apes. This apparently contributed to change his conception about the conformation of humankind's link with the other primates. Indeed, Broom (1942a) argued that if the human line retained more primitive features than the great apes—as seen in the monkey-like features—then the great apes must have been too specialized to constitute the stock from which humankind had sprung. The similarities between humans and the hominoid apes were, therefore, partly related to parallel evolution. Broom (1942b, 1946, 1950a, 1952; Broom and Robinson, 1950, 1952) now placed the dryopithecines within the radiation of the great apes exclusively on the basis of their teeth specializations (large canines, sectorial first lower premolars). On this new view, Broom established the split of the human line in the late Eocene or early Oligocene period from a very generalized hominoid or a prehominoid form whose conformation approached the gibbon-like *Propliopithecus*.[15]

In a reasoning similar to Broom's, Le Gros Clark managed to put the australopithecines in an intermediate evolutionary position between the living humans and a more ancient and generalized hominoid ape. Le Gros Clark (1950a, 1955, 1960a, 1964, 1967, 1971; Le Gros Clark and Leakey, 1951) promoted that the human branch had departed from the hominoid apes at the very base of this radiation in the Oligocene or Miocene period from a quite generalized form. *Proconsul* was believed to be sufficiently generalized to indicate how the evolutionary split between the specialized great apes and the more generalized humans could have occurred. From a *Proconsul*-like form, the human branch adapted early to a bipedal locomotion and avoided the development of many specialized ape-like structures seen in the living hominoid apes and their immediate ancestors. This evolutionary stage in human evolution, Le Gros Clark insisted, is seen in the australopithecines themselves.

Specialized ancestors. As is always the case, scholars are never unanimously agreed on the phylogenetic place of a fossil group, and the australopithecines are no exception to this rule. Whereas some of them believed that the australopithecines supported the thesis that the human line had departed from the other primates at a generalized evolutionary stage, others, on the contrary, saw in them evidence that this departure had occurred at a more specialized evolutionary stage. More precisely, these latter scholars saw in the australopithecines a proof that the human line shares a close relationship with the three great apes. Proponents of this view did not need to look for truly ancient ancestors which avoided going through any specialized hominoid phase of evolution. For them, it became possible to hold that the human line and the australopithecines arose from the other primates as recently as the Miocene or even the Pliocene period.

Weidenreich eventually saw in the australopithecines evidence that the human line was more closely related to the living gorillas than to any other great apes. At first, though, Weidenreich (1943b, 1945, 1946) recognized that the australopithecines were closely related to all the great apes and the living humans:

> I am of the opinion that they [australopithecines] are not in the human line but are a special group which has preserved some original characters of the common stock from which man, as well as the other anthropoids [hominoids], originated. These characters have been lost by that group which differentiated in the direction of the living anthropoids [hominoids], while they have been maintained and perfected in the line which led to man. (Weidenreich, 1946: 22)

Eventually, Weidenreich (1948) made clear that the human-like features of the australopithecines are signs of their past rather than of their future, meaning that such features are inherited from a common stock shared with humankind before they both went in their own evolutionary direction in the late Miocene period. Weidenreich now placed the australopithecines between the hominid line and the gorilla line on the basis of their morphological similarities, alluding to the possibility that the australopithecines could be a sort of pygmy gorilla. He held that the australopithecines branched off near the point where the hominids and the gorillas departed from the common hominoid ancestor.[16]

If Weidenreich was inclined to see a close relationship between the australopithecines, the humans and the gorillas, Weinert opted for a close link with the chimpanzees. It is true that Weinert (1932, 1938, 1941) once held that the australopithecines were not related to the human line. Yet, he was already convinced at that time that the australopithecines were part of a broad chimpanzoid group of which only one of its portions (*Dryopithecus rhenanus or germanicus*) was truly ancestral to humans (see above). Eventually, however, Weinert (1951) recognized that the australopithecines constituted a genuine phase leading to living humans which he called the *Propithecanthropus* phase.[17] Weinert continued to promote that the human line (including the australopithecines) evolved out of a very recent chimpanzoid stock which shared a last common ancestor with the chimpanzee line, but now placed this divergence time at a slightly earlier date in order to leave enough chronological room for the *Propithecanthropus* phase to occur. Whereas he had previously conceived this separation to be at the turn of the Pliocene/Pleistocene period, he now placed it at about the mid-Pliocene time.[18]

Unlike Weidenreich and Weinert, scholars like Gregory, Keith, and Simpson saw in the australopithecines a fossil group which permitted the establishment of a phylogenetic connection not with a great ape species in particular, but rather with all of them. For Gregory, who promoted the thesis that the human lineage had sprung from a hominoid stock, the discovery of a physical connection in the early Pleistocene period, as seen in the australopithecines, only contributed to bring further support to his thesis:

> [The] orang and man have diverged very profoundly and very rapidly from a more chimpanzee-like ancestor and that the Australopithecinae have such a mixture of characters because they were late survivors of the common *Dryopithecus* stock, and were truly related to all their cousins of the modern chimpanzee-gorilla, orang and human branches. (Gregory and Hellman, 1939a: 368)[19]

For Gregory and his colleagues, the human lineage was not the only one that sprang from the dryopithecine group to evolve toward the human direction. It has been argued that both *Ramapithecus* and *Australopithecus*, although simians by definition, evolved in this direction to the point where they almost reached the human threshold (Gregory, Hellman, and Lewis, 1938).[20]

Keith also turned toward the australopithecines in order to throw light on the split between the great apes and the human lines. Although Keith (1931) previously excluded the australopithecines from the hominid radiation (see above), he now held that they represented the nearest fossil group known to us which is akin to humankind (Keith, 1949). Keith explained the similarities between the australopithecines and the living great apes by a common and recent inheritance. Keith (1949: 209–210) stated:

> [The australopithecines], although anthropoidal in appearance and in size of brain, were yet human in their dentition and in carriage body . . . My scheme assumes that up to the end of the Oligocene period . . . the great apes (the gorilla, chimpanzee, and orang) and man were represented by a common ancestry, all being strictly arboreal in habit. It was during this stage . . . that the anthropoidal group which was ultimately to evolve into humanity became separated from the groups which were to remain anthropoids [hominoids] . . . [I]n the pre-human group the canines fell into abeyance . . . [B]efore the end of the Miocene period the lower limbs of the pre-human groups had become completely adapted for a life on the ground . . . The South African anthropoids [australopithecines] seem to me to represent the stage reached by our human ancestry in the Miocene period.

For Keith, the two distinct human and great ape branches had definitively departed from one another by the end of the Miocene period.

Simpson also eventually recognized that the recovery of the australopithecines permitted to conceive a phylogenetic link between the great apes and humankind. At first, Simpson (1945, 1949) conceived of the australopithecines as a small Pliocene radiation that sprang from the larger dryopithecine group which itself evolved in the direction of humankind in the Miocene period. Simpson remained at the time uncertain as to the exact place of the australopithecines, though he apparently believed that they were not, in all probability, directly leading to living humans. By the early 1960s, however, Simpson (1963a) was favoring the viewpoint that some of the australopithecines or forms near to them were directly ancestral to living humans. Simpson (1963a) now believed that the australopithecines reinforced the notion that humankind had shared a common ape-like ancestor with the great apes, although he insisted that this contributed in no way to bring some precision as to which of these living apes is the more closely related to humans.[21]

Whereas Gregory, Keith, and Simpson fostered the idea that the australopithecines could shed some light on the relationship between humankind and the three great apes exclusively, Washburn expanded this notion to include also the gibbon evolutionary line. Washburn held that the human line departed from the hominoid stock before the other hominoid apes diverged from one another (see Chapter 7). However, this did not prevent Washburn from arguing that this occurred at a fairly specialized evolutionary stage. For Washburn, the australopithecines played a pivotal role in his conception of humankind's place among the primates. Because he promoted the view that humankind sprang from an ape-like brachiating ancestor as recently as the very late Pliocene period, the discovery of australopithecine fossils in South Africa permitted him to either conceive or at least to strengthen this very conception. Washburn (1950: 67, 70) stated:

> [The bipedal australopithecines were] . . . derived from the forest-living apes. Morphologically they are ideal representatives of a stage in our evolution and chronologically they may be actual ancestors or the first cousins of the same . . . That is, these forms may be representative of populations which were directly ancestral to such humans as Java man [*Pithecanthropus*].

In Washburn's view, the human line split from all the other hominoid apes at the turn of the Pliocene/Pleistocene period.[22] Washburn recognized in the australopithecines many ape-like features of this evolutionary transition. For instance, the human-like pelvis of the australopithecines—which still presented some ape-like features—showed that human evolution started with the rise of a new mode of locomotion. Later, Washburn (1960, 1963a) favored the view that the australopithecines were not the representatives of a stable and long evolutionary stage, but rather a transitional form in the process of a rapid transformation from an ape-like to a human-like type.

The fate of the australopithecines. We now have a better understanding of how the australopithecine discoveries were exploited in order to establish a phylogenetic connection between the living humans and the other primates between 1935 and 1965. However, this is only half the story. We have already mentioned that the australopithecines played a key role in breaking the isolation between the two research areas respectively concerned with humankind's place among the primates and human phylogeny proper. Now that we understand better how the australo-pithecines relate to this first research area, we need to understand how they articulate with debates on human phylogeny proper. A more complete picture of the importance of the australopithecines in paleoanthropology can only emerge once this task is accomplished. Scholars who promoted that the australopithecines were part of the hominid radiation proposed two hypotheses to resolve this issue. In the first one, the australopithecines were believed to be an extinct side branch of the human evolutionary line. In the second hypothesis, the entire australopithecine group or at least a portion of it was believed to be directly ancestral to the living humans. The scholars were almost equally divided in this debate.

Evolutionary side branches. For a number of scholars, the known australopithecines were not directly ancestral to the living humans. Several scholars insisted that the australopithecines were just too late in time to have assumed this phyletic position. Although it was argued that the australopithecines evolved away from the main human line, it was nonetheless recognized that they contributed to throwing some light on questions such as: (1) The time horizon of the rise of the human line itself; (2) the geographical place of this event; (3) the physical conformation of humankind's direct ancestors; and (4) the intellectual capacity of the early hominids.

An interesting feature of the conception which placed the australopithecines on an extinct hominid side branch is that their human-like features could either have been explained by parallel evolution with the genuine human line or inherited from a common ancestor to both lines. This certainly contributed to reduce the importance of the so-called unique aspects of the human line. For instance, Vallois, Piveteau, and Genet-Varcin eventually recognized that the extinct australopithecine line was a tool-making one, thus sharing this specific attribute often judged important with the human line. From a different perspective, it was also sometimes argued that the australopithecine line was not the only one to have evolved in the human direction. For instance, von Koenigswald and Vallois once recognized in *Gigantopithecus* a form which shared with the humans a number of features. On this view, evolution produced several distinct evolutionary lines going down the path of humanity, without all reaching it.

Many reasons were simultaneously used to justify that the known australopithecines were not humankind's direct ancestors. Scholars never appealed to only one such factor in order to put them on an evolutionary side branch. But perhaps it is possible to identify one key factor which was apparently more important than the others in the phylogenetic analyses. For Hooton, for instance, brain size may have been such a key factor. Hooton (1946) held that the australopithecines developed in such a direction as to barely miss the human status. This being said, Hooton viewed the australopithecines as human-like apes rather than ape-like humans.

He insisted that their dentition resembled more closely the earliest known hominids than the living great apes or the fossil dryopithecines. Yet, rather than concluding that this similarity testified to their proximity with the living humans, Hooton concluded instead that one must be very cautious in tracing the human descent exclusively on the basis of dental anatomy, only because nature endowed the apes with human-like dentitions. Furthermore, considering that the australopithecines were apparently dated to the early Pleistocene period, Hooton (1946) believed these South African forms to be too late in time to be ancestral to humankind, as they lived in contemporaneity with genuine hominids (*Pithecanthropus*, *Sinanthropus*). But beyond questions of dating and dental anatomy,

Hooton's main reason for excluding the australopithecines from a direct kinship with the humans has apparently more to do with the assumption that humankind's ancestors in the Pliocene period had to be, above all, big-brained creatures:

> Although these Pleistocene apes of South Africa are undoubtedly much closer to man than any existing or extinct subhuman forms heretofore discovered, they lacked the brain overgrowth that is specifically human and perhaps should be the ultimate criterion of a direct ancestral relationship to man of a Pliocene precursor. Because they lacked brains, they remained apes, in spite of their humanoid teeth. (Hooton, 1946: 288)

Like Hooton, Piveteau apparently insisted on the notion that the australopithecines lacked the necessary progressive ability or intellectual capacity to have successfully gone down the path of humanity. For Piveteau (1954, 1957, 1958), the australopithecines were not directly ancestral to the living humans. It is true that they had acquired a bipedal gait and possessed a human-like dentition, key signs of the hominization process. Yet, such key features of the hominid line, insisted Piveteau, had already been developed in a much earlier time than the second half of the Pliocene or early Pleistocene period attributed to the known australopithecines. Indeed, it will be remembered that Piveteau saw traces of such key features in *Oreopithecus* of the late Miocene period (see Chapter 7).

Piveteau promoted that the australopithecines constituted an extinct side branch of the stem leading to the living humans because they were, among other things, too late in time to assume such an ancestral position. Irrespective of whether or not the australopithecines were restricted, geographically speaking, to the southern part of Africa only, or also inhabited South Asia, it was argued that they were nonprogressive forms living in refuge habitats. According to Piveteau, the assumed association between primitive stone tools and the australopithecines in South Africa was merely an unproven hypothesis as yet. Piveteau contended that it is not entirely impossible to imagine that unknown and more ancient representatives of the australopithecines in other regions of the world might have been truly ancestral to the humans. The known australopithecines were, therefore, a side line diverging away from the genuine human line with terminal twigs represented either by robust forms (*Paranthropus*) or by more human-like ones under the effect of convergent evolution.

Following the discovery of *Zinjanthropus* presumably in association with primitive stone tools, Piveteau (1962, 1963) eventually recognized that small-brained australopithecines were indeed toolmakers. He conjectured that perhaps their brains had already gone through a cerebral reorganization. In this new context, Piveteau still maintained that the australopithecines were not directly ancestral to the living humans. Now, he simply believed that they were barely able to cross the intellectual threshold usually associated with the human condition. Piveteau (1962: 53–54) stated:

> There are indeed some reasons to believe that the australopithecines, while being incontestably on the human side, were not a part of the main hominid stem, but rather belonged to a marginal branch which disappeared without leaving any traces although they managed to climb high enough to cross the threshold of self-reflection.

> The australopithecines are too close to us not to believe that, although they are excluded from our ancestry, our direct ancestors must have passed through a similar phase now represented by them.[23] [The translation is mine]

Notions other than an insufficient brain capacity or intellectual ability were used to exclude the australopithecines from human ancestry. For Genet-Varcin, von Koenigswald, Weidenreich, and Vallois the known australopithecines were just too specialized to have transformed into humans. This argument took on several distinct forms. For Genet-Varcin, for instance, the known australopithecines were not sufficiently pedomorphic or fetalized creatures to be directly ancestral to humankind. Genet-Varcin (1963, 1967, 1969a) held the australopithecines are situated on the marginal human stem which runs through the entire Tertiary era. However, the known remains of the australopithecines are not, in Genet-Varcin's view, directly ancestral to the living humans. Instead, she postulated that they represented an extinct offshoot which departed quite early. While Genet-Varcin (1963) first placed this separation time in the mid-Oligocene period, she (1969a) later opted for the mid-Miocene period.[24]

In her view, therefore, the known australopithecines of the late Pliocene and early Pleistocene period are merely the end products of a long separated branch that was originally represented by less specialized features. This is seen, she insisted, by the fact that the most recent australopithecines are the most robust and specialized creatures (*Australopithecus robustus*, *A. crassidens*, *A. boisei*) while the oldest ones are the most gracile and generalized creatures (*A. africanus*, *A. transvaalensis*, *A. habilis*). This being said, the robust and gracile australopithecines were not, for Genet-Varcin, successive evolutionary stages but rather two separate lineages which departed from each other in the Pliocene period. Although essentially known from South and East Africa, Genet-Varcin (1969a) recognized in *Meganthropus palaeojavanicus* a robust Indonesian australopithecine form which indicated that this fossil group was widely distributed in space.

Genet-Varcin (1966, 1967, 1969a, 1969b) insisted that the earliest and yet unknown representatives of the australopithecine line were pedomorphic or fetalized hominid forms, that is, forms which retained in adulthood the features that are usually only transient during infancy or fetal life. She imagined these early creatures to be small, standing upright, with legs and arms of similar proportions, and having reduced canines. It is only under this very primitive and generalized form that the earliest and hypothetical australopithecines were directly ancestral to the living humans. It was argued that *Australopithecus habilis* (*Homo habilis*) may shed some light on the conformation of these early unknown creatures. Once the australopithecines departed from the main human stem, they gradually underwent an elongation of the legs and thus acquired a more perfect bipedal gait that never reached its full development before their extinction. Like the other hominids, Genet-Varcin recognized that the australopithecines were stone toolmakers.

For his part, von Koenigswald excluded the australopithecines from a direct kinship with the living humans on the basis of a comparison with the pithecanthropines. What von Koenigswald looked for was a suitable ancestor for the pithecanthropines, an ancestor he could not find among the known australopithecines. Whereas the australopithecines were indeed part of the hominid radiation, their exact position in relation to the living humans is one of indirect kinship through a common ancestry (von Koenigswald, 1940, 1942, 1954, 1965).[25] The various forms of australopithecines, argued von Koenigswald, presented a number of specialized features which clearly excluded them from being our ancestors. In addition, their geological position in time was too recent for them to assume such an ancestral position, being contemporaneous with the oldest genuine human ancestors (pithecanthropines). Features such as small incisors, large molars, the presence of a sagittal crest, and a small brain capacity were believed to clearly indicate that the australopithecines were embarked on an evolutionary trend taking them away from the living humans toward a greater robusticity. This is true regardless of their human-like features which are largely associated to their bipedal locomotion.

Von Koenigswald (1965) held that the more ancient representatives of the australopithecines were the least robust of all (*Australopithecus africanus*), while the more recent were by far the most robust (*Paranthropus robustus, Zinjanthropus*). Humankind's direct ancestors, argued von Koenigswald, were embarked on a different evolutionary trend involving, instead, a less marked reduction of the incisors, a reduction of the molars and the premolars, and an important increase in brain capacity.

Von Koenigswald envisioned the hominid radiation as being broad and composed of several evolutionary branches showing some parallel evolution with humankind and the great apes, by presenting various combinations of human-like and ape-like features. Only one branch of this radiation managed to survive. In fact, besides the australopithecines von Koenigswald (1952, 1958) included in this broad hominid radiation—at least during the 1950s—a Pleistocene form such as *Gigantopithecus*. It was argued that regardless of their gigantic size, the teeth of *Gigantopithecus* presented many human-like features, to the point where von Koenigswald (1958) wondered if *Gigantopithecus* would not be an Asian equivalent of the South African australopithecines.[26] He (1954: 797) summarized his conception in the following words:

> [By the] end of the Pliocene period the early Hominidae were separated into several branches—Australopithecinae in Africa, *Gigantopithecus* . . . in China, Pithecanthropi in Asia—and that only one of them, the Pithecanthropi . . . gave rise to the Hominidae, of which group we are the most human members.

Although the australopithecines were thus far known to be geographically restricted to Africa, von Koenigswald (1952, 1956, 1960 [1962], 1968 [1976]) was inclined to believe that they may ultimately have sprung from an Asian ancestor common to all the branches, part of his broad hominid radiation. In fact, he insisted on a few large isolated fossil teeth from China that could have belonged to a robust australopithecine form not unlike *Paranthropus*, although he recognized there was as yet no unequivocal proof of their presence in Asia (Tobias and von Koenigswald, 1964). In von Koenigswald's (1952) view, both the australopithecines and *Gigantopithecus* are over-specialized hominid extinct side branches evolving toward a greater robusticity or size during the Pleistocene period.

At first, von Koenigswald (1956: 163; 1957) hinted that his broad hominid radiation had a common ancestor in the Middle or Upper Pliocene period, an ancestor that was characterized by its massiveness or robusticity. This latter feature was assumed to have been shared by all the branches of this radiation: the australopithecines, *Gigantopithecus*, and *Meganthropus palaeojavanicus* (the earliest pithecanthropines). After having decided to exclude *Gigantopithecus* from the hominid radiation, von Koenigswald (1963) hypothesized that the Lower or Middle Pliocene common ancestor to both the australopithecine and the human lines possessed features such as a brain somewhat smaller or equal in size to that of the more ancient and gracile australopithecines, a diastema (as seen in *Meganthropus*), and medium-size canines. It was hinted that this common ancestor may not be unlike *Ramapithecus*, a form not yet sufficiently known.

If Genet-Varcin and von Koenigswald once believed that the known australopithecines were far too specialized to assume a direct ancestral position to the living humans, Weidenreich and Vallois, for their part, inclined more toward the notion that they were just slightly too specialized for that phyletic position. For instance, Weidenreich (1943b, 1945, 1946) held that if the australopithecines were not directly ancestral to the human line, they nonetheless constituted an extinct evolutionary group which departed very near the human evolutionary line. It was argued that the australopithecines, during their evolutionary history, avoided going through an ape phase which is too specialized: "The common ancestor [of the hominids and the australopithecines] must have had a short face, small canines of the incisor type, bicuspid lower premolars . . ." (Weidenreich, 1945: 122). Although Weidenreich recognized a very close relationship between the human branch and the australopithecines, the latter were presented as ape-like creatures with remarkably human-like dentition. Weidenreich insisted that it should not be readily accepted that the australopithecines were bipedal creatures.

Like Weidenreich, Vallois found in the known australopithecines a fossil group that just barely missed the ancestral position of the human evolutionary line. Vallois (1955a, 1956, 1961) contended that key human features such as a bipedal gait, a reduced snout, and reduced frontal teeth and canines had developed quite early in human evolution, as seen in the combination of human-like and ape-like features in the australopithecines. Although Vallois (1961) insisted on the early rise of the bipedal gait, he held that the bipedal locomotion of the known australopithecines was probably not as perfect as ours. For him, the known australopithecines—which were on the verge of humanity, though they lacked the brain size—were certainly a good approximation of the conformation of humankind's early progenitors, meaning that the living humans departed from an australopithecine-like ancestor. On that count, Vallois (1956: 126) stated:

> But there is hardly any doubt that it is from similar forms of the yet known australopithecines, and somewhere in Africa or South-East Asia, that the human family differentiated. If the australopithecines are not our direct ancestors, they were close cousins of such ancestors; they could hardly have been very different. [The translation is mine][27]

However, owing to the contemporaneity of the latest australopithecines with more human-like and big-brained hominids in the early Pleistocene period (i.e., *Pithecanthropus*), Vallois held that the known australopithecines represented an extinct side branch of the hominid family tree.[28] He placed the separation of the human line from the assumed australopithecine line at about the early Pliocene period. For Vallois (1957), the australopithecines constituted a polymorphic group composed of small as well as large representatives that were not necessarily restricted, geographically speaking, to Africa. In fact, he recognized in *Meganthropus* of Java a member of the robust australopithecines (*Paranthropus*). But far from seeing in *Paranthropus* the largest members, Vallois hypothesized that *Gigantopithecus* of the Pleistocene of China may well represent a larger member still of this entire evolutionary group which presented a combination of ape-like and human-like features.[29] All these evolutionary branches, it was argued, underwent extinction, probably under the competition of humankind's direct ancestors. Vallois, who long doubted that the australopithecines were able to use and make tools, now recognized that at least some of them had been able to do so (Vallois, 1961).[30]

Direct ancestors. The scholars just reviewed believed that the australopithecines belonged to an extinct side branch which was not directly ancestral to the living humans. However, about as many scholars during the 1935–1965 period eventually came to embrace the idea that they were direct ancestors to the living humans. In reality, this time period turned out to be one of change for the proponents of this phylogenetic conception. All this started with a first series of important discoveries of South African australopithecines in the late 1930s and throughout the 1940s. This was followed next by a period of assessment and evaluation in the 1950s. In the late 1950s and early 1960s, more fossils were recovered in East Africa. The nature of these latest discoveries also needed to be assessed and evaluated. Under such circumstances, it is perhaps unsurprising to see that scholars' opinions about the place of the australopithecines were far from fixed. This state of flux is best seen among the proponents of the thesis that the australopithecines are ancestral to living humans. Indeed, not only were most scholars reviewed in this section previously against an ancestral role for australopithecines but their views regarding the detail of this role continued to change between the late 1940s and the early 1960s. By the mid-1960s, with perhaps the exception of Leakey, the australopithecines were strongly entrenched, in their minds, at the very base of the human family tree.

Already in the 1940s there was some divergence of opinion as to how the australopithecines were related to the living humans. An important characteristic of the debate at the time is that the australopithecines were treated as a single evolutionary unit or phase. It is true that several distinct forms had been recognized since the late 1930s, forms such as *Australopithecus*, *Plesianthropus* and *Paranthropus*. Yet, scholars holding the view that the australopithecines were at the base of the human lineage considered them as a single group in their phylogenetic investigations. For scholars like Broom and Le Gros Clark (before 1955), a certain ambiguity still surrounded the precise nature of this relationship. For Broom (1942b, 1946, 1950a, 1952), for instance, the known australopithecines of the Pliocene and Pleistocene periods were either the actual ancestors or the extinct descendants of an australopithecine branch, which itself evolved throughout the Pliocene period before giving rise to all the later hominids, including the living humans.[31] Here, the dating of the australopithecines was crucial in determining their place in human phylogeny. However, Broom was still unsettled on this question. At times, Broom seemed inclined to recognize that Africa had been the only cradle of the human line. At other times, he held that both Africa and Asia were entitled to this status. Regardless of the location of humankind's birthplace, Broom recognized in *Giganto-pithecus* from Asia a probable eastern australopithecine.

Not unlike Broom, Le Gros Clark also wavered on the question of whether or not the australopithecines were the ancestors of the living humans. Remember that Le Gros Clark denied, until the mid-1940s, the ancestral position of the australopithecines. Following the direct study of the australopithecine remains themselves in 1947, Le Gros Clark (1947a, 1947b, 1950a, 1950b) changed his mind and now promoted the notion of an australopithecine phase in human evolution, giving up on the notion that they were part of the ape radiation.[32] Now promoting that the morphological features of the australopithecines conformed to the theoretical postulates of an intermediate stage in human evolution, the question revolved around determining whether the known taxa were ancestral to living humans or whether an as yet undiscovered australopithecine was ancestral to humans. Le Gros Clark (1947a: 393–394) stated:

> [But because the australopithecines are no older than the late Pliocene and early Pleistocene], it must probably be assumed that . . . these extinct hominoids represent the little modified survivors of the ancestral stock from which, at a still earlier date, the line of human evolution originated.

On a purely morphological basis, then, the known australopithecines could well represent a genuine ancestral connection with the living humans. Indeed, Le Gros Clark insisted that the australopithecines showed no gross specializations precluding this possibility. Morphologically, the australopithecines were described in the following way: creatures of small stature; brains similar in size to that of the African great apes; massive jaws presenting many human-like features; a human type dentition with small frontal teeth (inscisors and canines) but with large back teeth (molars and premolars); limb proportions similar to that of the living humans indicating a bipedal locomotion, though perhaps not as perfect as ours.

According to Le Gros Clark, the combination of primitive cranial features with modern body features in the earliest members of *Homo* (i.e., pithecanthropines) in the Lower Pleistocene period rendered the phylogenetic connection between the australopithecines and the earliest *Homo* quite reasonable. It is the geological age of the known australopithecines which would determine whether or not they are the actual direct ancestors of the living humans.[33] If the known australopithecine remains proved eventually to be too late in time, Le Gros Clark simply stated that one has to postulate that a slightly different and undiscovered australopithecine type would constitute such a common ancestor to both the known australopithecines and the living humans.[34]

Unlike Broom and Le Gros Clark, Keith (1949) formulated a phylogenetic hypothesis which was devoid of any ambiguity in linking the australopithecines and the living humans. Keith's conception of the place of the australopithecines changed drastically in the 1940s, going from their complete exclusion of the hominid radiation to their direct link with each main living human race.[35] Keith now envisioned the australopithecines as an evolutionary phase which leads to the seperate and parallel human evolutionary lines known to exist in the Pleistocene period in Java (*Pithecanthropus*), China (*Sinanthropus*), Europe (Neandertals, Piltdown), and Africa (Kanam man, Rhodesian man).

For Keith, the transformation of the australopithecines into the distinct human branches was entirely conceivable to an anatomist through a process of an increased brain size and the loss of ape-like features in the face and the cranium.[36] It was argued that many features seen today among the living human races—such as tall versus pigmy statures and dolichocephalic versus brachycephalic head forms—were either directly inherited from the original diversity of the australopithecines or transmitted as genetic potentialities not yet developed among the latter. Keith (1949) held that the australopithecines or their ancestors probably arose in East Africa at the turn of the Miocene/Pliocene period before spreading out to all the tropical regions of the Old World. Keith (1949: 245) stated:

> . . . human-footed, ground-living anthropoids had been evolved in some part of Africa, and that during the long Pliocene period these primitive forms, which we are to speak of as 'Dartians' [australopithecines], spread slowly abroad, and so laid the foundation of humanity throughout the Old World.

Starting with the 1950s, the debate on the precise nature of the relationship between the australopithecines and the living humans took on a new dimension. It was now realized that the recognition of several distinct forms of australopithecines had important phylogenetic implications in the assessment of their direct ancestral position with the living humans. By so doing, scholars introduced a new level of phylogenetic resolution which certainly contributed to push forward the phylogenetic debate. This is seen in the changing opinions of Robinson, Le Gros Clark, Arambourg, and Leakey.

More than anybody else in the 1950s, Robinson contributed to crystalizing and formalizing the distinction between the gracile and the robust australopithecines. At first, Robinson (1953a, 1953b, 1954a, 1954b, 1955) held that the australopithecines constituted a distinct and ancestral evolutionary grade to the living humans. At the time, Robinson believed that none of the known fossil remains of australopithecines were directly ancestral to the living humans, although they were part of a small adaptive radiation which ultimately gave rise to them. He regrouped all of them in two main distinct evolutionary groups: *Australopithecus* and *Paranthropus*. While the former group comprised remains from South and East Africa formerly attributed to forms such as *Australopithecus*, *Plesianthropus*, and *Meganthropus africanus*, the latter group included remains from South Africa and Southeast Asia formerly classified as *Paranthropus* and *Meganthropus palaeojavanicus*. The evolutionary history of the australopithecines was not, for Robinson, exclusively confined to South Africa as seen especially in the more robust forms being positively represented in Java and only possibly in China (*Gigantopithecus*). In fact, Robinson (1953a: 33) even alluded at one time that the australopithecines had probably once inhabited Europe. Undoubtedly, this could only complicate the quest for the establishment of humankind's cradle.

Robinson recognized in these two distinct australopithecine groups evolutionary lines committed to bipedalism but not to the same life strategies. With their huge molar teeth, greatly reduced anterior teeth (especially the canines), a nonprojecting face, and well-developed bony crests for muscle attachments, *Paranthropus* was believed to be a vegetarian form eating hard food. With their somewhat smaller molars, larger anterior teeth and a more projecting face, *Australopithecus* was assumed to have had an omnivorous diet which might have included a certain amount of flesh. On the basis of such important evolutionary differences—and considering that *Paranthropus* and *Australopithecus* were more or less living contemporaneously during the Plio-Pleistocene period—Robinson held that the two forms must have separated from a common australopithecine ancestor some time ago, perhaps as early as the very early Pliocene period. According to this view, *Australopithecus* and *Paranthropus* diverged from a common ancestor and evolved in two different directions, although none of them directly contributed to the rise of the living humans before going extinct.

Also stemming from this hypothetical common australopithecine ancestor, Robinson recognized a third evolutionary line which by the time of the late Pliocene/early Pleistocene was already beyond the australopithecine evolutionary grade, as evidenced by *Telanthropus* of South Africa.[37] Robinson contrasted this third evolutionary line—believed to be characterized by a fast evolutionary rate—with the other two lines being presumably of a slower evolutionary rate. By being approximately of the same grade as *Pithecanthropus*, *Telanthropus* was taken as evidence that living humans arose from the australopithecines.

Indeed, Robinson directly compared *Telanthropus* to *Pithecanthropus robustus* of Java. At the time, *Telanthropus* was, for Robinson, an entirely independent product of the australopithecine radiation which presented similarities to both *Paranthropus* and *Australopithecus*, as well as novelties related to its non-australopithecine evolutionary grade. Robinson recognized that, morphologically speaking, *Telanthropus* was closer to *Australopithecus* than to *Paranthropus*. In addition, this latter form was assessed to probably be the primitive condition of the australopithecine group. This instituted a morphological series—*Paranthropus*, *Australopithecus*, *Telanthropus*, and living humans—that was quickly used by Robinson to rethink the phylogenetic link between the australopithecines and the living humans.

This rethinking started in 1956 and continued throughout the 1960s (Robinson, 1956, 1961, 1962, 1963, 1964, 1965, 1967, 1968). Robinson gradually modified his view in the direction of recognizing an ever closer relationship between the *Australopithecus* line and the line leading to the living humans. This was done to the point where Robinson completely fused the two in a single phyletic line within a single genus: *Homo*. This fusion process occurred in several steps. First, Robinson (1956: 171–175) recognized that *Australopithecus* was phylogenetically more closely related to *Telanthropus* than to *Paranthropus*. At that time, Robinson switched from a morphological similarity to a phylogenetic proximity.

Then, Robinson (1961) moved on to consolidate this phylogenetic proximity to the point of deriving *Telanthropus* directly from *Australopithecus*.[38] By that time, Robinson had formerly sunk the genus *Telanthropus* into *Homo erectus*. In order to explain the temporal overlap between *Homo erectus* (*Telanthropus*) and *Australopithecus*, Robinson simply mentioned that this is to be expected considering that not all the populations or demes of *Australopithecus* contributed to *Homo erectus*. The two forms were contemporaneous for a time until the various *Australopithecus* populations were driven to extinction by *Homo erectus*.

The last stage of Robinson's (1965, 1967, 1968) phylogenetic consolidation was the suggestion that the genus *Australopithecus* should be formally sunk into the genus *Homo*. By then, Robinson recognized three successive and somewhat arbitrarily delimited species in the genus *Homo*: *Homo transvaalensis* (the former *Australopithecus africanus*), *Homo erectus* (now including *Telanthropus*), and *Homo sapiens*.[39]

Remember that Robinson had previously insisted on the notion that the australopithecines constituted a distinct evolutionary grade from all the later hominids (*Homo erectus* and after). He now reduced this evolutionary distinction in favor of a new divide which distinguished between *Paranthropus* and *Homo* (including *Australopithecus*). This permitted him to establish a strong and direct phylogenetic link between living humans and the gracile australopithecines. In Robinson's new interpretation, the entire radiation of the australopithecines is conceived as originally deriving from a generalized *Paranthropus*-like form. This common ancestor of the early Pliocene period probably possessed larger canines and smaller molars than later *Paranthropus* taxa. Indeed, because Robinson recognized in *Paranthropus* a number of ape-like features (absence of forehead, primitive nasal area) and behaviors (a vegetarian diet), he assumed that the australopithecines all sprang from a similar form which was not as specialized. This evolution, it was argued, occurred in two distinct directions.

The slow-rate *Paranthropus* evolutionary line went down the path of specialization and extinction by exploiting its ecological niche in developing morphological adaptations to tough food and tool-using.[40] The fast-rate *Australopithecus* (now *Homo*) evolutionary line entered an omnivorous ecological niche. It was assumed that this fast-rate evolutionary line sprang from the *Paranthropus*-like form at a stage when the latter possessed larger canines than those seen in later *Paranthropus* taxa. By entering this new niche, the *Australopithecus* (now *Homo*) line began what turned out to be a series of anatomical and behavioral changes.

Perhaps under the impulse of Robinson's well-articulated distinction between the gracile and the robust australopithecines, Le Gros Clark no longer referred to them as a single evolutionary unit in his phylogenetic view. Although he agreed with Robinson on the close relationship between the gracile australopithecines and the human line, he did not support the interpretation that *Paranthropus* was closer to the ancestral condition than *Australopithecus*. Le Gros Clark (1955, 1964) now explicitly recognized that the australopithecines subsumed two distinct morphological components, but insisted they did not overlap temporally.[41]

Le Gros Clark believed that the australopithecines had changed over time with the earlier members being less robust and more generalized than the later ones. The more recent and more robust australopithecines would be more distantly related to modern humans, whereas the older and more gracile australopithecines would make a more plausible ancestor. Le Gros Clark was not convinced the transition from early and generalized australopithecines to the early *Homo* phase had necessarily occurred in Africa. Considering that robust australopithecine forms were known in Java (*Meganthropus palaeojavanicus*), it might be possible to conceive that gracile forms would also eventually be found in Asia. If this turned out to be true, continued Le Gros Clark, the gracile australopithecines of South Africa may only represent slightly modified survivors of a common ancestral stock shared with the living humans.

In a viewpoint which is not unlike that of Robinson and Le Gros Clark, Arambourg eventually placed the gracile australopithecines in a direct ancestral position relative to humankind. However, unlike Robinson and Le Gros Clark, Arambourg once apparently flirted with the idea that the known robust australopithecines might also be ancestral to the living humans. What is particularly interesting about Arambourg's view is that he kept adding more and more known australopithecine fossils at the base of the human line as the years went by. At first, Arambourg (1943a, 1945, 1947, 1948a, 1948b, 1952a) held that all the known australopithecine fossils were on an evolutionary line leading toward extinction.[42] Starting with the mid-1950s, Arambourg's conception of the australopithecines gradually changed to finally reach the point where he incorporated them at the base of the evolutionary line leading to living humans.[43] This shift occurred in several steps.

First, Arambourg (1955a: 120) recognized that some representatives of the australopithecine evolutionary line, like *Telanthropus*, presented morphological similarities as well as chronological proximity with the pithecanthropines, the earliest known evolutionary stage in human evolution at the time. Then, Arambourg held that a portion of the known australopithecine fossils represented an actual stage in human evolution.

Eventually, Arambourg (1959) included more of the known australopithecine fossils in humankind's earliest evolutionary stage. Forms such as *Australopithecus prometheus* and *Australopithecus transvaalensis* were now part of this evolutionary stage. Arambourg made clear that this change was motivated, in part at least, by the fact that such fossil forms were now associated with primitive stone tools.[44] At that time, the only australopithecines that were not directly ancestral to the living humans were, in Arambourg's view, the more robust ones which belonged to the genus *Paranthropus*. Arambourg insisted that regardless of their numerous humanoid features, the extinct

Paranthropus group had been unable to cross the intellectual threshold already reached by the tool-making *Australopithecus-Telanthropus* group.[45]

Following the discovery of the robust australopithecine specimen named *Zinjanthropus* in East Africa in 1959, Arambourg (1960, 1961) finally incorporated the robust australopithecines (*Paranthropus*, *Zinjanthropus*) in the earliest stage of human evolution.[46] Interestingly, *Zinjanthropus* was assumed to be associated with primitive stone tools. All the australopithecine forms—gracile and robust—were now viewed by Arambourg to have reached the intellectual threshold of material culture. This may have helped him to incorporate all of them at the very base of the human line. It is unclear if Arambourg intended at the time to promote the view that all the known australopithecine specimens (and not the forms) were directly ancestral to the living humans.

Arambourg (1965: 103) later made clear that the very specialized members of the culture-bearing australopithecine types such as *Paranthropus* probably left no descendants, in contradistinction to the more generalized and progressive forms such as *Telanthropus*. However, this latter clarification regarding the robust australopithecines left Arambourg's phylogenetic tree unchanged.[47] Apparently, Arambourg now conceived of the australopithecines as an evolving lineage comprising several distinct types, some of which may be more directly related to the living humans than others.

Perhaps more clearly than Arambourg, Tobias expressed how the robust australopithecines could have contributed, genetically speaking, to human ancestry without being the main contributors. Possible interbreeding between the gracile and the robust australopithecines was the suggested explanation. Tobias (1965a, 1965b, 1967, 1968) held that the two main australopithecine forms—the robust (*Australopithecus boisei*, *A. robustus*) and the gracile (*A. africanus*) ones—shared many similarities. No generic distinctions between them should therefore be retained but only specific ones. In fact, Tobias assessed that these two forms, which evolved throughout the Lower Pleistocene period, shared a common ancestor which probably dated back no earlier than to the early Pleistocene or to the very late Pliocene period. Their proximity was such that Tobias would not exclude the possibility that the two lines might have been able to interbreed:

> [W]e cannot exclude the chance of crossing between *A. africanus* and members of the *A. boisei-A. robustus* line. It is not outside the bounds of possibility that such crossing may have led to the "gracilisation" of *A. boisei* into the later and somewhat toned down *A. robustus*. Even among the australopithecine fossils already known, there is a suggestion of intermediates. (Tobias, 1967: 244)

Tobias promoted that the gracile forms are more likely to be the common ancestors of all later australopithecines, whereas Robinson favored the robust forms for this position. Indeed, Tobias argued that primate fossil evidence of the Mio-Pliocene period, such as seen in *Ramapithecus*, shows that these ancient remains shared more similarities in their jaw and teeth with *A. africanus* than with *A. boisei* or *A. robustus*. He contended that this supported the idea that the gracile forms represent the earliest evidence of the australopithecine grade. In this view, it is the *A. boisei–A. robustus* line which diverged away in the direction of a specialization towards a vegetarian diet from a form approaching *A. africanus*, and not the reverse. The more omnivorous and generalized *A. africanus* form—or a form closely akin to it—continued its evolution toward the hominization process.[48]

Tobias (1966b; Leakey et al. 1964) recognized in *Homo habilis* a form which permitted bridging the important morphological and behavioral gap that separated the australopithecine grade from the *Homo* grade. This transition process occurred in the Upper Pliocene or early Lower Pleistocene period. Tobias suggested there was no convincing evidence of australopithecines outside Africa. However, he suggested that the passage from the australopithecine grade to the early *Homo* grade could have occurred both in Africa and in Asia, as seen respectively in *Homo habilis* of Kenya and *Meganthropus palaeojavanicus* of Java (Tobias, 1965a; Tobias and von Koenigswald, 1964).[49]

Robinson, Le Gros Clark, Arambourg, and Tobias all agreed that the gracile australopithecines were directly ancestral to the living humans. Yet, they disagreed over the role of the robust australopithecines in human phylogeny. For a scholar like Leakey, however, the perspective was to be reversed: It was a robust australopithecine—*Zinjanthropus*—that was directly ancestral to the living humans, the other forms or types being extinct side branches. This is, at least, the view that Leakey promoted for a time. At first, Leakey (1953: 180–184) held that the australopithecines were neither directly ancestral to the living humans, nor were they representing some sort of ancient evolutionary stage through which the human stem had passed. In his mind, the australopithecines were both too late in time and too specialized morphologically to occupy any of these positions.[50]

By the late 1950s, Leakey had entirely changed his mind. He now held that the living humans were indeed directly derived from some generalized australopithecine form. This change of heart was brought about by the discovery of an australopithecine skull in East Africa believed to be different from the two South African australopithecines, *Australopithecus* and *Paranthropus*, dated to the Lower Pleistocene. Leakey (1959) named this new skull *Zinjanthropus boisei*. As it was presumably associated with primitive stone tools, it was argued that *Zinjanthropus* was the earliest known stone toolmaker. On the basis of some anatomical features showing specializations in the direction of the living humans (the length of the face and the conformation of the teeth and palate), Leakey thought it was now justified to put *Zinjanthropus* at the very base of the human line. The other australopithecine forms were judged to be too specialized to be ancestral to living humans, thus explaining their extinction. In Leakey's (1960a, 1961b) new conception, one should expect to eventually find an earlier and much more generalized australopithecine form in the Pliocene of Africa, a form truly ancestral to all the hominid lines: the extinct South African australopithecines (*Australopithecus*, *Paranthropus*), the living humans (through *Zinjanthropus*), and the extinct pithecanthropines and Neandertals.

In 1961 and after, Leakey somewhat retreated from his view that *Zinjanthropus* was surely ancestral to the living humans. This modification was instigated by new fossil discoveries (Leakey, 1961a, 1961d, 1961e). It was argued that another hominid type lived before or in contemporaneity with *Zinjanthropus* in East Africa. This new hominid form, eventually called *Homo habilis*, was described as having smaller and more human-like teeth than the australopithecines, in addition to having a larger brain capacity (Leakey et al. 1964). The stone tools once believed to be associated with *Zinjanthropus* were now assumed to be more probably the product of *Homo habilis*.

Leakey (1963, 1966) now pushed all the known australopithecines on extinct side branches, with a *Zinjanthropus*-like form as their earliest and possible common ancestor. It was promoted that a less specialized and more primitive form such as *Homo habilis* was probably directly ancestral to the living humans. On this new view, it is not entirely clear if Leakey ultimately derived the living humans from a still earlier and even more primitive australopithecine-like form than *Homo habilis* or if he derived the known australopithecines from a very primitive *Homo*-like creature. At this early evolutionary stage, perhaps all this was mainly a question of terminology. Leakey (1966: 1280) stated:

> [T]heir shared common ancestor [of *H. habilis*, *H. erectus* and some australopithecines] must be sought in the more remote past and that when examples of the parent stock are found they will not much resemble any one of the three subsequent branches.[51]

SCENARIOS OF HOMINIZATION: THE IMPACT OF THE AUSTRALOPITHECINES

It is clear from what has been presented thus far that the impact of the australopithecines on the field of human evolution has been an important one. Perhaps unexpectedly, their impact was also felt to some extent on attempts to reconstruct the scenarios of hominization. We have seen in the previous chapter how a number of nonhuman primate fossil discoveries were incorporated in such scenarios during the 1935–1965 period. Their use increased the scientific robustness of the scenarios by providing them with an empirical foundation, albeit an incomplete one. The same applies to the scenarios of hominization which fully exploited the australopithecine recoveries, with the difference that the quality of this fossil record was, by the late 1950s, already much better than that of the other nonhuman primate fossil groups.

Indeed, by that time the australopithecine fossil record comprised specimens of various developmental ages (juvenile, adolescent and adult) as well as specimens represented by cranial and postcranial parts, including several almost complete crania. It was estimated that at least sixty-five individuals were represented in this fossil sample and probably a substantially larger number (Robinson, 1954a: 183). It is argued here that scenarios proposed after the late 1940s which substantially exploited the australopithecines' fossil record took the process of scenario building to a new level of scientific credibility. Scholars like Weidenreich, Washburn, and Robinson took advantage of this remarkable empirical opportunity. By so doing, they were following in the footsteps of Raymond Dart, who had earlier proposed such a scenario without the advantage of an extensive fossil record.

Indeed, Dart's (1925a, 1926, 1934) conception of the hominization process was greatly influenced by the single recovery of the Taung child, *Australopithecus africanus*. Dart postulated that humankind ultimately sprang from an entirely arboreal creature. From this original state, the human line went through three evolutionary phases: (1) a semi-arboreal (semi-terrestrial) phase being represented today by the frugivorous living great apes; (2) a terrestrial man-ape phase upon which *Australopithecus* shed some light; (3) a terrestrial human-like phase. According to Dart, whereas the first and third phases are already well-known to us through their living counterparts, the second one was, until recently, entirely hypothetical. With the discovery of the Taung skull, continued Dart, this second phase is now revealed to us. Unhesitantly, Dart attempted to provide a picture of this phase of the hominization process.

Because *Australopithecus* lived in the dry environmental conditions of Southern Africa, it was argued that the human line had by that stage attained a degree of physical and intellectual advancement that separated it from the tropical great apes. It is by living in such harsh environmental conditions—which demanded a continuous operation of choice and cunning, and thus a greater intelligence—that *Australopithecus* severed itself from its tropical cousins. Dry and deforested conditions forced humankind's ancestor to adapt to a bipedal mode of locomotion, permitting the use of the upper limbs to fight or find a new way to make a living. In this context, the freed hands permitted development of more intelligence while more intelligence rendered the use of freed hands more adaptive. Equipped with freed hands and increased intelligence, *Australopithecus* managed to wean itself from the frugivorous diet of the great apes and entered the world of the omnivore diet which included meat.

Several years later, Dart (1949d, 1957; Dart and Craig, 1959) expanded on this notion of man-apes being hunting creatures by exposing what was believed to be the victims of the hunters and their associated tools made of bones, teeth, and antlers: the so-called osteodontokeratic culture. By that time, Dart put a greater stress than in the past on the idea that hunting was a powerful factor which instigated the bipedal locomotion, for it liberated the hands which made this activity possible.

Whereas Dart could originally rely on only a single immature australopithecine specimen, Weidenreich benefited from a substantially increased fossil record. Although Weidenreich held that the australopithecines were not directly ancestral to the living humans, they nonetheless constituted a useful source of information. Weidenreich (1943b, 1945, 1946) described the conformation of humankind's early ancestors on more than one occasion. He suggested the human line avoided the development of large canines and the projecting snouts typical of the great apes. Based on the australopithecine evidence, Weidenreich (1943b: 272) conceived the last common ancestor of humans and the three great apes to be more similar to the australopithecine type than to the living hominoid apes or any *Dryopithecus* forms. This ancestor was described as having human-like proportions of trunk and extremities, a short face, and small canines. It is from this ancestral condition that the *Homo sapiens* type was believed to have arisen before going through a brain enlargement.

Weidenreich (1941, 1947) made clear that the hominization process involves two fundamental specializations: bipedality and increased brain size. These changes both instigated a rapid evolutionary shift and channeled the human evolutionary trend in one direction, irrespective of environmental conditions. In Weidenreich's conception, form and function were tightly correlated so that a change in one region necessitated a change in all the related parts.

In this scenario, the evolution of a bipedal gait and of an increase in brain size triggered all other important morphological changes, such as the shift from a grasping foot to a supporting one, and the reduction in the prognathism of the face and teeth. Because Weidenreich believed that *Gigantopithecus*, *Meganthropus*, and the australopithecines were all forms closely related to the hominid line, he postulated that massiveness was a primitive condition of this evolutionary line. This implied that the reduction of this massiveness was an integral part of the late stages of the hominization process.

More than Dart and Weidenreich before him, Washburn exploited the australopithecine fossil record in the elaboration of his scenario of hominization. This is particularly obvious when changes in the interpretation of the assumed behavior of the australopithecines was immediately reflected in Washburn's scenario. At first, Washburn (1950) held that the hominization process was powerfully influenced by the development of tool use, but only after a certain evolutionary stage had been reached. If culture appeared later in the hominization process, what triggered the earlier changes? Washburn unhesitatingly pointed to the rise of a new mode of locomotion: bipedality. In Washburn's view, humankind's earliest representatives evolved from a brachiator to a biped. By so doing, he argued that these earliest ancestors faced new adaptive pressures which instigated a series of anatomical and behavioral changes.

Washburn described humankind's common ancestor with the other hominoids as an ape-like brachiating creature with longer arms and smaller thumbs than the living humans. Once humankind's ancestors became bipeds, the selective pressures on the legs and hands took those creatures away from tree-living creatures. Whereas the limbs and trunk attained a human status quite rapidly, the brain and the dentition reached their human shapes only later. Washburn contended that the selective pressure for the enlargement of the brain may be related to the later evolution of the use of tools.

According to Washburn (1950), the human-like pelvis of the australopithecines, which still presented some ape-like features, showed that human evolution started with the rise of a new mode of locomotion. When considering the reduced canines of the australopithecines, Washburn hypothesized that this could indicate that they were already tool users, although this was as yet unproven. Without big canines to defend themselves, reasoned Washburn, the australopithecines had to use other means to do so. This being said, Washburn (1957) was not convinced at the time that the australopithecines were tool users.

By the late 1950s and the 1960s, Washburn (1959, 1960, 1963a; Washburn and Howell, 1960; Washburn and Lancaster, 1968) was no longer suggesting that the impact of culture on human evolution only affected it at later stages. He now held that both bipedality and culture were key factors that conjointly molded the hominization process from the very beginning:

> Man began when populations of apes, about a million years ago, started the bipedal, tool-using way of life that gave rise to the man-apes of the genus *Australopithecus*. Most of the obvious differences that distinguish man from ape came after the use of tools (Washburn, 1960: 63).

On this new view, Washburn promoted the idea that tool use was both the cause and the effect of bipedal locomotion. From there, a positive feedback system between these two key elements was postulated: Partial bipedalism was enough to free the hands from locomotor functions so that tools could be used which in turn selected for more bipedalism, etc. What was the basis of this modified opinion? Washburn now recognized that the australopithecines had indeed been tool users. This new interpretation followed an assumed direct association between primitive stone tools and australopithecines both in East and South Africa.

Washburn (1959, 1960, 1963a; Washburn and Howell, 1960) brought some modifications and precise explanations regarding his view of the australopithecines. Now, the australopithecines were no longer viewed as the representatives of a stable and long evolutionary stage, but rather as a transitional stage in the process of a rapid transformation under a new selective pressure that was instigated by tool use. Indeed, whereas Washburn previously held that the australopithecines were fully bipedal creatures, he now insisted that these creatures were able to run but not to walk on two legs, thus establishing a distinction between bipedal running and bipedal walking. The australopithecines were incompletely adapted bipeds. However, over time the reduction of the canines no longer required for defense eventually favored the reduction of the snout. This was followed at a still later time by the enlargement of the brain. Washburn's new hypothesis involved many social and technological factors that interacted with greater complexity over time.

Even more than Washburn, Robinson turned to the australopithecine fossil record for the elaboration of his hominization scenario. This is not surprising given his first-hand knowledge of the fossil evidence. For Robinson, his distinction between the gracile and the robust australopithecines lies at the heart of the hominization process. He (1961, 1962, 1963) assumed that the first hominids arose from an ape-like form more closely related to the pongids (great apes) than to any other known primates. It was deduced that humankind's pongid-like ancestor was vegetarian, on the basis that the dentition of the early Miocene pongids is similar to that of their living vegetarian counterparts. From this original stock, which Robinson was inclined to recognize in *Oreopithecus*, it was believed that the hominization process went through two major adaptive shifts.

In the first shift, the earliest hominids acquired an erect posture. This was described as the result of changes in the pelvic region that were not originally directed toward a bipedal gait. However, these constituted a sort of preadaptation for an exclusively bipedal locomotion and an erect posture. Robinson envisioned these new biped creatures to be *Paranthropus*-like forms which were essentially adapted to a vegetarian diet.

The second major adaptive shift in the hominization process was largely instigated by environmental changes. The desiccation of Africa during the late Tertiary era opened up an arid environment which was more easily exploited by carnivorous creatures. In Robinson's view, the *Australopithecus* line emerged under such circumstances. Because they lacked canines of any significant size, creatures belonging to this second stage turned to tool-using in order to exploit their new feeding habit. Eventually, the combination of freed hands (bipedality) and tool use resulted in a selective pressure that favored an increased brain size and a shift from tool using to toolmaking. In Robinson's conception, this is how *Homo*-like creatures evolved out of an australopithecine phase.

Dart, Weidenreich, Wasburn, and Robinson believed that the australopithecines could shed much light on the hominization process. However, von Koenigswald entirely disagreed with them. Although the australopithecines are part of the hominid radiation, von Koenigswald insisted they were not ancestral to living humans. In his view, it is the pithecanthropines which shed light on this process. Von Koenigswald's view is interesting for it shows that it was still conceivable in the 1935–1965 period to propose a scenario of hominization which largely ignored the australopithecines. It should be noted that von Koenigswald reduced the importance of bipedality as a key feature in the hominization process, as this locomotion mode was, according to him, shared by several distinct hominid evolutionary lines. In von Koenigswald's (1942) scenario of hominization, the evolution of the teeth and of the brain went hand in hand but in opposite directions. While the brain increased in size during human evolution, the teeth got smaller and smaller, with the two being causally related under the same and single cause: culture. He (1942: 219–220) stated:

> After the invention of implements, [Man] no longer needed his teeth to tear his food to pieces, no big jaw muscles which pressed his braincase. . . . [His evolution can be explained by] the reduction of the dentition combined with an astonishing, progressive development of the brain—the two surely interdependent.

The australopithecines should be excluded from being directly ancestral to the living humans regardless of the fact that they were bipedal. For von Koenigswald (1940, 1942, 1954, 1957, 1965), the australopithecines went wrong on all counts: They were subjected to an increase in the size of their molars and premolars, they retained a small brain size which went through an insignificant increase, and they lacked in the capacity of making tools. The hominization process which took the human line away from the hominoid apes was clearly under way with the pithecanthropines, the earliest known tool-making hominids which also showed a significant increase in brain size and a decrease in molar size. In von Koenigswald's (1956, 1960 [1962], 1968 [1976]) view, it is the rise of culture—the invention of tools, weapons, and the mastery of fire—that liberated the hominids from the warm and vegetarian niches in which the hominoid apes were confined. This permitted our early ancestors to eventually roam throughout the world.[52]

CONCLUSION

The discovery of the australopithecines established a connection between research areas concerned with humankind's place among the primates and human phylogeny proper during the 1935–1965 period. The robustness of this link was made possible only because the australopithecines then known were open to a number of phylogenetic interpretations. In this context, it is remarkable that a solid majority of scholars between 1935 and 1965 saw in the australopithecines a link between the living humans and the other primates, whether or not they were thought to be directly ancestral to the living humans. The interpretative flexibility provided by the australopithecines at the time was fundamental to the success of the integrating process of these two research areas. It would not be an overstatement to claim that between 1935 and 1965 the field of paleoanthropology became, for the first time, a genuinely integrated field of research. It is true the various research areas and investigative methods were only loosely connected, yet human evolution was becoming a more coherent quest.

NOTES

1. The foundations of these two ideas (brain size in human evolution and the location of humankind's cradle, Africa or Asia?) have been ably presented in P.J. Bowler's *Theories of Human Evolution: A Century of Debate, 1844–1944* (Baltimore: Johns Hopkins University Press, 1986), pp. 161–185.
2. In 1925, Dart (1925b: 462) declared that he agreed almost entirely with Broom's (1925a: 571) phylogenetic tree of the hominoids, on which the place of *Australopithecus africanus* can be seen. In this phylogenetic tree, however, the three great apes all depart from the main hominoid stem before the rise of *Australopithecus*. Apparently, Dart (1929) changed his mind on this very question a few years later.
3. In one instance, Broom (1933: 123, 141) described *Autralopithecus* as being, at least, less quadrupedal than the living great apes.
4. In Broom's (1925a: 571; 1925b: 418) phylogenetic trees the directly ancestral position of *Australopithecus* at the very base of the human branch can thus be ambiguously interpreted either as the Taung child itself or as a group to which the Taung child belongs.
5. See Broom's primate family tree in *The Coming of Man: Was It Accident or Design?* (London: H.F. & G. Witherby, 1933), p. 116.
6. Alsberg explained the application of his "biological method" in a letter dated August 27, 1938, which he directly addressed to Broom. This letter is reproduced in R. Broom, *Finding the Missing Link* (London: Watts & Co., 1950a), pp. 79–81.
7. See O. Abel's family tree of the hominoids in "Das Verwandtschaftsverhältnis zwischen dem Menschen und höheren fossilen Primaten," *Zeitschrift für Morphologie und Anthropologie*, 34 (1934), p. 1.
8. Although, at first, Schwarz (1934) arrived at the conclusion that *Australopithecus* was a pygmy gorilla on the basis exclusively of the Taung specimen (*Australopithecus africanus*), he later (1936) benefited from the first discoveries of adult remains at Sterkfontein which started in 1936 as seen in *Australopithecus transvaalensis*.
9. By the early 1970s, Osman Hill (1972) made clear that he believed that the australopithecines were phylogenetically intermediate between *Ramapithecus* and *Homo*. See Osman Hill's hominid family tree in his *Evolutionary Biology of the Primates* (London: Academic Press, 1972), p. 194.
10. Consult Zuckerman's (1954: 349) precise statement on this question.
11. For a biographical note on John Talbot Robinson see P.V. Tobias, "The South African early fossil

hominids and John Talbot Robinson (1923–2001)," *Journal of Human Evolution*, 43 (2002): 563–576.

12. First, Robinson (1956: 164) was unconvinced about the hominid status of *Oreopithecus*. After a period of support of its hominid status, Robinson (1967) apparently returned to his original skepticism.

13. See the place of the australopithecines on the human stem in Genet-Varcin's phylogenetic trees, *Les singes actuels et fossiles* (Paris: N. Boubée & Cie, 1963), pp. 220–221, and *À la recherche du primate ancêtre de l'homme* (Paris: Boubée et Cie, 1969), p. 304.

14. See Broom's primate family trees in "Discovery of a Lower Molar of Australopithecus," *Nature*, 140 (1937a), p. 682; "The Dentition of the Transvaal Pleistocene Anthropoids, *Plesianthropus* and *Paranthropus*," *Annals of the Transvaal Museum*, 19 (1939), p. 313; "The Origin of Man," *Nature*, 148 (1941a), p. 13.

15. See Broom's new primate family tree in *The South African Fossil Ape-Men: The Australopithecinae*, Part I. The Occurrence and General Structure of the South African Ape-Men (Pretoria, Transvaal Museum Memoir No. 2, 1946), p. 139. Broom was apparently unsettled about whether or not the human line had split from the other hominoids just before or just after the gibbon line had departed. Unsure about the early representatives of this human line, Broom alluded at one time or another in the 1940s that generalized forms like *Pliopithecus*, *Limnopithecus*, and *Ramapithecus* might be near or part of it. Eventually, however, Broom dismissed all these presumed early hominids.

16. The place of the australopithecines in the primate family tree can be seen in F. Weidenreich, *Apes, Giants and Man* (Chicago: University of Chicago Press, 1946), p. 24.

17. This *Propithecanthropus* phase was envisioned by Weinert (1951) as being a widely polymorphic one with forms evolving in various directions, some of which probably interbred to some extent. Representatives of this evolutionary phase were dispersed throughout the Old World as possibly seen in South Africa (*Australopithecus*, *Plesianthropus*, *Paranthropus*), Java (*Meganthropus*) and China (*Gigantopitheus*). On this view, it becomes impossible for the moment to both pinpoint the cradle of humankind and to identify its precise ancestor. It will be remembered that Weinert had been strongly inclined by the past to place this cradle in Europe.

18. Compare Weinert's ancient and recent views in his hominoid phylogenetic trees in *Stammesentwicklung der Menschheit* (Braunschweig; F. Vieweg & Sohn, 1951), p. 205.

19. In 1930, Gregory (1930b: 650) was already strongly inclined to view the australopithecines, as then known only through the Taung skull, as a sort of missing link between the dryopithecines and the living humans. However, it is unclear if Gregory intended at the time to view this so-called missing link as merely a morphological connection or a genuine genealogical link.

20. For Gregory and his colleagues (Gregory, Hellman, and Lewis, 1938), the australopithecines show a mixture of human-like and ape-like features, especially in their dental anatomy. On this view, the australopithecines were, structurally and genetically speaking, the less progressive or conservative cousins of the contemporary human line, thus establishing a connection between the humans and the apes at a not too distant geological period, perhaps as recently as the early Pliocene (Gregory and Hellman, 1938, 1939b). Furthermore, Gregory's (1949) assessment that the australopithecines were the only bipedal striders of the open plains with the humans was yet another key feature that linked these two forms more closely. In fact, Gregory (1951) recognized the existence of a close relationship between the australopithecines in South Africa and the *Pithecanthropus-Meganthropus-Sinanthropus* group of Southeast Asia.

21. For Simpson's view on the place of the australopithecines see his phylogenewtic tree in "The Meaning of Taxonomic Statements." In S.L. Washburn (ed.), *Classification and Human Evolution* (Chicago: Aldine, 1963), p. 27.

22. See Washburn's place of the australopithecines in primate and human phylogeny in "Tools and Human Evolution," *Scientific American*, 203 (1960), p. 67.

23. The original text reads as follows: "Il y a assurément quelques raisons de croire que les Australopithèques, tout en étant incontestablement sur le versant humain, n'appartiennent pas au

rameau principal des Hominidés, mais à une branche marginale, disparue sans laisser de traces, ayant toutefois monté assez haut pour franchir le seuil du psychisme réfléchi. Et ils demeurent trop près de nous pour que nous ne puissions croire que même s'ils sont en dehors de notre ascendance, nos ancêtres directs ont dû passer par une phase proche de celle qu'ils expriment."

24. Genet-Varcin was not the only scholar to put, at one time, the separation of the australopithecine line from the hominid radiation as early as the Oligocene period. Schultz (1953) once placed this separation in the late Oligocene period. See Schultz's primate family tree in "Man's Place among the Primates." *Man*, 53 (1953), p. 8. Later, Schultz changed his mind and placed this separation in the mid-Pliocene period. See Schultz revised date in his hominoid family tree in *The Life of Primate* (New York: Universe Book, 1969), p. 251. See also the place of the australopithecines on the human stem in Genet-Varcin's phylogenetic trees, *Les singes actuels et fossiles* (Paris: N. Boubée & Cie, 1963), pp. 220–221, and *À la recherche du primate ancêtre de l'homme* (Paris: Boubée et Cie, 1969), p. 304.

25. The place attributed to the australopithecines in human phylogeny by von Koenigswald can be seen in his two phylogenetic trees. See *Meeting Prehistoric Man* (New York: Harper & Brothers, 1956), p. 202, and *The Evolution of Man* (Ann Arbor: University of Michigan Press, 1962), p. 131.

26. In von Koenigswald's (1958: 74) own words: ". . . on peut se demander si les *Gigantopithecinae* ne doivent pas être considérés comme un équivalent asiatique des *Australopithecinae* sud-africains, et classés parmi les <<*Praehomininae*>> plutôt que parmi les Anthropoïdes." At one time, before the actual discovery of jaws in the mid-1950s and not only of teeth, von Koenigswald (1952, 1956:63) conjectured that the conformation of the root of the upper canine might be indicative that *Gigantopithecus* had a face less prognathous than that of any other living hominoid apes.

27. The original text reads as follows: "Mais il n'y a guère de doute que ce ne soit aux dépens de formes voisines des Australopithèques jusqu'ici découverts, et quelque part en Afrique ou en Asie sud-orientale, que s'est différenciée la famille humaine. Si les Australopithèques ne sont pas nos ancêtres directs, ils étaient les proches cousins de ces ancêtres; ils ne devaient guère en différer."

28. The place of the australopithecines in the primate family tree can be seen in Vallois's "L'ordre des primates." In P.-P. Grassé (ed.), *Traité de zoologie: Anatomie, systématique, biologie*, Tome XVII, 2ième partie (Paris: Masson, 1955a), p. 2082 and "L'origine de l'homme: État actuel de la question." *Le Concours Médical*, 83 (1961), p. 4909.

29. It is unclear here if Vallois intended to classify *Gigantopithecus* among the australopithecines.

30. Although not explicit about the australopithecines being toolmakers, it is very likely that Vallois here had been influenced by the assumed correlation between the discovery of *Zinjanthropus* and stone tools in East Africa in 1959. This correlation was soon to be questioned.

31. See Broom's conception of the place of the australopithecines in his family tree, *The South African Fossil Ape-Men: The Australopithecinae*, Part I. The Occurrence and General Structure of the South African Ape-Men (Pretoria, Transvaal Museum Memoir No. 2, 1946), p. 139.

32. In fact, by 1946 Le Gros Clark (1946b) was apparently ready to revise his position on the place of the australopithecines, although at the time he had not yet seen the original material. Apparently, he had been greatly impressed by the monography published by R. Broom and G.W.H. Schepers on the australopithecines which appeared in 1946. Yet, Le Gros Clark's new view was, in 1946, not yet formulated. In the previous year, Le Gros Clark (1945) was still excluding the australopithecines from being part of the human line.

33. Was there perhaps another factor other than the geological age which pushed Le Gros Clark not to establish with certainty a direct genealogical connection between the known australopithecines and the living humans? After all, Le Gros Clark (1950a: 258) recognized that the australopithecines presented some specializations in their teeth, indicating slightly aberrant features. Similarly, Le Gros Clark (1950b: 51) recognized a few years later

that some dental features of *Pithecanthropus robustus* (the size of the canine and the presence of a diastema) resembled more the hominoid apes than the australopithecines. Le Gros Clark insisted, however, that more pithecanthropine fossils were needed in order to assess the variability of this group. Irrespective of whether the australopithecines are seen as slightly specialized or slightly generalized relative to the early members of *Homo*, the morphological connection between them was perhaps not as perfect as Le Gros Clark occasionally stated. It is only a few years later that Le Gros Clark (1955: 155; 1964: 167) made clear that he considered these so-called specializations to be of such minor importance so that they could easily be eliminated during the transformation process without doing violence to any known evolutionary principles. On this view, Le Gros Clark always maintained since 1947 that the geological age of the known australopithecines would be the sole criterion to establish whether the latter are directly or indirectly related to the living humans.

34. Le Gros Clark continually wavered throughout the years on the question of the exact phylogenetic position of the *known* australopithecines relative to the living humans. This is perfectly understandable considering that: (1) The datation of the australopithecines and the early members of *Homo* was not clearly established and was subjected to changes and to various interpretations; (2) new specimens of australopithecines and early *Homo* were continually being recovered, some in new geographical areas such as in East Africa (*Zinjanthropus*, "*Homo habilis*"). This empirical instability is reflected in Le Gros Clark's assessment of the phylogenetic place of the known australopithecines. For instance, Le Gros Clark (1954: 391; 1957: 120) once declared that if the known australopithecines were no older than the Early Pleistocene, then they are unlikely to be directly ancestral to living humans. In another place, Le Gros Clark (1960b: 76) recognized that because the known australopithecines were already showing a certain amount of structural diversification (several forms of them) by the Lower Pleistocene, this implied that the origin of the group as a whole would be found in the Upper Pliocene period, thus positioning it in a proper temporal sequence to be directly ancestral to the living humans. In yet another place, Le Gros Clark (1958: 143; 1964: 172) held that the evidence showed that the australopithecines were older than the other hominid groups, so that the entire group was properly positioned in time to be directly ancestral to the living humans.

35. See Keith's human family tree in *A New Theory of Human Evolution* (New York: Philosophical Library, 1949), p. 159.

36. This transformation of ape-like creatures into human-like creatures through a worldwide australopithecine phase that started in Africa could not be applied to the ancient Piltdown evolutionary line because of its modern-looking braincase. Keith suggested the following explanation: "The African theory . . . accounts very well for the pent-browed early types of humanity, but leaves unexplained such an aberrant type as that of Piltdown. To account for Piltdown man our theory must be modified in the following respects. So far it has been assumed that the pioneer groups were made up of individuals conforming to one type—namely, that of the South African anthropoids [australopithecines]. This may not have been the case—there may have been more than one type. Seeing the close relationship of the orang to the African chimpanzee and gorilla, it is probable that this anthropoid, too, is of African origin. If this were the case, then it is possible that among the early forerunners of mankind in Africa some had inherited the orang form of skull and forehead. This is what I am assuming. This modification of my theory involves two other assumptions: (1) that it was the orangoid forms that turned westward into Europe and ultimately reached England, where their further evolution continued; (2) that those characters of the human skull we count modern, such as the mastoid process and chin, have been evolved independently in several early races of mankind" (Keith, 1949: 231–232).

37. See Robinson's family tree of the australopithecines in, "The Genera and Species of the Australopithecinae," *American Journal of Physical Anthropology*, 12 (1954), p. 197.

38. Robinson derived *Telanthropus* (now called *Homo erectus*) directly from the *Australopithecus* branch. See his new hominid family tree presented in "The Australopithecines and Their

Bearing on the Origin of Man and of Stone Tool-Making," *South African Journal of Science*, 57 (1961), p. 12.

39. Robinson (1965, 1966) never recognized the validity of the species *Homo habilis* created in 1964. He argued that the fossil sample of this species was an amalgam of the latest representatives of *Australopithecus* and the earliest members of *Homo erectus*.

40. For Robinson (1960, 1961), the discovery of "*Zinjanthropus*" in East Africa in 1959 only confirmed that this was another specimen of *Paranthropus*.

41. The place attributed by Le Gros Clark to the australopithecines in the hominid and hominoid trees can be seen in *The Fossil Evidence for Human Evolution* (Chicago: University of Chicago Press, 1955), p. 8; *The Antecedents of Man* (Chicago: Quadrangle Books, 1960a), p. 344; *The Fossil Evidence for Human Evolution*, 2nd edition (Chicago: University of Chicago Press, 1964), p. 8; *The Antecedents of Man*, 3rd edition (Chicago: Quadrangle Books, 1971), p. 346.

42. For Arambourg, the time of divergence of the human and the australopithecine lines was placed between the late Miocene and the mid-Pliocene periods. See Arambourg's different ways of presenting the phylogeny of the australopithecines. Compare: *La genèse de l'humanité* (Paris: Presses Universitaires de France, 1943), p. 131, "L'état actuel de nos connaissances sur les origines de l'homme." *L'Année Biologique*, 23 (1947), p. 302 and "Observations sur la phylogénie des primates et l'origine des hominiens." In L.S.B. Leakey and S. Cole (eds.), Proceedings of the Pan-African Congress on Prehistory, 1947 (Oxford: Basil Blackwell, 1952), p. 118. However, Arambourg clearly indicated that this common ancestor was australopithecine-like in conformation, although of a less specialized conformation than the one known to us. For Arambourg, the australopithecines already announced the rise of the human type, in opposition to the ape type, as seen by a number of key features such as an increased in brain size, a human-like dentition, a reduced face and a bipedal gait. To my knowledge, Arambourg alluded to the only probable bipedal gait of the australopithecines only in 1947. See C. Arambourg, "L'état actuel de nos connaissances sur les origines de l'homme." *L'Année Biologique*, 23 (1947), p. 300. By 1948, Arambourg was fully convinced of the bipedality of the australopithecines.

43. This gradual incorporation of the australopithecines in the direct ancestry of the living humans is nicely captured by the changes in Arambourg's phylogenetic trees. Compare: *La genèse de l'humanité*, 5th edition (Paris: Presses Universitaires de France, 1957), p. 123; "Les données de la paléontologie humaine." In, A. Varagnac (ed.), *L'homme avant l'écriture* (Paris: Armand Colin, 1959), p. 57; *La genèse de l'humanité*, 6th edition (Paris: Presses Universitaires de France, 1961), p. 117.

44. Arambourg already suspected in 1957 that the australopithecines were the makers of primitive stone tools, although he recognized that no positive proof was yet known. See *La genèse de l'humanité*, 5th edition (Paris: Presses Universitaires de France, 1957), p. 114.

45. The phylogenetic isolation of the *Paranthropus* group from the other australopithecines is clearly seen in Arambourg's phylogenetic tree of 1959. See "Les données de la paléontologie humaine." In, A. Varagnac (ed.), *L'homme avant l'écriture* (Paris: Armand Colin, 1959), p. 57.

46. The incorporation of the robust australopithecines in the earliest stage of human evolution can be seen in Arambourg's phylogenetic tree. See *La genèse de l'humanité*, 6th edition (Paris: Presses Universitaires de France, 1961), p. 117.

47. This precision regarding the robust australopithecines left Arambourg's phylogenetic tree unchanged compared to his previous one of 1961. See *La genèse de l'humanité*, 7th edition (Paris: Presses Universitaires de France, 1965), p. 117.

48. See Tobias's family trees of the australopithecines in "Early Man in East Africa," *Science*, 149 (1965), p. 32, and *Olduvai Gorge: The Cranium and Maxillary Dentition of* Australopithecus (Zinjanthropus) boisei (Cambridge: Cambridge University Press, 1967), p. 241.

49. Tobias (1968: 296) was once tempted by the idea that *Telanthropus* of Swartkrans (South Africa) might be a representative of *Homo habilis* (see also Leakey et al., 1964: 9).

50. It is only possible to fully understand Leakey's conception of the place of the australopithecines at the time by turning to his primate phylogenetic tree. See Leakey's tree in *Adam's Ancestors*, 4th edition (London: Methuen, 1953), p. 212. According to Leakey, the australopithecines constituted an extinct side branch which departed in the early Pliocene period exclusively from the portion of the hominid branch which led to extinct forms such as the pithecanthropines and the Neandertals. On this view, the genuine human branch leading to the living humans is to be found in still deeper geological deposits, that is, in the late Miocene period. In other words, the australopithecines arrived too late on the scene to contribute to the ancestry of the living humans. At that time, Leakey refused to endorse the idea that the australopithecines were tool makers.

51. Leakey's position on the place of the australopithecines after 1961 was not merely a restatement of his previous view of 1953. For Leakey, after 1961, the evolutionary lines leading to both the living humans and the australopithecines converged in a not too distant past to reach a common state of dissolution. This inevitably brings the australopithecine line closer to the one leading to the living humans. This view of Leakey is perhaps not surprising when considering that in 1960 he was prepared to derive the living humans directly from *Zinjanthropus*. This certainly contributed to his appreciation of many similarities between the living humans and the australopithecines, something he was certainly not prepared to recognize in 1953.

52. However, von Koenigswald (1964: 74) once alluded that it is the bipedal locomotion which might have been responsible for the increase in the brain size and that the reduction of the canines was not caused by the use of implements. It is not possible to establish where this very short and elusive passage fits into von Koenigswald's conception of the hominization process.

9

Human Phylogeny, 1950–1965

INTRODUCTION

As stated in Chapter 6, research on human phylogeny had reached an unprecedented level of coherence between 1935 and 1950. By then, multilinear, parallel, and linear phylogenetic hypotheses constituted a spectrum of hypotheses grading into one another more or less seamlessly. All this provided a solid and robust scientific framework that was further enhanced during the 1950–1965 period.

This new level of coherence was achieved by the gradual abandonment of the notion of a modern-looking hominid ancestor leading to the living humans dated back to the Pliocene or to the Lower Pleistocene period. According to this new view, a strong majority of scholars now promoted the viewpoint that a modern-looking hominid ancestor did not appear until the Middle Pleistocene, perhaps not until the Upper Pleistocene. Coon, Heberer, Howells, Leakey, Le Gros Clark, Piveteau, and Vallois all changed their mind between 1935 and 1965 about the date of this modern-looking form by displacing it from the Lower to the Middle Pleistocene, or from the Middle to the Upper Pleistocene. This added additional coherence to the common structure of debates about human phylogeny. Now, a large majority of scholars derived the living humans from a primitive-looking ("ape-like") Lower Pleistocene ancestor, irrespective of their views regarding the contribution or the noncontribution of modern-looking ancestors to the living humans in the Middle or Upper Pleistocene. The move away from an early modern-looking ancestor is part of a historical trend which started earlier in the twentieth century. The continuation of this trend gradually pushed this modern-looking ancestor closer and closer to the present.

Several factors contributed to this historical trend during the 1935–1965 period. Some factors were external to the research area concerned with human phylogeny proper. This is not surprising considering that by the 1950s the separate research areas devoted to the establishment of humankind's place among the primates and to the investigation of human phylogeny proper were more and more integrated. By the 1950s, debates on humankind's place among the primates revolved around establishing if the human line had departed from the other primates at an early generalized prehominoid ape stage, at an early hominoid ape stage, or at a later and somewhat specialized hominoid ape stage (see Chapter 7). Irrespective of the position taken by individual scholars in this debate, it was agreed that the emergence of the human line from an ancient modern-looking ancestor was no longer an option.

This was further reinforced in the 1940s and 1950s by the debates about the role played by the australopithecines in human evolution (see Chapter 8). Whether or not the australopithecines were considered to be directly or indirectly ancestral to living humans, it was evident for a large majority of scholars that the former represented the type of creature that might have given rise to living humans. Although a number of so-called modern human-like features were identified among the australopithecines, nobody believed the latter were equivalent to the humans. The discovery of the australopithecines contributed to the demise of the notion of modern human-looking ancestors in the Pliocene or the Lower Pleistocene period. Furthermore, the recovery of the australopithecines helped to make the pithecanthropines seem more "modern". This modernization process made the pithecanthropines more suitable ancestors for modern humans, especially for scholars who preferred human ancestors less primitive or "ape-like".

A number of other factors were involved in the rejection of the hypothesis that modern-looking humans appeared early in human evolution. These were internal to the research area concerned with human phylogeny proper. First, the notion that primitive hominids (not ape-like hominids) were widespread in the Old World in the Lower and/or Middle Pleistocene was significantly bolstered in the 1940s, 1950s, and 1960s. Remember that the 1930s saw the recognition of pithecanthropine forms such as *Pithecanthropus*, *Sinanthropus*, and *Meganthropus* in South and East Asia. At the time, some researchers accepted that pithecanthropines were also found in Europe (Heidelberg man) and in East Africa (*Africanthropus*). Although the situation remained uncertain in Europe, the following decades saw the recovery of several pithecanthropine-like forms in Africa: *Telanthropus* in southern Africa, *Atlanthropus* in North Africa, and hominid Bed II at Olduvai in East Africa (e.g., Arambourg, 1954, 1955b, 1955c, 1955d; Arambourg and Biberson, 1955, 1956; Arambourg and Hoffstetter, 1954, 1955; Leakey, 1961f; Robinson, 1953b).

Such discoveries reinforced the notion that all Middle and Upper Pleistocene hominids were derived from primitive-looking Lower Pleistocene ancestors, as the known primitive hominids were probably older than all the modern-looking ones. Indeed, early modern-looking forms of the Middle Pleistocene such as Swanscombe and Fontéchevade were eventually all dated to the second portion of this latter period (Oakley, 1964b). Furthermore, modern-looking hominids once believed to date back to the Lower Pleistocene were now believed to be more recent than previously assumed. Some had been dismissed altogether as in the case of the Piltdown man, following its exposure as a hoax. Others, such as the Kanam jaw, were merely demoted to a much more recent time period after new dating methods were applied to them. Similarly, modern-looking forms once dated to the Middle Pleistocene like Kanjera and Galley Hill were now placed in the Upper Pleistocene and the Holocene period respectively (e.g., Oakley, 1953, 1964a, 1964b; Weiner et al., 1953). Clearly, it became more difficult in the 1950s and 1960s to defend the hypothesis that all living humans were exclusively descended from a modern-looking ancestor.

In the new empirical context of the 1950s and 1960s, it was believed that human phylogeny could best be explained by three main competing hypotheses. A first group of scholars promoted a multilinear hypothesis of the "Presapiens" kind. In this scheme, living humans are exclusively descended from an ancient modern-looking ancestor, with all the other primitive hominids being extinct side branches. The increasingly precarious empirical foundation of this position is clearly seen by the fact that Howells and Leakey eventually retreated from it in the 1960s. By so doing, they followed Le Gros Clark, who had already done so in the early 1940s. A second group of scholars promoted a parallel hypothesis in which both modern- and primitive-looking forms were directly contributing to the ancestry of the main living human races. They were later followed in this view, somewhat hesitantly, by Howells and Leakey in the late 1960s and early 1970s. We have already seen in Chapter 5 that some modern observers had assumed that it was not possible to hold that phylogenetic contributions to the living humans could be made by both modern- and primitive-looking forms. Not only was this tradition of interpretation well-represented before 1950, but it also continued to be so in the 1950s and 1960s. Finally, a third group of scholars promoted a linear hypothesis in which primitive-looking ancestors gradually gave rise to living humans. It will be seen how various versions of linear hypotheses permitted the accomodation of more or less ancient modern-looking ancestors in human phylogeny. Although this chapter is concerned mainly with the 1950–1965 period, it will sometimes be necessary to consider some developments in the late 1930s and throughout the 1940s in order to fully understand the extent to which some scholars modified their views.

A HISTORIOGRAPHICAL NOTE

It has been pointed out already in Chapter 5 that the traditional historiography interested in the history of paleoanthropology is wrongly biased toward the place of the Neandertals in human evolution. In the light of this traditional historiography, the development of the field is to be understood both in terms of a polarization between linear and multilinear hyptheses as well as in terms of the phylogenetic place of the Neandertals in these hypotheses. This historiography assumes that the Neandertals are directly ancestral to the living humans in the linear hypotheses, while they constitute an extinct side branch in the multilinear hypotheses. This study makes the case that the polarization between the linear and the multilinear hypotheses is too simplistic to permit the understanding of paleoanthropology before 1935. As far as the post-1935 period is concerned, the following comments are in order.

First, it is argued here that this polarization could be of some use for understanding the debates on human phylogeny after 1935 *provided that other types of hypotheses are incorporated in it*. This leaves us not with a simple dichotomy but with a less restrictive context in which the linear and the multilinear hypotheses are the two extremes of a spectrum of phylogenetic hypotheses. Moderated multilinear hypotheses, parallel hypotheses, and more or less linear hypotheses occupy the middle ground of this spectrum.

Second, the notion that the phylogenetic role of the Neandertals is tightly associated with one or other of the hypotheses is largely false. In light of our more broadly defined linear-multilinear dichotomy, this correlation is, at best, rather loose. It will be seen in this chapter that many scholars believed that there has been a certain amount of interbreeding between the specialized ("classic") Neandertals and the other hominids, irrespective of their phylogenetic hypotheses. Similarly, many scholars held that the specialized Neandertals went extinct regardless of the phylogenetic hypothesis they subscribed to. In order to understand properly the development of paleoanthropology in the post-1935 period, one must avoid the bias toward the place of the Neandertals. This is as true for the post-1935 period as it was for the pre-1935 one.

MULTILINEAR HYPOTHESES

Numerous scholars prior to 1935 held that several hominid groups were either too ape-like, too specialized, or too late in time to be ancestral to the living humans (see Chapters 4 and 5). These fossil groups were believed to represent extinct side branches on the human family tree. However, even though they were agreed on this, proponents of this interpretation before 1935 disagreed about whether humankind's direct ancestor was more ape-like or more human-like in conformation. This tradition of interpretation continued in the 1935–1965 period but was modified in two ways. First, many scholars, such as Keith, Hooton, Leakey, and Howells, all retreated, completely or partially, from it. Second, it became more difficult than in the past to hold that the living humans have exclusively sprung from an early modern-looking ancestor. This is probably why Le Gros Clark, Leakey, and Howells eventually gave up on this idea, while Vallois and Heberer placed this modern-looking ancestor in the Middle rather than in the Lower Pleistocene. In this new context, a number of scholars continued to promote in the 1950–1965 period a genuine multilinear hypotheses. Two versions of the multilinear hypothesis were suggested at the time: the "Presapiens" and the "non-presapiens."

Le Gros Clark initially proposed a Presapiens hypothesis but he retreated from it in the late 1930s. In the mid-1930s, Le Gros Clark (1935) held that the living humans descended from a modern human type that was discovered in the very early

Pleistocene period of Africa. Although he refrained from naming such discoveries, it is pretty clear that reference was made here to the East African remains of Kanam and Kanjera. With such hominid remains, continued Le Gros Clark, all the other archaic fossil types such as *Pithecanthropus*, *Sinanthropus*, and even *Eoanthropus* were in all probability unrelated to the rise of the living humans. In order to explain the late appearance in time of the specialized Neandertal extinct side branch, it was held that they arose as a secondary retrogression from a stock approaching *Homo sapiens*.

In the second half of the decade, however, Le Gros Clark retreated from the notion that the modern human type could be traced back to the Lower Pleistocene. This revision occurred in two steps. In the first one, Le Gros Clark (1936) excluded the Kanam and Kajera remains from human phylogeny.[1] He now no longer necessarily excluded Piltdown man nor *Sinanthropus* from being directly ancestral to the living humans. In fact, Le Gros Clark noted that both of these forms, which lived more or less in contemporaneity, approached, though differently, the modern human type by some of their features. However, it was denied that Piltdown man and *Sinanthropus* could both be directly ancestral to the living humans. If one form was truly ancestral, insisted Le Gros Clark, then the modern-looking features of the other could only be explained by parallel evolution. In 1936, then, Le Gros Clark was wavering over whether or not a Lower Pleistocene modern-looking ancestor was directly ancestral to the living humans. In the second step of his retreat from the notion of an ancient modern-looking ancestor, Le Gros Clark (1939a, 1940) no longer considered Piltdown man as a possible early Pleistocene ancestor to the living humans. Although this was done implicitly only and without any explanation, he later specified that:

> [Considering the Piltdown remains, it would be wise] to wait the time when further discoveries will show them in their true light. [Yet], they can hardly be dismissed so lightly, as Weidenreich seems disposed to do, by affirming categorically that the cranial fragments are those of *Homo sapiens*, and the jaw that of an ape. (Le Gros Clark, 1945: 5)

From that time on, Le Gros Clark's (1940, 1945, 1946a, 1950, 1954, 1955, 1964) conception of human phylogeny excluded the notion of a Lower Pleistocene modern-looking ancestor to humankind.[2] He now recognized an evolutionary line or trend from the earliest pithecanthropines to the living humans. However, this evolutionary line was not linear for it included a number of extinct side branches.[3] Le Gros Clark promoted the hypothesis that the pithecanthropine group provided the basis for the development of all the other hominid types. Although he was at first uncertain if the geographical distribution of the pithecanthropines was restricted only to Southeast Asia (*Pithecanthropus*, *Sinanthropus*, and *Meganthropus*), he later recognized its presence in Africa (*Africanthropus* and *Atlanthropus*) and possibly also in Europe (Heidelberg man). This early Pleistocene group was described as being characterized by a number of primitive features such as a small brain capacity, a retreating forehead, a developed supraorbital torus, and large teeth.

The precise nature of the phylogenetic connection between the pithecanthropines and the living humans is not entirely clear from Le Gros Clark's writings in the 1940s. At that time, he (1940, 1945) made clear that the pithecanthropine group was directly ancestral to the later hominids in the sense that a progressive pithecanthropine form gave rise to them, although he refrained from specifying if all or most of the pithecanthropines contributed to this movement. In the 1950s and 1960s, Le Gros Clark (1955, 1964) was more explicit only because his phylogenetic trees showed that the pithecanthropine stem continued to evolve on its own for some time toward extinction, after the later hominids had sprung from it at an earlier time.[4]

Le Gros Clark (1940, 1945, 1954, 1955, 1964) conceived the pithecanthropine group as embracing a sufficient amount of variation in brain size to have directly given rise to all the later hominid forms through a relatively modern-looking ancestor of the mid-Pleistocene:

> [A] primitive type of *H. sapiens* came into existence by the Middle Pleistocene, presumably from an earlier small-brained type represented by the *Pithecanthropus* stage of hominid evolution . . . [T]he progressive development of the brain in the *Pithecanthropus* group of hominids led eventually to the appearance of a type of *Homo* which, on morphological evidence, was apparently not specifically distinct from *H. sapiens*. (Le Gros Clark, 1955: 74)

If Le Gros Clark recognized that this ancestor was probably not sufficiently different from *Homo sapiens* to establish a distinct species, it should not be assumed that it was believed to be identical to the living humans.[5] Indeed, he saw in this form a generalized Neandertal type differing from the living humans by its strong supraorbital torus and by its great thickness of the cranial walls. Le Gros Clark included, at one time or another, the following remains as representatives of this relatively modern-looking fossil type: Steinheim, Fontéchevade, Swanscombe, Ehringsdorf, Saccopastore, Krapina, and Mount Carmel. The affinities of the remains found in the last two locations, however, were somewhat uncertain.

In Le Gros Clark's later conception of human phylogeny, this relatively modern-looking group was at the base of at least two main evolutionary branches: one leading directly to the living humans and the other to the collateral and extinct branch of the specialized Neandertals. In the former branch, progressive enlargement of the brain was accompanied by a reduction of the supraorbital torus, the reduction in size of the jaw and teeth, and the establishment of a more rounded cranium with a vertical forehead. In the specialized Neandertal branch—called *Homo neanderthalensis*—this progressive enlargement of the brain was associated with an exaggerated increase of the supraorbital torus, the rise of some specializations in the skull and teeth, and the pronounced curvatures and the massiveness of the limb bones. Although Le Gros Clark held that there were a number of morphological similarities between the pithecanthropines and *Homo neanderthalensis*, these similarities were not explained by a direct kinship but rather by a retrogressive evolution of the Neandertal evolutionary branch. He was apparently uncertain about whether or not Neanderthaloid forms like Solo man and Rhodesian man should be affiliated to the branch of *Homo neanderthalensis*. In 1950 at least, Le Gros Clark (1950a: 259) was prepared to recognize in Piltdown man another somewhat specialized collateral branch of the later hominid phase, although its phylogenetic place was not clearly presented.

If Le Gros Clark eventually entirely retreated from the Presapiens hypothesis, scholars like Vallois, Heberer and Genet-Varcin held on to this very type of multilinear hypothesis, but not in its original form. Indeed, Vallois now changed the antiquity of the Presapiens ancestor from the Lower Pleistocene to the Middle Pleistocene. We have already seen that during the 1930s and 1940s Vallois promoted a conception of human phylogeny which recognized several hominid lines evolving in parallel throughout the Pleistocene period (see Chapter 6). One such line consisted of modern-looking individuals similar though not identical to the living humans, while the other lines were represented by more primitive forms. Vallois continued to follow this view in the 1950s but proposed two modifications.

First, whereas he had previously believed the modern-looking line—now formally called by him Presapiens—was already constituted by the Lower Pleistocene as seen in Piltdown, he now reduced the antiquity of this line to the Middle Pleistocene. This process was first instituted after a new and more recent date for Piltdown itself (Vallois, 1952). Soon after was the dramatic debunking of the Piltdown morphological type in human evolution, after the realization that it has been a hoax (Vallois, 1954, 1955b).[6] This forced Vallois to base his support for the Presapiens hypothesis on the evidence from Swanscombe and Fontéchevade.

Second, Vallois was not as explicit as in the past in his recognition of the possiblity that some primitive hominid lines might also have given rise to some living human races. This was done by two subtle yet important changes of interpretation. First, Vallois (1952, 1955b) made clear he no longer believed that Solo man was necessarily a Neandertal type from Asia. Rather, he now was inclined to see it as a sort of evolved pithecanthropine. This contributed to increase the morphological gap between Solo man and the living humans, as the pithecanthropines were believed to be the most primitive hominids then known. Second, Vallois no longer held that the Preneandertals were at the root of both the more specialized or classic Neandertals and some living humans. Instead, he now put the Preneandertals exclusively on the line leading to these more specialized Neandertals. This contributed to cutting a genealogical route by which the Neandertals could have been transformed into living humans.[7]

Thus, Vallois had somewhat retreated from his previous view which recognized that at least some primitive hominid evolutionary lines could have contributed to the rise of some living human races. Logically, this modified position opened the door for a greater contribution on the part of some modern-looking hominids to the ancestry of the living humans.

Although Vallois was somewhat vague about several aspects of his general view of human phylogeny in the 1950s, it is possible to partly reconstruct it because in the 1950s he already had addressed the place of the australopithecines in the phylogeny of humankind (see Chapters 7 and 8). The parallel hominid evolutionary lines that Vallois recognized during the Pleistocene were ultimately derived from a single and common source. He (1955b) now identified at least four such evolutionary lines, although he expected that more would eventually be revealed. Vallois specified that it was not yet possible to determine precisely when such lines diverged from one another. However, it is perfectly clear from his writings that this occurred somewhere between the early Pliocene period, when the human stem departed from an australopithecine-like ancestor, and the late portion of the Lower Pleistocene period, when at least two distinct hominid lines had already made their appearance.

When considering the conformation of this common hominid ancestor, it is also clear that Vallois conceived it as a generalized and bipedal hominoid-like creature with a brain size larger than that of the living hominoid apes. In other words, although Vallois recognized in the Presapiens hypothesis an evolutionary line approaching the modern human type in the Middle Pleistocene, he did not interpret the common ancestor to all the hominid lines as modern and human-like. In fact, as these lines are followed back in time—that is, deeper into the Lower Pleistocene—the more they seem to converge toward a primitive ancestor approaching a pithecanthropine-like creature.[8] This is not surprising considering that Vallois often insisted on the numerous ape-like features of the oldest hominid line he recognized, the pithecanthropines (now also comprising Solo man). Similarly, the second oldest hominid line he identified started with the primitive and somewhat ape-like Heidelberg man of the Lower Pleistocene and was continued through the Preneandertals and still later through the classic Neandertals. Vallois (1958 [1962]) held that the Presapiens line of the Middle Pleistocene probably diverged from a common Lower Pleistocene ancestor shared with this Neandertal line.[9]

In Vallois's conception, the Neandertal line evolves toward an increasing specialization and eventually reaches an evolutionary dead end both in Europe and in Southern Africa during the Upper Pleistocene (Vallois, 1954, 1955a, 1958 [1962]). In Europe, the classic Neandertals or *Homo neanderthalensis* were superseded by *Homo sapiens*, the descendants of the Presapiens line. It is not impossible, he continued, that a certain amount of interbreeding occurred between these two groups, but not to the point where the hereditary potentialities of the newcomers (*Homo sapiens*) were modified. In Africa, Vallois also identified a Neanderthaloid line represented by the Rhodesian man and the Saldanha remains that was outcompeted by more modern representatives. Although he (1955b) clearly established only a single Presapiens line—the one leading to *Homo sapiens* (Aurignacian man) in Europe—he conjectured that other such unknown modern-looking lines might possibly have contributed to give rise to *Homo sapiens* in Asia and Africa.

Clearly, Vallois was, in the 1950s, more prepared than in the past to hold that ancient modern-looking ancestors made a major contribution to the rise of the living humans, although these modern-looking types were now dated to the Middle rather than to the Lower Pleistocene period. At one time, Vallois (1955a: 2193-2194) even alluded to the possibility that all the living humans might have sprung from only a single evolutionary line (presumably Presapiens), all the others being dead ends. This being said, he had to recognize that too little was known about the more ancient hominids of Asia and Africa. On this view, Vallois could not entirely deny the possibility that some primitive hominid lines might have directly contributed to the ancestry of the living humans. This is seen in two instances.

In the first case, Vallois (1958 [1962]) mentioned that it is still possible to conceive of a genealogical connection between the pithecanthropine line and some living human races such as the Australians and the Chinese. However, he pointed out that no decisive argument had been put forward yet to support this view. In the second instance, Vallois (1955a: 2165–2166) held that the Neanderthaloid group of Palestine documented a morphological transition between the Neandertals and *Homo sapiens*. Yet, Vallois was uncertain whether this Palestine group was the product of admixture between Neanderthals and modern humans or the transformation of the former into the latter.

Independently of the contribution or noncontribution of primitive hominid lines to the living human races, Vallois's (1962: 499) general conception of human phylogeny, although somewhat vague, may best be summarized in his own words:

> Our genealogical tree should not be compared to a poplar which rises in a single thrust high above the ground, but rather to a bush which spreads out at once in lateral branches, many of which come to an end, others subdividing to end in turn, with only a few reaching full growth. We do not know if the totality of races living today derives from a single branch or from several, but there is no doubt that the first appearance of the type which we call *Homo sapiens* was much older than we formerly imagined.

Needless to say, this last statement about the first appearance of the *Homo sapiens* type being older than formerly imagined should not be taken literally, especially when considering that Vallois himself now placed this type in the Middle rather than in the Lower Pleistocene.

Not unlike Vallois, Heberer's version of the Presapiens hypothesis was modified in the 1950s and 1960s. At first, Heberer (1950) conceived of a parallel evolution of three main hominid evolutionary lines throughout most of the Pleistocene period in more or less distinct geographical areas (especially for the Asian archanthropines).[10] He suggested that this entire hominid radiation was derived from an australopithecine phase at the Pliocene/Pleistocene boundary. This being said, Heberer made clear that each main hominid line was not independently derived from this australopithecine phase as two such lines (Presapiens and paleoanthropines) independently sprang from the base of the third one (archanthropines), possibly in the early portion of the Lower Pleistocene.

Heberer originally conceived of these lineages as evolving in opposite directions. Whereas the two primitive-looking ones evolved in the direction of ever more degenerate forms—as seen in their terminal forms such as Ngandong for the archanthropines and La Chapelle-aux-Saints for the paleoanthropines—the Presapiens line, for its part, evolved toward more modern-looking representatives. Although the early portion of the archanthropine line was fairly well documented with fossil remains such as Sangiran and Choukoutien, Heberer could not point to any certain early remains for the other two evolutionary lines. For instance, he was unsure if the Lower Pleistocene jaw found at Heidelberg should be placed with the archanthropines or the paleoanthropines, leaving open the possibility that no fossil remains dated to this early period were known in the paleoanthropine (Neandertal) line. The situation was even less certain for the Presapiens line, as Heberer identified Fontéchevade, Swanscombe, Galley Hill, and Quinzano as its earliest members, which were all dated to the early portion of the Middle Pleistocene. It seems that Heberer's conviction that the Presapiens line could possibly be traced back to the early portion of the Lower Pleistocene still awaited formal proofs. The Piltdown remains were of no significance because this Presapiens representative was dated by Heberer himself to the Upper Pleistocene.

By the late 1950s, however, Heberer (1959b) no longer supported a Lower Pleistocene divergence of the Presapiens and paleoanthropine lines from a common archanthropine ancestor. Now, he concluded that the separation was an early Middle Pleistocene event. In the mid-1960s there was no more attempts of deriving the paleoanthropine line from a form approaching more nearly the *sapiens* type than the Neandertal type, as once suggested by Heberer (1959b). Instead, Heberer (1965) reversed his perspective and derived the Presapiens line from a Neanderthaloid type of the Middle Pleistocene period. As an example, whereas Steinheim was placed squarely in the paleoanthropine line in 1950, this fossil was now believed to be near the divergence of the Presapiens and the paleoanthropine lines. Heberer's new phylogenetic tree not only indicated that the direct modern-looking ancestors of the living humans were not as ancient as previously believed, but also conveyed the impression that the conformation of these so-called modern-looking representatives were not as modern as once assumed.[11] The parallel evolution of the three distinct lineages was less and less clearly presented by Heberer. The hominid radiation even started to look a bit like three successive evolutionary waves in time (archanthropines, paleoanthropines, neanthropines), the first two being characterized by numerous extinct side branches.

Just as Vallois and Heberer changed their mind about the antiquity of the Presapiens ancestors, Genet-Varcin eventually did the same. However, she apparently still placed this modern-looking form in very ancient times. It is difficult to pinpoint the moment in time as well as the precise conformation of this ancestor because Genet-Varcin's writings are very vague on these important questions. At first, Genet-Varcin (1963) held that the hominid forms that both belonged to *Pithecanthropus* and *Homo*, which lived more or less in contemporaneity during the Pleistocene period, shared a last common ancestor as early as the Oligocene period.[12] In fact, Genet-Varcin (1963) derived an entire group of forms represented by *Oreopithecus*, *Ramapithecus*, *Australopithecus*, *Pithecanthropus*, and *Homo* from this common Oligocene ancestor. In her view, the extinct side branch of the Neandertals departed in the late Pliocene period from the evolutionary line leading to living humans (*Homo*), and not from the one leading to *Pithecanthropus*.

Genet-Varcin's view of human phylogeny changed during the 1960s. However, the basis for this change was not made explicit by her. By the late 1960s, Genet-Varcin (1967, 1969) now promoted a scheme in which archanthropines

(*Pithecanthropus*), *Homo neanderthalensis*, and *Homo sapiens* all independently departed from a common hominid ancestor in the late or middle Pliocene period. While the first two branches were without living representatives, the third one directly led to the living humans.[13] Genet-Varcin's conception entirely denied the assumed succession of evolutionary stages in human evolution, such as represented by the australopithecines, the archanthropines, the Neandertals, and the living humans.

Instead, her new view rested on the notion that only the earliest and more generalized representatives of both the archanthropine and the Neandertal lineages were closely related to the lineage which led to the living humans. Among the archanthropines, *Tchadanthropus* and *Telanthropus* may well represent such early and generalized forms. Among the Neandertals, the fossils of Steinheim, Swanscombe, and Fontéchevade could constitute less specialized forms. In other words, the more the evolutionary branches of the archanthropines and the Neandertals independently diverged from the main lineage leading to living humans during the Pliocene and Pleistocene, the more they specialized by developing massive structures such as heavy browridges. For Genet-Varcin (1967, 1969), the lineage leading to the living humans is a fetalized one, being characterized by forms which retained generalized and juvenile features in adulthood. Genet-Varcin's view continued to change in the 1970s to the point of nearly conforming with the other multilinear hypotheses of the period (see Chapter 10).

FROM MULTILINEAR TO PARALLEL HYPOTHESES?

Whereas a number of scholars thought it was justified to continue to promote genuine multilinear hypotheses during the 1950s and 1960s, others eventually changed their mind when confronted by the new empirical context. Howells's and Leakey's cases illustrate very well the challenges being posed at the time to the proponents of the multilinear hypotheses, especially of the Presapiens kind. Howells's and Leakey's phylogenetic conceptions were gradually and profoundly modified on two counts. First, they changed their phylogenetic views to the point where their original multilinear hypotheses were almost transformed into parallel hypotheses. These are two further examples of the constriction process of human phylogenetic hypothesis going on in paleoanthropology after 1935 (see also Chapter 6). Second, Howells and Leakey gradually retreated from the Presapiens hypothesis.

For instance, Howells (1942, 1944, 1950) initially promoted the view that human phylogeny had been characterized by an adaptive radiation, that is, the rise of several hominid evolutionary lines diverging from a common "ape-like" ancestor, some or all independently going through an increase in brain size. Although this common stock remained unspecified in Howells's mind, he insisted that you "can hardly accept both the Piltdown and Peking men in your genealogy" (Howells, 1944: 207).[14] Similarly, Howells held that the Neandertal lineage, as first appearing in Heidelberg man and later Steinheim, is not the ancestor of the living human races, regardless of the fact that there may have been a negligible amount of interbreeding between the former and the ancestors of the latter. Howells (1944: 161) conceived of the Neandertal lineage as running almost from the beginning of the Pleistocene to the end. He clearly recognized that several hominid lines went extinct, although he remained vague as to their total numbers and identity. Howells was looking for an ancient modern-looking ancestral form that showed thinning of the cranium and reduction of the face. Fossil remains such as Swanscombe, Galley Hill, Bury St. Edmunds, and Piltdown were possible indicators of the presence of such a lineage whose exact relationship with the others remained uncertain. Although Howells (1944: 194) recognized that clear and unequivocal evidence was still lacking, he was inclined to believe that the species *Homo sapiens* arrived on the scene as early as the Lower Pleistocene.

In the late 1950s and throughout the 1960s, Howells's view was to change substantially. He simultaneously retreated from the Presapiens hypothesis as well as from the concept of an adaptive radiation in human evolution. This retreat occurred in two distinct phases. In the late 1950s, Howells (1959) continued to promote a Presapiens hypothesis, although his basis for doing so changed entirely.

He made the following changes. First, he held that all the later hominids stemmed from a *Pithecanthropus*-like form and not from an unknown ancestor shared in common with *Pithecanthropus* and *Sinanthropus*. Second, he promoted that the rise of the *Homo sapiens* type occurred not before the Middle Pleistocene, if not later, rather than during the Lower Pleistocene. Third, Heidelberg and Steinheim were now classified among the early ancestors of the living humans and were no longer seen as representatives of the Neandertal line, thus contributing to the "demodernization" of the earliest ancestors of the living humans. Fourth, it was held that the Neandertal line had not evolved independently throughout most of the Pleistocene period, as previously argued, but rather that it branched off in the Middle or the Upper Pleistocene from either the pithecanthropine stock or the Presapiens stock.

Howells (1959) derived all the hominids from an australopithecine phase of evolution widely spread throughout the Old World. Two distinct hominid groups were recognized in the Lower Pleistocene period. One of them was a widely spread pithecanthropine group with representatives in East Asia (*Pithecanthropus* and *Sinanthropus*) as well as in North Africa (*Atlanthropus*). This evolutionary group persisted until the Upper Pleistocene, as seen at least in the Far East (Solo man) and only possibly in South Africa (Rhodesian man).[15]

The second evolutionary group recognized by Howells in the Lower Pleistocene made its appearance in the West of the Old World with Heidelberg man in Europe and *Telanthropus* in South Africa. This line was believed to have rapidly evolved out of a *Pithecanthropus*-like ancestor. Being at the base of the living humans, this evolutionary line was represented in the Middle Pleistocene period by the remains of Swanscombe and Steinheim, forms assessed to be only moderately modern-looking.[16] This modern-looking strain could be followed in the Upper Pleistocene of Europe (Fontéchevade), the Middle East (Skhul) and East Africa (Kanjera). Howells (1959: 229) insisted that the cranium of the *Homo sapiens* type was in the making by the late Middle Pleistocene (Steinheim, Swanscombe) and completed by the early Upper Pleistocene (Fontéchevade, Kanjera).[17]

A third and later hominid group recognized by Howells was the Neandertals. It is not entirely clear whether Howells derived them in the Middle or Upper Pleistocene from either the pithecanthropine stock or the Presapiens stock (Steinheim, Swanscombe). He did not accept the early Neandertals to be modern-looking, but he recognized that the later ones were more specialized than the earlier forms. In Howells's interpretation at the time, the evolutionary line leading to the living humans was evolving toward modernity, whereas the Neandertal line was simultaneously going through a "Neandertalization" process. Although Howells would not derive the living humans from the Neandertal line, he allowed for some interbreeding between strains of the Neandertal type (Tabun) and of the *Homo sapiens* type (Skhul), at least in the Middle East. By so doing, Howells explained the neanderthaloid features of the Skhul people; a secondary *Homo sapiens* strain not on the main evolutionary stem.

By the mid-1960s, Howells (1966, 1967) had completed his retreat from the concept of an adaptive radiation in human evolution. Now, his view of human phylogeny was closer to a parallel hypothesis with a number of minor evolutionary side branches evolving toward extinction. This new view only undermined further his support for the Presapiens hypothesis, thus replacing it with something closer to the Preneandertal hypothesis. In Howells's new view, all the later hominids were now viewed as stemming from a homogeneous, widespread and long-lasting evolutionary phase called *Homo erectus*. Previously, Howells (1959) entertained a certain ambiguity regarding the relationship between the pithecanthropines and all the other hominid lines. On his new view, Heidelberg man is no longer exclusively ancestral to the living humans but constitutes a subspecies of *Homo erectus*, while the ancestry of the Neandertals is probably linked to Heidelberg man through the Montmaurin jaw (France). Howells (1967) held that if the *Homo erectus* phase was rather homogeneous, this has not been the case in the succeeding phases during which more heterogeneity and evolutionary diversification is detectable. Indeed, Howells conceived that we have in Steinheim a form that could be ancestral to both the Neandertals and the modern human type. While continuing their evolution in direction of the living humans, these two hominid groups or strains interbred significantly in the Middle East (Tabun and Skhul) but not in Western Europe, thus explaining the morphological peculiarities of the later classic Neandertals of Europe and their ensuing extinction.

Remember that Howells (1959) once saw in Steinheim a form unrelated to the Neandertals. His new view not only contributed to establish a close proximity between the Neandertals and modern humans, but also contributed to "modernize" the ancestor of the Neandertals as well as to "demodernize" further the ancestors of the modern human type.[18] On that basis, it is now clear that the *Homo sapiens* morphological type did not make its appearance before the Upper Pleistocene. For Howells (1966, 1967), it was now irrelevant to raise the question of whether or not the Neandertals are directly and exclusively derived from the pithecanthropines by avoiding altogether the hominid group leading to the modern human type. Not content with the notion that *Homo erectus* gave rise to the living humans through some of the Neandertals and the modern human types (Fontéchevade), Howells (1967: 247) even alluded to the possibility that the conservative *Pithecanthropus*-Solo man strain in Java might have passed on some of their genes to the living aboriginal Australians, through admixtures with modern-looking Asian elements of the late Pleistocene period. Howells's comment here indicates that his human phylogenetic conception was, by the mid-1960s, perhaps closer to a parallel hypothesis than to a multilinear hypothesis.[19]

Like Howells, Leakey's conception of human phylogeny went through profound changes during the 1950s and 1960s. Leakey also retreated from a multilinear hypotheses of the Presapiens kind. At first, Leakey held that the modern human type, *Homo sapiens*, might be traced back to the Lower Pleistocene period. Leakey (1950: 196) stated that "*Homo sapiens* is a species at least as old as the oldest of these other stocks", these other stocks being the pithecanthropine and the Neandertal specimens of the Lower and Middle Pleistocene (see also Leakey, 1953: 210).[20] Leakey (1953) placed on the lineage leading to the living humans fossil specimens such as the Kanam jaw (Kenya) of the early portion of the Pleistocene while the Kanjera (Kenya), Swanscombe (England), and Fontéchevade (France) remains were dated to the Middle Pleistocene. The latter three were presented as surely being of the *Homo sapiens* type.

For Leakey, the development and the diversification of living humans had been a slow evolutionary process which had required at least the entire Pleistocene period. The living Australians and Tasmanians were not, for Leakey, directly derived from some sort of pithecanthropine or Neanderthaloid stocks but rather were showing some exaggerated specializations within the *Homo sapiens* type. In Leakey's view, all the pithecanthropine and the Neandertal specimens belonged to a separate and extinct evolutionary branch which was not evolving towards less and less primitive features but, on the contrary, was gradually diversifying toward ever increasing over-specializations.[21] It should be remembered that Leakey denied that the hominid stock evolved from an ape possessing specialized features such as a simian shelf and massive browridges. In this interpretation, it is not possible to hold that such specialized ape features were inherited by, and passed on to, the common hominid evolutionary stock.

After 1959, Leakey's view of human phylogeny changed profoundly. This occurred in several steps and were instigated by Leakey's identification of new fossil remains believed to be directly ancestral to the living humans. Indeed, these were not as modern-looking as he had previously assumed. First, Leakey (1959, 1960a, 1961b) argued that *Zinjanthropus*, an australopithecine form of the Lower Pleistocene, was directly ancestral to the living humans. Shortly after, Leakey (1961d, 1961f, 1963, 1966, 1971) excluded *Zinjanthropus* from this ancestral position and replaced it by a form eventually named *Homo habilis* and also dated to the Lower Pleistocene (Leakey et al., 1964). Eventually, Leakey (1966, 1971) came to promote the hypothesis that *Homo habilis* evolved into *Homo sapiens* with *Homo erectus* being a sort of Asian side branch. Leakey was no longer able to hold the view that the evolutionary line leading to the living humans was already modern-looking by the Lower Pleistocene. After all, *Homo habilis* was described as having a cranial capacity below that of *Homo erectus* (pithecanthropines) and teeth comparable in size or larger than *Homo erectus*. These fossil discoveries had important consequences for Leakey's conception of human phylogeny.

First, this led to the recognition that the *Homo sapiens* type appeared later in time, that is, in the Middle Pleistocene and not in the Lower Pleistocene. In fact, Leakey spoke less and less of *Homo sapiens* evolving throughout the entire Pleistocene period and more and more of the genus *Homo* in general. This permitted Leakey to put a relatively primitive form such as *Telanthropus* in the direct line leading to the living humans.

Second, the evolutionary pace at which the line leading to the living humans evolved was now believed to be quicker than expected. Whereas Leakey (1950, 1953) previously argued that most of the Pleistocene period had been required to give rise to the living human races, he now insisted that the pace of human evolution had been greatly accelerated under the effect of a self-domestication brought about by the fact that the tool-making hominids were living within a cultural environment (Leakey, 1960a, 1961a, 1961b).

Third, several hominid fossils previously assigned by Leakey (1953) to the pithecanthropine (*Africanthropus*) and the Neandertal (Rhodesian man, Steinheim) extinct evolutionary side branches were now inserted on the main branch leading to the living humans as direct contributors or specialized offshoots (Leakey, 1960a, 1961a, 1961b, 1963). The impact of this latter change is that the main line leading to the living humans was less and less exclusively modern-looking. Furthermore, this considerably reduced the taxonomic diversity as well as the geographical distribution of the hominids evolving toward extinction. Indeed, most of these so-called doomed hominids were now being mostly represented by a number of pithecanthropines (*Homo erectus*) from Asia. Leakey (1961b, 1966) argued that *Homo erectus* first arose in Africa and later moved eastward.

Fourth, the two main hominid evolutionary lines—one evolving toward the living humans and the other toward the extinct pithecanthropines and Neandertals—previously believed to have been diverging from one another for a long period were now thought to be close enough to have been able, maybe, to interbreed significantly. This concession was fundamental to Leakey's new view of human phylogeny.

Remember that Leakey (1953: 192) once conceded that only the modern-looking Neandertals from Palestine might have interbred with *Homo sapiens*, although it was recognized that this cross was perhaps sterile. Later, however, Leakey (1971) suggested that fossil forms such as the classic Neandertals of Europe, the Rhodesian man of Africa, and Solo man in Asia may well be the product of a cross-breeding between *Homo sapiens* and *Homo erectus*. Leakey now insisted that this unusual cross under natural conditions between distinct species might have been common in a self-domesticated animal such as humankind. According to this new view, Leakey's so-called multilinear view of human phylogeny was transformed into a kind of parallel hypothesis.

POLYMORPHIC ANCESTORS AND PARALLEL LINES

The human fossil record presented all sorts of challenges for someone interested in human phylogeny in the 1950s and 1960s. This is reflected in Howells's and Leakey's changing views during that time period. From well-defined multilinear hypotheses they move to the point of proposing parallel hypotheses in which modern-looking forms only appeared in the Middle Pleistocene or after. If it is true that no modern-looking hominids dated back to the Lower Pleistocene, it is also true that some modern hominid fossils were interpreted as being as early as the Middle Pleistocene.

Whereas scholars like Heberer, Vallois, and Genet-Varcin thought that this empirical situation could best be explained by a Presapiens hypothesis, others to whom we now turn believed that parallel hypotheses made a better fit with the fossil evidence. In so doing, these latter scholars continued a tradition of interpretation which was well-represented in the 1935–1950 period by Marett, Paterson, Poisson, Gates, Hooton, and Weidenreich. Proponents of this tradition hold that the main distinct living human races could trace their ancestry more or less independently throughout a large portion of the Pleistocene period. Ultimately, all the different parallel human evolutionary lines were derived from a common primitive ("ape-like") ancestor. However, this did not prevent the proponents of this tradition from arguing that some of the evolutionary lines arrived at the modern-looking stage before the others.

This interpretation of parallel and nonsynchronic lineages is grounded in the recognition of several ancestors passing through a series of evolutionary stages. The support for this concept can sometimes blur the distinction between the following two distinct hypotheses. First, that multiple lineages go through the same evolutionary stages but at different paces. Second, two distinct lineages (one modern-looking and one primitive-looking) contributed to living humans. Whereas Coon and Thoma chose the first option, Weckler preferred the second. In Osman Hill and Piveteau's conception, however, the distinct evolutionary stems which gave birth to the living humans were sometimes difficult to recognize because they were subjected to a series of complex evolutionary stages or waves.

In Weckler's view, for instance, the two main stems which gave rise to the living humans were easily recognized on the basis of their distinct morphology and different geographical distribution. Weckler (1954, 1957, 1964) derived all the living human races from a common primate ancestor that lived in Africa, India, or the Middle East in the Pliocene or Lower Pleistocene period.[22] From such a center of dispersal, Weckler conceived human evolution to have centered around two main evolutionary stems which were isolated throughout much of the Lower and the Middle Pleistocene by obstacles such as the Black and Caspian Seas, as well as the Caucasus and Himalaya mountains. It is by living under different environmental conditions that the hominids of these two provinces developed morphological and behavioral distinctions.

In one such geographical province—East Asia—hominids such as *Pithecanthropus*, *Sinanthropus*, Neanderthals (Solo man), and Wadjak man were part of a primitive lineage which contributed to regional, or racial, groups of living humans such as the Australians. While the early Neandertals first developed in this portion of the Old World into a form approaching the more recent classic Neandertals of Europe, its restricted geographical range limited the amount of racial diversification in the eastern region.

In the other geographical province—Africa, West Asia, and Europe—hominids such as Fontéchevade, Swanscombe, Heidelberg man, Kanam, and Kanjera were part of a modern strain which gave rise to several living human races. It is held that the differentiation of the *Homo sapiens* type into fairly independent breeding races occurred at the end of the Middle Pleistocene. Weckler insisted that this explained the significant morphological variability observed in both the Upper Pleistocene and the living human races. This being said, it should not be assumed that Weckler held that the *Homo sapiens* morphological type could be traced back early in the Pleistocene period. Rather, he believed that the early portion of this modern-looking strain might not be recognized as being *Homo sapiens*, because of its primitive condition (e.g., Heidelberg man).

According to Weckler, the two main hominid evolutionary stems which have long been separated eventually met and interbred in the Middle East and Europe during the late Middle Pleistocene or the Upper Pleistocene period. This breeding process was instigated by the westward migration of the primitive-looking hominid strain of East Asia.[23] This complex evolutionary process produced a variety of races ranging from robust modern types, Neandertaloid types, and progressive Neandertals. This is seen, among other places, in fossil evidence from Uzbekistan (Teshik-Tash), Palestine (Mount Carmel), and Germany (Steinheim). As far as the classic Neandertals of Europe are concerned, Weckler explained their peculiar morphology not so much by a local adaptation to extreme environmental conditions as by the result of a sustained inbreeding following their isolation from the modern-looking genetic strain.

Weckler promoted that the hominid races which were the products of the miscegenation between the modern-looking and the Neandertal strains directly or indirectly contributed to the genetic constitution of the living humans races. Indeed, he insisted that Australians were made up of a significant number of Neandertal genes as a result of their direct affiliation with the *Pithecanthropus*-Wadjak man stem in Java. He also thought it was possible this lineage received repeated infusions of *Homo sapiens* genes through India during its development. Weckler held that once the modern-looking hominid strain managed to assimilate some morphological traits and a number of cultural innovations from the Neandertals, this modern-looking strain finally pushed its dominion eastward into Asia and eventually colonized the New World.

In Weckler's conception of human phylogeny, the two distinct evolutionary stems which gave rise to the living humans were fairly easily recognized up to the point where they started to interbreed. In Osman Hill's and Piveteau's conceptions, however, the recognition of these two evolutionary stems was more difficult because each went through a series of complex evolutionary stages or waves which blurred the evolutionary patterns. For Osman Hill (1954), remember, several distinct large-brained apes contributed to give rise to distinct living human races (see Chapter 7). Osman Hill simultaneously believed in the successive stages and the parallel evolution of several living and extinct hominid lines:

> At any rate, we are in a position to state that, far from Man's lineage being a straight (or orthogenetic) one, it has been subject to phylogenetic radiation possibly from more than one starting point. Only the tips of certain branches of the radiations are represented in surviving populations; some lines became extinct long ago; others survived until relatively recent times; a few,—like the Tasmanians, have disappeared in historic times, whilst others are rapidly approaching the same fate. (Osman Hill, 1954: 116)

In this many-branched hominid family tree, Osman Hill recognized three evolutionary stages: pithecanthropine, Neandertal, and modern Man. At the pithecanthropine stage, several forms were recognized in Asia, such as *Pithecanthropus* (*erectus*, *robustus*, and *pekinensis*), *Meganthropus,* and *Gigantopithecus*. In Africa, *Africanthropus* was among the late survivors of the pithecanthropine stage. Osman Hill argued that an evolutionary trend toward gigantism characterized some of these early proto-human stocks. He believed that some of the Asian representatives of the pithecanthropines survived and evolved into living human forms.

From a generalized pithecanthropine predecessor, the following Neandertal stage developed in several local races or species that belonged either to a lightly-built form or a coarsely-built variety. Among the more massive Neandertals, probably only those affiliated to the Asian pithecanthropines-Australians line survived through Solo Man and Wadjak Man. On the other hand, the more progressive and lightly-built varieties of Neandertals such as those of Palestine show the possibility of their transformation into a modern form of the Cro-Magnon type. In Africa, Osman Hill was apparently inclined to recognize an evolutionary sequence linking *Africanthropus* and living humans (Florisbad and Boskop) through the Neandertal stage of Rhodesian man. He explained this as a case of parallel evolution with the Asian sequence under the cause of similar latent evolutionary trends.

When turning to the modern human stage, Osman Hill argued that many features shared in common among the living human races were probably due to an evolutionary convergence. On this view, it is clear that several more or less distinct evolutionary lines evolved toward the living human forms. One such line was an ancient modern-looking lineage represented by forms such as Piltdown (including the jaw) and Swanscombe. This latter line showed some similarities with the earliest and more progressive Neandertals. This ancient and modern-looking line was contrasted with the other lines. Osman Hill (1954: 143) stated:

> It would appear then, if this appraisal of Piltdown Man is correct, that two early types existed which underwent divergent evolution from the common pithecanthropine stock, (i) one exhibiting gerontomorphic evolutionary trends,—leading to the classic

> Neanderthal type and forms like Solo and Rhodesian Man; and (ii) the other showing paedomorphic tendencies, expressing themselves finally in modern, large-brained, small-jawed men. This latter radiation, contained on one of its lower branches, men of the Piltdown race and its allies.

As already explained (see Chapter 7), Osman Hill recognized in the human radiation, just as in the ape radiation, changes of shape which were caused by either the retention of juvenile features in adulthood (pedomorphism) or by the further development of mature features during this same adulthood (gerontomorphism).[24]

Not unike Osman Hill, Piveteau also believed that the two main distinct lines which gave rise to the living humans were complex evolutionary stems which went through a series of adaptive radiations or evolutionary waves. At first, Piveteau (1954, 1957, 1958) maintained that the rise of the living humans was achieved by two different routes, each route being already represented by fully thinking beings, as seen in their ability to manufacture stone tools. One such route saw the succession of three polymorphic waves of hominids starting in the early Pleistocene with the archanthropines (pithecanthropines) followed next by the Neandertals and ending in the modern human type. The transformation of this stem was characterized by the gradual loss of some ape-like features: a small brain, a slightly projecting face, a low and elongated skull cap, and a prominent supraorbital torus.

In Piveteau's view, many forms which belonged to these successive evolutionary waves constituted evolutionary dead ends. In the earliest wave, for instance, more primitive forms such as *Pithecanthropus robustus*, *Meganthropus*, and possibly *Gigantopithecus* had no descendants. This leaves *Pithecanthropus erectus* and *Sinanthropus* as possible contributors to the following wave. Similarly, many Neandertal forms were without descendants but the more progressive ones such as Steinheim and those from Palestine could well have contributed to the modern human type. For Piveteau, therefore, these three evolutionary waves are linked, genealogically speaking, but only through a tiny thread being constituted by the more progressive or evolved forms belonging to each wave.

The second route exploited by the hominids to give rise to the living humans was through a modern-looking stem which dated back to the Middle Pleistocene. Having its roots within the common progressive archanthropines and perhaps also through the intermediary of the Ehringsdorf and Steinheim types, this modern-looking and less expansive stem evolved through forms such as Swanscombe and Fontéchevade, the representatives of the so-called Presapiens group. Piveteau was anything but clear about whether or not these two distinct (modern- and primitive-looking) stems interbred during their parallel evolution.

By the early 1960s, however, Piveteau (1962, 1963) had retreated from any notion of ancient modern-looking hominids in the Middle Pleistocene. He no longer supported, implicitly or explicitly, elements of the Presapiens hypothesis. Piveteau now held that the rise of truly modern-looking hominids occurred only quite late in the Pleistocene. He (1962) continued to recognize the parallel evolution of two main hominid lineages which were geographically restricted. Now, however, these two lineages were both characterized by the gradual loss of some primitive features in favor of fully modern ones. If one line presented some slightly more modern forms than the other, it is merely because humankind presents such a level of diversity among its living representatives.

The first lineage comprised the Neandertal group and a group composed of forms with a mixture of Neandertal-like and modern-like features. The former group probably had either a few or no descendants. This lineage evolved in western Europe and in the Middle East and was represented by fossils such as Mauer, Steinheim, Swanscombe, and remains from Palestine. The second lineage, which lived in northern Africa and in East Asia, has its earliest representatives in *Pithecanthropus*, *Sinanthropus*, and *Atlanthropus* and leads both to the living Australians through *Homo soloensis* and to the living Africans through perhaps Rhodesian man and Florisbad man.

In Piveteau's new view, human phylogeny is entirely characterized by the succession of three evolutionary waves. Whereas he previously believed that such waves were phylogenetically connected by only a tiny thread, he now held that this link was more robust through a whole series of connections. This being said, Piveteau denied the idea of an entire evolutionary stage giving rise to the next one.[25]

Osman Hill and Piveteau believed that the two main evolutionary stems that gave rise to the living humans were complex evolutionary lineages with many ramifications. Nonetheless, they managed to find traces of them in different regions and at different time horizons. For scholars like Coon and Thoma, to whom we now turn, the hominid fossil record is best interpreted as representing more than two evolutionary lines genetically contributing to the living humans. But in contradistinction to Osman Hill and Piveteau, who postulated the relative separateness of these lines, Coon and Thoma saw them as being part of a single evolutionary trend going through a series of identical evolutionary stages. On this conception, the separateness of these evolutionary lines becomes even more difficult to establish than in Osman Hill's and Piveteau's conception. For Coon and Thoma, the disparity between the primitive- and modern-looking fossils is explained by evolutionary lines going through the same evolutionary stages but at different rates. As will be seen, Coon and Thoma appealed to different mechanisms in order to explain this disparity in evolutionary paces.

Coon (1939) previously promoted that both modern-looking and some primitive-looking hominid forms had contributed genetically to the living human races, although it is the modern strain which has been the most important contributor (see Chapter 6). For Coon, this modern-looking hominid line could be traced back to the Middle Pleistocene. Whereas Coon (1954) continued to promote this view of human phylogeny until about the mid-1950s, he added the notion that this modern-looking hominid line could be traced back to the very beginning of the Pleistocene period.

By the late 1950s and early 1960s, however, Coon (1959, 1962a, 1962b, 1965) had significantly modified his view. He now held that all or most of the primitive-looking hominid forms had contributed to the rise of the living human races. Whereas he had previously argued that the genetic contribution of these primitive-looking forms were indirect—having been absorbed in the modern evolutionary strain—he now argued that this genetic contribution was a direct one.[26] Coon now believed that the five main living human races he recognized[27]—Australoid, Congoid, Capoid, Mongoloid, and Caucasoid—were living in distinct geographical areas and were subjected to distinct selective pressures. These main racial groups, he continued, could be traced back at least to the Middle Pleistocene, if not to an earlier time.[28]

The Australoid racial line of Southeast Asia and Australia was said to be represented by the most archaic living humans, as seen in their pronounced and straight browridge and gradually sloping forehead. Such morphological features were traced back in time through several evolutionary grades as seen in Wadjak (*Homo sapiens*), Solo man, and *Pithecanthropus* (*Homo erectus*), and even possibly *Meganthropus* (australopithecine). The Congoid racial line of Africa was traced back to the *Homo erectus* grade through Broken Hill and Chellean 3 (Olduvai), and perhaps as far back as the australopithecine grade as seen in the numerous australopithecine fossils in Africa. This racial line was said to be characterized by well-developed browridges forming two arches, facial prognathism, and long legs. The Capoid racial line of Africa could not be clearly followed back in time, being possibly present in the Middle Pleistocene at Ternifine in North Africa before moving southward to the tip of the continent, where remnants of this racial line are found today.

According to Coon (1962b: 34–35), the three racial lines just presented only crossed the *erectus/sapiens* threshold quite late in the Upper Pleistocene. These racial groups were viewed as slow evolutionary lines which had lived in refuge areas of evolutionary lag situated in the Southern Hemisphere. This implied that *Homo sapiens* appeared in the world in different places and at different times.

Coon suggested that human evolution proceeded more rapidly in Europe, West Asia, and China during the Pleistocene period. Indeed, it was believed that the Mongoloid racial line of East Asia and the Americas had crossed the *erectus/sapiens* threshold near the turn of the Middle/Upper Pleistocene. This racial line could only be traced back to the Middle Pleistocene as seen in *Sinanthropus* (*Homo erectus*). Morphological features such as a high and angulated cheekbone, a flat face, large shovel-shaped incisors, and short long bones were believed to characterize this racial line. But by far the most dynamic racial line of all, according to Coon, was the Caucasoid which is presently distributed in West Asia, Europe, and North Africa. This line had reached the *Homo sapiens* grade as early as the mid-point of the Middle Pleistocene, as seen in the fossil remains of Steinheim and Swanscombe, although Heidelberg man may have pushed this evolutionary grade to the early Middle Pleistocene, unless it belongs already to the *erectus* grade.[29] This Caucasoid line could be traced back further still through the fossil remains at Ubeidiya (Israel) dated to the late Lower Pleistocene. These latter remains might either represent a *Homo erectus* grade or an australopithecine grade. Morphologically, this racial evolutionary line had been characterized by a flat face and small teeth. Coon placed all the Neandertals in the Upper Pleistocene portion of this Caucasoid line. He explained that the western Neandertals, which stemmed out of a *Homo sapiens* grade of evolution, developed their anatomical peculiarities as an adaptation to cold weather and closed inbreeding. This Neandertal branch avoided extinction by contributing genetically to the living Caucasoids. In other words, it was argued that the western Neandertals went extinct by absorption (Coon, 1962a: 549; 1962b: 41–42).

In Coon's (1959, 1962a, 1962b, 1965) view of human phylogeny, each of the main living human races has had its own evolutionary history without, however, having an entirely independent evolution. Indeed, Coon (1962a) pointed to a number of instances which might have implied contacts between them. For instance, the transition from *Homo erectus* to *Homo sapiens* in the Australoid line was caused by gene flow coming from the Mongoloid line; a view consistent with the fact that these two racial lines have constantly been in contact throughout human evolution. Similarly, the central geographical position of the Caucasoid line permitted contacts with the Australoid, Congoid, and Capoid racial lines.

Coon believed that there had been little or no contact between the Caucasoid and the Mongoloid lines during the Pleistocene, thus largely isolating the Congoid and the Capoid lines from non-Caucasoid elements. This being said, Coon would not exclude completely the possibility of a connection between the Caucasoid and Mongoloid lines through a mixture between *Sinanthropus*-descended Mongoloids and Neandertals, thus also opening a narrow channel with the Congoid and the Capoid lines. Furthermore, Coon wondered if the Mongoloid racial line had crossed the *erectus/sapiens* threshold alone by the effect of mutation and natural selection or through admixture with another racial line that had crossed this threshold at earlier times.

Far from evolving independently, Coon's five racial lines shared a common destiny by avoiding speciation. Indeed, a polytypic species composed of geographical races or subspecies could evolve into another species while retaining the same geographical races. The more or less independent evolution of the main living human races or subspecies managed to avoid speciation through enough intermittent gene flow—which preserved the unity of the entire species—although there was not enough of this gene flow to eliminate the subspecies (Coon, 1962a: 4). At first, Coon (1959: 1399) held that human evolution "has never had more than one species at a time". Later, he recognized that the two succeeding evolutionary grades in human evolution—*Homo erectus* and *Homo sapiens*—have not been crossed by all the main human races at the same time. Coon (1962a: 29–30) stated:

> Although the component populations of a polytypic species evolve as a unit, they cannot do so simultaneously since it takes time for a mutation to spread from one population to another . . . [W]e will see that related populations, which in our case are subspecies, passed from species A, which is *Homo erectus*, to species B, *Homo sapiens*, at different times, and the time at which each one crossed the line depended on who got the new trait first, who lived next to whom, and the rates of gene flow between neighboring populations.

Thus, the level of relative isolation between the main human races explains the differential evolutionary rates in each of them. This can be further reinforced by the isolation which is created between potential breeding populations: geographical isolation accompanying populations of low density living on large territories, or cultural isolation instigated by socially based segregation (Coon, 1965: 30–33).[30]

Not unlike Coon, Thoma (1962, 1965, 1971, 1973) conceived human phylogeny as a series of parallel evolutionary lines evolving toward the living humans through three successive Old World phases: archanthropic, paleoanthropic, and neanthropic. Thoma promoted that the living human races had deep genealogical roots. Whereas Coon recognized a *sapiens-erectus* transition, Thoma held that this entire portion of human evolution occurred within the framework of a single evolving gene pool or species called *Homo sapiens*.[31] He was able to clearly recognize at least three independent evolutionary lines.

One such evolutionary line, called *Homo sapiens australasiaticus*, led from *Pithecanthropus* (including *Meganthropus*) to the living Australians, through fossil remains such as Solo man and Wadjak. This evolutionary strain left Africa early and evolved in isolation from the other hominids in Southeast Asia.

The second evolutionary line recognized by Thoma led to *Homo sapiens eurafricanus*, the living Europeans and Africans. The fossil remains of Heidelberg, Vértesszöllös, Swanscombe, Steinheim, and Fontéchevade were all part of this complex and ramified strain which interbred on more than one occasion with some Neandertal elements both in Europe and in the Middle East. The living human races of Africa probably only departed from this main evolutionary strain quite late in the Upper Pleistocene, meaning that the African races of black complexion were the product of a recent evolutionary event.[32]

The third evolutionary line linked the archanthropine ancestor to *Homo sapiens mongolicus*, the living Mongolians. Having its origin in Africa as testified by fossil remains such as Rabat, this complex evolutionary strain gave rise to various Neandertal groups ranging from progressive ones in the Middle East (Shanidar) to highly specialized ones in Europe (La Chapelle-aux-Saints), the so-called classic Neandertals. These Neandertal groups both interbred to a variable extent among themselves and with some representatives of the evolutionary line leading to *Homo sapiens eurafricanus*. Whereas Thoma promoted that the living Mongolians derived directly from the progressive Neandertaloid forms of the Middle East, the classic Neandertals of Europe, for their part, went extinct but not without having transmitted some of their genes to the other evolutionary strain composed of Fontéchade, Swanscombe, and Steinheim (e.g., Thoma, 1962: 46).[33] The classic Neandertals thus somewhat contributed to the gene pool of some living human populations.

In order to explain how evolutionary strains or lines that were part of a single species called *Homo sapiens* could have more or less independently reached the modern or neanthropic phase of evolution—a process referred to as an intraspecific radiation—Thoma (1962: 67–78) appealed to a feedback loop between brain size and culture: A larger brain size contributed to a more sophisticated culture which, in turn, permitted the reduction of the robust or primitive anatomical features. It is because of this process of orthoselection that the evolutionary lines followed the same general evolutionary path. This being said, it should not be assumed that each and every evolutionary line evolved at a constant and identical pace, nor that they reached the neanthropic phase at the same time.

Thoma assumed that all the evolutionary lines were descended from a common African hypothetical form of the Lower Pleistocene period he called the primordial archanthropine.[34] This form was imagined to be of small and robust stature, with a brain size of about 750 cc, as well as with an enormous supraorbital torus and a diastema in the tooth row. From that evolutionary state, the various evolutionary lines spread in the Old World. In Thoma's view, the known fossils of the archanthropic phase (*Pithecanthropus*, *Sinanthropus*, *Atlanthropus*) were still fairly morphologically homogeneous because they shared a very recent common ancestry.

This divergence process continued and reached its climax during the next evolutionary phase, the palaeanthropic one. Three factors contributed to explain the morphological heterogeneity and the specializations at this evolutionary phase: (1) The time separating all the evolutionary lines from their common ancestor was important enough not to constitute any longer a homogenizing factor; (2) The evolutionary lines were subjected to the various adaptive cirscumstances and challenges in their distinct geographical areas; (3) the differential effect of the brain size/culture feedback loop on each evolutionary line was as yet neither powerful enough to reverse the divergence process in favor of a convergence process, nor equally applied in all evolutionary lines. This happened only later in the neanthropic phase of human evolution, although the traces of the past evolutionary events were still visible among the living human races.

At the later phase of human evolution, culture was sufficiently developed and homogenized as to forge similar anatomical responses on the part of all the hominid groups. Thus, it is easy to understand why some evolutionary lines presented either more modern-looking or more primitive-looking representatives during the palaeanthropic phase.[35] Noting that the primitive morphology of the classic Neandertals was not in step with the modernity of its large brain size, Thoma (1962: 89) explained that it took them too long to develop an appropriate cultural response to extreme environmental conditions. Where culture had failed to buffer the adaptive pressure, morphology had to respond accordingly.[36]

LINEAR HYPOTHESES

By enshrining the distinct evolutionary lines leading to the living humans within a single common evolutionary trend, Coon and Thoma were flirting with the concept of a linear evolution. However, they probably believed that the hominid fossil record was not sufficiently homogenous to conceive a single evolutionary line going through successive stages. This step was taken by another group of scholars. For them, the hominid fossil record could best be explained by appealing to a more or less linear phylogenetic hypothesis. This tradition of interpretation has been represented in the 1935–1950 period by Weinert and von Eickstedt. In this tradition, it is not necessarily held that human evolution followed a rigid evolutionary path. It is true that Brace insisted on a certain rigidity of these evolutionary stages. However, von Koenigswald conceived his evolutionary stages as reticulate events which could accommodate variable paces of evolutionary change, while Arambourg viewed them as being polymorphic stages (being composed of modern- and primitive-looking forms). Linear hypotheses should therefore not be equated with simple phylogenetic hypotheses, considering that some of them are rather complex explanations of the empirical reality.

For von Koenigswald, for instance, human phylogeny is characterized by the gradual transformation of ancient hominids presenting a number of primitive features into modern human types, through a series of more or less well-defined evolutionary stages. Indeed, von Koenigswald insisted on ape-like features within the oldest hominid group—the pithecanthropines of the Lower Pleistocene—as seen especially in their medium-sized brain, their fairly large canines and incisors, and their long vaulted and elongated crania with projecting browridges. With time, these ape-like features were gradually lost and replaced by modern-looking ones. As far as the evolutionary stages are concerned, von Koenigswald (1956: 205) recognized, at one time at least, four successive stages in Java only: *Meganthropus* (gigantism), *Pithecanthopus*, Neandertal (Solo man), and *Homo sapiens* (Wadjak and the living populations). Later, von Koenigswald (1960 [1962], 1968 [1976]) made clear that he believed that the second and third stages were widely distributed with representatives also found in Europe and Africa.[37] Each of these evolutionary stages were thought to be composed of several distinct morphological types.

For von Koenigswald, human phylogeny had been a complex process involving the migration, the division, and the fusion of many hominid fossil groups. It is worth quoting him at some length:

> Because of the nomadic existence of the hunting hordes, one group can seldom have remained isolated long enough to form a definite "species"; and even if this did happen and a group followed a particular line of specialization . . . we have to reckon with the possibility of another population group invading the area and interbreeding with the previous inhabitants . . . We shall therefore do best to represent man's family tree as a funnel with its tip in the earliest Pleistocene, a funnel into which we introduce the finds of ancient man according to their geological horizon. We shall then see that, as in Java, the geologically older forms are generally also the most primitive. Hence there is no reason to assume diverse "racial stocks" or any marked degree of "parallel evolution". When our knowledge of the various forms increases, it will probably transpire that the relationships between them can only be represented as a very complicated network. (von Koenigswald, 1956: 206–207)

According to von Koenigswald (1956, 1968 [1976]), the interbreeding between different hominid groups is well-illustrated by the remains of Palestine. In this instance, it was believed that populations of *Homo sapiens* and Neandertals met and interbred. Detailing his general view of human phylogeny, von Koenigswald (1962: 132) stressed that the evolution of humankind has not been a straightforward process:

> Certain differences—between, for instance, *Sinanthropus, Pithecanthropus*, and *Atlanthropus*—may have resulted from the breaking away of small splinter groups, which formed first a "race" and, with prolonged isolation, a special "species". This may be true of extreme Neanderthal man also. Most races, however, intermingled, and our fossils do not enable us to distinguish between what was still "race" and what had already become "species". As a result, our family tree . . . looks like a thicket, and

> it seems likely that man would never have achieved his pre-eminent position had his evolution proceeded in a perfectly straight line.[38]

As seen only implicitly in this passage, the reality of extinction in human evolution was certainly not ruled out. Indeed, von Koenigswald (1956, 1960 [1962], 1968 [1976]) clearly stated that the classic Neandertals of Europe (La Ferrassie, La Quina, La Chapelle-aux-Saints, Spy, etc.) constituted an evolutionary dead end which has not contributed to give rise to the living humans. Instead, one has to turn towards the more ancient and less specialized forms of the Middle Pleistocene, such as Steinheim and Swanscombe, in order to find a genealogical connection between the classic Neandertals and the living humans. Von Koenigswald referred to this less specialized group as the presapiens because they presented more features of *Homo sapiens* than of the Neandertals, although this designation was totally unrelated to the Presapiens hypothesis of some other scholars.[39] In fact, von Koenigswald (1956: 108) explicitly rejected the notion that the living humans are not descended from hominids presenting ape-like features (i.e., Neandertals, Heidelberg man, *Pithecanthropus*), and refused to see in all of them merely collateral branches not leading to the living humans. For him (1953), the modern human type appeared quite late in human evolution. Von Koenigswald would not exclude the possibility of extinctions among other hominid groups, but only in the context of his reticulate conception of human phylogeny.

Because of the complexity of this evolutionary process, von Koenigswald remained cautious about the possiblity of recognizing, with any certainty, direct evolutionary connections between some living human races and ancient hominid groups. He did explicitly recognize a direct genealogical link between the various hominid evolutionary stages, but he usually refrained from identifying precise connections. For instance, von Koenigswald (1956: 123; 1962: 103; 1976: 113) insisted that the proposed link between the living Australians and *Pithecanthropus* through the intermediary of Solo and Wadjak men was not sufficiently demonstrated as yet.[40] After all, how can a reticulate evolutionary process allow such a level of resolution in the phylogenetic analyses?

If von Koenigswald viewed human phylogeny as a complex and reticulate process, Arambourg proposed to view it as a series of polymorphic stages. Arambourg's (1943a, 1947, 1948c, 1955a, 1956, 1959) conception of human phylogeny was based on this kind of linear hypothesis.[41] He envisioned a series of human evolutionary stages characterized by an increase in brain size and the gradual loss of ape-like features since the late Pliocene or the early Pleistocene period: australopithecine, pithecanthropine, Neandertal, and *Homo sapiens*.[42] Except for the first and earliest evolutionary stage restricted to Africa, the following three stages were represented by fossil specimens spread throughout the Old World.[43]

According to Arambourg, the pithecanthropine and the Neandertal evolutionary stages constitute two morphological and phylogenetic links in the rise of the living humans. Each of these were described as being polymorphic and constituted of groups or twigs which presented differences of orders varying between those seen among races, species, and even possibly genera. Each evolutionary stage was being represented by hominid members or forms either more advanced or more primitive in conformation. In Arambourg's view at the time, only a number of groups or twigs in each evolutionary stage managed to advance to a new stage, thus becoming the founding members of the next evolutionary level.

This view implied that many races, species, and genera at each evolutionary stage left no descendants. For instance, we have already seen that Arambourg (1955a, 1959, 1965) eventually recognized that australopithecine forms such as *Telanthropus* and *Australopithecus* were among the founding members of the pithecanthropine stage, whereas *Paranthropus* was believed to have left no descendants (see Chapter 8). Similarly, Arambourg argued that *Pithecanthropus erectus, Sinanthropus*, and *Atlanthropus* were among the pithecanthropine groups which contributed to the rise of the Neandertal evolutionary stage, whereas gigantic forms such as *Pithecanthropus robustus, Meganthropus*, and possibly *Gigantopithecus* were among the extinct pithecanthropines. Furthermore, Arambourg held that the Neandertal forms such as those found in Palestine (Mount Carmel) presented many advanced features and alluded that they could well be the founding members of the next evolutionary stage, *Homo sapiens*.

By the early 1960s, Arambourg's (1961, 1965) conception of human phylogeny was slightly modified by a deeper adhesion to linear evolution. He was now no longer inclined to identify forms or twigs in each evolutionary stage which either moved on to the next stage or went extinct. In other words, Arambourg's evolutionary stages were now less polymorphic. It is not that he denied the diversity of forms in each evolutionary stage, it is simply that he believed them to be more homogeneous than in the past. This is clearly seen in his assessment of the morphological differences between the hominid fossils. Whereas Arambourg (1956, 1959) previously believed that such differences in the same evolutionary stage could be attributed to distinct species or genera, he now reduced the importance of such differences by attributing them to individual and racial distinctions only (Arambourg, 1961, 1965).

In fact, Arambourg now focused less on the morphological differences between hominid fossils and insisted more on the common thread binding all the evolutionary stages in human evolution: The increase of the brain size and its impact on all the aspects of the lives of the hominids, as seen especially in the increased complexity of material culture. Arambourg (1960) was now more prepared than in the past to couch the hominization process entirely in terms of a whole new intellectual vista opened up by the enlargement of the brain. Although it was recognized that the liberation of the hands which followed the development of a bipedal locomotion probably contributed to accelerate the pace of human evolution, Arambourg held that the increased brain size constituted the genuine evolutionary engine that instigated all the other anatomical changes. Under a view dominated by intellectual faculties and cultural innovations, it is, perhaps, not surprising to see that Arambourg now believed that all the pithecanthropines were much more similar to the living humans than to any hominoid apes. The humanness of most hominids might also explain why Arambourg was no longer inclined to identify extinct hominid twigs, with the exception of the robust australopithecines (*Paranthropus*).

Whereas Arambourg was gradually moving toward a more linear hypothesis, Brace unhesitatingly embraced this notion. Indeed, Brace (1962, 1964, 1967) held that all hominid fossils were part of a single evolutionary continuum leading to the living humans, with no strains or twigs being left out of it. Brace (1964, 1967) identified four distinct and successive morphological evolutionary stages in the Pleistocene period: australopithecines, pithecanthropines, Neandertals, and modern humans.

The australopithecine stage of the Lower Pleistocene was characterized by creatures with small canines who were dependant upon manufactured tools for their survival and possessed a bipedal locomotion that was not yet fully adapted for long distances. This evolutionary stage was further subdivided in two successive evolutionary phases: The earliest small-brained and small-bodied *Australopithecus*, and the later large-bodied *Paranthropus*, which went through an increase in brain size and acquired a more robust and larger masticatory apparatus (excluding the anterior portion of the dentition which was further reduced). While the earliest phase of the australopithecine stage was geographically restricted to Africa, as seen in the fossil discoveries in South and East Africa exclusively, the later *Paranthropus* phase covered the entire tropic regions of the Old World, as testified by the fossil remains of *Meganthropus* in Java. In Brace's conception, the *Paranthropus* phase linearly evolved out of an African *Australopithecus* phase only to successfully spread in the Old World as the sole hominid species on earth, thus providing the evolutionary basis for all subsequent hominid forms. By being culture-bearing creatures, Brace was strongly inclined to include all the australopithecines in the genus *Homo*, the early phase of this evolutionary stage thus being called *Homo africanus*.[44]

The second evolutionary stage Brace identified—the pithecanthropine stage of the Lower Pleistocene—was represented by a single species called *Homo erectus*, which was widespread, as seen by the fossil remains in Africa (Olduvai, Ternifine, and Sterkfontein), in Europe (Heidelberg, Verteszöllös), and in Asia (Java and China).[45] In comparison to the previous australopithecine stage, this new stage saw an important increase in brain size, a good adaptation to long-distance capabilities in locomotion, and a reduction of the posterior teeth and associated facial structures. This reduction was believed to be indicative that *Homo erectus* had somewhat turned away from a vegetarian diet—which required robust structures for the mastication process—by incorporating more meat in its diet.

The third evolutionary stage recognized by Brace is the Neandertal stage of the late Middle Pleistocene or early Upper Pleistocene. This stage was also widely geographically distributed with representatives in Southeast Asia (Solo and Mapa), in Africa (Broken Hill and Saldanha), in West Asia (Shanidar and Mount Carmel) and of course in Europe on many sites. In fact, Brace believed that Solo man of Java represented an evolutionary transition between the pithecanthropine and the Neandertal stages in Southeast Asia. He dismissed claims that modern humans existed in the Middle Pleistocene as seen in the remains of Steinheim, Swanscombe, and Fontéchevade. Brace was inclined to see in Steinheim an evolutionary transition between the pithecanthropine and the Neandertal stages in Europe, in Swanscombe a good Neandertal and in Fontéchevade an as yet unspecified form.

Brace was convinced that the only way to link the pithecanthropine stage to the living humans was through a Neandertal stage. The Neandertals were distinguished from the pithecanthropines mainly by their possession of brains of fully modern size, meaning that the Neandertals are distinguished from the modern humans merely by having a dentition and a face similar to the pithecanthropines. Considering such a morphological and behavioral proximity between the Neandertals and the living humans, Brace included the former in the species *Homo sapiens*, with at most a subspecific distinction.

The last evolutionary stage Brace identified is the modern human stage that started in the Upper Pleistocene and is still progressing today. This stage is characterized by a reduction in the robusticity of the body in general and a reduced dentition and flat face. Brace recognized several instances of transition between the Neandertal and the modern stages as seen especially in Palestine (Mount Carmel) and in Croatia (Krapina). In this conception of human evolution, the diversity among the living human races constituted a very recent evolutionary event. Brace held that this morphological diversity was modulated in accordance with the ability of the various living groups to face the selective pressures with different technologies. For instance, if the aboriginal Australians presented some remarkable similarities with some Neanderthaloids in the anatomy of the face, it is largely because the technological abilities of the former approached that of the latter.

Indeed, Brace's conception of human phylogeny must be understood in light of the role of culture as a buffer or a modulator of selective pressures on hominids. In this aspect, Brace's view is not unlike that of Thoma's, although they make a different use of this concept. The four evolutionary stages identified by Brace were involved in a complex interaction between biology and culture. Once the habitable portions of the Old World had been occupied during the *Paranthropus* phase of human evolution, the succeeding evolutionary stages occurred gradually and simultaneously throughout the entire occupied world rather than through a process of invasion and extinction. This is explained, in Brace's view, by the very nature of the cultural adaptive mechanism in human evolution. Indeed, considering that the hominids were culture-bound creatures depending on it for their survival, and because any cultural innovation would be eventually shared by all the hominids, it is postulated that similar selective forces would have been acting on all the hominids. This contributed to maintain their unity during each evolutionary stage. Similar forces produced similar morphological and behavioral effects in different geographical areas, irrespective of the gene flow between these areas. Brace explained his conception by contrasting it to Coon's view. He observed that Coon promoted that the changes from one evolutionary stage to another occurred both in isolation and at different evolutionary rates in various localities:

> [In my view] the diffusion of the cultural *reasons* for the specific physical changes which characterize the stages as having been rapid enough so that the unity of the human species was maintained at any one time. Development from one stage to the next, then, would have proceeded at approximately the same time and the same rate throughout the inhabited world. The probability that a given population will be genetically more like its precusors in the same locality is of course greater than the probability that it will

> be genetically closer to groups in adjacent areas, and this allows for the development of regional pecularities, but, at the same time, genetic material is continually being exchanged with adjacent areas. The result is that no human population has ever become different enough from the others to warrant taxonomic recognition. (Brace, 1967: 80–81) [Not my italics]

For Brace, the dependence of the hominids toward culture was such that culture became the ecological niche in which they lived. Only one hominid species at any one time period could live in this cultural niche because the competitive exclusion principle states that no two organisms can live in the same niche, unless of course they happen to be part of the same species.

EVOLUTIONARY THEORIES: THE EVOLUTIONARY SYNTHESIS

Now that we have a better understanding of how the debates on human phylogeny were conducted during the 1935–1965 period, the question of the impact of the evolutionary theories on them should be revisited. Remember that the impact of the evolutionary theories during the first third of the twentieth century had been limited (see Chapter 5). What was the situation during the 1935–1965 period? To put things bluntly, their impact was also fairly limited, although not necessarily or exclusively for the same reasons as in the past. This statement surely requires some elaboration and qualification.

The pre-1935 period was characterized by a number of widely divergent and competing evolutionary theories, such as Darwinism and Orthogenesis, among others (e.g., Bowler, 1983). One could argue that the field of paleoanthropology could not have been substantially influenced by the evolutionary theories of this earlier time period owing to the lack of a genuinely coherent evolutionary framework. With the constitution of a robust and widely embraced evolutionary framework under the umbrella of the evolutionary synthesis in the 1940s, 1950s, and 1960s—so the argument goes—paleoanthropologists could now either confidently rely on it, or at the least, no longer avoid taking it into consideration.

Although the evolutionary synthesis is a moving target—being defined somewhat differently from one author to the other (Smocovitis, 1996: 19–44)—most of them would agree that it was instigated between the late 1930s and the late 1940s as presented in a series of key publications such as Theodosius Dobzhansky's *Genetics and the Origin of Species* (1937), Ernst Mayr's *Systematics and the Origin of Species* (1942), and George Gaylord Simpson's *Tempo and Mode in Evolution* (1944). How were paleoanthropologists exposed to the evolutionary synthesis? A number of meetings organized at the time contributed to exposing scholars interested in human evolution to the ideas of the evolutionary synthesis: The *Congrès de Paris* of 1947 (Arambourg, 1950);[46] the Cold Spring Harbor Symposium of 1950, New York, on the theme *Origin and Evolution of Man* (Demerec, 1950);[47] and the symposium held at Burg Wartenstein (Austria) in 1962 on the theme *Classification and Human Evolution* (Washburn, 1963b).[48]

Were the paleoanthropologists converted to the evolutionary synthesis? This is a difficult question. It is now well-known that it took some time for the evolutionary synthesis to penetrate the ramified domain of evolutionary biology, including the field of paleoanthropology (e.g., Dobzhansky, 1963a, 1963b; Grimoult, 2000; Mayr, 1963; Mayr and Provine, 1980; Simpson, 1963a). In this scientific context, it was anything but obvious to the scholars at the time that the evolutionary synthesis would eventually turn out to dominate the evolutionary framework in the 1950s and 1960s. It is in hindsight only that one realizes that the evolutionary synthesis had some impact on the field of human evolution in the 1950s and 1960s. If this was so, how could paleoanthropologists have relied confidently and wholeheartedly on the evolutionary synthesis at the time? The question of whether or not scholars who were interested in human evolution could confidently rely on a robust and coherent evolutionary framework is perhaps not the most illuminating one in order to understand the possible impact of the evolutionary synthesis.

It is true that the evolutionary synthesis provided a fairly robust and coherent corpus of mechanisms and concepts that could be useful for the development of paleoanthropology. On that score, paleoanthropologists of the 1950s and 1960s were undoubtedly in a much better position than their counterparts of the pre-1935 period, regardless of the difficulties just raised for the post-1950 period (e.g., Delisle, 1995, 2001). This being said, the fundamental issue of the potential influence of the evolutionary theories on paleoanthropology seems to be elsewhere. We have claimed in this book that the field of paleoanthropology is not merely a by-product of distinct and specific evolutionary theories. It has been consistently argued in these pages that at the heart of the field of paleoanthropology since its inception lies the task of establishing humankind's place in nature through the taxonomic method—that is, the phylogenetic placing of new hominid fossil discoveries by comparing them to the other hominid fossils as well as to the living forms judged relevant. If this conception of the nature of paleoanthropology is accepted, then it becomes perfectly obvious why debates on evolutionary theories can never create profound and lasting impacts on its development. However, this is not the same as to state that changes in evolutionary theories cannot influence the field of human evolution.

While the taxonomic method is the backbone of paleoanthropology, fluctuations in evolutionary conceptions and theories can influence how this taxonomic procedure will be performed. If the reverse were true, the shell of paleoanthropology would be an empty one: If hominid fossils were merely enshrined in phylogenetic patterns suggested by evolutionary theories, this would negate or invalidate the notion that such fossils are attributed a phylogenetic place largely in accordance to their anatomical similarities and dissimilarities. If this latter view of paleoanthropology were true, its development ever since its inception would have been empirically incoherent by being entirely at the mercy of the changing evolutionary conceptions and theories. This is basically the view expounded by the historian of science Peter J. Bowler (1986), as seen in Chapter 5. It is clear from what we have seen thus far in this book that the field of paleoanthropology since 1860 does not comply to such an empirically incoherent sequence of development.

As the twentieth century progressed and as the fossil record improved, the diversity of phylogenetic hypotheses entertained about humankind's place in nature was drastically reduced. We have seen that the 1930–1950 period was especially important in this regard (see Chapters 6, 7, and 8). When considering the hominid fossil record, for instance, this brought a greater cohesion in the human phylogenetic hypotheses. This continued in the 1950s and 1960s under further fossil discoveries and new dating information. However, it must be recognized that this greater cohesion in human phylogenetic hypotheses after 1950 was partially supported by the evolutionary synthesis. This being said, the coherence of the research program seen in paleoanthropology during the 1950s and 1960s was not instigated by the evolutionary synthesis. The modern research structure in paleoanthropology was not borne from the evolutionary synthesis (Delisle, 2000b: 507–509). The fall of the polyphyletic thesis and the constriction of the human phylogenetic hypotheses were well under way before the evolutionary synthesis could have had any impact on paleoanthropology. But as these fossil discoveries and others continued to be assessed in the 1950s and 1960s, the evolutionary synthesis provided an evolutionary framework which was not necessarily inconsistent with the hypotheses promoted by many paleoanthropologists.

Was the evolutionary synthesis merely consistent with such hypotheses in the 1950s and 1960s or did it play a more active role in their rise? As will be seen, both cases are found. It is only by distinguishing clearly between these two possibilities that one can understand the nature of the impact of the evolutionary synthesis on paleoanthropology. This will be achieved by investigating three aspects: the new systematics, the evolutionary dynamics, and the cultural niche.

The new systematics. At the heart of the evolutionary synthesis lies the notion that natural selection plays on variations (ultimately encrypted in genes) carried by individuals living in populations. It is this evolutionary process which instigates the evolutionary change leading to adaptation either through phyletic evolution or speciation. This dynamic view of evolution required a proper conception of the biological entities being studied and classified. For that purpose, a "new systematics" was devised, one that conceived the species as inherently variable entities often composed of semi-isolated populations (polytypic species) constituted of breeding members and held together by gene flow. Species are therefore envisioned as isolated from one another by reproductive gaps and not by morphological differences. The evolutionary synthesis instituted a distinction between population thinking and typological thinking in systematics, the former being based on the notion that a population or a species is constituted of breeding members and the latter of members that are morphologically similar.

According to Mayr (1969: 24–29, 67), typologists would tend to exaggerate the constancy of taxa and the sharpness of the gaps separating them because variation is trivial and irrelevant in the typological way of thinking based on the existence of a limited number of types in nature. This is not the case for populationists, continued Mayr, from whom variability is merely an indication of a possible species distinction; morphology being subordinated to other biological factors (Mayr, 1942: 121). For the populationists, variability among individuals flows from their membership to a genetic unit, an ecological unit, and a reproductive community. Thus, it is easy to understand the phylogenetic consequences of both forms of thinking: populationists would be more inclined toward a taxonomic reduction or a linear hypothesis, whereas typologists would be more inclined toward a taxonomic inflation or a multilinear hypothesis.

The new systematics was actively applied in the field of human evolution in the 1950s and 1960s by a small number of scholars, some of whom figured as founding members of the evolutionary synthesis, such as Mayr himself.[49] As might have been expected, the original application of this approach in human evolution led to a taxonomic constriction of the phylogenetic hypotheses. For instance, Mayr insisted in 1950 that the problem of human origins depended largely on the proper definition and evaluation of the taxonomic categories (Mayr, 1950; Delisle, 1997a). He suggested at the time to reduce the bewildering diversity of genera attributed to fossil remains (*Australopithecus*, *Plesianthropus*, *Paranthropus*, *Pithecanthropus*, *Sinanthropus*, *Africanthropus*, *Javanthropus*, *Paleoanthropus*, etc.) to a single genus: *Homo*. Mayr conceived that the genus *Homo* had entered a new adaptive zone that increased selective pressure and accelerated the evolutionary changes that resulted in a phyletic evolution up to the living humans through three succeeding stages only: *Homo transvalensis*, *H. erectus*, and *H. sapiens*.

In Mayr's (1950: 112) own terms, "never more than one species of man existed on the earth at any one time". In accordance to the population thinking and the polytypic species concept, Mayr recognized geographical variation among populations within this single evolving lineage. He explained that although the living humans are relatively homogeneous owing to the importance of interbreeding between different races, the earlier hominids presented a greater amount of variability because they lived in small and more isolated groups. Although Mayr (1953, 1963) recognized a few years later at least one speciation event at the australopithecine level, he in no way at the time backed away from a hominid phylogenetic hypothesis approaching a linear conception (see also below).

If some founding members of the evolutionary synthesis directly applied the new systematics in human evolution, a nonmember and a paleoanthropologist like Breitinger (1957 [1962a], 1959 [1962b]) also enthusiastically embraced it.[50] Like Mayr, this also led him to view human evolution as a phylogenetic process which is essentially linear: "In the evolution of the hominids there has been only one *a priori* certain case of a complete speciation or splitting, namely that which explains their separation from Tertiary primate species" (Breitinger, 1962b: 188). Breitinger was not necessarily closed to the idea of recognizing in human evolution some instances of splitting of lineages whose fate could be extinction, but these probably occurred at the racial or subspecific levels, thus not implying a complete breakdown of gene flow between two or more contemporary hominid species. This latter event was judged by him to be rather improbable.

Breitinger was prepared to recognize a certain amount of morphological variability among the hominid material at any one time period, especially among the early hominids (like Mayr). By so doing, he repudiated the so-called typological thinking. Indeed, Breitinger complained that fossil hominids were still being classified in a formal manner, using taxonomic names as mere labels without any biological meaning and thus renouncing any biological significance and phylogenetic implications. "The only safe way out," insisted Breitinger (1962a: 445), is by "getting in step with the new knowledge and principles of taxonomy, which have led to a biologically based definition in place of the morphological definition of species." Investigations in paleoanthropology, continued Breitinger, should be based on the taxonomic level of the population, that is, on a natural breeding community sometimes presenting considerable geographical variation (polytypic species).

Two aspects of the impact of the new systematics on paleoanthropology are of special interest to us. In the first one, population thinking and its accompanying concept, the polytypic species concept, allow for the recognition that humankind's direct ancestors presented an important amount of morphological variation (geographical or otherwise), as seen in Mayr's and Breitinger's views. Was this conception new in the paleoanthropological studies? The answer is no.

We have already seen that several scholars prior to, or during, the constitution of the evolutionary synthesis promoted that the direct ancestors of the living humans were polymorphic in nature, being human-like and ape-like in conformation (e.g., Verneau, 1906a, 1924; Pycraft, 1925; Marett, 1936; Coon, 1939; Poisson, 1939; Paterson, 1940; Hooton, 1946; Gates, 1944, 1948). It is not argued here that these paleoanthropologists were either precursors of, or contributors to, the new systematics. After all, the application of the new systematics is based on categories with precise biological meanings which were generally lacking from the field of human evolution in the pre-1950 period. Nor is it argued that the founding members of the evolutionary synthesis would accept their hominid phylogenetic hypotheses. What is defended here, however, is that there has been in paleoanthropology a long tradition which accepted an important amount of variability among humankind's direct ancestors. This tradition arose well before the evolutionary synthesis and continued to be promoted in contemporaneity with the new systematics (e.g., Weckler, 1954; Osman Hill, 1954; Piveteau, 1957; Coon, 1962a; Thoma, 1962).

With the exception of Coon (1962a: 29–30), who was perhaps somewhat influenced by the new systematics as seen by his use of the polytypic species concept,[51] the other representatives of this tradition in the 1950s and 1960s were apparently not directly influenced by this new approach to systematics (see Thoma below). This means, of course, that they might have been indirectly influenced by it in one way or another. Irrespective of whether or not this was the case, it is clear that proponents of the new systematics in paleoanthropology arrived at conceptual developments which were not inconsistent to the views long promoted by a number of paleoanthropologists who recognized polymorphic ancestors to the living humans.

The second aspect of the impact of the new systematics on paleoanthropology relates to the constriction of the hominid phylogenetic hypotheses. By focusing on taxonomic entities at, or below, the species level (demes, races, subspecies), proponents of the new systematics like Mayr (1950, 1963) and Breitinger (1957 [1962a], 1959 [1962b]) could absorb all the variability observed among the known hominid fossils in a single or a very few evolving lineages, thus either entirely denying or greatly limiting the number of major extinct side branches. Was this taxonomic constriction new in paleoanthropology? The answer is again no.

Following the important fossil discoveries made in the 1930–1940 decade, several paleoanthropologists reduced the taxonomic diversity of their human phylogenetic hypotheses to varying degrees (e.g., Keith, 1931, 1936; Boule and Piveteau, 1935; Boule, 1937; Le Gros Clark, 1935, 1940; Hooton, 1931, 1946). Some of them joined the other paleoanthropologists who were already taking part in a long tradition which conceived that all or most of the hominid fossils were directly related to the living humans. Others continued to promote multilinear hypotheses although they now proposed constricted or less ramified phylogenetic hypotheses which were not as far apart from the linear hypotheses as they used to be. These changes occurred before or during the institution of the new systematics, and they continued in the 1950s and 1960s. What was the impact of the new systematics on this continued process of hominid phylogenetic constriction? Let us concentrate on two scholars only.

Le Gros Clark (1940, 1945, 1946a) had already reduced considerably the ramification of his multilinear hominid hypothesis by the 1940s. This early reduction cannot be attributed to the new systematics. By the 1950s and 1960s, Le Gros Clark further reduced his phylogenetic hypothesis, but this time under the influence of the new systematics. For instance, Le Gros Clark (1954, 1955) first held that the pithecanthropine group represented a genus—*Pithecanthropus*—distinct from all the later hominids included in the genus *Homo*. At least two distinct species were believed to belong to this former genus: *Pithecanthropus erectus* and *P. pekinensis*. Not long after, Le Gros Clark (1958, 1964) recognized that the tendency toward taxonomic individualization of almost every fossil specimen, by attributing each of them to a new species or genus, unnecessarily complicated the picture of human phylogeny. He now proposed to sink the genus *Pithecanthropus* into the genus *Homo*, as well as to downgrade the two former species *Pithecanthropus erectus* and *P. pekinensis* to two subspecies of *Homo erectus*.

Similar to Le Gros Clark, Leakey (1960, 1961b, 1966, 1971) also eventually reduced considerably the ramification of his multilinear hominid hypothesis. However, the main impetus for such a reduction came, for Leakey, not from the new sytematics as he himself attributed little biological meaning to taxonomic categories and procedures. Indeed, Leakey (1960b: 458) clearly stated that taxonomic issues are arbitrary: "Inevitably, different scientific workers have different ideas of what characters justify specific, generic, and even superfamilial rank. After all, this is purely a question of artificial labels."

This discussion illustrates well the different kinds of links observed between the constriction of the hominid phylogenetic hypotheses and the new systematics during the 1950s and 1960s. These can be divided into three possible types of link: (1) that the new systematics led to the constriction of the hominid phylogenetic hypotheses because of the direct influence of the proponents of the evolutionary synthesis; (2) the new systematics encouraged or reinforced such a constriction process among a number of paleoanthropologists; (3) the new systematics was merely consistent with such a constriction process that had already begun by the 1930s and continued in the following decades.

The evolutionary dynamics. The evolutionary synthesis required a proper conception of the biological entities being studied and classified. The new systematics constituted precisely this adapted methodological and conceptual framework. But beyond taxonomic questions, the evolutionary synthesis also carries at its heart a conception of how the evolutionary process occurs. This is referred to here as the evolutionary dynamics. Influenced by Sewall Wright's model of populations subdivided into more or less isolated groups evolving under natural selection and genetic drift, Dobzhansky (1937, 1955) conceived the gradual evolution of species (phyletic evolution) as a complex evolutionary process taking place in a genetically open system or racial web with strands continually diverging and rejoining through hybridization (e.g., Delisle, 1997c; Provine, 1986: 327–365). For Dobzhansky (1950), a species is not a static type but a changing population in a dynamic state of equilibrium between intra- and interpopulational variability, with race divergence taking place, but also sometimes being arrested by the melting down of their differences through genetic fusion. Simpson (1953: 379) managed to nicely capture this concept in a diagram illustrating a temporal segment of an evolving species. By looking closer at this species's segment, one sees a network of races and individuals. In this conception of the evolutionary dynamics, a species is not a monolithic and immutable type but rather a variable and changing entity.

This conception of the evolutionary dynamics was actively applied in the field of human evolution in the 1940s, 1950s, and 1960s by a small number of scholars, some of whom figured as founding members of the evolutionary synthesis like Dobzhansky himself. Perhaps unexpectedly, its original application led to the recognition of a single and complex evolving lineage in human evolution. For instance, Dobzhansky (1944, 1963a) classified all or most of the main hominid forms in distinct racial groups still potentially able to reproduce and exchange genes with each other. At most, it was argued, these forms represented distinct subspecies rather than distinct species. Dobzhansky (1944: 262) stood his ground and stated that all "the phylogenetic transformations in Hominidae were always taking place within a single genetic system, a species consisting of geographically, but not reproductively, isolated races."

As a paleoanthropologist and a nonfounding member of the evolutionary synthesis, Breitinger (1957 [1962a], 1959 [1962b]) also powerfully echoed this conception of the evolutionary dynamics in human evolution. In Breitinger's view, the phyletic evolution of the hominids was probably characterized by the parallel evolution of subspecific groups in distinct areas with phylogenetic changes taking place at unequal rates, punctuated by episodes of migrations, mixtures, and extinctions. According to Breitinger, this is what probably lies behind the successive evolutionary stages in human evolution (*Australopithecus*, *Homo erectus*, *H. neanderthalensis*, and *H. sapiens*).

The evolutionary dynamics accompanying the evolutionary synthesis promoted a conception of human phylogeny based on a complex model of reticulate racial evolution involving the splitting, migration, fusion, local evolution, and extinction of racial groups, as seen in Dobzhansky's and Breitinger's views. Again, was this conception new in the paleoanthropological studies? The answer must still be no.

A number of students in human evolution had already subscribed to it prior to the constitution of the evolutionary synthesis (e.g., Taylor, 1919, 1927; Dixon, 1923; von Eickstedt, 1934; Weidenreich, 1940). Again, it is not argued here that proponents of the evolutionary synthesis would necessarily agree with the way these hominid phylogenetic hypotheses were formulated, especially considering that they lacked the standardized framework that only came later with the new systematics. Yet, such hominid phylogenetic hypotheses were clearly founded on a similar evolutionary dynamics that was later associated with the evolutionary synthesis. During the 1950s and 1960s, this tradition of hominid phylogenetic hypotheses continued to be represented in paleoanthropology (e.g., von Koenigswald, 1956; 1960 [1962]; Arambourg. 1956, 1961; Coon, 1962a; Thoma, 1962). Were these phylogenetic views merely consistent with, encouraged by, or directly derived from, the evolutionary dynamics associated with the evolutionary synthesis? Coon (1962a: viii–ix) and Thoma (1962: 4–16) were at least partly encouraged by this latter evolutionary dynamics, as seen in some of their direct references to it. Arambourg's view, however, was merely consistent with it as he always remained skeptical of the explanatory power of the evolutionary synthesis (Grimoult, 2000: 60–64). The case of von Koenigswald remains unclear.

The cultural niche. Two of the pillars accompanying the evolutionary synthesis—the new systematics and its evolutionary dynamics—provided a basis for the conceiving of human phylogeny. These pillars were as valid in paleoanthropology as they were in other fields of evolutionary biology, in the sense that they were of universal value and not exclusively applicable in human evolution. However, proponents of the evolutionary synthesis like Mayr eventually developed evolutionary concepts uniquely applied in paleoanthropology. Such concepts which were originally borrowed from the corpus of the theoretical principles in evolutionary biology were adapted to suit the specific situation in human evolution.

It is in this context that the competitive exclusion principle, which states that no two species can occupy the same ecological niche because competition would prevent one or the other species from surviving, was combined with the conviction that cultural ability was a most efficient means of ecological niche exploitation. Armed with this conceptual apparatus, Mayr (1950: 116) could justify his conviction of the time that only one species of hominid has ever existed at any one time level:

> What is the cause for this puzzling trait of the hominid stock to stop speciating in spite of its eminent evolutionary success? . . . If the single species man occupies successfully all the niches that are open for *Homo*-like creatures [because of its cultural ability], it is obvious that he cannot speciate. . . .

Even when Mayr (1953) recognized a short time later that there was good morphological evidence of more than one contemporary hominid species at the australopithecine level, he insisted that this situation raised a serious problem of competition between species that needed to be addressed. Clearly, Mayr (1963: 336) had not totally relinquished his "hunch that there was no opportunity for the simultaneous existence of two separate hominid species of advanced tool makers."

Mayr's importation of the competitive exclusion principle in paleoanthropology would not fall on deaf ears, with respect to a number of scholars. Was the application of the concept of a cultural niche as elaborated from within the evolutionary synthesis new in paleoanthropology? Essentially, yes.

It is true that the notion of culture being a key element which either instigated or contributed to the hominization process is very old indeed (e.g., Lamarck, 1809; Darwin, 1871). Culture has long been viewed as both a unique and a key factor in human evolution. Yet, Mayr's application of the culture concept in human evolution, by enshrining it in the ecological principle of exclusion, instantaneously gave it an operational dimension that was lacking in the scenarios of hominization. Now, culture was not, scientifically speaking, only a vague explanatory argument in human evolution but rather a concept rendered theoretically testable and refutable by at least two distinct empirical sources: (1) the number of contemporaneous hominid lineages as interpreted in the fossil record; (2) the number of contemporaneous stone tool assemblages as interpreted in the archaeological record. This contributed to bring the fields of paleoanthropology and prehistoric archaeology into close contact; not an uncommon occurrence in the history of these two disciplines (e.g., Delisle, 2000a). Robinson and Brace both appealed to these empirical sources in order to either disprove or support the application of the competitive exclusion principle in human evolution.

For instance, Robinson responded to Mayr's challenge and tried to explain the presence of more than one contemporary species at the australopithecines level. He held that the fossil sample of this early time period contained at least two contemporary evolving branches of the australopithecine group. Not content with the anatomical dimension of his phylogenetic hypothesis, Robinson (1954a, 1963) felt compelled to discard the competitive exclusion principle. By so doing, Robinson indicated that he recognized the validity of this principle in human evolution. He explained that the early hominids had only a rudimentary culture which prevented the activation of the competitive exclusive principle, so that the slowing down of the speciation rate was not effective at this early stage of human evolution. According to Robinson, early hominids were not yet fully culture-bearing creatures and should therefore be evaluated as nonhominids by applying to them ordinary mammalian taxonomic standards.

Whereas Robinson tried to invalidate the applicability of the competitive exclusion principle in the early phases of human evolution, Brace (1967), for his part, promoted that even the earliest hominids belonged to a single evolving species only, as seen in their morphological variability. Although Brace's (1967: 56, 70) phylogenetic hypothesis was explicitly grounded in the competitive exclusion principle, he insisted on reinforcing it further by adding that the Old World stone tools of this early period were sufficiently homogeneous as to warrant their production from a single species only.

The concept of a cultural niche as elaborated within the evolutionary synthesis constituted a new input in the field of paleoanthropology. This concept had no antecedent in this field for reasons already mentioned. The obvious impact of the application of this concept in paleoanthropology was to encourage the constriction of the phylogenetic hypotheses. In fact, the potential influence of the entire evolutionary synthesis on the field of human evolution, presented here in three components—the new systematics, the evolutionary dynamics, and the cultural niche—invariably encouraged the elaboration of hominid phylogenetic trees with a single or the fewest possible number of distinct evolutionary branches of the species level. Was, then, the constriction process of phylogenetic hypotheses going on in the 1950s and 1960s in human evolution entirely the result of the evolutionary synthesis?

In a nutshell, the evolutionary synthesis was not the instigating factor in, nor the most important reason behind, the constriction of the hominid phylogenetic hypotheses between 1935 and 1965. Yet, it nevertheless constituted an important factor in either encouraging, sustaining, or even molding this process in the 1950s and 1960s. First, the evolutionary synthesis did not instigate the constriction process, as this was clearly achieved under the impetus which followed the hominid fossil discoveries of the 1930–1940 decade. Furthermore, the potential impact of the new systematics, as well as of the evolutionary dynamics accompanying the evolutionary synthesis, was greatly limited by the simple fact that some conceptual developments in paleoanthropology prior to 1950 had already anticipated those that came later with the evolutionary synthesis.

In fact, the perspective could well be reversed: The impact of the evolutionary synthesis on paleoanthropology in the 1950s and 1960s was made possible only because the conceptual developments accompanying it had already been anticipated by some pre-1950 developments in paleoanthropology. Although it is always risky to dwell upon hypothetical arguments, it is difficult to imagine that the evolutionary synthesis could have had any significant impact on the debates on human phylogeny during the 1910s and 1920s at the precise moment when such debates were being conducted in the perspective of three widely distinct interpretative frameworks (see Chapter 5). The evolutionary synthesis needed favorable conditions in order to penetrate the field paleoanthropology; these were reunited not before the 1940s. Even the genuinely new input of the cultural niche concept was largely dependent for its applicability upon the acceptance—from the part of a number of paleoanthropologists—that the hominid fossil record could be, after all, interpreted in a more or less linear fashion.

The evolutionary synthesis arrived on the scene when the field of paleoanthropology had just recently entered its early phase of maturity, as seen in its modern research structure. By that time, the fossil record was complete enough as to apply a lot of pressure on the number of hominid phylogenetic hypotheses believed to be defensible. In this scientific context, the impact of the evolutionary synthesis on paleoanthropology could only have been relatively limited. To say the contrary would be to promote that this field is largely a by-product of the evolutionary theories. The evolutionary synthesis would have been judged unacceptable by paleoanthropologists if it had promoted phylogenetic hypotheses which were not at least consistent with the hominid fossil record of the time.

Although it is fully recognized here that the evolutionary synthesis produced changes in hominid phylogenetic hypotheses, these were of a rather superficial kind when looked at from the perspective of the development of paleoanthropology between 1860 and 1950. The evolutionary synthesis would become an important source of inspiration mainly for scholars whose conception of human phylogeny was already consistent with it. However, this should not distract us from the fact that a number of students of human evolution always continued to promote multilinear hypotheses, unable as they were to resolve the discrepancies they observed between the fossil record and some of the prescriptions that emanated from the evolutionary synthesis at the time.

CONCLUSION

The field of human evolution is not a by-product of any specific evolutionary theories or conceptions, whether you consider Darwinism, Orthogenesis, or the Evolutionary Synthesis (Neo-Darwinism). Far from being an empty shell dependent upon the various evolutionary theories to inject life into it, the field of paleoanthropology has a nature of its own. The backbone of paleoanthropology is to be found in the ongoing interplay between the empirical data generated by comparative anatomy (living forms) and the fossil record. By 1965, the quest to establish humankind's place in nature had generated a rough picture. Fossil recoveries of nonhuman primates, australopithecines, and hominids made during the 1935–1965 period permitted the emergence of an incomplete but yet fairly coherent picture. At last, the various components of paleoanthropology—its distinct research areas—started to come together.

Researchers devoted to human phylogeny proper contributed two important elements to this enterprise. First, all human phylogenetic hypotheses formed a coherent set of propositions insensibly grading into one another from multilinear to parallel, and from parallel to linear hypotheses. The demise of the polyphyletic thesis in the 1930s centered the debate around the key notion of the unity of humankind. Second, most hominid phylogenetic hypotheses rested on the notion that a genuinely modern-looking ancestor to the living humans appeared only in the Middle Pleistocene or after. For most scholars, therefore, the common ancestor to all the main living human races had to be sought among primitive-looking ("ape-like") forms of the Lower Pleistocene period, should they be australopithecines or forms more or less closely akin to them. This could only have contributed to clarify: (1) the morphological sequence through which the human line had passed; (2) the time dimension of these various morphological stages; and (3) the polarity or the evolutionary direction of the morphological traits in the phylogenetic analyses.

NOTES

1. Le Gros Clark (1936) excluded the Kanam and Kanjera remains without explicitly saying so or naming them. He just stopped taking them into consideration in his following publications *when discussing their phylogeny* (for they still figured in his presentation of the hominid fossil discoveries). This may be related to the controversy that arose in the mid-1930s about the geological age of these remains. Indeed, Le Gros Clark (1949: 97; 1955: 56) later mentioned that the Kanam and Kanjera remains awaited confirmation of their geological dating.

2. Le Gros Clark (1949: 91–92; 1953: 91–92) repeatedly claimed that the Piltdown remains should be laid aside until more evidence becomes available. This happened when the Piltdown hoax was discovered (Weiner, Oakley, Le Gros Clark, 1953). Yet, in 1950 Le Gros Clark could not resist the temptation of commenting on Piltdown (Le Gros Clark, 1950a: 259). At that time, Le Gros Clark thought that the new dating of the Piltdown remains showed that it represented a somewhat specialized collateral branch which had persisted quite late in the Pleistocene.

3. See Le Gros Clark's hominid phylogenetic trees in, *The Fossil Evidence for Human Evolution* (Chicago: University of Chicago Press, 1955), p. 8; *The Antecedents of Man* (Chicago: Quadrangle Books, 1960a), p. 344; *The Fossil Evidence for Human Evolution*, 2nd edition (Chicago: University of Chicago Press, 1964), p. 8; *The Antecedents of Man*, 3rd edition (Chicago: Quadrangle Books, 1971), p. 346.

4. See Le Gros Clark's hominid phylogenetic trees in, *The Fossil Evidence for Human Evolution* (Chicago: University of Chicago Press, 1955), p. 8, and *The Fossil Evidence for Human Evolution*, 2nd edition (Chicago: University of Chicago Press, 1964), p. 8. The possible nature of the phylogenetic connection between the pithecanthropine stem and the later hominids was expressed by Le Gros Clark (1955: 106) in the following words: "There is, indeed, a general consensus of opinion that *Pithecanthropus* stands in an ancestral relationship to *Homo*. This does not mean . . . that the Far Eastern population of this genus was itself the actual ancestral group . . . [I]f so, of course, the transition from one to the other may have occurred in some other part of the world." It must be recognized that this comment is, at best, cryptic as far as phylogenetic inferences are concerned. That is why I argue that Le Gros Clark's phylogenetic trees bring more precision on this question. It is interesting to note that in Le Gros Clark's phylogenetic tree of 1964 the pithecanthropine stem continues its evolution towards extinction after the later hominids had sprung from it during a shorter time period than in his 1955 phylogenetic tree. This gives a general impression that his entire phylogenetic tree of 1964 is more compact, that is, with the distinct stems being more closely related than seen in 1955. This is perhaps not unrelated to the fact that in 1964 Le Gros Clark included all the pithecanthropines in the genus *Homo* as *Homo erectus*. This taxonomic shift contributed to reinforce a greater phylogenetic proximity.

5. Le Gros Clark (1955: 72) recognized that there may be enough morphological difference between the living humans and this mid-Pleistocene ancestor to include the latter in a subspecies of *Homo sapiens*.

6. Vallois always maintained that the Piltdown morphological type was constituted by both the crania and its accompanying jaw.

7. In the 1950s, Vallois recognized a fourth hominid line, in Africa this time. This Upper Pleistocene line was believed to be constituted of the Rhodesian man and of the remains of Saldanha at its very base. Although this evolutionary line was evolving in the direction of some living human races of black complexion, Vallois (1955a: 2192) clearly stated that this Neandertaloid line was not leading to living humans. As noted in Europe, continued Vallois, the Neanderthaloid forms of Africa were in an evolutionary dead end. For this new and fourth hominid evolutionary line, see Vallois's diagram in "L'ordre des primates." In, P.-P. Grassé (ed.), *Traité de zoologie: Anatomie, systématique, biologie*, Tome XVII, 2ième partie (Paris: Masson), p. 2193. Vallois had previously included the Rhodesian man within the classic Neandertal group.

8. A clear impression is given that Vallois's distinct hominid evolutionary lines of the Pleistocene are converging towards a common ape-like creature. See his diagram in *La grotte de Fontéchevade*, deuxième partie, anthropologie (Paris: Masson, 1958), p. 149. In fact, this diagram gives a fairly good impression that all the hominid lines are converging toward a common pithecanthropine-like ancestor near the turn of the Plio-Pleistocene.

9. It should be noted that Vallois's fifth chapter of *La grotte de Fontéchevade* (Paris: Masson, 1958) was translated into English as "The Origin of *Homo sapiens*." In, W.W. Howells (ed.), *Ideas on Human Evolution: Selected Essays, 1949–1961* (Cambridge: Harvard University Press, 1962), pp. 473–499.

10. See Heberer's hominid family tree in "Das Präsapiens-Problem." In, H. Grüneberg and W. Ulrich (eds.), *Moderne Biologie* (Berlin: F.W. Peters, 1950), p. 154.

11. See Heberer's modified hominid family tree in "Die Abstammung des Menschen." In, L. von Bertalanffy and F. Gessner (eds.), *Handbuch der Biologie*, Vol. 9, *Der Mensch und seine Stellung im Naturganzen* (Akademische Verlagsgesellschaft Athenaion Konstanz, 1965), p. 310.

12. Genet-Varcin's conception of human phylogeny at the time can only be glimpsed from her phylogenetic tree in *Les singes actuels et fossiles* (Paris: N. Boubée et Cie, 1963), pp. 220–221.

13. See Genet-Varcin's new conception of human phylogeny in her phylogenetic tree in *À la recherche du primate ancêtre de l'homme* (Paris: N. Boubée et Cie, 1969), p. 304.

14. Although Howells rejected *Pithecanthropus* and *Sinanthropus* as being direct ancestors to the living humans, he apparently believed that they were not too far removed from the line which gave rise to the living humans: "[T]he Far Eastern fossils [*Pithecanthropus* and *Sinanthropus*] are two examples of men in a primitive stage, but not too far from the line which our own descent must have followed; and they also happen to be closely related to each other, probably by common descent from a still earlier type" (Howells, 1944: 147).

15. It seems that Howells (1959) believed that if the Rhodesian man is not directly derived from the pithecanthropines than it probably comes from the Neandertnaloid stock.

16. Howells (1959: 336) made clear that the ancestors of the living humans in the Middle Pleistocene were not as modern-looking as he once expected: "[T]he birth of *Homo sapiens*. Now, we have seen that the argument is not as sharply drawn as once. Probably our modern species is neither tighly bound up with Neanderthals, nor so ancient as to let us expect that the Swanscombe Woman's forehead [missing] would have looked like one of ours. Obviously, sapient man developed from a more primitive ancestor, probably toward the middle of the Pleistocene; that is to say, our forebears gradually became more 'sapiens-like'. And the evidence does seem to show that the Neanderthal line became more extreme, or more Neanderthal-like."

17. Howells (1959: 179, 239) alluded to another hominid group leading to the living humans that might be represented by the Kanam jaw of East Africa in the Lower Pleistocene period, but he recognized that this source of information was an unreliable witness of *Homo sapiens*.

18. Concerning the "modernized" ancestor of the Neandertals and the "demodernized" ancestor of the modern human type in Howells's new view, Howells (1967: 220) stated: "How do you score her [Steinheim]? Fairly evenly as between sapiens and Neanderthal, but not specifically like either and rather more primitive than both. Take her as a common ancestress, if you wish, but remember that she goes back a tremendous number of generations. While she may resemble the Neanderthals by having

primitive features, it is perhaps surprising that she is not more primitive than she is."

19. In the post-1965 period, Howells's (1993) view of the phylogeny of the genus *Homo* was definitely a parallel hypothesis or a linear hypothesis of one kind or another.

20. There is a certain ambiguity in Leakey's writings in the early 1950s about whether *Homo sapiens* itself dates back to the earliest portions of the Pleistocene period or if merely an ancestral form approaching it existed at such an early time. In one instance, Leakey (1950: 198) was apparently inclined to recognize the existence of the *Homo sapiens* type in Lower and Middle Pleistocene deposits. A few years later, Leakey (1953: 203) named the Kanam jaw of the earliest portions of the Pleistocene *Homo kanamensis* and not *Homo sapiens* on the basis that, although it presents many features in common to the latter type, it also presents some differences such as large premolars and a general massiveness. My impression is that Leakey was tempted in 1950 to see a *Homo sapiens* type in the Kanam jaw although in 1934 and 1953 he preferred to recognize a distinct species (see Leakey, 1934: 207). This is part of a trend in Leakey's mind to push deeper and deeper in time the antiquity of *Homo sapiens.* This trend reached its peak around 1950. By 1953, Leakey started to subtly retreat from the viewpoint that the evolutionary line leading to the living human races had deep roots and was represented by modern-looking individuals. This retreat is much more obvious after 1959. See discussion in the main text. In 1953, Leakey still believed that *Homo sapiens* would eventually be found in the Lower Pleistocene period, although he recognized in the Kanam jaw a different species. There is no necessary contradiction in that. It should not be forgotten that the Lower Pleistocene is a long period. Leakey probably expected to find *Homo sapiens* in the latest portions of the Lower Pleistocene, the Kanam jaw (*Homo kanamensis*) being in the earliest portions.

21. See Leakey's hominid family tree in *Adam's Ancestors* (London: Methuen, 1953), p. 212.

22. It is not clear what kind of common ancestor Weckler had in mind for all the living humans. At first, Weckler (1954: 1004) was disposed to recognize in the australopithecines such an ancestor. Later, Weckler (1957: 93–94) insisted that the australopithecines probably had no direct connection with human evolution and spoke vaguely of a proto-men as a common ancestor to all living humans.

23. It is true that Weckler (1954, 1957) continually opposed the two strains "*Homo sapiens*" and Neandertals. However, Weckler (1964: 31) later made clear that the Neandertals were not a distinct species from the living humans: "If Brace defines a species as a collection of 'races' which can produce fertile offspring by interbreeding, then I go along with the idea that we and the Neanderthal belong to the same species." Weckler (1954, 1957) merely used the word "*Homo sapiens*" as representing a modern-looking morphology in opposition to a primitive-looking one (Neandertals).

24. By the early 1970s, Osman Hill (1972) had considerably simplified his conception of human phylogeny. He now recognized a linear series from *Australopithecus africanus, Homo habilis, Homo erectus,* followed by a split with, on the one hand, *Homo neanderthalensis* evolving toward extinction and, on the other hand, *Homo sapiens* leading to the living humans.

25. On this denial of the concept of evolutionary stages in human evolution, Piveteau (1963: 202) wrote: "Nous aurions ainsi des nappes successives, génétiquement liées. Chacune ne se transformerait pas, dans son ensemble, pour donner naissance à la suivante, mais en divers points, s'individualiseraient des pôles biologiquement plus actifs, par lesquels se perpétuerait le courant évolutif." This being said, Piveteau's (1973, 1983) view of the phylogeny of the genus *Homo* in the post-1965 period was pretty much a linear hypothesis of a kind or another, implying a certain recognition of successive evolutionary stages.

26. It will be remembered that Coon (1939: 28) had previously considered the possibility that several primitive-looking hominid lines might have contributed to the living human races (see Chapter 6). But this is certainly not comparable to the extent to which he recognized this idea after the late 1950s.

27. See the geographical distribution of the main five living human races in Coon's *The Origin of Races* (New York: Alfred A. Knopf, 1962), pp. 6–7.

28. The various hominid forms inserted in these five human races are presented in a chart in Coon's *The Origin of Races* (New York: Alfred A. Knopf, 1962), p. 335.

29. Previously, Coon (1954: 36–38) pushed the modern-looking strain of humanity as far back as the very early Pleistocene period through the fossil remains of Kanam (East Africa). Now, Coon (1962b: 38) no longer referred to the Kanam remains and was constrained to place this modern-looking hominid strain at no later than the Middle Pleistocene.

30. It should not be assumed that Coon promoted that gene flow between the five main human races had been minimal throughout the time. On the contrary. However, he believed that the evolutionary significance of this gene flow was reduced because external genes to a region are not always as advantageous as the local genes. After all, local populations usually carry advantageous genes because they have had a lot of time to reach an equilibrium with their environment. Coon (1962a: 663): stated: "[T]here has been enough gene flow over the clinal regions of the world during the last half million years to have homogenized us all had that been the evolutionary scheme of things, and had it not been advantageous to each of the geographical races for it to retain, for the most part, the adaptive elements in its genetic *status quo*."

31. See Thoma's human phylogenetic trees in "Le déploiement évolutif de l'*Homo sapiens*," *Anthropologia Hungarica*, 5 (1962), p. 16 and 88 and in "New Evidence for the Polycentric Evolution of *Homo sapiens*," *Journal of Human Evolution*, 2 (1973), p. 530.

32. In his human phylogenetic tree, Thoma (1973: 530) alluded to the possibility that the Khoisands of South Africa were not affiliated in the late Upper Pleistocene period with the other African races of black complexion. Rather, they might have been derived early and independently from the common archanthropine ancestor.

33. At one time, Thoma (1962) would not rule out the possibility that the classic Neandertals of Europe constituted a distinct species from *Homo sapiens*, *Homo neanderthalensis*. Later, Thoma (1965, 1971, 1973) made clear that the classic Neandertals were merely a subspecies of *Homo sapiens*. The important point here is that Thoma always maintained that the extinction of the classic Neandertals—whether considered to be a distinct species or merely a subspecies of *Homo sapiens*—was a minor event in human evolution since most of the known fossil hominids were on direct evolutionary lines leading to living human races. In fact, Thoma claimed that the extinction of the classic Neandertals was the only extinction event since the rise of the archanthropines.

34. At first, Thoma (1962: 18) derived all the archanthropines from a more ancient and less specialized group than the South African australopithecines. Later, Thoma (1971: 81; 1973: 529) derived the archanthropines from *Homo transvaalensis* as defined by John Robinson (see Chapter 8) to include the gracile australopithecines.

35. For Thoma, the morphological divergence between the modern-looking and the primitive-looking (Neanderthaloid) forms was not that important. The Swanscombe and Fontéchevade fossil remains were among such modern-looking forms of the palaeanthropic phase. In comparison, Thoma insisted that the Neanderthaloid forms differed from the modern-looking ones only in a number of specializations in the facial anatomy (Thoma, 1962: 81).

36. Thoma's (1985) view of the phylogeny of the genus *Homo* was unchanged in the mid-1980s.

37. At the *Pithecanthropus* level, von Koenigswald identified, in China, *Sinanthropus*, in Europe, Heidelberg man and, in Africa, *Atlanthropus* and some remains of "*Homo habilis*". It should be noted that von Koenigswald (1953) was once uncertain of the pithecanthropine affinity of Heidelberg man. At the Neandertal level, there were of course in Europe all the Neandertals and in Africa the remains such as Rhodesian man and Saldanha. Remember that as far as the *Meganthropus* level is concerned, von Koenigswald recognized in the australopithecines of South Africa forms approaching it, largely because of their common commitment to gigantism (see Chapter 7). Later, the comparison of the *Meganthropus* level or grade with a newly recognized African form called *Homo habilis* was made (Tobias and von Koenigswald, 1964; von Koenigswald, 1976 [1968]). Note that von Koenigswald considered that some remains attributed to *Homo habilis* should best be regarded as *Homo erectus*.

38. Von Koenigswald (1976 [1968]: 142) used these exact words to describe his view few years later. Von Koenigswald presented his conception of human phylogeny in two distinct types

of family trees, a simplified version and a detailed yet partial version. This latter version was directly borrowed from Emil Breitinger. See G.H.R. von Koenigswald, *The Evolution of Man* (Ann Arbor: University of Michigan Press, 1962), p. 115 and p. 131; also *The Evolution of Man* (Ann Arbor: University of Michigan Press, 1976), p. 125 and p. 141.

39. Von Koenigswald also recognized a hominid group he called "pre-Neanderthal". Composed of remains such as Ehringsdorf, Saccopastore, and Krapina this group was apparently exclusively on its way toward the classic Neandertals. Perhaps not totally isolated, genetically speaking, this pre-Neandertal group may well have been able to interbreed with the descendents of the presapiens group, as seen in the remains of Palestine. Von Koenigswald was not very explicit about this entire question.

40. Earlier, however, von Koenigswald (1940: 194) was perhaps more open to the possibility that Solo man constituted a genuine phylogenetic intermediate between *Pithecanthropus* and the living Australians.

41. See Arambourg's human family tree in *La genèse de l'humanité* (Paris: Presses Universitaire de France, 1943), p. 131 and *La genèse de l'humanité*, 6th edition (Paris: Presses Universitaire de France, 1961), p. 117.

42. The hominid members that constituted the pithecanthropine and the Neandertal evolutionary stages changed in Arambourg's mind during the 1950s. Those changes were either related to new datings of hominid fossil specimens or to a new anatomical assessments of them. For instance, *Africanthropus* was first attributed to the pithecanthropine stage and was later transferred to the Neandertal stage. Conversely, Steinheim, Broken Hill, and *Homo soloensis* were first associated to the Neandertal phase and were later transferred to the pithecanthropine one. Such changes had no impact on Arambourg's general conception of human phylogeny. Compare, C. Arambourg, *La genèse de l'humanité* (Paris: Presses Universitaires de France, 1943) and *La genèse de l'humanité*, 7th edition (Paris: Presses Universitaires de France, 1965).

43. It is true that Arambourg placed the australopithecines at the base of the human family tree only after the mid-1950s. However, the australopithecines represented a morphological link, though not a genealogical one, prior to that time. Furthermore, it should not be forgotten that before the mid-1950s Arambourg postulated that the human and the australopithecine lines had diverged from a common ancestor which was a generalized australopithecine-like creature.

44. It is unclear if Brace (1967: 62, 70) intended to refer to the second evolutionary phase of the australopithecine stage—the one that is attributed to *Paranthropus*—by the name of *Homo robustus*.

45. Brace (1967: 78) would not recognize the validity of the species *Homo habilis* of Olduvai (East Africa) which he included in his pithecanthropine stage, that is, within *Homo erectus*.

46. Among the participants to take part in the Congrès de Paris in 1947 were Camille Arambourg, J.B.S. Haldane, Jean Piveteau, George G. Simpson, and Henri V. Vallois.

47. The program for this Cold Spring Harbor Symposium of 1950 was worked out in collaboration with Theosodius Dobzhansky and Sherwood L. Washburn. Among the attending scholars were Joseph B. Birdsell, Carleton S. Coon, Theodosius Dobzhansky, Ernst A. Hooton, Francis C. Howell, William W. Howells, Ernst Mayr, Theodore D. McCown, Adolph H. Schultz, George G. Simpson, and Sherwood L. Washburn.

48. Among the participants at this symposium on Classification and Human Evolution in 1962 were Bernard G. Campbell, Theodosius Dobzhansky, Louis S.B. Leakey, Ernst Mayr, John Napier, Adolf H. Schultz, George G. Simpson, William L. Straus, Sherwood L. Washburn, and Joseph S. Weiner.

49. Other founding members of the evolutionary synthesis who applied the new systematics in paleoanthropology are Theodosius Dobzhansky and George Gaylord Simpson. Dobzhansky (1944: 257) wrote in a footnote that the scholars in human evolution were not properly using the taxonomic categories. We will discuss Dobzhansky's view of human phylogeny shortly. For his part, Simpson's (1963a; Delisle, 1997b) contribution was not so much directed at proposing a particular human phylogenetic hypothesis as to bring some clarification on the use of taxonomy. Simpson noted what he called

the chaos in hominid nomenclature, and pointed at two possibilities explaining this situation: (1) the failure to use consistent designations for specimens, populations, and taxa; (2) a lack of experience in evaluating taxonomic categories from the part of paleoanthropologists who have not worked extensively on larger groups of animal other than hominids. Simpson stressed the biological meaning of taxonomy and its importance as an unambiguous language for scientific communication. In so doing, he noted at the time the prevailing tendency in human evolution of naming individual fossils (typological thinking) without any reference to a population (population thinking), and the failure therein to understand the biological meaning of taxonomy.

50. Breitinger's paper "Zur phyletischen Evolution von *Homo sapiens*." *Anthropologischer Anzeiger*, 21 (1957), pp. 62–83 was translated as "On the Phyletic Evolution of *Homo sapiens*." In W.W. Howells (ed.), *Ideas on Human Evolution: Selected Essays, 1949–1961* (Cambridge: Harvard University Press, 1962), pp. 436–459. Breitinger's "Zur frühesten Phase der Hominiden-Evolution." In, E. Breitinger, J. Haeckel and R. Pittioni (eds.), *Beiträger Osterreichs zur Erforschung der Vergangenheit und Kulturegeschichte der Menschheit* (Wenner-Gren Foundation for Anthropological Research, 1959), pp. 205–235 was translated as "On the Earliest Phase of Hominid Evolution." In W.W. Howells (ed.), *Ideas on Human Evolution: Selected Essays, 1949–1961* (Cambridge: Harvard University Press, 1962), pp. 172–202.

51. Coon (1962a: viii–ix) recounted how he discovered the polytypic species concept. It is certainly interesting to note that Coon admitted that he first arrived at his hominid phylogenetic hypothesis through the fossil record only to look afterward for a theoretical justification. I have argued in this book that when paleoanthropologists have been influenced by evolutionary theories, it is usually through this mode, and not the reverse. Dobzhansky (1963a, 1963b) and Simpson (1963b) were not entirely convinced that Coon (1962a) had properly applied the rules of the new systematics.

10

Primate and Human Phylogeny, 1965–2000[1]

INTRODUCTION

We have reached the last stage of our inquiry. The purpose of this chapter is to present in a condensed manner the key developments related to the quest of humankind's place in nature between 1965 and 2000. On several occasions in this book we have had the opportunity to insist on a number of false assumptions carried by the traditional historiography interested in the history of paleoanthropology. Too often, proponents of this historiography have looked upon paleoanthropology with the expectation that its past developments would more or less conform with the modern ones. By so doing, modern scholars have shoehorned the past debates into a modern framework which is far too restrictive for their proper understanding. Not only has this procedure produced a distorted interpretation of the history of the field but, perhaps more importantly, it has also deprived the modern paleoanthropologists of a proper understanding of how progress came about, epistemologically speaking. This epistemological question will be treated more fully in the next chapter. It is no surprise then that the traditional historiography carried the notion—implicitly or explicitly—of a field of paleoanthropology largely at a standstill (see also Chapter 1). What is needed is not the reading of the past debates in light of the modern ones but the exact opposite. This chapter will review four key modern debates—humankind's place among the primates, the scenarios of hominization, the place of the australopithecines, and the rise of the living humans—with the intention of determining to what extent each of these quests has progressed in light of the past debates. It will be clearly seen that the general quest to establish humankind's place in nature during the 1965–2000 period continued to progress on several counts when compared to the pre-1965 period.

HUMANKIND'S PLACE AMONG THE PRIMATES

We have seen during 1935–1965 period that the debates on humankind's place among the primates were greatly simplified or circumscribed by exclusively revolving around the hominoid radiation. Indeed, the pre-1935 period saw phylogenetic debates which often involved nonhominoid primates, not to mention the polyphyletic hypotheses which established close phylogenetic links between one specific nonhuman primate species and one specific human race to the exclusion of the other human races (see Chapters 2, 4, and 5). In the 1935–1965 period, the debate was conducted in a more restricted framework: Had the departure of the human line from the other primates occurred before, in the early phase, or in the later phase of the hominoid radiation (see Chapter 7)? By that time, the polyphyletic hypotheses had been discarded. The 1965–2000 period saw the research agenda of this debate reduced further still. This is seen in two distinct manifestations.

First, the number of scholars ready to promote that the human line entirely avoided going through a hominoid ape phase of evolution seriously decreased, especially after 1980. Second, the notion that humankind had sprung from an early and very generalized hominoid ape phase in the Oligocene period as seen in *Propliopithecus*, *Aegyptopithecus*, or *Proconsul* was gradually abandoned after 1965. Now, the debate largely centered around the dryopithecines of the Miocene and the Pliocene periods. All this contributed to place the split of the human line from the other primates in a not too ancient time period, and among a frankly ape-like evolutionary group.

Many of the same primate fossil forms used in the 1935–1965 period to shed light on the rise of the human line were exploited after 1965, with the important difference that many more fossil discoveries were added to these same fossil groups, thus often changing the perception that scholars had about them. This is especially true of *Ramapithecus*, *Sivapithecus*, *Dryopithecus*, *Kenyapithecus*, *Gigantopithecus*, and *Oreopithecus*. This being said, some new primate fossil forms were added to the debates, notably *Lufengpithecus* (formerly *Sivapithecus*) and a form either called *Ouranopithecus* or *Graecopithecus*. In continuity with the 1935–1965 period, the post-1965 period offered the possibility of placing the birthplace of humankind almost anywhere in the Old World. Although Africa remained a popular location for such a cradle, the very widely distributed dryopithecine radiation, the Chinese location of *Lufengpithecus* and the Greek one for *Ouranopithecus*/*Graecopithecus*, and the not entirely settled question of the exclusive African rise of the australopithecines, all contributed to this uncertainty.

The incontestable novelty of the post-1965 period in the debates on humankind's place among the primates was the impact of the molecular studies. The increased importance of molecular studies since the 1960s contributed to the reversal of a historical trend in the field. We have seen that the importance of comparative anatomy (living forms) in the phylogenetic studies gradually declined throughout the twentieth century, although it always remained important. Indeed, scholars turned more and more to the improving primate fossil record to investigate phylogenetic questions that had not been resolved satisfactorily in the past by comparative anatomy only. With the rise of molecular anthropology in the 1960s, the value of neontological studies (living forms) in paleoanthropology made a comeback, not because of comparative anatomy but rather through the intermediary of the molecular studies. This reinstituted a sort of equilibrium between paleontological and neontological studies in the quest to establish humankind's place among the primates. This reinstated value of the neontological studies was not, however, associated with the ambiguities that often accompanied them in the past. The molecular studies all pointed to a very limited number of phylogenetic hypotheses all centered around humankind's close relationship with the two African great apes exclusively, as well as to a late departure or divergence time.

The fossil record. The conception that the human line avoided going through a hominoid ape phase during its evolution continued to be promoted during the 1965–2000 period, although this was largely done in the first half of this time period only. By postulating that human evolution bypassed the ape evolutionary phase, proponents of this view looked for a last common ancestor with the other nonhuman primates which dated back to the Oligocene period, if not at an earlier time. As most nonhuman anthropoid fossils discovered thus far were part of the Old World monkeys or of the hominoid ape radiations, and as all or most hominoid fossils were believed to be either too specialized or too ape-like in conformation, very few fossils were used to bolster this conception. For these scholars, the primate fossil record largely provided a negative proof of this conception, meaning that the hominoid ape fossils showed that the human line could not have sprung from within this group.

Kurtén (1972) was perhaps the one scholar who made the most extensive use of this fossil record by recognizing in *Propliopithecus*, *Ramapithecus*, and *Australopithecus* forms exclusively affiliated to the human line and not to the ape line. Kurtén held that the Old World monkeys, the hominoid apes, and the humans all derived from a primitive common stock of the Eocene period which had small canines and frontal teeth as well as unspecialized (nonsectorial) premolars. While the human line retained this primitive ancestral condition, continued Kurtén, the ape and monkey lines diverged from it toward specializations.

For her part, Genet-Varcin (1974, 1978) found in the New World monkeys a primitive stage through which the Old World monkeys, the pongids, and the humans all separately sprang from in the late Eocene period. *Apidium* and *Parapithecus* were thought to represent a side branch near this common anthropoid stock. Of all the Old World anthropoids, the human line alone retained the primitiveness and the generality of this New World monkey evolutionary phase.[2] Eventually, Genet-Varcin (1979) made clear that *Oreopithecus* represented an extinct side branch which departed from the human line exclusively in the Miocene period. By then, Genet-Varcin (1979) established the split between the human and the pongid lines in the very early Oligocene period, with the Old World monkeys being slightly more distant, phylogenetically and chronologically speaking.[3]

Similarly, Hürzeler (1978) placed *Oreopithecus* as an extinct side branch which exclusively departed from the human line in the Eocene period. The australopithecines also eventually departed from this human line in the early Miocene period evolving toward extinction. Like Kurtén and Genet-Varcin, Hürzeler insisted that the frontal portion of the dentition in apes and humans were different enough as to warrant that the two groups diverged from one another as early as the Paleocene period.[4]

Unlike the other scholars, Piveteau (1973, 1983) appealed to no primate fossils other than the australopithecines to hold that the hominoid apes and the humans had diverged from each other in the Oligocene period.[5] Piveteau conceived this last common ancestor as an anthropomorphous or preanthropomorphous creature which could be called neither a pongid nor a hominid. For Piveteau, the quadrupedal Old World monkeys, the brachiating hominoid apes, and the bipedal humans all exploited entirely different strategies of locomotion, meaning that the human line never went through either a quadrupedal or a brachiating stage of evolution.

The conception that the human line had avoided altogether a hominoid ape phase of evolution eventually became a truly marginal view in the late portion of the twentieth century. By then, the debate on humankind's place among the primates came to center almost exclusively around the nature of the relationship between the humans and the three great apes: the chimpanzees, the gorillas, and the orang-utans. Interestingly, one has to wait for the 1965–2000 period in order to see the gibbons entirely excluded from the phylogenetic considerations in human evolution. In fact, a large majority of scholars in the 1980s and the 1990s even narrowed their search further for humankind's ancestor to the relationship between the humans and the two African great apes exclusively, thereby excluding also the orang from these considerations. This is certainly not entirely unrelated to the impact of the molecular studies on this very question (see below). Perhaps expectedly, a vast majority of scholars now believed that humankind's last common ancestor with the other primates was a hominoid ape neither too generalized in conformation nor too ancient in time, being dated to the Miocene or the Pliocene period. By channeling the bulk of the intellectual activity within this newly restricted area of inquiry, questions reached an unprecedented level of refinement (e.g., Ciochon, 1983). It is worth mentioning several of these questions.

Was humankind's last common ancestor with the hominoid apes slightly specialized, moderately specialized, or fairly specialized? Was this ancestor still presenting features attributed to quadrupedalism, to quadrumanism, to brachiation, to knuckle-walking, or to bipedalism? Were analyses based on hominoid fossil dental and gnathic material a good reflection of the cranial and the postcranial anatomy? Is it possible to distinguish the primitive features from the derived ones and properly establish the polarity of the character states or the direction of the morphological change? Were parallel and convergent evolution prevalent among the evolution of the hominoids? How similar were the fossil hominoids in comparison to their living counterparts? These questions and others took on a vivid importance in an area of inquiry now being largely restricted to the large hominoid apes (excluding the gibbons and their ancestors). This acuteness was only further enhanced following more fossil discoveries, new approaches of investigation, and new philosophies of systematics (e.g., Beard, 2002; Begun, 2002a, 2002b; Ciochon and Corruccini, 1982; Corruccini and Ciochon, 1983; Harrison, 2002; Kelley, 2002; Pilbeam, 1979, 1997; Rasmussen, 2002; Simons, 1995; Simons and Covert, 1981; Ward and Duren, 2002). It is beyond the scope of this book to go into these developments. Suffice it to say that the widely embraced notion in the 1935–1965 period that the living great apes were evolving toward a greater specialization, whereas the humans retained more of the primitive and generalized condition, was believed to be less and less valid in the phylogenetic researches after 1965. Let us review four main phylogenetic hypotheses proposed in this new framework of analysis.

In a first phylogenetic hypothesis, it was believed that the human line had departed from the hominoid ape stock before the three great apes had diverged from one another. For instance, Eckhardt (1972) postulated that *Gigantopithecus* of the Pliocene period may represent the common ancestor from which stemmed the human line (through an australopithecine phase) and the great ape line. Eckhardt conceived *Gigantopithecus* as an ape which may have been moderately exploiting an open environment and tool use.[6]

For his part, Simons (1977) derived the human and the great ape lines from a not too specialized and widely distributed dryopithecine radiation in the Miocene period some 15 million years ago (mya). Simons saw in *Ramapithecus* the most ancient hominid yet known evolving between 12 and 8 mya toward the australopithecines and the living humans; evolutionary stages all probably widely distributed in the Old World, although formal proof of this was still wanting in the case of the australopithecines. From this not too specialized dryopithecine ancestor, the great apes developed a number of specializations.

Not unlike Simons, Pilbeam and a number of colleagues saw in the dryopithecines the common ancestor to the humans and the three great apes in the mid-Miocene period (Pilbeam et al., 1977). Although Simons recognized in *Sivapithecus* a form with close ties to *Ramapithecus*, Pilbeam and his colleagues saw in *Sivapithecus* a form which is probably exclusively ancestral to the living humans, a position undoubtedly occupied by *Ramapithecus*. It was believed that *Sivapithecus* and *Ramapithecus* probability both contributed to the rise of humankind through the australopithecines.[7]

In a second phylogenetic hypothesis, it was promoted that the human line is more closely related to the orang line than to the African great apes. For instance, Xu and Lu apparently derived the australopithecines and the humans (*Homo*) from distinct fossil apes found in China (Xu and Lu, 1979; Lu and Xu, 1981). Xu and Lu argued that *Proconsul* may have given rise to both *Sivapithecus* and *Ramapithecus*. From there, different species of *Sivapithecus* (including the Chinese form *S. yunnanensis*) apparently contributed to the ancestry of both the orang-utan and some or all of the australopithecines. On the other hand, it was held that *Ramapithecus lufengensis* may be the direct ancestor of the early members of the genus *Homo*, a genuine transition from the ape type to the human type. I assume that by not referring to the chimpanzee and the gorilla in their discussion, Xu and Lu conceived this phylogenetic scheme to the exclusion of the African great apes.

For his part, Schwartz (1984) insisted that what really counts in order to establish the phylogenetic relationship of forms is not necessarily the total number of features they share in common but rather the quality of these features, that is, the number of features uniquely shared by them to the exclusion of the others. On the basis of these cladistic principles, Schwartz held that the humans share unique features more frequently with the orang-utans than with the chimpanzees and/or the gorillas. He conceived that the humans and the orangs shared a last common ancestor to the exclusion of the African great apes. The australopithecines, *Gigantopithecus*, and *Sivapithecus* were believed to be part of this human/orang group (clade).[8]

In a third phylogenetic hypothesis, it is promoted that the orang-utans are excluded from any considerations regarding humankind's last common ancestor with the other primates. The human line, it is held, would have departed from a form shared in common with the two African great apes exclusively. For instance, Aguirre (1972) found in *Aegyptopithecus* of the Oligocene period a common ancestor to the living humans and the two African great apes. By the early Miocene period, the African great apes had acquired their independence after going through a *Proconsul* phase of evolution, whereas the human line avoided this more specialized phase by going instead through a *Kenyapithecus*/*Ramapithecus* phase, probably in Africa.[9] Aguirre inclined to believe that *Kenyapithecus* was more directly ancestral to the living humans than *Ramapithecus*.

For other scholars, however, the human line had split from the African great apes at a more specialized evolutionary stage and at a later time period than proposed by Aguirre. For instance, Greenfield (1980, 1983) denied that *Sivapithecus* (now including *Ramapithecus*) was exclusively ancestral to the humans. He saw in the dryopithecines of the mid-Miocene period—in *Sivapithecus* in particular—a common ancestor to the three great apes and the humans at 15 million years ago. From there, it was postulated that the two African great apes and the humans shared an exclusive common ancestor which must be dated to a later time period, somewhere between 14 and 6 mya. Greenfield believed this latter common ancestor to be fairly specialized considering the dryopithecine-like traits seen in the earliest hominids (*Australopithecus afarensis*).[10]

Other scholars eventually changed their mind and also decided to exclude the orang-utans from their phylogenetic hypotheses. Whereas Xu and Lu once apparently believed that the human line shared a most recent common ancestor with the orang line exclusively, they joined Wu Rukang in the mid-1980s in promoting that this common ancestor was not with the Asian great ape but with the two African great apes. While *Sivapithecus* from China was believed to be linked to the orangs, *Ramapithecus* of the same region was held to be related to the common ancestor shared with the humans (*Australopithecus*) and the two African great apes (Wu, 1984; Wu and Xu, 1985). *Ramapithecus* was described as a form presenting small canines and rounded cranial vault which essentially lacked bony ridges. Eventually, *Sivapithecus* and *Ramapithecus* from China were fused together in *Sivapithecus lufengensis* (Wu et al., 1986). Subscribing to this new view, these scholars argued that *Sivapithecus lufengensis* represented the branch which evolved toward the australopithecines (humans) and the African great apes. The orang evolutionary line was confined to ancestors in Turkey and Pakistan as seen in *Sivapithecus meteai* and *S. indicus* respectively. Wu, Xu, and Lu held that the divergence of the orang line occurred before the late Miocene period around 12 to 10 million years ago, thus implying that a split of the African great apes and the humans occurred after that period. *Sivapithecus lufengensis* was eventually renamed *Lufengpithecus lufengensis* (Wu, 1987). Like the previous scholars, Pilbeam (1985) also eventually recognized that the humans shared a last common ancestor with the African great apes exclusively. If the orang line had already been distinct by 15 to 12 mya, insisted Pilbeam, then the human line departed from the African great apes somewhere between 10 to 5 mya in Africa. Pilbeam conceived this common ancestor to be as arboreal (if not more) as the chimpanzee, although it was not as well adapted to knuckle-walking nor as quadrupedal as the chimpanzee when on the ground. Neither was this ancestor as bipedal as the australopithecines. Furthermore, Pilbeam believed that this common ancestor resembled *Proconsul*, *Sivapithecus*, and *Ramapithecus* as much as it did *Australopithecus* and the chimpanzee, while it also differed from all of them.

Whereas Pilbeam (1985) refrained from explicitly appealing to any fossil discovery to support his new phylogenetic hypothesis, de Bonis, Koufos, and their colleagues turned to *Ouranopithecus* (*Graecopithecus*) for that matter (de Bonis and Koufos, 1994; de Bonis and Koufos, 1995; de Bonis et al., 1990). In their view, *Ouranopithecus* from Greece, which dates back to 10 or 9 mya, is exclusively ancestral to the australopithecines and the living humans. If true, this implied that the human line had departed from the African great apes not before the late Miocene period around 12 mya. For his part, however, Andrews (1992) saw in *Graecopithecus* (*Ouranopithecus*) a form not uniquely ancestral to the living humans but rather the last common ancestor to the humans, the chimpanzees and the gorillas dated back at 10 mya.[11] A number of other scholars like Martin (1986) and Barriel (1991) supported, on the basis of cladistic analyses, the phylogenetic hypothesis which derived humankind from a last common ancestor shared with the African great apes exclusively. These analyses, which always include the living hominoid species, also sometimes incorporated the fossil species as well.[12]

In a fourth phylogenetic hypothesis, it was believed that the human line is closely related not to the two African great apes but only to the chimpanzee, with the gorilla being the second closest living relative to humankind. Again, Pilbeam (1986, 1996) modified his view to become a proponent of this hypothesis. By so doing, Pilbeam's continually changing perspective on the question illustrates well a trend in paleoanthropology since the 1960s. This trend consisted in gradually establishing a close and unique proximity between humankind and the chimpanzee by first removing the orang-utan from such phylogenetic considerations, followed later by removal of the gorilla. In Pilbeam's latest view, the gorilla line departed first at least 8 million years ago, leaving the human and the chimpanzee lines to diverge from one another at least 5 mya.[13] Pilbeam (1996, 1997) emphasized more and more that the common ancestor to the humans and the chimpanzees was chimpanzee-like in several features: short-legged, long-armed, adapted to arm-swinging arboreal habits and quadrupedal climbing, and walking in the trees as well as on the ground. Pilbeam pointed out that the earliest hominids like *Ardipithecus ramidus* and *Australopithecus afarensis* presented precisely a number of such chimpanzee-like features.

Like Pilbeam, Begun (1994, 2003) held that the gorilla line had been distinct by 9 million years ago, placing the divergence time between the human and chimpanzee lines near 6 mya. The last common ancestor to humankind and the chimpanzee was described as being a knuckle-walking chimpanzee-like form also socially and behaviorally like the chimpanzees.[14]

Molecular studies. Although it has never been possible to definitely resolve the debates on humankind's place among the primates with the fossil record, it must be recognized that by 1965 the area of inquiry concerning this question had been substantially reduced when compared to the previous time periods. By that time, the field of paleoanthropology was perhaps entering its most difficult phase which consisted in choosing among several distinct phylogenetic hypotheses, most of which were not that far apart from each other. It is one thing to select among widely divergent phylogenetic hypotheses, quite another to eliminate close ones, especially when considering the inherent problem of the incompleteness of the fossil record.

It is in this context that a different source of information entered the debate on humankind's place among the primates, a source coming from the genes themselves. If the study of the phenotype (anatomy) of the living and the fossil forms could not resolve the thorny issues of similarities related either to a direct kinship or to parallel evolution, perhaps a more direct study of the genotype (genes) could do the trick? After all, it is only the genes which are passed on to the next generations. When applied to human evolution, this new approach came to be designated as "molecular anthropology" (Zuckerkandl, 1963). From that time on, a new dimension was added to the search for human origins (e.g., Goodman, 1996; Goodman and Cronin, 1982; Marks, 1996a, 1997; Sarich, 1983). If molecular anthropology has deep roots in the twentieth century through the studies of blood groups (serology), it was not until the 1960s that it finally created a genuine impact on paleoanthropology.

The conclusions reached by molecular anthropology in the 1960s and 1970s were more or less at variance with those of traditional anthropology which were based on the anatomy of the living and the fossil forms. It is a widespread belief today that a huge chasm separated molecular and traditional anthropology at the time (e.g., Gribbin and Cherfas, 1983; Lewin, 1987). Instead of clarifying the issues—the story goes—molecular anthropology only contributed to entertain a greater level of confusion. Is this belief entirely founded? Studies in molecular anthropology in the 1960s promoted that humankind was more closely related to the two African great apes than to any other living hominoid apes. Furthermore, it was argued that the divergence time of the human line from the last common ancestor shared with the African great apes occurred perhaps as late as the Pliocene period.

These two conclusions somewhat differed from those reached by numerous paleoanthropologists—though not all—who approached the question from comparative anatomy and/or the fossil record. This being said, the real divide at the time was not between molecular and traditional anthropology but rather between the scholars who promoted that the human line entirely avoided going through a hominoid ape phase from those who held that humankind had sprung from a more or less specialized hominoid ape form. Whereas the former argued that the human line had by the Oligocene period (or before) been on its own, the latter variably placed this divergence time in the Oligocene, the Miocene, or even the Pliocene period. When viewed from this perspective, it is clear that the tension between molecular and traditional anthropology has not been a profound one.

It is tempting here to entirely reverse the perspective. I surmise that the tension between molecular and traditional anthropology was possible only because the phylogenetic conclusions they independently reached were not that far apart from each other. After all, would a number of traditional anthropologists bother to energetically refute the hypotheses of the molecular anthropologists if they had believed them to be entirely indefensible, scientifically speaking? Probably not. It is not my intention here to minimize the tensions between these two research areas. The rise of molecular anthropology brought an entirely new scientific dimension within paleoanthropology: a different empirical basis, new conceptual and theoretical foundations, unknown methodological principles and technical manipulations. It is only natural that this would have created a number of problems of integration between molecular and traditional anthropology.

Yet, I would argue that the most striking feature of this so-called tension is not in their divergence of viewpoints but rather in their convergence toward a more restricted or better cirscumcribed area of inquiry within which the debates on humankind's place among the primates should be conducted. The downfall of a number of phylogenetic hypotheses during the 1935–1965 period saw the field of paleoanthropology clearly developing toward this more cirscumcribed area of inquiry. It seems that molecular and traditional anthropology were, after 1965, only competing to define the limits of these new boundaries on distinct scientific foundations; boundaries which were significantly overlapping in their respective views.

Although, in principle, the genotype is a more direct source of information about descent, the procedures for extracting this information are not straightforward (e.g., Goodman and Cronin, 1982; Lewin, 1997; Marks, 1994). Several regions of the genotype or the genome can be used in molecular analyses: proteins which are themselves under the direct control of the genes; the morphology of the chromosomes or the position of the genes placed on them; the sequence of the constituent elements of the genes themselves (DNA), etc. This molecular information is housed in distinct places in the cell: in the nucleus, in the mitochondria, or in the ribosome. Several techniques were used or developed since the 1960s to extract this genetic information: immunodiffusion, electrophoresis, restriction mapping, DNA hybridization, etc. With these, similarities and dissimilarities among living species are established. The more genetic similarities there are the more likely is a close phylogenetic proximity.

The utilization of large data sets often generates conflicting hypotheses which need to be resolved and eliminated on the basis of parsimony. The difficulty of the molecular studies resides in establishing a phylogenetic hypothesis which reflects the evolutionary history of the species being compared and not just that part of the genome being analyzed. Because the genome constitutes a huge data base, a significant portion of it must be analyzed to ensure the validity of the phylogenetic conclusions that are reached. It has been discovered that—not unlike the anatomical features—the evolutionary history of molecules is somewhat cloaked by the variation within the same species (polymorphism) as well as parallel evolution within and between species.

Regardless of a scientific process fraught with obstacles, nearly all of the phylogenetic hypotheses generated by molecular anthropology since the 1960s has established a close relationship between humankind and the two African great apes, putting the orang-utans in a more distant position. This would imply that some of the morphological similarities uniting the two African great apes (chimpanzee, gorilla) and the Asian great ape (orang) are either primitive features not amenable to a direct kinship or features that were developed independently by parallel evolution. How can this be explained? Why is nature apparently sending different signals when it comes to the evolution of morphological features and of the genome?

It was originally assumed in the Neo-Darwinian conception of evolution that morphological and genomic changes were essentially evolving hand in hand: Changes at the morphological level indicated that changes at the genome level had surely occurred, although not all genomic changes needed to be immediately expressed in the phenotype (the recessive traits), though they would surely do so eventually. In this conception of evolution, the phenotype and the genotype are believed to be fairly tightly related. This view was challenged when it was discovered that the genotype contained more variability than the phenotype could make use of.

It was suggested that a lot of genetic changes, such as the mutations in the proteins, had no impact on the morphological level for the simple reason that such genetic changes were playing the same role in the phenotype (e.g., Kimura, 1968, 1979; King and Jukes, 1969). In more technical terms, it was held that many evolutionary changes at the molecular level were selectively neutral or equivalent. It is on that basis that the Neutral Theory of Molecular Evolution was proposed.

This theory holds that many molecular changes are simply invisible to natural selection for it cannot directly act on the molecular changes that are not being expressed at the phenotypic level. If many such molecular changes are not constrained under the action of natural selection, then variability at this level is free to vary according to chance processes such as genetic drift. Whereas the Neo-Darwinians originally viewed the genotype and the phenotype as two distinct evolutionary levels which are fairly tightly related, the Neutral Theory of Molecular Evolution encouraged viewing these two levels as being largely uncoupled. If this latter conception is correct, it is easy to understand why nature is sending different signals when its comes to the morphological and the genomic evolution of humankind and its closest living relatives (e.g., King and Wilson, 1975). Indeed, evolution is apparently working differently at the two levels.

Molecular anthropology made two distinct contributions to the debate on humankind's place among the primates. It is remarkable that these were, from the outset, made in the 1960s. Later studies only confirmed the validity of the general conclusions reached through the exploitation of other methods and techniques, although they may have questioned the details of such conclusions. The first contribution of these studies was of taxonomic nature: The orang-utans and the gibbons should be excluded from the search of humankind's closest living relatives. Humankind's last common ancestor with the other living hominoids was with the two African great apes exclusively, the chimpanzee and the gorilla (Goodman, 1962a, 1962b, 1963; Klinger et al., 1963). Scholars devoted the subsequent years to debates on the precise nature of this relationship.

A number of them held that the actual resolving power of the molecular method made it impossible as yet to disentangle the exact relationship involving the humans, the chimpanzees, and the gorillas (e.g., Ferris et al., 1981; Goodman, 1975; Goodman and Moore, 1971; Goodman et al., 1984; Hoyer et al., 1972; Marks et al., 1988; Smouse and Li, 1987). However, some of these scholars and others were eventually confident enough to believe that one hypothesis was more likely than the others.

In one hypothesis, it was argued that the human line had departed from an ancestor shared in common with both the chimpanzee and the gorilla (e.g., Benveniste and Todaro, 1976; Brown et al., 1982; Chaline et al., 1991; Dutrillaux and Couturier, 1986; Lucotte and Lefebvre, 1981; Marks, 1995; Rogers, 1993; Stanyon and Chiarelli, 1982; Templeton, 1985). In a second hypothesis, it was held that humankind shares a last common ancestor with the gorilla exclusively (e.g., Miller, 1977). In a third hypothesis, the chimpanzee was seen as the closest and the exclusive relative of the living humans (e.g., Bailey et al., 1992; Caccone and Powell, 1989; Gonzalez et al., 1990; Goodman et al., 1998; Horai et al., 1992; Kim and Takenaka, 1996; Koop et al., 1989; Miyamoto et al., 1987; Ruvolo, 1994, 1997; Sibley and Ahlquist, 1984, 1987; Takahata and Satta, 1997; Yunis and Prakash, 1982).

The second contribution of molecular anthropology in the debate on humankind's place among the primates came from its use as a tool to establish the absolute time of separation of the human line from its nearest living relatives. Remember that in light of the Neutral Theory of Molecular Evolution, evolutionary changes (mutations) at this level are postulated to be largely driven by chance processes such as genetic drift. If such mutations are not disturbed by the selecting and eliminating action of natural selection—for these mutations are invisible or selectively neutral—then perhaps the pace at which these molecular changes are occurring is regular enough as to provide a "molecular clock".

The reasoning is as follows: As two species diverge from a common ancestor they will accumulate mutations at a similar and constant rate, so that the genetic differences observed in their living counterparts since their separation can be used to establish the time of that separation. From there, what is needed is to convert the amount of observed molecular change in absolute time by selecting an event already dated in the fossil record. This is called calibrating the molecular clock.

The application of the molecular clock in paleoanthropology established that humankind had departed quite late in the Cenozoic era (Tertiary and the Quaternary eras) from his closest living relatives. It was proposed at first that humankind shared a last common ancestor with the African great apes somewhere between 5 and 3.5 million years ago (Sarich, 1968; Sarich and Wilson, 1967). On that basis, Sarich (1970: 199) concluded that "I now feel that the body of protein evidence on the *Homo-Pan* relationship is sufficiently extensive so that one no longer has the option of considering a fossil specimen older than about 8 million years as a hominid *no matter what it looks like*" [not my italics]. Scholars devoted the subsequent years in an effort to bring more precision to this absolute divergence time. In addition to the technical and the empirical aspects, the estimation of an absolute date of divergence also depends on whether or not the rate of molecular evolution is constant or fluctuating, as well as on chosen dates taken from the fossil record to convert the amount of observed molecular change in time (calibrating the molecular clock).

Indeed, a number of scholars questioned the reliability of the molecular clock (e.g., Ayala, 1997; Goodman, 1996). For instance, it was argued that different proteins within the same species yielded different evolutionary rates; that animals with longer generational time have slower evolutionary rates; that more complex organisms also have slower evolutionary rates; that adaptive radiations are correlated, which accelerated evolutionary rates, etc. These varying rates might be, after all, indicative of a certain action of natural selection at the molecular level.

Perhaps expectedly, more molecular studies provided a whole range of dates for the departure of the human line from the other living primates. It is convenient here to regroup them in three sets of hypotheses. In the first set, it was believed that this speciation event should be placed not before 10 but no later than 15 million years ago (e.g., Benveniste and Todaro, 1976; Read, 1975). The second group of hypotheses placed this separation in later times, that is, between 10 and 5 mya (e.g., Bailey et al., 1992; Caccone and Powell, 1989; Gonzalez et al., 1990; Goodman et al., 1998; Li and Tanimura, 1987; Sibley and Ahlquist, 1984, 1987). In a third group of hypotheses, a later time still of divergence was proposed at 5 mya or earlier (e.g., Edelstein, 1987; Excoffier and Yang, 1999; Gonzalez et al., 1990; Hasegawa et al., 1984; Hasegawa et al., 1987; Horai et al., 1992; Sarich and Cronin, 1976; Takahata and Satta, 1997).

The rise of molecular anthropology within paleoanthropology deserves a few comments. The first is to note a historical trend which started in the 1960s among the molecular anthropologists: The uncertainty that surrounded the nature of the relationship between the humans, the chimpanzees, and the gorillas gradually gave way. It was replaced by a polarization between proponents of a common ancestor equally shared with the two African great apes and the proponents of an ancestry shared with a single African great ape only, the chimpanzee. Very few molecular anthropologists are now prepared to establish an exclusive relationship between the humans and the gorillas.

The second comment concerns the time frame. Only a limited number of molecular anthropologists have been ready to place the departure time of the human line from the other primates beyond 10 million years ago, that is, in the mid-Miocene period or before. Undoubtedly, the development of molecular anthropology since the 1960s genuinely contributed to cirscumcribe this area of inquiry in the debates on humankind's place among the primates. As the exchange of information between molecular and traditional anthropology is still ongoing, it is beyond our capability to prejudge its outcome. Suffice it to restate that their disagreements, when there are some, are anything but fundamental when looked at from a historical perspective. Molecular and traditional anthropology were both involved in further reducing the area of inquiry in the debates on humankind's place in nature after 1965, a process which had already gained considerable impetus during the 1935-1965 period. Considering that these two approaches to human evolution are based on distinct empirical and theoretical foundations, it is only natural that they would not agree perfectly on how to define precisely the new boundaries of this newly reduced area of inquiry.

The third comment raises the question of the nature of the impact of the Neutral Theory of Molecular Evolution on paleoanthropology. We have already seen that the Synthetic Theory of Evolution created an impact on the debates on human phylogeny in the 1950s and 1960s but only to the extent that it was applied within the constraints imposed by the state of the fossil record at the time (see Chapter 9). Because the field of paleoanthropology is not a by-product of specific evolutionary theories, it is imperative that the application of such theories to the question pertaining to human phylogeny be at least consistent with the latest empirical developments in that field. This is a minimal requirement without which any evolutionary theory would be judged irrelevant in human evolution.

This is precisely the case of the Neutral Theory of Molecular Evolution as seen by its twin applications in paleoanthropology: a close link between humankind and the two African great apes and a late divergence time situated between the mid-Miocene and the late-Pliocene period. These ideas were received in paleoanthropology only because they were hardly new for a number of traditional anthropologists (see Chapters 7 and 8). For instance, Gregory, Patterson, von Koenigswald, Washburn, and Weinert held in the 1950s or the early 1960s that the human line had departed quite late from the other primates, that is, during a period ranging from the late Miocene to the late Pliocene. Furthermore, Weinert clearly promoted in the early 1950s that the chimpanzee was humankind's closest living relative, whereas Weidenreich was tempted to believe in the mid-1940s that the gorilla might have occupied this position. For his part, Simpson insisted in the early 1960s that the two African great apes were humankind's closest living relatives. Although these views represented a minority stance among the traditional anthropologists at the time, it clearly shows that the fossil record could be consistent with the conclusions that were eventually reached by the molecular studies in the 1960s and after. If some traditional anthropologists prepared the way for the molecular anthropologists, the latter, in counterpart, eventually attracted some traditional anthropologists to their side. Since then, the developments of traditional and molecular anthropology have been more or less intertwined: The systematic and the temporal frameworks provided by the molecular studies could encourage a reassessment of the hominoid fossil record (polarity of character states, etc.), while the increasing density and quality of the hominid fossil record of the past few million years—especially at the australopithecine level—might influence the elaboration of a time frame in the molecular studies (calibration of the molecular clock).

SCENARIOS OF HOMINIZATION

The scenarios of hominization proposed during the 1965–2000 period were circumscribed within more restricted limits than during the pre-1965 period. This is not entirely surprising when considering that better circumscribed phylogenetic debates could only impose a number of restrictions on the scenarios. It is true that, by definition, scenarios are conjectural propositions concerned with the causes and the sequence of the hominization process. However, this does not mean that their credibility has not been improving through the years. To hold that many constituent elements of scenarios (stone tools, bipedality, freed hands, language, increased brain size, etc.) have repeatedly been used since they were first proposed in the nineteenth century (e.g., Stoczkowski, 1994 [2002]), is of little value to assess whether or not their scientific robustness has been increasing since. What is especially crucial in this matter is the quality of their empirical foundation.

In the second half of the nineteeth century, scenarios of hominization were exclusively based on inferences drawn from comparing living forms (comparative anatomy). It was assumed then that a close relationship between humankind and other living primates indicated that human features such as bipedality, a big brain, reduced canines, freed hands, manufacturing of tools, etc., were features which had arisen gradually in time through a mutually reinforcing process (see Chapter 2). In the first third of the twentieth century, scenarios were caught in the midst of profoundly divergent phylogenetic hypotheses which disputed whether or not humankind's early ancestors were more ape-like or human-like in conformation, were small- or large-brained creatures, and had been early or lately committed to a fully bipedal gait (see Chapter 4). One has to wait until the 1935–1965 period to see a final rejection of a relatively big-brained human-like ancestor that was already bipedal. Since then, the debates largely centered around a generalized or a specialized hominoid-like or prehominoid-like ancestor. The primate fossil recoveries, including the australopithecines, were significant enough at the time as to create a sensible impact on the elaboration of the scenarios of hominization (see Chapters 7 and 8). The post-1965 period saw a further reduction of the theoretical possibilities for the scenarios as the debates largely centered around a relatively recent hominoid-like ancestor leading to the living humans.

Not only were the taxonomic and the temporal ranges relevant for the hominization process dramatically reduced after 1965, but the quality of the fossil record for such ranges has increased subtantially—especially in the case of the early hominids—although the phylogenetic connection between humankind and the other living hominoid apes is still largely eluding us. Yet, it cannot be denied that the scientific robustness of the scenarios has improved since the inception of paleoanthropology, no matter how unsatisfactory it still is. Indeed, a number of key constituent elements of the scenarios are sufficiently documented today in the fossil record as to no longer need to be merely inferred from the living forms.

For instance, it is no longer debated whether bipedality arose before, simultaneously, or after the increase of the brain size and the use of stone tools. It is now clear that bipedality preceded the evolution of a larger brain. Furthermore, it seems that stone tools and a significant increase in brain size appeared more or less synchronically in the late Pliocene, thus still offering the possibility of a causal link for their development. Throughout the Pleistocene period, brain size continued to increase while stone-tool technologies improved. In fact, a number of elements traditionally and exclusively incorporated in the scenarios of hominization are now sufficiently known to be also part of standard phylogenetic analyses. For instance, the organization of fossil brains (endocasts) left enough tangible traces in the hominid fossil record to be useful in phylogenetic analyses (e.g., Falk, 1986a, 1988; Saban, 1983). No doubt, studies of phylogeny and scenario are somewhat converging toward each another under this improving empirical context.

In order to evaluate the robustness of the scenarios of hominization, the following analysis will break them down into a number of constituent elements in order to analyze them individually. These elements are: locomotion, manipulative skills, increased brain size, and articulate language. Although stone tools are very commonly used in the scenarios, the empirical quality of this cultural record is such that it will not be insisted upon here (e.g., Bordes, 1968, 1988; Clark, 1970; Gamble, 1986; Harris, 1983; M.D. Leakey, 1971; Movius, 1948; Pei and Zhang, 1985; Schick and Toth, 1993; Tixier et al., 1980). When it is stated here that recent scenarios are more robustly built than in the past, it is not meant that each constituent element is fully and unequivocally grounded in a firm empirical basis. Rather, it is argued that there is enough empirical foundation about them so as to generate genuine interpretative debates. This was not often the case before.

The rise of bipedalism has become a multifaceted question now divided into a number of somewhat distinct debates along the ape-human evolutionary spectrum, each with its own empirical basis and investigating approaches. The interest for bipedality in scenario building has always been its assumed central position in either instigating the hominization process or accompanying the other elements in this process. Only a fully bipedal gait—the argument goes—can liberate the hands permanently so that they can be used for tool using and toolmaking, and thus contribute to increasing the brain size, etc. The debate on the cause of the rise of bipedalism is still very much a conjectural one. This is not surprising in the context of a poor fossil record directly relevant for this precise evolutionary phase (e.g., Langdon, 1985; McHenry and Temerin, 1979). For that reason, this debate largely rests on behavioral inferences extrapolated from both the living forms and the fossil remains before and after the very rise of bipedalism. To this are added speculations about the selective forces which could have instigated this new mode of locomotion.

Among the many causes proposed to explain this rise were the following: for defense, by permitting either the carrying and throwing of stones or the using of thorn branches (e.g., Fifer, 1987; Kelly, 2001; Kortlandt, 1980; Washburn, 1968); for protection, by offering the possibility of detecting predators far away over tall grasses (e.g., Ravey, 1978); as a feeding behavior, since this terrestrial posture is useful for reaching the lower tree branches and the small bushes or as a consequence of a pre-adaptation which consisted in squatting for small foodstuffs on the ground (e.g., Hunt, 1994; Jolly, 1970; Rose, 1976; Wrangham, 1980); for reducing the energy cost of traveling over long distances with scant resources (e.g., Foley and Elton, 1998; Isbell and Young, 1996); for increasing the energy input by permitting the carrying of food (e.g., Lovejoy, 1981); for display, in an attempt to scare away predators or competitors (e.g., Jablonski and Chaplin, 1993; Wescott, 1967).

Another debate on bipedalism investigated not the cause of its rise but rather the immediate morphological and behavioral state which permitted its development. Although the fossil record relevant to settle this question was frankly scarce, as already mentioned, its quest was less conjectural than the previous debate merely because it was not directly involved with speculations over causes and selective forces. This debate was therefore more descriptive in nature. Many distinct anatomical parts were studied to reconstuct this ancient morphological and behavioral state. After all, the clues to an animal's locomotion could be stamped all over its body, including the foot, the ankle, the knee, the pelvis, the shoulder, the elbow, the wrist, and the hand.

Although there are many subtleties in the scholars's viewpoints, it is useful to see them as proponents of two distinct hypotheses. In a first hypothesis, it was promoted that bipedalism directly developed out of some sort of terrestrial quadrupedal adaptation such as knuckle-walking or fist-walking (e.g., Begun, 1994, 2003; Corruccini, 1978; Corruccini and McHenry, 2001; Gebo, 1992, 1996; Marzke, 1971; Richmond and Strait, 2000, 2001; Washburn, 1968, 1971). This proposed adaptation does not preclude the ability to climb in the trees. In a second hypothesis, it was argued that bipedalism directly developed out of climbing or brachiating abilities in the trees, thus avoiding a formal adaptation to terrestrial quadrupedalism (e.g., Fleagle et al., 1981; Oxnard, 1969, 1975; Stern, 1975; Stern and Susman, 1981; Tuttle, 1969, 1974, 1975, 1981, 1994). This view does not preclude the possibility of covering some distances on the ground.

In yet another debate concerned with bipedalism, the locomotor system of the early hominids was directly investigated (e.g., Stern, 2000; Ward, 2002). In contradistinction to the previous two debates, this one could rely on postcranial fossil remains as a crucial additional source of information. However, this direct and rapidly improving source of information was insufficient to definitely settle the question. Several reasons may explain this. Although the relationship between a bony structure (form) and its function is a relatively tight one, it is not necessarily an absolute one. A body structure could potentially generate several distinct functions, although imperfectly. Also, as tissues such as muscles and ligaments are not preserved during the fossilization process, this can only entertain a level of uncertainty in the relationship between a fossilized form and its function. Furthermore, if the living forms are of great utility in the reconstruction of ancient behaviors this does not mean that the mode of locomotion of these ancient creatures was conforming perfectly with any living counterpart. Lastly, primitive morphological traits inherited from an ancestor are sometimes preserved in attenuated form without necessarily implying that they are indicative of a behavior that is still in use.

Keeping these limitations in mind, it cannot be denied that the improved empirical condition for the inquiry of the locomotion of the early hominids has powerfully contributed to the robustness of the proposed viewpoints. For instance, the bipedal activities of the early hominids are no longer questioned.[15] What is being debated instead is the extent of their bipedalism: Were the early hominids exclusively and fully bipedal or were they also simultaneously exploiting other modes of locomotion such as tree-climbing? There were two empirical aspects to this debate. The first one concerned the interpretation of the preserved footprints in Tanzania dated to about 3.5 million years ago. Many scholars believed them to clearly indicate a fully bipedal gait identical to, or strongly approaching, that of the living humans (e.g., Day and Wickens, 1980; Leakey and Hay, 1979; Tuttle, 1985; White, 1980; White and Suwa, 1987). However, this view was not unanimously shared as other scholars held that the type of bipedality observed in these prints differed in nature from that of the living humans (e.g., Deloison, 1992; Stern and Susman, 1983; Susman et al., 1984). The identity of the creatures who left their footprints remains uncertain.

The second empirical aspect to this debate involved the interpretation of the fossil remains themselves. This debate was conducted over fossilized anatomical parts which covered almost the entire postcranial body. This is a sure sign of the rapidly improving quality of the fossil record at the early hominid level. It is convenient to sort the scholars' viewpoints into two sets of distinct hypotheses. In one of them, it was held that whether or not all the early hominid forms shared the exact same locomotor system, it is clear that at least some of them were not perfectly efficient bipedal creatures as they kept a number of adaptations for tree climbing (e.g., Ashton, 1981; Bérillon, 2000; Berge, 1991; Clarke and Tobias, 1995; Deloison, 1995; Duncan et al., 1994; Lewis, 1989; Oxnard, 1975; Robinson, 1972; Senut, 1996; Senut et al., 2001; Stern and Susman, 1983; Susman et al., 1984; Tuttle, 1981). In another hypothesis, however, it was held that the early hominids were perfectly efficient bipeds and long-adapted to this exclusive mode of locomotion (e.g., Johanson and Edey, 1981; Latimer, 1991; Latimer and Lovejoy, 1987, 1989; Le Gros Clark, 1967; Lovejoy, 1975, 1988; Lovejoy et al., 1973). As this debate still continues, there is little doubt that more light will come from the recent fossil discoveries (e.g., Asfaw et al., 1999; Leakey et al., 1995; Senut et al., 2001; Ward et al., 2001; White et al., 1993).

The possibility that some or all australopithecine species might not be fully efficient bipedal creatures gave rise to a debate which also questioned the locomotor habit of the earliest representatives of the genus *Homo*. Were *Homo habilis* and *Homo rudolfensis* themselves fully adapted to bipedality? Recent discoveries may show that these creatures possessed limb proportions similar to the other early hominids, that is, short legs relative to long arms (e.g., Johanson et al., 1987; McHenry and Coffing, 2000). This could raise the possibility that a truly modern body proportion among the hominids—and thus a fully efficient bipedal gait—may have arisen only later with *Homo erectus* and/or *Homo ergaster* (e.g., Lewis, 1989; Richmond et al., 2002; Stern, 2000; Susman and Stern, 1982; Susman et al., 1984; Walker and Shipman, 1997). As postcranial fossil remains of the earliest *Homo* are scarce, this debate is not likely to be resolved for some time.

Leaving the debates on the rise of bipedalism behind, let us turn to manipulative skills. The interest of the manipulative skills in the scenarios of hominization is that although bipedality contributes to free the hands—so the argument goes—these must be skillful enough to be able to achieve complex and subtle operations in the preparation of stone tools, being either assisted in this task by a greater brain capacity or directly contributing to the increase of such a brain size (e.g., Piveteau, 1991). But beyond such speculations, scholars have been able to tackle head-on the apparently difficult question of determining the manual dexterity of the known fossil hand bones of the early hominids. The task consisted in inferring the functional capabilities or potentialities of these ancient hand bones with the help of living models (i.e., humans and other primates).

This debate revolved around two main alternatives. On the one hand, it was promoted that probably not all the early hominid forms had enough manual dexterity to make stone tools, whether it was the robust australopithecines such as *Paranthropus* (e.g., Robinson, 1972) or the most primitive australopithecines such as *Australopithecus afarensis* (e.g., Sussman, 1994, 1998). On the other hand, it was held that all the known early hominid forms probably had the potential manual dexterity to produce stone tools, although they were not necessarily stone-tool makers themselves nor had the full manual dexterity of the living humans (e.g., Leakey et al., 1964; Le Gros Clark, 1967; Marzke, 1983, 1997; Napier, 1962; Ricklan, 1987; Tuttle, 1981). Although not agreed on this question, all the scholars apparently recognized that at least some early hominid forms had the potential manual dexterity to make rudimentary stone tools.

Another constituent element commonly exploited in the scenarios of hominization is an increased brain size. The interest of this feature in the scenarios is that dexterous hands—it is supposed—imperatively need sufficient brain power to perform complex manipulative tasks such as making stone tools. Many distinctive evolutionary innovations were proposed as prime movers to a brain size increase: tools, hunting, gathering, social cooperation, food sharing, language, warfare, heat stress, etc. (e.g., Falk, 1980; Isaac, 1983). But in addition to these conjectures, the quest to understand the hominid trend toward a bigger brain could also rely on a more factual basis. Two main issues kept recurring in hominid paleoneurology.

The first one concerned the actual brain size of the main hominid taxa. It consisted in measuring the brain volume from the fossil skulls themselves. Interestingly, there was no profound disagreement on this question. All the scholars recognized that the early hominids had brain sizes that approached the living great ape condition while a significant increase occurred at the turn of the Plio-Pleistocene period, only to continue during a substantial portion of the Pleistocene until it reached its actual size, which is about three times that of the great apes (e.g., Begun and Walkey, 1993; Conroy et al., 1990, 1998; Falk, 1983a, 1985; Holloway, 1970; 1973, 1981a, 1981b; Tobias, 1971, 1981, 1987). However, scholars were not agreed about whether or not this brain increase has been a gradual process or a punctuated one (e.g., Blumenberg, 1983; Cronin et al., 1981; Falk, 1987; Godfrey and Jacobs, 1981; Hofman, 1983).

The second issue raised in hominid paleoneurology concerned not the size but the structural organization of the brain itself. Because the brain leaves an imprint inside a skull, it is possible to detect its superficial organization through artificial or natural endocasts. On that basis, it has been promoted that regardless of the small brain size of the early hominids, their brain organization was already human-like in configuration. This implied that a reorganization of the brain had preceded in geological time its size increase in human evolution (e.g., Holloway, 1972, 1974, 1981c, 1983, 1984, 1985, 1988; Holloway and De La Coste-Lareymondie, 1982; Holloway and Kimbel, 1986). Contesting this interpretation, other scholars believed that the brain organization of the early hominids was more ape-like than human-like in conformation, both implying that a brain increase preceded in time its reorganization while a new level of organization was only attained later with the rise of the genus *Homo* (e.g., Falk, 1983a, 1983b, 1985, 1986b, 1989; Falk et al., 1989; Tobias, 1987, 1994, 1998). Whatever their position in this debate, scholars have been speculating on the meaning of such a brain organization for the behavioral repertoire of the hominids. Surely, it cannot be denied that the evolutionary trend of an enlarging brain in human evolution is now a relatively well-documented phenomenon.

The last constituent element commonly used in the scenarios of hominization reviewed here is articulate language. The interest of this feature in the scenarios, it seems, is that it gives a large-brained species a means to rapidly and effectively exchange information between its members, thus providing this species with a powerful edge for adaptation and survival. In comparison to features such as bipedalism, manipulative skills, and brain size, articulate language is certainly the most conjectural one, being more remotely related to an empirical basis (e.g., Delisle, 2002). For instance, the cause of the rise of the language faculty itself is certainly a most difficult question to resolve. Some scholars held that this faculty gradually arose from preexisting and rudimentary structures and behaviors shared in common with other primates under the action of positively reinforcing selective pressures (e.g., Deacon, 1997; Lieberman, 1984, 1991; Pinker, 1994; Pinker and Bloom, 1990). Yet, other scholars believed that this faculty is too complex to have arisen through a direct selection process and suggested instead that it arose as a sort of by-product—an emergent property—of other structures and behaviors which were themselves selectively advantageous (e.g., Chomsky, 1972, 1980, 1982, 1988, 1990; Piattelli-Palmarini, 1989). This question is unlikely to be resolved any time soon. Yet, such difficulties did not discourage scholars from attempting to throw an indirect light on various components related to language during the hominization process by looking for empirical clues.

The main debate on the rise of articulated language centered on whether or not this occurred in the early phase of the genus *Homo* or only at a later evolutionary phase. Only two sources of information used in this debate will be insisted upon here. First, scholars investigated the vocal tract of the hominids in order to establish if this anatomical part was appropriate for a fully articulated language. This was done either by reconstructing the vocal tract from the base of the fossil skulls or by determining the shape and place of the fossil hyoid bone in the neck. On that basis, it was held that the vocal tract was transformed throughout the Pleistocene period only to reach its actual sound capabilities quite late. Indeed, it was argued that while the australopithecines could not talk and the early representatives of *Homo* probably could, the Neandertals certainly did so but without all the vocal capabilities offered by a modern vocal tract (e.g., Laitman and Reidenberg, 1988; Lieberman, 1994, 1995, 1998; Lieberman and Crelin, 1971; Lieberman et al., 1972). This viewpoint was criticized as far as the Neandertals were concerned, for it was argued that the vocal tract of the Neandertals was able to produce a range of sounds similar to that seen in the modern humans (e.g., Arensburg et al., 1990; Falk, 1975). Another source of information in this debate explored the structural organization of the fossil brains themselves (endocasts). On this empirical basis, a number of scholars promoted that a fully modern articulated language had appeared rather late in the Pleistocene period (e.g., Lieberman, 1985; Saban, 1993). In opposition to this view, other scholars insisted that articulated language arose at a much earlier time, probably with the rise of the genus *Homo* (e.g., Eccles, 1989; Falk, 1983a; Tobias, 1980a, 1987, 1998; Wilkins and Wakefield, 1995). Some proponents of an early rise of the articulated language even wondered if some australopithecine forms such as *Australopithecus africanus* might not have already been endowed with such a faculty, albeit perhaps in an attenuated form. Irrespective of the scholars' viewpoints in this debate, it must be appreciated that the very difficult question of articulated language in human evolution is not entirely devoid of an empirical basis.

What can be concluded of the quest to establish scenarios of hominization during the 1965–2000 period? It is pretty clear that each of the four features reviewed here finds some direct connections with an empirical reality in the fossil record. This empirical basis may not be strong enough as to prevent important debates about their expression or meaning, but it is no longer true that scenarios are merely conjectural explanations that are devoid of scientific constraints. Indeed, the framework within which the scenarios have been elaborated is getting narrower as the field of paleoanthropology matures. Of course, to have individual constituent elements more strongly grounded in empirical bases contributes little to the robustness of their causal connections that might or might not bind them. After all, scenarios of hominization are not based on isolated elements but rather focus on their causal relationships. Only causal explanations can satisfactorily explain the dynamic and sequential anatomical and behavioral transformations observed or postulated during the hominization process. Although the evolutionary causes and mechanisms at the heart of the scenarios of hominization may never find appropriate resolutions, as far as their robustness is concerned, it cannot be denied that the two levels of inquiry respectively concerned with scenario building and phylogenetic analyses had reached in the post-1965 period an unprecedented level of empirical convergence.

THE PLACE OF THE AUSTRALOPITHECINES

The research area concerned with the australopithecines, or the early hominids, has been a remarkably dynamic one during the 1965–2000 period (e.g., Aiello and Andrews, 2000; White, 2002). After an initial period of simplification and rationalization of the australopithecine forms in the 1950s and the early 1960s that led to the widely accepted distinction between the gracile and the robust australopithecines, the post-1965 period has been very much one of evaluation and assessment of an outstanding number of new African fossil discoveries that may or may not be related to the living humans. Although it cannot be ruled out that the *Homo* line arose outside of Africa (e.g., von Koenigswald, 1973; Campbell and Bernor, 1976; Franzen, 1985; Sartono, 1991), the discoveries of the past decades considerably bolstered the case of Africa as humankind's birthplace (e.g., Larick and Ciochon, 1996; Tattersall, 1997; Wood and Turner, 1995). This being said, it should not be forgotten that intensive research in Africa rather than in Asia may have contributed to introduce an empirical bias in favor of the former.

The recent African recoveries contributed to extending the geographical range of the early hominids by covering also Central Africa as well as expanding the time horizon to include the period between 6 and 1 million years ago. Among the most important fossil discoveries were: *Australopithecus afarensis* (Johanson et al., 1978; Johanson et al., 1982; White et al., 1993; Kimbel et al., 1994); *Australopithecus (aethiopicus) boisei* (Walker et al., 1986; Grine, 1988); *Ardipithecus* (White et al., 1994, 1995; Haile-Selassie, 2001); *Australopithecus anamensis* (Leakey et al., 1995); *Australopithecus bahrelghazali* (Brunet et al., 1995, 1996); *Australopithecus garhi* (Asfaw et al., 1999); *Kenyanthropus* (Leakey et al., 2001); *Orrorin* (Senut et al., 2001); and *Sahelanthropus* (Brunet et al., 2002).

These early hominid recoveries gradually introduced an element of complexity in the task of establishing their phylogenetic relationships. Indeed, it was found that the phylogeny of the australopithecines was not a simple one but rather a ramified one. It was increasingly recognized in the 1980s and the 1990s that two if not three distinct hominid species had to have lived in contemporaneity in each time period. This made clear that parallel evolution—the independent rise of similar features in two or more lineages not directly related—has not been uncommon among the early hominids. On this view, phylogenetic inferences are anything but straightforward as scholars must work their way through nature's mixed signals: similarities caused by descent or caused by parallel evolution (e.g., Grine, 1988; Kimbel et al., 1997; Suwa et al., 1996)?

Another factor which contributed to complicate the debate on the early hominids was the uncertainty which surrounded the earliest phase of the evolution of the genus *Homo* around 2 million years ago. Gradually in the 1970s and early 1980s, most scholars came to recognize that *Homo habilis* constituted the stock from which the living humans had sprung, a stock which may or may not have directly evolved from a known australopithecine. The taxonomic debate on whether or not the fossil sample called *Homo habilis* properly represented a single species was reactivated in the late 1980s and the 1990s (e.g., Dunsworth and Walker, 2002; Kramer et al., 1995; Groves, 1989; Lieberman et al., 1988, 1996; Miller, 1991, 2000; Prat, 1997; Rightmire, 1993; Stringer, 1986; Tattersall and Schwartz, 2000; Tobias, 1991; Wood, 1991, 2000). This was largely instigated by more fossil discoveries and new methods such as cladistics. This contributed to entertain a level of uncertainty regarding the exact phylogenetic connection between the earliest representatives of the genus *Homo* and the other early hominids.

As surprising as it seems, the research area relevant to establish the place of the australopithecines during the 1965–2000 period was further circumscribed when compared to the pre-1965 period. This is true even though there were several factors which introduced a new level of uncertainty. The recognition of a more ramified phylogeny of the australopithecines had only a limited impact on the debate concerned with the rise of the human line from the australopithecines or outside of them. Scholars were already divided in the 1935–1965 period on whether or not any of the known australopithecine remains were directly ancestral to the living humans (see Chapter 8). This debate continued during the 1965–2000 period but with two important differences.

First, any notion of a pre-Miocene rise of the australopithecines was eventually completely abandoned. Remember that Schultz (1953) and Genet-Varcin (1969) once held that the australopithecines had departed from the stem leading to the living humans during the Oligocene period. Now, this event was placed by these two scholars in the late Miocene or during the Pliocene period. This contributed to reducing the time frame within which this debate was taking place. Second, the proponents of the view that the known australopithecines are not directly ancestral to the living humans were, after 1965, less numerous in proposing a distant relationship between the known australopithecines and the human line. This contributed to reinforcing the phylogenetic proximity between the australopithecines and *Homo*, thus further reducing the theoretical possibilities defensible in the debate about the rise of the human line.

The reader should be warned that it will not be possible here to fully analyze the impact of the early hominid discoveries made in the 1965–2000 period on the field of paleoanthropology, as many of them were made in the past few years. Perhaps another decade will be needed before a clearer picture starts to emerge. What was, until recently, a very sketchy fossil record in Africa, especially between 14 and 4 million years ago (e.g., Hill and Ward, 1988), is now in the process of being filled in, although slowly.

Not from the known australopithecines. In the 1965–2000 period, a number of scholars continued to hold that the australopithecines were not directly ancestral to humankind. Although it was promoted that the australopithecines constituted an extinct side branch of the hominid family tree, it was nonetheless held that they threw much light on humankind's direct ancestor by indicating the presence of an ancestor shared in common between the former and the latter. Perhaps unsurprisingly, proponents of this viewpoint placed the rise of the human line at a time which is older than the other scholars, that is, between 10 and 4 million years ago. This timespan was consistent with the date proposed by most studies based on the molecular clock.

There were two different brands of phylogenetic hypotheses that excluded the known australopithecines from a direct ancestral position to the living humans. A first brand insisted on a relationship which was not too close. This is especially true of Oxnard's view, which established that the phylogenetic proximity between the humans and the australopithecines was about equidistant to that seen between the humans and the African great apes. Indeed, Oxnard (1985, 1987) held that the australopithecines could not be ancestral to the living humans because of their small brains, marked sexual dimorphism, and because their mode of locomotion was a compromise between tree climbing and a nonhuman type of bipedality. Oxnard conceived a hypothetical common ancestor around 10 mya that simultaneously gave rise to at least four main distinct evolutionary lines: the chimpanzee-gorilla line; the gracile australopithecine line; the robust australopithecine line, and the human line. It was believed that *Ramapithecus* was exclusively related to the human line, being near the base of this lineage.[16] Oxnard predicted that the earliest *Homo* forms would eventually be found as early as perhaps 5 million years ago.

For her part, Genet-Varcin (1978, 1979) held that the australopithecines were more closely related to the human line than to any other living or extinct evolutionary lines. Yet, she kept a certain distance between the known australopithecines and the human line. Genet-Varcin denied that the living humans ever went through an arboreal and hominoid ape evolutionary phase. She held that by avoiding this specialized phase, humankind's ancestors directly went from a quadrupedal locomotion to a bipedal one, which permitted the retention of primitive features such as a nonprojecting face and small frontal teeth. The australopithecines represented a somewhat specialized branch of the generalized humanoid radiation which shared a common ancestor with the human line in the mid-Pliocene period, perhaps some 4 mya.[17] According to Genet-Varcin, this assumed common ancestor is still entirely eluding us.

In a second brand of phylogenetic hypotheses excluding the known australopithecines from the human line, the link between the latter and the former was believed to be neither too remote nor entirely elusive. This is largely explained by the fact that a number of early hominid fossil remains sometimes attributed to the australopithecines (especially *Australopithecus afarensis*) were thought by these scholars to represent in reality an early portion of the human line, if not squarely an early *Homo* member itself. For instance, Olson (1981, 1985) analyzed the cranial remains of the so-called australopithecines and concluded that this entire fossil sample should be divided in two main lineages. Olson would not recognize in *Australopithecus afarensis*, dated between 4 and 3 million years ago, an ancestral form common to all the later hominids. Instead, he split this species into two new species: *Paranthropus africanus* which subsequently gave rise to the other australopithecines and *Homo aethiopicus* which was exclusively ancestral to the living humans. It was believed that the features shared in common between *Paranthropus africanus* and *Homo aethiopicus* indicated that they were bound by a very recent common ancestor some 5 or 4 mya. In light of this reevaluation, Olson also removed the so-called species *Australopithecus africanus* from among the australopithecines and placed it in the *Homo* lineage as *Homo africanus*, an assumed direct genealogical link between *H. aethiopicus* and *H. erectus*.[18]

Not unlike Olson, Ferguson (1983, 1984, 1986, 1987, 1989) divided the fossil population called *Australopithecus afarensis* in several distinct species: One such species was believed not to be a hominid at all but rather a generalized ape affiliated to the dryopithecines (*Praeanthropus*); a second species was associated with *Australopithecus africanus*; and a third species was not to be an australopithecine but instead an unspecialized early member of *Homo* called *Homo antiquus*, that is, a pre-*habilis* form ancestral to the living humans. Ferguson postulated the existence of an unspecialized hypothetical proto-hominid common ancestor which split in two distinct lineages, one evolving towards specialized teeth (*Australopithecus*) while the other largely retained the generalized ancestral condition (*Homo*). On this view, *Australopithecus africanus* is not ancestral to the living humans.

For her part, Senut (1996, 2001) excluded the australopithecines from human ancestry not on dental and cranial features but on postcranial ones only. She promoted that the early hominids were probably already committed to two different modes of locomotion: an exclusively bipedal mode and a dual mode combining bipedalism and climbing. All the hominid fossils dated between 4.5 and 3 million years ago (sometimes attributed to *Australopithecus afarensis* and *A. anamensis*) were regrouped in two distinct genera: *Australopithecus* and *Praeanthropus*. A common ancestor to these two genera was postulated at 6 or 5 mya. Only the exclusively bipedal *Praeanthropus* form was believed to be directly ancestral to *Homo* and the living humans. Soon, Senut placed the new find called *Orrorin* dated at 6 mya in a uniquely direct ancestral position to *Praeanthropus*, thus pushing further in the past the postulated common ancestor to the living humans and the known australopithecines to somewhere between 8 or 7 million years ago (Senut et al., 2001). *Orrorin* was presented as a fully bipedal chimpanzee-like form that retained abilities for climbing.[19]

A number of the scholars who once clearly promoted that the human line avoided going through an australopithecine phase eventually wavered. For instance, Richard Leakey (1976; 1981, Leakey and Lewin, 1977) once insisted that there were at least three distinct hominid evolutionary lines living in contemporaneity in Africa around 3 million years ago: *Homo habilis*, *Australopithecus africanus*, and *A. boisei*. At the time, Leakey would not derive the human line (*Homo*) from the australopithecines, as he believed that this advanced evolutionary line could be pushed further back in time as seen perhaps in some hominid remains at Hadar (Ethiopia) and Olduvai (Tanzania). It was held that a bipedal and ape-like creature not unlike

Ramapithecus was the common ancestor to all these distinct hominid lineages, which had departed from one another some 6 or 5 mya.[20] Several years later, however, Leakey was anything but explicit about the notion that the *Homo* line was not derived from an australopithecine stock (Leakey, 1989; Leakey and Lewin, 1992).[21]

More clearly than Leakey, Coppens changed his mind about the place of the australopithecines in human evolution. At first, Coppens (1981, 1983a, 1983b) would not derive the living humans from the known australopithecine remains. He conceived the early hominids as an adaptive radiation composed of at least three distinct evolutionary lines: pre-*Australopithecus* (*Australopithecus afarensis*), *Australopithecus* (*A. africanus, A. robustus, A. boisei*), and *Homo*. Coppens argued that the *Homo* line had sprung from an unknown common ancestor shared with the other two evolutionary lines somewhere between 5 and 4 million years ago. The *Homo* line is explicitly derived from a postulated and undiscovered *Australopithecus* stock which, itself, evolved from an undiscovered Pre-*Australopithecus* stock. The earliest representatives of the *Homo* line (Kanapoi, East Turkana, Omo, Hadar) were described as being almost fully bipedal creatures, with larger brains, fairly flat faces, and an omnivorous diet.[22] Several years later, however, Coppens (1994) made clear that he now believed that the *Homo* line had sprung directly from the *Australopithecus* line around 3 mya.[23]

Up from the australopithecines. While the number of scholars who did not derive the living humans from the australopithecines continued to decline during the 1965–2000 period—a historical trend which started in the late 1930s—those who did promote that humankind had indeed sprung from within the australopithecine radiation were facing an empirical situation that was becoming more complex. We have seen in Chapter 8 that the 1950s and the 1960s saw a trend among a number of scholars to place more and more of the known australopithecine fossils at the base of the human line. This movement reached a peak when Arambourg (1961), Tobias (1967), and Brace (1967), from different perspectives, conceived that all the australopithecines could have genetically contributed in one way or another to the rise of the living humans.[24] One version of this idea—the one of Brace (1967)—continued to be promoted in the late 1960s and the 1970s by Wolpoff (1968, 1971, 1973) under the name of the "single-species hypothesis". Wolpoff held that, morphologically speaking, there was no solid basis to support a specific distinction between the gracile and the robust australopithecines, since the variations were of an intraspecific nature only. All the known australopithecines were thus placed at the very base of the human line.

However, as possible instances of cohabitation of widely divergent hominid morphological types multiplied (e.g., Leakey and Walker, 1976), it became much more difficult to promote that there existed only a single species at each time level. Turning their back on this hypothesis, Brace and Wolpoff could no longer propose that all the known australopithecines were ancestral to the living humans. In this new scheme, Brace (1979, 1991) derived the living humans from *Australopithecus africanus* between 3 and 2 million years ago, putting all the robust australopithecines on an extinct side branch which directly sprang from the earlier lineage *Australopithecus afarensis*, a form that Brace thought might not necessarily be specifically distinct from *A. africanus*.[25] Similarly, Wolpoff (1980, 1999) derived the living humans from *Australopithecus africanus*, but insisted that this form was characterized by many robust features as it also gave rise to extinct robust australopithecines such as *A. robustus* and *A. boisei*.[26]

A majority of scholars in the 1965–2000 period always maintained that there was more than one australopithecine species at each time level. Therefore, they had to decide which australopithecine species was directly ancestral to the living humans. Regardless of the numerous recoveries of early hominids in the post-1965 period—especially during the 1990s—the debate largely revolved around finding such a direct ancestor among the so-called gracile australopithecines dated between 4 and 2 million years ago: *Australopithecus afarensis, A. africanus*, or *A. garhi.* This timespan—which was consistent with most molecular studies—contrasted from the one proposed by the scholars who held that the human line arose between 10 and 4 mya by avoiding going through a known australopithecine phase of evolution. However, the obvious impact of the numerous fossil discoveries made during the 1965–2000 period was to create a climate of instability in the precise identification of humankind's last ancestor among the gracile australopithecines. As will be seen, scholars often changed their mind.

Let us consider first the scholars who were, at one time or another, proponents of the ancestral position of *Australopithecus afarensis*. At first, Johanson, White, Kimbel, and Rak saw in *A. afarensis* of East Africa dated between 4 and 3 million years ago a common ancestor to both the living humans and the later robust australopithecines (Johanson and White, 1979; White et al., 1981; Kimbel et al., 1984; Rak, 1983, 1985a, 1985b). In their view, the younger and less primitive South African gracile form *A. africanus* was already too committed in the direction of the robust australopithecines to be ancestral to the living humans.[27] By the mid-1980s, the common view of these scholars started to erode.[28] For instance, Kimbel (1986) now considered that *A. africanus* could not necessarily be excluded from being the last common ancestor to the living humans and the robust australopithecines, in which case *A. afarensis* would be removed from occupying this direct ancestral position. For his part, Johanson (1985) continued to hold for some time to his original hypothesis, although he eventually became more nebulous about the exact relationship between *A. afarensis* and the later hominids (e.g., Johanson, 1996a, 1996b).[29] Similarly, Rak was anything but explicit about the nature of the relationship between *A. afarensis* and the genus *Homo*, a cautious attitude now also shared by Kimbel (e.g., Kimbel et al., 1994, 1997). After an apparent period of uncertainty, White eventually surmised that the newly discovered gracile form called *Australopithecus garhi* dated around 2.5 million years ago may turn out to be the direct and exclusive ancestor of the *Homo* line, a new form which was probably derived from *A. afarensis* (e.g., Asfaw et al., 1999).

While a number of scholars were retreating from a direct relationship between *A. afarensis* and the genus *Homo*, others were moving in the opposite direction.

For instance, Grine (1993) once argued that the discovery of the Black Skull in the mid-1980s (*Australopithecus [Paranthropus] aethiopicus*) showed a strong phylogenetic link between *A. afarensis* and the later robust australopithecines, thus determining that the similarities between *A. africanus* and the robust australopithecines were merely related to parallel evolution and not to common descent. It was postulated that a form close in morphology to *A. africanus* (after having evolved from *A. afarensis*) gave rise to the *Homo* line.[30] Not many years later, however, Grine joined Strait and Moniz in a reanalysis of early hominid phylogeny. Unable to present a definitive viewpoint, they wavered between two alternatives. One hypothesis derived the living humans and the robust australopithecines from a hypothetical form which was itself evolved out of *A. africanus*, this latter form being directly evolved from *A. afarensis*. It was argued that this *A. africanus*-like hypothetical ancestor may or may not be specifically distinct from *A. africanus*. The other hypothesis postulated that a hypothetical form which directly derived from *A. afarensis* was ancestral to both *A. africanus* and all the other hominids (*Homo* and the robust australopithecines). This hypothetical form which was also described to be *A. africanus*-like in conformation was believed to present many features in common with *A. afarensis*. These two hypotheses implied that the genus *Homo* appeared between 3 and 2.5 million years ago.[31]

Like Grine, Wood (1985) was at first inclined to derive humankind directly from *A. africanus*. More clearly than Grine, however, Wood later gave up on this idea. Wood (1991, 1992, 1996) now made clear that he believed that *A. africanus* was too specialized to be ancestral to *Homo*.[32] Apparently, studies of early African *Homo* fossils powerfully contributed to his reassessment. The living humans were now directly derived from *A. afarensis* around 3 million years ago, a form that may or may not also be ancestral to all the other hominids (e.g., Wood, 1996).

If *Australopithecus afarensis* has been considered at one time or another the last australopithecine ancestor leading to the living humans, *Australopithecus africanus* also attracted its share of proponents during the 1965–2000 period. For instance, Tobias always maintained that the living humans had sprung from *A. africanus*, although his basis for doing so has been slightly modified. At first at least, Tobias (1980b) would not recognize a specific distinction between the South African *A. africanus* and the East African *A. afarensis*. He held that the former was the earliest portion of a single polytypic and evolving lineage between 4 and 2 million years ago that should be called *A. africanus*. Only the later portion of this lineage gave rise to both the robust australopithecines and the *Homo* line some 2.5 to 2 mya.[33] Later, Tobias (1988, 1991) specified that the living humans were probably derived from a more evolved or derived form of *A. africanus* not yet known to us, although the Taung specimen may have somewhat approached this ancestral condition.

In the search of this more evolved and yet undiscovered *A. africanus* type, Tobias had followed the suggestion of McHenry and Skelton (McHenry, 1984, 1997; McHenry and Skelton, 1985; Skelton and McHenry, 1992; Skelton et al., 1986). Indeed, McHenry and Skelton conceived that a form either like the known *A. africanus* or an unknown type somewhat derived (evolved) relative to it, but still

A. africanus-like in conformation, gave rise to both the living humans and the robust australopithecine between 2.5 and 2 million years ago.[34] Although they once held that *A. africanus* had directly evolved from *A. afarensis*, they later inserted between the two a hypothetical *Australopithecus aethiopicus*-like evolutionary stage which was devoid, however, of overdeveloped features related to a powerful mastication. It should be noted that McHenry had previously collaborated with Corruccini in promoting that *A. afarensis* was more likely to be directly ancestral to *Homo* than *A. africanus* (McHenry and Corruccini, 1980; Corruccini and McHenry, 1980). More recently, McHenry wavered about the identity of humankind's ancestor. He now recognized that new discoveries of postcranial bones showed that the assumed direct phylogenetic link between *Australopithecus africanus* and *Homo* is perhaps not that obvious, as seen in the more human-like limb proportions of *A. afarensis* (McHenry and Berger, 1998).[35]

Delson and Tattersall were also among those who held that *A. africanus* was directly ancestral to the living humans. At first, though, the promotion of this view was not entirely without ambiguity since they proposed that the genus *Homo* may have been directly derived from a morphological form similar to the known *A. africanus* dated between 3 and 2 million years ago, although they placed the rise of the *Homo* line between 5 and 4 mya. Here, it was implicitly postulated that an undiscovered *A. africanus*-like form gave rise to the living humans (Delson, 1978; Delson et al., 1977; Tattersall and Eldredge, 1977).[36] Following the identification and naming of *Australopithecus afarensis* and *A. aethiopicus*, Delson (1981, 1986, 1987) made clear that he believed that the living humans directly sprang from *A. africanus* about 2.5 mya, this latter form being itself derived from *A. afarensis*.[37] Similarly, Tattersall (1993, 1998) maintained *A. africanus* in a direct ancestral position to *Homo* regardless of the new fossil discoveries made throughout the 1980s and most of the 1990s.[38] Yet, his position was valid until *Australopithecus garhi* was discovered. Now, Tattersall was unsure if the living humans should be directly derived from *A. africanus* or from *A. garhi* (e.g., Tattersall and Schwartz, 2000).[39]

This uncertainty regarding the exact identity of humankind's last ancestor among the australopithecines has grew through the 1990s, undoubtedly under the impact of the recent and numerous early hominid discoveries. Yet, this did not prevent the scholars from identifying this possible ancestor only among the gracile australopithecines dated between 4 and 2 million years ago. Another confirmation of this is Meave Leakey's and Walker's recent assessment that the living humans probably derived from a form similar to, or closely allied with, *A. africanus* around 2.5 mya, although they refrained from establishing a physical connection between *A. africanus* and the genus *Homo* in their phylogenetic tree (Leakey and Walker, 1997, 2003).[40]

Irrespective of the very dynamic state of the debate on the place of the australopithecines in the post–1965 period, scholars managed to reduce further the area of inquiry judged scientifically relevant to establish the rise of the human line when compared to the pre–1965 period. Indeed, very few scholars were now prepared to hold that the human line had entirely avoided going through an australopithecine-like phase of evolution. Furthermore, most scholars who refused to identify this ancestor among the *known* australopithecines recognized a very close phylogenetic proximity between them and the human line. They even sometimes postulated a common hypothetical australopithecine-like ancestor.

Perhaps more importantly, the chronological framework allowed to derive the human line from an early hominid form or another was now well within the 10 to 2 million years ago period, that is, no earlier than the mid-Miocene and no later than the late Pliocene. This is an important change in comparison to the much more extended chronological framework allowed during the 1935–1965 period. These new chronological figures were all consistent with the time range proposed in the various models of the molecular clock. Although much work remains to be done to establish with precision the genealogical root of the human line, it cannot be denied that the situation has considerably improved, empirically speaking.

THE RISE OF THE LIVING HUMANS: IN THE MIDST OF COMPETING EVOLUTIONARY CONCEPTIONS

It is sometimes argued that the present debate on the rise of the living humans has progressed very little since its inception, if at all, owing to the endless shuffling and reshuffling of the fossils into two opposite phylogenetic hypotheses (e.g., Willermet and Clark, 1995). We have seen in this book that nothing could be further from the truth, as this debate went through a series of very specific stages which crystallized in the post-1965 period (see Chapters 3, 5, 6, and 9). First restricted prior to 1900 to inserting the fossils in the immediate ancestry of the living Europeans exclusively, this debate allowed the insertion of such fossils in an outstanding diversity of hypotheses of worldwide implications in the first third of the twentieth century. One has to wait for the 1930s to see this debate reaching a state somewhat approaching the present one. Since that time, it has been presenting itself in a fairly coherent fashion with the phylogenetic hypotheses ranging from multilinear to unilinear hypotheses, with intermediate forms. However, the progress did not stop there. The whole spectrum of phylogenetic hypotheses has grown to incorporate a complex network of hypotheses grading more and more imperceptively into one another. Not only were the multilinear hypotheses proposed after 1935 less and less ramified—thus contributing to increase further the coherence of the entire spectrum of phylogenetic hypotheses—but the notion of a truly ancient and modern-looking human ancestor leading to all the living humans in the early Pleistocene period or before was increasingly abandoned to the point of almost having completely disappeared in the 1965–2000 period.

This is perhaps best seen in the changing view of Genet-Varcin. Genet-Varcin (1963) first held that the line leading to the living humans departed from the other advanced and extinct hominids such as the pithecanthropines and the Neandertals in the early Oligocene period and in the late Pliocene period respectively (see Chapter 9). Since that time, Genet-Varcin continually placed these divergence times in geological horizons which were less and less ancient. While in the late 1960s she reset the divergence times of all the hominid lines to the Pliocene period, she decided a decade later that the *Homo erectus* line (pithecanthropines) had departed at the turn of the Plio-Pleistocene period while the Neandertal line had split squarely in the Lower Pleistocene (cf., Genet-Varcin, 1969, 1979).[41] Although these still represented somewhat early dates of divergence when compared to the standard of the time, they were no longer entirely out of range from the majority's view.

Genet-Varcin (1967, 1969, 1973, 1975) continued to promote the view of a hominid radiation which saw the different evolutionary lines evolving away from a generalized state toward more specialized ones. Yet, her view had been tempered on two counts (Genet-Varcin, 1979). First, by now deriving all the advanced hominid lines from a common ancestor at the turn of the Plio-Pleistocene period rather than at a much earlier time, Genet-Varcin could no longer promote the hypothesis that living humans were directly derived from an ancestor that was generalized or modern-looking in conformation. Indeed, she now believed that this ancestor was also somewhat closely affiliated to *Homo erectus* and the Neanderdals. In fact, Genet-Varcin alluded that a form akin to *Homo habilis* may well be near the ancestral form common to all these advanced hominids. Second, Genet-Varcin's multilinear hypothesis was now so attenuated (or constricted) that she conceived that all the distinct evolutionary lines have probably been able to interbreed significantly with each other for long periods of time, at least until they had each reached a significant level of specialization. In her new view, this could also apply to the australopithecines. No doubt, this contributed to dilute the generalized or the modern-looking aspect of the ancestor directly leading to the living humans, not to mention the genetic input of the so-called extinct and less modern-looking hominid lines into the one leading to the living humans. In fact, Genet-Varcin now included in *Homo sapiens* forms like Steinheim, Neandertal man, Solo man, and Rhodesian man.

Once the general progressiveness of the debate on the rise of the living humans is acknowledged, it remains to be understood why its progression has been much slower in the past few decades, being apparently caught up in the midst of competing evolutionary conceptions and theories. At least three related factors are at play here. First, the slowdown of the progressiveness of this debate was not a sudden event but rather a gradual one. Whereas the 1930s and the 1940s were spectacular years for the resolution of that debate, progress has since been slower and will probably be slower still in the future. In a nutshell, it was relatively easy to discard a number of widely divergent phylogenetic hypotheses (polyphyletic, Presapiens, etc.) once the fossil record had reached a certain density. However, it will be much more difficult to decide between closely related hypotheses which can fit the present record. It is the details of a phylogeny which are difficult to work out, not the elimination of broad alternatives. This can be referred to as "a threshold of near empirical saturation". Eventually, all the other debates concerned with humankind's place in nature (humankind's place among the primates, the place of the australopithecines) will have arrived at this near empirical saturation.

Second, once the threshold of a near empirical saturation has been reached it might be tempting to try to break the apparent deadlock by turning to specific evolutionary theories or conceptions in order to promote or justify a view of human phylogeny. Does this mean that the debate on the rise of the living humans will be resolved in this way? Probably not. Human phylogenetic hypotheses proposed solely on the basis of evolutionary theories cannot stand the test of a rapidly improving fossil record *unless* they are consistent with that record at a particular moment. It is the quality of the empirical basis which establishes the constraints or the limits within which a debate can legitimately take place in paleoanthropology: The better the quality of the fossil record, the more restricted is the maneuver room for its interpretation. No doubt, scholars exploiting various evolutionary theories and approaches to assess human phylogeny have always been under such constraints. This has already been illustrated with the case of the Synthetic Theory of Evolution in the 1950s and 1960s (see Chapter 9). The debate on the rise of the living humans will not be resolved by appealing to specific evolutionary theories for there will always be competing theories which are consistent with the actual fossil record (see also Chapter 11). It could take a long time before this record improves sufficiently so as to permit the discarding of a number of evolutionary conceptions no longer consistent with it.[42]

Third, after 1965, of all the debates relevant to humankind's place in nature, the one on the rise of the living humans is by far the most closely associated with evolutionary theories and conceptions. This is easily explained. It is only during the later phases of human evolution that a significant increase in brain size and the complex development of stone-tools technologies are seen. These signs could be interpreted to mean that the later hominids were creatures whose adaptive strategies were not unlike that of the living humans, thus decreasing the possibility that there were any speciation events in this phase of human evolution. A number of scholars may be tempted to look for evolutionary theories and conceptions explaining or justifying this state of affairs. In contradistinction, other scholars may deny the notion of the impossibility of speciation events during this phase of human evolution on the basis of other evolutionary theories or conceptions, regardless of brain size and stone-tool technologies. Such a level of theoretical confrontation is seen today only among the scholars debating the last phases of human evolution. Owing to the state of a near empirical saturation in this debate, it is very unlikely that a crucial fossil discovery (or even a few of them) will settle the question. Rather, it seems that only a series of such discoveries will be needed to further trim down the number of competing phylogenetic hypotheses.

In comparison, things are different when the early hominids are concerned. In this debate, scholars are much more inclined to appeal almost exclusively to morphological and chronological arguments rather than to competing evolutionary conceptions. This is surely related to the fact that the early hominids were small-brained and had no or limited technological abilities. Remember that it was proposed in the 1960s and 1970s that all the australopithecines should be included in a single culture-bound species at the base of the human line. This hypothesis was discarded not by confronting alternative evolutionary conceptions but because of new fossil discoveries. Its refutation was made possible only because two conditions were simultaneously reunited: (1) The australopithecines were small-brained and clearly lacked the cultural abilities of the later hominids; (2) this debate had not nearly reached its threshold of near empirical saturation. Since these two conditions are missing in the current debates on the rise of the living humans, scholars are offered the possibility of appealing to evolutionary theories and conceptions for its resolution. As already alluded to, this appeal will in no way resolve the question.

Neither was the input of the molecular studies of great help for the resolution of this debate. Unlike its unambiguous contribution to the support of an exclusive link between the humans and the two African great apes exclusively, molecular anthropology has not yet been able to repeat this performance when dealing with the last phases of human evolution. Instead, molecular anthropologists became embroiled in internal debates which nearly mimicked those being conducted on the basis of the fossil record. It was realized that the use of molecular studies in an intraspecific context rather than an interspecific one yielded much more ambiguous results.

The fossil record. During the past two decades, considerable attention has been devoted to the rise of the living humans in light of two opposite alternatives, with intermediate positions: the Out of Africa model versus the Multiregional evolution model (e.g., Aiello, 1993; Lieberman and Jackson, 1995; Minugh-Purvis, 1995; Smith, 2002; Smith and Harrod, 1997; Smith et al., 1989). Whereas the Out of Africa model states that all the living humans are descended from a recent and modern-looking common African ancestor that dates back to no more than 200,000 years, the Multiregional Evolution model stipulates that the living humans are descended from much more ancient and archaic-looking ancestors that are not exclusively localized in Africa. Considering that our goal here is to understand the debate on the rise of the living humans after 1965 in light of the pre-1965 era, we will not be looking at it through the current tension between the Out of Africa and the Multiregional evolution models. Of course, this does not exclude a significant overlap in the two perpectives.

The 1965–2000 period saw both a number of important fossil discoveries and new chronological analyses of the fossil remains relevant to the last phases of human evolution (e.g., Arribas and Palmqvist, 2002; Arsuaga et al., 1993; Arsuaga et al., 1999; Bermudez de Castro et al., 1997; Brown et al., 1985; Delson, 1985; Gabunia et al., 2001; Howell, 1978; Howells, 1980; Jacob, 1973, 1975, 1981; Pilbeam, 1975; Pope and Cronin, 1984; Swisher et al., 1996; Tyler and Sartono, 2001; von Koenigswald, 1975; Walker and Leakey, 1993). Yet, it is not possible to identify fossil recoveries which created a profound impact on the phylogenetic debate. This is unsurprising when considering the threshold of near empirical saturation already alluded to. Yet, this is not to say that empirical facts played no role in the phylogenetic hypotheses. Each phylogenetic hypothesis rests on a good empirical basis, although the interpretation of that basis and/or the empirical content of it vary from one hypothesis to another (e.g., Willermet and Clark, 1995). Facing this apparent deadlock, supports or justifications for these hypotheses were sometimes sought outside the empirical realm.

This is well-illustrated in the uncertainties surrounding the status of the species "*Homo erectus*". In the early 1970s, most paleoanthropologists viewed *Homo erectus* as a widespread, long-lasting, and polytypic species which was directly ancestral to the living humans. Since then, scholars' opinions have been moving in opposite directions. One group eventually denied that *Homo erectus* transformed itself into *Homo sapiens* and/or split the *Homo erectus* fossil sample into a number of possible distinct species such as *Homo erectus* narrowly defined, *H. ergaster*, *H. heidelbergensis*, *H. steinheimensis*, *H. antecessor*, etc. (e.g., Andrews, 1984; Groves, 1989; Tattersall, 1986, 1998; Stringer, 1994; Wood, 1992). On the other hand, other scholars continued to maintain that *Homo erectus* as first defined is a valid species probably directly ancestral to the living humans (e.g., Kramer, 1993; Krantz, 1993; Turner and Chamberlain, 1989). Some even promoted that the boundary between *H. erectus* and *H. sapiens* is so arbitrary that *H. erectus* should simply be sunk or incorporated in *H. sapiens* (e.g., Jelinek, 1978; Tobias, 1995; Wolpoff et al., 1994a). Such diverging viewpoints about the taxonomic status of *Homo erectus* were largely explained not by new fossil discoveries but by differences of opinion over general evolutionary conceptions and approaches (e.g., Delisle, 2001). These will be reviewed here.

The post-1965 period was one of turmoil in evolutionary biology. A number of theoretical developments were made that raised questions about their compatibility with the theoretical corpus already developed in the evolutionary synthesis (cf., Gould, 1980; Stebbins and Ayala, 1981). It is against this uncertain theoretical background that the debate on the rise of the living humans was conducted. Because several aspects related to the evolutionary synthesis have already been presented in Chapter 9, these will not be repeated here. Our efforts, therefore, will be largely directed toward the presentation of the new theoretical developments, though not exclusively.

Three main theoretical developments converged after 1970 which could have been of some consequence for the phylogenetic debate in later phases of human evolution. While these developments were largely elaborated outside the realm of paleoanthropology, they all found their way into this field. A first development concerned a method of taxonomy called phylogenetic systematics or cladistics (e.g., Eldredge and Cracraft, 1980; Hennig, 1966; Wiley, 1981; see also Wood, this book). Cladistic analyses aim at establishing degrees of phylogenetic relationship within a given group of taxa (species, populations, individuals) by distinguishing among primitive features (plesiomorphies), shared derived features (synapomorphies) and uniquely derived features (autopomorphies). According to cladists, it is the sharing of derived morphological features and not of primitive ones which is indicative of an evolutionary relationship. The common and primitive features of three distinct species are of no use to establish which two are the most closely related. These must be identified by the morphological features they exclusively share in common; features which are not shared with a third species.

The application of cladistics to the phylogeny of the later hominids contributed to the promotion of multilinear hypotheses. Let us exemplify this situation with the help of two hypothetical but realistic cases. In the early 1970s, the genus *Homo* was considered by many scholars to be represented by a single, polytypic lineage evolving toward the living humans. Let us imagine for a moment that a cladist was to analyze only a portion (a temporal slice) of this lineage. That cladist might argue that this segment does not represent a single population because the constituent fossil specimens are not all bound together by the same derived features, but rather by a combination of primitive and derived ones. On that basis, our cladist might want to recognize two distinct lineages instead of a single one in this temporal slice.

The impact of the cladistics on the reconstruction of phylogenetic patterns can also be seen when relationships between known taxa are investigated on the basis of uniquely shared features (synapomorphies). Assuming that our cladist faces again a unilinear hypothesis (*Homo habilis–H. erectus–H. sapiens*), he or she might argue that, considering the great number of uniquely derived features (autopomorphies) present in *Homo sapiens*, in comparison with the relatively few present in its supposed ancestor *H. erectus*, it would be more convincing to establish a direct phylogenetic link between *H. sapiens* and *H. habilis* as these two species share more features in common, thus putting *H. erectus* on an extinct evolutionary side branch.

A second theoretical development which could have contributed to favor multilinear hypotheses in the later phases of human evolution was the renewed interest in species, speciation, and evolutionary events at and above the species level (species, genera, families). In fact, this second development constituted a network of theoretical developments on the theme of the "species". As already seen in Chapter 9, the constitution of the evolutionary synthesis in the 1940s and the 1950s directed considerable attention toward the evolutionary processes below the species level (subspecies, populations, individuals). When applied in human evolution, this approach encouraged the interpretation of morphological variability as differences among individuals within the same species, rather than as differences between distinct species. Now, a number of scholars became more and more interested in species rather than individual organisms, thus encouraging them to look for morphological differences between species in the fossil record. It was felt that evolutionary events at and above the species level were worth investigating, thus negating, in part at least, the notion that microevolution entirely explains macroevolution. Indeed, it was argued that perhaps not all evolutionary events above the species level could be explained by evolutionary mechanisms below the species level.

Eldredge (1979) formalized these two competing ways of looking at evolution by distinguishing between the "transformational approach" and the "taxic approach". The former approach claims that lower-level mechanisms as recognized by population genetics (i.e., natural selection, adaptation) sufficed to explain all evolutionary events at the species level and above, as promoted in the evolutionary synthesis (e.g., Bock, 1970, 1979; Charlesworth et al., 1982). The taxic approach, on the other hand, recognizes that species diversity (and that of genera, families, etc.) was itself a valid subject of study, since it was based on specific, but not necessarily distinct, evolutionary processes during speciation.

More clearly still, it was proposed that evolutionary patterns observed at and above the species level (macroevolution) were not exclusively, and perhaps not even predominantly, the result of processes below the species level (microevolution). It was held that species selection rather than individual selection could be the main macroevolutionary process (e.g., Stanley, 1975, 1979). This development opened the door to a new conception of evolution that suggested that evolutionary theories based on the extrapolation of microevolutionary processes to explain macroevolutionary patterns should be replaced by one explicitly embodying the notion of hierarchy, which may or may not involve distinct processes and patterns at each level (e.g., Gould, 1980; Vrba and Eldredge, 1984).

Another development related to the theme of the "species" concerned the pattern or mode of evolutionary change: Was change a continuous and gradual process, as promoted in the conception of phyletic gradualism, or was it episodic and sudden only to be followed by long periods of stasis, as proposed in the theory of punctuated equilibria? It was suggested on the basis of the paleontological evidence that episodic and sudden changes were common in the history of life (e.g., Eldredge and Gould, 1972). Although this debate was, at first, solely an empirical question, it soon took on a theoretical dimension (e.g., Gould, 1992; Hoffman, 1992; Ruse, 1992). It was argued that if the theory of punctuated equilibria was a valid one, this could mean that species are largely stable entities which can only change significantly during a speciation process. Here again, the theory of punctuated equilibria contributed to directing the attention toward evolutionary phenomena at the species level and not below the species level. Soon enough, the debate confronting punctuated equilibrium and phyletic gradualism was imported in paleoanthropology. This debate was especially directed at the later phases of human evolution, with paleoanthropologists sitting on both sides of the divide, although some proposed an intermediate position (e.g., Eldredge and Tattersall, 1975, 1982; Cronin et al., 1981; Rightmire, 1981; Tobias, 1985; Wolpoff, 1984).

Accompanying these developments on the theme of the "species" was the suggestion that species should perhaps not be regarded as classes (or groups) composed of individual organisms, as it was implicitly recognized in the evolutionary synthesis, but rather as entities or individuals themselves (e.g., Ghiselin, 1974; Hull, 1976). A new ontology of species defined as spatiotemporal entities was introduced to replace the other one based on arbitrarily delineated segments of an evolutionary continuum.

The third theoretical development which could have had an impact on the phylogenetic debate of the later hominids concerned the nature of the link between the evolutionary mechanisms (processes) and the evolutionary patterns. Let us go back for a moment to cladistics as a way to assess the phylogenetic relationships. The founding father of cladistics, Hennig (1981 [1969]), stressed the difficulties of mixing phylogenetic research on evolutionary patterns with causal research on evolutionary processes. In other words, Hennig questioned the feasibility of simultaneously investigating patterns and processes because one's view of the evolutionary process or mechanism might influence the interpretation of the evolutionary pattern or phylogeny. Indeed, some cladists were critical of the new systematics which accompanied the evolutionary synthesis precisely because investigations of patterns and processes are intertwined in this latter approach (see Chapter 9). It was promoted that the cladistic method, for its part, investigated the evolutionary patterns (phylogeny) independently of any evolutionary theory or process (e.g., Schafersman, 1985). It was believed that the investigation of phylogeny could be compromised if performed with the help of evolutionary theories; a pitfall which is avoided, it was contended, by the cladistic method. This idea was strongly expressed in the following words:

> Hennig established a criterion of demarcation between science and metaphysics at a time when neo-Darwinism [the evolutionary synthesis] had attained a sort of metaphysical pinnacle by imposing a burden of subjectivity and tautology on nature's observable hierarchy. Encumbered with vague and slippery ideas about adaptation, fitness, biological species, and natural selection, neo-Darwinism (summed up in the 'evolutionary' systematics [the new systematics] of Mayr and Simpson) not only lacked a definable investigatory method, but came to depend, both for evolutionary interpretation and classification, on consensus or authority. (Rosen, Nelson and Patterson, 1979: ix)

Similar criticisms found their way in paleoanthropology (e.g., Delson et al., 1977; Kimbel, 1991). At issue here was the notion that the reconstruction of phylogeny should be based solely on morphology (fossils), thus excluding any references to evolutionary processes or theories. Cladists who sharply distinguished between evolutionary patterns and evolutionary processes assumed that it was possible to research the former independently of the latter, thus considering that the two could be uncoupled (e.g., Cracraft, 1981). Only once the evolutionary patterns have been established should one turn to questions pertaining to evolutionary processes (e.g., Platnick, 1979; Schafersman, 1985).

This view was not shared by the proponents of the evolutionary synthesis (e.g., Bock, 1974; Mayr and Ashlock, 1991; Simpson, 1975). For them, taxonomic or morphological features were expressions of the entire biology of their carriers, being part of an integrated living system in relation to other organisms and environmental conditions. It was held that the evaluation of a particular morphological feature might change when other types of information were considered. The evolutionary processes could not, therefore, be uncoupled from the evolutionary patterns for the simple reason that the order found among organisms in phylogenies reflected their evolutionary histories, which, in turn, could only be understood by reference to the mechanisms of evolutionary change (e.g., Bock, 1977, 1981; Szalay, 1981, 1991). According to this view, a taxonomy and a phylogeny:

> . . . must be in agreement with the whole of evolutionary theory, including laws, mechanisms of change and subfactors thereof. By the whole of evolutionary theory, I mean . . . all studies of function, biological role, behaviour and environmental factors required to understand the evolutionary mechanisms . . . [as well as] factors of the formation of genetic mechanisms and of natural selections (Bock, 1977: 864).

This debate on the nature of the connection between the evolutionary patterns and the evolutionary processes was not entirely irrelevant for the later phases of human evolution. It is during these phases that a significant increase in brain size and a complexification in stone tools technologies were clearly seen. If morphology alone is used to establish this portion of human phylogeny, one might argue that the morphological variability observed in the fossil sample is too important to fit in a single evolutionary line leading to the living humans. On the other hand, if other biological and behavioral aspects are added to the morphological analysis, one might hold that big-brained and tool-making creatures were able to stand the pressure of the environment quite effectively so that a speciation event in this evolutionary line was unlikely. The morphological variability observed in this fossil sample could be interpreted in a different light.

To summarize, the turmoil in evolutionary biology after 1965 involved a number of interrelated theoretical issues: (1) the debate on the proper method of taxonomy which opposed the new systematics and cladistics; (2) the debate on whether all the evolutionary phenomena could be explained by mechanisms below the species level or required also mechanisms at and above the species level; and (3) the debate over whether or not it is possible or desirable to uncouple studies of evolutionary patterns and processes. We have alluded as to how such theoretical developments could have influenced the debate on the phylogeny of the later hominids in favor of either linear or multilinear hypotheses.

However, although it is against this theoretical background that the debate on the rise of the living humans was conducted, this is not to say that this debate was merely a by-product of this unstable epistemic and theoretical landscape. Certainly not. First, it should be remembered that it is the empirical context that imposes the limits within which the theoretical issues can be exploited. Second, once the limits are set empirically, the viewpoints of the scholars can either be: (1) largely derived from the theoretical conceptions, (2) only supported by some conceptions, or (3) merely consistent with them. It is rarely possible in the post-1965 period to unequivocally establish the nature of the link between a phylogenetic view and theoretical issues in the scholars' mind. For that reason, this will not be systematically attempted here.

A common feature of the debate on the rise of the living humans in the post-1965 period is that several scholars who promoted multilinear hypotheses posited that Africa constituted the cradle from which truly modern-looking hominids first arose in the late Middle or early Upper Pleistocene period before spreading throughout the Old World. In their view, this contributed to the extinction of the other hominids of less modern conformation. Another feature of this debate at the time was that several proponents of multilinear hypotheses have not been at first committed to this view of human phylogeny. Indeed, the late 1970s and 1980s saw a renewed interest for this conception of the later hominids, after a period during which a majority of scholars were committed to parallel and linear hypotheses in the late 1960s and early 1970s.

For instance, Tattersall was not at first prepared on the basis of cladistic principles to exclude the possibility that the later hominids represented by *Homo habilis*, *H. erectus*, the Neandertals, and *H. sapiens* should not be inserted in a multilinear hypothesis (Tattersall and Eldredge, 1977). Yet, Tattersall would not exclude a linear hypothesis from being the true pattern of human evolution. Remember that Tattersall promoted theoretical developments such as the cladistic method, punctuated modes of evolution, and an ontology of species based on discrete spatiotemporal entities (Eldredge and Tattersall, 1982). Eventually, Tattersall (1986) made clear that he believed that several distinct species of the Middle and Upper Pleistocene period (*Homo sapiens*, *H. neanderthalensis*, *H. heidelbergensis*, and *H. steinheimensis*) could not all be lineally related. At that time, however, Tattersall would not commit himself to a specific phylogenetic hypothesis. This was only done a few years later (Tattersall, 1993, 1997, 1998).[43]

By then, he held that *Homo sapiens* was directly evolved from *H. ergaster* through the intermediary of *H. heidelbergensis*, with *H. erectus* and *H. neanderthalensis* representing extinct side branches, each independently derived at different times from the stem leading to the living humans.[44] Tattersall was committed to the view that Eastern Asia (*Homo erectus*) and Europe (*H. neanderthalensis*) had been occupied until very recently by somewhat specialized forms which originally sprang up in Africa until they were supplanted by African emigrants, the direct ancestors of the living humans. Tattersall favored deriving all the living humans from a single and recent African source.

Like Tattersall, Wood eventually recognized that the number of species which comprised the genus *Homo* was greater than once believed. In the mid-1980s, Wood was strongly inclined to view the phylogeny of the later hominids as being characterized by at least one speciation event (Wood, 1984; Bilsborough and Wood, 1986).[45] On the basis of cladistic principles, Wood argued that it was impossible to decide whether *Homo habilis* or *H. erectus* had directly given rise to the living humans, to the exclusion of one or the other species. Irrespective of which view was the right one, Wood inclined to conceive *Homo erectus* as an extinct side branch not directly leading to *H. sapiens*, for the two probably shared a common ancestor. By the 1990s, Wood's (1992, 1996; Wood and Collard, 1999) multilinear hypothesis had crystallized in the recognition of several more species and extinct side branches in the genus *Homo*.[46] Deriving the living humans from *Homo ergaster* to the exclusion of *H. habilis* and *H. rudolfensis*, Wood (1992, 1996) believed this ancestral form to have independently given rise to both the extinct *H. erectus* and the surviving *H. sapiens*. Living humans evolved from *Homo ergaster* not directly but through the intermediary of *H. heidelbergensis*, a form which was also ancestral to the extinct *H. neanderthalensis*. Wood evaluated that the case for an African origin of the modern human type in the late Middle Pleistocene period was a strong one, although this was not fully proven as yet.

For his part, Groves (1989) depicted the evolution of the later hominids as a bush-like pattern characterized by speciation and quasi-speciation events. As a proponent of cladistics and punctuational models of evolution, Groves recognized a number of distinct species but also several distinct subspecies. In addition to *Homo sapiens* and *H. erectus,* which he defined narrowly, Groves identified *Homo ergaster* and an unnamed species of *Homo* of the *erectus* grade (level). Although Groves refrained from presenting a precise phylogenetic tree, it is pretty clear that he envisioned several complete speciation events at the level of the *erectus* grade—implying the parallel evolution of several extinct lines—followed later by incomplete speciation events involving essentially subspecies only.

Like Groves, Rightmire also embraced the cladistic method and a punctuational model of evolution. Until the mid-1980s, Rightmire (1985) held that the living humans had rapidly evolved in the last portion of the Pleistocene period from a segment of the long-lasting, stable, and widespread *Homo erectus* population. This constituted a linear hypothesis not of the gradual kind but of the punctuated kind. Soon, however, Rightmire (1986, 1988, 1990) wavered on the possibility that the rise of the living humans might have been a more complex evolutionary process than he had expected. He noted that there was no obvious connection between *Homo erectus* in Asia and the living local populations, while hominid remains of the Middle Pleistocene period in Africa and Europe may, after all, need to be regrouped in other species than *Homo erectus* and *H. sapiens*. In the 1990s, Rightmire (1991, 1994, 1996, 1998) arrived at a phylogenetic conception which derived the polytypic species *Homo erectus* from an unknown early *Homo* African form before spreading throughout the Old World. From there, a less specialized segment of *Homo erectus* gave rise in Africa to *H. heidelbergensis* in the Middle Pleistocene period—a form which eventually also occupied Europe—while a portion of the former species continued to evolve in Asia until quite recently, before its probable extinction. In the Middle Pleistocene period, *Homo heidelbergensis* independently gave rise to both *Homo neanderthalensis* in Europe and *Homo sapiens* in Africa, the latter form being probably the exclusive ancestor to all the living humans.[47]

Like several of his contemporaries, Stringer (1974, 1978) was not prepared at first to promote a multilinear hypothesis for the later hominids. Eventually, in the mid-1980s, Stringer (1985) clearly alluded to such a possibility by being tempted to classify the Neandertals (*Homo neandertahlensis*) in a distinct species from the living humans (*H. sapiens*). An infusion of cladistic principles into his researches apparently encouraged Stringer to pursue this line of reasoning. Although a proponent of cladistics, Stringer was not necessarily embracing a punctuational model of evolution nor the accompanying ontology of species based on discrete spatiotemporal entities. One has to wait for the 1990s in order to get a clear picture of Stringer's multilinear conception (Stringer, 1990, 1992, 1994; Stringer and Gamble, 1993; Stringer and McKie, 1996).

By that time, Stringer was maintaining that the living humans had descended from an early African *Homo erectus* form but not before having gone through a later *H. heidelbergensis* phase. This view implied that the East Asian portion of *Homo erectus* persisted until quite recently before being driven to extinction by more modern-looking forms. On their part, the Neandertals (*Homo neanderthalensis*), like *H. sapiens*, evolved out of the later *H. heidelbergensis* but were also driven to extinction in Europe and in West Asia.[48] According to Stringer, all the living humans can trace their origins to a single recent and modern-looking African source dated to the late Middle or early Upper Pleistocene period, as seen in fossil remains such as

Border cave and Klasies River Mouth in South Africa. While moving out of Africa to expand in the rest of the Old World, the early representatives of the modern-looking *Homo sapiens* competed successfully against the other hominid species, ultimately contributing to their extinction. Stringer recognized that a certain amount of interbreeding between the modern-looking and the more archaic-looking hominid species may have occurred during this replacement process. But if so, he continued, it was to a limited extent and had a negligible impact on the rise of the living humans. Stringer's view is to be counted among the proponents of the "Out of Africa" model.

Whereas a number of scholars linked a multilinear hypothesis with the notion of the rise of an African modern-looking ancestor to the living humans, it should be noted that there were no necessary connections between the two. For instance, Bräuer envisioned the phylogeny of the later hominids to be a complex evolutionary process, but a process which was probably devoid of any complete speciation events (Bräuer, 1984a, 1984a, 1989, 1990, 1992, 1994). Bräuer promoted that the rise of the living humans has been a slow process which lasted a large portion of the Pleistocene period during which *Homo erectus* was transformed in *H. sapiens* through a series of successive and intertwined evolutionary grades: primitive *Homo erectus*, developed *H. erectus*, early archaic *H. sapiens*, late archaic *H. sapiens*, and anatomically modern *H. sapiens*.[49]

For Bräuer, however, the pace at which these evolutionary grades were crossed was not uniformly spread throughout the Old World. While anatomically modern *Homo sapiens* arose fairly rapidly in Africa in the late Middle or early Upper Pleistocene period as seen in transitive forms such as Bodo, Broken Hill, Omo, Florisbad, Klasies River Mouth, etc., less modern-looking hominids were at the same time thriving elsewhere. In Europe, the Neandertals (*Homo sapiens neanderthalensis*) were eventually entirely replaced by anatomically modern *Homo sapiens* coming from Africa through varying levels of absorption and hybridization. In South and East Asia, the rise of the living humans was more complex still, for although gene flow from African anatomically modern *Homo sapiens* may have contributed to modernize the less modern-looking populations in this region, it seems that the Asian *H. erectus* population was already evolving locally toward more modern-looking forms. On this view, there is no need to hold that the Asian *Homo erectus* population constituted an extinct side branch of human evolution. In Bräuer's conception, named the "Afro-European *sapiens*" hypothesis, the replacement of archaic populations by modern-looking ones was anything but a radical process, for it occurred within the limits of a single evolving species.

Irrespective of whether or not the later phases of human evolution were characterized by speciations events, scholars like Tattersall, Wood, Rightmire, Stringer, and Bräuer all came to embrace a replacement model in which a modern-looking hominid form—after its rise in a localized geographical area—moved out of its cradle in order to replace completely or partially the other less modern-looking hominids. In this conception, all the living humans can entirely or largely trace back their origins to this originally localized modern-looking population.

Against this conception of human evolution, other scholars united their voices on several occasions to promote that the transformation of an archaic population into a modern-looking one occurred on more than one occasion and in several distinct geographical places, thus trading the concept of replacement for the concept of regional evolution (Frayer et al., 1993, 1994; Wolpoff et al., 1994b). For these scholars, the evolutionary process of the later hominids is not characterized by speciation events because it occurred within a single genetic system. In fact, their views were all consistent with several premises often associated with the evolutionary synthesis: the importance attributed to the infraspecific categories (individuals, populations, subspecies); the commitment to the biological species concept and the new systematics; an ontology of species based on classes composed of individual organisms and not on discrete spatiotemporal entities; and the assumption that the studies of evolutionary patterns and processes cannot or should not be uncoupled, thus implying the necessity of interpreting the later phases of human evolution in the light of evolutionary mechanisms (i.e., natural selection, gene flow, genetic drift, culture, etc.).

Two main phylogenetic hypotheses based on the concept of regional evolution were proposed at the time. In one such hypothesis developed by Smith (1984, 1985, 1991, 1992), enough evolutionary continuity is observed locally in Africa, Europe, and Asia between archaic and modern-looking hominid populations to refute a replacement process of any significant scale from the part of a single and originally localized modern-looking population. Smith explained the modernization process of the later hominids by a relaxation of the selective forces caused by improved technological factors and more effective behavioral strategies. However, Smith also explained this modernization process by gene flow coming from more modern-looking populations in Africa and Western Asia towards hominid forms in Europe, Eastern Asia, and Australia. Instead of a physical migration and replacement of modern-looking populations followed by some interbreeding with archaic populations, Smith proposed an assimilation of genes from the part of the latter populations through the migration process of the genes themselves from one neighboring population to the next. Smith is a proponent of a view called the "Assimilation" model. In Smith's hypothesis, all the archaic populations of the various geographical areas of the Old World contributed significantly to the gene pools of the local living populations, as there was sufficent independent local or regional evolution.

The second main phylogenetic hypothesis based on the concept of regional evolution was proposed by Thorne, Wolpoff, and Wu Xinzhi. It denies that gene flow coming from a single and localized modern-looking population contributed to modernize some other archaic hominid populations (Thorne and Wolpoff, 1981, 1992; Wolpoff et al., 1984; Wu, 1990, 1998). Instead, it was held that the anatomically modern human threshold was crossed collectively in several distinct geographical areas and not necessarily at the same time. The "Multiregional Evolution" model holds that ever since *Homo erectus* moved out of Africa for the first time in the Early Pleistocene period, human evolution constituted a single evolving polytypic species spread throughout the Old World and subjected to various evolutionary forces.

While selective pressures and genetic drift created regional distinctions in various areas, gene flow between these areas maintained enough cohesion to avoid the breakup of this species. Proponents of this hypothesis recognized morphological continuity between earlier (archaic) and later (modern) hominids in regions such as Africa, Europe and the Levant, East Asia, and Australasia.[50]

The Multiregional Evolution model is a form of parallel hypothesis[51]: The living humans have deep genealogical roots in their respective regions, thus explaining the features they share with their local ancestors. However, the distinct hominid evolutionary lines are not entirely independent from one another since they are bound by a network of gene flow which permits the sharing of some features and novelties between the geographical areas. In this model, the transition from *Homo erectus* to *H. sapiens* is a gradual one and is anything but a clean break.

As already alluded to, proponents of the concept of regional evolution are potential contributors to parallel phylogenetic hypotheses. The more it is held that several distinct hominid evolutionary lines independently contributed to the rise of the living humans, the more a view inclines towards a parallel hypothesis. On the other hand, the more it is held that the so-called distinct hominid evolutionary lines ancestral to the living humans were in contact (through hybridization or gene flow), the more a view inclines towards a linear hypothesis. Indeed, it could be argued that contacts between contemporaneous hominids in distinct geographical areas were so intense that it completely blurred the morphological differences between the regions, thus replacing the concept of parallel evolution by the concept of successive and morphologically homogeneous evolutionary stages.

As this example illustrates, the difference between a strict parallel hypothesis and a strict linear hypothesis relates to how much morphological variability, as well as isolation, is allowed between the geographical areas in a single temporal slice. In this theoretical spectrum of phylogenetic conceptions ranging imperceptibly from strict parallel to strict linear hypotheses, the Multiregional Evolution model represents a parallel hypothesis that allows enough gene flow between the distinct geographical areas to avoid the breakup of the species.

Let us now review a number of concepts which are perhaps more properly referred to as linear hypotheses, although a variable amount of regional evolution is implicitly or explicitly recognized in them. Before proceeding, however, it should be noted that there is no contradiction in promoting a linear hypothesis in the later hominids and yet recognizing at the same time a possible speciation event involving, for instance, the extinction of the Neandertals (e.g., Ferembach, 1979, 1986). As will be seen, linear hypotheses described a complex evolutionary process involving a great number of hominid populations since the Early Pleistocene period. No proponents of linear hypotheses were prepared to hold that all the populations that have taken part in this process have directly contributed to the genetic makeup of the living humans.

As a proponent of a linear hypothesis, Jelinek (1978, 1980, 1981, 1985) envisioned the last portion of human evolution as a single but complex evolutionary line following a gradual trend toward the living humans and characterized by variation of infraspecific order only. Denying that large-scale migration and extinction events could explain the morphological variability observed in the fossil record, Jelinek appealed instead to two other factors: (1) to mosaic evolution, that is, the notion that the archaic and progressive morphological features of a single individual change at different rates and to different degrees, thus explaining both the variability seen among the individuals belonging to the same population and among the individuals belonging to different populations of the same time horizon; (2) to local evolution over large geographical/ecological areas modulated by population density and genetic isolation. Unable to distinguish the transition between *Homo erectus* and *H. sapiens*, Jelinek suggested including them in a single species constituted of two successive subspecies: *Homo sapiens erectus* and *Homo sapiens sapiens*.

For his part, Bilsborough (1978, 1983, 1992) explained the variability observed in the fossil record of the later hominids by appealing to a host of evolutionary factors such as mosaic evolution, regional evolution, migration, varying levels of gene flow, and hybridization. Once a portion of *Homo erectus* expanded its range outside of Africa, it developed a greater level of morphological variability through an intraspecific radiation under the adaptive pressures generated by the new ecological conditions faced by the migrating members. Because novel advantageous features were rapidly shared from one region to the next through gene flow, the polytypic species *Homo erectus* went through a complex but rapid phyletic or anagenetic change up to the living humans. Bilsborough insisted that there were no obvious instances of speciation events throughout this later portion of human evolution. Instead, the continuity between *Homo erectus* and *H. sapiens* in several regions indicated that similar morphological trends occurred throughout the Old World. But in addition to regional evolution, local replacement of populations by others was also a part of this complex hominid evolutionary process, although replacement was compatible with continuity on a large continental scale. Unable to establish a clear demarcation between *Homo erectus* and *H. sapiens*, Bilsborough merely recognized an arbitrary distinction between these two successive species or chronospecies.

In yet another way to conceptualize the anagenetic transformation in the later hominids, Tobias (1978, 1991) appealed to the process of reticulate evolution. Ever since the hominids first moved out of Africa, the successive species *Homo erectus* and *H. sapiens* were composed of several subspecies spread throughout the Old World. Owing to a continual process of migration between the geographical areas coupled with sufficient mental capabilities to hybridize with mates presenting some differences of conformation, human evolution has since been a complex network of evolutionary strains or populations of infraspecific levels. In other words, this was not an adaptative radiation constituted of distinct species but of several subspecies. Tobias held that this complex evolutionary process of intertwined or reticulate evolutionary branches characterized the later phases of human evolution.

The last hypothesis reviewed here is the one proposed by Brace (1979, 1991, 1992, 1995). In Brace's view, no major migrational events occurred in the later stages of human evolution after the initial *Homo erectus* spread in the Old World, meaning that the rise and the transition of *H. sapiens* from *H. erectus* was not geographically localized but widespread throughout this territory and proceeded at approximately the same time and the same evolutionary rate everywhere. The relative morphological homogeneity of this transitional process was partly explained by a continous gene flow between the hominid populations living at the same time but, above all, by the similar selective pressures that these populations faced. Considering the swiftness with which new cultural innovations diffused from one population to the next, the various hominid groups were able to face the selective pressures equipped with the same cultural responses. This generated similar morphological adaptive responses. As the cultural abilities gradually improved in time—increasing the buffer against the selective forces and relaxing their impact—the skeletal robustness of the later hominids decreased. Although not denying the presence of minor regional distinction or evolution, Brace insisted above all upon the similar responses deployed by all the later hominids to face the adaptive challenges. On this view of human evolution, culture is the main ecological niche within which the later hominids were striving.

Molecular studies. While scholars were debating the phylogeny of the later hominids with the help of the fossil record—a debate that was being conducted against a background of theoretical tensions in evolutionary biology—molecular anthropologists entered the scene, especially after the mid-1980s. We have already seen that the fruitfulness of the molecular studies was demonstrated in the debates on humankind's place among the primates. Now, instead of investigating the nature of the phylogenetic relationship between humankind and the other primate species, it was suggested that the study of the genetic diversity among the living humans could reveal the evolutionary history of our species. The key idea is the following: Just as the divergence of two species from a common ancestor will permit the accumulation of genetic differences as time goes by—information which can be used to establish both the relationship (genetic distance) and the divergence time (molecular clock)—the genetic differences among the living human "races" or populations could be used to establish their time of divergence of one another from a common ancestor as well as their relative proximity.

Contrary to the successes of molecular anthropology in the previous debate, these studies were much more equivocal in the debate on the rise of the living humans. In the former debate, molecular anthropologists were investigating evolutionary entities (humans, chimpanzees, and gorillas) which have been genetically separated from one another for several millions of years. This is no longer the case when molecular anthropologists are working with the living human populations. Not only were these human populations derived from a fairly recent common ancestor (thus limiting the time of accumulation for the genetic differences), but they also constituted non isolated entities that were potentially able to exchange genes since their origins. In this new context, the genetic entities studied by the molecular anthropologists are not clearly distinguished from one another, thus introducing a lot of "noise" in the molecular analyses. This is only further complicated by the relatively low genetic diversity observed in the living human species. In short, molecular anthropologists faced a number of problems in their intraspecific analyses that were either absent or of limited consequence in their interspecific analyses.

A number of such difficulties are now better understood (e.g., Crubézy and Braga, 2003; Excoffier and Roessli, 1990; Langaney et al., 1990; Relethford, 1995, 1999; Stoneking, 1993).

1. It is unclear if the living humans constitute a valid and unbiased sample representing the entire genetic history of the species. After all, most of the individuals who genetically contributed to its history are no longer alive.

2. At least two distinct explanations can account for the low genetic diversity of the human species today: because the living humans are all derived from a very recent common ancestor or because the various populations always managed to exchange genes, thus avoiding a profound genetic divergence.

3. The greater genetic diversity of a living human population (i.e., Africans) over the others can be explained in more than one way: By being the oldest one it had more time to accumulate a higher genetic diversity (thus possibly implying that all the other populations are derived from this older population); by always having been represented by more individuals it was able to sustain a greater genetic diversity within its boundaries (thus not implying that the other smaller populations are derived from this larger one).

4. The greater genetic distance of a population in comparison to the others could either imply a greater time of divergence with the other populations or a lower level of gene flow received from the other populations.

5. The various portions of the genome used in the molecular studies yield different results of genetic proximity and divergence date.

6. For the molecular clock to be reliable, it must simultaneously be assumed that mutation rates are constant in a population while its size remains roughly similar during its entire evolutionary history. These two assumptions can be criticized on the basis that the size of the hominid populations has always been fluctuating in accordance to the challenges of the environment and of the competitors.

This survey of the main difficulties of the molecular studies as applied in an intraspecific context reveals that the genetic diversity among the living humans is explained by several factors which are rarely mutually exclusive: population size, mutation rate, gene flow, migration, hybridization, calibration of the clock, selective pressures, etc. All these factors provide a lot of flexibility for those who interpret the data. It is not surprising, therefore, that the results of the molecular studies were believed to fit competing views in traditional anthropology, such as the Out of Africa model (e.g., Stringer and Andrews, 1988; Stringer and Bräuer, 1994) and the Multiregional Evolution model (e.g., Frayer et al., 1993; Hawks and Wolpoff, 2001).

When applied to the debate on the rise of the living humans, molecular studies contributed to two distinct but closely related issues.[52] In the first one, molecular anthropologists were concerned with the relationships of the living human populations. This debate largely centered on whether or not the living Africans were more distantly related to all the other living human populations. A positive answer to this question might imply that by being the members of the oldest human population, the living Africans had more time for divergence from the other populations, thus accumulating more genetic differences. The possible implication accompanying this notion is that if the living Africans belonged to the oldest human population, then the other living humans (Europeans, Asians) could be derived from this African population. Many molecular studies have supported an African origin for the living humans (e.g., Ayala and Escalante, 1996; Bowcock et al., 1994; Cann et al., 1987; Horai et al., 1995; Long et al., 1990; Nei and Livshits, 1989; Vigilant et al., 1991; Wainscoat et al., 1986; Wilson and Cann, 1992). However, another hypothesis suggested that the level of genetic diversity among the living Africans was not sufficiently distinct from the other living human populations as to warrant the placing of the cradle of the truly modern human type exclusively in Africa. This was taken to imply that non-African populations have also contributed to the genetic makeup of the living humans (e.g., Relethford, 2001b; Rosalind et al., 1997; Templeton, 2002).

To hold that the African population is possibly the oldest stock from which stemmed all the others does little to settle the debate between the Out of Africa and the Multiregional Evolution models. After all, both models predicted that the living humans could trace back their ancestors to Africa. What distinguishes them, however, is the time frame of the last migration out of Africa. Whereas the proponents of the Out of Africa model assume a migration event in the late Middle Pleistocene or early Late Pleistocene period (between 200,000 and 100,000 years ago), the multiregionalists place it in the Early Pleistocene period (between 2 and 1 mya). It is therefore the timing of this migration event which is the key issue. Could the molecular clock be used to settle it?

This is precisely the other issue investigated by the molecular anthropologists. As in the previous issue, they were not able to reach a consensus. In a first hypothesis, it was proposed that the living human populations started to diverge from one another within the past 250,000 years (e.g., Ayala and Escalante, 1996; Cann et al., 1987; Goldstein et al., 1995; Hammer, 1995; Horai et al., 1995; Nei and Roychoudhury, 1974, 1982; Vigilant et al., 1991; Wilson and Cann, 1992). This hypothesis is consistent with the Out of Africa model and multilinear hypotheses which postulated that the earliest truly modern-looking fossil forms are to be found in this time range. Many molecular anthropologists interpreted these results as indicating that all the living humans had evolved from a common African ancestor.

In a second hypothesis, it was held that the genetic diversity observed among the living humans indicated a divergence time before 500,000 years ago (e.g., Harding et al., 1997; Kaessmann et al., 1999; Templeton, 2002; Wills, 1995). These results could be indicative that archaic hominid forms genetically contributed to the genetic makeup of the living humans, as no modern-looking forms are known from this ancient time range in the fossil record. This view is consistent with the

Multiregional Evolution model and the linear hypotheses which promoted that the later phases of human evolution occurred within a single genetic system, whether or not this system comprises two taxonomic groups (*Homo erectus* and *H. sapiens*) or only a single one (*H. sapiens* [including *H. erectus*]).

The molecular studies are consistent with both the Out of Africa and the Multiregional Evolution models, although molecular support for the latter has only come of late. It is unclear if this constitutes a new trend that will continue to gather more momentum in the near future. Whether or not this is case, it should not be forgotten that studies in traditional and molecular anthropology can be consistent with each other without necessarily implying that they bring support to the exact same phenomenon. Because the debate on the rise of the living humans was first based on the fossil record, it was perhaps tempting for the molecular anthropologists to read their findings through the lens of the original debate (e.g., Marks, 1996b). The impact of molecular anthropology in this debate was limited primarily because molecular anthropologists themselves were divided on this question. This offered the traditional anthropologists the possibility of supporting their competing views with a number of molecular studies, while rejecting at the same time the molecular studies that were not consistent with theirs. Irrespective of the successes of molecular anthropology in the debate on humankind's place among the primates, it seems that the ambiguities of the molecular studies on the rise of the living humans will need to be resolved through collaborations with the traditional anthropologists (e.g., Langaney et al., 1990; Relethford, 1995).

CONCLUSION

The quest to establish humankind's place in nature during the 1965–2000 period has made notable progress when compared to the 1935–1965 period. In the debate on humankind's place among the primates, for instance, the number of scholars who promoted that the human line entirely avoided going through a hominoid ape phase of evolution seriously decreased, especially after 1980. Furthermore, the notion that humankind had sprung from an early and very generalized hominoid ape phase in the Oligocene period or before was gradually abandoned after 1965. Now, the debate largely centered around the dryopithecines of the Mio-Pliocene period, thus placing the split of the human line from the other primates in a not too ancient time period and among a frankly ape-like evolutionary group. The molecular studies all pointed to a close relationship betwen humankind and the two African great apes exclusively, while supporting the thesis of a relatively late departure time. The molecular studies strongly contributed to reinforce the setting of this more restricted framework of analysis.

In light of this strongly reduced taxonomic and temporal framework, it is not surprising to see that the scenarios of hominization proposed during the 1965–2000 period were circumscribed within more restricted limits than in the past. Although the evolutionary causes at the heart of the scenarios of hominization will probably always remain conjectural, it is also clear that the constituent elements of the scenarios gained in scientific robustness by being more solidly grounded in the empirical reality of the fossil record. Under such circumstances, inquiries respectively concerned with scenario building and phylogenetic analyses have been converging toward one another, thus reducing the conjectural nature of the former.

If the scenarios of hominization were less speculative than in the past, it is largely under the impetus of a rapidly improving fossil record, especially for the early hominids. Undoubtedly, this could only have contributed to reduce further the investigative framework relevant to such studies. While very few scholars were now prepared to hold that the human line had entirely avoided going through an australopithecine-like phase of evolution (hypothetical or actually discovered), those who refused to identify this ancestor among the australopithecines recognized a very close phylogenetic proximity between them and the human line. In addition to a more constructed taxonomic perspective on the australopithecines, the post-1965 period also saw the rise of a more restrictive chronological framework. Indeed, the timespan allowed to derive the human line from an early hominid form was now within the fairly limited range of 10 to 2 million years ago, a time frame which was consistent with most of the dates proposed under the molecular clock.

If the post-1965 period was simply an outstanding one for the recovery of early hominids, things were not as spectacular for the later hominids. The progress has been much slower in this area of inquiry since it had already reached a threshold of a near empirical saturation. This is understandable considering that substantial empirical progress had already been achieved during the 1935–1965 period. Because of this situation, the debate on the rise of the living humans was caught up in the midst of competing evolutionary conceptions and theories after 1965. This being said, this debate was not entirely deprived of recent important scientific gains. Indeed, the whole spectrum of phylogenetic hypotheses has grown to incorporate a complex network of hypotheses grading imperceptibly into one another. In addition, the notion of a truly ancient and modern-looking human ancestor leading to all the living humans which has supposedly been dated to the Early Pleistocene period or before was increasingly abandoned to the point of almost having completely disappeared in the 1965–2000 period. The input of the molecular studies in this debate contributed little to its resolution as molecular anthropologists became embroiled in internal debates which nearly mimicked those being conducted on the basis of the hominid fossil record. The contribution of the molecular studies to the debate on the living humans is a very recent one; its full value probably lies only in the future.

In order to appreciate the progressiveness of the field of paleoanthropology since 1860, it must be remembered that the four main debates reviewed in this chapter were once almost entirely deprived of an empirical basis coming from the fossil record. At the very beginning, these debates largely rested on inferences extrapolated from the living forms, in addition to being conducted in relative isolation from one another. In this context, it is easy to understand why so many divergent phylogenetic hypotheses had been proposed at one time or another. Without a fossil record, the constraints imposed on the interpretations by the method of comparative anatomy alone were weak, to say the least. With the remarkable improvement of the fossil record and the new light shed by the molecular studies after 1960, not only have these four debates reached a state of near or partial integration but they also collectively circumscribe a very small portion of the tree of life believed to be relevant for the understanding of human evolution. Apparently, the quest to establish humankind's place in nature need not be conducted beyond these new limits.

NOTES

1. Many scholars have contributed to the debates on humankind's place in nature since 1965. Regrettably, it has not been possible in this chapter to do justice to them all. After all, developments in the 1965–2000 period could easily fill another book. As throughout this book, priority has been given to scholars who: (1) presented their views in an unambiguous fashion and embraced a broad perspective of primate or human phylogeny; (2) came from different countries; and (3) expounded viewpoints which were not necessarily mainstream. Keep in mind that the absolute priority of this book is to review the entire scientific spectrum of viewpoints held at one time or another about humankind's place in nature. Our main goal here is to identify what is and what is not scientifically defensible about human evolution during the various historical phases of the field of paleoanthropology. The authors reviewed in this chapter, most of whom are alive today, were selected for their viewpoints at a *particular moment* during the 1965–2000 period. For the reasons already enumerated, it has not always been possible to mention whether or not they have changed their mind since. The analysis of the 1965–2000 period was rendered more difficult by the increasing number of multi-authored articles. In this context, it is more difficult to follow the viewpoint of a single scholar without referring to his or her colleagues. I sincerely hope that paleoanthropologists will not be offended by the procedures and choices made in this chapter.

2. Remember that Genet-Varcin (1969: 304) once placed the separation of the human line from the other nonhuman primates in the Cretaceous period. See Genet-Varcin's new primate family tree in "Réflexion sur l'origine des hominidés." In, *Les origines humaines et les époques de l'intelligence* (Paris: Masson, 1978), p. 20.

3. See Genet-Varcin's most recent primate family tree in *Éléments de Primatologie: Les hommes fossiles, découvertes et travaux depuis dix années* (Paris: Boubée, 1979), p. 31.

4. See Hürzeler's hominoid family tree in "Les racines paléontologiques de l'humanité: Le mouvement primate vers l'homme." In, *Les origines humaines et les époques de l'intelligence* (Paris: Masson, 1978), p. 11. This phylogenetic tree is virtually identical to the one previously presented by Hürzeler (1968: 229).

5. At first, Piveteau (1973: 11–14) made clear that *Ramapithecus* is not within the human radiation but in the ape one, while he was uncertain as to the status of *Oreopithecus*. The human-like features of *Ramapithecus* were explained at the time by convergent evolution. Later, Piveteau (1983: 13–15) was not as certain as in the past that *Ramapithecus* should be confined to the ape radiation, while he remained as uncertain as in the past about the status of *Oreopithecus*.

6. See Eckhardt's hominoid family tree in "Population Genetics and Human Origins." *Scientific American*, 226 (1972), p. 97.

7. See the hominoid family tree of Pilbeam and his colleagues in "New Hominoid Primates From the Siwaliks of Pakistan and Their Bearing on Hominoid Evolution." *Nature*, 270 (1977), p. 692.

8. See Schwartz's cladogram of the hominoids in "The Evolutionary Relationships of Man and Orang-Utans." *Nature*, 308 (1984), p. 504.

9. See Aguirre's hominoid family tree in "Les rapports phylétiques de Ramapithecus et de Kenyapithecus et l'origine des hominidés." *L'Anthropologie*, 76 (1972), p. 521.

10. See Greenfield's hominoid family tree in "A Late Divergence Hypothesis." *American Journal of Physical Anthropology*, 52 (1980), p. 361.

11. See Andrews's hominoid family tree in "Evolution and Environment in the Hominoidea." *Nature*, 360 (1992), p. 644. Note that there is a mistake in this family tree. The "Human" should take the place of the "Orang", and the "Orang" the place of the "Human". The mistake has been corrected in P. Andrews, D.R. Begun, and M. Zylstra, "Interrelatioships Between Functional Morphology and Paleoenvironments in Miocene Hominoids." In, D.R. Begun, C.V. Ward and M. Rose (eds.), *Function, Phylogeny, and Fossils: Miocene Hominoid Evolution and Adaptations* (New York: Plenum Press, 1997), p. 51.

12. See Martin's cladogram in "Relationships Among Extant and Extinct Great Apes and Humans." In, B. Wood, L. Martin and P. Andrews (eds.), *Major Topics in Primate and Human Evolution* (Cambridge: Cambridge University Press), p. 181. See Barriel's cladogram (hypothesis # 2) in "Caractères ostéologiques et odontologiques chez les Hominoidea (Primate, Mammalia): Analyse de parcimonie." *Bulletins et Mémoires de la Société d'Anthropologie de Paris*, 3 (1991), p. 47.

13. See Pilbeam's hominoid family tree in "Hominoid Evolution and Hominoid Origins." *American Anthropologist*, 88 (1986), p. 308.

14. See Begun's hominoid family tree in "Planet of the Apes." *Scientific American*, 289 (2003), p. 80.

15. Sarmiento (1987, 1996) may have questioned the possibility of any form of bipedalism in the early hominids, but unfortunately his viewpoint was presented in a very laconic fashion not devoid of ambiguities.

16. See Oxnard's hominoid family tree in *Fossils, Teeth and Sex: New Perspectives on Human Evolution* (Seattle: University of Washington Press, 1987), p. 245.

17. See the place attributed to the australopithecines in Genet-Varcin's primate family tree in *Éléments de primatologie: Les hommes fossiles* (Paris: Boubée, 1979), p. 31. Previously, Genet-Varcin placed the split of the australopithecines from the human radiation in the Miocene period (1969: 304) and even in the Oligocene period (1963: 220–221).

18. See Olson's hominid family tree in "Basicranial Morphology of the Extant Hominoids and Pliocene Hominids: The New Material From the Hadar Formation, Ethiopia, and Its Significance in Early Human Evolution and Taxonomy." In, C.B. Stringer (ed.), *Aspects of Human Evolution* (London: Taylor and Francis, 1981), p. 124 and in "Cranial Morphology and Systematics of the Hadar Formation Hominids and *'Australopithecus' africanus*." In, E. Delson (ed.), *Ancestors: The Hard Evidence* (New York: Alan R. Liss, 1985), p. 117. Apparently, by 1987 Olson had given up on his entire hypothesis and now favored the idea that the *Homo* line had directly sprung from a form like *Australopithecus africanus* (e.g., Delson, 1987).

19. See Senut's phylogenetic tree of the australopithecines in "Pliocene Hominid Systematics and Phylogeny." *South African Journal of Science*, 92 (1996), p. 166 and in "First Hominid from the Miocene (Lukeino Formation, Kenya)." *Comptes Rendus de l'Académie des Sciences de Paris*, IIa, 332 (2001), p. 142.

20. See Leakey's hominid family tree in *Origins: What New Discoveries Reveal About the Emergence of Our Species and Its Possible Future* (New York: E.P. Dutton, 1977), pp. 84–85 and in *Human Origins* (New York: E.P. Dutton, 1982), pp. 50–51.

21. Leakey's changes are subtile but important (Leakey, 1989; Leakey and Lewin, 1992). First, the fossil remains recognized by Leakey as *Homo habilis* are now dated by him at 2 and not 3 million years ago. It is anticipated that the ancestor of *Homo habilis* may eventually be found before 2 million years ago but it is not clearly stated by Leakey that this ancestor will necessarily be a form of *Homo*. Second, Leakey now speaks of a common ancestor to all the hominids (including the *Homo* line) that could be dated at earlier than 3.5 million years and not at 6 or 5 million years as previously thought. This contributed to reduce the potential antiquity of the *Homo* line. The reduced antiquity of the genus *Homo* is apparently supported by the following statement: "Bipedal apes had been in existence for a long time when

Homo arrived. The human family emerged about 7.5 million years ago; *Homo* evolved sometime before two million years ago. There was a large evolutionary gap between the origin of the first hominid species and the origin of *Homo*, a gap as great as five million years" (Leakey and Lewin, 1992: 141). Third, an early *Ramapithecus*-like creature is no longer believed to be a common ancestor to all the later hominids. The *Homo* line is thus left without a known direct ancestor. Fourth, Leakey continued to hold that some fossil remains attributed to *Autralopithecus afarensis* by some scholars do not belong to this species but to another one, although he now refrained from identifying it, whereas in the past he called it *Homo* (Leakey, 1981: 70). Was this unidentified species *Homo* or australopithecine? On this view, it is clear that Leakey's view wavered in the late 1980s and early 1990s. I am not implying here that Leakey necessarily gave up on his early view entirely, although he was no longer able to promote it as clearly and as explicitly as in the past.

22. See Coppens's family tree of the australopithecines in "Le cerveau des hommes fossiles." *Comptes Rendus des Séances de l'Académie des Sciences de Paris*, 292 (Supplément d'Avril, 1981), p. 4 and in *Le singe, l'Afrique et l'homme* (Paris: Fayard, 1983), p. 115 and 118. Soon after, Coppens (1994) derived the *Homo* line directly from the known *Australopithecus* at about 3 million years ago.

23. See Coppens's new phylogenetic tree of the australopithecines in "East Side Story: The Origin of Humankind." *Scientific American*, 270 (1994): 62–69.

24. Remember that Tobias (1967: 244) promoted that the gracile australopithecines were in all probability at the very base of the line leading to the living humans, although he would not exclude the possibility of interbreeding between the gracile and the robust australopithecines. If there were interbreeding between the two, then it cannot be excluded that the robust australopithecines contributed genetically to the rise of the living humans.

25. See Brace's hominid family tree in *The Stages of Human Evolution*, 4th edition (New Jersey: Prentice Hall, 1991), p. 112.

26. See Wolpoff's hominid family tree in *Paleoanthropology*, 2nd edition (Boston: McGraw-Hill, 1999), p. 308.

27. See Johanson's and White's hominid family tree in "A Systematic Assessment of Early African Hominids." *Science*, 203 (1979), p. 328 and in "*Australopithecus africanus*: Its Phyletic Position Reconsidered." *South Africa Journal of Science*, 77 (1981), p. 466. See Rak's hominid phylogenetic tree in *The Australopithecine Face* (New York: Academic Press, 1983), p. 157.

28. Although Johanson, White, and Kimbel continued to publish articles together, the erosion of their common view is seen by the fact that their phylogenetic position is not clearly presented (e.g., Kimbel et al., 1988).

29. In 1989, Johanson stated that the hypothesis which places *A. afarensis* rather than *A. africanus* in a direct ancestral position to the *Homo* line has stood the test of time. Yet, he recognized that it is difficult to choose between different phylogenetic hypotheses (Johanson, 1989: 84). Two of the four hypotheses presented by Johanson placed *A. afarensis* as the sole and direct ancestor of *Homo*, while two hypotheses placed *A. africanus* in this position.

30. See Grine's hominid family tree in "Australopithecine Taxonomy and Phylogeny: Historical Background and Recent Interpretation." In, R.L. Ciochon and J.G. Fleagle (eds.), *The Human Evolution Source Book* (New Jersey: Prentice Hall, 1993), p. 207.

31. See Strait's, Grine's, and Moniz's two hominid family trees in "A Reappraisal of Early Hominid Phylogeny." *Journal of Human Evolution*, 32 (1997), p. 53 and p. 55.

32. In 1991, Wood favored *Australopithecus afarensis* as a direct ancestor to *Homo* but was not yet prepared to definitely exclude *A. africanus* from this position. See his hominid family tree in *Koobi Fora Research Project, Vol. 4, Hominid Cranial Remains* (Oxford: Clarendon Press, 1991), p. 280. However, Wood had done so by the following year, see his hominid phylogenetic tree in "Origin and Evolution of the Genus *Homo*." *Nature*, 355 (1992), p. 789.

33. See Tobias's hominid family tree in "'*Australopithecus afarensis* and *A. africanus*: Critique and an Alternative Hypothesis." *Palaeontologia Africana*, 23 (1980), p. 3.

34. See McHenry's and Skelton's phylogenetic trees of the australopithecines in "Phylogenetic Analysis of Early Hominids." *Current Anthropology*, 27 (1986), p. 33 and in "Evolutionary

Relationships Among Early Hominids." *Journal of Human Evolution*, 23 (1992), p. 340.

35. McHenry and Berger (1998: 20) stated that since "the two known associated partial skeletons of *H. habilis* appear to have the more primitive fore- to hindlimb proportions of *A. africanus*, the evolution of the human body is more complicated than previously understood". This situation opens up the possibility of parallel evolution in either craniodental features or limb proportions between *Homo* and autralopithecine forms.

36. See Tattersall's and Eldredge's two hominid phylogenetic trees in "Fact, Theory, and Fantasy in Human Paleontology." *American Scientist*, 65 (1977), p. 209; see Delson's model of the evolutionary history of the early hominids (and the explanation accompanying it) in "Models of Early Hominid Phylogeny." In, C.J. Jolly (ed.), *Early Hominids in Africa* (New York: Duckworth, 1978), p. 534.

37. See Delson's family tree of the australopithecines in "Human Phylogeny Revised Again." *Nature*, 322 (1986), p. 497.

38. See Tattersall's hominid family trees in *The Human Odyssey* (New York: Prentice Hall, 1993), p. 151, and in *Becoming Human* (New York: Harcourt Brace & Co., 1998), p. 185.

39. See Tattersall's new hominid family tree in *Extinct Humans* (Colorado: Westview Press, 2000), p. 244.

40. See Leakey's and Walker's phylogenetic tree of the australopithecines in "Early Hominid Fossils from Africa." *Scientific American*, 276 (1997), p. 76. This article was reproduced several years later but the phylogenetic tree was modified to incorporate some of the new fossil discoveries. However, the nature of the relationship between *Australopithecus africanus* and *Homo* remained unchanged, see "Early Hominid Fossils from Africa." *Scientific American*, special edition, 13 (2003), p. 16. At this stage, it is unclear if the discovery of *Kenyanthropus* will modify the view of this relationship, especially in the eyes of Meave Leakey (e.g., Leakey et al., 2001). It should be noted that few years earlier, Walker placed the rise of the *Homo* line not between 3 and 2 million years ago, but rather nearer to 4 million years ago, as he inclined to believe that the line leading to the living humans evolved out of the unknown direct ancestor of *Australopithecus africanus*. See Walker's and Shipman's hominid family tree in *The Wisdom of the Bones* (New York: Vintage Books, 1997), p. 150.

41. Compare Genet-Varcin's primate phylogenetic trees to see the continually changing dates of the split of the advanced hominid branches in *Les singes actuels et fossiles* (Paris: N. Boubée et Cie, 1963), pp. 220–221; *À la recherche du primate ancêtre de l'homme* (Paris: N. Boubée et Cie, 1969), p. 304; and *Éléments de primatologie: Les hommes fossiles* (Paris: Boubée, 1979), p. 31.

42. There will never be such a thing as a complete fossil record. Still, assuming that there would be such a thing, it is improbable that scholars would all agree on the exact same phylogenetic view. The completeness of that record would dramatically reduce the framework within which the phylogenetic debates could take place, but because fossilized bones are no substitute for real flesh and because it is impossible to directly observe the behavior of the hominids, it would always be possible to hold slightly different viewpoints.

43. Compare Tattersall's changing view of late hominid phylogeny in "Fact, Theory and Fantasy in Human Paleontology," *American Scientist*, 65 (1977), p. 209, and *The Human Odyssey* (New York: Prentice Hall, 1993), p. 151.

44. At one time, Tattersall was prepared to recognize another species, *Homo antecessor*, on the evolutionary line linking the living humans with *Homo ergaster*. See *Becoming Human* (New York: Harcourt Brance & Company, 1998), p. 185.

45. See Wood's human phylogenetic trees in "The Origin of *Homo erectus*." *Courier Forschungsinstitut Senckenberg*, 69 (1984), p. 106. Of the four proposed evolutionary trees, Wood favored hypothesis two or four. In 1986, Wood co-authored a paper with Bilsborough. However, both scholars had divergent views of human phylogeny. The distinct view of Bilsborough will be presented below.

46. See Wood's multilinear hypothesis of the genus *Homo* in "Human Evolution", *BioEssays*, 18 (1996), p. 947.

47. See Rightmire's phylogenetic tree in "Human Evolution in the Middle Pleistocene: The Role of *Homo heidelbergensis*." *Evolutionary Anthropology*, 6 (1998), p. 221.

48. See Stringer's simplified phylogenetic tree of the genus *Homo* in *African Exodus: The Origins*

of Modern Humanity (New York: Henry Holt, 1996), p. 53.

49. See Bräuer's phylogenetic tree of the later hominids in "A Cranial Approach to the Origin of Anatomically Modern *Homo sapiens* in Africa and Implications for the Appearance of Modern Europeans." In, F.H. Smith and F. Spencer (eds.), *The Origins of Modern Humans: A World Survey of the Fossil Evidence* (New York: Alan R. Liss, 1984), p. 394. See also Bräuer's diagram illustrating the complex succession of evolutionary grades in the later portion of human evolution in "Africa's Place in the Evolution of *Homo sapiens*." In, G. Bräuer and F.H. Smith (eds.), *Continuity or Replacement: Controversies in* Homo sapiens *evolution* (Rotterdam: A.A. Balkema, 1992), p. 88.

50. These various and more or less independent regional evolutionary hominid lines are presented in Thorne's and Wolpoff's diagram in "The Multiregional Evolution of Humans." *Scientific American*, 266 (1992), p. 32.

51. Wolpoff and Caspari explained how they believed the Multiregional model of evolution was distinct from the parallel hypotheses proposed earlier by Weidenreich and Coon. See Caspari and Wolpoff, "Weidenreich, Coon, and Multiregional Evolution." *Human Evolution*, 11 (1996): 261–268; and Wolpoff and Caspari, *Race and Human Evolution* (New York: Simon and Schuster, 1997).

52. In fact, another dimension brought by the molecular studies is the one called "ancient DNA". Of late, it has become possible to extract some genetic information from the hominid fossils themselves (e.g., Hagelberg, 1993–94; Kaestle and Horsburgh, 2002; Lengyel, 1981; Lowenstein, 1981). From a field first restricted to the comparison of the living forms, molecular anthropology is in a process of also acquiring a historical dimension, like paleontology has. Scholars were quick to exploit these new and still very partial results of ancient DNA. They got embroiled in debates on the phylogeny of the later phases of human evolution (e.g., Adcock et al., 2001; Beerli and Edwards, 2002; Krings et al., 1997; Krings et al., 1999; Krings et al., 2000; Ovchinnikov et al., 2000; Relethford, 2001a; Wolpoff, 1998). As the implications of these very recent developments are not clear, they will not be considered here.

11

The Nature of Paleoanthropology

INTRODUCTION

It is not easy not to be impressed by the progress made in the quest to establish humankind's place in nature since 1860. I would surmise that paleoanthropology might be among the most progressive scientific disciplines of this entire time period. Why should this be the case? After all, philosophers of science have insisted that disciplines are often characterized either by several competing viewpoints about the proper theoretical matrix upon which a discipline rests, or by a succession in time of such divergent and incommensurable (mutually exclusive) theoretical viewpoints. Are there any good reasons not to view the field of paleoanthropology in light of these epistemological frameworks or models? There are several reasons.

No particular epistemological model for paleoanthropology is proposed here. I contend that only a better understanding of paleoanthropology's nature will eventually permit us to select or forge a proper epistemological framework for it. It is true that a number of paleoanthropologists have already ventured to propose such epistemological models. Some favor applying a Kuhnian model which sees the field as being organized around one paradigm or more (e.g., Chamberlain and Hartwig, 1999). Others are more inclined toward a Popperian model which stresses the refutation of proposed hypotheses (e.g., Wolpoff, 1976, 1982). Still others suggest that a deductive-nomological model, under which particular evolutionary events are explained by general laws, would be the proper model for paleoanthropology (e.g., Cartmill, 1990). In light of these divergent assessments as well as by the insights gained in this book, we hold that it is premature to define the proper epistemological model for paleoanthropology. More reflection and more agreement on this important question are needed.

AVOIDING PRE-ESTABLISHED EPISTEMOLOGICAL MODELS

There is one good theoretical reason not to force the analysis of paleoanthropology into pre-established or ready-made epistemological models. To do so would be to assume that the scientific enterprise as a whole is guided by a single or a limited number of such epistemological frameworks; models which have by themselves been identified in other disciplines. To accept a ready-made epistemological model for paleoanthropology is to accept uncritically that its development is, epistemologically speaking, identical or conform, to the development of the other scientific disciplines which have already been analyzed by the philosophers of science.

To put things bluntly, philosophers of science have analyzed too few scientific disciplines to be in a position to know all the epistemological routes exploited at one time or another in the history of science. It would not be an exaggeration to say that the actual turmoil in the philosophy of science is largely the product of philosophical analyses applied to disciplines outside the realm of the physical sciences. The more philosophers of science study these other disciplines, the more it is realized that they are not complying to the known epistemological models. New epistemological models must therefore be established. This is not surprising when considering that the history of science teaches us that scientists had to continually build new epistemological frameworks to accommodate new scientific quests or research areas. It seems that we have not yet reached the point where scholars have exhausted the epistemological plurality associated with an expanding scientific enterprise.

In this context, it might be wise to reconsider the epistemological models developed for every scientific question or research area. This safety procedure might avoid applying the wrong epistemological analyses to the wrong scientific questions or research areas. It is far less damaging to multiply them unduly rather than forcing research areas into wrong models. In the first case, time would only show that several fields are complying to the same epistemological imperatives. In the other case, the understanding of the development of a discipline would be severely distorted.

THE NATURE OF PALEOANTHROPOLOGY

If there are good theoretical reasons not to analyze the field of paleoanthropology in light of pre-established epistemological models, its development as presented in this book also supports this cautious attitude. Paleoanthropology has been a very progressive research area because of both the accessibility and the intelligibility of its empirical basis. This statement may come as a surprise when considering that paleoanthropologists have been painfully extracting fossils embedded in ancient geological strata. The meaning of this statement can only be appreciated when compared to other disciplines.

Astronomers and cosmologists face major empirical problems because the reality they are studying is so far out in space that it directly impinges on the notion of time. Remember that under the Newtonian theory, time is the same (absolute) no matter where you are in space. It was argued, under Einstein's theory of relativity, that if this was a good approximation of the truth in circumscribed space (on earth, for instance), it entailed more serious deformations on a larger scale. In the theory of relativity, space and time are not isolated variables but rather are intertwined. This theory certainly constitutes anything but an intuitive theoretical context to understand the reality of the universe: The notion of a space traveler who carries his or her own time as he or she moves at great speed is strange indeed. Furthermore, the huge size of the universe not only restricts the quality and the quantity of the information obtained, but also has a direct effect on the intelligibility of the observed phenomena. The fact that technical instruments such as radio telescopes are used to study the universe also introduces another level of theoretical complexity in the interpretative process. The philosopher of science Gaston Bachelard remarked that a scientific instrument was, in essence, a theory which was presented in a material form, as this instrument was designed in accordance with a theoretical prediction of what would be found (Bachelard, 1933: 140–142).

On the other end of the spectrum, subatomic physicists are studying entities that are so small that when looked at from the classical theory of physics—originally designed to study macroscopic objects—matter at this level has a dual nature or ontology by being alternatively a particle or a wave, while it is impossible to simultaneously establish its location and speed, being one or the other. Physicists have devoted almost the entire twentieth century to elaborate a theory of subatomic particles, the quantum theory. The debate largely centered on whether or not the classical and the quantum theories were generating results that were compatible, or if one should be subsumed under the other. Needless to say, the study of the empirical reality at this subatomic level is done entirely through the intermediary of scientific instruments. This is true to the point where it was sometimes questioned if the observed phenomena were real or merely a by-product of the techniques that were used. Again, the subatomic reality poses important problems of intelligibility and can only be assessed through an imposing theoretical armature. There is absolutely nothing intuitive about it.

In comparison to these fields, paleoanthropology is a discipline at a human scale as far as its empirical basis is concerned. This is not surprising when considering that we are, after all, studying the remains of our ancestors! The relative accessibility and intelligibility of the empirical data in paleoanthropology has contributed powerfully to the swift resolution of many questions since 1860.

Paleoanthropology has been a successful research area also because of its single theoretical structure and its cumulative nature. By being committed to a general evolutionary conception of the living world—and not so much to specific evolutionary theories and conceptions—a strong majority of paleoanthropologists has devoted all their energy to resolve practical questions: humankind's closest relatives; the location of its cradle; the time horizon of the evolutionary events; the conformation of humankind's last common ancestor with his relatives; the most probable scenario of hominization, etc. The theoretical commitment toward a single theory contributed to avoid existential conflicts over the appropriate theoretical foundation needed to interpret paleoanthropology's empirical basis. This empirical basis was therefore largely cumulative, for it was not continually challenged and reinterpreted afresh under profoundly competing theories or successive theoretical changes. This is rarely the case in the physical sciences. The cumulative nature of the empirical basis in paleoanthropology is nicely illustrated in the three successive epistemological episodes through which the field has passed since 1860. This raises two important points.

First, it is clear that the development of paleoanthropology is not directed by the action of competing or successive theories. If this were the case, paleoanthropology would be rigidly constrained, or pulled apart, by these profound theoretical tensions. Instead, we see in the development of paleoanthropology a remarkable coherence and flexibility—a sort of plastic or organic fluidity—in the changing evolutionary hypotheses. For instance, at one time in the 1910s and 1920s unilinear and multilinear hominid phylogenetic hypotheses were part of the same conception of human evolution (interpretative framework). Later, while unilinear hypotheses fused with the parallel hominid phylogenetic hypotheses, a number of proponents of the multilinear hypotheses transformed their preferred hypotheses into parallel hypotheses, some of them even pushing the transformation to the point of approaching a linear hypothesis. Another example concerns the scholars who once hypothesized that the modern human type was of great antiquity. But as the twentieth century progressed, they gradually reduced this antiquity, in several steps, to the point where it was established at the end of the Pleistocene period. All these gradual changes in interpretation were possible only because they were not dependent upon genuinely distinct theories.

This type of cognitive and logical flexibility is not standard in disciplines characterized by competing or successive theories. This is understandable when considering that a change in theory will institute a change of interpretation in the empirical data, the converse also being true. After all, there must be some kind of link between a theory and its empirical foundation. Although a certain amount of flexibility between the prediction of a theory and its empirical basis should be allowed, there will be, eventually, a rupture if they are not changing with sufficient harmony. In paleoanthropology, the interpretation of the empirical basis keeps changing without instituting a break with the theoretical foundation. We promote that this has been the case because phylogenetic hypotheses have always been based on the same theoretical foundation: the general idea of biological evolution.

This fluidity of interpretation in paleoanthropology is such that there are almost as many participating scholars as there are different phylogenetic hypotheses at each moment in the history of the field. This profusion of distinct hypotheses certainly does not imply that there are as many theories as there are participating paleoanthropologists! Is it possible, then, to regroup closely related hypotheses under a small number of distinct theories or paradigms? We think not. This position is untenable considering that there are always intermediate hypotheses between two alleged groups of hypotheses. For instance, to view the debate between the Multiregional Evolution and the Out of Africa models as two distinct theories or paradigms, is to assume a cognitive and logical isolation between the two (e.g., Willermet and Clark, 1995). This assumption, however, breaks down when looking at the phylogenetic hypotheses which variously combine elements from both the Multiregional Evolution and the Out of Africa models (e.g., Smith and Harrold, 1997). These two conceptions, therefore, are merely the extreme poles of a spectrum of defensible hypotheses. The fact that phylogenetic hypotheses are blending into one another is very typical of the history of paleoanthropology. This is a part of its very nature. Were hominid phylogenetic hypotheses truly by-products of specific and competing evolutionary theories, as suggested by Bowler (1986), it would be impossible to understand both the so-called intermediate hypotheses and the ease with which scholars gradually modify their hypotheses over time.

The second important point that needs to be raised here concerns the nature of the relationship between the general conception of evolution at the base of paleoanthropology and the specific evolutionary theories. We have seen how evolutionary theories such as Darwinism, Orthogenesis, the Evolutionary Synthesis, the Neutral Theory of Molecular Evolution, and a host of developments in the post-1970 period had an impact on paleoanthropology. From time to time, some scholars derived from them inspiration for patterns and mechanisms in human evolution. Yet, it is clear that the development of paleoanthropology since 1860 was not mainly organized around the changes in specific evolutionary theories. This is not surprising when considering that paleoanthropology is not merely a by-product of specific evolutionary theories. Changes in such theories may have created some fluctuations in the development of paleoanthropology, but the core of the discipline was never centered around them.

The core of paleoanthropology rests on the general conception of evolution; a theoretical foundation which is more abstract and more neutral than any specific theory of evolution. It is on this theoretical foundation that the substance of paleoanthropology was founded by the complex interplay of the comparative method and of the fossil record. While the comparative method first generated a host of hominid phylogenetic hypotheses—essentially based on living forms—the fossil discoveries eventually contributed powerfully to reducing the number of such hypotheses. The complex dynamic instituted between the comparative method and the fossil record has been so productive as a means to generate knowledge about human evolution that hominid phylogenetic hypotheses entirely based on specific evolutionary theories could not endure for long the test of this powerful procedure. As already stated on more than one occasion, specific evolutionary conceptions and theories can be used to interpret the course of human evolution, but only to the extent that these viewpoints fit within the boundaries already set by the known empirical reality at a particular moment. As these boundaries were getting tighter and tighter with the development of paleoanthropology during the twentieth century, the room to maneuver only diminished for the theory-based phylogenetic hypotheses.

In what way then does paleoanthropology's nature differ from the other specialities of paleontology? It differs in no way since they are all bound by epistemological imperatives which are fundamentally identical. However, their specificities arise from the different portions of the tree of life they each try to reconstruct. Indeed, several factors can be at play in the development of each speciality. For instance, the random sequence of fossil discoveries in each tree's portion might at first have channelled the phylogenetic hypotheses in one direction or another. Furthermore, the morphological similarities or dissimilarities between the living forms and their ancestors also surely influenced the establishment of the phylogenetic hypotheses. The same would have applied to the geographical distribution of the living forms and their assumed ancestors. All these factors are involved in the process of building an identity for each speciality of paleontology. These fields, including paleoanthropology, are historical creations as each developed along a unique trajectory since the nineteenth century.

AN EXPANDED AND CHANGING NATURE FOR PALEOANTHROPOLOGY

The analysis of the development of paleoanthropology proposed in this book suggests viewing its nature in the way just presented. However, it is possible to expand on the conception of its nature. As the scientific enterprise is a complex network of ideas, paleoanthropology has been sharing with many other fields various kinds of connections, some being more superficial than others (e.g., Delisle, 2000a, 2001, 2002). Two examples will illustrate this.

Scenarios of hominization, for instance, are open to a host of disciplines such as evolutionary biology, physiology, ethology, sociology, ethnology, linguistics, archaeology, etc. It comes as no surprise that it has been difficult to anchor them in robust scientific explanations. It is indeed a complex task to work out these multiple connections and integrate them in a coherent explanatory structure. In another example, it was seen that the development of paleoanthropology was not profoundly influenced by specific evolutionary theories. However, this does not necessarily apply to all questions pertaining to human evolution. The field of paleoanthropology has been defined here as the quest to establish humankind's place in the tree of life. This definition excludes, for instance, any considerations on whether or not the rise of human beings in the history of life should be attributed to chance factors or to predetermined factors. This debate is powerfully related to specific theories of evolution such as Orthogenesis and Neo-Darwinism, among others, but involves also complex metaphysical issues. Traditionally, most paleoanthropologists have refrained from taking part in this debate, leaving it to the evolutionary theorists. One must go beyond the frontiers of paleoanthropology, as defined here, in order to tackle these questions.

The conception of the nature of paleoanthropology can be expanded by simply broadening the frontiers of this discipline. As we proceed, however, the entity called paleoanthropology becomes more and more nebulous, thus rendering the analysis of its development more difficult. It was decided here not to explore this avenue under the premise that it would be easier in the future to venture in this direction after having first defined paleoanthropology in a less diffuse way. Our strategy was to try to define the nature of paleoanthropology by identifying its core. This was done not by analyzing paleoanthropology at a particular time slice of its development (at a standstill) but since its inception around 1860. This dynamic and developmental view permits us to distinguish more clearly the foundation core from the more or less superficial and external influences.

As may now be clear, the recognition of paleoanthropology's nature largely depends on how its boundaries are set. There is no absolute essence corresponding to this discipline. Yet, this might not be the end of the story. Paleoanthropology's nature may not be necessarily immutable. One example will suffice to illustrate this point. We have seen that the relationship between specific evolutionary theories and paleoanthropology (as narrowly defined in this book) since 1860 has been more or less superficial. Such theories could not take the development of paleoanthropology off its main trajectory. On the contrary, specific evolutionary theories could create an impact on the field only when they were either reinforcing this main trajectory or being consistent with it. However, the nature of this relationship may change in the future.

As our knowledge about human phylogeny continues to improve, paleoanthropology may eventually prove to be in a better position either to receive deeper theoretical inputs from specific evolutionary theories or to contribute directly to their elaboration. In the first case, a firmly established hominid phylogenetic tree may prove to be particularly well explained by a specific evolutionary theory. This could institute ideal conditions for a deep perfusion of this theory into paleoanthropology, thus leading to a fusion of the two. In the other case, a firmly established hominid phylogenetic tree may allow the identification of a number of evolutionary processes which have been largely neglected in the evolutionary biology corpus. This might lead to an active participation of paleoanthropology in the elaboration of evolutionary theories. In both cases, the nature of paleoanthropology as defined in this book would be changed.

Some scholars hold that paleoanthropology has received deep theoretical inputs from specific evolutionary theories and/or has contributed to their elaboration (e.g., Tattersall, 1994, 2000; Wolpoff, 1994, this book). Considering the development of paleoanthropology in the past 150 years, I cannot agree with that. After all, the field has been influenced somewhat superficially by the specific evolutionary theories (e.g., Foley, 2001), not to mention its limited or passive role in their elaboration (e.g., Pilbeam, 1989). I surmise that paleoanthropology will not be in a position to do so until it reaches a greater degree of maturity than it has now. As long as humankind's phylogenetic tree will not be *firmly* established, it will always be possible to pretend that a specific evolutionary theory conforms well to an anticipated phylogenetic hypothesis. Similarly, as long as humankind's phylogenetic tree will not be *strongly* established, it will always be possible to pretend that an anticipated phylogenetic hypothesis contributes powerfully to the elaboration of a specific evolutionary theory. In either case, the exercise may well be stimulating and worthwhile but its value at this stage is, at best, equivocal. The debate on the rise of the living humans since the mid-1970s clearly illustrates this (see chapter 10).

The search for a proper epistemological model for paleoanthropology must be the focus of greater attention than it has yet received. While a better understanding of paleoanthropology's nature will contribute to identify or to forge this model, it will also contribute to tighten paleoanthropologists' grip on the destiny of their own discipline.

History Is Philosophy Learned from Examples

by Bernard Wood

(cited as a saying of Thucydides
by Dionysius of Halicarnassus
in *Ars Rhetorica XI [2]*)

Humankind has been deliberating rationally about its place in nature for more than two thousand years, but when paleoanthropology, the study of human prehistory, began to explore this as a scientific endeavor is a matter of legitimate debate. Richard Delisle's decision to begin his survey in 1860 will make sense to many because it begins the year after the publication of the first edition of Charles Darwin's *On the Origin of Species*. Darwin was not the first person to suggest that humans are both part of the natural world and the product of evolution, but he was the first person to provide a comprehensive exposition of a plausible mechanism for human evolution.

Richard Delisle (RD) sets out a simple thesis that should be heartening to paleoanthropologists. His interpretation of the history of paleoanthropology is that during the past 140 years it has made steady progress toward the goal of reconstructing the branching pattern of the part of the Tree of Life (TOL) that contains the human twig. He suggests that paleoanthropologists have been quick to recognize major advances in evolutionary theory, and that they incorporated them into their thinking at least as rapidly, and perhaps more rapidly, than many other biologists.

As I understand the argument, one of the main reasons for RD's generous grade for paleoanthropology is that through time he sees a steady reduction in the number and variety of viable hypotheses about the branching pattern of the higher primate part of the TOL. Instead of the investigational spotlight illuminating a large part of the Tree of Life, as RD correctly claims it did in the past, he sees it now focused on just the part of the TOL that contains the higher primates. This is not to say that the branching patterns of other parts of the TOL are well understood, but it does reflect the prevailing conventional wisdom that the closest living relatives of modern humans are almost certainly one of the three great apes. A few people (well, actually just one person—Jeff Schwartz) are fighting a hopeless rearguard action on behalf of the orang-utan, but most researchers now accept that the evidence is close to overwhelming that modern humans are more closely related to the African apes than to any other living creature. The vast majority of researchers go even further and accept the substantial body of evidence consistent with the hypothesis that modern humans are more closely related to chimpanzees than they are to any other higher primate.

I agree with RD that the spotlight is more narrowly focused than it was in the past, but where we differ is who should be given credit for this more precise focus. Whereas RD gives the credit to paleoanthropologists, I am more inclined to think that paleoanthropologists have done little more than pick up some of the crumbs that have fallen from the tables of the biochemists and the molecular biologists. The trail of biochemical crumbs began in the 1960s with the elegant analyses of hemoglobin and albumin by Emil Zuckerkandl and Morris Goodman, respectively. The DNA evidence has been accumulating steadily since the 1970s, and has been summarized by Ruvolo (1997) and more recently by Wildman et al (2003).

MAKING PROGRESS

If you want to make progress in any branch of paleontology, including paleoanthropology, you can do so in only a few ways. You can generate more data, or you can get better at interpreting the data you have. In paleoanthropology additional data comes from either finding new fossil evidence, or by extracting additional evidence from the existing fossil record. But no amount of fossil evidence will provide useful answers to questions unless researchers use appropriate methods to interpret the fossil evidence; thus new insights appear when appropriate innovative methods are applied to the existing evidence.

There is no doubt that the fossil evidence discovered in the past 140 years or so has made a major contribution to the progress that has been made in paleoanthropology in that time. But how much of that progress is due to the additional fossil evidence, and how much is due to improvements in the methods used to interpret the fossil record is anyone's guess. My hunch is that if paleoanthropology had chosen to ignore the analytical developments that were occurring in other areas of biology, and had continued to interpret its growing store of fossil evidence in much the same way as it did at the beginning of the twentieth century, then substantially less progress would have been made.

USING THE PRESENT TO UNDERSTAND THE PAST

It will not be too long before the "present" will become history, so it may help us understand how scientists thought and behaved in the past if we study the way scientists are coping with interpreting the present state of knowledge about human evolution.

The first thing to remember is that a better fossil record brings problems as well as benefits. Scenarios look simple and satisfactory when you have five fossils, but the picture becomes a good deal more complex when you have 500. As the fossil record improves, researchers have to be more concerned with taxonomy because they have to decide how many types of hominin are represented in their sample of 500 hominin fossils. Just as there is no point in trying to analyze the dialogue in a play unless you can link each line of dialogue with a character in the play, fossil evidence has to be assigned to a taxon in order for it to be incorporated in analyses. The way individual fossils are distributed among hominin taxa obviously affects the parameters of those taxa. It is these parameters that will be used by researchers to make inferences about early hominin taxa, including inferences about how the taxa are related to each other and to modern humans. These are the relationships that are captured in the pattern of the branches within the hominin clade.

Niles Eldredge (1993) suggested that species, extant and extinct, should be regarded as "individuals", each having its own "history". Each taxon's history begins with a speciation event, lasts as long as the species persists, and ends with either extinction or with that species' participation in another speciation event. The mean time between when a fossil mammal taxon is first seen in the fossil record, and when it disappears from the fossil record is around one million years. Thus, as the hominin fossil record for a particular period in human evolutionary history improves in both quality and quantity, it is possible that a species will be sampled not just once, but several times, during its history. This means that when paleoanthropologists are interpreting the fossil record one of the first things they must decide is whether they are looking at several samples belonging to the same taxon, or at single samples of several taxa. When paleoanthropologists make these taxonomic judgments they must avoid either grossly underestimating or extravagantly overestimating the actual number of species represented in the hominin fossil record.

One of the factors complicating these judgments is time. Researchers compare the amount of variation in their fossil sample with the variation they observe within living species. They do this by looking at collections of skeletons of these taxa in museums, and then combining them into a taxon sample. But even large samples of skeletons represent just a "snapshot" in the history of these extant taxa. Most comparative collections in museums were accumulated over a period of less than a hundred years, which is just a blink of an eye in terms of the geological timescale. In contrast, the combined samples of fossil hominin taxa, whether they come from several localities at one site or from localities at several sites, are almost always spread over time spans of tens of thousands of years, and in many cases they are spread over several hundred thousand years. Researchers who use comparative samples from museums as yardsticks for assessing the taxonomic significance of variation in their fossil samples do not know how they should adjust their observations of comparative samples to take into account temporal discrepancies between extant and fossil samples that may be several orders of magnitude.

Another factor paleoanthropologists have to take into account is that they are trying to reconstruct human evolutionary history with a fossil record that is confined to the remains of the hard tissues (i.e., the bones of the skeleton and teeth). We know from living animals (e.g., *Cercopithecus* species) that many uncontested species are difficult to distinguish if all there is to go on are their bones and teeth. Thus, some researchers have reached the conclusion that a hard tissue–bound fossil record is always likely to underestimate rather than overestimate the number of species. This is one of the reasons why paleoanthropologists favor recognizing more species in the fossil record than their colleagues do.

DIFFERENT INTERPRETATIONS

Although all scientific paleoanthropologists are united in their acceptance of the Darwinian paradigm, there is still scope within it for substantial differences in the way the details of that paradigm are interpreted. Taxonomies are hypotheses, and the types of taxonomic hypothesis researchers generate are inevitably going to be affected by their research philosophy. If you believe that most of hominin evolution occurred as the result of phyletic gradualism and anagenesis, then when you look at the hominin fossil record you will see and emphasize continuities and not discontinuities. You will recognize fewer taxa than researchers who place more emphasis on a punctuated equilibrium model of evolution, and who thus interpret the fossil evidence for hominin evolution as more consistent with cladogenesis. These researchers will tend to emphasize morphological discontinuities, and thus will tend to divide the hominin fossil record into a larger number of less inclusive taxa. You will also tend to recognize fewer taxa if you support the concept of allotaxa and thus allow a single species to manifest substantial regional geographic variation (e.g., Jolly, 2001; Antón, 2003). The more conservative taxonomic hypotheses that suggest a modest number of hominin fossil taxa are known informally as "lumping" hypotheses because they lump the fossil record into fewer, more inclusive, taxa. Supporters of the punctuated equilibrium model are referred to as splitters because they "split" the fossil record into a larger number of taxa.

There are also fundamental differences among paleoanthropologists with respect to what null-hypothesis to use when interpreting the hominin fossil record. If your prejudice is that the pattern of evolution was simple and linear, then you will be more comfortable with the metaphor of a ladder than with a bush. In the "ladder" scenario, if a researcher discovers a new fossil taxon that predates the existing hominin fossil record then they are inclined to regard the new fossil as being on one of the rungs of the ladder that connect the common ancestor of modern humans and chimpanzees with the existing hominin fossil record. In contrast, if you take the view that the higher primate part of the TOL was an adaptive radiation, the pattern of evolution would be more like a bush than a ladder. If a researcher with this systematic philosophy finds the fossil evidence of a hominin taxon that is older than the existing hominin fossil record they are less likely to assume they have stumbled upon the stem that connects the *Pan*/*Homo* recent common ancestor with modern humans, and more likely to assume the new fossil taxon belongs to one of the extinct side branches of the hominin bush.

RECONSTRUCTING PHYLOGENY

Richard Delisle makes the sensible assumption that there is a natural phylogeny. He is also optimistic that paleoanthropologists will be able to recover the pattern of this natural phylogeny. Other paleoanthropologists, especially those who are avid supporters of the principles that underpin Willi Hennig's method of "phylogenetic analysis", take the view that the methods currently available for phylogeny reconstruction will never be able to generate robust hypotheses about relationships, let alone robust hypotheses about ancestor/descendant relationships, because these are things we cannot ever "know" using evidence from the fossil record.

Researchers who are more optimistic point to the progress that has been made using genetic evidence to help resolve debates about relationships. Molecular biologists claim that both mitochondrial and nuclear DNA are capable of being used to recover information about relatedness. But the reality is that most of the hominin fossil record is a lot older than the age (e.g., 30–40 KYA) of the oldest hominin fossil from which mtDNA has been recovered. Thus, in the absence of DNA evidence, researchers have to investigate relatedness among taxa in the early part of the hominin fossil record by using hard tissue morphology as a proxy for genetic evidence. In theory, if there is a relatively close relationship between gross or microscopic hard tissue morphology and the genetic evidence, and providing any shared hard tissue morphology was inherited from a recent common ancestor, then it should be possible to reconstruct the branching pattern within the hominin clade.

But how do you validate a method for recovering phylogeny when it is being applied to extinct taxa whose phylogeny is unknown? Mark Collard and I (Collard and Wood, 2000) reasoned that the method could be validated by examining groups of living primates whose relationships have been established using DNA analysis. We suggested that we could mimic the investigation of fossil hominins if we restricted the analysis of the living taxa to the same craniodental hard tissue characters that are used to study the hominin fossil record. We could then compare the pattern of relationships determined from the DNA evidence with the pattern of relationships supported by the majority of the craniodental hard tissue characters. If the hard tissue characters generate a pattern of relationships that is consistent with the pattern generated by the DNA sequence data then the method is validated; if not, then there are legitimate grounds for questioning the utility of craniodental hard tissue characters for reconstructing hominin phylogeny.

In fact when this test was applied to both higher primates and to monkeys belonging to the tribe Papionini, in neither case did the craniodental hard tissue data generate a branching pattern resembling that generated using DNA evidence. Other researchers claim that they have been able to use characters based on craniodental hard tissue data to generate cladograms that are consistent with those generated using DNA sequence data, but only if the list of OTUs included in the cladistic analysis is expanded to include fossil hominin taxa (Strait and Grine, 2004). But is this good enough? We are not just seeking methods that will produce the correct answer in a particular set of circumstances (i.e., characters, OTUs, outgroups, etc.). We want any method to be robust enough so that even if you take a random sample of a smaller set of characters, or if you restrict the analysis to a subset of the fossil hominin taxa, then the method will still generate a cladogram that is consistent with the DNA evidence.

As yet, methods of phylogeny reconstruction that achieve this level of reliability have eluded researchers. Why have these methods failed to generate robust phylogenies? The short version of the answer is "homoplasy." A homoplasy is a piece of morphology that is shared between two taxa, but which is not present in their most recent common ancestor. Homoplasy is one of the main causes of the "noise" that presently prevents us from recovering human evolutionary history from craniodental hardtissue data with an acceptable level of reliability.

Richard Delisle's book focuses on the reconstruction of phylogeny, and this, together with the prerequisite taxonomy, is what I have concentrated on in this short review of current palaeoanthropological practice. It must be obvious to the reader that the type of research I have surveyed is both inter- and multidisciplinary, and it is intricately related to evolutionary and molecular biology. For a long time phylogeny reconstruction was the main if not the sole preoccupation of paleoanthropologists, so the history of attempts to reconstruct phylogeny *was* effectively the history of paleoanthropology. But for most of my professional lifetime paleoanthropology has involved a good deal more than phylogeny reconstruction. These days there are as many, if not more, paleoanthropologists involved in the reconstruction of the behavior and life history of extinct hominins, as there are engaged in the task of reconstructing hominin phylogeny.

Richard Delisle's magisterial survey of attempts to recover the structure of the hominin twig of the TOL has perhaps been kinder to paleoanthropology and to paleoanthropologists than I believe it and we deserve. Perhaps mine is an overly "bottle-half-empty" analysis, but I suggest that in general the scientists who are examining the hominin fossil record have been slow to validate their methods, and when they have gotten around to doing so, several methods have failed the validation tests.

Progress will be made if paleoanthropologists begin to be more resourceful about devising methods for generating hypotheses about human evolutionary history. They need to explore ways of generating sets of characters that have a high probability of recovering the "natural phylogeny". There is copious evidence from both evolutionary and molecular biology that homoplasy is rife. Until we can devise reliable methods for detecting and then correcting for homoplasy, the details of the branching structure of the modern human twig of the TOL will continue to elude us.

REFERENCES

Antón, S.C. (2003). "Natural history of *Homo erectus*." *Yearbook of Physical Anthropology,* 46: 126–169.

Collard, M.C. and B.A. Wood (2000). "How reliable are human phylogenetic hypotheses?" *Proceedings of the National Academy of Sciences,* 97: 5003–5006.

Eldredge, N. (1993). "What, if anything, is a species?" In, W.H. Kimbel, L.B. Martin (eds.), *Species, Species Concepts, and Primate Evolution,* (New York: Plenum Press), pp. 3–20.

Jolly, C.J. (2001). "A proper study for Mankind: Analogies from the Papionin monkeys and their implications for human evolution." *Yearbook of Physical Anthropology,* 44: 177–204.

Ruvolo, M. (1997). "Molecular phylogeny of the hominoids: Inferences from multiple independent DNA sequence data sets." *Molecular Biology and Evolution,* 14: 248–265.

Strait, D.S. and F.E. Grine (2004). "Inferring hominoid and early hominin phylogeny using craniodental characters: The role of fossil taxa." *Journal of Human Evolution,* 47: 399–452.

Wildman, D., M. Uddin, G. Liu, L.I. Grossman and M. Goodman (2003). "Implications of natural selection in shaping 99.4% nonsynonymous DNA identity between humans and chimpanzees: Enlarging genus *Homo*." *Proceedings of the National Academy of Sciences,* 100: 7181–7188.

Biographical Appendix

Abel, Othenio (1875–1946). Austrian paleontologist and evolutionary biologist, he worked in the geological laboratory of Eduard Suess from 1898 to 1907. He first became professor of paleontology and paleobiology at Vienna, Austria, from 1917 to 1934 and then at the University of Göttingen, Germany, from 1935 to 1940. He contributed to the foundation of the journal *Paläobiologica.*

Ameghino, Florentino (1854–1911). Argentinian archeologist, geologist, and paleontologist not formally trained in these disciplines, his continued field works earned him the position of professor of natural history at the University of Cordoba in 1884. In 1886, he became vice director of the Museo de La Plata, a position he retained for a year. He had to wait until 1902 before securing again a position as director of the Museo Nacional de Buenos Aires, a post he kept until his death.

Arambourg, Camille (1885–1969). French paleontologist, he originally trained in agronomy between 1903 and 1908. He became professor of geology at the Institute Agricole d'Alger, Algeria, in 1920. His continued field work with vertebrate fossils earned him the position of professor of paleontology, replacing Marcellin Boule, at the Muséum National d'Histoire Naturelle in Paris in 1936, a position he retired from in 1960.

Boule, Marcellin (1861–1942). French geologist and paleontologist, he trained in the laboratoires de pétrographie at the Collège de France and at the Muséum National d'Histoire Naturelle (MNHN) of Paris. He succeeded Albert Gaudry in paleontology at the MNHN where he became professor from 1902 to 1936. He was the first director of the Institut de Paléontologie Humaine in Paris in 1920, an institution created by Prince Albert the First of Monaco. He was also editor of *L'Anthropologie,* which he helped found, from 1893 to 1920.

Broca, Paul Pierre (1824–1880). French scholar, he trained in medicine in the 1840s at the Université de Paris. He held several positions in hospitals in pathology before accepting the chair of pathologie externe at the Faculty of Medicine in 1867. His interest in anthropology led him to found the Société d'Anthropologie de Paris in 1859.

Broom, Robert (1866–1951). Scottish paleontologist, he originally trained in science and medicine at the University of Glasgow in the late 1880s. He was professor of zoology and geology at Victorian College (later the University of Stellenbosch), South Africa, from 1903 to 1909. His contributions to the recovery of fossil mammal-like reptiles of South Africa in the early decades of the century eventually earned him a post at the Transvaal Museum at Pretoria.

Coon, Carleton Stevens (1904–1981). American anthropologist, he trained at Harvard University under E.A. Hooton. He held his professorship at Harvard until 1948, when he moved to the University of Pennsylvania where he became both professor and curator in the University Museum until his retirement in 1963.

Cope, Edward Drinker (1840–1899). American paleontologist, he worked with the U.S. Geological Survey beginning in 1872. He is the founder of the journal *American Naturalist.*

Dart, Raymond Arthur (1893–1988). Australian anatomist, he trained in medicine at the University of Sydney in the mid-1910s. He was demonstrator of anatomy under Grafton Elliot Smith at University College, London. He took an appointment as professor of anatomy at the University of the Witwatersrand in South Africa in 1922, where he became dean of the newly founded medical school between 1925 and 1943. His name is associated with the recovery of the Taung skull and the naming of a new species for it, *Australopithecus africanus.*

Darwin, Charles Robert (1809–1882). British naturalist, he first studied medicine at the University of Edinburgh from 1825 to 1827 before studying at Cambridge in preparation to become a clergyman. Having developed interests in botany and geology, he embarked on a world trip as a naturalist aboard the HMS Beagle from 1831 to 1835. Those years were instrumental in the reflections which led him to unofficially conceive the theory of natural selection in the late 1830s, a theory publicly expounded in 1859.

De Mortillet, Gabriel Louis Laurent (1821–1898). French prehistorian, he trained in engineering and geology at the Conservatoire des arts et métiers of Paris. In 1864, he founded the journal *Matériaux pour l'histoire positive et philosophique de l'homme*, which later fused with several other journals to form *L'Anthropologie* in 1890.

De Quatrefages, Jean Louis Armand (1810–1892). French scholar, he received his M.D. from the University of Strasbourg in 1833. He earned his living in Paris as a scientific illustrator and writer of popular scientific articles in the 1840s. He was appointed Chair of Anthropology at the Muséum National d'Histoire Naturelle in Paris in 1855.

Dixon, Roland B. (1875–1934). American cultural anthropologist, he trained in anthropology at Harvard University, where he spent his entire career. He organized a remarkable anthropological library at the Peabody Museum of Harvard University and contributed to make Harvard a leading training center for anthropologists.

Dobzhansky, Theodosius (1900–1975). Russian geneticist, he graduated in biology from the University of Kiev in 1921. After a short stay as a lecturer at the University of Leningrad, he joined T.H. Morgan's laboratory at Columbia University in 1927. While he followed Morgan to the California Institute of Technology from 1929 to 1940, he moved back to Columbia in 1940 where he remained professor until 1962.

Dubois, Marie Eugène François Thomas (1858–1940). Dutch anatomist, he trained in medicine at the University of Amsterdam from 1877 to 1884 where he was lecturer in 1886–1887. He left for the Dutch East Indies that year only to return in 1895, during which time he discovered *Pithecanthropus*. He was professor of geology and paleontology at the University of Amsterdam from 1899 to 1929.

Elliot Smith, Grafton (1871–1937). Australian anatomist, he trained in medicine at the University of Sydney. After having occupied the Chair of Anatomy in the Government School of Medicine in Cairo, Egypt, from 1900 to 1909, he accepted a similar position in England at Manchester University until 1919. After that, he became professor of anatomy at University College, London.

Fraipont, Jean-Joseph Julien (1857–1910). Belgian scholar, he trained in science at the Université de Liège. He became professor of paleontology in this same institution.

Frassetto, Fabio (1876–1953). Italian scholar, he graduated in the natural sciences from the University of Turin in 1901. He taught at the universities of Padua, Rome, and Bologna, respectively, only to become Chair of Anthropology at the University of Bologna in 1908, where he also founded the Institute of Anthropology and the Museum.

Gaudry, Albert Jean (1827–1908). French paleontologist, he trained in geology at the Muséum National d'Histoire Naturelle in Paris. He occupied the Chair of Paleontology at this institution after 1872. He took part in several field trips in the 1850s.

Gregory, William King (1876–1970). American zoologist, he first completed undergraduate studies in zoology at Columbia University from 1895 to 1899. While continuing his studies at Columbia, he took part in H.F. Osborn's program of vertebrate paleontology at the American Museum of Natural History, New York. He succeeded Osborn as professor of zoology at Columbia in 1909 until his retirement in 1944. He was the editor of the newly founded *American Museum Journal*, the ancestor of the journal *Natural History*.

Haeckel, Ernst Heinrich Phillip August (1834–1919). German zoologist, he trained in medicine at the Universities of Würzburg and Berlin from 1852 to 1857. He joined the department of zoology of the University of Jena in 1861, where he became full professor in 1865. He remained there until his retirement in 1909.

Hamy, Jules Ernest Théodore (1842–1908). French scholar, he trained in medicine in Paris before becoming P. Broca's assistant at the École Pratique des Hautes Études. He joined de Quatrefages at the Muséum National d'Histoire Naturelle (MNHN) in Paris in 1872, and performed these functions which were shared after 1880 with his post of conservator in the new ethnographic museum housed in the Palais du Trocadéro. He succeeded de Quatrefages as professor of anthropology at the MNHN in 1892.

Hervé, Georges (1855–1932). French scholar, he trained in medicine in Paris. He joined P. Broca's Laboratoire d'Anthropologie of the École Pratique des Hautes Études in 1881, where he became professor of zoological anthropology in 1888. In 1892, he switched chairs to become professor of ethnology. He was elected president of the Société d'Anthropologie de Paris in 1898.

Hill-Tout, Charles (1858–1944). Born in England, he graduated from the University of Oxford. He moved to Canada in 1891 where he became a private-school teacher in

Vancouver. He was made Corresponding Fellow of the Royal Anthropological Institute of Great Britain and Ireland in 1900 and Fellow of the American Ethnological Society in 1908.

Hooton, Earnest Albert (1887–1954). American anthropologist, he first received a Ph.D. in classics from the University of Wisconsin in 1911, before receiving additional diplomas in anthropology and literature from Oxford University, England, in 1912–1913. On his return, he became professor of anthropology at Harvard University in 1913, where he remained until his death. He trained many students who later founded anthropology departments in U. S. universities.

Hovelacque, Abel (1843–1896). French anthropologist and linguist, he occupied the Chair of Linguistic Anthropology at the École d'Anthropologie de Paris. Member and president of the Société d'Anthropologie, he contributed to the foundation of the *Revue de l'École d'Anthropologie* and the *Revue de linguistique et de philologie comparée.*

Howells, William White (b. 1908). American anthropologist, he received his Ph.D in anthropology under E.A. Hooton at Harvard University in 1934. He was research associate at the American Museum of Natural History, New York, from 1934 to 1939. He was professor of anthropology at the University of Wisconsin until 1954. He succeeded E.A Hooton at Harvard University that same year, and was given emeritus status in 1974.

Hrdlicka, Ales (1869–1943). Born in what is now the Czech Republic, he trained in medicine at the New York Homeopathic College in the early 1890s. After a stay in Paris in the physical anthropology circles of L. Manouvrier in 1896, he joined the field anthropologists of the American Museum of Natural History in 1899. He was for forty years head of the newly founded Division of Physical Anthropology at the Smithsonian Institution. He founded both the *American Journal of Physical Anthropology* in 1918 and the American Association of Physical Anthropologists in 1930.

Hubrecht, Ambrosius Arnold Wilhelm (1853–1915). Dutch zoologist, he graduated from the University of Utrecht in 1874. He became professor of zoology and entomology in this same institution. He visited the Dutch East Indies in 1890 in order to study the tree shrews.

Huxley, Thomas Henry (1825–1895). British naturalist, he trained in medicine at the Charing Cross Hospital Medical School from 1841 to 1845. His four-year cruise aboard HMS *Rattlesnake* as assistant surgeon in 1845 diverted him toward zoology. In 1854, he acquired a position as lecturer in natural history at the Government School of Mines, London. He was the president of the Royal Institution from 1883 to 1885.

Joleaud, Léonce (1880–1938). French naturalist, he trained in the earth sciences before extending his interest to paleontology and zoology. He was professor at the Faculté des Sciences de l'Université de Paris.

Keith, Arthur (1866–1955). Scottish anatomist, he trained in medicine at the University of Aberdeen from 1884 to 1888. He developed his interest for primate anatomy during a three-year stay as a medical officer in Thailand. This led him to defend a M.D. thesis on this subject in 1894. He was appointed senior demonstrator in anatomy at the Medical School of the London Hospital in 1895, and became conservator of the Royal College of Surgeons from 1908 to 1933.

Klaatsch, Hermann (1863–1916). German anatomist, he graduated in comparative anatomy from the University of Berlin in

1885. First professor at Heidelberg University, Germany, he switched to anatomy and anthropology at Breslau University (now in Poland) from 1907 to 1916.

Lamarck, Jean-Baptiste Pierre Antoine de Monet (1744–1829). French naturalist; he studied medicine at the École de Médecine and natural history at the Jardin du Roi in Paris. Buffon created a position at the Jardin du Roi for him before this institution was changed into the Muséum (National) d'Histoire Naturelle in 1793. He was appointed professor of invertebrate zoology.

Leakey, Louis Seymour Bazett (1903–1972). Born in Kenya from British missionary parents, he trained at St. John's College, Cambridge, England, in languages, archeology, and anthropology from 1922 to 1926 where he earned his Ph.D. Being constantly in the field in East Africa searching for archeological and paleontological finds, he contributed to the recoveries of *Zinjanthropus* in 1959 and *Homo habilis* in the early 1960s. He was affilated with the Coryndon Museum, Nairobi, Kenya, which was later renamed the National Museum(s) of Kenya.

Le Gros Clark, Wilfrid Edward (1895–1971). British anatomist, he trained in the medical school of St. Thomas's Hospital, England, from 1912 to 1920. From 1923 to 1934, he became reader and then professor in anatomy in the Hospitals of St. Bartholomew and St. Thomas. In 1934, he was appointed to the Chair of Anatomy at Oxford University where he remained until his retirement in 1962.

Lydekker, Richard (1849–1915). British naturalist, he trained in the natural sciences at Trinity College, Cambridge, starting in the late 1860s. He joined the Geological Survey of India in 1872, giving him the opportunity to explore vertebrate paleontology. Back in England in 1882, he became affiliated with the departments of Geology and Zoology at the Natural History Museum (British Museum) until his death.

Marett, Robert Ranulph (1866–1943). British anthropologist with a strong background in classical studies and philosophy, he trained at Victoria College, Jersey, and Balliol College, Oxford. He held positions in philosophy at Exeter College, Oxford, and in archeology at Oxford University, England. From 1910 to 1936 he was reader in social anthropology. In 1909, he contributed to the foundation of the Oxford University Anthropological Society.

Mayr, Ernst (1904–2005). German-born naturalist, he earned a Ph.D. in biology from the University of Berlin in 1926. After several expeditions to New Guinea and the Solomon Islands from 1928 to 1930, he became curator of birds at the American Museum of Natural History, New York, until 1953. After that, he was affiliated with Harvard University until his death, either as a professor of zoology, director of the Agassiz Museum of Comparative Zooloogy, or as professor emeritus.

Mivart, St. George Jackson (1827–1900). British naturalist, he originally trained in law before turning his attention toward natural history. He was professor of comparative anatomy at St. Mary's Hospital Medical School from 1862 to 1884.

Morton, Dudley Joy (1884–1960). American physician, he earned his M.D. from the Hahnemann Medical College, Philadelphia, in 1907, where he was instructor in surgery from 1910 to 1920. While he subsequently taught at Yale Medical School, he became professor of surgery at the College of Physicians and Surgeons, Columbia University, in 1928.

Osborn, Henry Fairfield (1857–1935). American paleontologist, he took part in a fossil-hunting expedition to the western United States and studied comparative anatomy and embryology in England with T.H. Huxley and F.M. Balfour from 1877 to 1880. He earned a Sc.D. from Princeton University in 1881, where he taught comparative anatomy and embryology. In 1891, he taught at Columbia University until 1909, when he became curator of the newly founded Department of Vertebrate Paleontology at the American Museum of Natural History (AMNH), New York. In 1908, he became president of the AMNH, a position he retained for twenty-five years.

Osman Hill, William Charles (1901–1975). British anatomist, he trained in the medical sciences at Birmingham University. He has been affiliated with several institutions. In 1930, he became professor of anatomy at the University of Ceylon. In 1945 he became reader in physical anthropology at the University of Edinburgh. Prosector of the Zoological Society of London between 1950 and 1962, he became that year Assistant Director of the Yerkes Primate Centre of Emory University (U.S.A.). He was later associated with the Centro di Primatologia of the Università di Torino (Italia) and with the Royal College of Surgeons (England).

Owen, Richard (1804–1892). British naturalist, he trained in the medical sciences at the University of Edinburgh, Scotland, from 1824 to 1827. That year, he was appointed assistant of the conservator at the Museum of the Royal College of Surgeons, London, where he became Hunterian Professor in 1836 and conservator in 1842. He became superintendent of the Departments of Natural History at the British Museum.

Pilgrim, Guy Ellock (1875–1943). British naturalist, he trained at the University College, London, from 1894 to 1908. Between 1902 and 1930, he worked for the Geological Survey of India.

Piveteau, Jean (1899–1991). French paleontologist, he succeeded to C. Arambourg at the Sorbonne's Chair of Paleontology in 1939. He was the former student of M. Boule.

Pycraft, William Plane (1868–1942). A specialist on the study of birds, he was the assistant of Smith Woodward at the British Museum of Natural History, London.

Retzius, Anders Adolf (1796–1860). Swedish naturalist, he studied anatomy and medicine at the University of Lund, Denmark, from 1816 to 1819. After a short appointment as lecturer at the Veterinary Institute (VI), Stockholm, in 1821, he became professor there from 1824 to 1840. Simultaneously, he took a position as professor of anatomy at the Karolinska Institute, which he kept after resigning from the VI.

RobinÏson, John Talbot (1923–2001). South African paleoanthropologist, he trained in zoology at the University of Cape Town from 1941 to 1955. In 1947 he joined R. Broom, in the Department of Palaeontology and Physical Anthropology of the Transvaal Museum, Pretoria, whom he replaced in 1951. He conducted excavations at major australopithecine sites in South Africa until 1963, when he left for the United States and where he became professor of zoology at the University of Wisconsin until 1985.

Schaaffhausen, Hermann (1816–1893). German naturalist, he trained in medicine at the Universities of Bonn and Berlin in the 1830s. He lectured in anatomy and anthropolology at the University of Bonn until he was appointed professor there in 1855. He cofounded the journal *Archiv für Anthropology* in 1866 and presided the Deutsche Anthropologische Gesellschaft founded in 1869.

Schultz, Adolph Hans (1891–1976). German anatomist, he trained in the natural sciences at the university of Zürich, Switzerland, from 1909 to 1916. He moved to the United States where he became a research associate at the Carnegie Institution's Embryology Research Laboratory in Baltimore from 1918 to 1925. In 1925, he became professor of anthropology at the Johns Hopkins University in Baltimore, where he remained until 1951. That year, Schultz moved back to the University of Zürich and became professor at the Anthropology Institute.

Schwalbe, Gustav (1844–1916). German scholar, he earned his M.D. from the University of Berlin in 1866. He conducted all sorts of researches in medical related fields at many institutions in Bonn, Amsterdam, Halle, Freiburg, etc. In 1883, he became professor of anatomy at the University of Strassbourg, a position he kept until his retirement in 1914.

Sera, Gioacchino Leo (1878–1960). Italian anthropologist, he trained in medicine at the University of Rome. From 1911 to 1925, he taught anthropology at the University of Pavia, only to become professor at the University of Naples in the mid-1920s. He founded the journal *Giornale per la Morfologia dell'Uomo e dei Primati* in the 1910s.

Sergi, Giuseppe (1841–1936). Italian anthropologist, he trained in comparative philology and philosophy at the University of Messina only to later turn his interests toward evolutionary questions. Having first taught anthropology at the University of Bologna in 1880, he occupied the Chair of Anthropology at the University of Rome from 1883 to 1916.

Simpson, George Gaylord (1902–1984). American paleontologist, he trained in geology at the Universities of Colorado and Yale from 1918 to 1926. In 1927, he became assistant curator in the Department of Vertabrate Paleontology at the American Museum of Natural History, New York, before being named chairman from 1945 to 1959. During the same time period, he was professor of geology at Columbia University. From 1959 to 1970, he was professor at Harvard University, before moving to the University of Arizona.

Strauss, William L. (1900–1981). American anatomist, he was professor of anthropology and anatomy at Johns Hopkins University. He was president of the American Association of Physical Anthropologists from 1952 to 1955.

Taylor, Griffith Thomas (1880–1963). Born in England, he successively trained at the University of Sydney, Australia, and at Cambridge University, England, during the 1890s and the 1900s. In the years 1911 to 1912 he was the Senior Geologist of the British Antarctic Expedition. He became professor of geography at the University of Sydney in 1920 and then at the University of Chicago from 1929 to 1935. He held the position of Head of the Department of Geography at the University of Toronto from 1935 until his retirement in 1951.

Topinard, Paul (1830–1911). French scholar, he trained in the Faculty of Medicine, Paris, from 1848 to 1860, during which time he worked in hospitals. In 1872, he became P. Broca's assistant at the Laboratoire d'Anthropologie of the École Pratique des Hautes Études, only to become assistant director from 1877 to 1900. He occupied the Chair of Biological Anthropology at the Ēcole d'Anthropologie from 1874 to 1889. While he was the first subeditor of the journal *Revue d'Anthropologie*, he became its sole editor from 1880 to 1890, when the journal was finally fused with others to create *L'Anthropologie*.

Vallois, Henri Victor (1889–1981). French scholar, he trained as a physician and a naturalist in Montpellier and Paris. He taught anatomy and zoology in the Faculty of Medecine at Toulouse, France, from 1922 to 1941. From 1941 until his retirement in 1960, he was professor at the Muséum National d'Histoire Naturelle in Paris. He was also director of the Institut de Paléontologie Humaine in Paris from 1942 to 1971 and director of the Musée de l'Homme in 1941–1945 and 1950–1960.

Verneau, René Pierre (1852–1938). French scholar, he trained in the medical sciences in Paris. In 1870, he was first instructor and then assistant of de Quatrefages's laboratory at the Muséum National d'Histoire Naturelle (MNHN) in Paris. From 1909 to 1927, he succeeded J. Hamy in both the Chair of Anthropology at the MNHN and as keeper at the Musée d'Ethnographie du Trocadéro.

Vogt, Carl (1817–1895). Born in Giessen, Germany, he trained in the medical sciences at the University of Bern, Switzerland, in the 1830s. He collaborated with the Swiss naturalist Louis Agassiz from 1839 to 1847. After a brief stay in Giessen during which he occupied the Chair of Zoology, he finally established himself at the University of Geneva, Switzerland, in the Chair of Geology in 1952. He also taught paleontology, zoology, and comparative anatomy.

Von Eickstedt, Egon (1892–1965). German anthropologist, he was first professor at Breslau University (now in Poland) before participating in the foundation of an Institute of Anthropology at the newly founded University of Mainz, Germany, after World War II.

Von Koenigswald, Gustav Heinrich Ralph (1902–1982). German scholar, he trained in several German Universities in geology and paleontology. He joined the Dutch Geological Survey in Java from 1931 to the Second World War. After a stay at the American Museum of Natural History in New York from 1946 to 1948, he accepted the Chair of Paleontology at the Rijksuniversiteit of Utrecht, Netherlands. In 1968, he moved back to his homeland, Germany, with a position at the Forschungsinstitut und Natur-Museum Senckenberg in Frankfurt.

Wallace, Alfred Russel (1823–1913). British naturalist with no formal scientific training, he learned in the field during two expeditions of natural history in South America and the Malay Archipelago from 1848 to 1862. He supported himself by writing on the subject of evolution and spent the year 1886 lecturing on this question in the United States. He is the co-discoverer of natural selection with C. Darwin.

Washburn, Sherwood L. (1911–2000). American anthropologist, he trained in physical anthropology and comparative primate anatomy in the United States and England at Harvard and Oxford universities during the 1930s. He was instructor of anatomy at Columbia University Medical School from 1939 to 1947, and professor of anthropology at the University of Chicago from 1947 to 1958. He then moved to the University of California, Berkeley, where he became emeritus in 1978.

Weidenreich, Franz (1873–1948). German scholar, he trained in medicine at the universities of Munich, Kiel, Berlin, and Strasburg in the 1890s. He became professor of anatomy at the University of Strasburg from 1904 to 1918, and then of anatomy and anthropology at the University of Heidelberg from 1921 to 1935. He left for China in 1935 where he became professor of anatomy at the Peking Union Medical College and director of the Cenozoic Research Laboratory. In 1941, he moved to the American Museum of Natural History, New York.

Weinert, Hans (1887–1967). German anthropologist, he trained in medicine and anthropology at the Universities of Göttingen, Leipzig, and Berlin. He was simultaneously lecturer at the University of Berlin and professor at the University of Munich from 1926 to 1935. After 1935, he became professor at the University of Kiel as well as director of the Kiel Institut für Anthropologie. He was the editor of the journal *Zeitschrift für Morphologie und Anthropology* from 1949 to 1957.

Wood Jones, Frederic (1879–1954). British anatomist, he trained in medicine at the London Hospitals from 1897 to 1904. He successively occupied many positions either in anatomy or anthropology at Manchester University in 1909, the University of Adelaide (Australia) in 1919, the Rockefeller Chair in Hawaii in 1927, and the Royal College of Surgeons in London.

Zuckerman, Solly (1904–1993). South African scholar, he trained in medicine at the University of Cape Town and the University College Hospital (London) in the 1920s. He was demonstrator in anatomy at the University College, London, from 1928 to 1932, and then at Oxford University, before being appointed professor at the University of Birmingham (UB) in 1945. After his retirement from UB, he became professor-at-large at the University of East Anglia from 1969 to 1993.

References

Abbott, C.C. (1881). *Primitive Industry* (Salem, Mass.: G.A. Bates).

Abel, O. (1934). "Das Verwandtschaftsverhältnis zwischen dem Menschen und höheren fossilen Primaten." *Zeitschrift für Morphologie und Anthropologie*, 34: 1–14.

Abel, W. (1931a). "Über *Australopithecus* und seine Stellung zu den Anthropoiden und Hominiden." *Verhandlungen der Zoologisch-Botanischen Gesellschaft in Wien*, 80: 92–99.

Abel, W. (1931b). "Kritische Untersuchungen über *Australopithecus africanus* Dart." *Gegenbaurs Morphologisches Jahrbuch*, 65: 539–640.

Adcock, G.J., E.S. Dennis, S. Easteal, G.A. Huttley, L. S. Jermiin, W. J. Peacock and A. Thorne (2001). "Mitochondrial DNA Sequences in Ancient Australians: Implications for Modern Human Origins." *Proceedings of the National Academy of Sciences* (USA), 98: 537–542.

Adloff, P. (1908). *Das Gebiss des Menschen und der Anthropomorphen. Vergleichend-anatomische Untersuchungen. Zugleich ein Beitrag zur menschlichen Stammesgeschichte* (Berlin: Julius Springer).

Adloff, P. (1932). "Das Gebiss von Australopithecus africanus Dart." *Zeitschrift für Anatomie und Entwicklungsgeschichte*, 87: 145–156.

Aguirre, E. (1972). "Les rapports phylétiques de *Ramapithecus* et de *Kenyapithecus* et l'origine de l'homme." *L'Anthropologie*, 76: 501–523.

Aiello, L. (1993). "The Fossil Evidence For Modern Human Origins in Africa: A Revised View." *American Anthropologist*, 95: 73–96.

Aiello, L.C. and P. Andrews (2000). "The Australopithecines in Review." *Human Evolution*, 15: 17–38.

Allbrook, D. and W.W. Bishop (1963). "New Fossil Hominoid Material From Uganda," *Nature*, 197: 1187–1190.

Alsberg, P. (1934). "The Taungs Puzzle: A Biological Essay." *Man*, 34: 154–159.

Ameghino, F. (1879). "L'homme préhistorique dans La Plata." *Revue d'Anthropologie*, 2e série, 2: 210–249.

Ameghino, F. (1891). "Los monos fosiles del eoceno de la Republica Argentina." *Revista Argentina de Historia Natural*, 1: 383–397.

Ameghino, F. (1897). "South America as the Source of the Tertiary Mammalia." *Natural Science*, 11: 256–264.

Ameghino, F. (1906). "Les formations sédimentaires du Crétacé supérieur et du Tertaire de Patagonie." *Anales del Museo Nacional de Buenos Aires*, 3rd series, 8: 1–568.

Ameghino, F. (1907). "Notas preliminares sobre el Tetraprothomo argenticus: Un precursor del hombre del Mioceno superior de Monte Hermoso." *Anales del Museo Nacional de Buenos Aires*, 3rd series, 9: 107–242.

Ameghino, F. (1909). "Le *Diprothomo platensis*: Un précurseur de l'homme du Pliocène inférieur de Buenos Aires." *Anales del Museo Nacional de Buenos Aires*, 3rd series, 12: 107–209.

Ameghino, F. (1910a). "Une nouvelle industrie lithique. L'industrie de la pierre fendue dans le Tertiaire de la région littorale au sud de Mar del Plata." *Anales del Museo Nacional de Buenos Aires*, 3ième série, 13: 189–204.

Ameghino, F. (1910b). "La industria de la Piedra Quebrada en el Mioceno superior de Monte Hermoso." *Congreso Cientifico Internacional Americano*, Buenos Aires 10 a 25 de julio, pp. 1–5.

Ameghino, F. (1910c). "Vestigios industriales en la formacion Entrerriana (Oligocene superior o Mioceno el mas inferior)." *Congreso Cientifico Internacional Americano*, Buenos Aires 10 a 25 de julio, pp. 6–12.

Andrews, P. (1984). "An Alternative Interpretation of the Characters Used to Define *Homo erectus*." In, P. Andrews and J. L. Franzen (eds.), *The Early Evolution of Man with Special Emphasis on Southeast Asia and Africa* (Courier Forschungs-Institut Senckenberg, 69), pp. 167–175.

Andrews, P. (1992). "Evolution and Environment in the Hominoidea." *Nature*, 360: 641–646.

Andrews, P., D.R. Begun and M. Zylstra (1997). "Interrelatioships Between Functional Morphology and Paleoenvironments in Miocene Hominoids." In, D.R. Begun, C.V. Ward and M. Rose (eds.), *Function, Phylogeny, and Fossils: Miocene Hominoid Evolution and Adaptations* (New York: Plenum Press), pp. 29–58.

Anonymous (1929a). "An Alleged Anthropoid Ape Existing in America." *Nature*, 123: 924.

Anonymous (1929b). "Ein neuer Menschenaffe." *Kosmos*, 26: 256–257.

Arambourg, C. (1943a). *La genèse de l'humanité* (Paris: Presses Universitaires de France).

Arambourg, C. (1943b). "Sur les affinités de quelques anthropoïdes fossiles d'Afrique et leurs relations avec la lignée humaine." *Comptes Rendus de l'Académie des Sciences*, 216: 593–595.

Arambourg, C. (1945). "L'Afrique, centre d'évolution, son rôle dans l'histoire paléontologique des hominiens." *Congrès de l'Association française pour l'Avancement des Sciences*, Paris, pp. 37–47.

Arambourg, C. (1947). "L'état actual de nos connaissances sur les origines de l'homme." *L'Année Biologique*, 23: 293–304.

Arambourg, C. (1948a). "Le rôle de l'Afrique dans l'histoire paléontologique de l'homme." *Revue Scientifique*, No. 3289: 77–82.

Arambourg, C. (1948b). "La classification des primates et particulièrement des hominiens." *Mammalia*, 12: 123–135.

Arambourg, C. (1948c). *La genèse de l'humanité*, 2nd edition (Paris: Presses Universitaires de France).

Arambourg, C. (1950, ed.). *Paléontologie et transformisme* (Paris: Albin Michel).

Arambourg, C. (1952a). *La genèse de l'humanité*, 3rd edition (Paris: Presses Universitaires de France).

Arambourg, C. (1952b). "Observations sur la phylogénie des primates et l'origine des hominiens." In, L.S.B. Leakey and S. Cole (eds.), *Proceedings of the Pan-African Congress on Prehistory, 1947* (Oxford: Basil Blackwell), pp. 116–119.

Arambourg, C. (1954). "L'hominien fossile de Ternifine (Algérie)." *Comptes Rendus de l'Académie des Sciences*, 239: 893–895.

Arambourg, C. (1955a). *La genèse de l'humanité*, 4th edition (Paris: Presses Universitaires de France).

Arambourg, C. (1955b). "A Recent Discovery in Human Paleontology: Atlanthropus of Ternifine (Algeria)." *American Journal of Physical Anthropology*, 13: 191–196.

Arambourg, C. (1955c). "Une nouvelle mandible d'*Atlanthropus du gisement de Ternifine.*" *Comptes Rendus de l'Académie des Sciences*, 241: 895–897.

Arambourg, C. (1955d). "Le pariétal de l'*Atlanthropus mauritanicus*." *Comptes Rendus de l'Académie des Sciences*, 241: 980–982.

Arambourg, C. (1956). "Considérations sur l'état actuel du problème des origines de l'homme." *Colloques Internationaux du Centre National de la Recherche Scientifique*, No. 60, *Problèmes actuels de Paléontologie*, Paris.

Arambourg, C. (1957). *La genèse de l'humanité*, 5th edition (Paris: Presses Universitaires de France).

Arambourg, C. (1959). "Les données de la paléontologie humaine." In, A. Varagnac (ed.), *L'homme avant l'écriture* (Paris: Armand Colin), pp. 10–59.

Arambourg, C. (1960). "Le Zinjanthropus et les données actuelles du problème des origines de l'Homme." *La Nature*, 88: 369–372.

ARAMBOURG, C. (1961). *La genèse de l'humanité*, 6th edition (Paris: Presses Universitaires de France).

ARAMBOURG, C. (1965). *La genèse de l'humanité*, 7th edition (Paris: Presses Universitaires de France).

ARAMBOURG, C. AND P. BIBERSON (1955). "Découverte de vestiges humains acheuléens dans la carrière de Sidi Abd-er-rahmann, prés de Casablanca." *Comptes Rendus de l'Académie des Sciences*, 240: 1661–1663.

ARAMBOURG, C. AND P. BIBERSON (1956). "The Fossil Human Remains From the Paleolithic Site of Sidi Abderrahman (Morocco)." *American Journal of Physical Anthropology*, 14: 467–489.

ARAMBOURG, C. AND R. HOFFSTETTER (1954). "Découverte, en Afrique du Nord, de restes humains du Paléolithique inférieur." *Comptes Rendus de l'Académie des Sciences*, 239: 72–74.

ARAMBOURG, C. AND R. HOFFSTETTER (1955). "Le gisement de Ternifine: Résultats des fouilles de 1955 et découverte de nouveaux restes d'*Atlanthropus*." *Comptes Rendus de l'Académie des Sciences*, 241: 431–433.

ARENSBURG, B., L.A. SCHEPARTZ, A.M. TILLIER, B. VANDERMEERSCH AND Y. RAK (1990). "A Reappraisal of the Anatomical Basis for Speech in Middle Palaeolithic Hominids." *American Journal of Physical Anthropology*, 83: 137–146.

ARRIBAS, A. AND P. PALMQVIST (2002). "The First Human Dispersal to Europe: Remarks on the Archaeological and Palaeoanthropological Record From Orce (Guadix-Baza Basin, Southern Spain)." *Human Evolution*, 17: 55–78.

ARLDT, T. (1915). "Die Stammesgeschichte der Primaten und die Entwicklung der Menschenrassen." *Fortschritte der Rassenkunde*, 1: 1–52.

ARLDT, T. (1917). "Zur Stammesgeschichte der Halbaffen und Menschenaffen." *Die Naturwissenschaften*, 5: 39–41.

ARSUAGA, J.-L., I. MARTINEZ, A. GRACIA, J.-M. CARRETERO AND E. CARBONELL (1993). "Three New Human Skulls From the Sima de los Huesos Middle Pleistocene Site in Sierra de Atapuerca, Spain." *Nature*, 362: 534–537.

ARSUAGA, J.-L., I. MARTINEZ, C. LORENZO AND A. GRACIA (1999). "The Human Cranial Remains From Gran Dolina Lower Pleistocene Site (Sierra de Atapuerca, Spain)." *Journal of Human Evolution*, 37: 431–457.

ASFAW, B., T. WHITE, O. LOVEJOY, B. LATIMER, S. SIMPSON AND G. SUWA (1999). "*Australopithecus garhi*: A New Species of Early Hominid from Ethiopia." *Science*, 284: 629–635.

ASHLEY-MONTAGU, F.M. (1929). "The Discovery of a New Anthropoid Ape in South America?" *The Scientific Monthly*, 29: 275–279.

ASHTON, E.H. (1981). "Primate Locomotion: Some Problems in Analysis and Interpretation." *Philosophical Transactions of the Royal Society of London*, B 292: 77–87.

AYALA, F.J. (1997). "Vagaries of the Molecular Clock." *Proceedings of the National Academy of Sciences* (USA), 94: 7776–7783.

AYALA, F.J. AND A.A. ESCALANTE (1996). "The Evolution of Human Populations: A Molecular Perspective." *Molecular Phylogenetics and Evolution*, 5: 188–201.

BACHELARD, G. (1933). *Les intuitions atomistiques* (Paris: Boivin).

BAILEY, W., K. HAYASAKA, C.G. SKINNER, S. KEHOE, L.C. SIEU, J.L. SLIGHTOM AND M. GOODMAN (1992). "Reexamination of the African Hominoid Trichotomy With Additional Sequences From the Primates B-Globin Gene Cluster." *Molecular Phylogenetics and Evolution*, 1: 97–135.

BALCH, E.S. (1917). "Early Man in America." *Proceedings of the American Philosophical Society*, 56: 473–483.

BARBOUR, E.H. (1907). "Evidence of Man in the Loess of Nebraska." *Science*, 25: 110–112.

BARNES, B., D. BLOOR AND J. HENRY (1996). *Scientific Knowledge: A Sociological Analysis* (Chicago: University of Chicago Press).

BARRELL, J. (1917). "Probable Relations of Climatic Change to the Tertiary Ape-Man." *Scientific Monthly*, 4: 16–26.

BARRIEL, V. (1991). "Caractères ostéologiques et odontologiques chez les Hominoidea (Primates, Mammalia): Analyse de parcimonie." *Bulletins et Mémoires de la Société d'Anthropologie de Paris*, 3: 45–72.

BEARD, K.C. (2002). "Basal Anthropoids." In, W.C. Hartwig (ed.), *The Primate Fossil Record* (Cambridge: Cambridge University Press), pp. 133–149.

Beerli, P. and S.V. Edwards (2002). "When Did Neanderthals and Modern Humans Diverge?" *Evolutionary Anthropology* (Supplement), 11: 60–63.

Begun, D.R. (1994). "Relations Among the Great Apes and Humans: New Interpretations Based on the Fossil Great Ape Dryopithecus." *Yearbook of Physical Anthropology*, 37: 11–63.

Begun, D.R. (2002a). "European Hominoids." In, W.C. Hartwig (ed.), *The Primate Fossil Record* (Cambridge: Cambridge University Press), pp. 339–368.

Begun, D.R. (2002b). "The Pliopithecoidae." In, W.C. Hartwig (ed.), *The Primate Fossil Record* (Cambridge: Cambridge University Press), pp. 221–240.

Begun, D.R. (2003). "Planet of the Apes." *Scientific American*, 289 (2): 75–83.

Begun, D.R. and A. Walker (1993). "The Endocast." In, A. Walker and R.E.F. Leakey (eds.), *The Nariokotome* Homo erectus *Skeleton* (Cambridge: Harvard University Press), pp. 326–358.

Benveniste, R.E. and G.J. Todaro (1976). "Evolution of the Type C Viral Genes: Evidence for an Asian Origin of Man." *Nature*, 261: 101–108.

Berge, C. (1991). "Quelle est la signification fonctionnelle du pelvis très large de *Australopithecus afarensis* (AL 288-1)? In, Y. Coppens and B. Senut (eds.), *Origine(s) de la bipédie chez les hominidés* (Paris: C.N.R.S.), pp. 113–119.

Bérillon, G. (2000). *Le pied des hominoïdes miocènes et des hominidés fossiles: Architecture, locomotion, évolution* (Paris: C.N.R.S.).

Bermudez de Castro, J.M., J.L. Arsuaga, E. Carbonell, A. Rosas, I. Martinez and M. Mosquera (1997). "A Hominid From the Lower Pleistocene of Atapuerca, Spain: Possible Ancestor to Neandertals and Modern Humans." *Science*, 276: 1392–1395.

Berry, R.J.A. and A.W.D. Robertson (1913–14). "The Place in Nature of the Tasmanian Aboriginal as Deduced From a Study of His Calvaria—Part II. His Relation to the Australian Aboriginal." *Proceedings of the Royal Society of Edinburgh*, 34: 144–189.

Bilsborough, A. (1978). "Some Aspects of Mosaic Evolution in Hominids." In, D.J. Chivers and K.A. Joysey (eds.), *Recent Advances in Primatology*, Vol. 3 (London: Academic Press), pp. 335–350.

Bilsborough, A. (1983). "The Pattern of Evolution Within the Genus *Homo*." In, V. Navaratnam and R.J. Harrison (eds.), *Progress in Anatomy*, Vol. 3 (Cambridge: Cambridge University Press), pp. 143–164.

Bilsborough, A. (1992). *Human Evolution* (London: Blackie Academic and Professional).

Bilsborough, A. and B. Wood (1986). "The Nature, Origin and Fate of *Homo erectus*." In, B. Wood, L. Martin and P. Andrews (eds.), *Major Topics in Primate and Human Evolution* (Cambridge: Cambridge University Press), pp. 295–316.

Black, D. (1925). "Asia and the Dispersal of Primates." *Bulletin of the Geological Society of China*, 4: 133–183.

Black, D. (1927). "On a Lower Molar Hominid Tooth From the Chou Kou Tien Deposit." *Palaeontologia Sinica*, series D, 7 (1): 1–28.

Black, D. (1934). "On the Discovery, Morphology, and Environment of *Sinanthropus pekinensis*." *Philosophical Transactions of the Royal Society of London*, series B, 223: 57–120.

Blake, C. (1862). "On the Crania of the Most Ancient Races of Men." *The Geologist*, 5: 205–233.

Blake, C. (1863). "Man and Beast." *Anthropological Review*, 1: 153–162.

Blake, C. (1864a). "On the Alleged Peculiar Characters, and Assumed Antiquity of the Human Cranium from the Neanderthal." *Journal of the Anthropological Society of London*, 2: cxxxix–clviii.

Blake, C. (1864b). "Comments on Wallace's Paper." *Journal of the Anthropological Society of London*, 2: clxxv–clxxvii.

Blake, C. (1865–1866). "On Certain 'Simious' Skulls, with especial reference to a skull from Louth, in Ireland." *Memoirs Read Before the Anthropological Society of London*, 2: 74–81.

Blake, C. (1867). "On a Human Jaw From the Cave of La Naulette, Near Dinant, Belgium." *Anthropological Review*, 5: 294–303.

Blanckaert, C. (1989a). "L'anthropologie personnifiée: Paul Broca et la biologie du genre humain," in P. Broca, *Mémoires d'Anthropologie* (Paris: Jean-Michel Place), pp. i–xliii.

Blanckaert, C. (1989b). "L'indice céphalique et l'ethnogénie européenne: A. Retzius, P. Broca, F. Pruner-Bey (1840–1870)." *Bulletins et Mémoires de la Société d'Anthropologie de Paris*, nouvelle série, 1: 165–202.

Blanckaert, C. (1995). "La question du singe et l'ordre des primates à la Société d'Anthropologie de Paris (1865–1870)." In, R. Corbey and B. Theunissen (eds.), *Ape, Man, Apeman: Changing Views since 1600* (Leiden University: Department of Prehistory), pp. 117–137.

Blanckaert, C. (1996). "Monogénisme et polygénisme." In, P. Tort (ed.), *Dictionnaire du Darwinisme et de l'évolution* (Paris: Presses Universitaires de France), pp. 3021–3037.

Blumenberg, B. (1983). "The Evolution of the Advanced Hominid Brain." *Current Anthropology*, 24: 589–623.

Bock, W.J. (1970). "Microevolutionary Sequences as a Fundamental Concept in Macroevolutionary Models." *Evolution*, 24: 704–722.

Bock, W.J. (1974). "Philosophical Foundation of Classical Evolutionary Classification." *Systematic Zoology*, 22: 375–392.

Bock, W.J. (1977). "Foundations and Methods of Evolutionary Classification." In, M.K. Hecht, P.C. Goody and B.M. Hecht (eds.), *Major Patterns in Vertebrate Evolution* (New York: Plenum Press), pp. 851–895.

Bock, W.J. (1979). "The Synthetic Explanation of Macroevolutionary Change: A Reductionistic Approach." In, J.H. Schwartz and H.B. Rollins (eds.), *Models and Methodologies in Evolutionary Theory* (Bulletin of Carnegie Museum of Natural History, 13), pp. 20–69.

Bock, W.J. (1981). "Functional-Adaptive Analysis in Evolutionary Classification." *American Zoologist*, 21: 5–20.

Bordes, F. (1968). *The Old Stone Age* (New York: McGraw-Hill).

Bordes, F. (1988). *Typologie du Paléolithique ancien et moyen* (Paris: C.N.R.S.).

Boule, M. (1908). "L'homme fossile de La Chapelle-aux-Saints (Corrèze)." *L'Anthropologie*, 19: 519–525.

Boule, M. (1911–13). "L'homme fossile de La Chapelle-aux-Saints." *Annales de Paléontologie*, 6: 109–172; 7: 21–56, 85–192; 8: 1–70.

Boule, M (1914). "L'*Homo neanderthalensis* et sa place dans la nature." *Congrès International d'Anthropologie et d'Archéologie Préhistoriques*, 14e session, vol. 2, pp. 392–395.

Boule, M. (1915). "La paléontologie humaine en Angleterre." *L'Anthropologie*, 26: 1–67.

Boule, M. (1921). *Les hommes fossiles: éléments de paléontologie humaine* (Paris: Masson).

Boule, M. (1925). "'L'homme-singe' du sud de l'Afrique." *L'Anthropologie*, 35: 123–130.

Boule, M. (1937). "Le Sinanthrope." *L'Anthropologie*, 47: 1–22.

Boule, M. and R. Anthony (1911). "L'encéphale de l'homme fossile de La Chapelle-aux-Saints." *L'Anthropologie*, 22: 129–196.

Boule, M. and J. Piveteau (1935). *Les fossiles: éléments de paléontologie* (Paris: Masson).

Boule, M. and H.V. Vallois (1946). *Les hommes fossiles: éléments de paléontologie humaine*, 3rd edition (Paris: Masson).

Boule, M. and H.V. Vallois (1952). *Les hommes fossiles: éléments de paléontologie humaine*, 4th edition (Paris: Masson).

Bourdelle, E. (1929). "Nouvelles espèces de grands singes." *Revue d'Histoire Naturelle*, 10: 251–253.

Bourgeois, M. L'abbé (1872). "Indices de l'existence de l'homme à l'époque tertiaire." *Congrès International d'Anthropologie et d'Archéologie Préhistoriques*, pp. 81–94.

Bowcock, A.M., A. Ruiz-Linares, J. Tomfohrde, E. Minch, J.R. Kidd and L.L. Cavalli-Sforza (1994). "High Resolution of Human Evolutionary Trees With Polymorphic Microsatellites." *Nature*, 368: 455–457.

Bowden, A.O. and I.A. Lopatin (1936). "Pleistocene Man in Southern California." *Science*, 84: 507–508.

Bowler, P.J. (1976). *Fossil and Progress: Paleontology and the Idea of Progressive Evolution in the Nineteenth Century* (New York: Science History Publications).

Bowler, P.J. (1983). *The Eclipse of Darwinism. Anti-Darwinian Evolution Theories in the Dacades around 1900* (Baltimore: Johns Hopkins University Press).

Bowler, P.J. (1986). *Theories of Human Evolution: A Century of Debate, 1844–1944* (Baltimore: Johns Hopkins University Press).

Bowler, P.J. (1996). *Life's Splendid Drama: Evolutionary Biology and the Reconstruction of Life's Ancestry, 1860–1940* (Chicago: University of Chicago Press).

Bowler, P.J. (1997). "Paleoanthropology Theory." In, F. Spencer (ed.), *History of Physical Anthropology:*

An Encyclopedia, vol. 2 (New York: Garland, 1997), pp. 785–790.

Brace, C.L. (1962). "Refocusing on the Neanderthal Problem." *American Anthropologist*, 64: 729–741.

Brace, C.L. (1964). "The Fate of the 'Classic' Neanderthals: A Consideration of Hominid Catastrophism." *Current Anthropology*, 5: 3–43.

Brace, C.L. (1967). *The Stages of Human Evolution* (New Jersey: Prentice Hall).

Brace, C.L. (1979). *The Stages of Human Evolution*, 2nd edition (New Jersey: Prentice Hall).

Brace, C.L. (1991). *The Stages of Human Evolution*, 4th edition (New Jersey: Prentice Hall).

Brace, C.L. (1992). *Modern Human Origins: Narrow Focus or Broad Spectrum*? (Indiana University: Department of Anthropology).

Brace, C.L. (1995). "Biocultural Interaction and the Mechanism of Mosaic Evolution in the Emergence of 'Modern' Morpholoy." *American Anthropologist*, 97: 711–721.

Bräuer, G. (1984a). "A Cranial Approach to the Origin of Anatomically Modern *Homo sapiens* in Africa and Implications for the Appearance of Modern Europeans." In, F.H. Smith and F. Spencer (eds.), *The Origins of Modern Humans: A World Survey of the Fossil Evidence* (New York: Alan R. Liss, 1984), pp. 327–410.

Bräuer, G. (1984b). "The 'Afro-European *sapiens*-hypothesis', and hominid evolution in East Asia During the Late Middle and Upper Pleistocene." In, P. Andrews and J. L. Franzen (eds.), *The Early Evolution of Man With Special Emphasis on Southeast Asia and Africa* (Courier Forschungs-Institut Senckenberg, 69), pp. 145–165.

Bräuer, G. (1989). "The Evolution of Modern Humans: A Comparison of the African and non-African Evidence." In, P. Mellars and C. Stringer (eds.), *The Human Revolution* (New Jersey: Princeton University Press, 1989), pp. 123–154.

Bräuer, G. (1990). "The Occurrence of Some Controversial *Homo erectus* Cranial Features in the Zhoukoudian and East African Hominids." *Acta Anthropological Sinica*, 9:350–358.

Bräuer, G. (1992). "Africa's Place in the Evolution of *Homo sapiens*." In, G. Bräuer and F.H. Smith (eds.), *Continuity or Replacement: Controversies in* Homo sapiens *evolution* (Rotterdam: A.A. Balkema, 1992), pp. 83–98.

Bräuer, G. (1994). "How Different are Asian and African *Homo erectus*?" In, J.L. Franzen (ed.), *100 Years of Pithecanthropus: The* Homo erectus *Problem* (Frankfurt am Main: Courier Forschungs-Institut Senckenberg, 171), pp. 301–318.

Breitinger, E. (1957). "Zur phyletischen Evolution von *Homo sapiens*." *Anthropologischer Anzeiger*, 21: 62–83.

Breitinger, E. (1959). "Zur frühesten Phase der Hominiden-Evolution." In, E. Breitinger, J. Haeckel and R. Pittioni (eds.), *Beiträger Osterreichs zur Erforschung der Vergangenheit und Kulturegeschichte der Menschheit* (Wenner-Gren Foundation for Anthropological Reserach), pp. 205–235.

Breitinger, E. (1962a). "On the Phyletic Evolution of *Homo sapiens*." In, W.W. Howells (ed.), *Ideas on Human Evolution: Selected Essays, 1949–1961* (Cambridge: Harvard University Press), pp. 436–459.

Breitinger, E. (1962b). "On the Earliest Phase of Hominid Evolution." In, W.W. Howells (ed.), *Ideas on Human Evolution: Selected Essays, 1949–1961* (Cambridge: Harvard University Press), pp. 172–202.

Broca, P. (1863a). "Observations sur le crâne de Néanderthal." *Bulletins de la Société d'Anthropologie de Paris*, 4: 322–323.

Broca, P. (1863b). "Sur les Crânes basques." *Bulletins de la Société d'Anthropologie de Paris*, 4: 38–62.

Broca, P. (1864a). "Discussion sur les origines indo-européennes." *Bulletins de la Société d'Anthropologie de Paris*, 5: 193–196.

Broca, P. (1864b). "Sur les origines européennes." *Bulletins de la Société d'Anthropologie de Paris*, 5: 303–316.

Broca, P. (1866). "Sur la mâchoire humaine de la Naulette (Belgique)." *Bulletins de la Société d'Anthropologie de Paris*, 2e série, 1: 593–601.

Broca, P. (1867). "Discours de M. Broca sur l'ensemble de la question." *Congrès International d'Anthropologie et d'Archéologie Préhistoriques*, 2e session, pp. 367–402.

Broca, P. (1868). "Sur les crânes et ossements des Eyzies." *Bulletins de la Société d'Anthropologie de Paris*, 2e série, 3: 350–392.

Broca, P. (1869). "L'ordre des primates. Parallèle anatomique de l'homme et des singes."

Bulletins de la Société d'Anthropologie de Paris, 2e série, 4: 228–401.

BROCA, P. (1870a). "Réponse aux observations de M. le professeur Richard Owen." *Bulletins de la Société d'Anthropologie de Paris*, 2e série, 5: 592–605.

BROCA, P. (1870b). "Le transformisme." *Bulletins de la Société d'Anthropologie de Paris*, 2e série, 5: 168–239.

BROCA, P. (1870c). "L'anthropologie en 1868." *Encyclopédie générale, Almanach de 1869* (Paris, 1870), pp. 49–54, reproduced in P. Broca, *Mémoires d'Anthropologie* (Paris: Jean-Michel Place, 1989), pp. 510–520.

BROCA, P. (1873). "Les crânes de la caverne de l'Homme-Mort (Lozère)." *Revue d'Anthropologie*, 2: 1–53.

BROCA, P. (1877). "Les races fossiles de l'Europe occidentale." *Association Française pour l'avancement des sciences*, Congrès du Havre, pp. 10–25.

BROOM, R. (1918). "The Evidence Afforded by the Boskop Skull of a New Species of Primitive Man (*Homo capensis*)." *Anthropological Papers of the American Museum of Natural History*, 23: 67–79.

BROOM, R. (1923). "A Contribution to the Craniology of the Yellow-Skinned Races of South Africa." *Journal of the Royal Anthropological Institute*, 53: 132–149.

BROOM, R. (1925a). "Some Notes on the Taungs Skull." *Nature*, 115: 569–571.

BROOM, R. (1925b). "On the Newly Discovered South African Man-Ape." *Natural History*, 25: 409–418.

BROOM, R. (1929). "Note on the Milk Dentition of *Australopithecus*." *Proceedings of the Zoological Society of London*, pp. 85–88.

BROOM, R. (1933). *The Coming of Man: Was It Accident or Design?* (London: H.F. & G. Witherby).

BROOM, R. (1936a). "A New Fossil Anthropoid Skull from South Africa." *Nature*, 138: 486–488.

BROOM, R. (1936b). "The Dentition of *Australopithecus*." *Nature*, 138: 719.

BROOM, R. (1937a). "Discovery of a Lower Molar of *Australopithecus*." *Nature*, 140: 681–682.

BROOM, R. (1937b). "On Australopithecus and Its Affinities." In, G.G. MacCurdy (ed.), *Early Man* (Freeport: Books for Librairies Press), pp. 285–292.

BROOM, R. (1938a). "More Discoveries of *Australopithecus*." *Nature*, 141: 828–829.

BROOM, R. (1938b). "The Pleistocene Anthropoid Apes of South Africa." *Nature*, 142: 377–379.

BROOM, R. (1938c). "Further Evidence on the Structure of the South African Pleistocene Anthropoids." *Nature*, 142: 897–899.

BROOM, R. (1939). "The Dentition of the Tranvaal Pleistocene Anthropoids, *Plesianthropus* and *Paranthropus*." *Annals of the Transvaal Museum*, 19: 303–314.

BROOM, R. (1941a). "The Origin of Man." *Nature*, 148: 10–14.

BROOM, R. (1941b). "Mandible of a Young Paranthropus Child." *Nature*, 147: 607–608.

BROOM, R. (1942a). "The Hand of the Ape-Man, *Paranthropus robustus*." *Nature*, 149: 513–514.

BROOM, R. (1942b). "Man's Place Among the Primates." *South African Medical Journal*, 16: 267–268.

BROOM, R. (1943). "South Africa's Part in the Solution of the Problem of the Origin of Man." *South African Journal of Science*, 40: 68–80.

BROOM, R. (1946). *The South African Fossil Ape-Men: The Australopithecinae*, Part I. The Occurrence and General Structure of the South African Ape-Men (Pretoria, Transvaal Museum Memoir No. 2), pp. 1–153.

BROOM, R. (1947a). "The Upper Milk Molars of the Ape-man, *Plesianthropus*." Nature, 159: 602.

BROOM, R. (1947b). "Discovery of a New Skull of the South African Ape-man, *Plesianthropus*." *Nature*, 159: 672.

BROOM, R. (1949). "Another New Type of Fossil Ape-man." *Nature*, 163: 57.

BROOM, R. (1950a). *Finding the Missing Link* (London: Watts & Co.).

BROOM, R. (1950b). "The Genera and Species of the South African Fossil Ape-Men." *American Journal of Physical Anthropology*, 8: 1–14.

BROOM, R. (1952). "The Fossil Ape-Men of South Africa." In, L.S.B. Leakey and S. Cole (eds.), *Proceedings of the Pan-African Congress on Prehistory, 1947* (New York: Philosophical Librairy), pp. 107–111.

BROOM, R. AND J.T. ROBINSON (1947a). "Jaw of the Male Sterkfontein Ape-men." *Nature*, 160: 153.

BROOM, R. AND J.T. ROBINSON (1947b). "Further Remains of the Sterkfontein Ape-man, Plesianthropus." *Nature*, 160: 430–431.

Broom, R. and J.T. Robinson (1949a). "A New Mandible of the Ape-Man Plesianthropus Transvaalensis." *American Journal of Physical Anthropology*, 7: 123–127.

Broom, R. and J.T. Robinson (1949b). "Thumb of the Swartkrans Ape-Man." *Nature*, 164: 841–842.

Broom, R. and J.T. Robinson (1949c). "The Lower End of the Femur of Plesianthropus." *Annals of the Transvaal Museum*, 21: 181–182.

Broom, R. and J.T. Robinson (1950a). *Sterkfontein Ape-Man: Plesianthropus*, Part I. Further Evidence of the Structure of the Sterkfontein Ape-Man Plesianthropus (Pretoria, Transvaal Museum Memoir No. 4), pp. 1–83.

Broom, R. and J.T. Robinson (1950b). "Note on the Skull of the Swartkrans Ape-Man Paranthropus crassidens." *American Journal of Physical Anthropology*, 8: 295–303.

Broom, R. and J.T. Robinson (1950c). "Notes on the Pelves of the Fossil Ape-Men." *American Journal of Physical Anthropology*, 8: 489–494.

Broom, R. and J.T. Robinson (1952). *Swartkrans Ape-Man:* Paranthropus crassidens (Pretoria, Transvaal Museum Memoir No. 6).

Brown, F., J. Harris, R. Leakey and A. Walker (1985). "Early *Homo erectus* Skeleton From West Lake Turkana, Kenya." *Nature*, 316: 788–792.

Brown, W.M., E.M. Prager, A. Wang and A.C. Wilson (1982). "Mitochondrial DNA Sequences of Primates: Tempo and Mode in Evolution." *Journal of Molecular Evolution*, 18: 225–239.

Brunet, M., A. Beauvilain, Y. Coppens, E. Heintz, A.H.E. Moutaye and D. Pilbeam (1995). "The First Australopithecine 2,500 Kilometers West of the Rift Valley (Tchad)." *Nature*, 378: 273–275.

Brunet, M., A. Beauvilain, Y. Coppens, E. Heintz, A.H.E. Moutaye and D. Pilbeam (1996). "*Australopithecus bahrelghazali*, une nouvelle espèce d'hominidé ancien de la région de Koro Toro (Tchad)." *Comptes Rendus de l'Académie des Sciences de Paris*, 322: 907–913.

Brunet, M., et al. (2002). "A New Hominid from the Upper Miocene of Chad, Central Africa." *Nature*, 418: 145–151.

Bryan, K. (1945). "Recent Work on Early man at the Gruta de Cadonga in the Argentine Republic." *American Antiquity*, 11: 58–60.

Burkitt, A.N. and J.I. Hunter (1922–23). "The Description of a Neanderthaloid Australian Skull, With Remarks on the Production of the Facial Characteristics of Australian Skulls in General." *Journal of Anatomy*, 57: 31–54.

Butler, P.M. and J.R.E. Mills (1959). "A Contribution to the Odontology of *Oreopithecus*." *Bulletin of the British Museum of Natural History*, 4: 1–26.

Caccone, A. and J.R. Powell (1989). "DNA Divergence Among Hominoids." *Evolution*, 43: 925–942.

Campbell, B.G. and R.L. Bernor (1976). "The Origin of the Hominidae: Africa or Asia?" *Journal of Human Evolution*, 5: 441–454.

Cann, R.L., M. Stoneking and A.C. Wilson (1987). "Mitochondrial DNA and Human Evolution." *Nature*, 325: 31–36.

Capellini, J. (1876). "Les traces de l'homme pliocène en Toscane." *Congrès International d'Anthropologie et d'Archéologie Préhistoriques*, pp. 46–63.

Cartmill, M. (1990). "Human Uniqueness and Theoretical Content in Paleoanthropology." *International Journal of Primatology*, 11: 173–192.

Cartmill, M., D. Pilbeam and G. Isaac (1986). "One Hundred Years of Paleoanthropology." *American Scientist*, 74: 410–420.

Caspari, R. and M.H. Wolpoff (1996). "Weidenreich, Coon, and Multiregional Evolution." *Human Evolution*, 11: 261–268.

Chaline, J., B. Dutrillaux, J. Couturier, A. Durand and D. Marchand (1991). "Un modèle chromosomique et paléobiogéographique d'évolution des primates supérieurs." *Geobios*, 24: 105–110.

Chamberlain, J.G. and W.C. Hartwig (1999). "Thomas Kuhn and Paleoanthropology." *Evolutionary Anthropology*, 8: 42–44.

Charlesworth, B., R. Lande and M. Slatkin (1982). "A Neo-Darwinian Commentary on Macroevolution." *Evolution*, 36: 474–498.

Chomsky, N. (1972). *Language and Mind*, 2nd edition (New York: Harcourt, Brace and Jovanovich).

Chomsky, N. (1980). "Discussion of Putnam's Comments." In, M. Piattelli-Palmarini (ed.), *Language and Learning* (Cambridge: Harvard University Press), pp. 310–324.

Chomsky, N. (1982). *The Generative Enterprise* (Dordrecht: Foris Publications).

Chomsky, N. (1988). *Language and Problems of Knowledge* (Cambridge: MIT Press).

Chomsky, N. (1990). "Language and Mind." In, D.H. Mellor (ed.), *Ways of Communicating* (Cambridge: Cambridge University Press), pp. 56–80.

Churchill, F.B. (1976). "Rudolf Virchow and the Pathologist's Criteria for the Inheritance of Acquired Characteristics." *Journal of the History of Medicine and Allied Sciences*, 31: 117–148.

Ciochon, R.L. (1983). "Hominoid Cladistics and the Ancestry of Modern Apes and Humans." In, R.L. Ciochon and R.S. Corruccini (eds.), *New Interpretations of Ape and Human Ancestry* (New York: Plenum Press), pp. 783–843.

Ciochon, R.L. and R.S. Corruccini (1982). "Miocene Hominoids and New Interpretations of Ape and Human Ancestry." In, A.B. Chiarelli and R.S. Corruccini (eds.), *Advanced Views in Primate Biology* (Berlin: Springer-Verlag), pp. 149–159.

Clark, J.D. (1970). *The Prehistory of Africa* (London: Thames and Hudson).

Clarke, R.J. and P.V. Tobias (1995). "Sterkfontein Member 2 Foot Bones of the Oldest South African Hominid." *Science*, 269: 521–524.

Cohen, C. and J.-J. Hublin (1989). *Boucher de Perthes, 1788–1868: les origines romantiques de la préhistoire* (Paris: Belin).

Colbert, E.H. (1937). "A New Primate From the Upper Eocene Pondaung Formation of Burma." *American Museum Novitates*, No. 951: 1–18.

Colbert, E.H. (1938). "Fossil Mammals From Burma in the American Museum of Natural History." *Bulletin of the American Museum of Natural History*, 74: 255–434.

Cole, S. (1975). *Leakey's Luck: The Life of Louis Seymour Bazett Leakey, 1903–1972* (London: Collins).

Conroy, G.C., M.W. Vannier and P.V. Tobias (1990). "Endocranial Features of *Australopithecus africanus* Revealed by 2- and 3-D Computed Tomography." *Science*, 247: 838–841.

Conroy, G.C., G.W. Weber, H. Seidler, P.V. Tobias, A. Kane and B. Brunsden (1998). "Endocranial Capacity in an Early Hominid Cranium From Sterkfontein, South Africa." *Science*, 280: 1730–1731.

Coon, C.S. (1939). *The Races of Europe* (New York: Macmillan).

Coon, C.S. (1954). *The Story of Man* (New York: Alfred A. Knopf).

Coon, C.S. (1959). "Review of W.W. Howells's *Manking in the Making*." *Science*, 130: 1399–1400.

Coon, C.S. (1962a). *The Origin of Races* (New York: Alfred A. Knopf).

Coon, C.S. (1962b). *The Story of Man*, 2nd edition (New York: Alfred A. Knopf).

Coon, C.S. (1965). *The Living Races of Man* (New York: Alfred A. Knopf).

Cook, H.J. (1927). "New Geological and Palaeontological Evidence Bearing on the Antiquity of Mankind in America." *Natural History*, 27: 240–248.

Cope, E.D. (1885). "The Lemuroidea and the Insectivora of the Eocene Period of North America." *American Naturalist*, 19: 457–471.

Cope, E.D. (1888). "Archaeology and Anthropology." *American Naturalist*, 22: 660–663.

Cope, E.D. (1893). "The Genealogy of Man." *American Naturalist*, 27: 321–335.

Coppens, Y. (1961a). "Découverte d'un Australopithéciné dans le Villafranchien du Tchad." *Comptes Rendus de l'Académie des Sciences*, 252: 3851–3852.

Coppens, Y. (1961b). "Un Australopithèque au Sahara (Nord-Tchad)." *Bulletin de la Société Préhistorique Française*, 58: 756–757.

Coppens, Y. (1962). "Découverte d'un australopithéciné dans le Villafranchien du Tchad." In, *Problèmes actuels de paléontologie, évolution des vertébrés*, No. 104 (Paris: Colloques internationaux du Centre National de la Recherche Scientifique), pp. 455–459.

Coppens, Y. (1965). "L'hominien du Tchad." *Comptes Rendus de l'Académie des Sciences*, 260: 2869–2871.

Coppens, Y. (1981). "Le cerveau des hommes fossiles." *Comptes Rendus des Séances de l'Académie des Sciences de Paris*, 292 (Supplément d'Avril): 3–17.

Coppens, Y. (1983a). *Le singe, l'Afrique et l'homme* (Paris: Fayard).

Coppens, Y. (1983b). "Systématique, phylogénie, environnment et culture des australopithèques: Hypothèses et synthèses." *Bulletins et Mémoires de la Société d'Anthropologie de Paris*, 10: 273–284.

Coppens, Y. (1994). "East Side Story: The Origin of Humankind." *Scientific American*, 270: 62–69.

Corruccini, R.S. (1978). "Comparative Osteometrics of the Hominoid Wrist Joint, With Special Reference to Knuckle-Walking." *Journal of Human Evolution*, 7: 307–321.

Corruccini, R.S. and R.L. Ciochon (1983). "Overview of Ape and Human Ancestry: Phyletic Relationships of Miocene and Later Hominoidea." In, R.L. Ciochon and R.S. Corruccini (eds.), *New Interpretations of Ape and Human Ancestry* (New York: Plenum Press), pp. 3–19.

Corruccini, R.S. and H.M. McHenry (1980). "Cladometric Analysis of Pliocene Hominids." *Journal of Human Evolution*, 9: 209–221.

Corruccini, R.S. and H.M. McHenry (2001). "Knuckle-Walking Hominid Ancestors." *Journal of Human Evolution*, 40: 507–511.

Cracraft, J. (1981). "The Use of Functional and Adaptive Criteria in Phylogenetic Systematics." *American Zoologist*, 21: 21–36.

Cressman, L.S. (1946). "Early Man in Oregon." *Scientific Monthly*, 62: 43–51.

Cronin, J.E., N.T. Boaz, C.B. Stringer and Y. Rak (1981). "Tempo and Mode in Hominid Evolution." *Nature*, 292: 113–122.

Crookshank, F.G. (1913). "Mongols." *Universal Medical Record*, 3: 12–29.

Crookshank, F.G. (1924). *The Mongol in Our Midst* (London: Kegan Paul, Trench, Trubner & Co.).

Crookshank, F.G. (1931). *The Mongol in Our Midst*, 3rd edition (London: Kegan Paul, Trench, Trubner & Co.).

Crubézy, E. and J. Braga (2003). "*Homo sapiens* prend de l'âge." *La Recherche*, 368: 30–35.

Crusafont-Pairo, M. and J. Hürzeler (1961). "Les Pongidés fossiles d'Espagne." *Comptes Rendus de l'Académie des Sciences*, 252: 582–584.

Dally, E. (1868). "Introduction," in T.H. Huxley, *De la Place de l'Homme dans la Nature* (Paris: J.B. Baillière), pp. 1–95.

Dart, R.A. (1923). "Boskop Remains from the South-east African Coast." *Nature*, 112: 623–625.

Dart, R.A. ((1925a). "*Australopithecus africanus*: The Man-Ape of South Africa." *Nature*, 115: 195–199.

Dart, R.A. (1925b). "The Taungs Skull." *Nature*, 116: 462.

Dart, R.A. (1926). "Taungs and Its Significance." *Natural History*, 26: 315–326.

Dart, R.A. (1929). "A Note on the Taungs Skull." *South African Journal of Science*, 26: 648–658.

Dart, R.A. (1934). "The Dentition of *Australopithecus africanus*." *Folia Anatomica Japonica*, 22: 207–221.

Dart, R.A. (1940a). "Recent Discoveries Bearing on Human History in Southern Africa." *Journal of the Royal Anthropological Institute*, 70: 13–27.

Dart, R.A. (1940b). "The Status of Australopithecus." *American Journal of Physical Anthropology*, 26: 167–186.

Dart, R.A. (1948a). "The Makapansgat Proto-Human Australopithecus prometheus." *American Journal of Physical Anthropology*, 6: 259–283.

Dart, R.A. (1948b). "The Adolescent Mandible of Australopithecus prometheus." *American Journal of Physical Anthropology*, 6: 391–411.

Dart, R.A. (1949a). "The Cranio-Facial Fragment of Australopithecus prometheus." *American Journal of Physical Anthropology*, 7: 187–213.

Dart, R.A. (1949b). "The First Pelvic Bones of Australopithecus prometheus: Preliminary Note." *American Journal of Physical Anthropology*, 7: 255–257.

Dart, R.A. (1949c). "Innominate Fragments of Australopithecus prometheus." *American Journal of Physical Anthropology*, 7: 301–332.

Dart, R.A. (1949d). "The Predatory Implemental Technique of Australopithecus." *American Journal of Physical Anthropology*, 7: 1–38.

Dart, R.A. (1954). "The Second, or Adult, Female Mandible of Australopithecus prometheus." *American Journal of Physical Anthropology*, 12: 313–343.

Dart, R.A. (1955). "Australopithecus prometheus and Telanthropus capensis." *American Journal of Physical Anthropology*, 13: 67–96.

Dart, R.A. (1957). "The Makapansgat Australopithecine Osteodontokeratic Culture." In, J. D. Clark and S. Cole (eds.), *Third Pan-African Congress on Prehistory, Livingstone 1955* (London: Chatto & Windus, 1957), pp. 161–171.

Dart, R.A and D. Craig (1959). *Adventures with the Missing Link* (New York: Harper & Brothers).

Darwin, C.R. (1859). *On the Origin of Species by Means of Natural Selection, or the Preservation of Favoured Races in the Struggle for Life* (London: John Murray).

Darwin, C.R. (1871). *The Descent of Man, and Selection in Relation to Sex*, Vol. 1 (London: John Murray).

Davis, B. (1863–64). "The Neanderthal Skull: its Peculiar Conformation explained Anatomically." *Memoirs Read Before the Anthropological Society of London*, 1: 281–295.

Davis, B (1864). "De la valeur réelle de la forme spéciale d'un fragment de crâne trouvé dans la caverne de Néanderthal." *Bulletins de la Société d'Anthropologique de Paris*, 5: 708–718.

Day, M.H. and E.H. Wickens (1980). "Laetoli Pliocene Hominid Footprints and Bipedalism." *Nature*, 286: 385–387.

Deacon, T.W. (1997). *The Symbolic Species: The Co-Evolution of Language and Brain* (New York: W.W. Norton).

De Bonis, L. and G.D. Koufos (1994). "Our Ancestors's Ancestor: Ouranopithecus Is a Greek Link in Human Ancestry." *Evolutionary Anthropology*, 3: 75–83.

De Bonis, L. and G.D. Koufos (1995). "Nouveaux documents sur les ancêtres de la lignée humaine." *L'Anthropologie*, 99: 18–28.

De Bonis, L., G. Bourvain, D. Geraads and G.D. Koufos (1990). "New Hominid Skull Material From the Late Miocene of Macedonia in Northern Greece." *Nature*, 345: 712–714.

Delisle, R.G. (1995). "Human Palaeontology and the Evolutionary Synthesis during the Decade 1950–1960." In, R. Corbey and B. Theunissen (eds.), *Ape, Man, Apeman: Changing Views since 1600* (Leiden: Leiden University), pp. 217–228).

Delisle, R.G. (1997a). "Mayr, Ernst (1904–)." In, F. Spencer (ed.), *History of Physical Anthropology*, Vol. 2 (New York: Garland), pp. 650–651.

Delisle, R.G. (1997b). "Simpson, George Gaylord (1902–1984)." In, F. Spencer (ed.), *History of Physical Anthropology*, Vol. 2 (New York: Garland), pp. 932–933.

Delisle, R.G. (1997c). "Dobzhansky, Theodosius (1900–1975)." In, F. Spencer (ed.), *History of Physical Anthropology*, Vol. 1 (New York: Garland), pp. 349–351.

Delisle, R.G. (1998). "Les origines de la paléontologie humaine: essai de réinterprétation." *L'Anthropologie*, 102: 3–19.

Delisle, R.G. (1999). *The Field of Human Evolution Within Evolutionary Biology and Anthropology: Historical and Epistemological Analyses since Inception*, Ph.D. thesis, University of the Witwatersrand, Johannesburg.

Delisle, R.G. (2000a). "The Biology/Culture Link in Human Evolution, 1750–1950: The Problem of Integration in Science." *Studies in History and Philosophy of Biological and Biomedical Sciences*, 31: 531–556.

Delisle, R.G. (2000b). "Construire l'arbre phylétique de l'Homme: fossiles, théories et cadres interprétatifs." *L'Anthropologie*, 104: 489–522.

Delisle, R.G. (2001). "Adaptationism Versus Cladism in Human Evolution Studies." In, R. Corbey and W. Roebroeks (eds.), *Studying Human Origins: Disciplinary History and Epistemology* (Amsterdam: Amsterdam University Press), pp. 107–121.

Delisle, R.G. (2002). "Evolutionary Biology and Linguistics: The Nature and Implication of a Disciplinary Integration." *Selection*, 3: 29–44.

Delisle, R. G. (2004). "Et l'homme quitta les singes. . ." *La Recherche*, No. 377: 46–51.

Deloison, Y. (1992). "Empreintes de pas à Laetoli (Tanzanie): Leur apport à une meilleure connaissance de la locomotion des Hominidés fossiles." *Comptes Rendus de l'Académie des Sciences de Paris*, série II, 315: 103–109.

Deloison, Y. (1995). "Le pied des premiers hominidés." *La Recherche*, 281: 52–55.

De Loys, F. (1929). "A Gap Filled in the Pedigree of Man?" *Illustrated London News*, June 15, p. 1040.

Delson, E. (1978). "Models of Early Hominid Phylogeny." In, C.J. Jolly (ed.), *Early Hominids in Africa* (New York: Duckworth, 1978), pp. 517–541.

Delson, E. (1981). "Paleoanthropology: Pliocene and Pleistocene Human Evolution." *Paleobiology*, 7: 298–305.

Delson, E. (1985). "Palaeobiology and Age of African *Homo erectus*." *Nature*, 316: 762–763.

Delson, E. (1986). "Human Phylogeny Revised Again." *Nature*, 322: 496–497.

Delson, E. (1987). "Evolution and Palaeobiology of Robust *Australopithecus*." *Nature*, 327: 654–655.

Delson, E., N. Eldredge and I. Tattersall (1977). Reconstruction of Hominid Phylogeny: A Testable Framework Based on Cladistic Analysis." *Journal of Human Evolution*, 6: 263–278.

Demerec, M. (1950). "Foreword." *Cold Spring Harbor Symposia on Quantitative Biology*, Vol. 15, pp. v–vi.

de Mortillet, G. (1873). "Le précurseur de l'homme." *Compte Rendu de l'Association Française pour l'Avancement des Sciences*, 2e session, Lyon, pp. 607–613.

de Mortillet, G. (1879). "Revue préhistorique." *Revue d'Anthropologie*, 2e série, 8: 114–118.

de Mortillet, G. (1883). *Le Préhistorique: antiquité de l'homme* (Paris: Reinwald).

de Mortillet, G. (1892). "L'Anthropopithèque." *Revue Mensuelle de l'École d'Anthropologie de Paris*, 2: 137–154.

de Mortillet, G. (1896). "Précurseur de l'homme et Pithécanthrope." *Revue Mensuelle de l'École d'Anthropologie de Paris*, 6: 305–317.

de Mortillet, G. and A. de Mortillet (1900). *Le Préhistorique: origine et antiquité de l'homme*, 3rd edition (Paris: C. Reinwald).

Denicker, P., A. de Quatrefages, J. Fraipont, L. Manouvrier and P. Topinard (1889). "Discussion." *Congrès International d'Anthropologie et d'Archéologie Préhistoriques*, 10e session, pp. 348–362.

de Quatrefages, A. (1860–1861). "Histoire naturelle de l'homme: Unité de l'espèce humaine." *Revue des Deux Mondes*, 30: 807–833; 31: 155–175, 412–435, 628–656, 938–969.

de Quatrefages, A. (1861). *Unité de l'espèce humaine* (Paris: Hachette).

de Quatrefages, A. (1867). *Rapport sur les progrès de l'anthropologie* (Paris: Imprimerie Impériale).

de Quatrefages, A. (1870). *Charles Darwin et ses précurseurs Français. Étude sur le transformisme* (Paris: Baillière).

de Quatrefages, A. (1883). *Hommes fossiles et hommes sauvages* (Paris, Jean-Michel Place, 1988).

de Quatrefages, A. (1894). *Les émules de Darwin*, Vol. 2 (Paris: Baillière).

de Quatrefages, A. (1905). *L'espèce humaine*, 14th edition (Paris: Alcan). This book was originally published in 1877.

de Quatrefages, A. and E.-T. Hamy (1873). "Races humaines fossiles—Race de Canstadt." *Bulletins de la Société d'Anthropologie de Paris*, 2e série, 8: 518–523.

de Quatrefages, A. and E.-T. Hamy (1874a). "La race de Cro-Magnon dans l'espace et dans le temps." *Bulletins de la Société d'Anthropologie de Paris*, 2e série, 9: 260–266.

de Quatrefages, A. and E.-T. Hamy (1874b). "Races humaines fossiles mésaticéphale et brachycéphales." *Bulletins de la Société d'Anthropologie de Paris*, 2e série, 9: 819–826.

de Quatrefages, A. and E.-T. Hamy (1875). "Les Crania Ethnica." *Bulletins de la Société d'Anthropologie de Paris*, 2e série, 10: 612–619.

De Quatrefages, A. and E.-T. Hamy (1882). *Crania Ethnica: Les crânes des races humaines* (Paris: J.B. Baillière).

Desmond, A. (1982). *Archetypes and Ancestors: Palaeontology in Victorian London, 1850–1875* (London: Blond & Briggs, 1982).

Desmond, A. (1985). "Richard Owen's Reaction to Transmutation in the 1830's." *British Journal for the History of Science*, 18: 25–50.

Dixon, R.B. (1923). *The Racial History of Man* (New York: Charles Scribner's Sons, 1923).

Dobzhansky, Th. (1937). *Genetics and the Origin of Species* (New York: Columbia University Press).

Dobzhansky, Th. (1944). "On Species and Races of Living and Fossil Man." *American Journal of Physical Anthropology*, 2: 251–265.

Dobzhansky, Th. (1950). "Human Diversity and Adaptation." *Cold Spring Harbor Symposia on Quantitative Biology*, 15: 385–400.

Dobzhansky, Th. (1955). *Evolution, Genetics, and Man* (New York: Wiley).

Dobzhansky, Th. (1963a). "Genetic Entities in Hominid Evolution." In, S.L. Washburn (ed.), *Clasification and Human Evolution* (Chicago: Aldine), pp. 347–362.

Dobzhansky, Th. (1963b). "A Debatable Account of the Origin of Races." *Scientific American*, 208: 169–171.

Drennan, M.R. (1935). "The Florisbad Skull." *South African Journal of Science*, 32: 601–602.

Dreyer, T.F. (1935). "A Human Skull from Florisbad, Orange Free State, with a note on the endocranial cast, by C.U. Ariëns Kappens." *Proceedings of the Section of Sciences of the Koninklijke Akademie van Wetenschappen*, 38: 119–128.

DREYER, T.F. (1936). "The Florisbad Skull in the Light of the Steinheim Discovery." *Zeitschrift für Rassenkunde*, 4: 320–322.

DUCKWORTH, W.L.H. (1912). *Prehistoric Man* (Cambridge: Cambridge University Press).

DUCKWORTH, W.L.H. (1925). "The Fossil Anthropoid Ape from Taungs." *Nature*, 115: 236.

DUBOIS, E. (1894). *Pithecanthropus erectus, eine menschenähnliche Uebergangsform aus Java* (Batavia).

DUBOIS, E. (1896a). "On *Pithecanthropus erectus*: A Transitional Form Between Man and the Apes." *Scientific Transactions of the Royal Dublin Society*, 6: 1–18.

DUBOIS, E. (1896b). "Le Pithecanthropus erectus et l'origine de l'homme." *Bulletins de la Société d'Anthropologie de Paris*, 4e série, 7: 460–467.

DUBOIS, E. (1896c). "The Place of Pithecanthropus in the Genealogical Tree." *Nature*, 53: 245.

DUBOIS, E. (1921). "The Proto-Australian Fossil Man of Wadjak, Java." *Proceedings of the Section of Sciences of the Koninklijke Akademie van Wetenschappen*, 23: 1013–1051.

DUNCAN, A.S., J. KAPPELMAN AND L.J. SHAPIRO (1994). "Matatarsophalangeal Joint Function and Positional Behavior in *Australopithecus afarensis*." *American Journal of Physical Anthropology*, 93: 67–81.

DUNSWORTH, H. AND A. WALKER (2002). "Early Genus *Homo*." In, W.C. Hartwig (ed.), *The Primate Fossil Record* (Cambridge: Cambrige University Press), pp. 419–435.

DUTRILLAUX, B. AND J. COUTURIER (1986). "Principes de l'analyse chromosomique appliquée à la phylogénie: l'exemple des Pongidae et des Hominidae." *Mammalia*, 50: 22–37.

ECCLES, J.C. (1989). *Evolution of the Brain: Creation of the Self* (London: Routledge).

ECKHARDT, R.B. (1972). "Population Genetics and Human Origins." *Scientific American*, 226: 94–103.

EDELSTEIN, S.J. (1987). "An Alternative Paradigm for Hominoid Evolution." *Human Evolution*, 2: 169–174.

ELDREDGE, N. (1979). "Alternative Approaches to Evolutionary Theory." In, J.H. Schwartz and H.B. Rollins (eds.), *Models and Methodologies in Evolutionary Theory* (Bulletin of Carnegie Museum of Natural History, 13), pp. 7–19.

ELDREDGE, N. AND J. CRACRAFT (1980). *Phylogenetic Patterns and the Evolutionary Process: Method and Theory in Comparative Biology* (New York: Columbia University Press).

ELDREDGE, N. AND S.J. GOULD (1972). "Punctuated Equilibria: An Alternative to Phyletic Gradualism." In, T.J.M. Schopf (ed.), *Models in Paleobiology* (San Francisco: Freeman and Cooper), pp. 82–115.

ELDREDGE, N. AND I. TATTERSALL (1975). "Evolutionary Models, Phylogenetic Reconstruction, and Another Look at Hominid Phylogeny." In, F.S. Szalay (ed.), *Approaches to Primate Paleobiology*, Vol. 5 (Basel: Karger), pp. 218–242.

ELDREDGE, N. AND I. TATTERSALL (1982). *The Myths of Human Evolution* (New York: Columbia University Press).

ELLIOT SMITH, G. (1924). *Essays on the Evolution of Man* (London: Oxford Univerity Press).

ELLIOT SMITH, G. (1925). "The Fossil Anthropoid Ape from Taungs." *Nature*, 115: 235.

ELLIOT SMITH, G. (1927). *Essays on the Evolution of Man*, 2nd edition (London: Oxford Univerity Press).

ELLIOT SMITH, G. (1930). "The Cradle of Mankind." *Scientia*, 47: 401–408.

EXCOFFIER, L. AND D. ROESSLI (1990). "Origine et évolution de l'ADN mitochondrial humain: le paradigme perdu." *Bulletins et Mémoires de la Société d'Anthropologie de Paris*, new series, 2: 25–42.

EXCOFFIER, L. AND Z. YANG (1999). "Substitution Rate Variation Among Sites in Mitochondrial Hypervariable Region I of Humans and Chimpanzees." *Molecular Biology and Evolution*, 16: 1357–1368.

FALK, D. (1975). "Comparative Anatomy of the Larynx in Man and the Chimpanzee: Implications for Language in Neanderthal." *American Journal of Physical Anthropology*, 43: 123–132.

FALK, D. (1980). "Hominid Brain Evolution: The Approach From Paleoneurology." *Yearbook of Physical Anthropology*, 23: 93–107.

FALK, D. (1983a). "Cerebral Cortices of East African Early Hominids." *Science*, 221: 1072–1074.

FALK, D. (1983b). "The Taung Endocast: A Reply to Holloway." *American Journal of Physical Anthropology*, 60: 479–489.

FALK, D. (1985). "Hadar AL 162–28 Endocast As Evidence That Brain Enlargement Preceded Cortical Reorganization in Hominid Evolution." *Nature*, 313: 45–47.

FALK, D. (1986a). "Evolution of Cranial Blood Drainage in Hominids: Enlarged Occipital/Marginal Sinuses and Emissary Foramina." *American Journal of Physical Anthropology*, 70: 311–324.

FALK, D. (1986b). "Endocast Morphology of Hadar Hominid AL 162–28." *Nature*, 321: 536–537.

FALK, D. (1987). "Hominid Paleoneurology." *Annual Review of Anthropology*, 16: 13–30.

FALK, D. (1988). "Enlarged Occipital/Marginal Sinuses and Emissary Foramina: Their Significance in Hominid Evolution." In, F.E. Grine (ed.), *Evolutionary History of the 'Robust' Australopithecines* (New York: Aldine de Gruyter), pp. 85–96.

FALK, D. (1989). "Ape-Like Endocast of 'Ape-Man' Taung." *American Journal of Physical Anthropology*, 80: 335–339.

FALK, D., C. HILDEBOLT AND M.W. VANNIER (1989). "Reassessment of the Taung Early Hominid From A Neurological Perspective." *Journal of Human Evolution*, 18: 485–492.

FALK, D. AND S. KASINGA (1983). "Cranial Capacity of a Female Robust Australopithecine (KNM-ER 407) From Kenya." *Journal of Human Evolution*, 12: 515–518.

FEREMBACH, D. (1958). "Les Limnopithèques du Kenya," *Annales de Paléontologie*, 44 (1958): 151–249.

FEREMBACH, D. (1979). "L'émergence du genre *Homo* et de l'espèce *Homo sapiens*: Les faits, les incertitudes." *Biométrie Humaine*, 14: 11–18.

FEREMBACH, D. (1986). "Proposition de phylogenèse et de taxonomie du genre *Homo*." *Anthropos*, 23: 127–138.

FERGUSON, W.W. (1983). "An Alternative Interpretation of *Australopithecus afarensis* Fossil Material." *Primates*, 24: 397–409.

FERGUSON, W.W. (1984). "Revision of Fossil Hominid Jaws from the Plio/Pleistocene of Hadar, in Ethiopia Including a New Species of the Genus *Homo* (Hominoidea: Homininae)." *Primates*, 25: 519–529.

FERGUSON, W.W. (1986). "The Taxonomic Status of *Praeanthropus africanus* (Primates: Pongidae) from the Late Pliocene of Eastern Africa." *Primates*, 27: 485–492.

FERGUSON, W.W. (1987). "Revision of the Subspecies of *Australopithecus africanus* (Primates: Hominidae), Including a New Subspecies from the Late Pliocene of Ethiopia." *Primates*, 28: 258–265.

FERGUSON, W.W. (1989). "Taxonomic Status of the Hominid Mandible KNM-ER TI 13150 from the Middle Pliocene of Tabarin, in Kenya." *Primates*, 30: 383–387.

FERRIS, S.D., A.C. WILSON AND W.M. BROWN (1981). "Evolutionary Tree for Apes and Humans Based on Cleavage Maps of Mitochondrial DNA." *Proceedings of the National Academy of Sciences* (USA), 78: 2432–2436.

FICHMAN, M. (1977). "Wallace: Zoogeography and the Problem of Land Bridges." *Journal of the History of Biology*, 10: 45–63.

FIFER, F.C. (1987). "The Adoption of Bipedalism by the Hominids: A New Hypothesis." *Human Evolution*, 2: 135–147.

FISCHER, J.-L. (1972). "Le concept expérimental dans l'oeuvre tératologique d'Étienne Geoffroy Saint-Hilaire." *Revue d'Histoire des Sciences*, 25: 347–364.

FLEAGLE, J.G. AND W.C. HARTWIG (1997). "Paleoprimatology." In, F. Spencer (ed.), *History of Physical Anthropology: An Encyclopedia*, Vol. 2 (New York: Garland), pp. 796–810.

FLEAGLE, J.G. AND W. L. JUNGERS (1982). "Fifty Years of Higher Primate Phylogeny." In, F. Spencer (ed.), *A History of American Physical Anthropology, 1930–1980* (New York: Academic Press), pp. 187–230.

FLEAGLE, J.G., J.T. STERN, W.L. JUNGERS AND R.L. SUSMAN (1981). "Climbing: A Biomechanical Link With Brachiation and With Bipedalism." *Symposia of the Zoological Society of London*, 48: 359–375.

FLOWER, W.H. AND R. LYDEKKER (1891). *An Introduction to the Study of Mammals Living and Extinct* (London: Adam and Charles Black).

FOLEY, R.A. (2001). "In the Shadow of the Modern Synthesis? Alternative Perspectives on the Last Fifty Years of Paleoanthropology." *Evolutionary Anthropology*, 10: 5–14.

FOLEY, R.A. AND S. ELTON (1998). "Time and Energy: The Ecological Context for the Evolution of Bipedalism." In, E. Strasser, J. Fleagle, A. Rosenberger and H. McHenry (eds.), *Primate Locomotion: Recent Advances* (New York: Plenum Press), pp. 419–433,

FOSTER, J.W. (1873). *Pre-historic races of the United States of America* (Chicago: Griggs).

FOURTEAU, R. (1918). *Contribution à l'étude des vertébrés miocènes de l'Égypte* (Cairo: Government Press).

FRAIPONT, J. (1889). "Discussion." *Congrès International d'Anthropologie et d'Archéologie Préhistoriques*, 10e session, pp. 358–359.

FRAIPONT, J. AND M. LOHEST (1887). "La race de Neanderthal ou de Canstadt en Belgique." *Archives de Biologie*, 7: 587–757.

FRANZEN, J.L. (1985). "Asian Australopithecines?" In, P.V. Tobias (ed.), *Hominid Evolution: Past, Present and Future* (New York: Alan R. Liss), pp. 255–263.

FRASSETTO, F. (1927). "New Views on the Dawn Man of Piltdown (Sussex)." *Man*, 27: 121–124.

FRAYER, D.W., M.H. WOLPOFF, A.G. THORNE, F.H. SMITH, AND G.G. POPE (1993). "Theories of Modern Human Origins: The Paleontological Test." *American Anthropologist*, 95: 14–50.

FRAYER, D.W., M.H. WOLPOFF, A.G. THORNE, F.H. SMITH, AND G.G. POPE (1994). "Getting It Straight." *American Anthropologist*, 96: 424–438.

GABUNIA, L., S.C. ANTON, D. LORDKIPANIDZE, A. VEKUA, A. JUSTUS AND C.C. SWISHER (2001). "Dmanisi and Dispersal." *Evolutionary Anthropology*, 10: 158–170.

GALLOWAY, A. (1937). "Man in Africa in the Light of Recent Discoveries." *South African Journal of Science*, 34: 89–120.

GALLOWAY, A. (1937–38a). "The Characteristics of the Skull of the Boskop Physical Type." *American Journal of Physical Anthropology*, 23: 31–47.

GALLOWAY, A. (1937–38b). "The Nature and Status of the Florisbad Skull as Revealed by Its Non-Metrical Features." *American Journal of Physical Anthropology*, 23: 1–17.

GAMBLE, C. (1986). *The Palaeolithic Settlement of Europe* (Cambridge: Cambridge University Press).

GATES, R.R. (1944). "Phylogeny and Classification of Hominids and Anthropoids." *American Journal of Physical Anthropology*, 2: 279–292.

GATES, R.R. (1948). *Human Ancestry From a Genetical Point of View* (Cambridge: Harvard University Press).

GAUDRY, A. (1878). *Les enchaînements du monde animal dans les temps géologiques. Mammifères tertiaires* (Paris: Hachette).

GAUDRY, A. (1890). "Le Dryopithèque." *Mémoires de la Société Géologique de France*, 1: 5–11.

GEBO, D.L. (1992). "Plantigrady and Foot Adaptation in African Apes: Implications for Hominid Origins." *American Journal of Physical Anthropology*, 89: 29–58.

GEBO, D.L. (1996). "Climbing, Brachiation, and Terrestrial Quadrupedalism: Historical Precursors of Hominid Bipedalism." *American Journal of Physical Anthropology*, 101: 55–92.

GENET-VARCIN, E. (1963). *Les singes actuels et fossiles* (Paris: N. Boubée et Cie).

GENET-VARCIN, E. (1966). "Conjectures sur l'allure générale des Australopithèques." *Bulletin de la Société Préhistorique Française*, 63: cvi–cvii.

GENET-VARCIN, E. (1967). "De quelques problèmes posés par les australopithèques." In, *Problèmes actuels de paléontologie (Évolution des Vertébrés)*, Colloques internationaux du Centre National de la Recherche Scientifique, No. 163 (Paris: C.N.R.S.), pp. 649–653.

GENET-VARCIN, E. (1969a). *À la recherche du primate ancêtre de l'homme* (Paris: N. Boubée et Cie).

GENET-VARCIN, E. (1969b). "Structure et comportement des australopithèques d'après certains os post-crâniens." *Annales de Paléontologie* (Vertébrés), 55: 139–148.

GENET-VARCIN, E. (1973). "*Homo sapiens*, le plus original des primates." *Bulletins et Mémoires de la Société d'Anthropologie de Paris*, 10: 297–300.

GENET-VARCIN, E. (1974). "Platyrrhine Contribution to the Phylogeny of the Primates." *Journal of Human Evolution*, 3: 259–263.

GENET-VARCIN, E. (1975). "Conjectures sur l'évolution des primates." In, *Problèmes actuels de paléontologie (Évolution des Vertébrés)*, Colloques internationaux du Centre National de la Recherche Scientifique, No. 218 (Paris: C.N.R.S.), pp. 829–838.

GENET-VARCIN, E. (1978). "Réflexion sur l'origine des hominidés." In, *Les origines humaines et les époques de l'intelligence* (Paris: Masson, 1978), pp. 13–36.

GENET-VARCIN, E. (1979). *Éléments de primatologie: Les hommes fossiles* (Paris: Boubée et Cie).

GHISELIN, M.T. (1974). "A Radical Solution to the Species Problem." *Systematic Zoology*, 23: 536–544.

GINSBURG, L. (1961). "Découverte de *Pliopithecus antiquus* Bl. dans le falun savignéen de

Noyant-ous-le-Lude (Maine-et-Loire)." *Comptes Rendus de l'Academie des Sciences*, 252: 585–587.

Giuffrida-Ruggeri, V. (1911). "Il supposito centro antropogenico sud-americano." *Monitore Zoologico Italiano*, 22: 269–286.

Giuffrida-Ruggeri, V. (1918). "Unicità del Philum umano con pluralità dei centri specific." *Rivista Italiana di Paleontologia*, 24: 3–15.

Godfrey, L. and K.H. Jacobs (1981). "Gradual, Autocatalytic and Punctuational Models of Hominid Brain Evolution: Cautionary Tale." *Journal of Human Evolution*, 10: 255–272.

Goldstein, D.B., A.R. Linares, L.L. Cavalli-Sforza and M.W. Feldman (1995). "Genetic Absolute Dating Based on Microsatellites and the Origin of Modern Humans." *Proceedings of the National Academy of Sciences* (USA), 92: 6723–6727.

Gonzalez, I.L., J.E. Sylvester, T.F. Smith, D. Stambolian and R.D. Schmickel (1990). "Ribosomal RNA Gene Sequences and Hominoid Phylogeny." *Molecular Biology and Evolution*, 7: 203–219.

Goodman, M. (1962a). "Evolution of the Immunologic Species Specificity of Human Serum Proteins." *Human Biology*, 34: 104–150.

Goodman, M. (1962b). "Immunochemistry of the Primates and Primate Evolution." *Annals of the New York Academy of Sciences*, 102: 219–234.

Goodman, M. (1963). "Man's Place in the Phylogeny of the Primates as Reflected in Serum Proteins." In, S.L. Washburn (ed.), *Classification and Human Evolution* (Chicago: Aldine), pp. 204–234.

Goodman, M. (1975). "Protein Sequence and Immunological Specificity: Their Role in Phylogenetic Studies of Primates." In, W.P. Luckett and F.S. Szalay (eds.), *Phylogeny of the Primates: A Multidisciplinary Approach* (New York: Plenum Press), pp. 219–248.

Goodman, M. (1996). "A Personal Account of the Origins of a New Paradigm." *Molecular Phylogenetics and Evolution*, 5: 269–285.

Goodman, M. and J.E. Cronin (1982). "Molecular Anthropology: Its Development and Current Directions." In, F. Spencer (ed.), *A History of American Physical Anthropology, 1930–1980* (New York: Academic Press), pp. 105–146.

Goodman, M. and G.M. Moore (1971). "Immunodiffusion Systematics of the Primates I: The Catarrhini." *Systematics Zoology*, 20: 19–62.

Goodman, M., J. Czelusniak and J.E. Beeber (1984). "Phylogeny of Primates and Other Eutherian Orders: A Cladistic Analysis Using Amino Acid and Nucleotide Sequence Data." *Cladistics*, 1: 171–185.

Goodman, M., C.A. Porter, J. Czelusniak, S.L. Page, H. Schneider, J. Shoshani, G. Gunnell and C.P. Groves (1998). "Toward a Phylogenetic Classification of Primates Based on DNA Evidence Complemented by Fossil Evidence." *Molecular Phylogenetics and Evolution*, 9: 585–598.

Gould, S.J. (1977). *Ontogeny and Phylogeny* (Cambridge: Harvard University Press).

Gould, S.J. (1980). "Is a New and General Theory of Evolution Emerging?" *Paleobiology*, 6: 119–130.

Gould, S.J. (1992). "Punctuated Equilibrium in Fact and Theory." In, A. Somit and S.A. Peterson (eds.), *The Dynamics of Evolution: The Punctuated Equilibrium Debate in the Natural and Social Sciences* (Ithaca: Cornell University Press), pp. 54–84.

Gray, J. (1911). "The Differences and Affinities of Palaeolithic Man and the Anthropoid Apes." *Man*, 11: 117–120.

Grayson, D.K. (1983). *The Establishment of Human Antiquity* (New York: Academic Press).

Grayson, D.K. (1986). "Eoliths, Archaeological Ambiguity, and the Generation of Middle-Range Research." In, D.J. Meltzer, D.D. Fowler and J.A. Sabloff (eds.), *American Archaeology: Past and Future* (Washington: Smithsonian Institution Press), pp. 77–133.

Greenfield, L.O. (1980). "A Late Divergence Hypothesis." *American Journal of Physical Anthropology*, 52: 351–365.

Greenfield, L.O. (1983). "Toward the Resolution of Discrepancies Between Phenetic and Paleontological Data Bearing on the Question of Human Origins." In, R.L. Ciochon and R.S. Corruccini (eds.), *New Interpretations of Ape and Human Ancestry* (New York: Plenum Press), pp. 695–703.

Gregory, W.K. (1916). "Studies on the Evolution of the Primates." *Bulletin of the American Museum of Natural History*, 35: 239–355.

Gregory, W.K. (1922). *The Origin and Evolution of the Human Dentition* (Baltimore: Williams & Wilkins).

Gregory, W.K. (1925). "The Biogenetic Law and the Skull Form of Primitive Man." *American Journal of Physical Anthropology*, 8: 373–378.

Gregory, W.K. (1927a). "Hesperopithecus Apparently Not An Ape Nor A Man." *Science*, 66: 579–581.

Gregory, W.K. (1927b). "How Near is the Relationship of Man to the Chimpanzee-Gorilla Stock?" *Quarterly Review of Biology*, 2: 549–560.

Gregory, W.K. (1930a). "A Critique of Professor Osborn's Theory of Human Origins." *American Journal of Physical Anthropology*, 14: 133–164.

Gregory, W.K. (1930b). "The Origin of Man From a Brachiating Anthropoid Stock." *Science*, 71: 645–650.

Gregory, W.K. (1934). *Man's Place among the Anthropoids: Three Lectures on the Evolution of Man from the Lower Vertebrates* (Oxford: Clarendon Press).

Gregory, W.K. (1938). "Man's Place Among the Primates." *Palaeobiologica*, 6: 208–213.

Gregory, W.K. (1949). "The Bearing of the Australopithecinae Upon the Problem of Man's Place in Nature." *American Journal of Physical Anthropology*, 7: 4 85–512.

Gregory, W.K. (1951). *Evolution Emerging: A Survey of Changing Patterns from Primeval Life to Man*, Vol.1 (New York: Macmillan).

Gregory, W.K. and M. Hellman (1923a). "Notes on the Type of *Hesperopithecus Haroldcookii* Osborn." *American Museum Novitates*, No.53: 1–16.

Gregory, W.K. and M. Hellman (1923b). "Further Notes on the Molars of Hesperopithecus and of Pithecanthropus." *Bulletin of the American Museum of Natural History*, 48: 509–530.

Gregory, W.K. and M. Hellman (1938). "Evidence of the Australopithecine Man-Apes on the Origin of Man." *Science*, 88: 615–616.

Gregory, W.K. and M. Hellman (1939a). "The Dentition of the Extinct South African Man-Ape *Australopithecus (Plesianthropus) transvaalensis* Broom. A Comparative and Phylogenetic Study." *Annals of the Transvaal Museum*, 19: 339–373.

Gregory, W.K. and M. Hellman (1939b). "Fossil Man-Apes of South Africa." *Nature*, 143: 25–26.

Gregory, W.K., M. Hellman and G. Edward Lewis (1938). "Fossil Anthropoids of the Yale-Cambridge India Expedition of 1935." *Carnegie Institution of Washington Publication No. 495* (Washington), pp. 1–27.

Gribbin, J. and J. Cherfas (1982). *The Monkey Puzzle: Reshaping the Evolutionary Tree* (New York: Pantheon Books).

Grimoult, C. (2000). *Histoire de l'évolutionnisme contemporain en France, 1945–1995* (Genève: Librairie Droz).

Grine, F.E. (1988, ed.). *Evolutionary History of the 'Robust' Australopithecines* (New York: Aldine de Gruyter).

Grine, F.E. (1993). "Australopithecine Taxonomy and Phylogeny: Historical Background and Recent Interpretation." In, R.L. Ciochon and J.G. Fleagle (eds.), *The Human Evolution Source Book* (New Jersey: Prentice Hall), pp. 198–210.

Groves, C.P. (1989). *A Theory of Human and Primate Evolution* (Oxford: Clarendon Press).

Gruber, H.E. (1974). *Darwin on Man* (New York: E.P. Dutton).

Haeckel, E. (1866). *Generelle Morphologie der Organismen*, Vol. 2 (Berlin: Georg Reimer).

Haeckel, E. (1868). *Natürliche Schöpfungsgeschichte* (Berlin: Georg Reimer).

Haeckel, E. (1874). *Anthropogenie oder Entwickelungs-geschichte des Menschen* (Leipzig: Wilhelm Englemann).

Haeckel, E. (1876). *The History of Creation: Or the Development of the Earth and Its Inhabitants by the Action of Natural Causes*, Vol. 2 (London: H.S. King).

Haeckel, E. (1896). *The Evolution of Man: A Popular Exposition of the Principal Points of Human Ontogeny and Phylogeny*, Vol. 2 (New York: Appleton).

Haeckel, E. (1898). "On our present knowledge of the origin of man." *Annual Report of the Smithsonian Institution of 1898*, pp. 461–480.

Hagelberg, E. (1993–94). "Ancient DNA Studies." *Evolutionary Anthropology*, 2: 199–207.

Haile-Selassie, Y. (2001). "Late Miocene Hominids from the Middle Awash, Ethiopia." *Nature*, 412: 178–181.

Hammer, M.F. (1995). "A Recent Common Ancestry For Human Y Chromosomes." *Nature*, 378: 376–378.

HAMMOND, M (1988). "The Shadow Man Paradigm in Paleoanthropology, 1911–1945." In, G.W. Stocking (ed.), *Bones, Bodies, Behavior: Essays on Biological Anthropology* (Madison: University of Wisconsin Press), pp. 117–137.

HARDING, R.M., S.M. FULLERTON, R.C. GRIFFITHS, J. BOND, M.J. COX, J.A. SCHNEIDER, D.S. MOULIN AND J.B. CLEGG (1997). "Archaic African and Asian Lineages in the Genetic Ancestry of Modern Humans." *American Journal of Human Genetics*, 60: 772–789.

HARRIS, J.W.K. (1983). "Cultural Beginnings: Plio-Pleistocene Archaeological Occurrences from the Afar." *The African Archaeological Review*, 1: 3–31.

HARRISON, T. (2002). "Late Oligocene to Middle Miocene Catarrhines From Afro-Arabia." In, W.C. Hartwig (ed.), *The Primate Fossil Record* (Cambridge: Cambridge University Press), pp. 311–338.

HARTMANN, R. (1883). *Die menschenähnlichen Affen und ihre Organization im Vergleich zur menschlichen* (Leipzig: F.A. Brockhaus).

HARTMANN, R. (1885). *Anthropoid Apes* (London: Kegan Paul, Trench & Co.).

HARTWIG, W.C. (1995). "*Protopithecus*: Rediscovering the First Fossil Primate." *History and Philosophy of the Life Sciences*, 17: 447–460.

HARTWIG, W.C. (2002, ed.). *The Primate Fossil Record* (Cambridge: Cambridge University Press)

HARVEY, J. (1983). "Evolutionism Transformed: Positivists and Materialists in the *Société d'Anthropologie de Paris* from the Second Empire to Third Republic." In, D. Oldroyd and I. Langham (eds.), *The Wider Domain of Evolutionary Thought* (Dordrecht: D. Reidel, 1983), pp. 289–310.

HASEGAWA, M., T.-A. YANO AND H. KISHINO (1984). "A New Molecular Clock of Mitochondrial DNA and the Evolution of Hominoids." *Proceedings of the Japan Academy*, series B, 60: 95–98.

HASEGAWA, M., H. KISHINO AND T.-A. YANO (1987). "Man's Place in Hominoidea as Inferred from Molecular Clocks of DNA." *Journal of Molecular Evolution*, 26: 132–147.

HAWKS, J.D. AND M.H. WOLPOFF (2001). "The Four Faces of Eve: Hypothesis Compatibility and Human Origins." *Quaternary International*, 75: 41–50.

HAY, O.P. (1918). "Further Consideration of the Occurrence of Human Remains in the Pleistocene Deposits at Vero, Florida." *American Anthropologist*, 20: 1–36.

HEBERER, G. (1950). "Das Präsapiens-Problem." In, H. Grüneberg and W. Ulrich (eds.), *Moderne Biologie* (Berlin: F.W. Peters), pp. 131–162.

HEBERER, G. (1952). "Fortschritte in der Erforschung der Phylogenie der Hominoidea." *Ergebnisse der Anatomie und Entwicklungsgeschichte*, 34: 499–637.

HEBERER, G. (1955). "Das moderne Bild der Abstammungsgeschichte des Menschen." *Berliner Blätter für Vor- und Frühgeschichte*, 4: 3–7.

HEBERER, G. (1956). "Die Fossilgeschichte der Hominoidea." In, H. Hofer, A.H. Schultz and D. Starck (eds.), *Primatologia: Handbuch der Primatenkunde* (Basel: S. Karger), pp. 379–560.

HEBERER, G. (1959a). "Die subhumane Abstammungsgeschichte des Menschen." In, G. Heberer (ed.), *Die Evolution der Organismen*, 2nd edition (Stuttgart: G. Fischer Verlag), pp. 1110–1142. Translated in English in 1962.

HEBERER, G. (1959b). "The Descent of Man and the Present Fossil Record." *Cold Spring Harbor Symposia on Quantitative Biology*, 24: 235–244.

HEBERER, G. (1962). "The Subhuman Evolutionary History of Man." In, W.W. Howells (ed.), *Ideas on Human Evolution: Selected Essays, 1949–1961* (Cambridge: Harvard University Press), pp. 203–241. Originally published in German in 1959.

HEBERER, G. (1965). "Die Abstammung des Menschen." In, L. von Bertalanffy and F. Gessner (eds.), *Handbuch der Biologie*, Vol. 9, *Der Mensch und seine Stellung im Naturganzen* (Akademische Verlagsgesellschaft Athenaion Konstanz, 1965), pp. 245–328.

HEILBORN, A. (1923). "Introduction." English translation of H. Klaatsch's *The Evolution and Progress of Mankind* (London: T. Fisher Unwin, 1923), pp. 15–29.

HEMPEL, C.G. (1966). *Philosophy of Natural Science* (New Jersey: Prentice Hall).

HENNIG, W. (1966). *Phylogenetic Systematics* (Urbana: University of Illinois Press).

HENNIG, W. (1981). *Insect Phylogeny* (New York: John Wiley). First published in 1969.

HERVÉ, G. (1886). "L'homme descend-t-il d'un animal grimpeur." *L'Homme*, 3: 513–523.

Hervé, G. (1889). "Les prétendus Quadrumanes." *Bulletins de la Société d'Anthropologie de Paris*, 3e série, 12: 680–717.

Hill, A. and S. Ward (1988). "Origin of the Hominidae: The Record of African Large Hominoid Evolution Between 14 My and 4 My." *Yearbook of Physical Anthropology*, 31: 49–83.

Hill-Tout, C. (1921). "The Phylogeny of Man from a New Angle." *Transactions of the Royal Society of Canada*, 15: 47–82.

Hinton, M.A.C., et al. (1938). "Report on the Swanscombe Skull." *Journal of the Royal Anthropological Institute*, 68: 17–98.

His, W. (1864). "Sur la population rhétique." *Bulletins de la Société d'Anthropologie de Paris*, 5: 868–880.

Hoffman, A. (1992). "Twenty Years Later: Punctuated Equilibrium in Retrospect." In, A. Somit and S.A. Peterson (eds.), *The Dynamics of Evolution: The Punctuated Equilibrium Debate in the Natural and Social Sciences* (Ithaca: Cornell University Press), pp. 121–138.

Hofman, M.A. (1983). "Encephalization in Hominids: Evidence for the Model of Punctuationalism." *Brain, Behavior and Evolution*, 22: 102–117.

Holloway, R.L. (1970). "New Endocranial Values for the Australopithecines." *Nature*, 227: 199–200.

Holloway, R.L. (1972). "New Australopithecine Endocast, SK 1585, From Swartkrans, South Africa." *American Journal of Physical Anthropology*, 37: 173–186.

Holloway, R.L. (1973). "New Endocranial Values for the East African Early Hominids." *Nature*, 243: 97–99.

Holloway, R.L. (1974). "The Casts of Fossil Hominid Brains." *Scientific American*, 231(7): 106–115.

Holloway, R.L. (1981a). "Volumetric and Asymmetry Determinations on Recent Hominid Endocasts: Spy I and II, Djebel Ihround I, and the Salè *Homo erectus* Specimens, With Some Notes on Neandertal Brain Size." *American Journal of Physical Anthropology*, 55: 385–393.

Holloway, R.L. (1981b). "The Indonesian *Homo erectus* Brain Endocasts Revisited." *American Journal of Physical Anthropology*, 55: 503–521.

Holloway, R.L. (1981c). "Revisiting the South African Taung Australopithecine Endocast: The Position of the Lunate Sulcus As Determined by the Stereoplotting Technique." *American Journal of Physical Anthropology*, 56: 43–58.

Holloway, R.L. (1983). "Cerebral Brain Endocast Pattern of *Australopithecus afarensis* Hominid." *Nature*, 303: 420–422.

Holloway, R.L. (1984). "The Taung Endocast and the Lunate Sulcus: A Rejection of the Hypothesis of Its Anterior Position." *American Journal of Physical Anthropology*, 64: 285–287.

Holloway, R.L. (1985). "The Past, Present, and Future Significance of the Lunate Sulcus in Early Hominid Evolution." In, P.V. Tobias (ed.), *Hominid Evolution: Past, Present and Future* (New York: Alan R. Liss), pp. 47–62.

Holloway, R.L. (1988). "'Robust' Australopithecine Brain Endocasts: Some Preliminary Observtions." In, F.E. Grine (ed.), *Evolutionary History of the 'Robust' Australopithecines* (New York: Aldine de Gruyter), pp. 97–105.

Holloway, R.L. and M.C. De La Coste-Lareymondie (1982). "Brain Endocast Asymmetry in Pongids and Hominids: Some Preliminary Findings on the Paleontology of Cerebral Dominance." *American Journal of Physical Anthropology*, 58: 101–110.

Holloway, R.L. and W.H. Kimbel (1986). "Endocast Morphology of Hadar Hominid AL 162–28." *Nature*, 321: 536.

Honoré, F. (1929). "Un nouveau singe à facies humain." *L'Illustration*, 13 avril, p. 451.

Hooijer, D.A. (1948). "Prehistoric Teeth of Man and of the Orang-Utan From Central Sumatra, With Notes on the Fossil Orang-Utan from Java and Southern China." *Zoologische Mededeelingen*, 29: 175–301.

Hooijer, D.A. (1949). "Some Notes on the Gigantopithecus Question." *American Journal of Physical Anthropology*, 7: 513–518.

Hooijer, D.A. (1951). "Questions Relating to a New Large Anthropoid Ape From the Mio-Pliocene of the Siwaliks." *American Journal of Physical Anthropology*, 9: 79–94.

Hooton, E.A. (1930). "Doubts and Suspicions Concerning Certain Functional Theories of Primate Evolution." *Human Biology*, 2: 223–249.

Hooton, E.A. (1931). *Up From the Ape* (New York: Macmillan).

Hooton, E.A. (1935). "Homo Sapiens—Whence and Whither." *Science*, 82: 19–31.

Hooton, E.A. (1937). *Apes, Men, and Morons* (New York: G.P. Putnam's Sons).

Hooton, E.A. (1940). *Why Men Behave like Apes and Vice Versa or Body and Behavior* (Princeton: Princeton University Press).

Hooton, E.A. (1946). *Up From the Ape*, 2nd edition (New York: Macmillan).

Hopwood, A.T. (1932–1934). "Miocene Primates From Kenya." *Journal of the Linnean Society of London*, 38: 437–464.

Horai, S., K. Hayasaka, R. Konso, K. Tsugane and N. Takahata (1995). "Recent African Origin of Modern Humans Revealed By Complete Sequences of Hominoid Mitochondrial DNAs." *Proceedings of the National Academy of Sciences* (USA), 92: 532–536.

Horai, S., Y. Satta, K. Hayasaka, R. Kondo, T. Inoue, T. Ishida, S. Hayashi and N. Takahata (1992). "Man's Place in Hominoidea Revealed by Mitochondrial DNA Genealogy." *Journal of Molecular Evolution*, 35: 32–43.

Horst, M. (1913). *Die natürlichen Grundstämme der Menschheit* (Hildburghausen: Thüringische Verlags-Anstalt).

Horst, M. (1918/19). *Die natürlichen Grundstämme der Menschheit*, 2nd edition (Berlin: Psychologish-Soziologischer Verlag).

Houzé, E. (1895–96). "Le Pithecanthropus erectus: discussion." *Revue de l'Université de Bruxelles*, 1: 401–438.

Hovelacque, A. (1875). *Lettre sur l'homme préhistorique du type le plus ancien; sur la structure de ses restes et sur son origine* (Paris: Reinwald).

Hovelacque, A. (1877). "Notre ancêtre: recherches d'anatomie et d'ethnologie sur le précurseur de l'homme." *Revue d'Anthropologie*, 6: 62–99.

Hovelacque, A. and G. Hervé (1887). *Précis d'Anthropologie* (Paris: A. Delahaye et E. Lecrosnier).

Howard, E.B., et al. (1936). "Early Man in America With Particular Reference to the Southwestern United States." *American Naturalist*, 70: 313–371.

Howell, F.C. (1978). "Hominidae." In, V.J. Maglio and H.B.S. Cooke (eds.), *Evolution of African Mammals* (Cambridge: Harvard University Press), pp. 154–248.

Howells, W.W. (1942). "Fossil Man and the Origin of Races." *American Anthropologist*, 44: 182–193.

Howells, W.W. (1944). *Mankind So Far* (New York: Doubleday).

Howells, W.W. (1950). "Origin of the Human Stock." *Cold Spring Harbor Symposia on Quantitative Biology*, 15: 79–86.

Howells, W.W. (1959). *Mankind in the Making: The Story of Human Evolution* (New York: Doubleday).

Howells, W.W. (1966). "*Homo erectus.*" *Scientific American*, 215: 46–53.

Howells, W.W. (1967). *Mankind in the Making: The Story of Human Evolution*, 2nd edition (New York: Doubleday).

Howells, W.W. (1980). "*Homo erectus*—Who, When and Where: A Survey." *Yearbook of Physical Anthropology*, 23: 1–23.

Howells, W.W. (1993). *Getting Here: The Story of Human Evolution* (Washington, D.C.: Compass Press).

Hoyer, B.H., N.W. van de Velde, M. Goodman and R.B. Roberts (1972). "Examination of Hominid Evolution by DNA Sequence Homology." *Journal of Human Evolution*, 1: 645–649.

Hrdlicka, A. (1907). *Skeletal Remains Suggesting or Attributed to Early Man in North America* (Smithsonian Institution No. 33, Washington, D.C.).

Hrdlicka, A. (1914). "The Most Ancient Skeletal Remains of Man." *Annual Report, Smithsonian Institution* of 1913, pp. 491–552.

Hrdlicka, A. (1918). *Recent Discoveries Attributed to Early Man in America*, Bulletin 66 (Smithsonian Institution, Washington, D.C.).

Hrdlicka, A. (1921). "The Peopling of Asia." *Proceedings of the American Philosophical Society*, 60: 535–545.

Hrdlicka, A. (1925). "The Taungs Ape." *American Journal of Physical Anthropology*, 8: 379–392.

Hrdlicka, A. (1926). "The Peopling of the Earth." *Proceedings of the American Philosophical Society*, 65: 150–156.

Hrdlicka, A. (1927). "The Neanderthal Phase of Man." *Journal of the Royal Anthropological Institute*, 57: 249–274.

Hrdlicka, A. (1930). *The Skeletal Remains of Early Man* (Washington: Smithsonian Miscellaneous Collections Vol. 83).

Hrdlicka, A. (1937). "Early Man in America: What Have the Bones to Say?" In, G.G. MacCurdy (ed.), *Early Man* (New York: Freeport), pp. 93–104.

HRDLICKA, A., W.H. HOLMES, B. WILLIS, F.E. WRIGHT AND C.N. FENNER (1912). *Early Man in South America* (Smithsonian Institution No 102, Washington, D.C.).

HUBRECHT, A.A.W. (1897). *The Descent of the Primates* (New York: Charles Scribner's Sons).

HULL, D.L. (1976). "Are Species Really Individuals?" *Systematic Zoology*, 25: 174–191.

HUNT, J. (1864). "Editor's Preface." In, C. Vogt, *Lectures on Man: His Place in Creation, and in the History of the Earth* (London: Longman, Green, Longman, and Roberts).

HUNT, J. (1866). "On the Application of the Principle of Natural Selection to Anthropology." *Anthropological Review*, 4: 320–340.

HUNT, J. (1867). "On the Doctrine of Continuity Applied to Anthropology." *Anthropological Review*, 5: 110–120.

HUNT, K.D. (1994). "The Evolution of Human Bipedality: Ecology and Functional Morphology." *Journal of Human Evolution*, 26: 183–202.

HÜRZELER, J. (1949). "Neubeschreibung von Oreopithecus bambolii Gervais." *Schweizerische Palaeontologische Abhandlungen*, 66: 1–20.

HÜRZELER, J. (1952). "Contribution à l'étude de la dentition de lait d'Oreopithecus bambolii Gervais." *Eclogae Geologicae Helvetiae*, 44: 404–411.

HÜRZELER, J. (1954a). "Zur systematischen Stellung von *Oreopithecus*." *Verhandlungen der Naturforschenden Gesellschaft in Basel*, 65: 88–95.

HÜRZELER, J. (1954b). "Contribution à l'odontologie et à la phylogénèse du Genre *Pliopithecus* Gervais." *Annales de Paléontologie*, 40: 5–63.

HÜRZELER, J. (1956). "*Oreopithecus*, un point de repère pour l'histoire de l'humanité à l'ère tertiaire." In, *Problèmes actuels de paléontologie*, No. 60 (Paris: Colloques internationaux du Centre National de la Recherche Scientifique), pp. 115–121.

HÜRZELER, J. (1958). *Oreopithecus bambolii* Gervais: A Preliminary Report." *Verhandlungen der Naturforschenden Gesellschaft in Basel*, 69: 1–48.

HÜRZELER, J. (1960). "Signification de l'Oréopithèque dans la phylogénie humaine." *Triangle*, 4: 164–174.

HÜRZELER, J. (1962). "Quelques réflexions sur l'histoire des anthropomorphes." In, *Problèmes actuels de paléontologie, évolution des vertébrés*, No. 104 (Paris: Colloques internationaux du Centre National de la Recherche Scientifique), pp. 441–450.

HÜRZELER, J. (1968). "Questions et réflexions sur l'histoire des anthropomorphes." *Annales de Paléontologie*, 54: 195–233.

HÜRZELER, J. (1978). "Les racines paléontologiques de l'humanité: Le mouvement primate vers l'homme." In, *Les origines humaines et les époques de l'intelligence* (Paris: Masson, 1978), pp. 5–12.

HUXLEY, T.H. (1861). "On the Zoological Relations of Man with the Lower Animals." *Natural History Review*, 1: 67–84.

HUXLEY, T.H. (1863). *Evidence as to Man's Place in Nature* (London: Williams & Norgate).

HUXLEY, T.H. (1864). "Further Remarks Upon the Human Remains from the Neanderthal." *Natural History Review*, 4: 430–437.

HUXLEY, T.H. (1865). "On the Methods and Results of Ethnology," *Fortnightly Review*, reprinted in *Collected Essays (1893–1894)*, Vol. 7 (London: Macmillan, 1894), pp. 209–252.

HUXLEY, T.H. (1868). "On the Distribution of the Races of Mankind, and Its Bearing on the Antiquity of Man." *Congrès International d'Anthropologie et d'Archéologie Préhistoriques*, 3e session, pp. 92–97.

HUXLEY, T.H. (1890). "The Aryan Question and Prehistoric Man." *Nineteenth Century* (November). Reprinted in *Thomas Henry Huxley. Collected Essays (1893–1894)*, Vol. VII (Georg Olms Verlag: Hildesheim, 1970), pp. 271–328.

HUXLEY, T.H. (1894). *Evidence as to Man's Place in Nature* [1863], reprinted in *Collected Essays (1893–1894)*, Vol. 7 (London: Macmillan).

ISAAC, G.L. (1983). "Aspects of Human Evolution." In, D.S. Bendall (ed.), *Evolution From Molecules to Men* (Cambridge: Cambridge University Press), pp. 509–543.

ISBELL, L.A. AND T.P. YOUNG (1996). "The Evolution of Bipedalism in Hominids and Reduced Group Size in Chimpanzees: Alternative Responses to Decreasing Resource Availability." *Journal of Human Evolution*, 30: 389–397.

JABLONSKI, N.G. AND G. CHAPLIN (1993). "Origin of Habitual Terrestrial Bipedalism in the Ancestor of the Hominidae." *Journal of Human Evolution*, 24: 259–280.

JACOB, T. (1973). "Palaeoanthropological Discoveries in Indonesia With Special Reference to the

Finds of the Last Two Decades." *Journal of Human Evolution*, 2: 473–485.

JACOB, T. (1975). "Morphology and Paleoecology of Early Man in Java." In, R.H. Tuttle (ed.), *Paleoanthropology: Morphology and Paleoecology* (The Hague: Mouton), pp. 311–325.

JACOB, T. (1981). "Solo Man and Peking Man." In, B.A. Sigmon and J.S. Cybulski (eds.), *Homo erectus: Papers in Honor of Davidson Black* (Toronto: University of Toronto Press), pp. 87–104.

JENKS, A.E. (1932). "Pleistocene Man in Minnesota." *Science*, 75: 607–608.

JELINEK, J. (1978). "*Homo erectus* or *Homo sapiens*?" In, D.J. Chivers and K.A. Joysey (eds.), *Recent Advances in Primatology*, Vol. 3 (London: Academic Press), pp. 419–429.

JELINEK, J. (1980). "European *Homo erectus* and the Origin of *Homo sapiens*." In, L.-K. Königsson (ed.), *Current Argument on Early Man* (Oxford: Pergamon Press), pp. 137–144.

JELINEK, J. (1981). "Was *Homo erectus* Already *Homo sapiens*?" In, D. Ferembach (ed.), *Les processus de l'hominisation* (Paris: C.N.R.S.), pp. 85–89.

JELINEK, J. (1985). "The European, Near East and North African Finds After *Australopithecus* and the Principal Consequences for the Picture of Human Evolution." In, P.V. Tobias (ed.), *Hominid Evolution: Past, Present and Future* (New York: Alan R. Liss), pp. 341–354.

JOHANSON, D.C. (1985). "The Most Primitive *Australopithecus*." In, P.V. Tobias (ed.), *Hominid Evolution: Past, Present and Future* (New York: Alan R. Liss), pp. 203–212.

JOHANSON, D.C. (1989). "The Current Status of *Australopithecus*." In, G. Giacobini (ed.), *Hominidae: Proceedings of the 2nd International Congress of Human Paleontology* (Milan: Editoriale Jaca Book), pp. 77–96.

JOHANSON, D.C. (1996a). "Face-to-Face With Lucy's Family." *National Geographic*, 189(3): 96–117.

JOHANSON, D.C. (1996b). "The Strategy of Paleoanthropology: Early African Hominids Annual Luncheon Address." *Yearbook of Physical Anthropology*, 39: 1–10.

JOHANSON, D.C. AND M. EDEY (1981). *Lucy: The Beginnings of Humankind* (New York: Simon and Schuster).

JOHANSON, D.C., F.T. MASAO, G.G. ECK, T.D. WHITE, R.C. WALTER, W.H. KIMBEL, B. ASFAW, P. MANEGA, P. NDESSOKIA AND G. SUWA (1987). "New Partial Skeleton of *Homo habilis* from Olduvai Gorge, Tanzania." *Nature*, 327: 205–209.

JOHANSON, D.C., M. TAIEB AND Y. COPPENS (1982, eds.). "Pliocene Hominids from Hadar, Ethiopia." *American Journal of Physical Anthropology*, 57: 373–719.

JOHANSON, D.C. AND T.D. WHITE (1979). "A Systematic Assessment of Early African Hominids." *Science*, 203: 321–330.

JOHANSON, D.C., T.D. WHITE AND Y. COPPENS (1978). "A New Species of the Genus Australopithecus (Primates: Hominidae) from the Pliocene of Eastern Africa." *Kirtlandia*, 28: 1–14.

JOLEAUD, L. (1929). "A propos du grand singe du Vénézuéla." *Revue Scientifique*, 67: 269–273.

JOLLY, C.J. (1970). "The Seed-Eaters: A New Model of Hominid Differentiation Based on a Baboon Analogy." *Man*, 5: 5–26.

KAESSMANN, H., F. HEISSIG, A. VON HAESELER AND S. PÄÄBO (1999). "DNA Sequence Variation in a Non-Coding Region of Low Recombination on the Human X Chromosome." *Nature Genetics*, 22: 78–81.

KAESTLE, F.A. AND K.A. HORSBURGH (2002). "Ancient DNA in Anthropology: Methods, Applications, and Ethics." *Yearbook of Physical Anthropology*, 45: 92–130.

KEITH, A. (1895). "Pithecanthropus erectus—A Brief Review of Human Fossil Remains." *Science Progress*, 3 (1895): 348–369.

KEITH, A. (1910). "A New Theory of the Descent of Man." *Nature*, 85: 206.

KEITH, A. (1911a). *Ancient Types of Man* (London: Harper).

KEITH, A. (1911b). "Klaatsch's Theory of the Descent of Man." *Nature*, 85: 509–510.

KEITH, A. (1912). "The Relationship of Neanderthal Man and Pithecanthropus to Modern Man." *Nature*, 89: 155–156.

KEITH, A. (1915). *The Antiquity of Man* (London: William and Norgate).

KEITH, A. (1925a). *The Antiquity of Man*, 2 Vols. 2nd edition (London: William and Norgate).

KEITH, A. (1925b). "The New Missing Link." *The British Medical Journal*, February 14, pp. 325–326.

KEITH, A. (1925c). "The Fossil Anthropoid Ape from Taungs." *Nature*, 115: 234–235.

KEITH, A. (1925d). "The Taungs Skull." *Nature*, 116: 11.

KEITH, A. (1925e). "The Taungs Skull." *Nature*, 116: 462–463.

KEITH, A. (1929). "The Alleged Discovery of an Anthropoid of South America." *Man*, 29: 135–136.

KEITH, A. (1931). *New Discoveries Relating to the Antiquity of Man* (London: Williams and Norgate).

KEITH, A. (1934). *The Construction of Man's Family Tree* (London: Watts & Co.).

KEITH, A. (1935). "Conceptions of Man's Ancestry." *Nature*, 135: 705–708.

KEITH, A. (1936). "Origins of Modern Races of Mankind." *Nature*, 138: 194.

KEITH, A. (1937–38). "The Florisbad Skull and Its Place in the Sequence of South African Human Fossil Remains." *Journal of Anatomy*, 72: 620–621.

KEITH, A. (1938–39). "A Resurvey of the Anatomical Features of the Piltdown Skull With Some Observations on the Recently Discovered Swanscombe Skull." *Journal of Anatomy*, 73: 155–185, 234–254.

KEITH, A. (1944a). "Pre-Neanderthal Man in the Crimea." *Nature*, 153: 515–517.

KEITH, A. (1944b). "Evolution of Modern Man (*Homo sapiens*)." *Nature*, 153: 742.

KEITH, A. (1947). "Australopithecinae or Dartians?" *Nature*, 159: 377.

KEITH, A. (1949). *A New Theory of Human Evolution* (New York: Philosophical Library).

KEITH, A. AND T.D. MCCOWN (1937). "Mount Carmel Man. His Bearing on the Ancestry of Modern Races." In, G.G. MacCurdy (ed.), *Early Man* (New York: Freeport), pp. 41–52.

KELLEY, J. (2002). "The Hominoid Radiation in Asia." In, W.C. Hartwig (ed.), *The Primate Fossil Record* (Cambridge: Cambridge University Press), pp. 369–384.

KELLY, R.E. (2001). "Tripedal Knuckle-Walking: A Proposal for the Evolution of Human Locomotion and Handedness." *Journal of Theoretical Biology*, 213: 333–358.

KENNEDY, K.A.R. AND R.L. CIOCHON (1999). "A Canine Tooth From the Siwaliks: First Recorded Discovery of a Fossil Ape?" *Human Evolution*, 14: 231–253.

KERN, H.M. AND W.L. STRAUS (1949). "The Femur of *Plesianthropus transvaalensis*." *American Journal of Physical Anthropology*, 7: 53–77.

KIM, H.-S. AND O. TAKENAKA (1996). "A Comparison of TSPY Genes From Y-Chromosomal DNA of the Great Apes and Humans: Sequence, Evolution, and Phylogeny." *American Journal of Physical Anthropology*, 100: 301–309.

KIMBEL, W.H. (1986). *The Calvarial Remains of Australopithecus afarensis: A Comparative Phylogenetic Study*, Ph.D. Dissertation, Kent State University, Kent, Ohio.

KIMBEL, W.H. (1991). "Species, Species Concepts and Hominid Evolution." *Journal of Human Evolution*, 20: 355–371.

KIMBEL, W.H., D.C. JOHANSON AND Y. RAK (1994). "The First Skull and Other New Discoveries of *Australopithecus afarensis* at Hadar, Ethiopia." *Nature*, 368: 449–451.

KIMBEL, W.H., D.C. JOHANSON AND Y. RAK (1997). "Systematic Assessment of a Maxilla of *Homo* from Hadar, Ethiopia." *American Journal of Physical Anthropology*, 103: 235–262.

KIMBEL, W.H., T.D. WHITE AND D.C. JOHANSON (1984). "Cranial Morphology of *Australopithecus afarensis*: A Comparative Study Based on a Composite Reconstruction of the Adult Skull." *American Journal of Physical Anthropology*, 64: 337–388.

KIMBEL, W.H., T.D. WHITE AND D.C. JOHANSON (1988). "Implications of KNM-WT 17000 for the Evolution of 'Robust' *Australopithecus*." In, F.E. Grine (ed.), *Evolutionary History of the 'Robust' Australopithecines* (New York: Aldine de Gruyter), pp. 259–268.

KIMURA, M. (1968). "Evolutionary Rate at the Molecular Level." *Nature*, 217: 624–626.

KIMURA, M. (1979). "The Neutral Theory of Molecular Evolution." *Scientific American*, 241(5): 98–126.

KING, J.L. AND T.H. JUKES (1969). "Non-Darwinian Evolution." *Science*, 164: 788–798.

KING, M.-C. AND A.C. WILSON (1975). "Evolution at Two Levels in Humans and Chimpanzees." *Science*, 188: 107–116.

KING, W. (1864). "The Reputed Fossil Man of the Neanderthal." *Quarterly Journal of Science*, 1: 88–97.

KLAATSCH, H. (1899). "Des gegenwärtige Stand der Pithecanthropus-Frage." *Zoologisches Zentralblatt*, 6: 217–235.

KLAATSCH, H. (1902). "Entstehung und Entwickelung des Menschengeschlechtes." In, H. Kraemer (ed.), *Weltall und Menscheit: Geschichte der Erforschung der Natur und der Verwertung der Naturkräfte im Dienste der Völker*, Vol. 2 (Berlin: Bong & Co.), pp. 1–338.

KLAATSCH, H. (1905). "Le genre humain: Ses origines et son évolution." In, H. Kraemer (ed.), *L'Univers et l'Humanité: Histoire des différents systèmes appliqués à l'étude de la Nature. Utilisation des forces naturelles au service des peuples*, Vol. 2 (Paris: Bong & Co.), pp. 1–370.

KLAATSCH, H. (1908). "The Skull of the Australian Aboriginal." *Reports from the Pathological Laboratory of the Lunacy Department*, New South Wales Government, vol. 1, Part III, pp. 43–167.

KLAATSCH, H. (1910a). "Menschenrassen und Menschenaffen." *Korrespondenz-Blatt der Deutschen Gesellschaft für Anthropologie, Ethnologie und Urgeschichte*, 41: 91–101.

KLAATSCH, H. (1910b). "Die Aurignac-Rasse und ihre Stellung im Stammbaum der Menschheit." *Zeitschrift für Ethnologie*, 42: 513–577.

KLAATSCH, H. (1920). *Der Werdegang der Menschheit und die Entstehung der Kultur* (Berlin: Bong & Co., 1920).

KLAATSCH, H. (1923). *The Evolution and Progress of Mankind* (London: T. Fisher Unwin).

KLINGER, H.P., J.L. HAMERTON, D. MUTTON AND E.M. LANG (1963). "The Chromosomes of the Hominoidea." In, S.L. Washburn (ed.), *Classification and Human Evolution* (Chicago: Aldine), pp. 235–242.

KOLLMANN, J. (1895). "Dubois' Pithecanthropus erectus, betrachtet als eine wirkliche Uebergangsform und als Stammform des Menschen." *Zeitschrift für Ethnologie*, 27: 740–744.

KOOP, B.F., D.A. TAGLE, M. GOODMAN AND J.L. SLIGHTOM (1989). "A Molecular View of Primate Phylogeny and Important Systematic and Evolutionary Questions." *Molecular Biology and Evolution*, 6: 580–612.

KORTLANDT, A. (1980). "How Might Early Hominids Have Defended Themselves Against Large Predators and Food Competitors?" *Journal of Human Evolution*, 9: 79–112.

KRAMER, A. (1993). "Human Taxonomic Diversity in the Pleistocene: Does *Homo erectus* Represent Multiple Species?" *American Journal of Physical Anthropology*, 91: 161–171.

KRAMER, A., S.M. DONNELLY, J.H.KIDDER, S.D. OUSLEY AND S.M. OLAH (1995). "Craniometric Variation in Large-Bodied Hominoids: Testing the Single-Species Hypothesis for *Homo habilis*." *Journal of Human Evolution*, 29: 443–462.

KRANTZ, G.S. (1993). "The Subspecies of *Homo erectus*." *Human Evolution*, 8: 275–279.

KRAUSE, W. (1895). "Dubois' Pithecanthropus erectus, eine menschenähnliche Uebergangsform aus Java." *Zeitschrift für Ethnologie*, 27 (1895): 78–81.

KRINGS, M., C. CAPELLI, F. TSCHENTSCHER, H. GEISERT, S. MEYER, A. VON HAESELER, K. GROSSCHMIDT, G. POSSNERT, M. PAUNOVIC AND S. PÄÄBO (2000). "A View of Neanderthal Genetic Diversity." *Nature Genetics*, 26: 144–146.

KRINGS, M., H. GEISERT, R.W. SCHMITZ, H. KRAINITZKI AND S. PÄÄBO (1999). "DNA Sequence of the Mitochondrial Hyperviable Region II From the Neandertal Type Specimen." *Proceedings of the National Academy of Sciences* (USA), 96: 5581–5585.

KRINGS, M., A. STONE, R.W. SCHMITZ, H. KRAINITZKI, M. STONEKING AND S. PÄÄBO (1997). "Neandertal DNA Sequences and the Origin of Modern Humans." *Cell*, 90: 19–30.

KUHN, T.S. (1970). *The Structure of Scientific Revolutions*, 2nd edition (Chicago: University of Chicago Press).

KURTÉN, B. (1972). *Not From the Apes* (New York: Pantheon Books).

KURTÉN, B. (1981). "The 'Gestalt' of Hominid Evolution." In, D. Ferembach (ed.), *Les processus de l'hominisation* (Paris: C.N.R.S.), pp. 61–65.

KURZ, G.E. (1924). "Das Gehirn des Gelben und die mehrstämmige Abkunft der Menschenarten." *Anatomischer Anzeiger*, 58: 107–117.

LAITMAN, J.T. AND J.S. REIDENBERG (1988). "Advances in Understanding the Relationship Between the Skull Base and Larynx With Comments on the Origins of Speech." *Human Evolution*, 3: 99–109.

LAKATOS, I. (1978). *The Methodology of Scientific Research Programmes*, Philosophical Papers, Vol. 1 (Cambridge: Cambridge University Press).

LAMARCK, J.-B. (1802). *Recherches sur l'organisation des corps vivants* (Paris: Maillard).

LAMARCK, J.-B. (1809). *La philosophie zoologique*, Vol. 1 (Paris: Dentu).

LAMARCK, J.-B. (1820). *Système analytique des connaissances positives de l'homme* (Paris: A. Belin).

LANGANEY, A., N.M. VAN BLYENBURGH AND R. NADOT (1990). "L'histoire génétique des mille derniers siècles et ses mécanismes: une revue." *Bulletins et Mémoires de la Société d'Anthropologie de Paris*, new series, 2: 43–56.

LANGDON, J.H. (1985). "Fossils and the Origin of Bipedalism." *Journal of Human Evolution*, 14: 615–635.

LARICK, R. AND R.L. CIOCHON (1996). "The African Emergence and Early Asian Dispersals of the Genus *Homo*." *American Scientist*, 84(6): 538–551.

LATIMER, B. (1991). "Locomotor Adaptations in *Australopithecus afarensis*: The Issue of Arboreality." In, Y. Coppens and B. Senut (eds.), *Origine(s) de la bipédie chez les hominidés* (Paris: C.N.R.S.), pp. 169–176.

LATIMER, B. AND C.O. LOVEJOY (1989). "The Calcaneous of *Australopithecus afarensis* and Its Implications for the Evolution of Bipedality." *American Journal of Physical Anthropology*, 78: 369–386.

LATIMER, B., J.C. OHMAN AND C.O. LOVEJOY (1987). "Talocrural Joint in African Hominoids: Implications for *Australopithecus afarensis*." *American Journal of Physical Anthropology*, 74: 155–175.

LAUDAN, L. (1977). *Progress and Its Problems: Towards a Theory of Scientific Growth* (Berkeley: University of California Press).

LAURENT, G. (1977). "Le cheminement d'Étienne Geoffroy Saint-Hilaire (1772–1844) vers un transformisme scientifique." *Revue d'Histoire des Sciences*, 30: 43–70.

LAURENT, G. (1987). *Paléontologie et évolution en France de 1800 à 1860: Une histoire des idées de Cuvier et Lamarck à Darwin* (Paris: Édition du C.T.H.S.).

LAURENT, G. (1995a). "Idées sur l'origine animale de l'homme en France au XIXe siècle." In, R. Corbey and B. Theunissen (eds.), *Ape, Man, Apeman: Changing Views since 1600* (Leiden University: Department of Prehistory), pp. 157–171.

LAURENT, G. (1995b). "Les idées sur l'origine de l'homme au début du XXe siècle: Les conceptions de Marcellin Boule (1861–1942)." In, *Nature, Histoire, Société: Essais en hommage à Jacques Roger* (Paris: Klincksieck), pp. 433–442.

LEAKEY, L.S.B. (1934). *Adam's Ancestors: An Up-To-Date Outline of What is Known About the Origin of Man*, 2nd edition (London: Methuen).

LEAKEY, L.S.B. (1936a). "Fossil Human Remains from Kanam and Kanjera, Kenya Colony." *Nature*, 138: 643.

LEAKEY, L.S.B. (1936b). "A New Fossil Skull from Eyassi, East Africa." *Nature*, 138: 1082–1084.

LEAKEY, L.S.B. (1943). "A Miocene Anthropoid Mandible from Rusinga, Kenya." *Nature*, 152: 319–320.

LEAKEY, L.S.B. (1946). "Fossil Finds in Kenya: Ape or Primitive Man?" *Antiquity*, 20: 201–204.

LEAKEY, L.S.B. (1948). "Fossil and Sub-Fossil Hominoidea in East Africa." In, A.L. Du Toit (ed.), *Robert Broom Commemorative Volume* (Cape Town: Royal Society of South Africa), pp. 165–170.

LEAKEY, L.S.B. (1950). "The Age of Homo sapiens." *Mankind*, 4: 196–200.

LEAKEY, L.S.B. (1953). *Adam's Ancestors: An Up-To-Date Outline of the Old Stone Age (Palaeolithic) and What is Known About Man's Origin and Evolution*, 4th edition (London: Methuen).

LEAKEY, L.S.B. (1959). "A New Fossil Skull From Olduvai." *Nature*, 184: 491–493.

LEAKEY, L.S.B. (1960a). "The Origin of the Genus *Homo*." In, S. Tax (ed.), *Evolution After Darwin*, Vol. II (Chicago: University of Chicago Press), pp. 17–32.

LEAKEY, L.S.B. (1960b). "Comments on 'The Affinities of the New Olduvai Australopithecine' by J.T. Robinson." *Nature*, 186: 458.

LEAKEY, L.S.B. (1961a). *The Progress and Evolution of Man in Africa* (London: Oxford University Press).

LEAKEY, L.S.B. (1961b). "Africa's Contribution to the Evolution of Man." *South African Archaeological Bulletin*, 16: 3–7.

LEAKEY, L.S.B. (1961c). "A New Lower Pliocene Fossil Primate From Kenya." *Annals and Magazine of Natural History*, 4: 689–696.

LEAKEY, L.S.B. (1961d). "The Juvenile Mandible From Olduvai." *Nature*, 191: 417–418.

LEAKEY, L.S.B. (1961e). "Exploring 1,750,000 Years Into Man's Past." *The National Geographic*, 120: 564–589.

Leakey, L.S.B. (1961f). "New Finds at Olduvai Gorge." *Nature*, 189: 649–650.

Leakey, L.S.B. (1962). "L'évolution des primates supérieurs et de l'homme." In, *Problèmes actuels de paléontologie, évolution des vertébrés*, No. 104 (Paris: Colloques internationaux du Centre National de laRecherche Scientifique), pp. 451–453.

Leakey, L.S.B. (1963). "East African Fossil Hominoidea and the Classification Within this Super-Family." In, S.L. Washburn (ed.), *Classification and Human Evolution* (Chicago: Aldine), pp. 32–49.

Leakey, L.S.B. (1966). "*Homo habilis, Homo erectus* and the Australopithecines." *Nature,* 209: 1279–1281.

Leakey, L.S.B. (1967). "An Early Miocene Member of Hominidae." *Nature*, 213: 155–163.

Leakey, L.S.B. (1968a). "Lower Dentition of *Kenyapithecus africanus*." *Nature*, 217: 827–830.

Leakey, L.S.B. (1968b). "Bone Smashing by Late Miocene Hominidae." *Nature*, 218: 528–530.

Leakey, L.S.B. (1968c). "Upper Miocene Primates From Kenya." *Nature*, 218: 527–528.

Leakey, L.S.B. (1970). "The Relationship of African Apes, Man, and Old World Monkeys." *Proceedings of the National Academy of Sciences*, 67: 746–748.

Leakey, L.S.B. (1971). "*Homo sapiens* in the Middle Pleistocene and the Evidence of *Homo sapiens*' Evolution." In, F. Bordes (ed.), *The Origin of* Homo sapiens (Paris: Unesco), pp. 25–29.

Leakey, L.S.B. (1974). *By the Evidence: Memoirs, 1932–1951* (New York: Harcourt, Brace and Jovanovich).

Leakey, L.S.B. and M.D. Leakey (1964). "Recent Discoveries of Fossil Hominids in Tanganyika at Olduvai or Near Lake Natron." *Nature*, 202: 5–7.

Leakey, L.S.B., P.V. Tobias and J.R. Napier (1964). "A New Species of the Genus *Homo* From Olduvai Gorge." *Nature*, 202: 7–9.

Leakey, M.D. (1971). *Olduvai Gorge: Excavations in Beds I and II, 1960–1963*, Vol. 3 (Cambridge: Cambridge University Press).

Leakey, M.D. and R.L. Hay (1979). "Pliocene Footprints in the Laetoli Beds at Laetoli, Northern Tanzania." *Nature*, 278: 317–323.

Leakey, M.G., C.S. Feibel, I. McDougall and A. Walker (1995). "New Four-Million-Year-Old Hominid Species from Kanapoi and Allia Bay, Kenya." *Nature*, 376: 565–571.

Leakey, M.G., F. Spoor, F.H. Brown, P.N. Gathogo, C. Kiarie, L.N. Leakey and I. McDougall (2001). "New Hominin Genus from Eastern Africa Shows Diverse Middle Pliocene Lineages." *Nature*, 410: 433–440.

Leakey, M.G. and A. Walker (1997). "Early Hominid Fossils from Africa." *Scientific American*, 276(6): 74–79.

Leakey, M.G. and A. Walker (2003). "Early Hominid Fossils from Africa." *Scientific American*, special edition, 13(2): 14–19.

Leakey, R.E.F. (1976). "Hominids in Africa." *American Scientists*, 64: 174–179.

Leakey, R.E.F. (1981). *The Making of Mankind* (New York: E.P. Dutton).

Leakey, R.E.F. (1982). *Human Origins* (New York: E.P. Dutton).

Leakey, R.E.F. (1989). "Recent Fossil Finds from East Africa." In, J.R. Durant (ed.), *Human Origins* (Oxford: Clarendon Press), pp. 53–62.

Leakey, R.E.F. and R. Lewin (1977). *Origins: What New Discoveries Reveal About the Emergence of Our Species and Its Possible Future* (New York: E.P. Dutton).

Leakey, R.E.F. and R. Lewin (1992). *Origins Reconsidered: In Search of What Makes Us Human* (New York: Doubleday).

Leakey, R.E.F. and A. Walker (1976). "*Australopithecus, Homo erectus* and the Single-Species Hypothesis." *Nature*, 261: 572–574.

LeGrand, H.E. (1988). *Drifting Continents and Shifting Theories* (Cambridge: Cambridge University Press).

Le Gros Clark, W.E. (1934). *Early Forerunners of Man: A Morphological Study of the Evolutionary Origin of the Primates* (Baltimore: William Wood).

Le Gros Clark, W.E. (1935). "Man's Place Among the Primates." *Man*, 35: 1–6.

Le Gros Clark, W.E. (1936). "Evolutionary Parallelism and Human Phylogeny." *Man*, 36: 4–8.

Le Gros Clark, W.E. (1939a). "The Scope and Limitations of Physical Anthropology." *The Advancement of Science*, 1: 52–75.

Le Gros Clark, W.E. (1939b). "The Interpretation of Human Fossils." *The Modern Quarterly*, 2: 115–127.

Le Gros Clark, W.E. (1940). "Palaeontological Evidence Bearing on Human Evolution." *Biological Reviews*, 15: 202–230.

Le Gros Clark, W.E. (1945). "Pithecanthropus in Peking." *Antiquity*, 19: 1–5.

Le Gros Clark, W.E. (1946a). "Immediate Problems of Human Palaeontology." *Man*, 46: 80–84.

Le Gros Clark, W.E. (1946b). "Significance of the Australopithecinae." *Nature*, 157: 863–865.

Le Gros Clark, W.E. (1947a). "The Importance of the Fossil Australopithecinae in the Study of Human Evolution." *Science Progress*, 35: 377–395.

Le Gros Clark, W.E. (1947b). "Observations on the Anatomy of the Fossil Australopithecinae." *Journal of Anatomy*, 81: 300–333.

Le Gros Clark, W.E. (1949). *History of the Primates: An Introduction to the Study of Fossil Man* (London: Trustees of the British Museum).

Le Gros Clark, W.E. (1950a). "New Palaeontological Evidence Bearing on the Evolution of the Hominoidea." *Quarterly Journal of the Geological Society of London*, 105: 225–264.

Le Gros Clark, W.E. (1950b). "Hominid Characters of the Australopithecine Dentition." *Journal of the Royal Anthropological Institute*, 80: 37–54.

Le Gros Clark, W.E. (1953). *History of the Primates: An Introduction to the Study of Fossil Man*, 3rd edition (London: Trustees of the British Museum).

Le Gros Clark, W.E. (1954). "The Antiquity of *Homo sapiens* in Particular and of the Hominidae in General." *Science Progress*, 42: 377–395.

Le Gros Clark, W.E. (1955). *The Fossil Evidence for Human Evolution: An Introduction to the Study of Paleoanthropology* (Chicago: University of Chicago Press).

Le Gros Clark, W.E. (1957). *History of the Primates: An Introduction to the Study of Fossil Man*, 5th edition (Chicago: Phoenix Books). This book was first edited by the Trustees of the British Museum.

Le Gros Clark, W.E. (1958). "Bones of Contention." *Journal of the Royal Anthropological Institute*, 88: 131–145.

Le Gros Clark, W.E. (1960a). *The Antecedents of Man: An Introduction to the Evolution of the Primates* (Chicago: Quadrangle Books). First edited by Edinburgh University Press in 1959.

Le Gros Clark, W.E. (1960b). *History of the Primates: An Introduction to the Study of Fossil Man*, 7th edition (London: Trustees of the British Museum).

Le Gros Clark, W.E. (1964). *The Fossil Evidence for Human Evolution: An Introduction to the Study of Paleoanthropology*, 2nd edition (Chicago: University of Chicago Press).

Le Gros Clark, W.E. (1967). *Man-Apes or Ape-Men? The Story of Discoveries in Africa* (New York: Holt, Rinehart and Winston).

Le Gros Clark, W.E. (1971). *The Antecedents of Man: An Introduction to the Evolution of the Primates*, 3rd edition (Chicago: Quadrangle Books).

Le Gros Clark, W.E. and L.S.B. Leakey (1951). "The Miocene Hominoidea of East Africa." *Fossil Mammals of Africa*, 1: 1–117.

Leguebe, A. (1986). "Importance des découvertes de Néandertaliens en Belgique pour le développement de la paléontologie humaine." *Bulletin de la Société Royale Belge d'Anthropologie et de Préhistoire*, 97: 13–31.

Lengyel, I. (1981). "Serological Examinations of Some *Homo erectus* Finds." In, D. Ferembach (ed.), *Les processus de l'hominisation* (Paris: C.N.R.S.), pp. 295–298.

Lenoir, E.-R. (1926). "L'homme et le gibbon." *Revue anthropologique*, 36: 427–460.

Lewin, R. (1987). *Bones of Contention: Controversies in the Search for Human Origins* (New York: Simon & Schuster).

Lewin, R. (1997). *Patterns in Evolution: The New Molecular View* (New York: Scientific American Library).

Lewis, G.E. (1934). "Preliminary Notice of New Man-Like Apes From India." *American Journal of Science*, 27: 161–179.

Lewis, G.E. (1936). "A New Species of Sugrivapithecus." *American Journal of Science*, 31: 450–452.

Lewis, G.E. (1937). "Taxonomic Syllabus of Siwalik Fossil Anthropoids." *American Journal of Science*, 34: 139–147.

Lewis, O.J. (1989). *Functional Morphology of the Evolving Hand and Foot* (Oxford: Clarendon Press).

Li, W.-H. and M. Tanimura (1987). "The Molecular Clock Runs More Slowly in Man Than in Apes and Monkeys." *Nature*, 326: 93–96.

LIEBERMAN, D.E., D.R. PILBEAM AND B.A. WOOD (1988a). "A Probabilistic Approach to the Problem of Sexual Dimorphism in *Homo habilis*: A Comparison of KNM-ER 1470 and KNM-ER 1813." *Journal of Human Evolution*, 17: 503–511.

LIEBERMAN, D.E., D.R. PILBEAM AND B.A. WOOD (1988b). "Homoplasy and Early *Homo*: An Analysis of the Evolutionary Relationships of *H. habilis sensu stricto* and *H. rudolfensis*." *Journal of Human Evolution*, 30: 97–120.

LIEBERMAN, L. AND F.L.C. JACKSON (1995). "Race and Three Models of Human Origin." *American Anthropologist*, 97: 231–242.

LIEBERMAN, P. (1984). *The Biology and Evolution of Language* (Cambridge: Harvard University Press).

LIEBERMAN, P. (1985). "On the Evolution of Human Syntactic Ability: Its Pre-Adaptive Bases—Motor Control and Speech." *Journal of Human Evolution*, 14: 657–668.

LIEBERMAN, P. (1991). *Uniquely Human: The Evolution of Speech, Thought, and Selfless Behavior* (Cambridge: Harvard University Press).

LIEBERMAN, P. (1994). "Hyoid Bone Position and Speech: Reply to Dr. Arensburg et al. (1990)." *American Journal of Physical Anthropology*, 94: 275–278.

LIEBERMAN, P. (1995). "Manual Versus Speech Motor Control and the Evolution of Language." *Behavioral and Brain Sciences*, 18: 197–198.

LIEBERMAN, P. (1998). *Eve Spoke: Human Language and Human Evolution* (New York: W.W. Norton).

LIEBERMAN, P. AND E.S. CRELIN (1971). "On the Speech of Neanderthal Man." *Linguistic Inquiry*, 2: 203–222.

LIEBERMAN, P., E.S. CRELIN AND D.H. KLATT (1972). "Phonetic Ability and Related Anatomy of the Newborn and Adult Human, Neanderthal Man, and the Chimpanzee." *American Journal of Physical Anthropology*, 74: 287–307.

LONG, J.C., A. CHAKRAVARTI, C.D. BOEHM, S. ANTONARAKIS AND H.H. KAZAZIAN (1990). "Phylogeny of Human B-Globin Haplotypes and Its Implications For Recent Human Evolution." *American Journal of Physical Anthropology*, 81: 113–130.

LOVEJOY, C.O. (1975). "Biomechanical Perspectives on the Lower Limb of Early Hominids." In, R.H. Tuttle (ed.), *Primate Functional Morphology and Evolution* (The Hague: Mouton), pp. 291–326.

LOVEJOY, C.O. (1981). "The Origin of Man." *Science*, 211: 341–350.

LOVEJOY, C.O. (1988). "Evolution of Human Walking." *Scientific American*, 259 (11): 118–125.

LOVEJOY, C.O., K.G. HEIPLE AND A.H. BURSTEIN (1973). "The Gait of *Australopithecus*." *American Journal of Physical Anthropology*, 38: 757–780.

LOWENSTEIN, J.M. (1981). "Immunological Reactions From Fossil Material." *Philosophical Transactions of the Royal Society of London*, B 292: 143–149.

LU, Q. AND Q. XU (1981). "Preliminary Research on the Cranium of Sivapithecus Yunnanensis." *Vertebrata Palasiatica*, 19: 101–106.

LUCOTTE, G. AND J. LEFEBVRE (1981). "Distances électrophorétiques entre l'homme, le chimpanzée (Pan troglodytes) et le gorilla (Gorilla gorilla) basées sur la mobilité des enzymes érythrocytaires." *Human Genetics*, 57: 180–184.

LULL, R.S. (1917). *Organic Evolution* (New York: Macmillan).

LULL, R.S. (1929). *Organic Evolution*, revised edition (New York: Macmillan).

LYDEKKER, R. (1879). "Further Notices of Siwalik Mammalia." *Records of the Geological Survey of India*, 11: 33–57.

LYDEKKER, R. (1886). "Indian Tertiary and Post-Tertiary Vertebrata. Siwalik Mammalia—Supplement I." *Memoirs of the Geological Survey of India*, 10th series, 4: 1–21.

LYDEKKER, R. (1895). "Comments on *Pithecanthropus erectus*." *Nature*, 51: 291.

MACINNES, D.G. (1943). "Notes on the East African Miocene Primates." *Journal of the East Africa and Uganda Natural History Society*, 17: 141–181.

MAHOUDEAU, P.-G. (1904). "Indication des principales étapes de la phylogénie des hominiens." *Revue de l'École d'Anthropologie de Paris*, 14: 1–20.

MAHOUDEAU, P.-G. (1912). "Le Pithécanthrope de Java." *Revue Anthropologique*, 22: 453–472.

MAHOUDEAU, P.-G. (1914). "La recherche du début de l'Ère humaine." *Revue Anthropologique*, 24: 323–341.

MANOUVRIER, L. (1895). "Deuxième étude sur le Pithecanthropus erectus comme précurseur présumé de l'homme." *Bulletins de la Société d'Anthropologie de Paris*, 4e série, 6: 553–651.

MANOUVRIER, L. (1896). "Réponse aux objections contre le Pithecanthopus." *Bulletins de la Société d'Anthropologie de Paris*, 4e série, 7: 396–460.

MARETT, J.R. DE LA H. (1936). *Race, Sex, and Environment: A Study of Mineral Deficiency in Human Evolution* (London: Hutchinson).

MARKS, J. (1994). "Blood Will Tell (Won't It?): A Century of Molecular Discourse in Anthropological Systematics." *American Journal of Physical Anthropology*, 94: 59–79.

MARKS, J. (1995). "Learning to Live With a Trichotomy." *American Journal of Physical Anthropology*, 98: 211–213.

MARKS, J. (1996a). "The Legacy of Serological Studies in American Physical Anthropology." *History and Philosophy of the Life Sciences*, 18: 345–362.

MARKS, J. (1996b). "Molecular Anthropology in Retropect and Prospect." In, E. Meikle, F.C. Howell and N.G. Jablonski (eds.), *Contemporary Issues in Human Evolution* (San Francisco: California Academy of Sciences 21), pp. 167–186.

MARKS, J. (1997). "Molecular Anthropology." In, F. Spencer (ed.), *History of Physical Anthropology: An Encyclopedia*, Vol. 2 (New York: Garland), pp. 672–679.

MARKS, J., C.W. SCHMID AND V.M. SARICH (1988). "DNA Hybridization as a Guide to Phylogeny: Relations of the Hominoidea." *Journal of Human Evolution*, 17: 769–786.

MARSH, O.C. (1896). "The Ape-Man From the Tertiary of Java." *Science*, new series, 3: 789–793.

MARSTON, A.T. (1937). "The Swanscombe Skull." *Journal of the Royal Anthropological Institute*, 67: 339–406.

MARTIN, L. (1986). "Relationships Among Extant and Extinct Great Apes and Humans." In, B. Wood, L. Martin and P. Andrews (eds.), *Major Topics in Primate and Human Evolution* (Cambridge: Cambridge University Press), pp. 161–187.

MARTIN, R. (1895). "Kritische Bedenken gegen den Pithecanthropus erectus Dubois." *Globus*, 67: 213–217.

MARZKE, M.W. (1971). "Origin of the Human Hand." *American Journal of Physical Anthropology*, 34: 61–84.

MARZKE, M.W. (1983). "Joint Function and Grips of the *Australopithecus afarensis* Hand, With Special Reference to the Region of the Capitate." *Journal of Human Evolution*, 12: 197–211.

MARZKE, M.W. (1997). "Precision Grips, Hand Morphology, and Tools." *American Journal of Physical Anthropology*, 102: 91–110.

MAYER, F. (1864). "Ueber die fossilen Ueberreste eines menschlichen Schädels und Skeletes in einer Felsenhöhle des Düssel- oder Neander-Thales." *Archiv für Anatomie, Physiologie und Wissenschaftliche Medicin*, 1: 1–26.

MAYR, E. (1942). *Systematics and the Origin of Species* (New York: Columbia University Press).

MAYR, E. (1950). "Taxonomic Categories in Fossil Hominids." *Cold Spring Harbor Symposia on Quantitative Biology*, 15: 109–118.

MAYR, E. (1953). "Comments on Evolutionary Literature." *Evolution*, 7: 273–281.

MAYR, E. (1963). "The Taxonomic Evaluation of Fossil Hominids." In, S.L. Washburn (ed.), *Clasification and Human Evolution* (Chicago: Aldine), pp. 332–346.

MAYR, E. (1969). *Principles of Systematic Zoology* (New York: McGraw-Hill).

MAYR, E. AND P.D. ASHLOCK (1991). *Principles of Systematic Zoology*, 2nd edition (New York: McGraw-Hill).

MAYR, E. AND W.B. PROVINE (1980, eds.). *The Evolutionary Synthesis: Perspectives on the Unification of Biology* (Cambridge: Harvard University Press).

MCCOWN, T.D. AND A. KEITH (1939). *The Stone Age of Mount Carmel. The Fossil Human Remains from the Levalloiso-Mousterian*, Vol. II (Oxford: Clarendon Press).

MCHENRY, H.M. (1984). "Relative Cheek-Tooth Size in *Australopithecus*." *American Journal of Physical Anthropology*, 64: 297–306.

MCHENRY, H.M. (1997). "'Robust' Australopithecines, Our Family Tree, and Homoplasy." In, C.R. Ember, M. Ember and P.N. Peregrine (eds.), *Research Frontiers in Anthropology, Vol. 3, Physical Anthropology* (New Jersey: Prentice Hall), pp. 233–252.

MCHENRY, H.M. AND L.R. BERGER (1998). "Body Proportions in *Australopithecus afarensis* and *A. africanus* and the Origin of the Genus *Homo*." *Journal of Human Evolution*, 35: 1–22.

MCHENRY, H.M. AND K. COFFING (2000). "*Australopithecus* to *Homo*: Transformations in Body and

Mind." *Annual Review of Anthropology*, 29: 125–146.

McHenry, H.M. and R.S. Corruccini (1980). "On the Status of *Australopithecus afarensis*." *Science*, 207: 1103–1104.

McHenry, H.M. and R.R. Skelton (1985). "Is *Australopithecus africanus* Ancestral to *Homo*?" In, P.V. Tobias (ed.), *Hominid Evolution: Past, Present and Future* (New York: Alan R. Liss), pp. 221–226.

McHenry, H.M. and A. Temerin (1979). "The Evolution of Hominid Bipedalism: Evidence From the Fossil Record." *Yearbook of Physical Anthropology*, 22: 105–131.

Melchers, F. (1910). "Der Ursprung der Menschenrassen." *Der Zeitgeist* (Beiblatt zum *Berliner Tageblatt*), Nummer 25, 20 Juni. Front page.

Meltzer, D.J. (1983). "The Antiquity of Man and the Development of American Archeology." In, M.B. Schiffer (ed.), *Advances in Archaeological Method and Theory*, Vol. 6 (New York: Academic Press), pp. 1–51.

Mendes-Corrêa, A.A. (1923). "La généalogie humaine et le polyphylétisme." *L'Anthropologie*, 33: 147–155.

Miller, G.S. (1928). "The Controversy over Human Missing Links." *Annual Report of the Smithsonian Institution* for 1928, pp. 413–465.

Miller, D.A. (1977). "Evolution of Primate Chromosomes." *Science*, 198: 1116–1124.

Miller, J.A. (1991). "Does Brain Size Variability Provide Evidence of Multiple Species in *Homo habilis*?" *American Journal of Physical Anthropology*, 84: 385–398.

Miller, J.A. (2000). "Craniofacial Variation in *Homo habilis*: An Analysis of the Evidence for Multiple Species." *American Journal of Physical Anthropology*, 112: 103–128.

Minugh-Purvis, N. (1995). "The Modern Human Origins Controversy: 1984–1994." *Evolutionary Anthropology*, 4: 140–147.

Mivart, St. George (1873). *Man and Apes, an Exposition of Structural Resemblances and Differences Bearing Upon Questions of Affinity and Origin* (London: Robert Hardwicke).

Miyamoto, M.M., J.L. Slightom and M. Goodman (1987). "Phylogenetic Relations of Humans and African Apes from DNA Sequences in the un-Globin Region." *Science*, 238: 369–373.

Moir, J.R. (1919). *Pre-Palaeolithic Man* (Ipswich: Harrison).

Moir, J.R. (1927). *The Antiquity of Man in East Anglia* (Cambridge: Cambridge University Press).

Moir, J.R. and A. Keith (1912). "An Account of the Discovery and Characters of a Human Skeleton Found Beneath a Stratum of Chalky Boulder Clay Near Ipswich." *Journal of the Royal Anthropological Institute*, 42: 345–379.

Montandon, G. (1928). *L'ologenèse humaine* (Paris: Alcan).

Montandon, G. (1929a). "Un singe d'apparence anthropoïde en Amérique du Sud." *Comptes Rendus hebdomadaires des Séances de l'Académie des Sciences*, 188: 815–817.

Montandon, G. (1929b). "Un singe anthropoïde actuel en Amérique." *Revue Scientifique*, 67: 268–269.

Montandon, G. (1929c). "Découverte d'un singe d'apparence anthropoïde en Amérique du Sud." *Journal de la Société des Américanistes de Paris*, 21: 183–195.

Montandon, G. (1929d). "L'ologénisme ou ologenèse humaine." *L'Anthropologie*, 39: 103–122.

Montandon, G. (1930). "Précision relatives au grand singe de l'Amérique du Sud." *Archivio Zoologico Italiano*, 14: 441–459.

Montandon, G. (1933). *La race, les races* (Paris: Payot).

Morell, V. (1995). *Ancestral Passions: The Leakey Family and the Quest for Humankind's Beginnings* (New York: Simon and Schuster).

Morton, D.J. (1927). "Human Origin: Correlation of Previous Studies of Primate Feet and Posture With Other Morphologic Evidence." *American Journal of Physical Anthropology*, 10: 173–203.

Movius, H. (1948). "The Lower Palaeolithic Cultures of Southern and Eastern Asia." *Transactions of the American Philosophical Society*, 38: 328–420.

Nagel, E. (1979). *The Structure of Science: Problems in the Logic of Scientific Explanation*, 2nd edition (Indianapolis: Hackett).

Napier, J. (1962). "Fossil Hand Bones From Olduvai Gorge." *Nature*, 196: 409–411.

Napier, J.R. and P.R. Davis (1959). "The Fore-Limb Skeleton and Associated Remains of Proconsul Africanus." *Fossil Mammals of Africa*, 16: 1–69.

Nei, M. and G. Livshits (1989). "Genetic Relationships of Europeans, Asians and Africans and the Origin of Modern *Homo sapiens*." *Human Heredity*, 39: 276–281.

Nei, M. and A.K. Roychoudhury (1974). "Genic Variation Within and Between the Three Major Races of Man; Caucasoids, Negroids, and Mogoloids." *American Journal of Human Genetics*, 26: 421–443.

Nei, M. and A.K. Roychoudhury (1982). "Genetic Relationship and Evolution of Human Races." *Evolutionary Biology*, 14: 1–59.

Oakley, K.P. (1953). "Dating Fossil Human Remains." In, A.L. Kroeber (ed.), *Anthropology Today: An Encyclopedic Inventory* (Chicago: University of Chicago Press), pp. 43–56.

Oakley, K.P. (1964a). "The Problem of Man's Antiquity: An Historical Survey." *Bulletin of the British Museum (Natural History)*, Geology, 9: 85–155.

Oakley, K.P. (1964b). *Frameworks for Dating Fossil Man* (Chicago: Aldine).

Olson, T.R. (1981). "Basicranial Morphology of the Extant Hominoids and Pliocene Hominids: The New Material From the Hadar Formation, Ethiopia, and Its Significance in Early Human Evolution and Taxonomy." In, C.B. Stringer (ed.), *Aspects of Human Evolution* (London: Taylor and Francis), pp. 99–128.

Olson, T.R. (1985). "Cranial Morphology and Systematics of the Hadar Formation Hominids and *'Australopithecus' africanus*." In, E. Delson (ed.), *Ancestors: The Hard Evidence* (New York: Alan R. Liss), p. 102–119.

Oppenheim, St. (1929). "Nochmals Ameranthropoides Loysi (Montandon)." *Die Naturwissenschaften*, 17: 689.

Oppenoorth, W.F.F. (1937). "The Place of Homo Soloensis Among Fossil Men." In, G.G. MacCurdy (ed.), *Early Man* (New York: Freeport, 1937), pp. 349–360.

Osborn, H.F. (1915). *Men of the Old Stone Age: Their Environment, Life and Art* (New York: Charles Scribner's Sons).

Osborn, H.F. (1922a). "*Hesperopithecus*, the First Anthropoid Primate Found in America." *American Museum Novitates*, No.37: 1–5.

Osborn, H.F. (1922b). "Hesperopithecus, the Anthropoid Primate of Western Nebraska." *Nature*, 110: 281–283.

Osborn, H.F. (1926). "Why Central Asia?" *Natural History*, 26: 263–269.

Osborn, H.F. (1927a). "Recent Discoveries Relating to the Origin and Antiquity of Man." *Proceedings of the American Philosophical Society*, 66: 373–389.

Osborn, H.F. (1927b). *Man Rises to Parnassus: Critical Epochs in the Prehistory of Man* (Princeton: Princeton University Press).

Osborn, H.F. (1929). "Is the Ape-Man a Myth?" *Human Biology*, 1: 4–9.

Osborn, H.F. (1930). "The Discovery of Tertiary Man." *Science*, 71: 1–7.

Osman Hill, W.C. (1950). "Man's Relation to the Apes." *Man*, 50: 161–162.

Osman Hill, W.C. (1954). *Man's Ancestry: A Primer of Human Phylogeny* (London: W. Heinemann).

Osman Hill, W.C. (1972). *Evolutionary Biology of the Primates* (London: Academic Press).

Ospovat, D. (1976). "The Influence of Karl Ernst von Baer's Embryology, 1828–1859: A Reappraisal in Light of Richard Owen's and William B. Carpenter's Palaeontological Application of Von Baer' Law." *Journal of the History of Biology*, 9: 1–28.

Ovchinnikov, I.V., A. Götherström, G.P. Romanova, V.M. Kharitonov, K. Lidén and W. Goodwin (2000). "Molecular Analysis of Neanderthal DNA From the Northern Caucasus." *Nature*, 404: 490–493.

Owen, R. (1857). "On the Characters, Principles of Division, and Primary Groups of the Class Mammalia." *Journal of the Proceedings of the Linnean Society of London*, Zoology, 2: 1–37.

Owen, R. (1861). "The Gorilla and the Negro." *The Athenaeum*, pp. 395–396, 467.

Owen, R. (1863). "On the Aye-aye." *Transactions of the Zoological Society of London*, 5: 33–101.

Owen, R. (1868). *On the Anatomy of Vertebrates. Mammals*, Vol. 3 (London: Longmans, Green, and Co.).

Oxnard, C.E. (1969). "Evolution of the Human Shoulder: Some Possible Pathways." *American Journal of Physical Anthropology*, 30: 319–332.

Oxnard, C.E. (1975). *Uniqueness and Diversity in Human Evolution: Morphometric Studies of Australopithecines* (Chicago: University of Chicago Press).

Oxnard, C.E. (1985). *Humans, Apes and Chinese Fossils: New Implications for Human Evolution* (Hong Kong: Hong Kong University Press).

Oxnard, C.E. (1987). *Fossils, Teeth and Sex: New Perspectives on Human Evolution* (Seattle: University of Washington Press).

Paterson, T.T. (1940). "Geology and Early Man." *Nature*, 146: 12–15, 49–52.

Patterson, B. (1954). "The Geologic History of Non-Hominid Primates in the Old World." *Human Biology*, 26: 191–209.

Pautrat, J.-Y. (1993). "*Le Préhistorique* de G. de Mortillet: une histoire géologique de l'homme." *Bulletin de la Société Préhistorique Française*, 90: 50–59.

Pei, W.C. (1936). "Peking Man." *Nature*, 138: 1056.

Pei, W.C. (1937). "The Fifth Skull of Peking Man." *Nature*, 139: 109–110.

Pei, W.C. (1957). "Giant Ape's Jaw Bone Discovered in China." *American Anthropologist*, 59: 834–838.

Pei, W.C. and Y.-H. Li (1959). "Discovery of a Third Mandible of *Gigantopithecus* in Liu-Cheng, Kwangsi, South China." *Vertebrata Palasiatica*, 2: 198–200.

Pei, W.C. and S. Zhang (1985). "A Study on Lithic Artifacts of *Sinanthropus*." *Palaeontologia Sinica*, 168: 1–277.

Pettit, A. (1895). "Le Pithecanthrope erectus." *L'Anthropologie*, 6: 65–69.

Piattelli-Palmarini, M.L. (1989). "Evolution, Selection and Cognition: From Learning to Parameter Setting in Biology and the Study of Language." *Cognition*, 31: 1–44.

Pilbeam, D.R. (1967). "Man's Earliest Ancestors." *Science Journal*, 3 (2): 47–53.

Pilbeam, D.R. (1968). "The Earliest Hominids." *Nature*, 219: 1335–1338.

Pilbeam, D.R. (1970). *The Evolution of Man* (London: Thames and Hudson).

Pilbeam, D.R. (1975). "Middle Pleistocene Hominids." In, K.W. Butzer and G.LL. Isaac (eds.), *After the Australopithecines: Stratigraphy, Ecology and Culture Change in the Middle Pleistocene* (The Hague: Mouton), pp. 809–856.

Pilbeam, D.R. (1979). "Recent Finds and Interpretations of Miocene Hominoids." *Annual Review of Anthropology*, 8: 333–352.

Pilbeam, D.R. (1985). "Patterns of Hominoid Evolution." In, E. Delson (ed.), *Ancestors: The Hard Evidence* (New York: Alan R. Liss), pp. 51–59.

Pilbeam, D.R. (1986). "Hominoid Evolution and Hominoid Origins." *American Anthropologist*, 88: 295–312.

Pilbeam, D.R. (1989). "Human Fossil History and Evolutionary Paradigms." In, M.K. Hecht (ed.), *Evolutionary Biology at the Crossroads* (Flushing: Queens College Press), pp. 117–138.

Pilbeam, D.R. (1996). "Genetic and Morphological Records of the Hominoidea and Hominid Origins: A Synthesis." *Molecular Phylogenetics and Evolution*, 5: 155–168.

Pilbeam, D.R. (1997). "Research on Miocene Hominoids and Hominid Origins." In, D.R. Begun, C.V. Ward and M.D. Rose (eds.), *Function, Phylogeny, and Fossils: Miocene Hominoid Evolution and Adaptations* (New York: Plenum Press), pp. 13–28.

Pilbeam, D.R. and E.L. Simons (1965). "Some Problems of Hominid Classification." *American Scientist*, 53: 237–259.

Pilbeam, D.R., G.E. Meyer, C. Badgley, M.D. Rose, M.H.L. Pickford, A.K. Behrensmeyer and S.M. Ibrahim Shah (1977). "New Hominoid Primates From the Siwaliks of Pakistan and Their Bearing on Hominoid Evolution." *Nature*, 270: 689–695.

Pilgrim, G.E. (1915). "New Siwalik Primates and Their Bearing on the Question of the Evolution of Man and the Anthropoidea." *Records of the Geological Survey of India*, 45: 1–74.

Pilgrim, G.E. (1927). "A Sivapithecus Palate and other Primate Fossils from India." *Memoirs of the Geological Survey of India, Palaeontologia Indica*, 14: 1–26.

Pinker, S. (1994). *The Language Instinct* (New York: William Morrow and Co.).

Pinker, S. and P. Bloom (1990). "Natural Language and Natural Selection." *Behavioral and Brain Sciences*, 13: 707–784.

Piveteau, J. (1954). "L'évolution humaine." *Bulletin de l'Académie internationale de Philosophie des Sciences*, série A, 8: 49–61.

Piveteau, J. (1957). *Traité de Paléontologie, Primates et Paléontologie humaine*, Tome VII (Paris: Masson).

Piveteau, J. (1958). "La paléontologie de l'hominisation." In, *Les processus de l'hominisation* (Paris: Centre National de la Recherche Scientifique), pp. 167–178.

PIVETEAU, J. (1962). *L'origine de l'Homme* (Paris: Hachette).

PIVETEAU, J. (1963). *Des premiers vertébrés à l'homme* (Paris: Albin Michel).

PIVETEAU, J. (1973). *Origine et destinée de l'homme* (Paris: Masson).

PIVETEAU, J. (1983). *Origine et destinée de l'homme*, 2nd edition (Paris: Masson).

PIVETEAU, J. (1991). *La main et l'hominisation* (Paris: Masson).

PLATNICK, N.I. (1979). "Philosophy and the Transformation of Cladistics." *Systematic Zoology*, 28: 537–546.

POISSON, G. (1939). *Le peuplement de l'Europe: état actuel, origines et évolution* (Paris: Payot).

POLIAKOV, L. (1971). *The Aryan Myth: A History of Racist and Nationalist Ideas in Europe* (London: Chatton & Windus).

POPE, G.G. AND J.E. CRONIN (1984). "The Asian Hominidae." *Journal of Human Evolution*, 13: 377–396.

POPKIN, R.H. (1978–79). "Pre-Adamism in 19th Century American Thought: Speculative Biology and Racism." *Philosophia*, 8: 205–239.

PRASAD, K.N. (1962). "Fossil Primates From the Siwalik Beds Near Haritalyangar, Himachal Pradesh, India." *Journal of the Geological Society of India*, 3: 86–96.

PRASAD, K.N. (1964). "Upper Miocene Anthropoids From the Siwalik Beds of Haritalyangar, Himachal Pradesh, India." *Palaeontology*, 7: 124–134.

PRAT, S. (1997). "Problème taxinomique des premiers représentants du genre *Homo*: Études crâniennes des individus d'Olduvai et de Koobi Fora." *Bulletins et Mémoires de la Société d'Anthropologie de Paris*, 9: 251–266.

PRESTWICH, J. (1892). "On the Primitive Characters of the Flint Implements of the Chalk Plateau of Kent." *Journal of the Anthropological Institute*, 21: 246–262.

PROVINE, W.B. (1986). *Sewall Wright and Evolutionary Biology* (Chicago: University of Chicago Press).

PRUNER-BEY, F. (1863). "Observations sur le crâne de Néanderthal." *Bulletins de la Société d'Anthropologie de Paris*, 4: 318–322.

PRUNER-BEY, F. (1866a). "Sur la mâchoire humaine de la Naulette (Belgique)." *Bulletins de la Société d'Anthropologie de Paris*, 2e série, 1: 584–593.

PRUNER-BEY, F. (1866b). "Sur le maxillaire humain fossile trouvé par M. Dupont et présenté par M. Pruner-Bey." *Bulletins de la Société d'Anthropologie de Paris*, 2e série, 1: 616–620.

PRUNER-BEY, F. (1867). "Discours de M. Pruner-Bey sur la question anthropologique." *Congrès International d'Anthropologie et d'Archéologie Préhistoriques*, 2e session, pp. 345–360.

PRUNER-BEY, F. (1868a). "Sur les ossements humains des Eyzies." *Bulletins de la Société d'Anthropologie de Paris*, 2e série, 3: 416–432.

PRUNER-BEY, F. (1868b). "Les crânes des Eyzies et la théorie esthonienne." *Bulletins de la Société d'Anthropologie de Paris, 2e série*, 3: 511–514.

PRUNER-BEY, F. (1869). "Discussion sur le transformisme." *Bulletins de la Société d'Anthropologie de Paris*, 2e série, 4: 647–682.

PYCRAFT, W.P. (1922). "The Nebraska Tooth." *Nature*, 110: 707–708.

PYCRAFT, W.P. (1925). "On the Calvaria Found at Boskop, Transvaal, in 1913, and its Relationship to Cromagnard and Negroid Skulls." *Journal of the Royal Anthropological Institute*, 55: 179–198.

PYCRAFT, W.P. (1928). "Rhodesian Man. Description of the Skull and Other Human Remains from Broken Hill." In, W.P. Pycraft et al. (eds.), *Rhodesian Man and Associated Remains* (London: British Museum of Natural History), pp. 1–51.

RAINGER, R. (1985). "Paleontology and Philosophy: A Critique." *Journal of the History of Biology*, 18: 267–287.

RAINGER, R. (1988). "Vertebrate Paleontology as Biology: Henry Fairfield Osborn and the American Museum of Natural History." In, R. Rainger, K.R. Benson and J. Maienschein (eds.), *The American Development of Biology* (Philadelphia: University of Pennsylvania Press), pp. 219–256.

RAK, Y. (1983). *The Australopithecine Face* (New York: Academic Press).

RAK, Y. (1985a). "Australopithecine Taxonomy and Phylogeny in Light of Facial Morphology." *American Journal of Physical Anthropology*, 66: 281–287.

RAK, Y. (1985b). "Systematic and Functional Implications of the Facial Morphology of *Australopithecus* and *Homo*." In, E. Delson (ed.), *Ancestors: The Hard Evidence* (New York: Alan R. Liss), pp. 168–170.

Rasmussen, D.T. (2002). "Early Catarrhines of the African Eocene and Oligocene." In, W.C. Hartwig (ed.), *The Primate Fossil Record* (Cambridge: Cambridge University Press), pp. 203–220.

Rasmussen, N. (1991). "The Decline of Recapitulationism in Early Twentieth-Century Biology: Disciplinary Conflict and Consensus on the Battleground of Theory." *Journal of the History of Biology*, 24: 51–89.

Ravey, M. (1978). "Bipedalism: An Early Warning System for Miocene Hominoids." *Science*, 199: 372.

Read, D.W. (1975). "Primate Phylogeny, Neutral Mutations, and 'Molecular Clocks'." *Systematic Zoology*, 24: 209–221.

Reader, J. (1981). *Missing Links: The Hunt for Earliest Man* (London: Collins).

Reed, C.A. (1983). "A Short History of the Discovery and Early Study of the Australopithecines: The First Find to the Death of Robert Broom (1924–1951)." In, K.J. Reichs (ed.), *Hominid Origins: Inquiries Past and Present* (Washington: University Press of America), pp. 1–77.

Relethford, J.H. (1995). "Genetics and Modern Human Origins." *Evolutionary Anthropology*, 4: 53–63.

Relethford, J.H. (1999). "Models, Predictions, and the Fossil Record." *Evolutionary Anthropology*, 48: 7–10.

Relethford, J.H. (2001a). "Absence of Regional Affinities of Neandertal DNA With Living Humans Does Not Reject Multiregional Evolution." *American Journal of Physical Anthropology*, 115: 95–98.

Relethford, J.H. (2001b). *Genetics and the Search for Modern Human Origins* (New York: Wiley-Liss).

Remane, A. (1929). "Ameranthropoides, der angebliche Anthropoide Südamerikas." *Die Naturwissenschaften*, 17: 626.

Retzius, A. (1850). "On Certain American, Celtic, Cimbric, Roman and Ancient British Skulls." *Report of the Nineteenth Meeting of the British Association for the Advancement of Science, Notices and Abstracts* (London: J. Murrey), p. 86.

Retzius, G. (1874). "Sur l'étude craniologique des races humaines." *Congrès International d'Anthropologie et d'Archéologie Préhistoriques*, 7e session, pp. 693–740.

Ribeiro, C. (1880). "L'homme tertiaire en Portugal." *Congrès International d'Anthropologie et d'Archéologie Préhistoriques*, pp. 81–117.

Richard, N. (1993). "La fabrique du précurseur." In, C. Blanckaert (ed.), *Des sciences contre l'homme*, vol.1 (Paris: Autrement, 1993), pp. 64–79.

Richards, E. (1987). "A Question of Property Rights: Richard Owen's Evolutionism Reassessed." *British Journal for the History of Science*, 20: 129–171.

Richmond, B.G., L.C. Aiello and B.A. Wood (2002). "Early Hominin Limb Proportions." *Journal of Human Evolution*, 43: 529–548.

Richmond, B.G. and D.S. Strait (2000). "Evidence That Humans Evolved From a Knuckle-Walking Ancestor." *Nature*, 404: 382–385.

Richmond, B.G. and D.S. Strait (2001). "Knuckle-Walking Hominid Ancestor: A Reply to Corruccici and McHenry." *Journal of Human Evolution*, 40: 513–520.

Ricklan, D.E. (1987). "Functional Anatomy of the Hand of *Australopithecus africanus*." *Journal of Human Evolution*, 16: 643–664.

Rightmire, G.P. (1981). "Patterns in the Evolution of *Homo erectus*." *Paleobiology*, 7: 241–246.

Rightmire, G.P. (1985). "The Tempo of Change in the Evolution of Mid-Pleistocene *Homo*." In, E. Delson (ed.), *Ancestors: The Hard Evidence* (New York: Alan R. Liss), pp. 255–264.

Rightmire, G.P. (1986). "Species Recognition and *Homo erectus*." *Journal of Human Evolution*, 15: 823–826.

Rightmire, G.P. (1988). "*Homo erectus* and Later Middle Pleistocene Humans." *Annual Review of Anthropology*, 17: 239–259.

Rightmire, G.P. (1990). *The Evolution of* Homo erectus*: Comparative Anatomical Studies of An Extinct Human Species* (Cambridge: Cambridge University Press).

Rightmire, G.P. (1991). "The Dispersal of *Homo erectus* From Africa and the Emergence of More Modern Humans." *Journal of Anthropological Research*, 47: 177–191.

Rightmire, G.P. (1993). "Variation Among Early *Homo* Crania from Olduvai Gorge and the Koobi Fora Region." *American Journal of Physical Anthropology*, 90: 1–33.

Rightmire, G.P. (1994). "The Relationship of *Homo erectus* to Later Middle Pleistocene Hominids."

In, J.L. Franzen (ed.), *100 Years of Pithecanthropus: The* Homo erectus *Problem* (Courier Forschungs-Institut Senckenberg, 171), pp. 319–326.

Rightmire, G.P. (1996). "The Human Cranium From Bodo, Ethiopia: Evidence For Speciation in the Middle Pleistocene?" *Journal of Human Evolution*, 31: 21–39.

Rightmire, G.P. (1998). "Human Evolution in the Middle Pleistocene: The Role of *Homo heidelbergensis*." *Evolutionary Anthropology*, 6: 218–227.

Robinson, J.T. (1953a). "Meganthropus, Australopithecines and Hominids." *American Journal of Physical Anthropology*, 11: 1–38.

Robinson, J.T. (1953b). "Telanthropus and its Phylogenetic Significance." *American Journal of Physical Anthropology*, 11: 445–501.

Robinson, J.T. (1954a). "The Genera and Species of the Australopithecinae." *American Journal of Physical Anthropology*, 12: 181–200.

Robinson, J.T. (1954b). "Prehominid Dentition and Hominid Evolution." *Evolution*, 8: 324–334.

Robinson, J.T. (1955). "Further Remarks on the Relationship Between 'Meganthropus' and Australopithecines." *American Journal of Physical Anthropology*, 13: 429–445.

Robinson, J.T. (1956). *The Dentition of the Australopithecinae* (Pretoria: Transvaal Museum Memoir No. 9).

Robinson, J.T. (1960). "The Affinities of the New Olduvai Australopithecine." *Nature*, 186: 456–458.

Robinson, J.T. (1961). "The Australopithecines and Their Bearing on the Origin of Man and of Stone Tool-Making." *South African Journal of Science*, 57: 3–13.

Robinson, J.T. (1962). "The Origin and Adaptive Radiation of the Australopithecines." In, G. Kurth (ed.), *Evolution and Hominisation* (Stuttgart: Gustav Fisher Verlag), pp. 120–140.

Robinson, J.T. (1963). "Adaptive Radiation in the Australopithecines and the Origin of Man." In, F.C. Howell and F. Bourlière (eds.), *African Ecology and Human Evolution* (Chicago: Aldine), pp. 385–316.

Robinson, J.T. (1964). "Some Critical Phases in the Evolution of Man." *South African Archaeological Journal*, 19: 3–12.

Robinson, J.T. (1965). "*Homo habilis* and the Australopithecines." *Nature*, 205: 121–124.

Robinson, J.T. (1966). "The Distinctiveness of *Homo habilis*." *Nature*, 209: 957–960.

Robinson, J.T. (1967). "Variation and the Taxonomy of the Early Hominids." *Evolutionary Biology*, 1: 69–100.

Robinson, J.T. (1968). "The Origin and Adaptive Radiation of the Australopithecines." In, G. Kurth (ed.), *Evolution and Hominisation*, 2nd edition (Stuttgart: Gustav Fisher Verlag), pp. 150–175.

Robinson, J.T. (1972). *Early Hominid Posture and Locomotion* (Chicago: University of Chicago Press).

Rogers, J. (1993). "The Phylogenetic Relationships Among *Homo*, *Pan* and *Gorilla*: A Population Genetics Perspective." *Journal of Human Evolution*, 25: 201–215.

Romer, A.S. (1930). "Australopithecus not a Chimpanzee." *Science*, 71: 482–483.

Romer, A.S. (1933). *Man and the Vertebrates* (Chicago: University of Chicago Press).

Romer, A.S. (1941). *Man and the Vertebrates*, 3rd edition (Chicago: Chicago University Press).

Rosa, D. (1918). *Ologenesi. Nuova teoria dell'evoluzione e della distribuzione geografica dei viventi* (Firenze: Bemporad).

Rosa, D. (1923). "Qu'est-ce que l'ologénèse?" *Scientia*, 33: 113–124.

Rosa, D. (1931). *L'ologénèse. Nouvelle théorie de l'évolution et de la distribution géographique des êtres vivants* (Paris: Alcan).

Rose, M.D. (1976). "Bipedal Behavior of Olive Baboons (*Papio anubis*) and Its Relevance to an Understanding of the Evolution of Human Bipedalism." *American Journal of Physical Anthropology*, 44: 247–262.

Rosen, D.E., G. Nelson and C. Patterson (1979). *Foreword to a Reprint of W. Hennig* Phylogenetic Systematics (Urbana: University of Illinois Press, [1966]).

Roujou, M. (1867). "L'homme miocène." *Bulletins de la Société d'Anthropologie de Paris*, 2e série, 2: 662–664.

Roujou, M. (1873). "Sur l'homme tertiaire." *Bulletins de la Société d'Anthropologie de Paris*, 2e série, 86: 75–678.

Rusconi, C. (1935). "Las especies de primates del oligoceno de Patagonia (gen. Homunculus)."

Revista argentina de paleontologia y antropologia, Ameghinia, 1: 71–123.

Ruse, M. (1992). "Is the Theory of Punctuated Equilibria a New Paradigm?" In, A. Somit and S.A. Peterson (eds.), *The Dynamics of Evolution: The Punctuated Equilibrium Debate in the Natural and Social Sciences* (Ithaca: Cornell University Press), pp. 139–167.

Rutot, A. (1900–01). "Sur l'Homme Préquaternaire." *Bulletins et Mémoires de la Société d'Anthropologie de Bruxelles*, 19: 1–19.

Rutot, A. (1904–05). "Toujours les éolithes." *Bulletins et Mémoires de la Société d'Anthropologie de Bruxelles*, 24: clxiii–clxxxiii.

Rutot, A. (1909). "Une industrie éolithique antérieure à l'Oligocène supérieur ou Aquitanien." *Congrès Préhistoriques de France, Compte rendu de la Quatrième Session, Chambéry 1908*, pp. 90–104.

Rutot, A. (1918). *La Préhistoire: Introduction à l'étude de la préhistoire de la Belgique*, Partie 1 (Bruxelles: Les naturalistes belges).

Ruvolo, M. (1994). "Molecular Evolutionary Processes and Conflicting Gene Trees: The Hominoid Case." *American Journal of Physical Anthropology*, 94: 89–113.

Ruvolo, M. (1997). "Molecular Phylogeny of the Hominoid: Inferences From Multiple Independent DNA Sequence Data Sets." *Molecular Biology and Evolution*, 14: 248–265.

Saban, R. (1983). "Les veines méningées moyennes des australopithèques." *Bulletins et Mémoires de la Société d'Anthropologie de Paris*, 10: 313–324.

Saban, R. (1993). *Aux sources du langage articulé* (Paris: Masson).

Sarasin, F. (1924). "Sur les relations des Néo-Calédoniens avec le groupe de l'*Homo neanderthalensis*." *L'Anthropologie*, 34: 193–227.

Sarich, V.M. (1968). "Hominid Origins: An Immunological View." In, S.L. Washburn and P.C. Jay (eds.), *Perspectives on Human Evolution* (New York: Holt, Rinehart & Winston), pp. 94–121.

Sarich, V.M. (1970). "Primate Systematics With Special Reference to Old World Monkeys." In, J.R. Napier and P.H. Napier (eds.), *Old World Monkeys: Evolution, Systematics, and Behavior* (New York: Academic Press), pp. 175–226.

Sarich, V.M. (1983). "Retrospective on Hominoid Macromolecular Systematics." In, R.L. Ciochon and R.S. Corruccini (eds.), *New Interpretations of Ape and Human Ancestry* (New York: Plenum Press), pp. 137–150.

Sarich, V.M. and J.E. Cronin (1976). "Molecular Systematics of the Primates." In, M. Goodman, R.E. Tashian and J.H. Tashian (eds.), *Molecular Anthropology: Genes and Proteins in the Evolutionary Ascent of the Primates* (New York: Plenum Press), pp. 141–170.

Sarich, V.M. and A.C. Wilson (1967). "Immunological Time Scale for Hominid Evolution." *Science*, 158: 1200–1203.

Sarmiento, E.E. (1987). "Long Bone Torsions of the Lower Limb and Its Bearing Upon the Locomotor Behavior of Australopithecines." *American Journal of Physical Anthropology*, 72: 250–251.

Sarmiento, E.E. (1996). "Quadrupedalism in the Hominid Lineage: 11 Years After." *American Journal of Physical Anthropology*, Supplement 22: 210.

Sarmiento, E.E. (1996). "Long Bone Torsions of the Lower Limb and Its Bearing Upon the Locomotor Behavior of Australopithecines." *American Journal of Physical Anthropology*, 72: 250–251.

Sartono, S. (1991). "*Homo (Pithecanthropus) erectus*: Le débat sans fin." *L'Anthropologie*, 95: 123–136.

Schaaffhausen, H. (1861). "On the Crania of the Most Ancient Races of Man." Translated from Müller's Archiv (1858) with remarks by G. Busk, *Natural History Review*, 1: 155–176.

Schaaffhausen, H. (1868). "On the Primitive Form of the Human Skull." *Anthropological Review*, 6: 412–431.

Schafersman, S.D. (1985). "Anatomy of a Controversy: Halstead Versus the British Museum (Natural History)." In, L.R. Godfrey (ed.), *What Darwin Began: Modern Darwinian and Non-Darwinian Perspectives on Evolution* (Boston: Allyn and Bacon), pp. 186–219.

Schepers, G.W.H. (1946). *The South African Fossil Ape-Men: The Australopithecinae, Part II, The Endocranial Casts of the South African Ape-Men* (Pretoria: Transvaal Museum Memoir No. 2, 1946), pp. 165–275.

Schick, K.D. and N. Toth (1993). *Making Silent Stones Speak: Human Evolution and the Dawn of Technology* (New York: Touchstone).

Schlosser, M. (1888). "Die Affen, Lemuren, Chiropteren, Insectivoren, Marsupialier, Creodonten und Carnivoren des Europäischen Tertiärs."

Beiträge zur Paläontologie Österreich-Ungarns und des Orients, 6: 1–224.

SCHLOSSER, M. (1911). "Beiträge zur Kenntniss der Oligozänen Landsäugetiere aus dem Fayum: Ägypten." *Beiträge zur Paläontologie und Geologie Österreich-Ungarns und des Orients*, 24: 51–167.

SCHMIDT, O. (1873). *Descendenzlehre und Darwinismus* (Leipzig).

SCHMIDT, O. (1884). *Die Saügethiere in ihrem Verhältniss zur Vorwelt* (Leipzig: F.A. Brockhaus).

SCHMIDT, O. (1887). *The Doctrine of Descent and Darwinism*, 7th edition (London: Kegan Paul, Trench).

SCHULTZ, A.H. (1924). "Growth Studies on Primates Bearing Upon Man's Evolution." *American Journal of Physical Anthropology*, 7: 149–164.

SCHULTZ, A.H. (1927). "Studies on the Growth of Gorilla and of Other Higher Primates With Special Reference to a Fetus of Gorilla, Preserved in the Carnegie Museum." *Memoirs of the Carnegie Museum*, 11: 1–86.

SCHULTZ, A.H. (1930). "The Skeleton of the Trunk and Limbs of Higher Primates." *Human Biology*, 2: 303–438.

SCHULTZ, A.H. (1936). "Characters Common to Higher Primates and Characters Specific for Man." *Quarterly Review of Biology*, 11: 259–283, 425–455.

SCHULTZ, A.H. (1950a). "The Specializations of Man and His Place Among the Catarrhine Primates." *Cold Spring Harbor Symposia on Quantitative Biology*, 15: 37–53.

SCHULTZ, A.H. (1950b). "The Physical Distinctions of Man." *Proceedings of the American Philosophical Society*, 94: 428–449.

SCHULTZ, A.H. (1953). "Man's Place among the Primates." *Man*, 53: 7–9.

SCHULTZ, A.H. (1963). "Age Changes, Sex Differences, and Variability as Factors in the Classification of Primates." In, S.L. Washburn (ed.), *Classification and Human Evolution* (Chicago: Aldine), pp. 85–115.

SCHULTZ, A.H. (1965). "Die rezenten Hominoidea." In, G. Heberer (ed.), *Menschliche Abstammungslehre* (Stuttgart, G. Fischer), pp. 56–102.

SCHULTZ, A.H. (1968). "The Recent Hominoid Primates." In, S.L. Washburn and P.C. Jay (eds.), *Perspectives on Human Evolution* (New York: Holt, Rinehart and Winston, 1968), pp. 122–195. Translated and revised from Schultz (1965).

SCHULTZ, A.H. (1969). *The Life of Primates* (New York: Universe Book).

SCHWALBE, G. (1899). "Studien über Pithecanthropus erectus Dubois." *Zeitschrift für Morphologie und Anthropologie*, 1: 16–240.

SCHWALBE, G. (1906). *Studien zur Vorgeschichte des Menschen* (Stuttgart: E. Schweizerbartsche).

SCHWALBE, G. (1909). "The Descent of Man." In, A.C. Seward (ed.), *Darwin and Modern Science* (Cambridge: Cambridge University Press), pp. 112–136.

SCHWALBE, G. (1910). "Studien zur Morphologie der südamerikanischen Primatenformen." *Zeitschrift für Morphologie und Anthropologie*, 13: 209–258.

SCHWARTZ, J.H. (1984). "The Evolutionary Relationships of Man and Orang-Utans." *Nature*, 308: 501–505.

SCHWARTZ, J.H AND I. TATTERSALL (2002–2005, eds.). *The Human Fossil Record*, 4 vols. (New York: Wiley-Liss).

SCHWARZ, E. (1934). "On the Local Races of the Chimpanzee." *Annals and Magazine of Natural History*, 13: 576–583.

SCHWARZ, E. (1936). "The Sterkfontein Ape." *Nature*, 138: 969.

SEAL, B. (1911). "Meaning of Race, Tribe, Nation." In, G. Spiller (ed.), *Papers on Inter-Racial Problems* (London: P.S. King & Son), pp. 3–13.

SELLARDS, E.H. (1916). "On the Discovery of Fossil Human Remains in Florida in Association with Extinct Vertebrates." *American Journal of Science*, 192: 1–18.

SENUT, B. (1996). "Pliocene Hominid Systematics and Phylogeny." *South African Journal of Science*, 92: 165–166.

SENUT, B. (2001). "L'émergence de la famille de l'homme." In, Y. Coppens and P. Picq (eds.), *Aux origines de l'humanité*, Vol. 1 (Paris: Fayard), p. 166–199.

SENUT, B., M. PICKFORD, D. GOMMERY, P. MEIN, K. CHEBOI AND Y. COPPENS (2001). "First Hominid from the Miocene (Lukeino Formation, Kenya)." *Comptes Rendus de l'Académie des Sciences de Paris*, series IIa, 332: 137–144.

SERA, G.L. (1918). "I caratteri della faccia e il polifiletismo dei primati." *Giornale per la Morfologia dell'Uomo e dei Primati*, 2: 1–296.

SERGI, G. (1908). *Europa* (Milano: Fratelli Bocca).

SERGI, G. (1909–10). "L'apologia del mio poligenismo." *Atti della Società Romana di Antropologia*, 15: 187–195.

SERGI, G. (1910). "Paléontologie sud-américaine." *Scientia*, 8: 465–475.

SERGI, G. (1911). *L'Uomo* (Torino: Fratelli Bocca).

SERGI, G. (1912). "Tasmanier und Australier. Hesperanthropus tasmanianus, spec." *Archiv für Anthropologie*, 11: 201–231.

SERGI, G. (1913). *Le origini umane: Ricerche paleontologiche* (Torino: Fratelli Bocca).

SERGI, G. (1914). *L'Evoluzione Organica e le Origini Umane: Induzioni paleontologiche* (Torino: Fratelli Bocca).

SIBLEY, C.G. AND J.E. AHLQUIST (1984). "The Phylogeny of the Hominoid Primates, as Indicated by DNA-DNA hybridization." *Journal of Molecular Evolution*, 20: 2–15.

SIBLEY, C.G. AND J.E. AHLQUIST (1987). "DNA Hybridization Evidence of Hominoid Phylogeny: Results From an Expanded Data Set." *Journal of Molecular Evolution*, 26: 99–121.

SIMONS, E.L. (1961). "The Phyletic Position of *Ramapithecus*." *Postilla*, 57: 1–9.

SIMONS, E.L. (1962). "Two New Primate Species From the African Oligocene." *Postilla*, 64: 1–12.

SIMONS, E.L. (1963). "Some Fallacies in the Study of Hominid Phylogeny." *Science*, 141: 879–889.

SIMONS, E.L. (1964a). "On the Mandibule of *Ramapithecus*." *Proceedings of the National Academy of Sciences*, 51: 528–535.

SIMONS, E.L. (1964b). "The Early Relatives of Man." *Scientific American*, 211: 50–62.

SIMONS, E.L. (1965). "New Fossil Apes from Egypt and the Initial Differentiation of Hominoidea." *Nature*, 205: 135–139.

SIMONS, E.L. (1967). "The Earliest Apes." *Scientific American*, 217: 28–35.

SIMONS, E.L. (1977). "Ramapithecus." *Scientific American*, 236 (5): 28–35.

SIMONS, E.L. (1995). "Egyptian Oligocene Primates: A Review." *Yearbook of Physical Anthropology*, 38: 199–238.

SIMONS, E.L. AND H.H. COVERT (1981). "Paleoprimatological Research Over the Last 50 Years: Foci and Trends." *American Journal of Physical Anthropology*, 56: 373–382.

SIMONS, E.L. AND D.R. PILBEAM (1965). "Preliminary Revision of the Dryopithecinae (Pongidae, Anthropoidea)." *Folia Primatologia*, 3: 81–152.

SIMPSON, G.G. (1944). *Tempo and Mode in Evolution* (New York: Columbia University Press).

SIMPSON, G.G. (1945). "The Principles of Classification and a Classification of Mammals." *Bulletin of the American Museum of Natural History*, 85: 1–350.

SIMPSON, G.G. (1949). *The Meaning of Evolution: A Study of the History of Life and of Its Significance for Man* (New Haven: Yale University Press).

Simpson, G.G. (1953). *The Major Features of Evolution* (New York: Columbia University Press).

SIMPON, G.G. (1962–63). "Primate Taxonomy and Recent Studies of Nonhuman Primates." *Annals of the New York Academy of Sciences*, 102: 497–514.

SIMPSON, G.G. (1963a). "The Meaning of Taxonomic Statements." In, S.L. Washburn (ed.), *Classification and Human Evolution* (Chicago: Aldine), p. 1–31.

SIMPSON, G.G. (1963b). "The Origin of Races by Carleton S. Coon." *Perspectives in Biology and Medicine*, 6: 268–272.

SIMPSON, G.G. (1966). "The Biological Nature of Man." *Science*, 152: 472–478.

SIMPSON, G.G. (1975). "Recent Advances in Methods of Phylogenetic Inference." In, W.P. Luckett and F.S. Szalay (eds.), *Phylogeny of the Primates* (New York: Plenum Press), pp. 3–19.

SKELTON, R.R. AND H.M. MCHENRY (1992). "Evolutionary Relationships Among Early Hominids." *Journal of Human Evolution*, 23: 309–349.

SKELTON, R.R., H.M. MCHENRY AND G.M. DRAWHORN (1986). "Phylogenetic Analysis of Early Hominids." *Current Anthropology*, 27: 21–43.

SMITH, F.H. (1984). "Fossil Hominids From the Upper Pleistocene of Central Europe and the Origin of Modern Europeans." In, F.H. Smith and F. Spencer (eds.), *The Origins of Modern Humans: A World Survey of the Fossil Evidence* (New York: Alan R. Liss, 1984), pp. 137–209.

SMITH, F.H. (1985). "Continuity and Change in the Origin of Modern *Homo sapiens*." *Zeitschrift für Morphologie und Anthropologie*, 75: 197–222.

SMITH, F.H. (1987). "Gustav Schwalbe: Neandertal Morphology and Systematics, 1899–1916." *Physical Anthropology News*, 6: 1–5.

SMITH, F.H. (1991). "The Neandertals: Evolutionary Dead Ends or Ancestors of Modern People?" *Journal of Anthropological Research*, 47: 219–238.

SMITH, F.H. (1992). "The Role of Continuity in Modern Human Origins." In, G. Bräuer and F.H. Smith (eds.), *Continuity or Replacement: Controversies in* Homo sapiens *evolution* (Rotterdam: A.A. Balkema, 1992), pp. 145–156.

SMITH, F.H. (1997a). "Neandertals." In, F. Spencer (ed.), *History of Physical Anthropology: An Encyclopedia*, vol. 2 (New York: Garland), pp. 711–722.

SMITH, F.H. (1997b). "Schwalbe, Gustav (1844–1916)." In, F. Spencer (ed.), *History of Physical Anthropology: An Encyclopedia*, vol. 2 (New York: Garland Publishing), pp. 916–918.

SMITH, F.H. (2002). "Migrations, Radiations and Continuity: Patterns in the Evolution of Middle and Late Pleistocene Humans." In, W.C. Hartwig (ed.), *The Primate Fossil Record* (Cambridge: Cambridge University Press), pp. 437–456.

SMITH, F.H., A.B. FALSETTI AND S.M. DONNELLY (1989). "Modern Human Origins." *Yearbook of Physical Anthropology*, 32: 35–68.

SMITH, S.L. AND F.B. HARROLD (1997). "A Paradigm's Worth of Difference? Understanding the Impasse Over Modern Human Origins." *Yearbook of Physical Anthropology*, 40: 113–138.

SMITH, S.A. (1918). "The Fossil Human Skull Found at Talgai, Queensland." *Philosophical Transactions of the Royal Society of London*, series B, 208: 351–387.

SMITH WOODWARD, A. (1908). "The Evolution of Mammals in South America." In *The Darwin-Wallace Celebration Held on Thursday, 1st July* (London: Linnean Society), pp. 79–80.

SMITH WOODWARD, A. (1921). "A New Cave Man from Rhodesia, South Africa." *Nature*, 108: 371–372.

SMITH WOODWARD, A. (1922). "A Supposed Ancestral Man in North America." *Nature*, 109: 750.

SMITH WOODWARD, A. (1925). "The Fossil Anthropoid Ape from Taungs." *Nature*, 115: 235–236.

SMOCOVITIS, V.S. (1996). *Unifying Biology: The Evolutionary Synthesis and Evolutionary Biology* (Princeton: Princeton University Press).

SMOUSE, P.E. AND W.-H. LI (1987). "Likelihood Analysis of Mitochondrial Restriction-Cleavage Patterns For the Human-Chimpanzee-Gorilla Trichotomy." *Evolution*, 41: 1162–1176.

SOLLAS, W.J. (1908). "On the Cranial and Facial Characters of the Neandertal Race." *Philosophical Transactions of the Royal Society of London*, series B, 199: 281–339.

SOLLAS, W.J. (1925). "The Taungs Skull." *Nature*, 115: 908–909.

SOLLAS, W.J. (1926). "On a Sagittal Section of the Skull of *Australopithecus africanus*." *Quarterly Journal of the Geological Society of London*, 82: 1–11.

SPENCER, F. (1984). "The Neandertals and Their Evolutionary Significance: A Brief Historical Survey." In, F.H. Smith and F. Spencer (eds.), *The Origins of Modern Humans: A World Survey of the Fossil Evidence* (New York: Alan R. Liss), pp. 1–49.

SPENCER, F. (1988). "Prologue to a Scientific Forgery: The British Eolithic Movement from Abbeville to Piltdown." In, G. Stocking (ed.), *Bones, Bodies, Behavior: Essays on Biological Anthropology* (Madison: University of Wisconsin Press), pp. 84–119.

SPENCER, F. (1990). *Piltdown: A Scientific Forgery* (Oxford: Oxford University Press).

SPENCER, F. (1997, ed.). *History of Physical Anthropology: An Encyclopedia*, 2 vols (New York: Garland).

SPENCER, F. AND F.H. SMITH (1981). "The Significance of Ales Hrdlicka's Neanderthal Phase of Man: A Historical and Current Assessment." *American Journal of Physical Anthropology*, 56: 435–459.

SPRING, A. (1864). "Les hommes d'Engis et les hommes de Chauvaux." *Bulletin de l'Académie royale des sciences, des lettres et des beaux-arts de Belgique*, 2e série, 18: 479–515.

STANLEY, S.M. (1975). "A Theory of Evolution Above the Species Level." *Proceedings of the Natural Academy of Sciences* (USA), 72: 646–650.

STANLEY, S.M. (1979). *Macroevolution: Pattern and Process* (San Francisco: W.H. Freeman).

STANYON, R. AND B. CHIARELLI (1982). "Phylogeny of the Hominoidea: The Chromosome Evidence." *Journal of Human Evolution*, 11: 493–504.

STEBBINS, G.L. AND F.J. AYALA (1981). "Is a New Evolutionary Synthesis Necessary?" *Science*, 213: 967–971.

STERN, J.T. (1975). "Before Bipedality." *Yearbook of Physical Anthropology*, 19: 59–68.

STERN, J.T. (2000). "Climbing to the Top: A Personal Memoir of *Australopithecus afarensis*." *Evolutionary Anthropology*, 9: 113–133.

STERN, J.T. AND R.L. SUSMAN (1981). "Electromyography of the Gluteal Muscles in *Hylobates, Pongo,* and *Pan*: Implications For the Evolution of Hominid Bipedality." *American Journal of Physical Anthropology*, 55: 153–166.

STERN, J.T. AND R.L. SUSMAN (1983). "The Locomotor Anatomy of *Australopithecus afarensis*." *American Journal of Physical Anthropology*, 60: 279–317.

STEWART, J.A. (1990). *Drifting Continents and Colliding Paradigms: Perspectives on the Geoscience Revolution* (Bloomington: Indiana University Press).

STOCK, C. (1924). "A Recent Discovery of Ancient Human Remains in Los Angeles, California." *Science*, 60: 2–5.

STOCZKOWSKI, W. (1994). *Anthropologie naïve, anthropologie savante: De l'origine de l'homme, de l'imagination et des idées reçues* (Paris: C.N.R.S.). Translated in English in 2002.

STOCZKOWSKI, W. (2002). *Explaining Human Origins: Myth, Imagination and Conjecture* (Cambridge: Cambridge University Press).

STOLYHWO, K. (1911). "Contribution à l'étude de l'homme fossile sud-américain et de son prétendu précurseur le Diprothomo platensis." *Bulletins et Mémoires de la Société d'Anthropologie de Paris*, 6ième série, 2: 158–168.

STOLYHWO, K. (1912). "Zur Frage einer neuen polygenistischen Theorie der Abstammung des Menschen." *Zeitschrift für Ethnologie*, 44: 97–104.

STONEKING, M. (1993). "DNA and Recent Human Evolution." *Evolutionary Anthropology*, 2: 60–73.

STRAIT, D.S., F.E. GRINE AND M.A. MONIZ (1997). "A Reappraisal of Early Hominid Phylogeny." *Journal of Human Evolution*, 32: 17–82.

STRAUS, W.L. (1940). "The Posture of the Great Ape Hand in Locomotion, and Its Phylogenetic Implications." *American Journal of Physical Anthropology*, 27: 199–207.

STRAUS, W.L. (1948a). "The Limb Bones of Australopithecines." *American Journal of Physical Anthropology*, 6: 237–238.

STRAUS, W.L. (1948b). "The Humerus of *Paranthropus robustus*." *American Journal of Physical Anthropology*, 6: 285–311.

STRAUS, W.L. (1949). "The Riddle of Man's Ancestry." *Quarterly Review of Biology*, 24: 200–223.

STRAUS, W.L. (1953). "Primates." In, *Anthropology Today: An Encyclopedic Inventory*, A.L. Kroeber (ed.), Chicago: University of Chicago Press, pp. 77–92.

STRAUS, W.L. (1957). "*Oreopithecus bambolii*." *Science*, 126: 345–346.

STRAUS, W.L. (1961). "Primate Taxonomy and *Oreopithecus*." *Science*, 133: 760–761.

STRAUS, W.L. (1962). "The Riddle of Man's Ancestry [1949], with Additional Notes." In, *Ideas on Human Evolution: Selected Essays, 1949–1961*, W.W. Howells (ed.), Cambridge, Harvard University Press, pp. 69–104.

STRAUS, W.L. (1963). "The Classification of *Oreopithecus*." In, S.L. Washburn (ed.), *Classification and Human Evolution* (Chicago, Aldine), pp. 146–177.

STRINGER, C.B. (1974). "Population Relationships of Later Pleistocene Hominids: A Multivariate Study of Available Crania." *Journal of Archaeological Science*, 1: 317–342.

STRINGER, C.B. (1978). "Some Problems in Middle and Upper Pleistocene Hominid Relationships." In, D.J. Chivers and K.A. Joysey (eds.), *Recent Advances in Primatology*, Vol. 3 (New York: Academic Press), pp. 395–418.

STRINGER, C.B. (1985). "Middle Pleistocene Hominid Variability and the Origin of Late Pleistocene Humans." In, E. Delson (ed.), *Ancestors: The Hard Evidence* (New York: Aland R. Liss), pp. 289–295.

STRINGER, C.B. (1986). "The Credibility of *Homo habilis*." In, B. Wood, L. Martin and P. Andrews (eds.), *Major Topics in Primate and Human Evolution* (Cambridge: Cambridge University Press), pp. 266–294.

STRINGER, C.B. (1990). "The Emergence of Modern Humans." *Scientific American*, 263: 98–104.

STRINGER, C.B. (1994). "Out of Africa: A Personal History." In, M.H. Nitecki and D.V. Nitecki (eds.), *Origins of Anatomically Modern Humans* (New York: Plenum Press), pp. 149–172.

STRINGER, C.B. AND P. ANDREWS (1988). "Genetic and Fossil Evidence for the Origin of Modern Humans." *Science*, 239: 1263–1268.

STRINGER, C.B. AND G. BRÄUER (1994). "Methods, Misreading, and Bias." *American Anthropologist*, 96: 416–424.

Stringer, C.B. and C. Gamble (1993). *In Search of the Neanderthals: Solving the Puzzle of Human Origins* (London: Thames and Hudson).

Stringer, C.B. and R. McKie (1996). *African Exodus: The Origins of Modern Humanity* (New York: Henry Holt).

Susman, R.L. (1994). "Fossil Evidence for Early Hominid Tool Use." *Science*, 265: 1570–1572.

Susman, R.L. (1998). "Hand Function and Tool Behavior in Early Hominids." *Journal of Human Evolution*, 35: 23–46.

Susman, R.L. and J.T. Stern (1982). "Functional Morphology of *Homo habilis*." *Science*, 217: 931–933.

Susman, R.L., J.T. Stern and W.L. Jungers (1984). "Arborality and Bipedality in the Hadar Hominids." *Folia Primatologia*, 43: 113–156.

Suwa, G., T.D. White and F.C. Howell (1996). "Mandibular Postcanine Dentition from the Shungura Formation, Ethiopia: Crown Morphology, Taxonomic Allocations, and Plio-Pleistocene Hominid Evolution." *American Journal of Physical Anthropology*, 101: 247–282.

Swisher, C.C., W.J. Rink, S.C. Anton, H.P. Schwarcz, G.H. Curtis, A. Suprijo, and Widiasmoro (1996). "Latest *Homo erectus* of Java: Potential Contemporaneity With *Homo sapiens* in Southeast Asia." *Science*, 274: 1870–1874.

Szalay, F.S. (1981). "Functional Analysis and the Practice of the Phylogenetic Method as Reflected by Some Mammalian Studies." *American Zoologist*, 21: 37–45.

Szalay, F.S. (1991). "The Unresolved World Between Taxonomy and Population Biology: What Is, and What Is Not, Macroevolution." *Journal of Human Evolution*, 20: 271–280.

Szalay, F.S. and E. Delson (1979). *Evolutionary History of the Primates* (New York: Academic Press).

Takahata, N. and Y. Satta (1997). "Evolution of the Primate Lineage Leading to Modern Humans: Phylogenetic and Demographic Inferences From DNA Sequences." *Proceedings of the National Academy of Sciences* (USA), 94: 4811–4815.

Tattersall, I. (1986). "Species Recognition in Human Paleontology." *Journal of Human Evolution*, 15: 165–175.

Tattersall, I. (1993). *The Human Odyssey: Four Million Years of Human Evolution* (New York: Prentice Hall).

Tattersall, I. (1994). "How Does Evolution Work?" *Evolutionary Anthropology*, 3: 2–3.

Tattersall, I. (1995). *The Fossil Trail: How We Know What We Think We Know about Human Evolution* (Oxford: Oxford University Press).

Tattersall, I. (1997). "Out of Africa Again . . . and Again?" *Scientific American*, 276(4): 60–67.

Tattersall, I. (1998). *Becoming Human: Evolution and Human Uniqueness* (New York: Harcourt Brace & Co.).

Tattersall, I. (2000). "Paleoanthropology: The Last Half-Century." *Evolutionary Anthropology*, 9: 2–16.

Tattersall, I. and N. Eldredge (1977). "Fact, Theory, and Fantasy in Human Paleontology." *American Scientist*, 65: 204–211.

Tattersall, I. and J.H. Schwartz (2000). *Extinct Humans* (Colorado: Westview Press).

Taylor, G. (1919). "Climatic Cycles and Evolution." *The Geographical Review*, 8: 289–328.

Taylor, G. (1921). "The Evolution and Distribution of Race, Culture, and Language." *Geographical Review*, 11: 54–119.

Taylor, G. (1927). *Environment and Race: A Study of the Evolution, Migration, Settlement, and Status of the Races of Man* (Oxford: Oxford University Press).

Taylor, G. (1930). "Racial Migration-Zones and their Significance." *Human Biology*, 2: 34–62.

Taylor, G. (1934). "The Ecological Basis of Anthropology." *Ecology*, 15: 223–242.

Taylor, G. (1936). "The Zones and Strata Theory—A Biological Classification of Races." *Human Biology*, 8: 348–367.

Taylor, G. (1937). *Environment, Race, and Migration: Fundamentals of Human Distribution* (Toronto: University of Toronto Press).

Taylor, G. (1945). *Environment, Race and Migration*, 2nd edition (Toronto: University of Toronto Press).

Templeton, A.R. (1985). "The Phylogeny of the Hominoid Primates: A Statistical Analysis of the DNA-DNA Hybridization Data." *Molecular Biology and Evolution*, 2: 420–433.

Templeton, A.R. (2002). "Out of Africa Again and Again." *Nature*, 416: 45–51.

Thenius, E. (1958). "Tertiärstratigraphie und tertiäre Hominoidenfunde." *Anthropologischer Anzeiger*, 22: 66–77.

THEUNISSEN, B. (1989). *Eugène Dubois and the Ape-Man from Java: The History of the First 'Missing Link' and its Discoverer* (Dordrecht: Kluwer Academic Publishers).

THOMA, A. (1962). "Le déploiement évolutif de l'*Homo sapiens*." *Anthropologia Hungarica*, 5: 1–111.

THOMA, A. (1965). "La définition des néanderthaliens et la position des hommes fossiles de Palestine." *L'Anthropologie*, 69: 519–534.

THOMA, A. (1971). "L'évolution polycentrique de l'*Homo sapiens*." In, F. Bordes (ed.), *Origine de l'homme moderne* (Paris: Unesco), pp. 81–85. With an English summary.

THOMA, A. (1973). "New Evidence for the Polycentric Evolution of *Homo sapiens*." *Journal of Human Evolution*, 2: 529–536.

THOMA, A. (1985). *Éléments de paléoanthropologie* (Louvain-La-Neuve: Institut supérieur d'archéologie et d'histoire de l'art).

THORNE, A.G. AND M.H. WOLPOFF (1981). "Regional Continuity in Australasian Pleistocene Hominid Evolution." *American Journal of Physical Anthropology*, 55: 337–349.

THORNE, A.G. AND M.H. WOLPOFF (1992). "The Multiregional Evolution of Humans." *Scientific American*, 266: 28–33.

THURNAM, J. (1863–1864a). "On the Two Principal Forms of Ancient British and Gaulish Skulls." *Memoirs Read Before the Anthropological Society of London*, 1: 120–168.

THURNAM, J. (1863–1864b). "On the two principal forms of Ancient British and Gaulish Skulls. Part II." *Memoirs Read Before the Anthropological Society of London*, 1: 459–519.

TIXIER, J., M.L. INIXAN AND H. ROCHE (1980). *Préhistoire de la pierre taillée* (Valbonne: Cercle de Recherches et d'Études Préhistoriques).

TOBIAS, P.V. (1965a). "Early Man in East Africa." *Science*, 149: 22–33.

TOBIAS, P.V. (1965b). "New Discoveries in Tanganyika: Their Bearing on Hominid Evolution." *Current Anthropology*: 6: 391–411.

TOBIAS, P.V. (1966a). "Fossil Hominid Remains From Ubeidiya, Israel." *Nature*, 211: 130–133.

TOBIAS, P.V. (1966b). "The Distinctiveness of *Homo habilis*." *Nature*, 209: 953–957.

TOBIAS, P.V. (1967). *Olduvai Gorge, Vol. 2: The Cranium and Maxillary Dentition of* Australopithecus (Zinjanthropus) boisei (Cambridge: Cambridge University Press).

TOBIAS, P.V. (1968). "The Taxonomy and Phylogeny of the Australopithecines." In, B. Chiarelli (ed.), *Taxonomy and Phylogeny of Old World Primates With References to the Origin of Man* (Torino: Rosenberg & Sellier), pp. 277–315.

TOBIAS, P.V. (1971). *The Brain in Hominid Evolution* (New York: Columbia University Press).

TOBIAS, P.V. (1978). "Primatology, Palaeoanthropology and Reticulate Evolution." In, D.J. Chivers and K.A. Joysey (eds.), *Recent Advances in Primatology*, Vol. 3 (London: Academic Press), pp. 507–509.

TOBIAS, P.V. (1980a). "L'évolution du cerveau humain." *La Recherche*, 109: 282–292.

TOBIAS, P.V. (1980b). "'*Australopithecus afarensis*' and *A. africanus*: Critique and an Alternative Hypothesis." *Palaeontologia Africana*, 23: 1–17.

TOBIAS, P.V. (1981). "The Emergence of Man in Africa and Beyond." *Philosophical Transactions of the Royal Society of London*, B 292: 43–56.

TOBIAS, P.V. (1984). *Dart, Taung and the 'Missing Link'* (Johannesburg: Witwatersrand University Press).

TOBIAS, P.V. (1985). "Punctuational and Phyletic Evolution in the Hominids." In, E.S. Vrba (ed.), *Species and Speciation* (Pretoria: Transvaal Museum Monograph No. 4), pp. 131–141.

TOBIAS, P.V. (1987). "The Brain of *Homo habilis*: A New Level of Organization in Cerebral Evolution." *Journal of Human Evolution*, 16: 741–761.

TOBIAS, P.V. (1988). "Numerous Apparently Synapomorphic Features in *Australopithecus robustus*, *Australopithecus boisei* and *Homo habilis*: Support for the Skelton-McHenry-Drawhorn Hypothesis." In, F.E. Grine (ed.), *Evolutionary History of the 'Robust' Australopithecines* (New York: Aldine de Gruyter), pp. 293–308.

TOBIAS, P.V. (1991). *Olduvai Gorge, Vol. 4. The Skulls, Endocasts and Teeth of* Homo habilis (Cambridge: Cambridge University Press).

TOBIAS, P.V. (1992). "Piltdown: An Appraisal of the Case against Sir Arthur Keith." *Current Anthropology*, 33: 243–293.

TOBIAS, P.V. (1994). "The Craniocerebral Interface in Early Hominids." In, R.S. Corruccini and R.L. Ciochon (eds.), *Integrative Paths to the Past* (New Jersey: Prentice Hall), pp. 185–203.

Tobias, P.V. (1995). "The Place of *Homo erectus* in Nature With A Critique of the Cladistic Approach." In, J.R.F. Bower and S. Sartono (eds.), *Human Evolution in Its Ecological Context*, Vol. 1, *Palaeo-anthropology: Evolution and Ecology of* Homo erectus (Leiden: Pithecanthropus Centennial Foundation), pp. 31–41.

Tobias, P.V. (1998). "Evidence for the Early Beginnings of Spoken Language." *Cambridge Archaeological Journal*, 8: 72–78.

Tobias, P.V. (2002). "The South African early fossil hominids and John Talbot Robinson (1923–2001)." *Journal of Human Evolution*, 43: 563–576.

Tobias, P.V. and von Koenigswald, G.H.R. (1964). "A Comparison Between the Olduvai Hominines and Those of Java and Some Implications for Hominid Phylogeny." *Nature*, 204: 515–518.

Topinard, P. (1876). *L'Anthropologie* (Paris: Reinwald).

Topinard, P. (1886). "Les caractères simiens de la mâchoire de la Naulette." *Revue d'Anthropologie*, 3e série, 1: 385–431.

Topinard, P. (1888). "Les dernières étapes de la généalogie de l'homme." *Revue d'Anthropologie*, 3: 298–332.

Topinard, P. (1890). *Anthropology*, 2nd edition (London: Chapman and Hall).

Topinard, P. (1891). *L'Homme dans la nature* (Paris, Félix Alcan).

Topinard, P. (1892). "De l'évolution des molaires et prémolaires chez les primates et en particulier chez l'homme." *L'Anthropologie*, 3: 641–710.

Topinard, P. (1895). "Revue de Turner sur la description de M. Dubois des restes récemment trouvés à Java et attribués par lui à un Pithecanthropus erectus." *L'Anthropologie*, 6: 605–607.

Trigger, B.G. (1989). *A History of Archaeological Thought* (Cambridge: Cambridge University Press).

Trinkaus, E. and P. Shipman, (1993). *The Neandertals: Changing the Image of Mankind* (New York: Alfred A. Knopf).

Trouessart, E. (1892). "Les primates tertiaires et l'homme fossile sud-américain." *L'Anthropologie*, 3: 257–274.

Turner, A. and A. Chamberlain (1989). "Speciation, Morphological Change and the Status of African *Homo erectus*." *Journal of Human Evolution*, 18: 115–130.

Turner, W. (1864a). "On Human Crania Allied in Anatomical Characters to the Engis and Neanderthal Skulls." *Quarterly Journal of Science*, 1: 250–259.

Turner, W. (1864b). "Additional Note on the Neanderthal Skull." *Quarterly Journal of Science*, 1: 758–760.

Turner, W. (1895). "On M. Dubois' Description of Remains Recently Found in Java, Named By Him *Pithecanthropus erectus*. With Remarks on So-called Transitional Forms Between Apes and Man." *Journal of Anatomy and Physiology*, 29: 424–445.

Tuttle, R.H. (1969). "Knuckle-Walking and the Problem of Human Origins." *Science*, 166: 953–961.

Tuttle, R.H. (1974). "Darwin's Apes, Dental Apes, and the Descent of Man: Normal Science in Evolutionary Anthropology." *Current Anthropology*, 15: 389–426.

Tuttle, R.H. (1975). "Parallelism, Brachiation, and Hominoid Phylogeny." In, W.P. Luckett and F.S. Szalay (eds.), *Phylogeny of the Primates* (New York: Plenum Press), pp. 447–480.

Tuttle, R.H. (1981). "Evolution of Hominis Bipedalism and Prehensible Capabilities." *Philosophical Transactions of the Royal Society of London*, B 292: 89–94.

Tuttle, R.H. (1985). "Ape Footprints and Laetoli Impressions: A Response to the Suny Claims." In, P.V. Tobias (ed.), *Hominid Evolution: Past, Present and Future* (New York: Alan R. Liss), pp. 129–133.

Tuttle, R.H. (1994). "Up From Electromyography: Primate Energetics and the Evolution of Human Bipedalism." In, R.S. Corruccini and R.L. Ciochon (eds.), *Integrative Paths to the Past* (New Jersey: Prentice Hall), pp. 269–284.

Tyler, D.E. and S. Sartono (2001). "A New *Homo erectus* Cranium From Sangiran, Java." *Human Evolution*, 16: 13–25.

Urbain, A. and P. Rode (1948). *Les singes anthropoïdes*, 2nd edition (Paris: Presses Universitaires de France).

Vallois, H.V. (1927). "Y a-t-il plusieurs souches humaines?" *Revue générale des Sciences pures et appliquées*, 38: 201–209.

VALLOIS, H.V. (1929). "Les preuves anatomiques de l'origine monophylétique de l'homme." *L'Anthropologie*, 39: 77–101.

VALLOIS, H.V. (1935). "Le Javanthropus." *L'Anthropologie*, 45: 71–84.

VALLOIS, H.V. (1949a). "L'origine de l'*Homo sapiens*." *Comptes Rendus des Séances de l'Académie des Sciences*, 228: 949–951.

VALLOIS, H.V. (1949b). "The Fontéchevade Fossil Men." *American Journal of Physical Anthropology*, 7: 339–362.

VALLOIS, H.V. (1950). "La paléontologie et l'origine de l'homme." In, *Paléontologie et transformisme* (Paris: Albin Michel), pp. 53–86.

VALLOIS, H.V. (1952). "Monophyletism and Polyphyletism in Man." *South African Journal of Science*, 49: 69–79.

VALLOIS, H.V. (1954). "Neandertals and Praesapiens." *Journal of the Royal Anthropological Institute*, 84: 111–130.

VALLOIS, H.V. (1955a). "L'ordre des primates." In, P.-P. Grassé (ed.), *Traité de zoologie: Anatomie, systématique, biologie*, Tome XVII, 2ième partie (Paris: Masson), pp. 1854–2206.

VALLOIS, H.V. (1955b). "A propos de l'énigme de Piltdown." *Atomes*, 10: 81–86.

VALLOIS, H.V. (1956). "Les théories sur l'origine de l'homme." *La Nature*, 84: 121–127.

VALLOIS, H.V. (1957). "Les singes géants fossiles de la Chine quaternaire." *La Nature*, 85: 386–390.

VALLOIS, H.V. (1958). *La grotte de Fontéchevade*. Deuxième partie, Anthropologie, Archives de l'Institut de Paléontologie Humaine, mémoire 29 (Paris: Masson).

VALLOIS, H.V. (1961). "L'origine de l'homme: État actuel de la question." *Le Concours Médical*, 83: 4745–4751, 4907–4914.

VALLOIS, H.V. (1962). "The Origin of Homo sapiens." In, W.W. Howells (ed.), *Ideas on Human Evolution: Selected Essays, 1949–1961* (Cambridge: Harvard University Press), pp. 473–499. English translation of Chapter 5 of *La Grotte de Fontéchevade* (1958).

VAN DÜBEN, G. (1865). "Sur les crânes de l'âge de pierre, en Suède." *Bulletins de la Société d'Anthropologie de Paris*, 6: 168–170.

VAN RIPER, A.B. (1993). *Men Among the Mammoths: Victorian Science and the Discovery of Human Prehistory* (Chicago: University of Chicago Press).

VERNEAU, R. (1886). "La race de Cro-Magnon: ses migrations, ses descendants." *Revue d'Anthropologie*, 3e série, 1: 10–24.

VERNEAU, R. (1902). "Les fouilles du Prince de Monaco aux Baoussé-Roussé: un nouveau type humain." *L'Anthropologie*, 13: 561–585.

VERNEAU, R. (1906a). Les grottes de Grimaldi: résumé et conclusions des études anthropologiques." *L'Anthropologie*, 17: 291–320.

VERNEAU, R. (1906b). "La race de Spy ou de Néanderthal." *Revue de l'École d'Anthropologie de Paris*, 16: 388–400.

VERNEAU, R. (1924). "La race de Néanderthal et la race de Grimaldi; leur rôle dans l'humanité." *Journal of the Royal Anthropological Institute*, 54: 211–320.

VIGILANT, L., M. STONEKING, H. HARPENDING, K. HAWKES, AND A.C. WILSON (1991). "African Populations and the Evolution of Human Mitochondrial DNA." *Science*, 253: 1503–1507.

VIRCHOW, R. (1867). "Sur les anciens crânes du nord-est de l'Allemagne et sur la méthode pour juger leurs particularités." *Congrès International d'Anthropologie et d'Archéologie Préhistoriques*, 2e session, pp. 406–407.

VIRCHOW, R. (1872). "Untersuchung des Neanderthal-Schädels." *Verhandlungen der Berliner Gesellschaft für Anthropologie, Ethnologie und Urgeschichte*, pp. 157–165.

VIRCHOW, R. (1874). "Discussion." *Congrès International d'Anthropologie et d'Archéologie Préhistoriques*, 7e session, pp. 327–328.

VIRCHOW, R. (1882). "Der Kiefer aus der Schipka-Höhle und der Kiefer von La Naulette." *Zeitschrift für Ethnologie*, 14: 277–310.

VIRCHOW, R. (1895). "On Pithecanthropus." *Zeitschrift für Ethnologie*, 27: 81–88, 435–440, 648–657, 744–747.

VOGT, C. (1864a). *Lectures on Man: His Place in Creation, and in the History of the Earth* (London: Longman, Green, Longman, and Roberts).

VOGT, C. (1864b). *Vorlesungen über den Menschen, seine Stellung in der Schöpfung und in der Geschichte der Erde*, 2 Vols. (Giessen).

VOGT, C. (1867a). *Mémoire sur les microcéphales ou hommes-singes* (Genève-Bâle: H. Georg).

VOGT, C. (1867b). "The Primitive Period of the Human Species." *Anthropological Review*, 5: 204–221, 334–350.

VOGT, C. AND F. SPECHT (1882). *Die Säugethiere in Wort und Bild* (München).

VOGT, C. AND F. SPECHT (1887). *The Natural History of Animals (Mammalia) in Word and Picture*, Vol. 1 (London: Blackie & Son).

VON BONIN, G. (1911). "Klaatsch's Theory of the Descent of Man." *Nature*, 85: 508–509.

VON BUTTEL-REEPEN, H. (1913). *Man and His Forerunners* (London: Longmans, Green and Co.).

VON EICKSTEDT, E. (1934). *Rassenkunde und Rassengeschichte der Menschheit* (Stuttgart: F. Enke).

VON EICKSTEDT, E. (1950). "The Science and History of the Human Races." In, E.W. Count (ed.), *This Is Race: An Anthology Selected from the International Literature on the Races of Man* (New York: Henry Schuman), pp. 489–514.

VON KOENIGSWALD, G.H.R. (1935). "Eine fossile Säugetierfauna mit Simia aus Südchina." *Proceedings of the Section of Sciences*, 38: 872–879.

VON KOENIGSWALD, G.H.R. (1937). "A Review of the Stratigraphy of Java and its Relations to Early Man." In, G.G. MacCurdy (ed.), *Early Man* (New York: Freeport), pp. 23–32.

VON KOENIGSWALD, G.H.R. (1940). "Neue Pithecanthropus-Funde, 1936–1938: Ein Beitrag zur Kenntnis der Praehominiden." *Wetenschappelijke Mededeelingen*, 28: 1–234.

VON KOENIGSWALD, G.H.R. (1942). "The South African Man-Apes and Pithecanthropus." *Carnegie Institution of Washington Publication* No. 530 (Washington, D.C.), pp. 205–222.

VON KOENIGSWALD, G.H.R. (1949). "The Discovery of Early Man in Java and Southern China." In, W.W. Howells (ed.), *Early Man in the Far East* (American Anthropological Association), pp. 83–98.

VON KOENIGSWALD, G.H.R. (1951). "Remarks on Indopithecus: A Reply." *American Journal of Physical Anthropology*, 9: 461–464.

VON KOENIGSWALD, G.H.R. (1952). "*Gigantopithecus blacki* von Koenigswald, a Giant Fossil Hominoid from the Pleistocene of Southern China." *Anthropological Papers of the American Museum of Natural History*, 43: 293–325.

VON KOENIGSWALD, G.H.R. (1953). "Die Phylogenie des Menschen." *Die Naturwissenschaften*, 40: 128–137.

VON KOENIGSWALD, G.H.R. (1954). "*Pithecanthropus, Meganthropus* and the Australopithecinae." *Nature*, 173: 795–797.

VON KOENIGSWALD, G.H.R. (1955). "Remarks on Oreopithecus." *Rivista di Scienze Preistoriche*, 10: 1–11.

VON KOENIGSWALD, G.H.R. (1956). *Meeting Prehistoric Man* (New York: Harper and Brothers).

VON KOENIGSWALD, G.H.R. (1957). "Meganthropus and the Australopithecinae." *Third Pan-African Congress on Prehistory*, Livingston 1955 (London: Chatto & Windus), pp. 158–160.

VON KOENIGSWALD, G.H.R. (1958). "L'hominisation de l'appareil masticateur et les modifications du régime alimetaire." In, *Les processus de l'hominisation*, Colloques Internationaux du Centre National de la Recherche Scientifique (Paris: C.N.R.S.), pp. 59–78.

VON KOENIGSWALD, G.H.R. (1960). *Die Geschichte des Menschen* (Berlin: Springer-Verlag).

VON KOENIGSWALD, G.H.R. (1962). *The Evolution of Man* (Ann Arbor: University of Michigan Press).

VON KOENIGSWALD, G.H.R. (1963). "Zur Systematic der Hominiden." *Zeitschrift für Morphologie und Anthropologie*, 53: 124–138.

VON KOENIGSWALD, G.H.R. (1964). "Early Man: Facts and Fantasy." *Journal of the Royal Anthropological Institute*, 94: 67–79.

VON KOENIGSWALD, G.H.R. (1965). "Die phylogenetische Stellung der Australopithecinen." *Anthropologischer Anzeiger*, 27: 273–277.

VON KOENIGSWALD, G.H.R. (1968). *Die Geschichte des Menschen*, 2nd edition (Berlin: Springer-Verlag).

VON KOENIGSWALD, G.H.R. (1973). "*Australopithecus, Meganthropus* and *Ramapithecus*." *Journal of Human Evolution*, 2: 487–491.

VON KOENIGSWALD, G.H.R. (1975). "Early Man in Java: Catalogue and Problems." In, R.H. Tuttle (ed.), *Paleoanthropology: Morphology and Paleoecology* (The Hague: Mouton), pp. 303–309.

VON KOENIGSWALD, G.H.R. (1976). *The Evolution of Man*, 2nd edition (Ann Arbor: University of Michigan Press).

Von Koenigswald, G.H.R. and F. Weidenreich (1939). "The Relationship Between Pithecanthropus and Sinanthropus." *Nature*, 144: 926–929.

Von Zittel, K. (1893a). *Handbuch der Palaeontologie*, Vol. 4 (Leipzig: R. Oldenbourg).

Von Zittel, K. (1893b). "The Geological Development, Descent, and Distribution of the Mammalia." *Geological Magazine*, 10: 401–412, 455–468, 501–514.

Von Zittel, K. (1926). *Textbook of Palaeontology*, Vol. 3 (London: Macmillan).

Vrba, E.S. and E. Eldredge (1984). "Individuals, Hierarchies and Processes: Towards a More Complete Evolutionary Theory." *Paleobiology*, 10: 146–171.

Wadia, D.N. and N.K.N. Aiyengar (1938). "Fossil Anthropoids of India: A List of the Fossil Material Hitherto Discovered From the Tertiary Deposits of India." *Record of the Geological Survey of India*, 72: 467–494.

Wainscoat, J.S., A.V.S. Hill, A.L. Boyce, J. Flint, M. Hernandez, S.L. Thein, J.M. Old, J.R. Lynch, A.G. Falusi, D.J. Weatherall and J.B. Clegg (1986). "Evolutionary Relationships of Human Populations From an Analysis of Nuclear DNA Polymorphisms." *Nature*, 319: 491–493.

Walker, A. and R.E.F. Leakey (1993, eds.). *The Nariokotome* Homo erectus *Skeleton* (Cambridge: Harvard University Press).

Walker, A., R.E.F. Leakey, J.M. Harris and F.H. Brown (1986). "2.5-Myr *Australopithecus boisei* from West of Lake Turkana, Kenya." *Nature*, 322: 517–522.

Walker, A. and P. Shipman (1997). *The Wisdom of the Bones: In Search of Human Origins* (New York: Vintage Books).

Wallace, A.R. (1864). "The Origin of Human Races and the Antiquity of Man deduced from the Theory of 'Natural Selection'." *Journal of the Anthropological Society of London*, 2: clviii–clxxxvii.

Wallace, A.R. (1889). *Darwinism: An Exposition of the Theory of Natural Selection With Some of its Applications* (London: Macmillan).

Ward, C.V. (2002). "Interpreting the Posture and Locomotion of *Australopithecus afarensis*: Where Do We Stand?" *Yearbook of Physical Anthropology*, 45: 185–215.

Ward, C.V., M.G. Leakey and A. Walkey (2001). "Morphology of *Australopithecus anamemsis* From Kanapoi and Allia Bay, Kenya." *Journal of Human Evolution*, 41: 255–368.

Ward, S.C. and D.L. Duren (2002). "Middle and Late Miocene African Hominoids." In, W.C. Hartwig (ed.), *The Primate Fossil Record* (Cambridge: Cambridge University Press), pp. 385–397.

Washburn, S.L. (1950). "The Analysis of Primate Evolution With Particular Reference to the Origin of Man." *Cold Spring Harbor Symposia on Quantitative Biology*, 15: 67–78.

Washburn, S.L. (1957). "Australopithecines: The Hunters or the Hunted?" *American Anthropologist*, 59: 612–614.

Washburn, S.L. (1959). "Speculations on the Interrelations of the History of Tools and Biological Evolution." *Human Biology*, 31: 21–31.

Washburn, S.L. (1960). "Tools and Human Evolution." *Scientific American*, 203 (3): 63–75.

Washburn, S.L. (1963a). "Behavior and Human Evolution." In, S.L. Washburn (ed.), *Classification and Human Evolution* (Chicago: Aldine), pp. 190–203.

Washburn, S.L. (1963b). "Preface." In, S.L. Washburn (ed.), *Classification and Human Evolution* (Chicago: Aldine), p. v.

Washburn, S.L. (1968). "Speculations on the Problem of Man's Coming to the Ground." In, B. Rothblatt (ed.), *Changing Perepctives on Man* (Chicago: University of Chicago Press), pp. 193–206.

Washburn, S.L. (1971). "The Study of Human Evolution." In, P. Dolhinow and V. Sarich (eds.), *Background For Man: Readings in Physical Anthropology* (Boston: Little, Brown and Company), pp. 82–117.

Washburn, S.L. (1985). "Human Evolution After Raymond Dart." In, P.V. Tobias (ed.), *Hominid Evolution: Past, Present and Future* (New York: Alan R. Liss), pp. 3–18.

Washburn, S.L. and F.C. Howell (1960). "Human Evolution and Culture." In, S. Tax (ed.), *The Evolution of Man: Man, Culture and Society* (Chicago: University of Chicago Press), pp. 33–56.

Washburn, S.L. and C.S. Lancaster (1968). "The Evolution of Hunting." In, R.B. Lee and I. DeVore (eds.), *Man the Hunter* (New York: Aldine), pp. 293–303.

WECKLER, J.E. (1954). "The Relationships Between Neanderthal Man and Homo sapiens." *American Anthropologist*, 56: 1003–1025.

WECKLER, J.E. (1957). "Neanderthal Man." *Scientific American*, 197: 89–96.

WECKLER, J.E. (1964). "Comments on Brace's 'The Fate of the Classic Neanderthals." *Current Anthropology*, 5: 31–32.

WEGNER, R.N. (1910). "A New Theory of the Descent of Man." *Nature*, 85: 119–121.

WEIDENREICH, F. (1940). "Some Problems Dealing With Ancient Man." *American Anthropologist*, 42: 375–383.

WEIDENREICH, F. (1941). "The Brain and its Rôle in the Phylogenetic Transformation of the Human Skull." *Transactions of the American Philosophical Society*, New Series, 31: 321–442.

WEIDENRIECH, F. (1943a). "The Skull of Sinanthropus Pekinensis: A Comparative Study on a Primitive Hominid Skull." *Palaeontologia Sinica*, New Series D, 10: 1–289.

WEIDENREICH, F. (1943b). "The 'Neanderthal Man' and the Ancestors of '*Homo sapiens*'." *American Anthropologist*, 45: 39–49.

WEIDENREICH, F. (1945). "Giant Early Man From Java and South China." *Anthropological Papers of the American Museum of Natural History*, 40: 5–134.

WEIDENREICH, F. (1946a). *Apes, Giants and Man* (Chicago: University of Chicago Press).

WEIDENREICH, F. (1946b). "Generic, Specific and Subspecific Characters in Human Evolution." *American Journal of Physical Anthropology*, 4: 413–431.

WEIDENREICH, F. (1947a). "Facts and Speculations Concerning the Origin of *Homo sapiens*." *American Anthropologist*, 49: 187–203.

WEIDENREICH, F. (1947b). "The Trend of Human Evolution." *Evolution*, 1: 221–236.

WEIDENREICH, F. (1948). "About the Morphological Character of the Australopithecinae Skull." In, A.L. Du Toit (ed.), *Robert Broom Commemorative Volume* (Cape Town: Royal Society of South Africa), pp. 153–158.

WEIDENREICH, F. (1951). "Morphology of Solo Man." *Anthropological Papers of the American Museum of Natural History*, 43: 203–290.

WEINER, J.S. (1955). The Piltdown Forgery (London: Oxford University Press).

WEINER, J.S., K.P. OAKLEY AND W.E. LE GROS CLARK (1953). "The Solution to the Piltdown Problem." *Bulletin of the British Museum of Natural History (Geology)*, 2: 141–146.

WEINERT, H. (1932). *Ursprung der Menschheit: über den engeren Anschluss des Menschengeschlechts an die Menschenaffen* (Stuttgart: F. Enke).

WEINERT, H. (1938). *Entstehung der Menschenrassen* (Stuttgart: F. Enke).

WEINERT, H. (1939a). "*Africanthropus njarensis*." *Zeitschrift für Morphologie und Anthropologie*, 37: 18–24.

WEINERT, H. (1939b). *L'homme préhistorique: des préhumains aux races actuelles* (Paris: Payot).

WEINERT, H. (1940). *Der geistige Aufstieg der Menschheit: Vom Ursprung bis zur Gegenwart* (Stuttgart: F. Enke).

WEINERT, H. (1941). *Entstehung der Menschenrassen*, 2nd edition (Stuttgart: F. Enke).

WEINERT, H. (1944). *L'homme préhistorique: des préhumains aux races actuelles*, 2nd edition (Paris: Payot).

WEINERT, H. (1946). *L'ascension intellectuelle de l'humanité: Des origines aux temps présents* (Paris: Payot).

WEINERT, H. (1951). *Stammesentwicklung der Menschheit* (Braunschweig: Friedr. Vieweg & Sohn).

WELCKER, H. (1868). "Sur les caractères des crânes esthoniens." *Bulletins de la Société d'Anthropologie de Paris*, 2e série, 3: 578–584.

WERTH, E. (1928). *Der fossile Mensch: Grundzüge einer Paläanthropologie* (Berlin: G. Borntraeger).

WESCOTT, R.W. (1967). "Hominid Uprightness and Primate Display." *American Anthropologist*, 69: 738.

WHITE, T.D. (1980). "Evolutionary Implications of Pliocene Hominid Footprints." *Science*, 208: 175–176.

WHITE, T.D. (2002). "Earliest Hominids." In, W.C. Hartwig (ed.), *The Primate Fossil Record* (Cambridge: Cambridge University Press), pp. 407–417.

WHITE, T.D., D.C. JOHANSON AND W.H. KIMBEL (1981). "*Australopithecus africus*: Its Phyletic Position Reconsidered." *South Africa Journal of Science*, 77: 445–470.

WHITE, T.D. AND G. SUWA (1987). "Hominid Footprints at Laetoli: Facts and Interpretations." *American Journal of Physical Anthropology*, 72: 485–514.

White, T.D., G. Suwa, W.K. Hart, R.C. Walter, G. WoldeGabriel, J. de Heinzelin, J.D. Clark, B. Asfaw and E. Vrba (1993). "New Discoveries of *Australopithecus* at Maka in Ethiopia." *Nature*, 366: 261–265.

White, T.D., G. Suwa and B. Asfaw (1994). "*Australopithecus ramidus*, a New Species of Early Hominid from Aramis, Ethiopia." *Nature*, 371: 306–312.

White, T.D., G. Suwa and B. Asfaw (1995). "*Australopithecus ramidus*, a New Species of Early Hominid from Aramis, Ethiopia." *Nature*, 375: 88.

Wiley, E.O. (1981). *Phylogenetics: The Theory and Practice of Phylogenetic Systematics* (New York: John Wiley and Sons).

Wilkins, W.K. and J. Wakefield (1995). "Brain Evolution and Neurolinguistic Preconditions." *Behavioral and Brain Sciences*, 18: 161–226.

Willermet, C.M. and G.A. Clark (1995). "Paradigm Crisis in Modern Human Origins Research." *Journal of Human Evolution*, 29: 487–490.

Wills, C. (1995). "When Did Eve Live? An Evolutionary Detective Story." *Evolution*, 49: 593–607.

Wilson, A.C. and R.L. Cann (1992). "The Recent African Genesis of Humans." *Scientific American*, 266: 68–73.

Wolpoff, M.H. (1968). "'Telanthropus' and the Single Species Hypothesis." *American Anthropologist*, 70: 477–493.

Wolpoff, M.H. (1971). "Competitive Exclusion Among Lower Pleistocene Hominids." *Man*, 6: 601–617.

Wolpoff, M.H. (1973). "The Evidence for Two Australopithecine Lineages in South Africa." *Yearbook of Physical Anthropology*, 17: 113–139.

Wolpoff, M.H. (1976). "Data and Theory in Paleoanthropological Controversies." *American Anthropologist*, 78: 94–96.

Wolpoff, M.H. (1980). *Paleoanthropology* (New York: Alfred A. Knopf).

Wolpoff, M.H. (1982). "*Ramapithecus* and Hominid Origins." *Current Anthropology*, 23: 501–522.

Wolpoff, M.H. (1984). "Evolution in *Homo erectus*: The Question of Stasis." *Paleobiology*, 10: 389–406.

Wolpoff, M.H. (1994). "How Does Evolution Work?" *Evolutionary Anthropology*, 3: 4–5.

Wolpoff, M.H. (1998). "Concocting a Divisive Theory." *Evolutionary Anthropology*, 7: 1–13.

Wolpoff, M.H. (1999). *Paleoanthropology*, 2nd edition (Boston: McGraw-Hill).

Wolpoff, M.H. and R. Caspari (1997). *Race and Human Evolution* (New York: Simon and Schuster).

Wolpoff, M.H., A.G. Thorne, J. Jelinek and Zhang Yinyun (1994a). "The Case For Sinking *Homo erectus*: 100 Years of Pithecanthropus is Enough!" In, J.L. Franzen (ed.), *100 Years of* Pithecanthropus: *The* Homo erectus *Problem* (Frankfurt am Main: Courier Forschung-Institut Senckenberg, 171), pp. 341–361.

Wolpoff, M.H., A.G. Thorne, F.H. Smith, D.W. Frayer and G.G. Pope (1994b). "Multiregional Evolution: A World-Wide Source for Modern Human Populations." In, M.H. Nitecki and D.V. Nitecki (eds.), *Origins of Anatomically Modern Humans* (New York: Plenum Press), pp. 175–199.

Wolpoff, M.H., Wu Xinzhi and A.G. Thorne (1984). "Modern *Homo sapiens* Origins: A General Theory of Hominid Evolution Involving the Fossil Evidence From East Asia." In, F.H. Smith and F. Spencer (eds.), *The Origins of Modern Humans: A World Survey of the Fossil Evidence* (New York: Alan R. Liss, 1984), pp. 411–483.

Woo, J.-K. (1957). "*Dryopithecus* Teeth From Keiyuan, Yunnan Province." *Vertebrata Palasiatica*, 1: 25–31.

Woo, J.-K. (1958). "New Materials of *Dryopithecus* From Keiyuan, Yunnan." *Vertebrata Palasiatica*, 2: 38–42.

Woo, J.-K. (1962). "The Mandibles and Dentition of Gigantopithecus." *Palaeontologia Sinica*, 146: 63–94.

Wood, B. (1984). "The Origin of *Homo erectus*." In, P. Andrews and J.L. Franzen (eds.), *The Early Evolution of Man With Special Emphasis on Southeast Asia and Africa* (Courier Forschungs-Institut Senckenberg, 69), pp. 99–111.

Wood, B. (1985). "A Review of the Definition, Distribution and Relationships of *Australopithecus africanus*." In, P.V. Tobias (ed.), *Hominid Evolution: Past, Present and Future* (New York: Alan R. Liss), pp. 227–232.

Wood, B. (1991). *Koobi Fora Research Project, Vol. 4, Hominid Cranial Remains* (Oxford: Clarendon Press).

WOOD, B. (1992). "Origin and Evolution of the *Genus* Homo." *Nature*, 355: 783–790.

WOOD, B. (1996). "Human Evolution." *BioEssays*, 18: 945–954.

WOOD, B. (2000). "The History of the Genus *Homo*." *Human Evolution*, 15: 39–49.

WOOD, B. AND M. COLLARD (1999). "The Human Genus." *Science*, 284: 65–71.

WOOD, B. AND A. TURNER (1995). "Out of Africa and Into Asia." *Nature*, 378: 239–249.

WOOD JONES, F. (1918). *The Problem of Man's Ancestry* (London: Society for Promoting Christian Knowledge).

WOOD JONES, F. (1919). "The Origin of Man." In, A. Dendy (ed.), *Animal Life and Human Progress* (New York: D. Appleton), pp. 99–131.

WOOD JONES, F. (1929). *Man's Place Among the Mammals* (London: Edward Arnold & Co.).

WOOD JONES, F. (1948). *Hallmarks of Mankind* (London: Baillière, Tindall and Cox).

WRANGHAM, R.W. (1980). "Bipedal Locomotion as a Feeding Adaptation in Gelada Baboons, and Its Implications for Hominid Evolution." *Journal of Human Evolution*, 9: 329–331.

WU, RUKANG (1984). "The Crania of *Ramapithecus* and *Sivapithecus* From Lufeng, China." In, P. Andrews and J. L. Franzen (eds.), *The Early Evolution of Man With Special Emphasis on Southeast Asia and Africa* (Courier Forschungsinstitut Senckenberg, 69), pp. 41–48.

WU, RUKANG (1987). "A Revision of the Classification of the Lufeng Great Apes." *Acta Anthropologica Sinica*, 6: 265–271.

WU, RUKANG AND Q. XU (1985). "*Ramapithecus* and *Sivapithecus* from Lufeng, China." In, R. Wu and J.W. Olsen (eds.), *Palaeoanthropology and Palaeolithic Archaeology in the People's Republic of China* (New York: Academic Press), pp. 43–68.

WU, RUKANG, Q. XU AND Q. LU (1986). "Relationship Between Lufeng *Sivapithecus* and *Ramapithecus* and Their Phylogenetic Position." *Acta Anthropologica Sinica*, 5: 1–30.

WU, XINZHI (1990). "The Evolution of Humankind in China." *Acta Anthropologica Sinica*, 9: 312–321.

WU, XINZHI (1998). "Continuity or Replacement: Viewed From Source of Certain Features of Modern Humans in China." In, K. Omoto and P.V. Tobias (eds.), *The Origins and Past of Modern Humans: Towards Reconciliation* (Singapore: World Scientific), pp. 139–144.

XU, Q. AND Q. LU (1979). "The Mandibles of *Ramapithecus* and *Sivapithecus* From Lufeng, Yunnan." *Vertebrata Palasiatica*, 17: 1–13.

YUNIS, J.J. AND O. PRAKASH (1982). "The Origin of Man: A Chromosomal Pictorial Legacy." *Science*, 215: 1525–1530.

ZABOROWSKI, S. (1881). *Les grands singes* (Paris: Librairie Germer Baillière).

ZAPFE, H. (1958). "The Skeleton of Pliopithecus (Epipliopithecus) Vindobonensis Zapfe and Hürzeler," *American Journal of Physical Anthropology*, 16: 441–455.

ZAPFE, H. (1960a). "A New Fossil Anthropoid From the Miocene of Austria," *Current Anthropology*, 1: 428–429.

ZAPFE, H. (1960b). "Die Primaten funde aus den miozänen Spaltenfüllung von Neudorf on der Maach (Devinska Nova Ves), Tschechoslowakier," *Schweizerische Paläontologische Abhandlungen*, 78: 1–293.

ZAPFE, H. (1961). "Ein Primatenfund aus der miozänen Molasse von Oberösterreich," *Zeitschrift für Morphologie und Anthropologie*, 51 (1961): 247–267.

ZIHLMAN, A.L. (2001). "In Memoriam: Sherwood Washburn, 1911–2000." *American Journal of Physical Anthropology*, 116: 181–183.

ZUCKERKANDL, E. (1963). "Perspectives in Molecular Anthropology." In, S.L. Washburn (ed.), *Classification and Human Evolution* (Chicago: Aldine), pp. 243–272.

ZUCKERMAN, S. (1928). "Age-Changes in the Chimpanzee, With Special Reference to Growth of Brain, Eruption of Teeth, and Estimation of Age; With a Note on the Taungs Ape." *Proceedings of the Zoological Society of London*, 1928: 1–42.

ZUCKERMAN, S. (1933). *Functional Affinities of Man, Monkeys, and Apes* (London: Kegan Paul, Trench, Trubner & Co.).

ZUCKERMAN, S. (1950). "Taxonomy and Human Evolution." *Biological Reviews*, 25: 435–485.

ZUCKERMAN, S. (1954). "Correlation of Change in the Evolution of Higher Primates." In, J. Huxley, A.C. Hardy and E.B. Ford (eds.), *Evolution as a Process* (London: Allen and Unwin), pp. 300–352.

Index